WORD PICTURES
IN THE
NEW TESTAMENT

BOOKS BY PROFESSOR A. T. ROBERTSON

The English New Testament as a Whole:
SYLLABUS FOR NEW TESTAMENT STUDY
THE STUDENT'S CHRONOLOGICAL NEW TESTAMENT
STUDIES IN THE NEW TESTAMENT
NEW TESTAMENT HISTORY (AIRPLANE VIEW)

The Greek New Testament:
WORD PICTURES IN THE NEW TESTAMENT (IN SIX VOLS.)
A NEW SHORT GRAMMAR OF THE GREEK TESTAMENT
A GRAMMAR OF THE GREEK NEW TESTAMENT IN THE LIGHT
  OF HISTORICAL RESEARCH (FIFTH EDITION)
THE MINISTER AND HIS GREEK NEW TESTAMENT
AN INTRODUCTION TO THE TEXTUAL CRITICISM OF THE NEW
  TESTAMENT
STUDIES IN THE TEXT OF THE NEW TESTAMENT

The Gospels and Jesus:
A HARMONY OF THE GOSPELS FOR STUDENTS OF THE LIFE OF
  CHRIST
A COMMENTARY ON MATTHEW
STUDIES IN MARK'S GOSPEL
LUKE THE HISTORIAN IN THE LIGHT OF RESEARCH
A TRANSLATION OF LUKE'S GOSPEL
THE DIVINITY OF CHRIST IN THE GOSPEL OF JOHN
JOHN THE LOYAL (THE MINISTRY OF THE BAPTIST)
THE PHARISEES AND JESUS (STONE LECTURES FOR 1916)
EPOCHS IN THE LIFE OF JESUS
KEYWORDS IN THE TEACHING OF JESUS
THE TEACHING OF JESUS CONCERNING GOD THE FATHER
THE CHRIST OF THE LOGIA (PORTRAITS OF CHRIST IN Q AND
  THE GOSPELS)
THE MOTHER OF JESUS: HER PROBLEMS AND HER GLORY

Paul:
PAUL AND THE INTELLECTUALS (EPISTLE TO THE COLOSSIANS)
EPOCHS IN THE LIFE OF PAUL
PAUL THE INTERPRETER OF CHRIST
PAUL'S JOY IN CHRIST (EPISTLE TO THE PHILIPPIANS)
THE GLORY OF THE MINISTRY (II COR. 2:12–6:10)
THE NEW CITIZENSHIP

Other Studies in the New Testament:
SOME MINOR CHARACTERS IN THE NEW TESTAMENT
STUDIES IN THE EPISTLE OF JAMES
MAKING GOOD IN THE MINISTRY (SKETCH OF JOHN MARK)
TYPES OF PREACHERS IN THE NEW TESTAMENT

Biography:
LIFE AND LETTERS OF JOHN ALBERT BROADUS

WORD PICTURES
IN THE
NEW TESTAMENT

BY

ARCHIBALD THOMAS ROBERTSON
A. M., D. D., LL. D., Litt. D.
PROFESSOR OF NEW TESTAMENT INTERPRETATION
IN THE
SOUTHERN BAPTIST THEOLOGICAL SEMINARY
OF
LOUISVILLE, KENTUCKY

VOLUME VI
THE GENERAL EPISTLES
and
THE REVELATION OF JOHN

BROADMAN PRESS
NASHVILLE, TENNESSEE

PRINTED IN THE UNITED STATES OF AMERICA

To

DR. ADOLF DEISSMANN

of Berlin

WHO HAS DONE SO MUCH
TO MAKE THE WORDS OF THE
NEW TESTAMENT GLOW WITH LIFE

CONTENTS

THE GENERAL EPISTLES

BY WAY OF INTRODUCTION

Not a Happy Title

There are various explanations of the term catholic (*katholikai epistolai*) as applied to this group of seven short letters by four writers (one by James, two by Peter, one by Jude, three by John). The Latin for *katholikos* is *generalis*, though the Vulgate terms these letters *Catholicae*. The meaning is not orthodox as opposed to heretical or canonical, though they are sometimes termed *Epistolae canonicae*. As a matter of fact five of the seven (all but First Peter and First John) Eusebius placed among the "disputed" (*antilegomena*) books of the New Testament. "A canonical book is primarily one which has been measured and tested, and secondarily that which is itself a measure or standard" (Alfred Plummer). Canon is from *kanōn* (cane) and is like a yardstick cut to the right measure and then used as a measure. Some see in the term *katholikos* the idea that these Epistles are meant for both Jews and Gentiles, but the Epistle of James seems addressed to Jewish Christians. There were two other chief groups of New Testament writings in the old Greek manuscripts (the Gospels and Acts, then the Epistles of Paul). This group of seven Epistles and the Apocalypse constitute the remainder of the New Testament. The usual interpretation of the term *katholikos* here is that these seven Epistles were not addressed to any particular church, but are general in their distribution. This is clearly true of I Peter, as is shown by the language in I Peter 1:1, where seven Roman provinces are mentioned. The language of II Peter 3:1 bears the same idea. Apparently the Epistle of Jude is general also as is I John. But

II John is addressed to "an elect lady" (verse 1) and III John to Gaius (verse 1), both of them individuals, and therefore in no sense are these two brief letters general or catholic. The earliest instance of the word *katholikos* is in an inscription (B.C. 6) with the meaning "general" (*tēi katholikēi mou prothesei*, my general purpose). It was common after that. The earliest example of it in Christian literature is in Ignatius' Epistle to the Church of Smyrna (VIII) where he has "the catholic church" (*hē katholikē ekklēsia*), "the general church," not a local body. Clement of Alexandria (*Strom.* IV. xv) applies this adjective to the letter sent to the Gentile Christians "in Antioch and Syria and Cilicia" from the Jerusalem Conference (Acts 15:23).

Order and Dates

The oldest Greek manuscripts give these General Epistles immediately after the Acts, and Westcott and Hort so print them in their Greek New Testament. But the English Versions follow the Textus Receptus and put them just before the Apocalypse. The order of the seven letters varies greatly in the different manuscripts, though usually James comes first and Jude last (as the last accepted and the least known of the four authors). It is possible that the order of James, Peter, and John (omitting Jude) represented a sort of chronological precedence in some minds. It is possible also that no importance is to be attached to this order. Certainly John wrote last and after the destruction of Jerusalem, while the others come before that great event if they are genuine, as I believe, though there are difficulties of a serious nature concerning II Peter. James may be very early. If so, these seven Epistles are scattered all the way from A.D. 45 to 90. They have no connection with one another save in the case of the Epistles of Peter and Jude.

IMPORTANCE OF THE GENERAL EPISTLES

Without them we should be deprived of much concerning three outstanding personalities in early Christianity. We should know much less of "James, and Cephas, and John, they who were reputed to be pillars" (Gal. 2:9). We should know less also of the Judaic (not Judaizing) form of Christianity seen in the Epistles of James and Jude in contrast with, though not opposed to, the Pauline type. In Peter's Epistles we see, indeed, a mediating position without compromise of principle, for Peter in the Jerusalem Conference loyally supported Paul and Barnabas even if he did flicker for a moment later in Antioch. In the Johannine Epistles we see the great Eagle soar as in his Gospel in calm serenity in spite of conflict with the Gnostics who struck at the very life of Christianity itself. "The only opposition which remains worthy of a Christian's consideration is that between light and darkness, truth and falsehood, love and hate, God and the world, Christ and Antichrist, life and death" (Plummer). So we can be grateful for the preservation of these little Epistles which reveal differences in the development of the great Christian leaders and the adaptation of the gospel message to changing world conditions then and now.

THE EPISTLE OF JAMES
BEFORE A.D. 50

BY WAY OF INTRODUCTION

He claims to be James, and so the book is not anonymous. It is either genuine or pseudonymous. He does not claim to be the brother of the Lord Jesus, as one might expect. James the brother of John was put to death by Herod Agrippa I about A.D. 44 (Acts 12:2). But James the brother of Jesus (Gal. 1:19) was still alive and became a leader of the church in Jerusalem (Acts 12:17), presiding over the Conference in Jerusalem (Acts 15:13–21) and apparently writing the message from the Conference to the Gentile churches (15:22–29), and was still the leading elder in Jerusalem on Paul's last visit (21:18–25). James does not claim here to be an apostle and he was not one of the twelve apostles, and the dispute about accepting it of which Eusebius spoke was about its apostolicity since James was only an apostle by implication (Gal. 1:19) in the general sense of that term like Barnabas (Acts 14:14), perhaps Silas and Timothy (I Thess. 2:7), certainly not on a par with Paul, who claimed equality with the twelve. James, like the other brothers of Jesus, had once disbelieved his claims to be the Messiah (John 7:6f.), but he was won by a special vision of the Risen Christ (I Cor. 15:7) and was in the upper room before the great pentecost (Acts 1:14). It is plain that he had much to overcome as a zealous Jew to become a Christian, though he was not a mere cousin of Jesus or a son of Joseph by a former marriage. He was strictly the half-brother of Jesus, since Joseph was not the actual father of Jesus. There is no reason to believe that he was a Nazirite. We know that he was married (I Cor. 9:5). He came to be

3

called James the Just and was considered very devout. The Judaizers had counted on him to agree with them against Paul and Barnabas, but he boldly stood for Gentile freedom from the ceremonial law. The Judaizers still claimed him at Antioch and used his name wrongly to frighten Peter thereby (Gal. 2:12). But to the end he remained the loyal friend to Paul and his gospel rightly understood (Acts 21:18–25). Clement of Alexandria (*Hypot.* vii) says that, when he bore strong testimony to Jesus as the Son of man, they flung him down from the gable of the temple, stoned him, and beat him to death with a club. But Josephus (*Ant.* XX. ix. 1) says that the Sadducees about A.D. 62 had James and some others brought before the Sanhedrin (Ananus presiding) and had them stoned as transgressors of the law. At any rate he won a martyr's crown like Stephen and James the brother of John.

The Date

If the Epistle is genuine and James was put to death about A.D. 62, it was clearly written before that date. There are two theories about it, one placing it about A.D. 48, the other about A.D. 58. To my mind the arguments of Mayor for the early date are conclusive. There is no allusion to Gentile Christians, as would be natural after A.D. 50. If written after A.D. 70, the tone would likely be different, with some allusion to that dreadful calamity. The sins condemned are those characteristic of early Jewish Christians. The book itself is more like the Sermon on the Mount than the Epistles. The discussion of faith and works in chapter 2 reveals an absence of the issues faced by Paul in Rom. 4 and Gal. 3 after the Jerusalem Conference (A.D. 49). Hence the date before that Conference has decidedly the better of the argument. Ropes in his Commentary denies the genuineness of the Epistle and locates it between A.D. 75 and 125, but Hort holds that the evidence for a late date rests "on very slight and intangible grounds." So we place the book before A.D. 49. It may indeed be the earliest New Testament book.

THE READERS

The author addresses himself "to the twelve tribes which are of the Dispersion" (James 1:1). Clearly, then, he is not writing to Gentiles, unless he includes the spiritual children of Abraham in the term *Diaspora* as Paul does for believers (Gal. 3:29; Rom. 9:6f.). The word *diaspora* occurs elsewhere in the N.T. only in John 7:35; I Pet. 1:1. It apparently has the spiritual significance in I Pet. 1:1, but in John 7:35 the usual meaning of Jews scattered over the world. The use here of "the twelve tribes" makes the literal sense probable here. Clearly also James knew nothing of any "lost" tribes, for the Jews of the Dispersion were a blend of all the twelve tribes. It is probable also that James is addressing chiefly the Eastern Dispersion in Syria, Mesopotamia, and Babylonia as Peter writes to five provinces in the Western Dispersion in Asia Minor. It is possible that James has in mind Christian and non-Christian Jews, not wholly non-Christian Jews as some hold. He may have in mind merely Christian Jews outside of Palestine, of whom there were already many scattered since the great pentecost. The use of synagogue as a place of worship (2:2) like church (5:14) argues somewhat for this view. He presents the Mosaic law as still binding (2:9–11; 4:11). As the leading elder of the great church in Jerusalem and as a devout Jew and half-brother of Jesus, the message of James had a special appeal to these widely scattered Jewish Christians.

THE PURPOSE

If James is writing solely to non-Christian Jews, the purpose is to win them to Christ, and so he puts the gospel message in a way to get a hearing from the Jews. That is true, whether he has them in mind or not, though he does not do it by the suppression of the deity of Jesus Christ. In the very first verse he places him on a par with God as "the Lord Jesus Christ." In 2:1 he presents Jesus as the object of faith: "as you believe in our Lord Jesus Christ, who is the Glory" (Moffatt's Translation), where Jesus is termed the Shekinah Glory of God. It is true that there is no discussion in the Epistle of the cross and the resurrection of Jesus, but there is an allusion to the murder of Jesus in 5:6 and the second coming in 5:8. The chief aim of the Epistle is to strengthen the faith and loyalty of the Jewish Christians in the face of persecution from rich and over-bearing Jews who were defrauding and oppressing them. It is a picture of early Christian life in the midst of difficult social conditions between capital and labor which also exist today. So then it is a very modern message even if it is the earliest New Testament book. The glory of the New Testament lies precisely at this point in that the revelation of God in Christ meets our problems today because it did meet those of the first century A.D. Christian principles stand out clearly for our present-day living.

THE STYLE

James assumes the doctrinal features of Christianity, but he is concerned mainly with the ethical and social aspects of the gospel that Jewish followers of Christ may square their lives with the gospel which they believe and profess. But this fact does not justify Luther in calling the Epistle of James "a veritable Epistle of straw." Luther imagined that James contradicted Paul's teaching of justification by faith. That is not true and the criticism of Luther is unjust. We shall see that, though James and Paul use the same words (faith, works, justify), they mean different things by them. It is possible that both Paul and Peter had read the Epistle of James, though by no means certain. M. Jones (*New Testament in the Twentieth Century*, p. 316) thinks that the author was familiar with Stoic philosophy. This is also possible, though he may have learned it only indirectly through the Wisdom of Solomon and Philo. What is true is that the author writes in the easy and accurate *Koiné* Greek of a cultivated Jew (the literary *Koiné*, not the vernacular), though not the artificial or stilted language of a professional stylist. Principal Patrick (*James the Lord's Brother*, p. 298) holds that he "had a wide knowledge of Classical Greek." This does not follow, though he does use the manner "of the Hellenistic diatribe" (Ropes, *Int. and Crit. Comm.*, p. 19) so common at that time. Ropes (pp. 10 to 22) points out numerous parallels between James and the popular moral addresses of the period, familiar since the days of Socrates and at its height in Seneca and Epictetus. The use of an imaginary interlocutor is one instance (James 2:18f.; 5:13f.) as is the presence of paradox (1:2, 10; 2:5; etc.). But the style of James is even more kin to that seen in the Jewish wisdom literature like Proverbs, the Wisdom of Solomon, etc. It is thus both tract and Epistle, a brief Christian sermon on a high plane for a noble purpose. But it is all natural and not artificial. The metaphors are many, but brief and remind one constantly of the Master's use of them in the Sermon on the Mount. Did not Mary the mother of Jesus and James make frequent use of such homely parables? The author shows acquaintance with the LXX, but there are few Hebraisms in the language, though the style is Hebraic, as is the whole tone of the book (Hebraic and Christian). "The style is especially remarkable for constant hidden allusions to our Lord's sayings, such as we find in the first three Gospels" (Hort).

RECENT BOOKS ON JAMES

BALJON, J. M. S., *Comm. op de katholieke brieven* (1904).
BARDENHEWER, O., *Der Brief des hl. Jakobus* (1928).
BARTMANN, *St. Paulus und St. Jakobus*.

BELSER, J. E., *Epistel des hl. Jakobus* (1909).

BEYSCHLAG, W., *Der Brief des Jakobus.* Meyer Komm. 6 Aufl. (1898).

BROWN, CHARLES, *The General Epistle of James.* 2nd ed. (1907).

CAMERLINCK, *Commentarius in epistolas catholicas* (1909).

CARPENTER, W. BOYD, *The Wisdom of James the Just* (1903).

CARR, ARTHUR, *The General Epistle of James.* Cambridge Greek Testament. New ed. (1905).

CHAINE, J., *L'Épître de S. Jacques* (1927).

DALE, R. W., *Discourses on the Epistle of James* (1895).

DEEMS, C. F., *The Gospel of Common Sense.*

DIBELIUS, M., *Meyer's Comm.* 7 Aufl. (1921).

FEINE, *Der Jakobusbrief*, etc. (1893).

FITCH, *James the Lord's Brother.*

GAUGUSCH, L., *Der Lehrgehalt der Jakobus-epistel* (1914).

GRAFE, *Stellung und Bedeutung des Jakobusbriefes* (1904).

GROSHEIDE, F. W., *De brief aan de Hebreën en de brief des Jakobus* (1927).

HAUCK, F., *Der Br. d. Jak. in Zahn's Komm.* (1926).

HOLLMANN, G., *Die Schriften d. N.T.* 3 Aufl. (1917).

HOLTZMANN, O., *Das N.T. II* (1926).

HORT, F. J. A., *The Epistle of James as far as 4:7* (1909).

HUTHER, J. E., *Meyer's Komm.* 3 Aufl. (1870).

JOHNSTONE, R., *Lectures Exegetical and Practical.* 2nd ed. (1889).

KNOWLING, R. J., *Comm. on the Epistle of St. James* (1904). Westminster Series.

MAYOR, J. B., *The Epistle of St. James.* 3rd ed. (1910).

MEINERTZ, *Der Jakobusbrief und sein Verfasser* (1905).

MEYER, A., *Das Rätsel des Jak.* (1930).

MOFFATT, JAMES, *The General Epistles (James, Peter, and Judas)* (1928).

OSTERLEY, W. E., *The Epistle of St. James.* Expos. Gk. Test. (1910).

PARRY, J., *The General Epistle of James* (1904).

PATRICK, W., *James, the Lord's Brother* (1906).

PLUMMER, A., *The General Epistle of St. James.* Expos. Bible (1891).

RENDALL, G. H., *The Epistle of St. James and Judaic Christianity* (1927).

ROBERTSON, A. T., *Studies in the Epistle of James.* 3rd ed. (1923). First in 1915 as *Pract. and Social Aspects of Christianity.*

ROPES, J. H., *A Crit. and Exeget. Comm. on the Epistle of St. James.* Int. and Crit. Comm. (1916).

SMITH, H. M., *The Epistle of James* (1925).

SODEN, H. VON, *Der Brief des Jakobus.* Hand-Comm. (1893).

SPITTA, F., *Der Brief des Jakobus untersucht* (1896).

TAYLOR, J. F., *The Apostle of Patience* (1907).

WEISS, B., *Die Katholische Briefe* (1902).

————, *Der Jakobusbrief und die neuere Kritik* (1904).

WINDISCH, H., *Die Katholische Briefe. Handbuch zum N.T.*, 2 Aufl. (1930).

CHAPTER I

1. *James* (*Iakōbos*). Grecised form (nominative absolute) of the Hebrew *Iakōb* (so LXX). Common name among the Jews, and this man in Josephus (*Ant.* XX.9.1) and three others of this name in Josephus also. *Servant* (*doulos*). Bond-servant or slave as Paul (Rom. 1:1; Phil. 1:1; Tit. 1:1). *Of the Lord Jesus Christ* (*kuriou Iēsou Christou*). Here on a par with God (*theou*) and calls himself not *adelphos* (brother) of Jesus, but *doulos*. The three terms here as in 2:1 have their full significance: Jesus is the Messiah and Lord. James is not an Ebionite. He accepts the deity of Jesus his brother, difficult as it was for him to do so. The word *kurios* is frequent in the LXX for *Elohim* and *Jahweh* as the Romans applied it to the emperor in their emperor worship. See I Cor. 12:3 for *Kurios Iēsous* and Phil. 2:11 for *Kurios Iēsous Christos*. *To the twelve tribes* (*tais dōdeka phulais*). Dative case. The expression means "Israel in its fulness and completeness" (Hort), regarded as a unity (Acts 26:7) with no conception of any "lost" tribes. *Which are of the Dispersion* (*tais en tēi diasporāi*). "Those in the Dispersion" (repeated article). The term appears in Deut. 28:25 (LXX) and comes from *diaspeirō*, to scatter (sow) abroad. In its literal sense we have it in John 7:34, but here and in I Pet. 1:1 Christian Jews are chiefly, if not wholly, in view. The Jews at this period were roughly divided into Palestinian Jews (chiefly agriculturists) and Jews of the Dispersion (dwellers in cities and mainly traders). In Palestine Aramaic was spoken as a rule, while in the Western Diaspora the language was Greek (*Koiné*, LXX), though the Eastern Diaspora spoke Aramaic and Syriac. The Jews of the Diaspora were compelled to compare their religion with the

various cults around them (comparative religion) and had a wider outlook on life. James writes thus in cultural *Koinē* but in the Hebraic tone. *Greeting* (*chairein*). Absolute infinitive (present active of *chairō*) as in Acts 15:23 (the Epistle to Antioch and the churches of Syria and Galatia). It is the usual idiom in the thousands of papyri letters known to us, but in no other New Testament letter. But note *chairein legete* in II John 10 and 11.

2. *Count it* (*hēgēsasthe*). First aorist middle imperative of *hēgeomai*, old verb to consider. Do it now and once for all. *All joy* (*pāsan charan*). "Whole joy," "unmixed joy," as in Phil. 2:29. Not just "some joy" along with much grief. *When* (*hotan*). "Whenever," indefinite temporal conjunction. *Ye fall into* (*peripesēte*). Second aorist active subjunctive (with the indefinite *hotan*) from *peripiptō*, literally to fall around (into the midst of), to fall among as in Luke 10:30 *lēistais periepesen* (he fell among robbers). Only other N.T. example of this old compound is in Acts 27:41. Thucydides uses it of falling into affliction. It is the picture of being surrounded (*peri*) by trials. *Manifold temptations* (*peirasmois poikilois*). Associative instrumental case. The English word temptation is Latin and originally meant trials whether good or bad, but the evil sense has monopolized the word in our modern English, though we still say "attempt." The word *peirasmos* (from *peirazō*, late form for the old *peiraō* as in Acts 26:21, both in good sense as in John 6:6, and in bad sense as in Matt. 16:1) does not occur outside of the LXX and the N.T. except in Dioscorides (A.D. 100?) of experiments on diseases. "Trials" is clearly the meaning here, but the evil sense appears in verse 12 (clearly in *peirazō* in verse 13) and so in Heb. 3:8. Trials rightly faced are harmless, but wrongly met become temptations to evil. The adjective *poikilos* (manifold) is as old as Homer and means variegated, many coloured as in Matt.

4:24; 2 Tim. 3:6; Heb. 2:4. In I Pet. 1:6 we have this same phrase. It is a bold demand that James here makes.

3. *Knowing* (*ginōskontes*). Present active participle of *ginōskō* (experimental knowledge, the only way of getting this view of "trials" as "all joy"). *The proof* (*to dokimion*). Now known (Deissmann, *Bible Studies*, pp. 259ff.) from the papyri examples of *dokimios* as an adjective in the same sense (good gold, standard gold) as *dokimos* proved or tested (James 1:12). The use of *to dokimion* (neuter article with neuter single adjective) here and in I Pet. 1:7, clearly means "the genuine element in your faith," not "crucible" nor "proving." Your faith like gold stands the test of fire and is approved as standard. James here, as in verse 6; 2:1; 5:15, regards faith (*pistis*) like Paul "as the very foundation of religion" (Mayor). *Worketh* (*katergazetai*). Present (durative) middle indicative of the compound verb with the perfective sense of *kata* as in Phil. 2:12, which see. *Patience* (*hupomonēn*). Old and common word for remaining under (*hupomenō*), "staying power" (Ropes), as in Col. 1:11.

4. *Let have* (*echetō*). Present active imperative of *echō*, let it keep on having. *Perfect* (*teleion*). See Rom. 5:3f. for a like chain of blessings. Carry on the work to the end or completion (from *telos*, end) as in John 17:4 (*to ergon teleiōsas*, having finished the work). *That ye may be* (*hina ēte*). Purpose clause with *hina* and present active subjunctive of *eimi*. This is the goal of patience. *Perfect and entire* (*teleioi kai holoklēroi*). Perfected at the end of the task (*telos*) and complete in all parts (*holoklēroi*, *holos* whole and *klēros* lot or part). "Perfected all over." These two adjectives often occur together in Philo, Plutarch, etc. See Acts 3:16 for *holoklērian* (perfect soundness). *Lacking in nothing* (*en mēdeni leipomenoi*). Present passive participle of *leipō* to leave. Negative statement of the preceding positive as often in James (cf. 1:6). There is now a digression (verses 5 to 8) from the discussion of *peirasmos*, which is taken up

again in verse 9. The word *leipomenoi* (lacking) suggests the digression.

5. *Lacketh wisdom* (*leipetai sophias*). Condition of first class, assumed as true, *ei* and present passive indicative of *leipō* to be destitute of, with ablative case *sophias*. "If any one falls short of wisdom." A banking figure, to have a shortage of wisdom (not just knowledge, *gnōseōs*, but wisdom *sophias*, the practical use of knowledge). *Let him ask* (*aiteitō*). Present active imperative of *aiteō*, "let him keep on asking." *Of God* (*para tou theou*). "From (from beside) God," ablative case with *para*. *Liberally* (*haplōs*). This old adverb occurs here only in the N.T. (from *haplous*, single-fold, Matt. 6:22, and *haplotēs*, simplicity, generosity, is common—II Cor. 8:2; Rom. 12:8). But the adverb is common in the papyri by way of emphasis as simply or at all (Moulton and Milligan's *Vocabulary*). Mayor argues for the sense of "unconditionally" (the logical moral sense) while Hort and Ropes agree and suggest "graciously." The other sense of "abundantly" or "liberally" suits the idea in *haplotēs* in II Cor. 8:2 and Rom. 12:8, but no example of the adverb in this sense has been found unless this is one here. See Is. 55:1 for the idea of God's gracious giving and the case of Solomon (I Kings 3:9–12; Prov. 2:3). *Upbraideth not* (*mē oneidizontos*). Present active participle of *oneidizō* (old verb to reproach, to cast in one's teeth, Matt. 5:11) in the ablative case like *didontos* agreeing with *theou* and with the usual negative of the participle (*mē*). This is the negative statement of *didontos haplōs* (giving graciously). The evil habit of giving stinging words along with the money is illustrated in Sirach 41:22 and Plutarch (*De adulat.*, p. 64A). Cf. Heb. 4:16. *And it shall be given him* (*kai dothēsetai autōi*). First future passive of *didōmi*, a blessed promise in accord with the words of Jesus (Matt. 7:7, 11; Luke 11:13), meaning here not only "wisdom," but all good gifts, including the

Holy Spirit.   There are frequent reminiscences of the words
of Jesus in this Epistle.

6. *In faith* (*en pistei*).   Faith here "is the fundamental
religious attitude" (Ropes), belief in God's beneficent activity and personal reliance on him (Oesterley).   *Nothing
doubting* (*mēden diakrinomenos*).   Negative way of saying
en pistei (in faith), present passive participle of *diakrinō*, old
verb to separate (*krinō*) between (*dia*), to discriminate as
shown clearly in Acts 11:12, 15:9, but no example of the
sense of divided against oneself has been found earlier than
the N.T., though it appears in later Christian writings.   It
is like the use of *diamerizomai* in Luke 11:18 and occurs in
Matt. 21:21; Mark 11:23; Acts 10:20; Rom. 2:4; 4:20; 14:23.
It is a vivid picture of internal doubt.   *Is like* (*eoiken*).
Second perfect active indicative with the linear force alone
from *eikō* to be like.   Old form, but in N.T. only here and
verse 23 (a literary touch, not in LXX).   *The surge of the
sea* (*kludōni thalassēs*).   Old word (from *kluzō* to wash
against) for a dashing or surging wave in contrast with *kuma*
(successive waves), in N.T. only here and Luke 8:24.   In
associative instrumental case after *eoiken*.   In Eph. 4:14 we
have *kludonizō* (from *kludōn*), to toss by waves.   *Driven by
the wind* (*anemizomenōi*).   Present passive participle (agreeing in case with *kludōni*) of *anemizō*, earliest known example
and probably coined by James (from *anemos*), who is fond
of verbs in *-izō* (Mayor).   The old Greek used *anemoō*.   In
Eph. 4:14 Paul uses both *kludonizō* and *peripherō anemōi*.
It is a vivid picture of the sea whipped into white-caps by
the winds.   *Tossed* (*ripizomenōi*).   Present passive participle
also in agreement with *kludōni* from *ripizō*, rare verb (Aristophanes, Plutarch, Philo) from *ripis* (a bellows or fire-fan),
here only in N.T.   It is a picture of "the restless swaying
to and fro of the surface of the water, blown upon by shifting breezes" (Hort), the waverer with slight rufflement.

7. *That man* (*ho anthrōpos ekeinos*).   Emphatic use of

ekeinos. *Of the Lord* (*para tou kuriou*). Ablative case with *para* like *theou* in verse 5.

8. *Man* (*anēr*). Instead of *anthrōpos* (general term) in verse 7, perhaps for variety (Ropes), but often in James (1:12, 23; 2:2; 3:2), though in other Epistles usually in distinction from *gunē* (woman). *Double-minded* (*dipsuchos*). First appearance of this compound known and in N.T. only here and 4:8. Apparently coined by James, but copied often in early Christian writings and so an argument for the early date of James' Epistle (Moulton and Milligan's *Vocabulary*). From *dis* twice and *psuchē* soul, double-souled, double-minded, Bunyan's "Mr. Facing-both-ways." Cf. the rebuke to Peter (*edistasas*) in Matt. 14:31. *Unstable* (*akatastatos*). Late double compound (alpha privative and *katastatos* verbal from *kathistēmi*), in LXX once (Is. 54:11) and in Polybius, in N.T. only here and 3:8. It means unsteady, fickle, staggering, reeling like a drunken man. Surely to James such "doubt" is no mark of intellectuality.

9. *But* (*de*). Return to the point of view in verse 2. *Of low degree* (*ho tapeinos*). "The lowly" brother, in outward condition (Luke 1:52), humble and poor as in Ps. 9:39; Prov. 30:14, not the spiritually humble as in Matt. 11:29; James 4:6. In the LXX *tapeinos* was used for either the poor in goods or the poor in spirit. Christianity has glorified this word in both senses. Already the rich and the poor in the churches had their occasion for jealousies. *Glory in his high estate* (*kauchasthō en tōi hupsei autou*). Paradox, but true. In his low estate he is "in his height" (*hupsos*, old word, in N.T., also in Luke 1:78; Eph. 3:1; etc.).

10. *In that he is made low* (*en tēi tapeinōsei autou*). "In his low estate." Play on *tapeinōsis* (from *tapeinoō*, Phil. 3:7), like *tapeinos* of verse 9, old word in various senses, in N.T. only here, Luke 1:48; Acts 8:33; Phil. 3:21. The Cross of Christ lifts up the poor and brings down the high. It is the great leveller of men. *As the flower of the grass*

(*hōs anthos chortou*). From the LXX (Is. 40:6). *Chortos* means pasture, then grass (Mark 6:39) or fodder. *Anthos* is old word, in N.T. only here, verse 11, and I Pet. 1:24 (same quotation). This warning is here applied to "the rich brother," but it is true of all. *He shall pass away* (*pareleusetai*). Future middle indicative (effective aoristic future, shall pass completely away from earth).

11. *Ariseth* (*aneteilen*). Gnomic or timeless aorist active indicative of the old compound *anatellō*, used here of plants (cf. *anathallō* in Phil. 4:10), often of the sun (Matt. 13:6). *With the scorching wind* (*sun tōi kausōni*). Associative instrumental case with *sun*. In the LXX this late word (from *kausos*) is usually the sirocco, the dry east wind from the desert (Job 1:19). In Matt. 20:12 and Luke 12:55 it is the burning heat of the sun. Either makes sense here. *Withereth* (*exēranen*). Another gnomic aorist active indicative (Robertson, *Grammar*, p. 837) of *xērainō*, old verb (from *xēros*, dry or withered, Matt. 12:10), to dry up. Grass and flowers are often used to picture the transitoriness of human life. *Falleth* (*exepesen*). Another gnomic aorist (second aorist active indicative) of *ekpiptō* to fall out (off). *The grace* (*hē euprepeia*). Old word (from *euprepēs* well-looking, not in the N.T.), only here in N.T. Goodly appearance, beauty. *Of the fashion of it* (*tou prosōpou autou*). "Of the face of it." The flower is pictured as having a "face," like a rose or lily. *Perisheth* (*apōleto*). Another gnomic aorist (second aorist middle indicative of *apollumi*, to destroy, but intransitive here, to perish). The beautiful rose is pitiful when withered. *Shall fade away* (*maranthēsetai*). Future passive indicative of *marainō*, old verb, to extinguish a flame, a light. Used of roses in Wisdom 2:8. *Goings* (*poreiais*). Old word from *poreuō* to journey, in N.T. only here and Luke 13:22 (of Christ's journey toward Jerusalem). The rich man's travels will come to "journey's end."

12. *Endureth* (*hupomenei*). Present active indicative of

hupomenō. Cf. verse 3. *Temptation (peirasmon).* Real temptation here. See verse 2 for "trials." *When he hath been approved (dokimos genomenos).* "Having become approved," with direct reference to *to dokimion* in verse 3. See also Rom. 5:4 for *dokimē* (approval after test as of gold or silver). This beatitude (*makarios*) is for the one who has come out unscathed. See I Tim. 6:9. *The crown of life (ton stephanon tēs zōēs).* The same phrase occurs in Rev. 2:10. It is the genitive of apposition, life itself being the crown as in I Pet. 5:4. This crown is "an honourable ornament" (Ropes), with possibly no reference to the victor's crown (garland of leaves) as with Paul in I Cor. 9:25; II Tim. 4:8, nor to the linen fillet (*diadēma*) of royalty (Ps. 20:3, where *stephanos* is used like *diadēma*, the kingly crown). *Stephanos* has a variety of uses. Cf. the thorn chaplet on Jesus (Matt. 27:29). *The Lord.* Not in the oldest Greek MSS., but clearly implied as the subject of *epēggeilato* (*he promised,* first aorist middle indicative).

13. *Let no one say (mēdeis legetō).* Present active imperative, prohibiting such a habit. *When he is tempted (peirazomenos).* Present passive participle of *peirazō,* here in evil sense of tempt, not test, as in Matt. 4:1. Verses 12 to 18 give a vivid picture of temptation. *I am tempted of God (apo theou peirazomai).* The use of *apo* shows origin (*apo* with ablative case), not agency (*hupo*), as in Mark 1:13, of Satan. It is contemptible, but I have heard wicked and weak men blame God for their sins. Cf. Prov. 19:3; Sirach 15:11f. Temptation does not spring "from God." *Cannot be tempted with evil (apeirastos kakōn).* Verbal compound adjective (alpha privative and *peirazō*), probably with the ablative case, as is common with alpha privative (Robertson, *Grammar,* p. 516), though Moulton (*Prolegomena,* p. 74) treats it as the genitive of definition. The ancient Greek has *apeiratos* (from *peiraō*), but this is the earliest example of *apeirastos* (from *peirazō*) made on the

same model. Only here in the N.T. Hort notes *apeiratos kakōn* as a proverb (Diodorus, Plutarch, Josephus) "free from evils." That is possible here, but the context calls for "untemptable" rather than "untempted." *And he himself tempteth no man* (*peirazei de autos oudena*). Because "untemptable."

14. *When he is drawn away by his own lust* (*hupo tēs idias epithumias exelkomenos*). *Epithumia* is old word for craving (from *epithumeō*, to have a desire for) either good (Phil. 1:23) or evil (Rom. 7:7) as here. Like a fish drawn out from his retreat. *Enticed* (*deleazomenos*). Present passive participle of *deleazō*, old verb from *delear* (bait), to catch fish by bait or to hunt with snares and Philo has *huph' hēdonēs deleazetai* (is enticed by pleasure). In N.T. only here and II Pet. 2:14, 18. Allured by definite bait.

15. *Then* (*eita*). The next step. *The lust* (*hē epithumia*). Note article, the lust (verse 14) which one has. *When it hath conceived* (*sullabousa*). Second aorist active participle of *sullambanō*, old word to grasp together, in hostile sense (Acts 26:21), in friendly sense of help (Phil. 4:3), in technical sense of a woman taking a man's seed in conception (Luke 1:24), here also of lust (as a woman), "having conceived." The will yields to lust and conception takes place. *Beareth sin* (*tiktei hamartian*). Present active indicative of *tiktō* to bring forth as a mother or fruit from seed, old verb, often in N.T., here only in James. Sin is the union of the will with lust. See Ps. 7:14 for this same metaphor. *The sin* (*hē hamartia*). The article refers to *hamartia* just mentioned. *When it is full-grown* (*apotelestheisa*). First aorist passive participle of *apoteleō*, old compound verb with perfective use of *apo*, in N.T. only here and Luke 13:32. It does not mean "full-grown" like *teleioō*, but rather completeness of parts or functions as opposed to rudimentary state (Hort) like the winged insect in contrast with the chrysalis or grub (Plato). The sin at birth is fully equipped

for its career (Rom. 6:6; Col. 3:5). *Bringeth forth death* (*apokuei thanaton*). Late compound (*kueō* to be pregnant, perfective use of *apo*) to give birth to, of animals and women, for normal birth (papyrus example) and abnormal birth (Hort). A medical word (Ropes) rather than a literary one like *tiktō*. The child of lust is sin, of sin is death, powerful figure of abortion. The child is dead at birth. For death as the fruit of sin see Rom. 6:21–23; 8:6. "The birth of death follows of necessity when one sin is fully formed" (Hort).

16. *Be not deceived* (*mē planāsthe*). Prohibition with *mē* and the present passive imperative of *planaō*, common verb to lead astray. This is the way of sin to deceive and to kill (Rom. 7:7–14). The devil is a pastmaster at blinding men's eyes about sin (II Cor. 4:4; Rom. 1:27; Eph. 4:14; etc.).

17. *Gift* (*dosis*)—*boon* (*dōrēma*). Both old substantives from the same original verb (*didōmi*), to give. *Dosis* is the act of giving (ending -*sis*), but sometimes by metonymy for the thing given like *ktisis* for *ktisma* (Col. 1:15). But *dōrēma* (from *dōreō*, from *dōron* a gift) only means a gift, a benefaction (Rom. 5:16). The contrast here argues for "giving" as the idea in *dosis*. Curiously enough there is a perfect hexameter line here: *pāsa do / sis aga / thē kai / pān dō / rēma te / leion*. Such accidental rhythm occurs occasionally in many writers. Ropes (like Ewald and Mayor) argues for a quotation from an unknown source because of the poetical word *dōrēma*, but that is not conclusive. *From above* (*anōthen*). That is, from heaven. Cf. John 3:31; 19:11. *Coming down* (*katabainon*). Present active neuter singular participle of *katabainō* agreeing with *dōrēma*, expanding and explaining *anōthen* (from above). *From the Father of lights* (*apo tou patros tōn phōtōn*). "Of the lights" (the heavenly bodies). For this use of *patēr* see Job 38:28 (Father of rain); II Cor. 1:3; Eph. 1:17. God is the Author of light and lights. *With whom* (*par' hōi*).

For *para* (beside) with locative sense for standpoint of God see *para tōi theōi* (Mark 10:27; Rom. 2:11; 9:14; Eph. 6:9. *Can be no* (*ouk eni*). This old idiom (also in Gal. 3:28; Col. 3:11) may be merely the original form of *en* with recessive accent (Winer, Mayor) or a shortened form of *enesti*. The use of *eni en* in I Cor. 6:5 argues for this view, as does the use of *eine* (*einai*) in Modern Greek (Robertson, *Grammar*, p. 313). *Variation* (*parallagē*). Old word from *parallassō*, to make things alternate, here only in N.T. In Aristeas in sense of alternate stones in pavements. Dio Cassius has *parallaxis* without reference to the modern astronomical parallax, though James here is comparing God (Father of the lights) to the sun (Mal. 4:2), which does have periodic variations. *Shadow that is cast by turning* (*tropēs aposkiasma*). *Tropē* is an old word for "turning" (from *trepō* to turn), here only in N.T. *Aposkiasma* is a late and rare word (*aposkiasmos* in Plutarch) from *aposkiazō* (*apo, skia*) a shade cast by one object on another. It is not clear what the precise metaphor is, whether the shadow thrown on the dial (*aposkiazō* in Plato) or the borrowed light of the moon lost to us as it goes behind the earth. In fact, the text is by no means certain, for Aleph B papyrus of fourth century actually read *hē tropēs aposkiasmatos* (the variation of the turning of the shadow). Ropes argues strongly for this reading, and rather convincingly. At any rate there is no such periodic variation in God like that we see in the heavenly bodies.

18. *Of his own will* (*boulētheis*). First aorist passive participle of *boulomai*. Repeating the metaphor of birth in verse 15, but in good sense. God as Father acted deliberately of set purpose. *He brought us forth* (*apekuēsen*). First aorist active indicative of *apokueō* (verse 15), only here of the father (4 Macc. 15:17), not of the mother. Regeneration, not birth of all men, though God is the Father in the sense of creation of all men (Acts 17:28f.). *By the word of*

truth (*logōi alētheias*). Instrumental case *logōi*. The reference is thus to the gospel message of salvation even without
the article (II Cor. 6:7) as here, and certainly with the
article (Col. 1:5; Eph. 1:13; II Tim. 2:15). The message
marked by truth (genitive case *alētheias*). *That we should
be* (*eis to einai hēmās*). Purpose clause *eis to* and the infinitive *einai* with the accusative of general reference *hēmās*
(as to us). *A kind of first-fruits* (*aparchēn tina*). "Some
first-fruits" (old word from *aparchomai*), of Christians of
that age. See Rom. 16:5.

19. *Ye know this* (*iste*). Or "know this." Probably the
perfect active indicative (literary form as in Eph. 5:5; Heb.
12:17, unless both are imperative, while in James 4:4 we
have *oidate*, the usual vernacular *Koiné* perfect indicative).
The imperative uses only *iste* and only the context can decide which it is. *Esto* (let be) is imperative. *Swift to hear*
(*tachus eis to akousai*). For this use of *eis to* with the infinitive after an adjective see I Thess. 4:9. For *eis to* after
adjectives see Rom. 16:19. The picture points to listening
to the word of truth (verse 18) and is aimed against violent
and disputatious speech (chapter 3:1–12). The Greek moral-
ists often urge a quick and attentive ear. *Slow to speak*
(*bradus eis to lalēsai*). Same construction and same ingressive aorist active infinitive, slow to begin speaking, not
slow while speaking. *Slow to anger* (*bradus eis orgēn*). He
drops the infinitive here, but he probably means that slow-
ness to speak up when angry will tend to curb the anger.

20. *The wrath of man* (*orgē andros*). Here *anēr* (as opposed to *gunē* woman), not *anthrōpos* of verse 19 (inclusive
of both man and woman). If taken in this sense, it means
that a man's anger (settled indignation in contrast with
thumos, boiling rage or fury) does not necessarily work God's
righteousness. There is such a thing as righteous indignation, but one is not necessarily promoting the cause of God
by his own personal anger. See Acts 10:35 for "working

righteousness," and James 2:9 for "working sin" (*ergazomai* both times).

21. *Wherefore* (*dio*). Because of this principle. See Eph. 4:25. *Putting away* (*apothemenoi*). Second aorist middle participle of *apotithēmi*, to put off, metaphor of removing clothing as in Rom. 13:12; Col. 3:8; Eph. 4:22, 25; I Pet. 2:1. *Filthiness* (*ruparian*). Late word (Plutarch) from *ruparos*, dirty (James 2:2), here only in N.T. Surely a dirty garment. *Overflowing of wickedness* (*perisseian kakias*). *Perisseia* is a late word (from *perissos*, abundant, exceeding), only four times in N.T., in II Cor. 8:2 with *charas* (of joy), in Rom. 5:17 with *charitos* (of grace). *Kakia* (from *kakos*, evil) can be either general like *ruparia* (filthiness, naughtiness), or special like "malice." But any of either sense is a "superfluity." *With meekness* (*en praütēti*). In docility. "The contrast is with *orgē* rather than *kakias*" (Ropes). *The implanted word* (*ton emphuton logon*). This old verbal adjective (from *emphuō* to implant, to grow in), only here in N.T., meaning properly ingrown, inborn, not *emphuteuton* (engrafted). It is "the rooted word" (verse 18), sown in the heart as the soil or garden of God (Matt. 13:3–23; 15:13; I Cor. 3:6). *Able to save* (*dunamenon sōsai*). Cf. I Pet. 1:9; James 2:14; 4:12; 5:20; Rom. 1:16. Ultimate salvation (effective aorist active infinitive *sōsai* from *sōzō*).

22. *But be ye* (*ginesthe de*). Rather, "But keep on becoming" (present middle imperative of *ginomai*). *Doers of the word* (*poiētai logou*). Old word for agent (-*tēs*) from *poieō* to do as in 4:11; Rom. 2:13, but in Acts 17:28 our "poet" (long regarded as a "doer" or "maker"). *Hearers* (*akroatai*). Old word for agent again from *akroamai* (to be a hearer), in N.T. only here and Rom. 2:13. *Deluding yourselves* (*paralogizomenoi heautous*). Present middle (direct) participle of *paralogizomai*, to reckon aside (*para*) and so wrong, to cheat, to deceive. Redundant reflexive *heautous*

with the middle. In N.T. only here and Col. 2:4. Such a man does not delude anyone but himself.

23. *And not a doer* (*kai ou poiētēs*). Condition of first class, assumed as true, and *ou* (rather than *mē*) contrasts *poiētēs* with *akroatēs*. *Unto a man beholding* (*andri kata-noounti*). Associative instrumental case after *eoiken* as in 1:6. Note *andri* as in 1:8 in contrast with *gunaiki* (woman), not *anthrōpōi* (general term for man). Present active participle of *katanoeō* to put the mind down on (*kata, nous*), to consider attentively, to take note of, as in verse 24 (*katenoēsen*). *His natural face* (*to prosōpon tēs geneseōs autou*). "The face of his birth" (origin, lineage, nativity). For this use of *genesis* see 3:6; Matt. 1:1, 18; Luke 1:13. *In a mirror* (*en esoptrōi*). Old word (from *eis, optō*) in N.T. only here and I Cor. 13:12. The mirrors of the ancients were not of glass, but of polished metal (of silver or usually of copper and tin). See *katoptrizomai* in II Cor. 3:18.

24. *He beholdeth himself* (*katenoēsen heauton*). Usually explained as gnomic aorist like those in 1:11, but the ordinary force of the tenses is best here. "He glanced at himself (*katenoēsen* aorist) and off he has gone (*apelēluthen* perfect active) and straightway forgot (*epelatheto*, second aorist middle indicative of *epilanthanomai*) what sort of a man he was" (*hopoios ēn*, back in the picture, imperfect tense). The tenses thus present a vivid and lifelike picture of the careless listener to preaching (Christ's wayside hearer).

25. *He that looketh into* (*ho parakupsas*). First aorist active articular participle of *parakuptō*, old verb, to stoop and look into (John 20:5, 11), to gaze carefully by the side of, to peer into or to peep into (I Pet. 1:12). Here the notion of beside (*para*) or of stooping (*kuptō*) is not strong. Sometimes, as Hort shows, the word means only a cursory glance, but the contrast with verse 24 seems to preclude that here. *The perfect law* (*nomon teleion*). For *teleion* see 1:17. See Rom. 7:12 for Paul's idea of the law of God. James here

refers to the word of truth (1:18), the gospel of grace (Gal.
6:2; Rom. 12:2). *The law of liberty (ton tēs eleutherias).*
"That of liberty," explaining why it is "perfect" (2:12
also), rests on the work of Christ, whose truth sets us free
(John 8:32; II Cor. 3:16; Rom. 8:2). *And so continueth
(kai parameinas).* First aorist active articular participle
again of *paramenō*, parallel with *parakupsas*. *Paramenō* is
to stay beside, and see Phil. 1:25 for contrast with the
simplex *menō*. *Being (genomenos).* Rather, "having become" (second aorist middle participle of *ginomai* to become). *Not a hearer that forgetteth (ouk akroatēs epilēsmonēs).*
"Not a hearer of forgetfulness" (descriptive genitive, marked
by forgetfulness). *Epilēsmonē* is a late and rare word (from
epilēsmōn, forgetful, from *epilanthomai*, to forget, as in verse
24), here only in N.T. *But a doer that worketh (alla poiētēs
ergou).* "But a doer of work," a doer marked by work
(descriptive genitive *ergou*), not by mere listening or mere
talk. *In his doing (en tēi poiēsei autou).* Another beatitude
with *makarios* as in 1:12, like the Beatitudes in Matt.
5:3–12. *Poiēsis* is an old word (from *poieō* for the act of
doing), only here in N.T.

26. *Thinketh himself to be religious (dokei thrēskos einai).*
Condition of first class *(ei-dokei).* *Thrēskos* (of uncertain etymology, perhaps from *threomai*, to mutter forms of prayer)
is predicate nominative after *einai*, agreeing with the subject of *dokei* (either "he seems" or "he thinks"). This
source of self-deception is in saying and doing. The word
thrēskos is found nowhere else except in lexicons. Hatch
(*Essays in Biblical Greek*, pp. 55–57) shows that it refers
to the external observances of public worship, such as
church attendance, almsgiving, prayer, fasting (Matt. 6:1–
18). It is the Pharisaic element in Christian worship. *While
he bridleth not his tongue (mē chalinagōgōn glōssan heautou).*
"Not bridling his own tongue." A reference to verse 19
and the metaphor is repeated in 3:12. This is the earliest

known example of the compound *chalinagōgeō* (*chalinos*, bridle *agō*, to lead). It occurs also in Lucian. The picture is that of a man putting the bridle in his own mouth, not in that of another. See the similar metaphor of muzzling (*phimoō*) one's mouth (Matt. 22:12 *ephimōthē*). *Deceiveth* (*apatōn*). Present active participle from *apatē* (deceit). He plays a trick on himself. *Religion* (*thrēskeia*). Later form of *thrēskiē* (Herodotus) from *thrēskos* above. It means religious worship in its external observances, religious exercise or discipline, but not to the exclusion of reverence. In the N.T. we have it also in Acts 26:5 of Judaism and in Col. 2:18 of worshipping angels. It is vain (*mataios*, feminine form same as masculine) or empty. Comes to nothing.

27. *Pure religion and undefiled* (*thrēskeia kathara kai amiantos*). Numerous examples in papyri and inscriptions of *thrēskeia* for ritual and reverential worship in the Roman Empire (Moulton and Milligan's *Vocabulary*; Deissmann, *St. Paul*, p. 251). As Hort shows, this is not a definition of religion or religious worship, but only a pertinent illustration of the right spirit of religion which leads to such acts. *Before our God and Father* (*para tōi theōi kai patri*). By the side of (*para*) and so from God's standpoint (Mark 10:27). *Amiantos* (compound verbal adjective, alpha privative, *miainō* to defile), puts in negative form (cf. 1:4, 6) the idea in *kathara* (pure, clean). This (*hautē*). Feminine demonstrative pronoun in the predicate agreeing with *thrēskeia*. *To visit* (*episkeptesthai*). Epexegetic (explaining *hautē*) present middle infinitive of *episkeptomai*, common verb to go to see, to inspect, present tense for habit of going to see. See Matt. 25:36, 43 for visiting the sick. *The fatherless and widows* (*orphanous kai chēras*). "The natural objects of charity in the community" (Ropes). *Orphanos* is old word for bereft of father or mother or both. In N.T. only here and John 14:18. Note order (orphans before widows). *Unspotted* (*aspilon*). Old adjective (alpha privative and *spilos*,

spot), spotless. This the more important of the two illustrations and the hardest to execute. *To keep* (*tērein*). Present active infinitive, "to keep on keeping oneself unspecked from the world" (a world, *kosmos*, full of dirt and slime that bespatters the best of men).

CHAPTER II

1. *My brethren* (*adelphoi mou*). Transition to a new topic as in 1:19; 2:5, 14; 3:1; 5:7. *Hold not* (*mē echete*). Present active imperative of *echō* with negative *mē*, exhortation to stop holding or not to have the habit of holding in the fashion condemned. *The faith of our Lord Jesus Christ* (*tēn pistin tou kuriou hēmōn Iēsou Christou*). Clearly objective genitive, not subjective (faith of), but "faith in our Lord Jesus Christ," like *echete pistin theou* (Mark 11:22), "have faith in God." See the same objective genitive with *pistis* in Acts 3:6; Gal. 2:16; Rom. 3:22; Rev. 14:12. Note also the same combination as in 1:1 "our Lord Jesus Christ" (there on a par with God). *The Lord of Glory* (*tēs doxēs*). Simply "the Glory." No word for "Lord" (*kuriou*) in the Greek text. *Tēs doxēs* clearly in apposition with *tou kuriou Iēsou Christou*. James thus terms "our Lord Jesus Christ" the Shekinah Glory of God. See Heb. 9:5 for "the cherubim of Glory." Other New Testament passages where Jesus is pictured as the Glory are Rom. 9:4; II Cor. 4:6; Eph. 1:17; Heb. 1:3. Cf. II Cor. 8:9; Phil. 2:5-11. *With respect of persons* (*en prosōpolēmpsiais*). A Christian word, like *prosōpolēmptēs* (Acts 10:34) and *prosōpolēmpteite* (James 2:9), not in LXX or any previous Greek, but made from *prosōpon lambanein* (Luke 20:21; Gal. 2:6), which is a Hebrew idiom for *panim nasa*, "to lift up the face on a person," to be favorable and so partial to him. See *prosōpolēmpsia* in this sense of partiality (respect of persons) in Rom. 2:11; Col. 3:25; Eph. 6:9 (nowhere else in N.T.). Do not show partiality.

2. *For* (*gar*). An illustration of the prohibition. *If there come in* (*ean eiselthēi*). Condition of third class (supposable

27

case) with *ean* and second (ingressive) aorist active subjunctive of *eiserchomai*. *Into your synagogue* (*eis sunagōgēn
humōn*). The common word for the gathering of Jews for
worship (Luke 12:11) and particularly for the building where
they met (Luke 4:15, 20, 28, etc.). Here the first is the
probable meaning as it clearly is in Heb. 10:25 (*tēn episuna-
gōgēn heautōn*), where the longer compound occurs. It may
seem a bit odd for a Christian church (*ekklēsia*) to be termed
sunagōgē, but James is writing to Jewish Christians and
this is another incidental argument for the early date.
Epiphanius (*Haer*. XXX. 18) states that the Ebionites call
their church *sunagōgē*, not *ekklēsia*. In the fourth century
an inscription has *sunagōgē* for the meeting-house of certain
Christians. *A man with a gold ring* (*anēr chrusodaktulios*).
"A gold-fingered man," "wearing a gold ring." The word
occurs nowhere else, but Lucian has *chrusocheir* (gold-
handed) and Epictetus has *chrusous daktulious* (golden seal-
rings). "Hannibal, after the battle of Cannae, sent as a
great trophy to Carthage, three bushels of gold-rings from
the fingers of Roman knights slain in battle" (Vincent).
In fine clothing (*en esthēti lamprāi*). "In bright (brilliant)
clothing" as in Luke 23:11; Acts 10:30; Rev. 18:41. In
contrast with "vile clothing" (*en ruparāi esthēti*), "new
glossy clothes and old shabby clothes" (Hort). *Ruparos*
(late word from *rupos*, filth, I Pet. 3:21) means filthy, dirty.
In N.T. only here and Rev. 22:11 (filthy). *Poor man*
(*ptōchos*). Beggarly mendicant (Matt. 19:21), the opposite
of *plousios* (rich).

3. *And ye have regard to* (*epiblepsēte de epi*). First aorist
active subjunctive (still with *ean* of verse 2) of *epiblepō*,
followed by repeated preposition *epi*, to gaze upon, old compound, in N.T. only here and Luke 1:48; 9:38. *Weareth*
(*phorounta*). "Wearing," present active participle of the
old frequentative verb *phoreō* (from *pherō*), to bear constantly, to wear (Matt. 11:8). Note repeated article *tēn*

(the) with *esthēta* pointing to verse 2. *And say (kai eipēte)*. Continuing the third-class condition with *ean* and second aorist active subjunctive of *eipon*. *Sit thou here in a good place (su kathou hōde kalōs)*. Emphatic position of *su*, "Do thou sit here in a good place." Present middle imperative of *kathēmai* to sit for the literary *kathēso*. See Matt. 23:6 for the first seats in the synagogue (places of honour). *And ye say to the poor man (kai tōi ptōchōi eipēte)*. Third class condition with *ean* continued as before (*eipēte*). Note article *tōi* pointing to verse 2. *Stand thou there (su stēthi ekei)*. Second aorist (intransitive) active imperative of *histēmi*, to place. Ingressive aorist, Take a stand. *Su* emphatic again. The MSS. vary in the position of *ekei* (there). *Or sit under my footstool (ē kathou hupo to hupopodion mou)*. For this use of *hupo* "down against" or "down beside" see Ex. 19:17 *hupo to oros* ("at the foot of the mountain") and *hupo se* ("at thy feet") (Deut. 33:3). Conquerors often placed their feet on the necks of the victims (Luke 20:43).

4. *Are ye not divided in your own mind? (ou diekrithēte en heautois;)*. First aorist (gnomic) passive indicative of *diakrinō*, to separate, conclusion of the third-class condition (future) in a rhetorical question in the gnomic aorist (as if past) with *ou* expecting an affirmative answer. For this idiom (gnomic aorist) in a conclusion of the third-class condition see I Cor. 7:28. "Were ye not divided in (among) yourselves?" Cf. 1:6; Matt. 21:21. *Judges with evil thoughts (kritai dialogismōn ponērōn)*. Descriptive genitive as in 1:25. *Dialogismos* is an old word for reasoning (Rom. 1:21). Reasoning is not necessarily evil, but see Matt. 15:19 (*ponēroi*) and Mark 7:21 (*kakoi*) for evil reasonings, and I Tim. 2:8 without an adjective. See James 1:8 and 4:8 for *dipsuchos*. They are guilty of partiality (a divided mind) as between the two strangers.

5. *Did not God choose? (ouch ho theos exelexato;)*. Affirmative answer expected. First aorist middle (indirect, God

chose for himself) indicative of *eklegō*, the very form used
by Paul three times of God's choice in I Cor. 1:27f. *As to
the world* (*tōi kosmōi*). The ethical dative of interest, as
the world looks at it as in Acts 7:20; I Cor. 1:18; II Cor.
10:4; James 4:4. By the use of the article (the poor) James
does not affirm that God chose all the poor, but only that
he did choose poor people (Matt. 10:23–26; I Cor. 1:26–28).
Rich in faith (*plousious en pistei*). Rich because of their
faith. As he has shown in 1:9f. *Which he promised* (*hēs
epeggeilato*). Genitive of the accusative relative *hēn* attracted to the case of the antecedent *basileias* (the Messianic
kingdom), the same verb and idea already in 1:12 (*epēggeilato*). Cf. the beatitude of Jesus in Matt. 5:3 for the
poor in spirit.

6. *But ye have dishonoured the poor man* (*humeis de ēti-
masate ton ptōchon*). First aorist active indicative of *ati-
mazō*, old verb from *atimos*, dishonoured (Matt. 13:57). In
the act of partiality pictured in 2:3. *Oppress you* (*kata-
dunasteuousin humōn*). Not very common compound (*kata-
dunasteuō*, present active indicative, from *kata* and *dunastēs*,
potentate, Luke 1:52), used of the devil in Acts 10-38 (only
other N.T. example). Examples in papyri of harsh treatment by men in authority. Already poor Christians are
feeling pressure from rich Jews as overlords. *Drag you*
(*helkousin humas*). Old and vigorous word for violent treatment, as of Paul in Acts 16:19; 21:30. Cf. such violence in
Luke 12:58; Acts 8:3. *Before the judgment-seats* (*eis kritēria*).
"To courts of justice" as in I Cor. 6:2, 4 (only other N.T.
examples). Common in the papyri in this sense. From
krinō to judge, *kritēs* (judge), place where judgment is given

7. *Blaspheme* (*blasphēmousin*). Present active indicative
of common verb *blasphēmeō* (from *blasphēmos*, speaking evil,
blax or *blaptō* and *phēmē*), as in Luke 22:65. *The honourable
name* (*to kalon onoma*). "The beautiful name." *By the
which ye were called* (*to epiklēthen eph' humās*). "The one

called upon you" (first aorist passive articular participle
of *epikaleō*, to put a name upon, to give a surname to, as
Acts 10:18). What name is that? Almost certainly the
name of Christ as we see it in Acts 11:26; 26:28; I Pet.
4:14, 16. It was blasphemy to speak against Christ as some
Jews and Gentiles were doing (Acts 13:45; 18:6; 26:11; I
Cor. 12:3; I Tim. 1:13). Cf. Acts 15:17.

8. *Howbeit* (*mentoi*). Probably not adversative here, but
simply confirmatory, "if now," "if indeed," "if really."
Common in Xenophon in this sense. See the contrast (*de*)
in verse 9. *If ye fulfil* (*ei teleite*). Condition of first class,
assumed as true with *ei* and present active indicative of
teleō, old verb, to bring to completion, occurring in Rom.
2:27 also with *nomos* (law). Jesus used *plēroō* in Matt.
4:17. James has *tēreō* in 2:10. *The royal law* (*nomon basil-
ikon*). Old adjective for royal, regal (from *basileus* king),
as of an officer (John 4:46). But why applied to *nomos*?
The Romans had a phrase, *lex regia*, which came from the
king when they had kings. The absence of the article is
common with *nomos* (4:11). It can mean a law fit to guide
a king, or such as a king would choose, or even the king of
laws. Jesus had said that on the law of love hang all the
law and the prophets (Matt. 22:40), and he had given the
Golden Rule as the substance of the Law and the prophets
(Matt. 7:12). This is probably the royal law which is
violated by partiality (James 2:3). It is in accord with the
Scripture quoted here (Lev. 19:18) and ratified by Jesus
(Luke 10:28).

9. *But if ye have respect of persons* (*ei de prosōpolēmpteite*).
Condition of first class by contrast with that in verse 8.
For this verb (present active indicative), formed from *prosōpon lambanō*, here alone in the N.T., see in 2:1. A direct
reference to the partiality there pictured. *Ye commit sin*
(*hamartian ergazesthe*). "Ye work a sin." A serious charge,
apparently, for what was regarded as a trifling fault. See

Matt. 7:23, *hoi ergazomenoi tēn anomian* (ye that work iniquity), an apparent reminiscence of the words of Jesus there (from Ps. 6:8). *Being convicted* (*elegchomenoi*). Present passive participle of *elegchō*, to convict by proof of guilt (John 3:20; 8:9, 46; I Cor. 14:24). *As transgressors* (*hōs parabatai*). For this word from *parabainō*, to step across, to transgress, see Gal. 2:18; Rom. 2:25, 27. See this very sin of partiality condemned in Lev. 19:15; Deut. 1:17; 16:19. To the law and to the testimony.

10. *Whosoever shall keep* (*hostis tērēsēi*). Indefinite relative clause with *hostis* and aorist active subjunctive of *tēreō*, old verb, to guard (from *tēros* guarding), as in Matt. 27:36, without *an* (though often used, but only one example of modal *ean = an* in James, *viz.*, 4:4). This modal *an* (*ean*) merely interprets the sentence as either more indefinite or more definite (Robertson, *Grammar*, p. 957f.). *And yet stumble in one point* (*ptaisēi de en heni*). First aorist active subjunctive also of *ptaiō*, old verb, to trip, as in 3:2 and Rom. 11:11. "It is incipient falling" (Hort). *He is become* (*gegonen*). Second perfect indicative of *ginomai*, "he has become" by that one stumble. *Guilty of all* (*pantōn enochos*). Genitive of the crime with *enochos*, old adjective from *enechō* (to hold on or in), held in, as in Mark 3:29. This is law. To be a lawbreaker one does not have to violate all the laws, but he must keep all the law (*holon ton nomon*) to be a law-abiding citizen, even laws that one does not like. See Matt. 5:18f. for this same principle. There is Talmudic parallel: "If a man do all, but omit one, he is guilty for all and each." This is a pertinent principle also for those who try to save themselves. But James is urging obedience to all God's laws.

11. *He that said* (*ho eipōn*)—*said also* (*eipen kai*). The unity of the law lies in the Lawgiver who spoke both prohibitions (*mē* and the aorist active subjunctive in each one, *moicheusēis, phoneusēis*). The order here is that of B in

Ex. 20 (Luke 18:20; Rom. 13:9), but not in Matt. 5:21, 27 (with *ou* and future indicative). *Now if thou dost not commit adultery, but killest* (*ei de ou moicheueis, phoneueis de*). Condition of first class with *ou* (not *mē*) because of the contrast with *de*, whereas *ei mē* would mean "unless," a different idea. So *ou* in 1:23. *A transgressor of the law* (*parabatēs nomou*) as in verse 9. Murder springs out of anger (Matt. 5:21–26). People free from fleshly sins have often "made their condemnation of fleshly sins an excuse for indulgence towards spiritual sins" (Hort).

12. *So speak ye, and so do* (*houtōs laleite kai houtōs poieite*). Present active imperatives as a habit. For the combination see 1:19–21 contrasted with 1:22–25, and 1:26 with 1:27. *By a law of liberty* (*dia nomou eleutherias*). The law pictured in 1:25, but law, after all, not individual caprice of "personal liberty." See Rom. 2:12 for this same use of *dia* with *krinō* in the sense of accompaniment as in Rom. 2:27; 4:11; 14:20. "Under the law of liberty."

13. *Without mercy* (*aneleos*). Found here only save a doubtful papyrus example (*aneleōs*) for the vernacular *anileōs* and the Attic *anēleēs*. For this principle of requital see Matt. 5:7; 6:14; 7:1f.; 18:33. *Glorieth against* (*katakauchātai*). Present middle indicative of the old compound verb *katakauchaomai*, to exult over (down), in N.T. only here, 3:14; Rom. 11:18. Only mercy can triumph over justice with God and men. "Mercy is clothed with the divine glory and stands by the throne of God" (Chrysostom). See Rom. 8:31–39; Matt. 9:13; 12:7.

14. *What doth it profit?* (*ti ophelos;*). Rhetorical question, almost of impatience. Old word from *ophellō*, to increase, in N.T. only here, verse 16, and I Cor. 15:32. "*Ti ophelos* was a common expression in the vivacious style of a moral diatribe" (Ropes). *If a man say* (*ean legēi tis*). Condition of third class with *ean* and the present active subjunctive of *legō*, "if one keep on saying." *He hath faith* (*pistin*

echein). Infinitive in indirect assertion after *legei*. *But have not works* (*erga de mē echēi*). Third-class condition continued, "but keeps on not having (*mē* and present active subjunctive *echēi*) works." It is the spurious claim to faith that James here condemns. *Can that faith save him?* (*mē dunatai hē pistis sōsai auton;*). Negative answer expected (*mē*). Effective aorist active infinitive *sōsai* (from *sōzō*). The article *hē* here is almost demonstrative in force as it is in origin, referring to the claim of faith without works just made.

15. *If a brother or sister be naked* (*ean adelphos ē adelphē gumnoi huparchōsin*). Condition again of third class (supposable case) with *ean* and present active subjunctive of *huparchō*, to exist, in the plural though *ē* (or) is used and not *kai* (and). Hence *gumnoi* is masculine plural in the predicate nominative. It does not here mean absolutely naked, but without sufficient clothing as in Matt. 25:36ff.; John 21:7; Acts 19:16. *In lack of daily food* (*leipomenoi tēs ephēmerou trophēs*). Present passive participle of *leipō* and ablative case *trophēs* like *leipetai sophias* (1:5). The old adjective *ephēmeros* (*ho epi hēmeran ōn*, that which is for a day) occurs here only in the N.T., though *ephēmeria* (daily routine) is found in Luke 1:5, 8. This phrase occurs in Diodorus, but not in LXX.

16. *And one of you say unto them* (*eipēi de tis autois ex humōn*). Third-class condition again continued from verse 15 with second aorist active subjunctive *eipēi*. *Go in peace* (*hupagete en eirēnēi*). Present active imperative of *hupagō*. Common Jewish farewell (Judges 18:6; I Sam. 1:17; 20:42; II Sam. 15:9). Used by Jesus (Mark 5:34; Luke 7:50). *Be ye warmed and filled* (*thermainesthe kai chortazesthe*). Present imperative either middle (direct) or passive. We have *thermainomai* as a direct middle in John 18:18 (were warming themselves) and that makes good sense here: "Warm yourselves." *Chortazō* was originally used for pas-

turing cattle, but came to be used of men also as here. "Feed yourselves" (if middle, as is likely). Instead of warm clothes and satisfying food they get only empty words to look out for themselves. *And yet ye give not* (*mē dōte de*). Third-class condition with *de* (and yet) and *mē* and the second aorist active subjunctive of *didōmi*, to give, cold deeds with warm words. *The things needful to the body* (*ta epitēdeia tou sōmatos*). "The necessities of the body" (the necessaries of life). Old adjective from adverb *epitēdes* (enough), only here in N.T. *What doth it profit?* (*ti ophelos;*). As in verse 14 and here the conclusion (apodosis) of the long condition begun in verse 15.

17. *If it have not works* (*ean mē echēi erga*). Another condition of the third class with *ean* and *mē* and the present active subjunctive of *echō*, "if it keep on not having works." *In itself* (*kath' heautēn*). In and of itself (according to itself), inwardly and outwardly dead (*nekra*). Same idiom in Acts 28:16; Rom. 14:22. It is a dead faith.

18. *Yea, a man will say* (*all' erei tis*). Future active of *eipon*. But *all'* here is almost certainly adversative (But some one will say), not confirmatory. James introduces an imaginary objector who speaks one sentence: "Thou hast faith and I have works" (*Su pistin echeis kagō erga echō*). Then James answers this objector. The objector can be regarded as asking a short question: "Hast thou faith?" In that case James replies: "I have works also." *Show me thy faith apart from thy works* (*deixon moi tēn pistin sou chōris tōn ergōn*). This is the reply of James to the objector. First aorist active imperative of *deiknumi*, tense of urgency. The point lies in *chōris*, which means not "without," but "apart from," as in Heb. 11:6 (with the ablative case), "the works that properly belong to it and should characterise it" (Hort). James challenges the objector to do this. *And I by my works will shew thee my faith* (*kagō soi deixō ek tōn ergōn mou tēn pistin*). It is not faith *or* works, but proof

of real faith (live faith *vs.* dead faith). The mere profession
of faith with no works or profession of faith shown to be
alive by works. This is the alternative clearly stated. Note
pistin (faith) in both cases. James is not here discussing
"works" (ceremonial works) as a means of salvation as
Paul in Gal. 3 and Rom. 4, but works as proof of faith.

19. *Thou believest that God is one* (*su pisteueis hoti heis
theos estin*). James goes on with his reply and takes up
mere creed apart from works, belief that God exists (there
is one God), a fundamental doctrine, but that is not belief
or trust in God. It may be mere creed. *Thou doest well*
(*kalōs poieis*). That is good as far as it goes, which is not
far. *The demons also believe* (*kai ta daimonia pisteuousin*).
They go that far (the same verb *pisteuō*). They never
doubt the fact of God's existence. *And shudder* (*kai phris-
sousin*). Present active indicative of *phrissō*, old onomatopoetic verb to bristle up, to shudder, only here in N.T.
Like Latin *horreo* (horror, standing of the hair on end with
terror). The demons do more than believe a fact. They
shudder at it.

20. *But wilt thou know?* (*theleis de gnōnai?*). "But dost
thou wish to know?" Ingressive aorist active infinitive of
ginōskō (come to know). James here introduces a new argument like Rom. 13:3. *O vain man* (*ō anthrōpe kene*). Goes
on with the singular objector and demolishes him. For
"empty" (deficient) Paul uses *aphrōn* (fool) in I Cor. 15:36
and just *anthrōpe* in Rom. 2:1; 9:20. *Barren* (*arge*). See
II Pet. 1:8 (not idle nor unfruitful) and Matt. 12:36, but
Hort urges "inactive" as the idea here, like money with no
interest and land with no crops.

21. *Justified by works* (*ex ergōn edikaiōthē*). First aorist
passive indicative of *dikaioō* (see Galatians and Romans for
this verb, to declare righteous, to set right) in a question
with *ouk* expecting an affirmative answer. This is the phrase
that is often held to be flatly opposed to Paul's statement in

Rom. 4:1–5, where Paul pointedly says that it was the faith of Abraham (Rom. 4:9) that was reckoned to Abraham for righteousness, not his works. But Paul is talking about the faith of Abraham before his circumcision (4:10) as the basis of his being set right with God, which faith is symbolized in the circumcision. James makes plain his meaning also. *In that he offered up Isaac his son upon the altar* (*anenegkas Isaak ton huion autou epi to thusiastērion*). They use the same words, but they are talking of different acts. James points to the offering (*anenegkas* second aorist—with first aorist ending—active participle of *anapherō*) of Isaac on the altar (Gen. 22:16f.) as *proof* of the faith that Abraham already had. Paul discusses Abraham's faith as the basis of his justification, that and not his circumcision. There is no contradiction at all between James and Paul. Neither is answering the other. Paul may or may not have seen the Epistle of James, who stood by him loyally in the Conference in Jerusalem (Acts 15 and Gal. 2).

22. *Thou seest* (*blepeis*). Obvious enough with any eyes to see. This may be a question, seest thou? *Wrought with* (*sunergei*). Imperfect active of *sunergeō*, old verb for which see Rom. 8:28. Followed by associative-instrumental case *ergois*. Faith coöperated with the deed of offering up Isaac. *Was made perfect* (*eteleiōthē*). First aorist passive indicative of *teleioō*, to carry to the end, to complete like love in I John 4:18. See James 1:4 for *teleion ergon*.

23. *Was fulfilled* (*eplērōthē*). First aorist passive indicative of *plēroō*, the usual verb for fulfilling Scripture. So James quotes Gen. 15:6 as proving his point in verse 21 that Abraham had works with his faith, the very same passage that Paul quotes in Rom. 4:3 to show that Abraham's faith preceded his circumcision and was the basis of his justification. And both James and Paul are right, each to illustrate a different point. *And he was called the friend of God* (*kai philos theou eklēthē*). First aorist passive indicative

of *kaleō*. Not a part of the Scripture quoted. Philo calls
Abraham the friend of God and see *Jubilees* 19:9; 30:20.
The Arabs today speak of Abraham as God's friend. It
was evidently a common description before James used it,
as in Is. 41:8; II Chron. 20:7.

24. *Ye see* (*horāte*). Present indicative active of *horaō*.
Now he uses the plural again as in 2:14. *Is justified* (*dikai-
outai*). Present passive indicative of *dikaioō*, here not "is
made righteous," but "is shown to be righteous." James
is discussing the proof of faith, not the initial act of being
set right with God (Paul's idea in Rom. 4:1–10). *And not
only by faith* (*kai ouk ek pisteōs monon*). This phrase clears
up the meaning of James. Faith (live faith) is what we must
all have (2:18), only it must shew itself also in deeds as
Abraham's did.

25. *Rahab the harlot* (*Raab hē pornē*). Her vicious life
she left behind, but the name clung to her always. For our
purposes the argument of James may seem stronger without the example of Rahab (Josh. 2:1–21, 6:17, 22–25; Matt.
1:5; Heb. 11:31). It is even said in Jewish Midrash that
Rahab married Joshua and became an ancestor of Jeremiah
and Ezekiel. *In that she received* (*hupodexamenē*). First
aorist middle participle of *hupodechomai*, to welcome. *The
messengers* (*tous aggelous*). Original meaning of *aggelos*
(Matt. 11:10). In Heb. 11:31 we have *kataskopous* (spies,
scouts). *Sent out* (*ekbalousa*). Second aorist active participle of *ekballō*, to hurl out. *Another way* (*heterāi hodōi*).
"By another way" (instrumental case), by a window instead of a door (Josh. 2:15f.).

26. *Apart from the spirit* (*chōris pneumatos*). "Apart from
breath" (the breath of life). It is not easy to tell when one
is dead, but the absence of a sign of breath on a glass before
the mouth and nose is proof of death. Startling picture of
dead faith in our churches and church members with only
a name to live (Rev. 3:2).

CHAPTER III

1. *Be not many teachers (mē polloi didaskaloi ginesthe).*
Prohibition with *mē* and present middle imperative of *ginomai.* "Stop becoming many teachers" (so many of you).
There is thus a clear complaint that too many of the Jewish
Christians were attempting to teach what they did not
clearly comprehend. There was a call for wise teachers
(verses 13f.), not for foolish ones. This soon became an
acute question, as one can see in I Cor. 12 to 14. They were
not all teachers (I Cor. 12:28f.; 14:26). The teacher is
here treated as the wise man (3:13–18) as he ought to be.
The rabbi was the teacher (Matt. 23:7f.; John 1:38; 3:10;
20:16). Teachers occupied an honourable position among
the Christians (Eph. 4:11; Acts 13:1). James counts himself a teacher (we shall receive, 3:1) and this discussion is
linked on with 1:19–27. Teachers are necessary, but in-
competent and unworthy ones do much harm. *Heavier
judgment (meizon krima).* "Greater sentence." See Mark
12:40 and Luke 20:47 for *perrisoteron krima* (the sentence
from the judge, Rom. 13:2). The reason is obvious. The
pretence of knowledge adds to the teacher's responsibility
and condemnation.

2. *In many things (polla).* Accusative neuter plural either
cognate with *ptaiomen* or accusative of general reference.
On *ptaiomen* (stumble) see on 2:10. James includes himself in this list of stumblers. *If not (ei-ou).* Condition of
first class with *ou* (not *mē*) negativing the verb *ptaiei. In
word (en logōi).* In speech. The teacher uses his tongue
constantly and so is in particular peril on this score. *The
same (houtos).* "This one" (not *ho autos* the same). *A
perfect man (teleios anēr).* "A perfect husband" also, for

anēr is husband as well as man in distinction from woman (*gunē*). The wife is at liberty to test her husband by this rule of the tongue. *To bridle the whole body also* (*chalinagōgēsai kai holon to sōma*). See 1:26 for this rare verb applied to the tongue (*glōssan*). Here the same metaphor is used and shown to apply to the whole body as horses are led by the mouth. The man follows his own mouth whether he controls the bridle therein (1:26) or someone else holds the reins. James apparently means that the man who bridles his tongue does not stumble in speech and is able also to control his whole body with all its passions. See Titus 1:11 about stopping people's mouths (*epistomizō*).

3. *If we put* (*ei ballomen*). Condition of the first class assumed as true. *The horses' bridles* (*tōn hippōn tous chalinous*). *Hippōn* (genitive plural of *hippos*, horse, old word, in N.T. only here except in the Apocalypse), put first because the first of the several illustrations of the power and the peril of the tongue. This is the only N.T. example of *chalinos*, old word for bridle (from *chalaō* to slacken, let down), except Rev. 14:20. *That they may obey us* (*eis to peithesthai autous hēmin*). Present middle infinitive of *peithō* with *eis to* as a purpose clause with the dative *hēmin* after *peithesthai* and *autous* the accusative of general reference. *We turn about* (*metagomen*). Present active indicative of *metagō*, late compound to change the direction (*meta, agō*), to guide, in N.T. only here and verse 4. The body of the horse follows his mouth, guided by the bridle.

4. *The ships also* (*kai ta ploia*). Old word from *pleō*, to sail (Matt. 4:21). Another metaphor like "horses" (*hippoi*). "There is more imagery drawn from mere natural phenomena in the one short Epistle of James than in all St. Paul's epistles put together" (Howson). *Though they are so great* (*tēlikauta onta*). Concessive participle of *eimi*. The quantitative pronoun *tēlikoutos* occurs in the N.T. only here, II Cor. 1:10; Heb. 2:3; Rev. 16:18. If James had only seen

the modern mammoth ships. But the ship on which Paul went to Malta carried 276 persons (Acts 27:37). *And are driven* (*kai elaunomena*). Present passive participle of *elaunō*, old verb, in this sense (II Pet. 2:17) for rowing (Mark 6:48; John 6:19). *Rough* (*sklēron*). Old adjective (from *skellō*, to dry up), harsh, stiff, hard (Matt. 25:24). *Are yet turned* (*metagetai*). Present passive indicative of the same verb, *metagō*, in verse 3. James is fond of repeating words (1:13f.; 2:14, 16; 2:21, 25). *By a very small rudder* (*hupo elachistou pēdaliou*). For the use of *hupo* (under) with things see Luke 8:14; II Pet. 2:7. There is possibly personification in the use of *hupo* for agency in James 1:14; 2:9; Col. 2:18. *Pēdaliou* (from *pēdon*, the blade of an oar) is an old word, in N.T. only here and Acts 27:40. *Elachistou* is the elative superlative as in I Cor. 4:3 (from the Epic *elachus* for *mikros*). *The impulse* (*hē hormē*). Old word for rapid, violent motion, here of the hand that worked the rudder, in N.T. only here and Acts 14:5 (rush or onset of the people). *Of the steersman* (*tou euthunontos*). Present active genitive articular participle of *euthunō*, old verb, to make straight (from *euthus*, straight, level, Mark 1:3), in N.T. only here and John 1:23. Used also of the shepherd, the charioteer, and today it would apply to the chauffeur. "The twin figure of the control of horse and of ship are frequently found together in later Greek writers" (Ropes). As in Plutarch and Philo. *Willeth* (*bouletai*). Present middle indicative of *boulomai*, common verb to will. Here intention of the steersman lies back of the impact of the hand on the rudder.

5. *A little member* (*mikron melos*). *Melos* is old and common word for members of the human body (I Cor. 12:12, etc.; Rom. 6:13, etc.). *Boasteth great things* (*megala auchei*). Present active indicative of *aucheō*, old verb, here only in N.T. The best MSS. here separate *megala* from *aucheō*, though *megalaucheō* does occur in Æschylus, Plato, etc.

Megala is in contrast with *mikron*. *How much—how small* (*hēlikon—hēlikēn*). The same relative form for two indirect questions together, "What-sized fire kindles what-sized forest?" For double interrogatives see Mark 15:24. The verb *anaptei* is present active indicative of *anaptō*, to set fire to, to kindle (Luke 12:49, only other N.T. example except some MSS. in Acts 28:2). *Hulēn* is accusative case, object of *anaptei*, and occurs here only in N.T., though old word for forest, wood. Forest fires were common in ancient times as now, and were usually caused by small sparks carelessly thrown.

6. The tongue is a fire (*hē glōssa pur*). So necessarily since there is no article with *pur* (apparently same word as German *feuer*, Latin *purus*, English pure, fire). This metaphor of fire is applied to the tongue in Prov. 16:27; 26:18–22; Sirach 28:22. *The world of iniquity* (*ho kosmos tēs adikias*). A difficult phrase, impossible to understand according to Ropes as it stands. If the comma is put after *pur* instead of after *adikias*, then the phrase may be the predicate with *kathistatai* (present passive indicative of *kathistēmi*, "is constituted," or the present middle "presents itself"). Even so, *kosmos* remains a difficulty, whether it means the "ornament" (I Pet. 3:3) or "evil world" (James 1:27) or just "world" in the sense of widespread power for evil. The genitive *adikias* is probably descriptive (or qualitative). Clearly James means to say that the tongue can play havoc in the members of the human body. *Which defileth the whole body* (*hē spilousa holon to sōma*). Present active participle of *spiloō* late Koiné, verb, to stain from *spilos* (spot, also late word, in N.T. only in Eph. 5:27; II Pet. 2:13), in N.T. only here and Jude 23. Cf. 1:27 *aspilon* (unspotted). *Setteth on fire* (*phlogizousa*). Present active participle of *phlogizō*, old verb, to set on fire, to ignite, from *phlox* (flame), in N.T. only in this verse. See *anaptei* (verse 5). *The wheel of nature* (*ton trochon geneseōs*). Old word for wheel

(from *trechō*, to run), only here in N.T. "One of the hardest passages in the Bible" (Hort). To what does *trochon*
refer? For *geneseōs* see 1:23 apparently in the same sense.
Vincent suggests "the wheel of birth" (cf. Matt. 1:1, 18).
The ancient writers often use this same phrase (or *kuklos,*
cycle, in place of *trochos*), but either in a physiological or a
philosophical sense. James may have caught the metaphor
from the current use, but certainly he has no such Orphic
or Pythagorean doctrine of the transmigration of souls, "the
unending round of death and rebirth" (Ropes). The wheel
of life may be considered either in motion or standing still,
though setting on fire implies motion. There is no reference
to the zodiac. *And is set on fire by hell* (*kai phlogizomenē
hupo gehennēs*). Present passive participle of *phlogizō*, giving the continual source of the fire in the tongue. For the
metaphor of fire with *gehenna* see Matt. 5:22.

7. *Kind* (*phusis*). Old word from *phuō*, order of nature
(Rom. 1:26), here of all animals and man, in II Pet. 1:4
of God and redeemed men. *Of beasts* (*thēriōn*). Old word
diminutive from *thēr* and so "little beasts" originally, then
wild animals in general (Mark 1:13), or quadrupeds as here.
These four classes of animals come from Gen. 9:2f. *Birds*
(*peteinōn*). Old word for flying animals (from *petomai*, to
fly), as in Matt. 13:4. *Creeping things* (*herpetōn*). Old
word from *herpō*, to crawl (Latin *serpo*), hence serpents.
Things in the sea (*enaliōn*). Old adjective (*en, hals*, sea,
salt) in the sea, here only in N.T. The four groups are
put in two pairs here by the use of *te kai* with the first two
and the second two. See a different classification in Acts
10:12; 11:6. *Is tamed* (*damazetai*). Present passive indicative of *damazō*, old verb kin to Latin *dominus* and English
tame, in N.T. only in this passage and Mark 5:4. The
present tense gives the general picture of the continuous
process through the ages of man's lordship over the animals
as stated in Gen. 1:28. *Hath been tamed* (*dedamastai*). Per-

fect passive indicative of the same verb, repeated to present the state of conquest in some cases (domestic animals, for instance). *By mankind* (*tēi phusei tēi anthrōpinēi*). Instrumental case with repeated article and repetition also of *phusis*, "by the nature the human." For *anthrōpinos* see Acts 17:25.

8. *No one* (*oudeis*). Especially his own tongue and by himself, but one has the help of the Holy Spirit. *A restless evil* (*akatastaton kakon*). Correct reading, not *akatascheton*, for which see 1:8. The tongue is evil when set on fire by hell, not evil necessarily. *Full of deadly poison* (*mestē iou thanatēphorou*). Feminine adjective agreeing with *glōssa*, not with *kakon* (neuter). *Iou* (poison here, as in Rom. 3:13, but rust in 5:3, only N.T. examples), old word. Genitive case after *mestē* (full of). *Thanatēphorou*, old compound adjective (from *thanatos*, death, *pherō*, to bear or bring), death-bringing. Here only in N.T. Like the restless death-bringing tongue of the asp before it strikes.

9. *Therewith* (*en autēi*). This instrumental use of *en* is not merely Hebraistic, but appears in late *Koiné* writers (Moulton, *Prol.*, pp. 11f., 61f.). See also Rom. 15:6. *We bless* (*eulogoumen*). Present active indicative of *eulogeō*, old verb from *eulogos* (a good word, *eu*, *logos*), as in Luke 1:64 of God. "This is the highest function of speech" (Hort). *The Lord and Father* (*ton kurion kai patera*). Both terms applied to God. *Curse we* (*katarōmetha*). Present middle indicative of the old compound verb *kataraomai*, to curse (from *katara* a curse), as in Luke 6:28. *Which are made after the likeness of God* (*tous kath' homoiōsin theou gegonotas*). Second perfect articular participle of *ginomai* and *homoiōsis*, old word from *homoioō* (to make like), making like, here only in N.T. (from Gen. 1:26; 9:6), the usual word being *homoiōma*, resemblance (Phil. 2:7). It is this image of God which sets man above the beasts. Cf. II Cor. 3:18.

10. *Ought not* (*ou chrē*). The only use of this old im-

personal verb (from *chraō*) in the N.T. It is more like *prepei* (it is appropriate) than *dei* (it is necessary). It is a moral incongruity for blessing and cursing to come out of the same mouth. *So to be* (*houtōs ginesthai*). "So to keep on happening," not just "to be," present middle infinitive of *ginomai*.

11. *The fountain* (*hē pēgē*). Old word for spring (John 4:14). *Opening* (*opēs*). Old word for fissure in the earth, in N.T. only here and Heb. 11:38 (caves). *Send forth* (*bruei*). Present active indicative of *bruō*, old verb, to bubble up, to gush forth, here only in N.T. The use of *mēti* shows that a negative answer is expected in this rhetor ical question. *The sweet and the bitter* (*to gluku kai to pikron*). Cognate accusatives with *bruei*. Separate articles to distinguish sharply the two things. The neuter singular articular adjective is a common way of presenting a quality. *Glukus* is an old adjective (in N.T. only here and Rev. 10:9f.), the opposite of *pikron* (from old root, to cut, to prick), in N.T. only here and verse 14 (sharp, harsh).

12. *Can?* (*mē dunatai;*). Negative answer expected. See the same metaphor in Matt. 7:16f. *Fig-tree* (*sukē*). Old and common word (Matt. 21:19f.). *Figs* (*suka*). Ripe fruit of *hē sukē*. *Olives* (*elaias*). Elsewhere in the N.T. for olive-trees as Matt. 21:1. *Vine* (*ampelos*). Old word (Matt. 26:29). *Salt water* (*halukon*). Old adjective from *hals* (*halas* salt), here only in N.T.

13. *Who* (*Tis*). Rhetorical interrogative like Luke 11:11. Common in Paul and characteristic of the diatribe. James here returns to the standpoint of verse 1 about many teachers. Speech and wisdom are both liable to abuse (I Cor. 1:5, 17; 2:1–3:20). *Wise and understanding* (*sophos kai epistēmōn*). *Sophos* is used for the practical teacher (verse 1), *epistēmōn* (old word from *epistamai*, here only in N.T.) for an expert, a skilled and scientific person with a tone of superiority. In Deut. 1:13, 15; 4:6, the two terms are prac-

tically synonyms. *Let him shew* (*deixatō*). First aorist active imperative of *deiknumi*, old verb to show. As about faith in 2:18. Emphatic position of this verb. *By his good life* (*ek tēs kalēs anastrophēs*). For this literary *Koiné* word from *anastrephomai* (walk, conduct) see Gal. 1:13. Actions speak louder than words even in the case of the professional wise man. Cf. I Pet. 1:15. *In meekness of wisdom* (*en prautēti sophias*). As in 1:21 of the listener, so here of the teacher. Cf. Matt. 5:5; 11:29 and Zach. 9:9 of King Messiah quoted in Matt. 21:5. Startling combination.

14. *Bitter jealousy* (*zēlon pikron*). *Zēlos* occurs in N.T. in good sense (John 2:17) and bad sense (Acts 5:17). Pride of knowledge is evil (I Cor. 8:1) and leaves a bitter taste. See "root of bitterness" in Heb. 12:14 (cf. Eph. 4:31). This is a condition of the first class. *Faction* (*erithian*). Late word, from *erithos* (hireling, from *eritheuō* to spin wool), a pushing forward for personal ends, partisanship, as in Phil. 1:16. *In your heart* (*en tēi kardiāi humōn*). The real fountain (*pēgē*, verse 11). *Glory not* (*mē katakauchāsthe*). Present middle imperative of *katakauchaomai*, for which see 2:13. Wisdom is essential for the teacher. Boasting arrogance disproves the possession of wisdom. *Lie not against the truth* (*pseudesthe kata tēs alētheias*). Present middle imperative of *pseudomai*, old verb, to play false, with *mē* carried over. Lying against the truth is futile. By your conduct do not belie the truth which you teach; a solemn and needed lesson. Cf. Rom. 1:18f., 2:18, 20.

15. *This wisdom* (*hautē hē sophia*). All talk and disproved by the life, counterfeit wisdom, not real wisdom (1:5; 3:17). *Coming down from above* (*katerchomenē anōthen*). As in 1:5, 17. All true wisdom comes from God. *Earthly* (*epigeios*). Old adjective, on earth (*epi, gē*), as in John 3:12, then with earthly limitations (Phil. 3:19), as here. *Sensual* (*psuchikē*). Old adjective, belonging to the *psuchē*, the sensuous or animal life (I Cor. 2:14 and here). *Devilish* (*daimoniōdēs*).

Late adjective from *daimonion* (demon) and so demoniacal or demon-like, here only in N.T.

16. *Confusion* (*akatastasia*). Late word (from *akatastatos*, 1:8; 3:8), a state of disorder (I Cor. 14:33). *Vile* (*phaulon*). Kin to German *faul*, first slight, ordinary, then bad. The steps are cheap, paltry, evil. Opposed to *agatha* (good) in John 5:39.

17. *First pure* (*prōton men hagnē*). First in rank and time. *Hagnos* is from the same root as *hagios* (holy), old adjective, pure from fault, not half-good and half-bad, like that above. *Then peaceable* (*epeita eirēnikē*). Old adjective from *eirēnē* (peace), loving peace here, bringing peace in Heb. 12:11 (only N.T. examples). But clearly great as peace is, purity (righteousness) comes before peace and peace at any price is not worth the having. Hence Jesus spurned the devil's peace of surrender. *Gentle* (*epieikēs*). Old adjective (from *eikos*, reasonable, fair), equitable (Phil. 4:5; I Pet. 2:18). No English word renders it clearly. *Easy to be entreated* (*eupeithēs*). Old adjective (*eu*, *peithomai*), compliant, approachable. Only here in N.T. *Mercy* (*eleous*). Practical help (2:13, 16). *Good fruits* (*karpōn agathōn*). *Kaloi karpoi* in Matt. 7:17f. Good deeds the fruit of righteousness (Phil. 1:11). *Without variance* (*adiakritos*). Late verbal adjective (from alpha privative and *diakrinō*, to distinguish). "Unhesitating," not doubting (*diakrinomenos*) like the man in 1:6. Here only in N.T. This wisdom does not put a premium on doubt. *Without hypocrisy* (*anupokritos*). Late and rare verbal adjective (alpha privative and *hupokrinō*). Not hypocritical, sincere, unfeigned (Rom. 12:9).

18. *Is sown in peace* (*en eirēnēi speiretai*). Present passive indicative of *speirō*, to sow. The seed which bears the fruit is sown, but James catches up the metaphor of *karpos* (fruit) from verse 17. Only in peace is the fruit of righteousness found. *For them that make peace* (*tois poiousin*

eirēnēn). Dative case of the articular participle of *poieō*. See Eph. 2:15 for this phrase (doing peace), and Col. 1:20 for *eirēnopoieō*, of Christ, and Matt. 5:9 for *eirēnopoioi* (peacemakers). Only those who act peaceably are entitled to peace.

CHAPTER IV

1. *Whence (pothen)*. This old interrogative adverb (here twice) asks for the origin of wars and fights. James is full of interrogatives, like all diatribes. *Wars (polemoi)—fightings (machai)*. War *(polemos,* old word, Matt. 24:6) pictures the chronic state or campaign, while *machē* (also old word, II Cor. 7:5) presents the separate conflicts or battles in the war. So James covers the whole ground by using both words. The origin of a war or of any quarrel is sometimes hard to find, but James touches the sore spot here. *Of your pleasures (ek tōn hēdonōn humōn)*. Old word from *hēdomai*. Ablative case here after *ek*, "out of your sinful, sensual lusts," the desire to get what one does not have and greatly desires. *That war (tōn strateuomenōn)*. Present middle articular participle (ablative case agreeing with *hēdonōn*) of *strateuō*, to carry on a campaign, here as in I Pet. 2:11 of the passions in the human body. James seems to be addressing nominal Christians, "among you" *(en humin)*. Modern church disturbances are old enough in practice.

2. *Ye lust (epithumeite)*. Present active indicative of *epithumeō*, old word (from *epi, thumos,* yearning passion for), not necessarily evil as clearly not in Luke 22:15 of Christ, but usually so in the N.T., as here. Coveting what a man or nation does not have is the cause of war according to James. *Ye kill and covet (phoneuete kai zēloute)*. Present active indicatives of *phoneuō* (old verb from *phoneus,* murderer) and *zēloō,* to desire hotly to possess (I Cor. 12:31). It is possible (perhaps probable) that a full stop should come after *phoneuete* (ye kill) as the result of lusting and not having. Then we have the second situation: "Ye covet

and cannot obtain (*epituchein*, second aorist active infinitive of *epitugchanō*), and (as a result) ye fight and war." This punctuation makes better sense than any other and is in harmony with verse 1. Thus also the anticlimax in *phoneuete* and *zēloute* is avoided. Mayor makes the words a hendiadys, "ye murderously envy." *Ye have not, because ye ask not (ouk echete dia to mē aiteisthai humas).* James refers again to *ouk echete* (ye do not have) in verse 2. Such sinful lusting will not obtain. "Make the service of God your supreme end, and then your desires will be such as God can fulfil in answer to your prayer" (Ropes). Cf. Matt. 6:31–33. The reason here is expressed by *dia* and the accusative of the articular present middle infinitive of *aiteō*, used here of prayer to God as in Matt. 7:7f. *Humās* (you) is the accusative of general reference. Note the middle voice here as in *aiteisthe* in 3. Mayor argues that the middle here, in contrast with the active, carries more the spirit of prayer, but Moulton (*Prol.*, p. 160) regards the distinction between *aiteō* and *aiteomai* often "an extinct subtlety."

3. *Because ye ask amiss (dioti kakōs aiteisthe).* Here the indirect middle does make sense, "ye ask for yourselves" and that is "evilly" or amiss (*kakōs*), as James explains. *That ye may spend it in your pleasures (hina en tais hēdonais humōn dapanēsēte).* Purpose clause with *hina* and the first aorist subjunctive of *dapanaō*, old verb from *dapanē*, cost (Luke 14:28 only in N.T.), to squander (Luke 15:14). God does not hear prayers like this.

4. *Ye adulteresses (moichalides).* *Moichoi kai* (ye adulterers) is spurious (Syrian text only). The feminine form here is a common late word from the masculine *moichoi*. It is not clear whether the word is to be taken literally here as in Rom. 7:3, or figuratively for all unfaithful followers of Christ (like an unfaithful bride), as in II Cor. 11:1f.; Eph. 5:24–28 (the Bride of Christ). Either view makes sense in this

context, probably the literal view being more in harmony with the language of verses 2f. In that case James may include more than Christians in his view, though Paul talks plainly to church members about unchastity (Eph. 5:3–5). *Enmity with God* (*echthra tou theou*). Objective genitive *theou* with *echthra* (predicate and so without article), old word from *echthros*, enemy (Rom. 5:10), with *eis theon* (below and Rom. 8:7). *Whosoever therefor? would be* (*hos ean oun boulēthēi*). Indefinite relative clause with *hos* and modal *ean* and the first aorist passive (deponent) subjunctive of *boulomai*, to will (purpose). *A friend of the world* (*philos tou kosmou*). Predicate nominative with infinitive *einai* agreeing with *hos*. See 2:23 for *philos theou* (friend of God). *Maketh himself* (*kathistatai*). Present passive (not middle) indicative as in 3:6, "is constituted," "is rendered." *An enemy of God* (*echthros tou theou*). Predicate nominative and anarthrous and objective genitive (*theou*).

5. *The Scripture* (*hē graphē*). Personification as in Gal. 3:8 and James 2:23. But no O.T. passage is precisely like this, though it is "a poetical rendering" (Ropes) of Ex. 20:5. The general thought occurs also in Gen. 6:3–5; Is. 63:8–16, etc. Paul has the same idea also (Gal. 5:17, 21; Rom. 8:6, 8). It is possible that the reference is really to the quotation in verse 6 from Prov. 3:34 and treating all before as a parenthesis. There is no way to decide positively. *In vain* (*kenōs*). Old adverb (Aristotle) from *kenos* (2:20), here alone in N.T. "Emptily," not meaning what it says. *Made to dwell* (*katōikisen*). First aorist active of *katoikizō*, old verb, to give a dwelling to, only here in N.T. *Long unto envying* (*pros phthonon epipothei*). A difficult phrase. Some even take *pros phthonon* with *legei* rather than with *epipothei*, as it naturally does go, meaning "jealously." But even so, with God presented as a jealous lover, does *to pneuma* refer to the Holy Spirit as the subject of *epipothei* or to man's spirit as

the object of *epipothei?* Probably the former and *epipothei* then means to yearn after in the good sense as in Phil. 1:8.

6. *More grace (meizona charin).* "Greater grace." Greater than what? "Greater grace in view of the greater requirement" (Ropes), like Rom. 5:20f. God does this. *Wherefore (dio).* To prove this point James quotes Prov. 3:34. *God resisteth the proud (ho theos huperēphanois antitassetai).* Present middle (direct) indicative of *antitassō,* old military term, to range in battle against, with dative case (Rom. 13:2) as in 5:6. *Huperēphanois (huper, phainomai)* is like our vernacular "stuck-up folks" (Rom. 1:30), "haughty persons." *But giveth grace to the humble (tapeinois de didōsin charin).* Anarthrous adjective again, "to humble or lowly persons," for which word see 1:9f. Cf. 2:5–7; 5:1–6.

7. *Be subject therefore unto God (hupotagēte oun tōi theōi).* Second aorist (ingressive) passive imperative of *hupotassō,* old verb, to range under (military term also). Same form in I Pet. 2:23; 5:5. With the dative case *theōi* (unto God). The aorist has the note of urgency in the imperative. Note the ten aorist imperatives in verses 7 to 10 (*hupotagēte, antistēte, eggisate, katharisate, hagnisate, talaipōrēsate, penthēsate, klausate, metatrapētō, tapeinōthēte*). *But resist the devil (antistēte de tōi diabolōi).* Second aorist (ingressive) active (intransitive) imperative of *anthistēmi,* "take a stand against." Dative case *diabolōi.* Result of such a stand is that the devil will flee (*pheuxetai,* future middle of *pheugō*). See I Pet. 5:8f.; Eph. 6:11f.; Luke 10:17.

8. *Draw nigh to God (eggisate tōi theōi).* First aorist active imperative of *eggizō,* late verb from *eggus* (near) as in Matt. 3:2. With dative case again of personal relation. The priests in the sanctuary drew nigh to God (Ex. 19:22), as we should now. *Cleanse your hands (katharisate cheiras).* First aorist active imperative of *katharizō,* to cleanse, from dirt in a ritual sense (Ex. 30:19–21; Mark 7:3, 19). Here it is figurative, as in Hos. 1:16; Ps. 24:4. If we always had clean (from

sin) hands and hearts? *Ye sinners* (*hamartōloi*). A sharp term to strike the conscience, "a reproach meant to startle and sting" (Ropes). *Purify your hearts* (*hagnisate kardias*). First aorist active imperative of *hagnizō*, old verb from *hagnos* (James 3:17), ceremonially (Acts 21:24, 26), but here morally as in I Pet. 1:22; I John 3:3. Anarthrous use of *kardias* as of *cheiras* (wash hands, purify hearts). *Ye double-minded* (*dipsuchoi*). As in 1:8.

9. *Be afflicted* (*talaipōrēsate*). First aorist active imperative *talaipōreō*, old verb from *talaipōros* (Rom. 7:24), to endure toils, here only in N.T. Cf. *talaipōriais* in 5:1. *Mourn* (*penthēsate*). First aorist active imperative of *pentheō*, old verb from *penthos* (mourning, 4:9), as in Matt. 5:4f. Often in N.T. joined as here with *klaiō*, to weep (Mark 16:10; Luke 6:25). A call to the godly sorrow spoken of in II Cor. 7:10 (Mayor), like an O.T. prophet. *Weep* (*klausate*). First aorist active imperative of *klaiō*. *Laughter* (*gelōs*). Old word from Homer down, only here in N.T. as *gelaō*, to *laugh* (opposite of *klaiō*), in N.T. only in Luke 6:21, 25, but *katagelaō* in Luke 8:53 (=Mark 5:40=Matt. 9:24). *Be turned* (*metatrapētō*). Second aorist passive imperative of *metatrepō*, old word, to turn about, to transmute, in Homer (not in Attic), here only in N.T. *Heaviness* (*katēpheian*). Old word from *katēphēs* (of a downcast look, from *kata*, *phaē* eyes), hanging down of the eyes like the publican in Luke 18:13, here only in N.T.

10. *Humble yourselves* (*tapeinōthēte*). First aorist passive imperative of *tapeinoō*, old verb from *tapeinos* (1:9), as in Matt. 18:4. The passive here has almost the middle or reflexive sense. The middle voice was already giving way to the passive. See I Pet. 5:6 for this same form with the same promise of exaltation. *He shall exalt you* (*hupsōsei humas*). Future active indicative of *hupsoō*, common verb from *hupsos* (height), used by Jesus in contrast with *tapeinoō* as here (Matt. 23:12; Luke 14:11; 18:14).

11. *Speak not one against another* (*mē katalaleite allēlōn*).
Prohibition against such a habit or a command to quit doing
it, with *mē* and the present imperative of *katalaleō*, old compound usually with the accusative in ancient Greek, in N.T.
only with the genitive (here, I Pet. 2:12; 3:16). Often harsh
words about the absent. James returns to the subject of the
tongue as he does again in 5:12 (twice before, 1:26; 3:1–12).
Judgeth (*krinōn*). In the sense of harsh judgment as in
Matt. 7:1; Luke 6:37 (explained by *katadikazō*). *Not a doer
of the law, but a judge* (*ouk poiētēs nomou, alla kritēs*). This
tone of superiority to law is here sharply condemned. James
has in mind God's law, of course, but the point is the same
for all laws under which we live. We cannot select the laws
which we will obey unless some contravene God's law, and so
our own conscience (Acts 4:20). Then we are willing to give
our lives for our rebellion if need be.

12. *One only* (*heis*). No "only" in the Greek, but *heis*
here excludes all others but God. *The lawgiver* (*ho nomo-
thetēs*). Old compound (from *nomos, tithēmi*), only here in
N.T. In Ps. 9:20. Cf. *nomotheteō* in Heb. 7:11; 8:6. *To save*
(*sōsai*, first aorist active infinitive of *sōzō*) *and to destroy* (*kai
apolesai*, first aorist active infinitive of *apollumi* to destroy).
Cf. the picture of God's power in Matt. 10:28, a common
idea in the O.T. (Deut. 32:39; I Sam. 2:16; II Kings 5:7).
But who art thou? (*su de tis ei;*). Proleptic and emphatic
position of *su* (thou) in this rhetorical question as in Rom.
9:20; 14:4. *Thy neighbour* (*ton plēsion*). "The neighbour"
as in James 2:8.

13. *Go to now* (*age nun*). Interjectional use of *age* (from
agō) as in 5:1 (only N.T. instances) with a plural verb (*hoi
legontes*, present active articular participle, ye that say) as is
common in ancient Greek like *ide nun ēkousate* (Matt. 26:65).
Today or tomorrow (*sēmeron ē aurion*). Correct text (Aleph
B), not *kai* (and). *Into this city* (*eis tēnde tēn polin*). Old
demonstrative *hode*, rare in N.T. (Luke 10:39) save in neuter

plural *tade* (these things Acts 21:11). One would point out
the city on the map (Mayor) as he made the proposal (we
will go, *poreusometha*). *And spend a year there* (*kai poiē-
somen ekei eniauton*). Another future (active of *poieō*). "We
will do a year there." *And trade* (*kai emporeusometha*). Future
middle of *emporeuomai* (*en, poreuomai*, to go in), old verb
from *emporos* (a merchant or trader, a drummer, one going in
and getting the trade, Matt. 13:45), a vivid picture of the
Jewish merchants of the time. *And get gain* (*kai kerdēsomen*).
Future (Ionic form) active of *kerdainō*, old verb from *kerdos*
(gain, Phil. 1:21), as in Matt. 16:26.

14. *Whereas ye know not* (*hoitines ouk epistasthe*). The
longer relative *hostis* defines here more precisely (like Latin
qui) *hoi legontes* (ye who say) of verse 13 in a causal sense,
as in Acts 10:47, "who indeed do not know" (present middle indicative of *epistamai*). *What shall be on the morrow*
(*tēs aurion*). Supply *hēmeras* (day) after *aurion*. This is
the reading of B (Westcott) "on the morrow" (genitive of
time), but Aleph K L cursives have *to tēs aurion* ("the
matter of tomorrow"), while A P cursives have *ta tēs aurion*
("the things of tomorrow"). The sense is practically the
same, though *to tēs aurion* is likely correct. *What is your
life?* (*poia hē zōē humōn*). Thus Westcott and Hort punctu-
ate it as an indirect question, not direct. *Poia* is a qualitative interrogative (of what character). *A vapour* (*atmis*).
This is the answer. Old word for mist (like *atmos*, from which
our "atmosphere"), in N.T. only here and Acts 2:19 with
kapnou (vapour of smoke (from Joel 2:30). *For a little
time* (*pros oligon*). See same phrase in I Tim. 4:8, *pros
kairon* in Luke 8:13, *pros hōran* in John 5:35. *That appear-
eth and then vanisheth away* (*phainomenē epeita kai aphani-
zomenē*). Present middle participles agreeing with *atmis*,
"appearing, then also disappearing," with play on the two
verbs (*phainomai, aphanizō* as in Matt. 6:19, from *aphanēs*

hidden Heb. 4:13) with the same root *phan* (*phainō, a-phan-ēs*).

15. *For that ye ought to say* (*anti tou legein humās*). "Instead of the saying as to you" (genitive of the articular infinitive with the preposition *anti* and the accusative of general reference with *legein*), "instead of your saying." *If the Lord will* (*ean ho kurios thelēi*). Condition of the third class with *ean* and the present active subjunctive (or first aorist active *thelesēi* in some MSS). The proper attitude of mind (Acts 18:21; I Cor. 4:19; 16:7; Rom. 1:19; Phil. 2:19, 24; Heb. 6:3), not to be uttered always in words like a charm. This Hellenistic formula was common among the ancient heathen, as today among modern Arabs like the Latin *deo volente*. *This or that* (*touto ē ekeino*). Applicable to every act.

16. *In your vauntings* (*en tais alazoniais humōn*). Old word for braggart talk (from *alazoneuomai*, to act the *alazōn* empty boaster Rom. 1:30), common in Aristophanes, in N.T. only here and I John 2:16. *Glorying* (*kauchēsis*). Act of glorying, late word from *kauchaomai*, good if for Christ (I Thess. 2:19), bad if for self as here.

17. *To him that knoweth* (*eidoti*). Dative case of second perfect participle *eidōs* (from *oida*), and with the infinitive to know how, "to one knowing how." *To do good* (*kalon poiein*). "To do a good deed." *And doeth it not* (*kai mē poiounti*). Dative again of the present active participle of *poieō*, "and to one not doing it." Cf. "not a doer" (1:23) and Matt. 7:26. *Sin* (*hamartia*). Unused knowledge of one's duty is sin, the sin of omission. Cf. Matt. 23:23.

CHAPTER V

1. *Come now, ye rich (age nun hoi plousioi).* Exclamatory interjection as in 4:13. Direct address to the rich as a class as in I Tim. 6:17. Apparently here James has in mind the rich as a class, whether believer, as in 1:10f., or unbeliever, as in 2:1f., 6. The plea here is not directly for reform, but a warning of certain judgment (5:1–6) and for Christians "a certain grim comfort in the hardships of poverty" (Ropes) in 5:7–11. *Weep and howl (klausate ololuzontes).* "Burst into weeping (ingressive aorist active imperative of *klaiō* as in 4:9), howling with grief" (present active participle of the old onomatopoetic verb *ololuzō*, here only in N.T., like Latin *ululare*, with which compare *alalazō* in Matt. 5:38. *For your miseries (epi tais talaipōriais humōn).* Old word from *talaipōros* (Rom. 7:24) and like *talaipōreō* in James 4:9 (from *tlaō* to endure and *pōros* a callus). *That are coming upon you (tais eperchomenais).* Present middle participle of the old compound *eperchomai* to come upon, used here in futuristic prophetic sense.

2. *Riches (ho ploutos).* Masculine singular, but occasionally neuter *to ploutos* in nominative and accusative (II Cor. 8:2). Apparently *pleotos* fulness (from *pleos* full, *pimplēmi* to fill). "Wealth." *Are corrupted (sesēpen).* Second perfect active indicative of *sēpō* (root *sap* as in *sapros*, rotten), to corrupt, to destroy, here intransitive "has rotted." Only here in N.T. On the worthlessness of mere wealth see Matt. 6:19, 24. *Are moth-eaten (sētobrōta gegonen).* "Have become (second perfect indicative of *ginomai*, singular number, though *himatia*, neuter plural, treated collectively) moth-eaten" (*sētobrōta*, late and rare compound from *sēs*, moth, Matt. 6:19f. and *brōtos*, verbal adjective of *bibrōskō*

57

to eat John 6:13. This compound found only here, Job
13:28, Sibyll. Orac. *Proem*. 64). Rich robes as heirlooms,
but moth-eaten. Vivid picture. Witness the 250 "lost
millionaires" in the United States in 1931 as compared
with 1929. Riches have wings.

3. *Are rusted* (*katiōtai*). Perfect passive indicative (singular for *chrusos* and *arguros* are grouped as one) of *katioō*,
late verb (from *ios*, rust) with perfective sense of *kata*, to
rust through (down to the bottom), found only here, Sir.
12:11, Epictetus (*Diss*. 4, 6, 14). *Rust* (*ios*). Poison in
James 3:8; Rom. 3:13 (only N.T. examples of old word).
Silver does corrode and gold will tarnish. Dioscorides (V.91)
tells about gold being rusted by chemicals. Modern chem-
ists can even transmute metals as the alchemists claimed.
For a testimony (*eis marturion*). Common idiom as in Matt.
8:4 (use of *eis* with accusative in predicate). *Against you*
(*humin*). Dative of disadvantage as in Mark 6:11 (*eis
marturion autois*) where in the parallel passage (Luke 9:5)
we have *eis marturion ep' autous*. "To you" will make
sense, as in Matt. 8:4; 10:18, but "against" is the idea here
as in Luke 21:13. *Shall eat* (*phagetai*). Future middle (late
form from *ephagon*) of defective verb *esthiō*, to eat. *Your
flesh* (*tas sarkas*). The plural is used for the fleshy parts
of the body like pieces of flesh (Rev. 17:16; 19:18, 21).
Rust eats like a canker, like cancer in the body. *As fire*
(*hōs pur*). Editors differ here whether to connect this phrase
with *phagetai*, just before (as Mayor), for fire eats up more
rapidly than rust, or with the following, as Westcott and
Hort and Ropes, that is the eternal fire of Gehenna which
awaits them (Matt. 25:41; Mark 9:44). This interpretation
makes a more vivid picture for *ethēsaurisate* (ye have laid
up, first aorist active indicative of *thēsaurizō*, Matt. 6:19
and see Prov. 16:27), but it is more natural to take it with
phagetai.

4. *The hire* (*ho misthos*). Old word for wages (Matt.

20:8). *Labourers* (*ergatōn*). Any one who works (*ergazo-mai*), especially agricultural workers (Matt. 9:37). *Who mowed* (*tōn amēsantōn*). Genitive plural of the articular first aorist active participle of *amaō* (from *hama*, together), old verb, to gather together, to reap, here only in N.T. *Fields* (*chōras*). Estates or farms (Luke 12:16). *Which is of you kept back by fraud* (*ho aphusterēmenos aph' humōn*). Perfect passive articular participle of *aphustereō*, late compound (simplex *hustereō* common as Matt. 19:20), to be behindhand from, to fail of, to cause to withdraw, to defraud. Pitiful picture of earned wages kept back by rich Jews, old problem of capital and labour that is with us yet in acute form. *The cries* (*hai boai*). Old word from which *boaō* comes (Matt. 3:3), here only in N.T. The stolen money "cries out" (*krazei*), the workers cry out for vengeance. *That reaped* (*tōn therisantōn*). Genitive plural of the articular participle first aorist active of *therizō* (old verb from *theros*, summer, Matt. 24:32), to reap, to harvest while summer allows (Matt. 6:26). *Have entered* (*eiselēluthan*). Perfect active third person plural indicative of *eiserchomai*, old and common compound, to go or come into. This late form is by analogy of the aorist for the usual form in *-asi*. *Of the Lord of Sabaoth* (*Kuriou Sabaōth*). "Of the Lord of Hosts," quotation from Is. 5:9 as in Rom. 9:29, transliterating the Hebrew word for "Hosts," an expression for the omnipotence of God like *Pantokratōr* (Rev. 4:8). God hears the cries of the oppressed workmen even if the employers are deaf.

5. *Ye have lived delicately* (*etruphēsate*). First aorist (constative, summary) active indicative of *truphaō*, old verb from *truphē* (luxurious living as in Luke 7:25, from *thruptō*, to break down, to enervate), to lead a soft life, only here in N.T. *Taken your pleasure* (*espatalēsate*). First aorist (constative) active indicative of *spatalaō*, late and rare verb to live voluptuously or wantonly (from *spatalē*, riotous liv-

ing, wantonness, once as bracelet), in N.T. only here and I Tim. 5:6. *Ye have nourished* (*ethrepsate*). First aorist (constative) active indicative of *trephō*, old verb, to feed, to fatten (Matt. 6:26). They are fattening themselves like sheep or oxen all unconscious of "the day of slaughter" (*en hēmerāi sphagēs*, definite without the article) ahead of them. For this use of *sphagēs* see Rom. 8:36 (*probata sphagēs*, sheep for the slaughter, *sphagē* from *sphazō*, to slay), consummate sarcasm on the folly of sinful rich people.

6. *Ye have condemned* (*katedikasate*). First aorist active indicative of *katadikazō*, old verb (from *katadikē*, condemnation, Acts 25:15). The rich controlled the courts of justice. *Ye have killed the righteous one* (*ephoneusate ton dikaion*). First aorist active indicative of *phoneuō* (2:11; 4:2). "The righteous one" (*ton dikaion*) is the generic use of the singular with article for the class. There is probably no direct reference to one individual, though it does picture well the death of Christ and also the coming death of James himself, who was called the Just (Eus. *H.E.* ii. 23). Stephen (Acts 7:52) directly accuses the Sanhedrin with being betrayers and murderers (*prodotai kai phoneis*) of the righteous one (*tou dikaiou*). *He doth not resist you* (*ouk antitassetai humin*). It is possible to treat this as a question. Present middle indicative of *antitassō*, for which see James 4:6. Without a question the unresisting end of the victim (*ton dikaion*) is pictured. With a question (*ouk*, expecting an affirmative answer) God or Lord is the subject, with the final judgment in view. There is no way to decide definitely.

7. *Be patient therefore* (*makrothumēsate oun*). A direct corollary (*oun*, therefore) from the coming judgment on the wicked rich (5:1-6). First aorist (constative) active imperative of *makrothumeō*, late compound (Plutarch, LXX) from *makrothumos* (*makros*, *thumos*, of long spirit, not losing heart), as in Matt. 18:26. The appeal is to the oppressed brethren. Catch your wind for a long race (long-tempered

as opposed to short-tempered). See already the exhortation to patience (*hupomonē*) in 1:3f., 12 and repeated in 5:11. They will need both submission (*hupomenō* 5:11) and steadfastness (*makrothumia* 5:10). *Until the coming of the Lord* (*heōs tēs parousias*). The second coming of Christ he means, the regular phrase here and in verse 8 for that idea (Matt. 24:3, 37, 39; I Thess. 2:19, etc.). *The husbandman* (*ho geōrgos*). The worker in the ground (*gē*, *ergō*) as in Matt. 21:33f. *Waiteth for* (*ekdechetai*). Present middle indicative of *ekdechomai*, old verb for eager expectation as in Acts 17:16. *Precious* (*timion*). Old adjective from *timē* (honor, price), dear to the farmer because of his toil for it. See I Pet. 1:19. *Being patient over it* (*makrothumōn ep' autōi*). Present active participle of *makrothumeō* just used in the exhortation, picturing the farmer longing and hoping over his precious crop (cf. Luke 18:7 of God). *Until it receive* (*heōs labēi*). Temporal clause of the future with *heōs* and the second aorist active subjunctive of *lambanō*, vividly describing the farmer's hopes and patience. *The early and latter rain* (*proïmon kai opsimon*). The word for rain (*hueton* Acts 14:17) is absent from the best MSS. The adjective *proïmos* (from *prōï*, early) occurs here only in N.T., though old in the form *proïmos* and *prōïs*. See Deut. 11:14; Jer. 5:24, etc. for these terms for the early rain in October or November for the germination of the grain, and the latter rain (*opsimon*, from *opse*, late, here only in N.T.) in April and May for maturing the grain.

8. *Ye also* (*kai humeis*). As well as the farmers. *Stablish* (*stērixate*). First aorist active imperative of *stērizō*, old verb, (from *stērigx*, a support) to make stable, as in Luke 22:32; I Thess. 3:13. *Is at hand* (*ēggiken*). Present perfect active indicative of *eggizō*, common verb, to draw near (from *eggus*), in James 4:8, for drawing near. Same form used by John in his preaching (Matt. 3:2). In I Pet. 4:7 the same word appears to have an eschatological sense as apparently here.

How "near" or "nigh" did James mean? Clearly, it could only be a hope, for Jesus had distinctly said that no one knew when he would return.

9. *Murmur not* (*mē stenazete*). Prohibition with *mē* and the present active imperative of *stenazō*, old verb, to groan. "Stop groaning against one another," as some were already doing in view of their troubles. In view of the hope of the Second Coming lift up your heads. *That ye be not judged* (*hina mē krithēte*). Negative purpose clause with *hina mē* and the first aorist passive subjunctive of *krinō*. As already indicated (2:12f.; 4:12) and repeated in 5:12. Reminiscence of the words of Jesus in Matt. 7:1f. *Standeth before the doors* (*pro tōn thurōn hestēken*). Perfect active indicative of *histēmi*, "is standing now." Again like the language of Jesus in Matt. 24:33 (*epi thurais*) and Mark 13:29. Jesus the Judge is pictured as ready to enter for the judgment.

10. *For an example* (*hupodeigma*). Late word for the old *paradeigma*, from *hupodeiknumi*, to copy under, to teach (Luke 6:47), here for copy to be imitated as in John 13:15, as a warning (Heb. 4:11). Here predicate accusative with *tous prophētas* (the prophets) as the direct object of *labete* (second aorist active imperative of *lambanō*). *Of suffering* (*tēs kakopathias*). Old word from *kakopathēs* (suffering evil, *kakopatheō* in verse 13 and II Tim. 2:3, 9), here only in N.T. *Of patience* (*makrothumias*). Like *makrothumeō* in 5:7. See both *makrothumia* and *hupomonē* in II Cor. 4:6; Col. 1:11 (the one restraint from retaliating, the other not easily succumbing). *In the name of* (*en tōi onomati*). As in Jer. 20:9. With the authority of the Lord (Deissmann, *Bible Studies*, p. 198).

11. *We call blessed* (*makarizomen*). Old word (present active indicative of *makarizō*), from *makarios* (happy), in N.T. only here and Luke 1:48. "We felicitate." As in 1:3, 12 and Dan. 12:12. *Ye have heard* (*ēkousate*). First aorist (constative) active indicative of *akouō*. As in Matt.

5:21, 27, 33, 38, 43. Ropes suggests in the synagogues. *Of Job* (*Iōb*). Job did complain, but he refused to renounce God (Job 1:21; 2:10; 13:15; 16:19; 19:25f.). He had become a stock illustration of loyal endurance. *Ye have seen* (*eidete*). Second aorist (constative) active indicative of *horaō*. In Job's case. *The end of the Lord* (*to telos kuriou*). The conclusion wrought by the Lord in Job's case (Job 42:12). *Full of pity* (*polusplagchnos*). Late and rare compound (*polus*, *splagchnon*), only here in N.T. It occurs also in Hermas (*Sim.* v. 7. 4; *Mand.* iv, 3). "Very kind." *Merciful* (*oiktirmōn*). Late and rare adjective (from *oikteirō* to pity), in N.T. only here and Luke 6:36.

12. *Above all things* (*pro pantōn*). No connection with what immediately precedes. Probably an allusion to the words of Jesus (Matt. 5:34–37). It is not out of place here. See the same phrase in I Pet. 4:8. Robinson (*Ephesians*, p. 279) cites like examples from the papyri at the close of letters. Here it means "But especially" (Ropes). *Swear not* (*mē omnuete*). Prohibition of the habit (or to quit doing it if guilty) with *mē* and the present active imperative of *omnuō*. The various oaths (profanity) forbidden (*mēte*, thrice) are in the accusative case after *omnuete*, according to rule (*ouranon*, *gēn*, *horkon*). The Jews were wont to split hairs in their use of profanity, and by avoiding God's name imagine that they were not really guilty of this sin, just as professing Christians today use "pious oaths" which violate the prohibition of Jesus. *Let be* (*ētō*). Imperative active third singular of *eimi*, late form (I Cor. 16:22) for *estō*. "Your yea be yea" (and no more). A different form from that in Matt. 5:37. *That ye fall not under judgment* (*hina mē hupo krisin pesēte*). Negative purpose with *hina mē* and the second aorist active subjunctive of *piptō*, to fall. See *hina mē krithēte* in verse 9. *Krisis* (from *krinō*) is the act of judging rather than the judgment rendered (*krima* James 3:1).

13. *Is any suffering?* (*kakopathei tis*;). See verse 10 for

kakopathia. The verb in N.T. occurs only here and in II Tim. 2:3, 9; 4:5. The lively interrogative is common in the diatribe and suits the style of James. *Among you* (*en humin*). As in 3:13. *Let him pray* (*proseuchesthō*). Present middle imperative, "let him keep on praying" (instead of cursing as in verse 12). *Is any cheerful* (*euthumei;*). Present active indicative of *euthumeō*, old verb from *euthumos* (Acts 27:36), in N.T. only here and Acts 27:22, 25. *Let him sing praise* (*psalletō*). Present active imperative of *psallō*, originally to twang a chord as on a harp, to sing praise to God whether with instrument or without, in N.T. only here, I Cor. 14:15; Rom. 15:9; Eph. 5:19. "Let him keep on making melody."

14. *Is any among you sick?* (*asthenei tis en humin;*). Present active indicative of *astheneō*, old verb, to be weak (without strength), often in N.T. (Matt. 10:8). *Let him call for* (*proskalesasthō*). First aorist (ingressive) middle imperative of *proskaleō*. Note change of tense (aorist) and middle (indirect) voice. Care for the sick is urged in I Thess. 5:14 ("help the sick"). Note the plural here, "elders of the church," as in Acts 20:17; 15:6, 22; 21:18; Phil. 1:1 (bishops). *Let them pray over him* (*proseuxasthōsan ep' auton*). First aorist middle imperative of *proseuchomai*. Prayer for the sick is clearly enjoined. *Anointing him with oil* (*aleipsantes elaiōi*). First aorist active participle of *aleiphō*, old verb, to anoint, and the instrumental case of *elaion* (oil). The aorist participle can be either simultaneous or antecedent with *proseuxasthōsan* (pray). See the same use of *aleiphō elaiōi* in Mark 6:13. The use of olive oil was one of the best remedial agencies known to the ancients. They used it internally and externally. Some physicians prescribe it today. It is clear both in Mark 6:13 and here that medicinal value is attached to the use of the oil and emphasis is placed on the worth of prayer. There is nothing here of the pagan magic or of the later practice of "extreme unction" (after the

eighth century). It is by no means certain that *aleiphō* here and in Mark 6:13 means "anoint" in a ceremonial fashion rather than "rub" as it commonly does in medical treatises. Trench (N.T. Synonyms) says: "*Aleiphein* is the mundane and profane, *chriein* the sacred and religious, word." At bottom in James we have God and medicine, God and the doctor, and that is precisely where we are today. The best physicians believe in God and want the help of prayer.

15. *The prayer of faith* (*hē euchē tēs pisteōs*). Cf. 1:6 for prayer marked by faith. *Shall save* (*sōsei*). Future active of *sōzō*, to make well. As in Matt. 9:21f.; Mark 6:56. No reference here to salvation of the soul. The medicine does not heal the sick, but it helps nature (God) do it. The doctor coöperates with God in nature. *The sick* (*ton kamnonta*). Present active articular participle of *kamnō*, old verb, to grow weary (Heb. 12:3), to be sick (here), only N.T. examples. *The Lord shall raise him up* (*egerei auton ho kurios*). Future active of *egeirō*. Precious promise, but not for a professional "faith-healer" who scoffs at medicine and makes merchandise out of prayer. *And if he have committed sins* (*kàn hamartias ēi pepoiēkōs*). Periphrastic perfect active subjunctive (unusual idiom) with *kai ean* (crasis *kàn*) in condition of third class. Supposing that he has committed sins as many sick people have (Mark 2:5ff.; John 5:14; 9:2f.; I Cor. 11:30). *It shall be forgiven him* (*aphethēsetai autōi*). Future passive of *aphiēmi* (impersonal passive as in Matt. 7:2, 7; Rom. 10:10). Not in any magical way, not because his sickness has been healed, not without change of heart and turning to God through Christ. Much is assumed here that is not expressed.

16. *Confess therefore your sins one to another* (*exomologeisthe oun allēlois tas hamartias*). Present middle (indirect) of *exomologeō*. Confession of sin to God is already assumed. But public confession of certain sins to one another in the meetings is greatly helpful in many ways. This is not con-

fessing to one man like a priest in place of the public confession. One may confess to the pastor without confessing
to God or to the church, with little benefit to anybody.
Pray for one another (*proseuchesthe huper allēlōn*). Present
middle imperative. Keep this up. *That ye may be healed*
(*hopōs iathēte*). Purpose clause with *hopōs* and the first
aorist passive subjunctive of *iaomai*. Probably of bodily
healing (verse 14), though *iaomai* is used also of healing of
the soul (Matt. 13:15; I Pet. 2:24; Heb. 12:13) as Mayor
takes it here. *Availeth much* (*polu ischuei*). "Has much
force." Present active indicative of *ischuō* (from *ischus*,
strength). *In its working* (*energoumenē*). Probably the
present middle participle of *energeō* as Paul apparently uses
it in Gal. 5:6; II Cor. 4:12; II Thess. 2:7, meaning "when
it works." The passive is possible, as is the usual idiom
elsewhere. Mayor argues strongly for the passive here,
"when it is exercised" (Ropes).

17. *Of like passions with us* (*homoiopathēs hēmin*). Associative-instrumental case *hēmin* as with *homoios*. This old
compound adjective (*homoios, paschō*), suffering the like with
another, in N.T. only here and Acts 14:15. *He prayed
fervently* (*proseuchēi prosēuxato*). First aorist middle indicative of *proseuchomai* and the instrumental case *proseuchēi* (cognate substantive), after idiom for intensity in classical Greek, like *pheugein phugēi*, to flee with all speed
(*figura etymologica*), but particularly frequent in the LXX
(Gen. 2:17; 31:30) in imitation of the Hebrew infinitive
absolute. So Luke 22:15; John 3:29; Acts 4:17. *That it
might not rain* (*tou mē brexai*). Genitive of the articular
infinitive (*brexai*, first aorist active of *brechō*, old verb, to
moisten, Luke 7:38, to rain, Matt. 5:45) with negative *mē*
used either for direct purpose, for an object clause as here
and Acts 3:12; 15:20, or even for result. *For three years and
six months* (*eniautous treis kai mēnas hex*). Accusative of
extent of time.

18. *Gave rain* (*hueton edōken*). This idiom is in the LXX of God as here of heaven (I Sam. 12:17; I Kings 18:1) and also in Acts 14:17 instead of *ebrexen* of verse 17. *Hueton* is old word for rain (from *huō*, to rain), genuine here, but not in verse 7. *Brought forth* (*eblastēsen*). First aorist active of *blastanō*, old verb, to sprout (intransitive as Mark 4:27), here as occasionally in later Greek transitive with accusative *karpon*.

19. *If any one among you do err* (*ean tis en humin planē-thēi*). Third-class condition (supposed case) with *ean* and the first aorist passive subjunctive of *planaō*, old verb, to go astray, to wander (Matt. 18:12), figuratively (Heb. 5:2). *From the truth* (*apo tēs alētheias*). For truth see 1:18; 3:14; John 8:32; I John 1:6; 3:18f. It was easy then, and is now, to be led astray from Christ, who is the Truth. *And one convert him* (*kai epistrepsēi tis auton*). Continuation of the third-class condition with the first aorist active subjunctive of *epistrephō*, old verb, to turn (transitive here as in Luke 1:16f., but intransitive often as Acts 9:35).

20. *Let him know* (*ginōsketō*). Present active imperative third person singular of *ginōskō*, but Westcott and Hort read *ginōskete* (know ye) after B. In either case it is the conclusion of the condition in verse 19. *He which converteth* (*ho epistrepsas*). First aorist active articular participle of *epistrephō* of verse 19. *From the error* (*ek planēs*). "Out of the wandering" of verse 19 (*planē*, from which *planaō* is made). See I John 4:6 for contrast between "truth" and "error." *A soul from death* (*psuchēn ek thanatou*). The soul of the sinner (*hamartōlon*) won back to Christ, not the soul of the man winning him. A few MSS. have *autou* added (his soul), which leaves it ambiguous, but *autou* is not genuine. It is ultimate and final salvation here meant by the future (*sōsei*). *Shall cover a multitude of sins* (*kalupsei plēthos hamartiōn*). Future active of *kaluptō*, old verb, to hide, to veil. But whose sins (those of the converter or the

converted)? The Roman Catholics (also Mayor and Ropes) take it of the sins of the converter, who thus saves himself by saving others. The language here will allow that, but not New Testament teaching in general. It is apparently a proverbial saying which Resch considers one of the unwritten sayings of Christ (Clem. Al. *Paed*. iii. 12). It occurs also in I Pet. 4:8, where it clearly means the sins of others covered by love as a veil thrown over them. The saying appears also in Prov. 10:12: "Hatred stirs up strife, but love hides all transgressions"—that is "love refuses to see faults" (Mayor admits). That is undoubtedly the meaning in I Pet. 4:8 and James 5:20.

THE FIRST EPISTLE GENERAL OF PETER

ABOUT A.D. 65

BY WAY OF INTRODUCTION

The Epistle is not anonymous, but claims to be written by "Peter, an apostle of Jesus Christ" (1:1), that is Cephas (Simon Peter). If this is not true, then the book is pseudonymous by a late writer who assumed Peter's name, as in the so-called Gospel of Peter, Apocalypse of Peter, etc. "There is no book in the New Testament which has earlier, better, or stronger attestation, though Irenæus is the first to quote it by name" (Bigg). Eusebius (*H.E.* iii. 25.2) places it among the acknowledged books, those accepted with no doubt at all. We here assume that Simon Peter wrote this Epistle or at any rate dictated it by an amanuensis, as Paul did in Romans (16:22). Bigg suggests Silvanus (Silas) as the amanuensis or interpreter (I Pet. 5:12), the obvious meaning of the language (*dia*, through). He may also have been the bearer of the Epistle. It happens that we know more of Peter's life than of any of the twelve apostles because of his prominence in the Gospels and in the first fifteen chapters of the Acts. In the *Student's Chronological New Testament* I have given a full list of the passages in the Gospels where Peter appears with any clearness and the material is rich and abundant. The account in Acts is briefer, though Peter is the oustanding man in the first five chapters during his career in Jerusalem. After the conversion of Saul he begins to work outside of Jerusalem and after escaping death at the hands of Herod Agrippa I (Acts 12:3ff.) he left for a while, but is back in Jerusalem at the Conference called by Paul and Barnabas (Acts 15:6–14; Gal. 2:1–10). After that we have no more about him in Acts, though he reappears in Antioch and is rebuked by Paul for cowardice because of the Judaizers (Gal. 11–21). He travelled for the Gospel among the Jews of the Dispersion (Gal. 2:9) with his wife (I Cor. 9:5), and went to Asia Minor (I Pet. 1:1) and as far as Babylon or Rome (I Pet. 5:13). Besides Silvanus he had John Mark with him also (I Pet. 5:13), who was said by the early Christian writers to have been Peter's "interpreter" in his preaching, since Peter was not expert in the Greek (Acts 4:13), and who also wrote his Gospel under the inspiration of Peter's preaching. We are not able to follow clearly the close of his life or to tell precisely the time of his death. He was apparently put to death in A.D. 67 or 68, but some think that he was executed in Rome in A.D. 64.

THE DATE

This question is tied up with that of the genuineness of the Epistle, the time of Peter's death, the use of Paul's Epistles, the persecution referred to in the Epistle. Assuming the genuineness of the Epistle and the death of Peter about A.D. 67 or 68 and the persecution to be not that under Domitian or Trajan, but under Nero, the date can be assumed to be about A.D. 65.

THE USE OF PAUL'S EPISTLES

There are two extremes about the relation of Peter to Paul. One is that of violent antithesis, with Peter and Paul opposing one another by exaggerating and prolonging Paul's denunciation of Peter's cowardice in Antioch (Gal. 2:11–21) and making Peter also the exponent of a Jewish type of Christianity (practically a Judaizing type). This view of Baur once had quite a following, but it has nearly disappeared. Under its influence Acts and Peter's Epistles were considered not genuine, but documents designed to patch up the disagreement between Peter and Paul. The other

extreme is to deny any Pauline influence on Peter or of
Peter on Paul. Paul was friendly to Peter (Gal. 1:18), but
was independent of his ecclesiastical authority (Gal. 2:1–10)
and Peter championed Paul's cause in the Jerusalem Conference (Acts 15:7–13). Peter was certainly not a Judaizer
(Acts 11:1–18), in spite of his temporary defection in Antioch. Undoubtedly Peter was won back to cordial relations
with Paul if any confidence can be placed in II Pet. 3:15f.
There is no reason for doubting that Peter was familiar
with some of Paul's Epistles as there indicated. There is
some indication of Peter's use of Romans and Ephesians in
this Epistle. It is not always conclusive to find the same
words and even ideas which are not formally quoted, because there was a Christian vocabulary and a body of
doctrinal ideas in common though with personal variations
in expression. Peter may have read James, but not the
Pastoral Epistles. There are points of contact with Hebrews
which Von Soden considers sufficiently accounted for by
the fact that Peter and the author of Hebrews were contemporaries.

The Persecution Pictured in the Epistle

Peter himself knew what persecution was at the hands
of the Sanhedrin and of Herod Agrippa I (both church and
state). If First Peter was written A.D. 65, there was time
enough for the persecution of Nero in Rome in A.D. 64 to
spread to Asia Minor. The province easily imitated the
capital city. Paul's life in the Acts and his Epistles abundantly show how early persecution arose in Asia Minor.
The Apocalypse, written during the reign of Domitian,
shows that persecution from the state had been on hand
long before and was an old burden. We know too little of
the history of Christianity in Asia Minor from A.D. 60 to
70 to deny that the fiery trials and suffering as a Christian

(I Pet. 4:16) can be true of this period. So we locate the persecution at this time as an echo from Rome.

The Place of Writing

Peter states that he is in Babylon (I Pet. 5:13), apparently with his wife (I Cor. 9:5). It is not certain whether he means actual Babylon, where Jews had been numerous, or mystical Babylon (Rome) as in the Apocalypse. We do not know when Rome began to be called Babylon. It may have started as a result of Nero's persecution of the Christians after the burning of Rome. The Christians were called "evil-doers" (I Pet. 2:12) in the time of Nero (Tacitus, *Ann.* XV. 44). So we can think of Rome as the place of writing and that Peter uses "Babylon" to hide his actual location from Nero. Whether Peter came to Rome while Paul was still there we do not know, though John Mark was there with Paul (Col. 4:10). "At the time when it was written Babylon had not yet unmasked all its terrors, and the ordinary Christian was not in immediate danger of the *tunica ardens*, or the red-hot iron chair, or the wild beasts, or the stake" (Bigg).

The Readers

Peter writes "to the elect who are sojourners of the Dispersion in Pontus, Galatia, Cappadocia, Asia, and Bithynia" (1:1). These five Roman provinces are naturally given from the standpoint of Babylon. In Galatia and Asia Paul had labored, though not all over these provinces. At any rate, there is no reason to wonder that Peter should himself work in the same regions where Paul had been. In a general way Paul and Peter had agreed on separate spheres of activity, Paul to the Gentiles and Peter to the Jews (Gal. 21:7ff.), though the distinction was not absolute, for Paul usually began his work in the Jewish synagogue. Probably the readers are mainly Jewish Christians. but not to the exclusion of Gentiles. Peter has clearly Paul's idea that Christianity is the true Judaism of God's promise (I Pet. 2:4–10).

THE PURPOSE

Evidently Peter's object is to cheer and strengthen the Christians in these five provinces who are undergoing fiery trials (1:7f.). There is every reason why Peter, as the leading apostle to the circumcision, should write to these believers in the provinces, especially since Paul's long imprisonment in Cæsarea and Rome had removed him from his accustomed activities and travel.

THE STYLE AND VOCABULARY

Like Peter's discourses in the Acts, the Epistle is mainly hortatory, with a minimum of argument and little of the closely knit reasoning seen in Romans. There is frequent use of the LXX and the Greek is decent *Koiné* with little of the uncouth Aramaic of the Galilean (Matt. 26:73), or of the vernacular *Koiné* as seen in the papyri or in II Peter (Acts 4:13). This fact may be accounted for by the help of Silvanus as amanuensis. There are sixty-two words in the Greek of the Epistle not occurring elsewhere in the N.T. There is verbal iteration as in II Peter. "One idea haunts the whole Epistle; to the author, as to the patriarch Jacob, life is a pilgrimage; it is essentially an old man's view" (Bigg). But it is an old man who has lived long with Christ. Peter has learned the lesson of humility and patience from Jesus his Lord.

SOME BOOKS

ALFORD, H., Vol. IV. 1 of his *Greek Testament* (1870).
BALDWIN, *The Fisherman of Galilee* (1923).
BARNES, *St. Peter in Rome and His Tomb on the Vatican Hill.*
BECK, J. T., *Erklärung der Briefe Petri* (1895).

BENNETT, W. H., *New-Century Bible* (1901).

BIGG, C., *Intern. Crit. Comm.* (1901).

BIRKS, *Studies in the Life and Character of St. Peter* (1887).

BLENKIN, *The First Ep. General of St. Peter* (1915).

CAMERLINCK, *Commentarius in epistolas catholicas* (1909).

COOKE and LUMBY, *Speaker's Comm.* (1881).

COUARD, *Commentaire* (1895).

COUARD, *Simon Petrus der Apostel des Herrn.*

DAVIDSON, *St. Peter and His Training.*

ELERT, *Die Religiosität des Petrus* (1911).

ERBES, *Die Todestage der Apostels Paulus and Petrus* (1899).

FOAKES-JACKSON, F. J., *Peter Prince of Apostles* (1927).

FOSTER, ORA D., *The Literary Relations of the First Epistle of Peter* (1913).

FOUARD, C., *St. Peter and the First Years of Christianity* (1892).

GALLAGHER, M., *Was the Apostle Peter Ever at Rome?* (1894).

GOUTARD, *Essai critique et historique sur la prem. épître de S. Pierre* (1905).

GREEN, S. G., *The Apostle Peter: His Life and Letters* (1880).

GUIGNEBERT, *La Primauté de Pierre et la Venue de Pierre à Rome* (1909).

GUNKEL, H., *Die Schriften d. N.T.* 3 Aufl. (1917).

HART, J. H. A., *Expos. Greek Test.* (1910).

HENRIOTT, *Saint Pierre* (1891).

HORT, F. J. A., *The First Epistle of St. Peter 1:1–2:17* (1898).

HOWSON, J., *Horæ Petrinæ* (1883).

JENKINS, R. C., *The Apostle Peter. Claims of Catholics* (1875).

JOHNSTONE, *The First Epistle of Peter* (1888).

KASTEREN, VAN, *De Eerste Brief Van d. Ap. Petrus* (1911).

KEIL, C. F., *Comm. über die Briefe des Petrus und Juda* (1883).

KNOPF, R., *Die Briefe Petri und Juda* (1912).

KÖGEL, J., *Die Gedankenheit des Ersten Briefes Petri* (1902).

KÜHL, E., *Die Briefe Petri und Judae* (Meyer Komm., 6 Aufl., 1897).

LIETZMANN, *Petrus and Paulus in Rom.*

LUMBY, J. R., *Expositor's Bible* (1893).

MASTERMAN, J. H. B., *Epistles of St. Peter* (1900).

McINNIS, J. M., *Simon Peter Fisherman and Philosopher* (1928).

MEYER, F. B., *Peter: Fisherman, Disciple, Apostle* (1920).

MOFFATT, JAMES, *Moffatt Comm. on N.T.* (1930).

MONNIER, J., *La première épître de l'apôtre Pierre* (1900).

PERDELWITZ, *Die Mysterienreligion und das Problem des ersten Petrusbriefes* (1911).

PLUMPTRE, *Cambridge Bible* (1879).

REAGAN, *The Preaching of Peter, the Beginning of Christian Apologetics* (1922).

ROBINSON, C. G., *Simon Peter: His Life and Times* (1889).

ROSS, J. M. E., *The First Epistle of Peter* (1913).

SALMOND, A. D. F., *Schaff's Comm.* (1883).

SCHARFE, *Die petrinische Strömung der neut. Literatur* (1893).

SCHMID, *Petrus in Rome* (1879).

SEELEY, *The Life and Writings of St. Peter.*

SODEN, VON, H., *Hand-Komm.* (3 Aufl., 1899).

TAYLOR, W. M., *Peter the Apostle* (1876).

THOMAS, W. H., GRIFFITH, *The Apostle Peter* (2nd ed., 1905).

THOMPSON, *Life-Work of Peter the Apostle.*

UPHAM, *Simon Peter Shepherd* (1910).

USTERI, J. M., *Wiss. und prakt. Komm. über den 1 Petrusbrief* (1887).

VÖLTER, D., *Der 1 Petrusbrief* (1906).

WEISS, B., *Die erste Petrusbrief und die Kritik* (1906).

————, *Der petrinische Lehrbegriff* (1855).

WILLIAMS, N. M., *American Comm.*

WINDISCH, H., *Die Katholische Briefe. Handbuch zum N.T.* (2 Aufl., 1930).

WOHLENBERG, G., *Der erste und zweite Petrusbrief und der Judasbrief.* (Zahn Komm., 2 Aufl., 1915.)

CHAPTER I

1. *Peter* (*Petros*). Greek form for the Aramaic (Chaldaic) *Cēphās*, the nickname given Simon by Jesus when he first saw him (John 1:42) and reaffirmed in the Greek form on his great confession (Matt. 16:18), with an allusion to *petra*, another form for a rock, ledge, or cliff. In II Peter 1:1 we have both *Simōn* and *Petros*. Paul in his Epistles always terms himself Paul, not Saul. So Peter uses this name, not Cephas or Simon, because he is writing to Christians scattered over Asia Minor. The nominative absolute occurs here as in James 1:1, but without *chairein* as there, the usual form of greeting in letters (Acts 23:26) so common in the papyri. *An apostle of Jesus Christ* (*apostolos Iēsou Christou*). This is his official title, but in II Pet. 1:1 *doulos* is added, which occurs alone in James 1:1. In II and III John we have only *ho presbuteros* (the elder), as Peter terms himself *sunpresbuteros* in I Pet. 5:1. Paul's usage varies greatly: only the names in I and II Thessalonians, the title *apostolos* added and defended in Galatians and Romans as also in I and II Corinthians and Colossians and Ephesians and II Timothy with "by the will of God" added, and in I Timothy with the addition of "according to the command of God." In Philippians Paul has only "*doulos* (slave) *Christou Iēsou*," like James and Jude. In Romans and Titus Paul has both *doulos* and *apostolos*, like II Peter, while in Philemon he uses only *desmios* (prisoner) *Iēsou Christou*. *To the elect* (*eklektois*). Without article (with the article in Matt. 24:22, 24, 31) and dative case, "to elect persons" (viewed as a group). Bigg takes *eklektois* (old, but rare verbal adjective from *eklegō*, to pick out, to select) as an adjective describing the next word, "to elect sojourn-

78

ers." That is possible and is like *genos eklekton* in 2:9. See the distinction between *klētoi* (called) and *eklektoi* (chosen) in Matt. 22:14. *Who are sojourners (parepidēmois).* Late double compound adjective (*para, epidēmountes*, Acts 2:10, to sojourn by the side of natives), strangers sojourning for a while in a particular place. So in Polybius, papyri, in LXX only twice (Gen. 23:4; 38 or 39 12), in N.T. only here, 2:11; Heb. 11:13. The picture in the metaphor here is that heaven is our native country and we are only temporary sojourners here on earth. *Of the Dispersion (diasporās).* See John 7:35 for literal sense of the word for scattered (from *diaspeirō*, to scatter abroad, Acts 8:1) Jews outside of Palestine, and James 1:1 for the sense here to Jewish Christians, including Gentile Christians (only N.T. examples). Note absence of the article, though a definite conception (of the Dispersion). The Christian is a pilgrim on his way to the homeland. These five Roman provinces include what we call Asia Minor north and west of the Taurus mountain range (Hort). Hort suggests that the order here suggests that Silvanus (bearer of the Epistle) was to land in Pontus from the Euxine Sea, proceed through Galatia, Cappadocia, Asia, to Bithynia, where he would re-embark for Rome. This, he holds, explains the separation of Pontus and Bithynia, though the same province. Only Galatia and Asia are mentioned elsewhere in the N.T. as having Christian converts, but the N.T. by no means gives a full account of the spread of the Gospel, as can be judged from Col. 1:6, 23.

2. *According to (kata).* Probably to be connected with *eklektois* rather than with *apostolos* in spite of a rather loose arrangement of words and the absence of articles in verses 1 and 2. *The foreknowledge (prognōsin).* Late substantive (Plutarch, Lucian, papyri) from *proginōskō* (1:20), to know beforehand, only twice in N.T. (here and Acts 2:23 in Peter's sermon). In this Epistle Peter often uses substantives

rather than verbs (cf. Rom. 8:29). *Of God the Father (theou patros)*. Anarthous again and genitive case. See *patēr* applied to God also in 1:3, 17 as often by Paul (Rom. 1:7, etc.). Peter here presents the Trinity (God the Father, the Spirit, Jesus Christ). *In sanctification of the Spirit (en hagiasmōi pneumatos)*. Clearly the Holy Spirit, though anarthrous like *theou patros*. Late word from *hagiazō*, to render holy (*hagios*), to consecrate, as in 1 Thess. 4:7. The subjective genitive here, sanctification wrought by the Spirit as in 2 Thess. 2:13 (where the Trinity mentioned as here). *Unto obedience (eis hupakoēn)*. Obedience (from *hupakouō*, to hear under, to hearken) to the Lord Jesus as in 1:22 "to the truth," result of "the sanctification." *And sprinkling of the blood of Jesus Christ (rantismon haimatos Iēsou Christou)*. Late substantive from *rantizō*, to sprinkle (Heb. 9:13), a word used in the LXX of the sacrifices (Numb. 19:9, 13, 20, etc.), but not in any non-biblical source so far as known, in N.T. only here and Heb. 12:24 (of the sprinkling of blood). Reference to the death of Christ on the Cross and to the ratification of the New Covenant by the blood of Christ as given in Heb. 9:19f.; 12:24 with allusion to Ex. 24:3–8. Paul does not mention this ritual use of the blood of Christ, but Jesus does (Matt. 26:28 = Mark. 14:24). Hence it is not surprising to find the use of it by Peter and the author of Hebrews. Hort suggests that Peter may also have an ulterior reference to the blood of the martyrs as in Rev. 7:14f.; 12:11, but only as illustration of what Jesus did for us, not as having any value. The whole Epistle is a commentary upon *prognōsis theou, hagiasmos pneumatos, haima Christou* (Bigg). Peter is not ashamed of the blood of Christ. *Be multiplied (plēthuntheiē)*. First aorist passive optative (volitive) of *plēthunō*, old verb (from *plēthus*, fulness), in a wish. So in II Pet. 1:2 and Jude 2, but nowhere else in N.T. salutations. Grace and peace (*charis kai eirēnē*) occur together in II Pet. 1:2, in II John 2 (with *eleos*), and in all Paul's Epistles (with *eleos* added in I and II Timothy).

3. *Blessed be* (*eulogētos*). No copula in the Greek (*estō*, let be, or *estin*, is, or *eiē*, may be). The verbal adjective (from *eulogeō*) occurs in the N.T. only of God, as in the LXX (Luke 1:68). See also II Cor. 1:3; Eph. 1:3. *The God and Father of our Lord Jesus Christ* (*ho theos kai patēr tou kuriou hēmōn Iēsou Christou*). This precise language in II Cor. 1:3; Eph. 1:3; and part of it in II Cor. 11:31, Rom. 15:6. See John 20:17 for similar language by Jesus. *Great* (*polu*). Much. *Begat us again* (*anagennēsas hēmās*). First aorist active articular (*ho*, who) participle of *anagennaō*, late, and rare word to beget again, in Aleph for *Sirach* (*Prol.* 20), in Philo, in Hermetic writings, in N.T. only here and verse 23. "It was probably borrowed by the New Paganism from Christianity" (Bigg). The Stoics used *anagennēsis* for *palingenesia* (Titus 3:5). If *anōthen* in John 3:3 be taken to mean "again," the same idea of regeneration is there, and if "from above" it is the new birth, anyhow. *Unto a living hope* (*eis elpida zōsan*). Peter is fond of the word "living" (present active participle of *zaō*) as in 1:23; 2:4, 5, 24; 4:5, 6. The Pharisees cherished the hope of the resurrection (Acts 23:6), but the resurrection of Jesus gave it proof and permanence (I Cor. 15:14, 17). It is no longer a dead hope like dead faith (James 2:17, 26). This revival of hope was wrought "by the resurrection of Jesus Christ" (*dia anastaseōs*). Hope rose up with Christ from the dead, though the disciples (Peter included) were slow at first to believe it.

4. *Unto an inheritance* (*eis klēronomian*). Old word (from *klēronomos*, heir) for the property received by the heir (Matt. 21:38), here a picture of the blessedness in store for us pilgrims (Gal. 3:18). *Incorruptible* (*aphtharton*). Old compound adjective (alpha privative and *phtheirō*, to corrupt), imperishable. So many inheritances vanish away

before they are obtained. *Undefiled* (*amianton*). Old verbal adjective (note alliteration) from alpha privative and *miainō*, to defile, without defect or flaw in the title, in N.T. only here, James 1:27; Heb. 13:4. *That fadeth not away* (*amaranton*). Alliterative and verbal adjective again from alpha privative and *marainō* (to dry up, to wither, as in James 1:11), late and rare word in several inscriptions on tombs, here only in N.T. These inscriptions will fade away, but not this inheritance in Christ. It will not be like a faded rose. *Reserved* (*tetērēmenēn*). Perfect passive participle of *tēreō*, old verb, to take care of, to guard. No burglars or bandits can break through where this inheritance is kept (Matt. 6:19f.; John 17:11f.). Cf. Col. 1:5, where "laid away" (*apokeimenēn*) occurs. *For you* (*eis humas*). More graphic than the mere dative.

5. *By the power of God* (*en dunamei theou*). No other *dunamis* (power) like this (Col. 1:3). *Are guarded* (*phrouroumenous*). Present (continuous process) passive articular (*tous*) participle of *phroureō*, to garrison, old verb (from *phrouros* sentinel), a military term (Acts 9:24; II Cor. 11:32), used of God's love (Phil. 4:7) as here. "The inheritance is kept; the heirs are guarded" (Bengel). *Through faith* (*dia pisteōs*). Intermediate agency (*dia*), the immediate being (*en*, in, by) God's power. *Unto a salvation* (*eis sōtērian*). Deliverance is the goal (*eis*) of the process and final salvation here, consummation as in I Thess. 5:8, from *sōtēr* (Saviour, from *sōzō*, to save). *Ready* (*hetoimēn*). Prepared awaiting God's will (Gal. 3:23; Rom. 8:18). *To be revealed* (*apokaluphthēnai*). First aorist passive infinitive of *apokaluptō*, to unveil. Cf. Col. 3:4 for *phaneroō* (to manifest) in this sense. *In the last time* (*en kairōi eschatōi*). This precise phrase nowhere else, but similar ones in John 6:39; Acts 2:17; James 5:3; II Tim. 3:1; II Pet. 3:3; Heb. 1:2; Jude 18; I John 2:18. Hort translates it here "in a

season of extremity," but it is usually taken to refer to the Day of Judgment. That day no one knows, Jesus said.

6. *Wherein* (*en hōi*). This translation refers the relative *hōi* to *kairōi*, but it is possible to see a reference to *Christou* (verse 3) or to *theou* (verse 5) or even to the entire content of verses 3 to 5. Either makes sense, though possibly *kairōi* is correct. *Ye greatly rejoice* (*agalliāsthe*). Present middle indicative (rather than imperative) of *agalliaomai*, late verb from *agallomai*, to rejoice, only in LXX, N.T., and ecclesiastical literature as in Matt. 5:12. *Now for a little while* (*oligon arti*). Accusative case of time (*oligon*) probably as in Mark 6:31, though it can be used of space (to a small extent) as in Luke 5:3. *If need be* (*ei deon*). Present active neuter singular participle of *dei* (it is necessary). Some MSS. have *estin* after *deon* (periphrastic construction). Condition of first class. *Though ye have been put to grief* (*lupēthentes*). First aorist passive participle (concessive circumstantial use) of *lupeō*, to make sorrowful (from *lupē*, sorrow), old and common verb. See II Cor. 6:10. *In manifold temptations* (*en poikilois peirasmois*). Just the phrase in James 1:2, which see for discussion. "Trials" clearly right here as there. Seven N.T. writers use *poikilos* (varied).

7. *The proof of your faith* (*to dokimion humōn tēs pisteōs*). The identical phrase in James 1:3 and probably derived from there by Peter. See there for discussion of *to dokimion* (the test or touchstone of faith). *Being more precious* (*polutimoteron*). No word for "being" (*on*) in the Greek. The secondary uncials have *polu timiōteron*. The text is the comparative of *polutimos*, late adjective (Plutarch) from *polu* and *timē* (of great price) as in Matt. 13:46. *Than gold* (*chrusiou*). Ablative case after the comparative adjective. *That perisheth* (*tou apollumenou*). Present middle articular participle of *apollumi* to destroy. Even gold perishes (wears away). *Though it is proved by fire* (*dia puros de dokimazo-*

menou). Present passive articular participle (in the ablative like *chrusiou*) of *dokimazō* (common verb for testing metals) with *de*, which gives a concessive sense to the participle Faith stands the test of fire better than gold, but even gold is refined by fire. *That might be found* (*hina heurethēi*). Purpose clause with *hina* and the first aorist passive subjunctive of *heuriskō*, common verb, to find. As in II Pet. 3:14, this is the result of the probation by God as the Refiner of hearts. *Unto praise and glory and honour* (*eis epainon kai doxan kai timēn*). Here probably both to God and man in the result. Cf. Matt. 5:11f.; Rom. 2:7, 10; I Tim. 1:17. *At the revelation of Jesus Christ* (*en apokalupsei Iēsou Christou*). So also in 1:13; 4:13; II Thess. 1:7; I Cor. 1:7; Luke 17:30 of the second coming of Christ as the Judge and Rewarder (Bigg).

8. *Whom* (*hon*). Relative referring to Christ just before and accusative case, object of both *idontes* and *agapate* (ye love). *Not having seen* (*ouk idontes*). Second aorist active participle of *horaō*, to see, with *ouk* rather than *mē* because it negatives an actual experience in contrast with *mē horōntes* (though not seeing, hypothetical case). On whom (*eis hon*) with *pisteuontes* common construction for "believing on" (*pisteuō eis*). It is possible that Peter here has in mind the words of Jesus to Thomas as recorded in John 20:29 ("Happy are those not seeing and yet believing"). Peter was present and heard the words of Jesus to Thomas, and so he could use them before John wrote his Gospel. *Ye rejoice greatly* (*agalliāte*). Same form as in verse 6, only active here instead of middle. *With joy* (*charāi*). Instrumental case (manner). *Unspeakable* (*aneklalētōi*). Late and rare double compound verbal (alpha privative and *eklaleō*), here only in N.T., in Dioscorides and Heliodorus, "unutterable," like Paul's "indescribable" (*anekdiēgētos*) gift (II Cor. 9:15, here alone in N.T.). *Full of glory* (*dedoxasmenēi*). Perfect passive participle of *doxazō*, to glorify, "glorified joy," like the glorified face of Moses (Ex. 34:29ff.; II Cor. 3:10).

9. *Receiving* (*komizomenoi*).   Present middle participle of
komizō, old verb, to receive back, to get what is promised
(5:4; Heb. 10:36).   *The end of your faith* (*to telos tēs pisteōs*).
The conclusion, the culmination of faith (II Cor. 3:13; Rom.
2:21f.; 10:4).   See Heb. 12:2 of Jesus as "Pioneer and Perfecter of Faith."   *Even the salvation of your souls* (*sōtērian
psuchōn*).   No "even" in the text, just the accusative of
apposition with *telos*, viz., final salvation.

10. *Concerning which salvation* (*peri hēs sōtērias*).   Another
relative clause (taking up *sōtēria* from verse 9 and incorpo-
rating it) in this long sentence (verses 3 to 12, inclusive, all
connected by relatives).   Peter lingers over the word *sōtēria*
(salvation) with something new to say each time (Bigg).
Here it is the general sense of the gospel of grace.   *Sought*
(*exezētēsan*).   First aorist active indicative of *ekzēteō*, to seek
out (Acts 15:17), late and rare compound, only in LXX and
N.T. save once in Aristides.   *Searched diligently* (*exēraunē-
san*).   First aorist active indicative of *exeraunaō*, old and
common compound (*exereunaō*), to search out diligently,
here only in N.T.   Both of these words occur together in
I Macc. 9:26.   *Of the grace that should come unto you* (*peri tēs
eis humas charitos*).   "Concerning the for you grace" (meant
for you).

11. *Searching* (*eraunōntes*).   Present active participle of
eraunaō, late form for older *ereunaō* (both in the papyri),
uncompounded verb (John 7:52), the compound occurring in
verse 10 above.   *What time or what manner of time* (*eis tina ē
poion kairon*).   Proper sense of *poios* (qualitative interrogative) kept here as in I Cor. 15:35, Rom. 3:27, though it is
losing its distinctive sense from *tis* (Acts 23:34).   The
prophets knew what they prophesied, but not at what time
the Messianic prophecies would be fulfilled.   *The Spirit of
Christ which was in them* (*to en autois pneuma Christou*).
Peter definitely asserts here that the Spirit of Jesus Christ
(the Messiah) was in the Old Testament prophets, the Holy

Spirit called the Spirit of Christ and the Spirit of God (Rom. 8:9), who spoke to the prophets as he would speak to the apostles (John 16:14). *Did point unto* (*edēlou*). Imperfect active of *dēloō*, to make plain, "did keep on pointing to," though they did not clearly perceive the time. *When it testified beforehand* (*promarturomenon*). Present middle participle of *promarturomai*, a late compound unknown elsewhere save in a writer of the fourteenth century (Theodorus Mech.) and now in a papyrus of the eighth. It is neuter here because *pneuma* is neuter, but this grammatical gender should not be retained as "it" in English, but should be rendered "he" (and so as to Acts 8:15). Here we have predictive prophecy concerning the Messiah, though some modern critics fail to find predictions of the Messiah in the Old Testament. *The sufferings of Christ* (*ta eis Christon pathēmata*). "The sufferings for (destined for) Christ" like the use of *eis* in verse 10 (*eis humas* for you). *The glories that should follow them* (*tas meta tauta doxas*). "The after these things (sufferings) glories." The plural of *doxa* is rare, but occurs in Ex. 15:11; Hos. 9:11. The glories of Christ followed the sufferings as in 4:13; 5:1, 6.

12. *To whom* (*hois*). Dative plural of the relative pronoun. To the prophets who were seeking to understand. Bigg observes that "the connexion between study and inspiration is a great mystery." Surely, but that is no argument for ignorance or obscurantism. We do the best that we can and only skirt the shore of knowledge, as Newton said. *It was revealed* (*apekaluphthē*). First aorist passive indicative of *apokaluptō*, old verb, to reveal, to unveil. Here is revelation about the revelation already received, revelation after research. *Did they minister* (*diēkonoun*). Imperfect active of *diakoneō*, old verb, to minister, "were they ministering." *Have been announced* (*anēggelē*). Second aorist passive indicative of *anaggellō*, to report, to bring back tidings (John 4:25). *Through them* (*dia tōn*). Intermediate agent

(*dia*), "the gospelizers" (*tōn euaggelisamenōn*, articular first aorist middle participle of *euaggelizō*, to preach the gospel). *By the Holy Ghost* (*pneumati hagiōi*). Instrumental case of the personal agent, "by the Holy Spirit" (without article). *Sent forth from heaven* (*apostalenti*). Second aorist passive participle of *apostellō* in instrumental case agreeing with *pneumati hagiōi* (the Spirit of Christ of verse 11). *Desire* (*epithumousin*). Eagerly desire (present active indicative of *epithumeō*, to long for). *To look into* (*parakupsai*). First aorist active infinitive of *parakuptō*, old compound to peer into as in Luke 24:12; John 20:5, 11; James 1:25, which see. For the interest of angels in the Incarnation see Luke 2:13f.

13. *Wherefore* (*dio*). "Because of which thing," the glorious free grace opened for Gentiles and Jews in Christ (verses 3–12). *Girding up* (*anazōsamenoi*). First aorist middle participle of *anazōnnumi*, late and rare verb (Judges 18:16; Prov. 29:35; 31:17), here only in N.T., vivid metaphor for habit of the Orientals, who quickly gathered up their loose robes with a girdle when in a hurry or starting on a journey. *The loins* (*tas osphuas*). Old word for the part of the body where the girdle (*zōnē*) was worn. Metaphor here as in Luke 12:35; Eph. 6:14. *Mind* (*dianoias*). Old word for the faculty of understanding, of seeing through a thing (*dia*, *noeō*) as in Matt. 22:37. *Be sober* (*nēphontes*). "Being sober" (present active participle of *nēphō*, old verb, but in N.T. always as metaphor (I Thess. 5:6, 8, etc., and so in 4:7). *Perfectly* (*teleiōs*). Adverb, old word (here alone in N.T.), from adjective *teleios* (perfect), connected with *elpisate* (set your hope, first aorist active imperative of *elpizō*) in the Revised Version, but Bigg, Hort, and most modern commentators take it according to Peter's usual custom with the preceding verb, *nēphontes* ("being perfectly sober," not "hope perfectly"). *That is to be brought* (*tēn pheromenēn*). Present passive articular participle of *pherō*, picturing the

process, "that is being brought." For "revelation" (*apoka-lupsei*) see end of verse 7.

14. *As children of obedience* (*hōs tekna hupakoēs*). A common Hebraism (descriptive genitive frequent in LXX and N.T., like *huioi tēs apeitheias*, children of disobedience, in Eph. 2:2) suggested by *hupakoēn* in verse 2, "children marked by obedience." *Not fashioning yourselves* (*mē sunschēmatizomenoi*). Usual negative *mē* with the participle (present direct middle of *sunschēmatizō*, a rare (Aristotle, Plutarch) compound (*sun, schēmatizō*, from *schēma* from *echō*), in N.T. only here and Rom. 12:2 (the outward pattern in contrast with the inward change *metamorphoō*). See Phil. 2:6f. for contrast between *schēma* (pattern) and *morphē* (form). *According to your former lusts* (*tais proteron epithumiais*). Associative instrumental case after *sunschēmatizomenoi* and the bad sense of *epithumia* as in 4:2; II Pet. 1:4; James 1:14f. *In the time of your ignorance* (*en tēi agnoiāi humōn*). "In your ignorance," but in attributive position before "lusts." *Agnoia* (from *agnoeō*, to be ignorant) is old word, in N.T. only here, Acts 3:17; 17:30; Eph. 4:18.

15. *But like as he which called you is holy* (*alla kata ton kalesanta humas hagion*). This use of *kata* is a regular Greek idiom (here in contrast with *sunschēmatizomenoi*). "But according to the holy one calling you or who called you" (first aorist articular participle of *kaleō*, to call). God is our standard or pattern (*kata*), not our lusts. *Be ye yourselves also holy* (*kai autoi hagioi genēthēte*). First aorist (ingressive) passive imperative of *ginomai*, to become with allusion (*kai* also) to *kata* (God as our example), "Do ye also become holy." For *anastrophē* (manner of life) see verse 18; 2:12; 3:1–16; James 3:13; II Pet. 2:7. Peter uses *anastrophē* eight times. The original meaning (turning up and down, back and forth) suited the Latin word *conversatio* (*converto*), but not our modern "conversation" (talk, not walk).

16. *Because it is written* (*dioti gegraptai*). "Because (*dioti*

stronger than *hoti* below) it stands written" (regular formula
for O.T. quotation, perfect passive indicative of *graphō*).
The quotation is from Lev. 11:44; 19:2; 20:7. Reënforced
by Jesus in Matt. 5:48. The future *esesthe* here is volitive like
an imperative.

17. *If ye call* (*ei epikaleisthe*). Condition of first class and
present middle indicative of *epikaleō*, to call a name on, to
name (Acts 10:18). *As Father* (*patera*). Predicate accusative in apposition with *ton—krinonta*. *Without respect of
persons* (*aprosōpolēmptōs*). Found nowhere else except in
the later Ep. of Clem. of Rome and Ep. of Barn., from
alpha privative and *prosōpolēmptēs* (Acts 10:34. See James
2:9 for *prosōpolēmpteō* and 2:1 for *prosōpolēmpsia*) from
prosōpon lambanō (in imitation of the Hebrew). *According
to each man's work* (*kata to hekastou ergon*). "According to
the deed of each one" God judges (*krinonta*) just as Christ
judges also (II Cor. 5:10). *Pass* (*anastraphēte*). Second
aorist passive imperative of *anastrephō*, metaphorical sense
as in II Cor. 1:12; 2 Pet. 2:18. *The time* (*ton chronon*).
Accusative case of extent of time. *Of your sojourning* (*tēs
paroikias humōn*). A late word, found in LXX (Ps. 119:5)
and in N.T. only here and Acts 13:17 and in ecclesiastical
writers (one late Christian inscription). It comes from
paroikeō, old verb, to dwell beside (in one's neighbourhood),
and so of pilgrims or strangers (*paroikos* Acts 7:6) as of
Jews away from Palestine or of Christians here on earth,
then of a local region (our "parish"). Peter here recurs
to 1:1 ("sojourners of the Dispersion"). *In fear* (*en phoboi*).
Emphatic position at beginning of the clause with *anastraphēte* at the end.

18. *Knowing* (*eidotes*). Second perfect active participle
of *oida*, causal participle. The appeal is to an elementary
Christian belief (Hort), the holiness and justice of God with
the added thought of the high cost of redemption (Bigg).
Ye were redeemed (*elutrōthēte*). First aorist passive indica--

tive of *lutroō*, old verb from *lutron* (ransom for life as of a slave, Matt. 20:28), to set free by payment of ransom, abundant examples in the papyri, in N.T. only here, Luke 24:21; Titus 2:14. The ransom is the blood of Christ. Peter here amplifies the language in Is. 52:3f. *Not with corruptible things* (*ou phthartois*). Instrumental case neuter plural of the late verbal adjective from *phtheirō* to destroy or to corrupt, and so perishable, in N.T. here, verse 23; I Cor. 9:25; 15:53f.; Rom. 1:23. *Arguriōi ē chrusiōi* (silver or gold) are in explanatory apposition with *phthartois* and so in the same case. Slaves were set free by silver and gold. *From your vain manner of life* (*ek tēs mataias humōn anastrophēs*). "Out of" (*ek*), and so away from, the pre-Christian *anastrophē* of verse 15, which was "vain" (*mataias*. Cf. Eph. 4:17–24). *Handed down from your fathers* (*patroparadotou*). This adjective, though predicate in position, is really attributive in idea, like *cheiropoiētou* in Eph. 2:11 (Robertson, *Grammar*, p. 777), like the French idiom. This double compound verbal adjective (*pater, para, didōmi*), though here alone in N.T., occurs in Diodorus, Dion. Halic. and in several inscriptions (Moulton and Milligan's *Vocabulary*; Deissmann, *Bible Studies*, pp. 266f.). The Jews made a wrong use of tradition (Matt. 15:2ff.), but the reference here seems mainly to Gentiles (1 Pet. 2:12).

19. *But with precious blood* (*alla timiōi haimati*). Instrumental case of *haima* after *elutrōthēte* (repeated from verse 18). Peter here applies the old adjective *timios* (from *timē*, of Christ in I Pet. 2:7) to Christ as in 1:7 *polutimoteron* to testing of faith. The blood of anyone is "precious" (costly), far above gold or silver, but that of Jesus immeasurably more so. *As of a lamb* (*hōs amnou*). This word occurs in Lev. 12:8; Numb. 15:11; Deut. 14:4 of the lamb prescribed for the passover sacrifice (Ex. 12:5). John the Baptist applies it to Jesus (John 1:29, 36). It occurs also in Acts 8:32 quoted from Is. 53:7f. Undoubtedly both the Baptist

and Peter have this passage in mind. Elsewhere in the N.T. *arnion* is used of Christ (Rev. 5:6, 12). Jesus is the Paschal Lamb. Peter sees clearly that it was by the blood of Christ that we are redeemed from sin. *Without blemish* (*amōmou*). Without (alpha privative) spot (*mōmos*) as the paschal lamb had to be (Lev. 22:21). So Heb. 9:14. *Without spot* (*aspilou*). Without (alpha privative) stain (*spilos* spot) as in James 1:27; II Pet. 3:14; I Pet. 6:14. *Even the blood of Christ* (*Christou*). Genitive case with *haimati*, but in unusual position for emphasis and clearness with the participles following.

20. *Who was foreknown indeed* (*proegnōsmenou men*). Perfect passive participle (in genitive singular agreeing with *Christou*) of *proginōskō*, old verb, to know beforehand (Rom. 8:29; II Pet. 3:17). See *prognōsin theou* in verse 2. *Before the foundation of the world* (*pro katabolēs kosmou*). This precise curious phrase occurs in John 17:24 in the Saviour's mouth of his preincarnate state with the Father as here and in Eph. 1:4. We have *apo katabolēs kosmou* in Matt. 25:34 (*kosmou* omitted in Matt. 13:35); Luke 11:50; Heb. 4:3; 9:26; Rev. 13:8; 17:8. *Katabolē* (from *kataballō*) was originally laying the foundation of a house (Heb. 6:1). The preincarnate Messiah appears in the counsels of God also in I Cor. 2:7; Col. 1:26f.; Eph. 1:9f.; 3:9–11; Rom. 16:25; I Tim. 1:9. *But was manifested* (*phanerōthentos de*). First aorist (ingressive) passive participle of *phaneroō*, referring to the Incarnation in contrast with the preëxistence of Christ (cf. John 1:31; I John 3:5, 8). *At the end of the times* (*ep' eschatou tōn chronōn*). Like *ep' eschatou tōn hēmerōn* (Heb. 1:2). The plural *chronoi*, doubtless referring to successive periods in human history until the fullness of the time came (Gal. 4:4). *For your sake* (*di' humās*). Proof of God's love, not of their desert or worth (Acts 17:30f.; Heb. 11:39f.).

21. *Who through him are believers in God* (*tous di' autou*

pistous eis theon). Accusative case in apposition with *humās* (you), "the through him (that is Christ as in 1:8 and Acts 3:16) believers (*pistous* correct text of A B) in God." *Which raised* (*ton egeiranta*). Accusative singular articular (agreeing with *theon*) first aorist active participle of *egeirō* (cf. *di' anastaseōs Iēsou* in verse 3). *Gave glory to him* (*doxan autōi donta*). Second aorist active participle of *didōmi* agreeing also with *theon*. See Peter's speech in Acts 3:13 about God glorifying (*edoxasen*) Jesus and also the same idea by Peter in Acts 2:33–36; 5:31. *So that your faith and hope might be in God* (*hōste tēn pistin humōn kai elpida eis theon*). *Hōste* with the infinitive (*einai*) and the accusative of general reference (*pistin kai elpida*) is used in the N.T. as in the *Koiné* for either purpose (Matt. 10:1) or usually result (Mark 4:37). Hence here result (so that is) is more probable than design.

22. *Seeing ye have purified* (*hēgnikotes*). Perfect active participle of *hagnizō*, old verb from *hagnos* (pure), here with *psuchas* (souls), with *kardias* (hearts) in James 4:8 as in I John 3:3 of moral cleansing also. See the ceremonial sense of the word as in LXX in John 11:55; Acts 21:24, 26; 24:18. *In your obedience* (*en tēi hupakoēi*). With repetition of the idea in 1:2, 2:14 (children of obedience). *To the truth* (*tēs aletheias*). Objective genitive with which compare John 17:17, 19 about sanctification in the truth and 2 Thess. 2:12 about believing the truth. There is cleansing power in the truth of God in Christ. *Unfeigned* (*anupokriton*). Late and rare double compound, here alone in Peter, but see James 3:17; II Cor. 6:6, etc. No other kind of *philadelphia* (brotherly love) is worth having (I Thess. 4:9; Heb. 13:1; II Pet. 1:7). *From the heart fervently* (*ek kardias ektenōs*). Late adverb (in inscriptions, Polybius, LXX). The adjective *ektenēs* is more common (I Pet. 4:8).

23. *Having been begotten again* (*anagegennēmenoi*). Perfect passive participle of *anagennaō*, which see in verse 2.

Not of corruptible seed (*ouk ek sporās phthartēs*). Ablative with *ek* as the source, for *phthartos* see verse 18, and *sporās* (from *speirō* to sow), old word (sowing, seed) here only in N.T., though *sporos* in Mark 4:26f., etc. For "incorruptible" (*aphthartou*) see verse 4, 3:4. *Through the word of God* (*dia logou theou*). See James 1:18 for "by the word of truth," verse 25 here, and Peter's use of *logos* in Acts 10:36. It is the gospel message. *Which liveth and abideth* (*zōntos kai menontos*). These present active participles (from *zaō* and *menō*) can be taken with *theou* (God) or with *logou* (word). In verse 25 *menei* is used with *rēma* (word). Still in Dan. 6:26 both *menōn* and *zōn* are used with *theos*. Either construction makes sense here.

24f. Quotation from Is. 40:6–8 (partly like the LXX, partly like the Hebrew). *For* (*dioti*). As in verse 16 (*dia* and *hoti*), "for that." So in 2:6. See a free use of this imagery about the life of man as grass and a flower in James 1:11. The best MSS. here read *autēs* (thereof) after *doxa* (glory) rather than *anthrōpou* (of man). *Withereth* (*exēranthē*). First aorist (gnomic, timeless) passive indicative of *xērainō* (see James 1:11). *Falleth* (*exepesen*). Second aorist (gnomic, timeless) active indicative of *ekpiptō* (see James 1:11). In verse 25 note *eis humās* (unto you) like *eis humās* in 1:4 (=*humin* dative).

CHAPTER II

1. *Putting away therefore (apothemenoi oun)*. Second aorist middle participle of *apotithēmi*, old and common verb, in metaphorical sense either to cleanse defilements (3:21; James 1:21) or to put off clothing (Rom. 13:12; Col. 3:5ff.; Eph. 4:22). Either sense suits here. Therefore *(oun)* because of the new birth (1:23) and the new life demanded. *Wickedness (kakian)*. This old word, from *kakos* (evil), in the ancients meant vice of any kind and note *pāsan* (all) here. *Guile (dolon)*. Old word (from *delō*, to catch with bait), deceit. *Hypocrisies (hupokriseis)*. Singular *(hupokrisin)* in the best MSS. See 1:22 *(anupokriton)* and Mark 7:6f. for Christ's denunciation of hypocrites which the disciples did not understand, including Peter (Matt. 15:16ff.). *Envies (phthonous)*. Genuine here, not *phonous* (murders), as B has it. For the word see Matt. 27:18. *Evil speakings (katalalias)*. Late word (from *katalalos*, defamer, Rom. 1:30), in N.T. only here and II Cor. 12:20. "Backbitings." For verb see 2:12.

2. *As newborn babes (hōs artigennēta brephē)*. *Brephos*, old word, originally unborn child (Luke 1:41, 44), then infant (Luke 2:12), here figuratively, like *nēpioi*. *Artigennēta* is a late and rare compound (Lucian, imperial inscription) from *arti* and *gennaō*, with evident allusion to *anagegennēmenoi* in 1:23, probably meaning that they were recent converts, possibly slight proof that the Epistle written before Romans by Paul (Kühl). *Long for (epipothēsate)*. First aorist (constative) active imperative of *epipotheō*, old verb for intense yearning (Phil. 2:26). *The spiritual milk which is without guile (to logikon adolon gala)*. *Gala* is old word for milk as in I Cor. 9:7 and as metaphor in I Cor. 3:2.

94

Adolos is an old compound (here alone in N.T.) adjective (alpha privative and *dolos* deceit), unadulterated milk which, alas, is so hard to get. *Logikon* is an old adjective in *-ikos*, from *logos* (reason, speech), in N.T. only here and Rom. 12:1, used here with allusion to *logou* (1:23) and *rēma* (1:25), "the sincere milk of the word" ("the milk belonging to the word," either the milk which is the word or the milk contained in the word, that is Christ). So Bigg holds. But in Rom. 12:1 Paul uses *logikon* in the sense of "rational" or "spiritual," and that idea is possible here as Hort holds. In the Pelagia legend (Usener) we have the phrase *tōn logikōn probatōn tou Christou* (the spiritual or rational sheep of Christ). *That ye may grow thereby* (*hina en autōi auxēthēte*). Purpose clause with *hina* and the first aorist passive subjunctive of *auxanō*, old and common verb to grow. See this same metaphor in Col. 2:19; Eph. 4:15. Peter uses the word of God as the food for growth, especially for babes in Christ, not emphasizing the distinction from solid food (*brōma*) made in I Cor. 3:2; Heb. 5:13. Salvation (*sōtērian*) here is final salvation.

3. *If ye have tasted* (*ei egeusasthe*). Condition of first class with *ei* and first aorist middle indicative of *geuō* in figurative sense as in Heb. 6:4f. "A taste excites the appetite" (Bengel). *Gracious* (*chrēstos*). Quotation from Ps. 33(34):9. The Hebrew for the LXX *chrēstos* is simply *tobh* (good). Plato used the word for food also, and Peter carries out the metaphor in *gala* (milk) as in Luke 5:39.

4. *Unto whom* (*pros hon*). The Lord, carrying on the imagery and language of the Psalm. *Coming* (*proserchomenoi*). Present middle participle masculine plural of *proserchomai* (*proselthate* in the Psalm) agreeing with the subject of *oikodomeisthe*. *A living stone* (*lithon zōnta*). Accusative case in apposition with *hon* (whom, the Lord Christ). There is apparent an intentional contradiction between "living" and "stone." Cf. "living hope" in 1:3 and "living word"

in 1:23. *Rejected indeed of men* (*hupo anthrōpōn men apode-dokimasmenon*). Perfect passive participle of *apodokimazō*, old verb to repudiate after test (Luke 9:22), in the accusative case agreeing with *lithon*. *But with God* (*para de theōi*). "By the side of God," as he looks at it, in contrast with the rejection "by men" (*hupo anthrōpōn*). *Elect* (*eklekton*). From Is. 28:6 as in *entimon* (precious, for which see Luke 7:2) rather than *dokimon* (proved) expected after *apodedoki-masmenon* as meaning far more in God's sight, "a pre-eminence of position with" (Hort).

5. *Ye also as living stones* (*kai autoi hōs lithoi zōntes*). Peter applies the metaphor about Christ as the living stone to the readers, "ye yourselves also." *Are built up a spiritual house* (*oikodomeisthe oikos pneumatikos*). Present passive indicative second person plural of *oikodomeō*, the very verb used by Jesus to Peter in Matt. 16:18 (*oikodomēsō*) of building his church on the rock. If the metaphor of a house of living stones seems "violent" (Vincent), it should be remembered that Jesus employed the figure of a house of believers. Peter just carried it a bit farther and Paul uses a temple for believers in one place (I Cor. 3:16) and for the kingdom of God in general (Eph. 2:22), as does the author of Hebrews (3:6). This "spiritual house" includes believers in the five Roman provinces of 1:1 and shows clearly how Peter understood the metaphor of Christ in Matt. 16:18 to be not a local church, but the church general (the kingdom of Christ). *To be a holy priesthood* (*eis hierateuma hagion*). Late word (from *hierateuō*, to serve as priest, Luke 1:8 alone in N.T.), in LXX (Ex. 19:6), in N.T. only here and verse 9, either the office of priest (Hort) or an order or body of priests. At any rate, Peter has the same idea of Rev. 1:6 (*hiereis*, priests) that all believers are priests (Heb. 4:16) and can approach God directly. *To offer up* (*anenegkai*). First aorist active infinitive (of purpose here) of *anapherō*, the usual word for offering sacrifices (Heb. 7:27). Only these are "spiritual"

(pneumatikas) as pictured also in Heb. 13:15f. *Acceptable* *(euprosdektous)*. Late (Plutarch) double compound verbal adjective *(eu, pros, dechomai)* as in II Cor. 6:2.

6. *It is contained (periechei)*. Present active (here intransitive, to contain, only N.T. example) of *periechō*, old verb, to surround, transitive in Luke 5:9 to seize (only other N.T. example). The formula with *periechei* is in Josephus (Ant. XI. 7). This Scripture *(en graphēi)* is Is. 28:16 with some changes. Peter had in verse 4 already quoted *eklekton* and *entimon*. Now note *akrogōniaion* (a chief corner stone), a word apparently invented by Isaiah (from *akros*, highest, and *gōniaios*, Attic word for corner stone). Paul in Eph. 2:20 uses the same word, making Christ the chief corner stone (the only other N.T. example). In Isaiah the metaphor is rather a foundation stone. Peter and Paul make it "the primary foundation stone at the structure" (W. W. Lloyd). *On him (ep'autōi)*. That is, "on it" (this corner stone, that is, Christ). *Shall not be put to shame (ou mē kataischunthēi)*. Strong negatives *ou mē* with first aorist passive subjunctive of *kataischunō*, old verb, to put to shame (Rom. 5:5).

7. *The preciousness (hē timē)*. Or "the honour." Explanation of *entimon* and *ou mē kataischunthēi* and only true "for you which believe" *(tois pisteuousin* ethical dative of articular present active participle of *pisteuō* to believe). *But for such as disbelieve (apistousin de)*. Dative present active participle again of *apisteō*, opposite of *pisteuō* (Luke 24:11). *Was made the head of the corner (egenēthē eis kephalēn gōnias)*. This verse is from Ps. 118:22 with evident allusion to Is. 28:16 *(kephalēn gōnias = akrogōniaion)*. See Matt. 21:42 = Mark 12:10 = Luke 20:17, where Jesus himself quotes Ps. 118:22 and applies the rejection of the stone by the builders *(hoi oikodomountes*, the experts) to the Sanhedrin's conduct toward him. Peter quoted it also (and applied it as Jesus had done) in his speech at the Beautiful Gate (Acts 4:11). Here he quotes it again to the same purpose.

8. *And* (*kai*). Peter now quotes Is. 8:14 and gives a new turn to the previous quotation. To the disbelieving, Christ was indeed "a stone of stumbling (*lithos proskommatos*) and rock of offence (*petra skandalou*)," quoted also by Paul in Rom. 9:32f., which see for discussion. *Proskomma* (from *proskoptō*, to cut against) is an obstacle against which one strikes by accident, while *skandalon* is a trap set to trip one, but both make one fall. Too much distinction need not be made between *lithos* (a loose stone in the path) and *petra* (a ledge rising out of the ground). *For they* (*hoi*). Causal use of the relative pronoun. *Stumble at the word, being disobedient* (*proskoptousin tōi logōi apeithountes*). Present active indicative of *proskoptō* with dative case, *logōi*, and present active participle of *apeitheō* (cf. *apistousin* in 2:7) as in 3:1. *Tōi logōi* can be construed with *apeithountes* (stumble, being disobedient to the word). *Whereunto also they were appointed* (*eis ho kai etethēsan*). First aorist passive indicative of *tithēmi*. See this idiom in I Tim. 2:7. "Their disobedience is not ordained, the penalty of their disobedience is" (Bigg). They rebelled against God and paid the penalty.

9. *But ye* (*humeis de*). In contrast with the disobedient ones. *An elect race* (*genos eklekton*). From Is. 43:20. The blood relation of the spiritual Israel (not the Jewish race) through the new birth (1:23). *A royal priesthood* (*basileion hierateuma*). From Ex. 19:6 (cf. Rev. 1:6; 5:10). The official in Christian churches is *presbuteros* = *episcopos*, not *hiereus*. We are all *hiereis* (priests). Cf. 2:5. *A holy nation* (*ethnos hagion*). Also from Ex. 19:6, but here applied, not to the national Israel, but to the spiritual Israel of believers (both Jews and Gentiles). *A people for God's own possession* (*laos eis peripoiēsin*). The idea here occurs in Ex. 19:5; Deut. 7:6; 14:2; 26:18, where we have *laos periousios* as in Titus 2:14 (alone in the N.T.), and in Mal. 3:17 we find *eis peripoiēsin* (for a possession). *Periousios laos* is a people over and above the others and *peripoiēsis* is a possession in a

special sense (Eph. 1:14). See Paul's use of *periepoiēsato* in Acts 20:28. The old rendering, "a peculiar people," had this idea of possession, for "peculiar" is from *pecus* (Latin for flock). *That ye may shew forth* (*hopōs exaggeilēte*). Purpose clause with *hopōs*, rather than *hina*, with the first aorist active subjunctive of *exaggellō*, old verb, to tell out, here alone in N.T. *The excellencies* (*tas aretas*). From Is. 43:21. Old word for any preëminence (moral, intellectual, military), often for "virtue," but not in that sense in the O.T. or the N.T. The word has the sense of moral worth in II Pet. 1:3, 5; Phil. 4:8; and the Apocrypha. In Isaiah (here quoted) it means praise and glory to God. So also Is. 42:12. See Acts 2:11 *ta megaleia tou theou* (the mighty works of God). *Darkness* (*skotous*). Heathenism. *His marvellous light* (*to thaumaston autou phōs*). Christianity. For *thaumaston* (from *thaumazō*) see Matt. 21:42. For the change from heathenism to Christianity see Col. 1:12; Eph. 5:8–14.

10. *Which in time past* (*hoi pote*). "Who once upon a time." *No people* (*ou laos*). This phrase from Hos. 2:23. Note use of *ou* (not *oudeis*) with *laos* like Hebrew negative. *Which had not obtained mercy* (*hoi ouk eleēmenoi*). Perfect passive articular participle of *eleeō* and the emphatic negative *ou*, with which compare Paul's use of Hos. 1 and 2 in Rom. 9:25, which may have been known to Peter or not. *But now have obtained mercy* (*nun de eleēthentes*). Change to first aorist passive participle from "the long antecedent state" to "the single event of conversion which ended it" (Hort).

11. *As sojourners and pilgrims* (*hōs paroikous kai parepidēmous*). This combination from the LXX (Gen. 33:4; Ps. 39:13). See 1:1 for *parepidēmos* and 1:17 for *paroikia* and Eph. 2:19 for *paroikos* (only there and here in N.T., Christians whose fatherland is heaven). *To abstain from* (*apechesthai*). Present middle (direct) infinitive of *apechō*, old verb, to hold back from (I Thess. 4:3). In indirect command (to keep on abstaining from) after *parakalō* (I beseech).

With the ablative case *tōn sarkikōn epithumiōn*, the grosser sins of the flesh (for *sarkikos* see I Cor. 3:3) like the list in 4:3. *Which* (*haitines*). "Which very ones." Like Latin *quippe qui*. *War against the soul* (*strateuontai kata tēs psuchēs*). Present middle indicative of *strateuō*, to carry on a campaign (James 4:1). See this struggle between the flesh and the spirit vividly pictured by Paul in Gal. 5:16–24.

12. *Seemly* (*kalēn*). Predicate adjective with *anastrophēn*, for which see 1:15, 18. The Gentiles are on the watch for slips in moral conduct by the Christians. *That* (*hina*). Final conjunction with *doxasōsin* (they may glorify, first aorist active subjunctive of *doxazō*, the purpose of the Christians about the Gentiles. *Wherein* (*en hōi*). "In what thing." *As evil-doers* (*hōs kakopoiōn*). As they did and do, old word (from *kakon* and *poieō*, John 18:30), in N.T. only here and verse 14 in correct text. Heathen talk against us (*katalalousin*) gleefully. *By your good works* (*ek tōn kalōn ergōn*). "Out of (as a result of) your good (beautiful) deeds." *Which they behold* (*epopteuontes*). Present active participle of *epopteuō*, old verb (from, *epoptēs*, overseer, spectator, II Pet. 1:16), to be an overseer, to view carefully, in N.T. only here and 3:2. *In the day of visitation* (*en hēmerāi episkopēs*). From Is. 10:33. Cf. its use in Luke 19:44, which see for the word *episkopē* (from *episkopeō*, to inspect (Heb. 12:15). Clear echo here of Matt. 5:16.

13. *Be subject to* (*hupotagēte*). Second aorist passive imperative second person plural of *hupotassō*, to subject to, as in 3:22. *Every ordinance of man* (*pasēi anthrōpinēi ktisei*). Dative case of old and common word *ktisis* (from *ktizō*, to create, to found), act of creation (Rom. 1:20), a creature or creation (Rom. 1:25), all creation (Col. 1:15), an institution as here (in Pindar so). *For anthrōpinos* (human) see James 3:7. Peter here approves no special kind of government, but he supports law and order as Paul does (Rom. 13:1–8) unless it steps in between God and man (Acts 4:20). *For the Lord's*

sake (*dia ton kurion*). For Jesus' sake. That is reason
enough for the Christian not to be an anarchist (Matt. 22:21).
The heathen were keen to charge the Christians with any
crime after Nero set the fashion. "It should not be forgotten that, in spite of the fine language of the philosophers, the
really popular religions in Greece and Rome were forms of
devil-worship, intimately blended with magic in all its
grades" (Bigg). *As supreme* (*hōs huperechonti*). Dative
singular of present active participle of *huperechō*, old verb
(intransitive), to stand out above (to have it over), as in
Rom. 13:1. It is not the divine right of kings, but the fact
of the king as the outstanding ruler.

14. *Unto governors* (*hēgemosin*). Dative again of *hēgemōn*,
a leader (from *hēgeomai*, to lead), old and common word (Matt.
10:18). *As sent by him* (*hōs di' autou pempomenois*). Present
passive participle of *pempō*. *Di'autou* is "by God," as Jesus
made plain to Pilate; even Pilate received his authority ultimately "from above" (John 18:11). *For vengeance on evil-
doers* (*eis ekdikēsin kakopoiōn*). Objective genitive with
ekdikēsin, for which see Luke 18:7f. *For praise to them that
do well* (*epainon agathopoiōn*). Objective genitive again,
agathopoios, a late word (Plutarch, Sirach) from *agathon* and
poieō here only in N.T. Found in a magical papyrus.

15. *By well-doing* (*agathopoiountas*). Present active participle of *agathopoieō*, only in LXX and N.T. (Mark 3:4).
In accusative case agreeing with *humās* understood, accusative of general reference with *phimoin*, present active infinitive (epexegetic infinitive after *to thelēma tou theou*, the will of
God), late and rare verb (from *phimos* muzzle), as in Matt.
22:12. *The ignorance of foolish men* (*tēn tōn aphronōn
anthrōpōn agnōsian*). *Agnōsia* is late and rare word (in the
papyri) from alpha privative and *gnōsis* (knowledge), in
N.T. only here and I Cor. 15:24 (disgraceful ignorance in
both instances). Note alliteration.

16. *As free* (*hōs eleutheroi*). Note nominative again con-

nected with *hupotagēte* in verse 13, not with *phimoin* in verse 14 (a parenthesis in fact). For this ethical sense of *eleutheros* see Gal. 4:26. *And not using your freedom (kai mē echontes tēn eleutherian).* "And not holding your liberty" (present active participle of *echō*, with usual negative *mē* with participle. *For a cloke of wickedness (hōs epikalumma tēs kakias). Epikalumma* (from *epikaluptō* Rom. 4:7) is a rare word (Aristotle, LXX) for veil, here only in N.T. and in figurative sense for pretext to do wickedness under, a thing, alas, that sometimes happens. *But as bondservants of God (all' hōs theou douloi).* Paul's proud title. There is no such thing as absolute freedom (personal freedom), for that is anarchy. Cf. Rom. 6:22 "enslaved to God."

17. *Honour all men (pantas timēsate).* Not with the same honour. Constative use of the aorist imperative. *Love the brotherhood (tēn adelphotēta agapāte).* Present active imperative of *agapaō*, keep on doing it. Note the abstract *adelphotēs* (from *adelphos*, brother) in the collective sense, rare save in ecclesiastical literature, though in I Macc. 12:10; IV Macc. 10:3, and in late papyri. It is a word for all Christians. *Fear God (ton theon phobeisthe).* In both senses of reverence and dread, and keep it up (present middle imperative). *Honour the king (ton basilea timāte).* Keep that up also. A fine motto in this verse.

18. *Servants (hoi oiketai).* Note article with the class as with *andres* (3:7), though not with *gunaikes* (3:1). *Oiketēs*, old word from *oikos* (house), means one in the same house with another (Latin *domesticus*), particularly house servants (slaves) in distinction from the general term *doulos* (slave). "Ye domestics." See similar directions to Christian servants (slaves) in Col. 3:22–25; Eph. 6:5–7; I Tim. 6:1f.; Titus 2:9f. *Oiketēs* in N.T. occurs only here, Luke 16:13; Acts 10:7; Rom. 14:4. *Be in subjection (hupotassomenoi).* Present middle participle of *hupotassō*. common late compound to subject oneself to one (Luke 2:51). Either the

participle is here used as an imperative (so in 3:1, 7) as in Rom. 12:16f., or the imperative *este* has to be supplied (Robertson, *Grammar*, p. 945). *To your masters* (*tois despotais*). Dative case of *despotēs*, old word for absolute owner in contrast with *doulos*. It is used also of God (Luke 2:29; Acts 4:24, 29) and of Christ (II Pet. 2:1; Jude 4). *Kurios* has a wider meaning and not necessarily suggesting absolute power. *To the good and gentle* (*tois agathois kai epieikesin*). Dative case also with the article with class. For *epieikēs* see on James 3:17. There were slave-owners (masters) like this as there are housekeepers and employers of workmen today. This is no argument for slavery, but only a sidelight on a condition bad enough at its best. *To the froward* (*tois skoliois*). "To the crooked." Old word, also in Luke 3:5; Acts 2:40; Phil. 2:15. Unfortunately there were slaveholders as there are employers today, like this group. The test of obedience comes precisely toward this group.

19. *For this is acceptable* (*touto gar charis*). "For this thing (neuter singular *touto*, obedience to crooked masters) is grace" (*charis* is feminine, here "thanks" as in Rom. 7:25). "Acceptable" calls for *euprosdekton* (2:5), which is not the text here. *If a man endureth griefs* (*ei huopherei tis lupas*). Condition of first class with *ei* and present active indicative of *hupopherō*, old verb, to bear up under, in N.T. only here, I Cor. 10:13; II Tim. 3:11. Note plural of *lupē* (grief). *For conscience toward God* (*dia suneidēsin theou*). Suffering is not a blessing in and of itself, but, if one's duty to God is involved (Acts 4:20), then one can meet it with gladness of heart. *Theou* (God) is objective genitive. For *suneidēsis* (conscience) see on Acts 23:1; I Cor. 8:7. It occurs again in I Pet. 3:16. *Suffering wrongfully* (*paschōn adikōs*). Present active participle of *paschō* and the common adverb *adikōs*, unjustly, here alone in N.T. This is the whole point, made clear already by Jesus in

Matt. 5:10–12, where Jesus has also "falsely" (pseudo-menoi). See also Luke 6:32–34.

20. *For what glory* (*poion gar kleos*). Qualitative interrogative (what kind of glory). "What price glory?" *Kleos* is old word from *kleō* (*kaleō*, to call), report, praise, glory, here only in N.T. *If ye shall take it patiently* (*ei hupomeneite*). First-class condition with *ei* and future active indicative of *hupomenō*, for which see James 1:12. Same condition also in next sentence (*all' ei*, etc.). *When ye sin* (*hamartanontes*). Present active participle of *hamartanō* (continued repetition). *And are buffeted for it* (*kai kolaphizomenoi*). Present passive participle of *kolaphizō*, late word (from *kolaphos* fist), only in N.T. (cf. Matt. 26:67) and ecclesiastical writers. Repeated action again. No posing as a martyr allowed here. Christians do sometimes deserve persecution, as Jesus implied (Matt. 5:10–12). *When ye do well* (*agathopoiountes*). Present active participle of *agathopoieō* as in verse 15. *And suffer for it* (*kai paschontes*). Present active participle of *paschō* (verse 19). No "for it" in the Greek here or in the previous sentence. *This is acceptable with God* (*touto charis para theōi*). "This thing (neuter) is thanks (verse 19) by the side of (*para*) God (as God looks at it)."

21. *For hereunto were ye called* (*eis touto gar eklēthēte*). First aorist indicative of *kaleō*, to call. They were called to suffer without flinching (Hort), if need be. *Because* (*hoti*). The fact that Christ suffered (*epathen*) lifts their suffering to a new plane. *Leaving you an example* (*humin hupolimpanōn hupogrammon*). Present active participle of the late Ionic verb *hupolimpanō* (in the papyri) for the common *hupoleipō*, to leave behind (under), here only in N.T. *Hupogrammos* is also a late and rare word (from *hupographō*, to write under), a writing-copy for one to imitate, in II Macc. 2:28; Philo, Clement of Rome, here only in N.T. Clement of Alex. (*Strom.* V. 8. 49) uses it of the copy-head at the

top of a child's exercise book for the child to imitate, including all the letters of the alphabet. The papyri give many examples of *hupographē* and *hupographō* in the sense of copying a letter. *That ye should follow his steps* (*hina epakolouthēsēte tois ichnesin autou*). Purpose clause with *hina* and first aorist active subjunctive of *epakoloutheō*, old verb, to follow closely upon, with the associative-instrumental (I Tim. 5:10, 24) or the locative here. *Ichnos* is old word (from *hikō*, to go), tracks, footprints, in N.T. only here, II Cor. 12:18; Rom. 4:12. Peter does not mean that Christ suffered only as an example (1:18), but he did leave us his example for our copying (I John 2:6).

22. *Who did no sin* (*hos hamartian ouk epoiēsen*). Quotation from Is. 53:9. He has already expressed the sinlessness of Christ in 1:19. The next clause is a combination of Is. 53:9 and Zeph. 3:13. For "guile" (*dolos*) see verse 1. *Was found* (*heurethē*). First aorist passive indicative of *heuriskō*. Christ's guilelessness stood the test of scrutiny (Vincent), as Peter knew (Matt. 26:60; John 18:38; 19:4, 6).

23. *When he was reviled* (*loidoroumenos*). Present passive participle of *loidoreō*, old verb (from *loidoros*, reviler, I Cor. 5:11) as in John 9:28. *Reviled not again* (*ouk anteloidorei*). Imperfect active (for repeated incidents) of *antiloidoreō*, late and rare compound (Plutarch, Lucian, one papyrus example with compound following the simplex verb as here, Moulton and Milligan's *Vocabulary*), here only in N.T. Idiomatic use of *anti* (in turn, return, back). *Threatened not* (*ouk ēpeilei*). Imperfect again (repeated acts) of *apeileō*, old compound (from *apeilē*, threat, Acts 9:1), in N.T. only here and Acts 4:17. *But committed himself* (*paredidou de*). Imperfect active again (kept on committing himself) of *paradidōmi*, to hand over, usually of one to a judge, but here not of another (as the Sanhedrin), but himself (supply *heauton*), for Jesus uses this very idea in Luke 23:46 as he dies. Jesus thus handed himself and his cause over to the

Father who judges righteously (*tōi krinonti dikaiōs*, dative of present active articular participle of *krinō*).

24. *Who his own self* (*hos autos*). Intensive pronoun with the relative referring to Christ (note relatives also in verses 22 and 23). *Bare our sins* (*anēnegken tas hamartias hēmōn*). Second aorist active indicative of *anapherō*, common verb of bringing sacrifice to the altar. Combination here of Is. 53:12 and Deut. 21:23. Jesus is the perfect sin offering (Heb. 9:28). For Christ's body (*sōma*) as the offering see I Cor. 11:24. "Here St. Peter puts the Cross in the place of the altar" (Bigg). *Upon the tree* (*epi to xulon*). Not tree here as in Luke 23:31, originally just wood (I Cor. 3:12), then something made of wood, as a gibbet or cross. So used by Peter for the Cross in Acts 5:30; 10:39; and by Paul in Gal. 3:13 (quoting Deut. 21:23). *Having died unto sins* (*tais hamartiais apogenomenoi*). Second aorist middle participle of *apoginomai*, old compound to get away from, with dative (as here) to die to anything, here only in N.T. *That we might live unto righteousness* (*hina tēi dikaiosunēi zēsōmen*). Purpose clause with *hina* and the first aorist active subjunctive of *zaō* with the dative (cf. Rom. 6:20). Peter's idea here is like that of Paul in Rom. 6:1–23, especially verses 2, 10f.). *By whose stripes ye were healed* (*hou tōi mōlōpi iathēte*). From Is. 53:5. First aorist passive indicative of *iaomai*, common verb to heal (James 5:16) and the instrumental case of *mōlōps*, rare word (Aristotle, Plutarch) for bruise or bloody wound, here only in N.T. Cf. 1:18. Writing to slaves who may have received such stripes, Peter's word is effective.

25. *For ye were going astray like sheep* (*ēte gar hōs probata planōmenoi*). Brought from Is. 53:6, but changed to periphrastic imperfect indicative with *ēte* and present middle participle of *planaō*, to wander away. Recall the words of Jesus in Luke 15:4–7. *But are now returned* (*alla epestraphēte*). Second aorist passive indicative of *epistrephō*, old verb,

to turn, to return (Matt. 10:13). *Unto the Shepherd and Bishop of your souls* (*epi ton poimena kai episkopon tōn psuchōn humōn*). Jesus called himself the Good Shepherd (John 10:11, and see also Heb. 13:20). Here alone is Christ called our "Bishop" (overseer). See both ideas combined in Ezek. 34:11. Philo calls God *Episcopos*. Jesus is also *Apostolos* Heb. 3:1) and he deserves all other titles of dignity that we can give him.

CHAPTER III

1. *In like manner* (*homoiōs*). Adverb closely connected with *hupotassomenoi*, for which see 2:18. *Ye wives* (*gunaikes*). Without article. About wives see also Col. 3:18; Eph. 5:22; Titus 2:4. *To your own husbands* (*tois idiois andrasin*). *Idiois* occurs also in Ephesians and Titus, but not in Colossians. It strengthens the idea of possession in the article *tois*. Wives are not enjoined to be in subjection to the husbands of other women, as some think it fine to be (affinities!) *Even if any obey not the word* (*kai ei tines apeithousin tōi logōi*). Condition of first class and dative case of *logos* (1:23, 25; 2:8), that is, remain heathen. *That they be gained* (*hina kerdēthēsontai*). Purpose clause with *hina* and first future passive indicative of *kerdainō*, old verb, to gain (from *kerdos*, gain, interest) as in Matt. 18:15. See the future with *hina* also in Luke 20:10; Rev. 3:9. *Without the word* (*aneu logou*). Probably here "word from their wives" (Hart), the other sense of *logos* (talk, not technical "word of God"). *By the behaviour of their wives* (*dia tēs tōn gunaikōn anastrophēs*). Won by pious living, not by nagging. Many a wife has had this blessed victory of grace.

2. *Beholding* (*epopteusantes*). First aorist active participle of *epopteuō*, for which see 2:12. See 2:12 also for *anastrophēn* (manner of life). *Chaste* (*hagnēn*). Pure because "in fear" (*en phobōi*), no word in the Greek for "coupled," fear of God, though in Eph. 5:33 fear (reverence for) of the husband is urged.

3. *Whose adorning* (*hōn kosmos*). Genitive plural of the relative referring to *gunaikōn* (wives). *Kosmos* has here its old meaning of ornament (cf. our cosmetics), not the common one of world (John 17:5) considered as an orderly

whole. *Mundus* in Latin is used in this double sense (ornament, world). *Let it be (estō)*. Imperative third singular of *eimi*. *Not the outward adorning of plaiting the hair (ouch ho exōthen emplokēs trichōn)*. The use of *ouch* here rather than *mē* (usual negative with the imperative) because of the sharp contrast in verse 4 (*all'*). The old adverb *exōthen* (from without) is in the attributive position like an adjective. *Emplokē* is a late word (from *emplekō*, to inweave, II. Tim. 2:4; II Pet. 2:20) in Strabo, but often in the papyri for struggle as well as plaiting, here only in N.T. *Of wearing (peritheseōs)*. Late and rare word (Galen, Arrian) from *peritithēmi* (Matt. 27:28), to put around, a placing around. Ornaments of gold were worn round the hair as nets and round the finger, arm, or ankle. *Or of putting on (enduseōs)*. Old word from *enduō* (to put on), here only in N.T. Peter is not forbidding the wearing of clothes and ornaments by women, but the display of finery by contrast. Cf. I Tim. 2:9–13 and Is. 3:16ff.

4. *But the hidden man of the heart (all' ho kruptos tēs kardias anthrōpos)*. Here *anthrōpos* is in contrast with *kosmos* just before. See Paul's use of *anthrōpos* for the outer and old, the inner and new man (II Cor. 4:16; Rom. 7:22; Col. 3:9; Eph. 3:16; 4:22, 24). See also the Jew *en kruptōi* (Rom. 2:29) and what Jesus said about God seeing "in secret" (Matt. 6:4, 6). *In the incorruptible apparel of a meek and quiet spirit (en tōi aphthartōi tou hēsuchiou kai praeōs pneumatos)*. No word in the Greek for "apparel" (*kosmōi*). For *aphthartos* see 1:4, 23. For *praus* see Matt. 5:5; 11:29. *Pneuma* (spirit) is here disposition or temper (Bigg), unlike any other use in the N.T. In 3:18, 19; 4:6 it means the whole inner man as opposed to *sarx* or *sōma*, very much as *psuchē* is used as opposed to *sōma*. *Which (ho)*. Spirit just mentioned. *Of great price (poluteles)*. Old word (from *polu* and *telos*, cost), in N.T. only here, Mark 14:3; I Tim. 2:9.

5. *Adorned themselves (ekosmoun heautas)*. Imperfect active

of customary action, "used to adorn themselves." *Kosmeō* is old verb from *kosmos* in the sense in verse 3. See Heb. 11:11, 35 for like tribute to holy women of the O.T. The participle *hupotassomenai* repeats verse 1.

6. *As Sarah* (*hōs Sarra*). *Obeyed Abraham* (*hupēkouen tōi Abraam*). Imperfect active of *hupakouō*, "used to obey" (with dative). *Calling him lord* (*kurion auton kalousa*). Present active participle of *kaleō*. See Gen. 18:12. *Whose children ye now are* (*hēs egenēthēte tekna*). First aorist passive indicative of *ginomai*, "whose children ye became." *If ye do well* (*agathopoiousai*). Present active feminine plural participle of *agathopoieō* (2:15), "doing good." *And are not put in fear by any terror* (*kai mē phoboumenai mēdemian ptoēsin*). Free quotation from Prov. 3:25, "and not fearing any terror" (cognate accusative of *ptoēsis*, after *phoboumenai*, present middle participle, late and rare word from *ptoeō*, to terrify, as in Luke 21:9, here only in N.T.). Perhaps Peter regards Sarah's falsehood as the yielding to a sudden terror (Hart). Hannah could also be named along with Sarah. The women somehow do not organize "daughters of Sarah" societies.

7. *Ye husbands likewise* (*hoi andres homoiōs*). Probably "likewise" here refers to honouring all men (2:17), not "likewise" of 3:1. *Dwell with* (*sunoikountes*). Present active participle of *sunoikeō*, old verb for domestic association, here only in N.T. Used as imperative here like the participle in 2:18; 3:1. *According to knowledge* (*kata gnōsin*). "With an intelligent recognition of the nature of the marriage relation" (Vincent). *Giving honour unto the woman as unto the weaker vessel* (*hōs asthenesterōi skeuei tōi gunaikeiōi aponemontes timēn*). Present active participle of *aponemō*, old verb, to assign, to portion out (or off), here only in N.T. *Skeuos* is an old and common word for vessel, furniture, utensil (Matt. 12:29; II Tim. 2:20). Here both husband and wife are termed vessels or "parts of the furniture of God's house" (Bigg). See Paul's use of *skeuos* for ministers (II Cor. 4:7). *Gunai-*

keiōi here is an adjective (female, feminine) from *gunē* (woman, wife). She is termed "the weaker" (*tōi astheneste-rōi*), not for intellectual or moral weakness, but purely for physical reasons, which the husband must recognize with due consideration for marital happiness. *Joint-heirs of the grace of life* (*sunklēronomoi charitos zōēs*). Late double compound found in an Ephesian inscription and the papyri, in N.T. only here, Rom. 8:17; Eph. 3:6; Heb. 11:9. God's gift of life eternal belongs to woman as well as to man. In the eyes of God the wife may be superior to the husband, not merely equal. *To the end that your prayers be not hindered* (*eis to mē egkoptesthai tas proseuchas humōn*). Purpose clause with *eis to* and the present passive infinitive (with negative *mē*) of *egkoptō*, to cut in, to interrupt, late verb (Polybius), as in Rom. 15:22, etc. Very vivid to us now with our telephones and radios when people cut in on us. *Proseuchas* (prayers) is the accusative of general reference. Husbands surely have here cause to consider why their prayers are not answered.

8. *Finally* (*to telos*). Adverbial accusative. Conclusion, not of the Epistle, but only of the addresses to various classes. No verb (*este* imperative, be) here. *Likeminded* (*homophrones*). Old compound (*homos, phrēn*), here only in N.T. *Compassionate* (*sumpatheis*). Old adjective (*sun, paschō*), in N.T. only here and Rom. 12:15. Our "sympathetic" in original sense. *Loving as brethren* (*philadelphoi*). Old compound (*philos, adelphos*), here only in N.T. *Tenderhearted* (*eusplagchnoi*). Late and rare compound (*eu* and *splagchnon*), in Hippocrates, Apocrypha, in N.T. only here and Eph. 4:32. *Humble minded* (*tapeinophrones*). Late compound (*tapeinos, phrēn*), in Plutarch, Prov. 29:23, here only in N.T.

9. *Not rendering evil for evil* (*mē apodidontes kakon anti kakou*). *Mē* and the present active participle of *apodidōmi*, to give back. The same phrase in Rom. 12:17 and the same

idea in I Thess. 5:15. Peter may have obtained it from Paul or both from Prov. 17:13; 20:22, "an approximation to Christ's repeal of the *lex talionis* (Matt. 5:38ff.) which Plato first opposed among the Greeks" (Hart). Common use of *anti* for exchange. *Reviling for reviling* (*loidorian anti loidorias*). Allusion to 2:23 (Christ's own example). *But contrariwise blessing* (*tounantion de eulogountes*). Adverbial accusative and crasis (*to enantion*) of the neuter article and the adjective *enantios* (*en, antios,* opposite, Matt. 14:24), "on the contrary." For *eulogountes* (present active participle of *eulogeō*) see Luke 6:28; Rom. 12:14 (imperative *eulogeite*). *For hereunto were ye called* (*hoti eis touto eklēthēte*). See 2:21 for this verb and use of *eis touto* (pointing to the preceding argument). *That ye should inherit a blessing* (*hina eulogian klēronomēsēte*). Purpose clause with *hina* and the first aorist active subjunctive of *klēronomeō*, a plain reference to Esau, who wanted "to inherit the blessing" (Heb. 12:17) after he had sold his birthright. Christians are the new Israel (both Gentiles and Jews) and are the spiritual descendants of Isaac (Gal. 4:22ff.).

10. *For* (*gar*). Reason for the entire exhortation in verses 8 and 9 and introducing in verses 10 to 12 a quotation from Ps. 34:13–17 with some slight changes. *Would love life* (*thelōn zōēn agapāin*). "Wishing to love life." This present life. The LXX expressions are obscure Hebraisms. The LXX has *agapōn* (participle present active of *agapaō*, not the infinitive *agapāin*. *Let him refrain* (*pausatō*). Third person singular first aorist active imperative of *pauō* to make stop, whereas the LXX has *pauson* (second person singular). *His tongue* (*tēn glōssan*). See James 3:1–12. *That they speak no guile* (*tou mē lalēsai dolon*). Purpose clause with genitive article *tou* (negative *mē*) and the first aorist active infinitive of *laleō*. But it can also be explained as the ablative case with the redundant negative *mē* after a verb of

hindering (*pausatō*) like Luke 4:42. See Robertson, *Grammar*, p. 1061. "Let him refrain his lips from speaking guile."

11. *Let him turn away* (*ekklinatō*). First aorist active imperative third person singular of *ekklinō*, where the LXX has *ekklinon* (second person singular). Old verb, in N.T. only here, Rom. 3:12; 16:17. Peter adapted the passage all through to his own construction and use. So as to *poiēsatō* (let him do) for *poiēson* (do thou), *zētēsatō* (let him seek) for *zētēson* (do thou seek), *diōxatō* (let him pursue) for *diōxon* (do thou pursue), all first aorist active imperatives (of *poieō*, *zēteō*, *diōkō*). See Heb. 12:14 for "pursuing peace." If men only did!

12. *Upon* (*epi*). In the case of righteous (*dikaious*, in the O.T. sense like *dikaion Lot* in II Pet. 2:7) for their good, but in the case of men "that do evil" (*epi poiountas kaka*, "upon men doing evil things") "the face of the Lord" (*prosōpon kuriou*) is not for their good, *epi* here approaching "against" in idea.

13. *That will harm you* (*ho kakōsōn humas*). Future active articular participle of *kakoō*, old verb (from *kakos*, bad) as in Acts 7:6, 19. Any real hurt, either that wishes to harm you or that can harm. See the words in Is. 50:9. *If ye be* (*ean genēsthe*). Rather, "if ye become" (condition of third class with *ean* and second aorist middle subjunctive of *ginomai*). *Zealous of that which is good* (*tou agathou zēlōtai*). "Zealots for the good" (objective genitive after *zēlōtai* (zealots, not zealous), old word from *zēloō* (I Cor. 12:12).

14. *But and if ye should suffer* (*all' ei kai paschoite*). "But if ye should also (or even) suffer." Condition of the fourth class with *ei* and the optative (undetermined with less likelihood), a rare condition in the vernacular *Koiné*, since the optative was a dying mode. If matters, in spite of the prophetic note of victory in verse 13, should come to actual suffering "for righteousness' sake" (*dia dikaiosunēn*) as in Matt. 5:10 (*heneken*, not *dia*), then "blessed" (*makarioi*, the

very word of Jesus there which see, a word meaning "happy," not *eulogētoi*) "are ye" (not in the Greek). If the conclusion were expressed regularly, it would be *eiēte an* (ye would be), not *este* (ye are). It is interesting to note the third-class condition in verse 13 just before the fourth-class one in verse 14. *Fear not their fear* (*ton phobon autōn mē phobēthēte*). Prohibition with *mē* and the first aorist (ingressive) passive subjunctive of *phobeomai*, to fear, and the cognate accusative *phobon* (fear, terror). "Do not fear their threats" (Bigg). Quotation from Is. 8:12f. *Neither be troubled* (*mēde taraxthēte*). Prohibition with *mēde* and the first aorist (ingressive) subjunctive of *tarassō*, to disturb (Matt. 2:6; John 12:27). Part of the same quotation. Cf. 3:6.

15. *Sanctify* (*hagiasate*). First aorist active imperative of *hagiazō*. This instead of being afraid. *Christ as Lord* (*kurion ton Christon*). *Ton Christon*, direct object with article and *kurion* predicate accusative (without article). This is the correct text, not *ton theon* of the *Textus Receptus*. An adaptation to Christ of Is. 8:13. *Being ready always* (*hetoimoi aei*). No participle in the Greek, old adjective (Tit. 3:1). *To give answer* (*pros apologian*). "For an apology," the old sense of *apologia*, an answer back, a defence (not excuse), as in Acts 22:1, from *apologeomai* to defend (not to apologize). *A reason concerning the hope that is in you* (*logon peri tēs en humin elpidos*). Original sense of *logon* (accusative of the thing with *aitounti* with *humās*, accusative of the person) "concerning the in you hope." Ready with a spoken defence of the inward hope. This attitude calls for an intelligent grasp of the hope and skill in presenting it. In Athens every citizen was expected to be able to join in the discussion of state affairs. *Yet with meekness and fear* (*alla meta prautētos kai phobou*). Of God (2:18; 3:2, 4), not of man.

16. *Having a good conscience* (*suneidēsin echontes agathēn*). Present active participle of *echō*. See 2:18 for *suneidēsin*

and 3:21 for *suneidēsis agathē* again ("a quasi-personifica-
tion," Hart). *That they may be put to shame* (*hina katai-
schunthōsin*). Purpose clause with *hina* and the first aorist
passive subjunctive of *kataischunō*, old verb, to put to shame
(Luke 13:17; I Pet. 2:6). *Wherein ye are spoken against* (*en
hōi katalaleisthe*). Present passive indicative of *katalaleō*,
for which see 2:12 with *en hōi* also. Peter may be recalling
(Hart) his own experience at Pentecost when the Jews first
scoffed and others were cut to the heart (Acts 2:13, 37).
Who revile (*hoi epēreazontes*). Articular present active participle of *epēreazō*, old verb (from *epēreia*, spiteful abuse),
to insult, in N.T. only here and Luke 6:28. *In Christ* (*en
Christōi*). Paul's common mystical phrase that Peter has
three times (here, 5:10, 14), not in John, though the idea is
constantly in John. Peter here gives a new turn (cf. 2:12)
to *anastrophē* (manner of life). "Constantly the apostle
repeats his phrases with new significance and in a new light"
(Bigg).

17. *Better* (*kreitton*). Comparative of *kratus* as in II Pet.
2:21; Heb. 1:4. Patient endurance not only silences cal-
umny (verse 16), is Christlike (verse 18), but it has a value
of its own (verse 17). *If the will of God should so will* (*ei
theloi to thelēma tou theou*). Condition of the fourth class
again (*ei—theloi*) with *ei* and the optative. For a like
pleonasm see John 7:17. *For well-doing than for evil-doing*
(*agathopoiountas ē kakopoiountas*). Accusative plural agreeing with *humās* understood (accusative of general reference
with the infinitive *paschein* (to suffer) of the participles from
agathopoieō (see 2:15) and *kakopoieō* (Mark 3:4, and see
I Pet. 2:14 for *kakopoios*).

18. *Because Christ also died* (*hoti kai Christos apethanen*).
So the best MSS.; later ones *epathen* (suffered). The example of Christ should stir us to patient endurance. *For sins*
(*peri hamartiōn*). "Concerning sins" (not his, but ours,
1:18). *Peri* (around, concerning) with *hamartias* in the

regular phrase for the sin offering (Lev. 5:7; 6:30), though *huper hamartias* does occur (Ezek. 43:25). So in the N.T. we find both *peri hamartiōn* (Heb. 5:3) and *huper hamartiōn* (Heb. 5:1). *Once (hapax)*. Once for all (Heb. 9:28), not once upon a time (*pote*). *The righteous for the unrighteous (dikaios huper adikōn)*. Literally, "just for unjust" (no articles). See I Pet. 2:19 for the sinlessness of Christ as the one perfect offering for sin. This is what gives Christ's blood value. He has no sin himself. Some men today fail to perceive this point. *That he might bring us to God (hina hēmās prosagagēi tōi theōi)*. Purpose clause with *hina*, with second aorist active subjunctive of *prosagō* and the dative case *tōi theōi*. The MSS. vary between *hēmās* (us) and *humās* (you). The verb *prosagō* means to lead or bring to (Matt. 18:24), to approach God (cf. *prosagōgēn* in Eph. 2:18), to present us to God on the basis of his atoning death for us, which has opened the way (Rom. 3:25; Heb. 10:19f.) *Being put to death in the flesh (thanatōtheis men sarki)*. First aorist passive participle of *thanatoō*, old verb (from *thanatos* death), to put to death. *Sarki* is locative case of *sarx*. *But quickened in the spirit (zōopoiētheis de pneumati)*. First aorist passive participle of *zōopoieō* rare (Aristotle) verb (from *zōopoios* making alive), to make alive. The participles are not antecedent to *apethanen*, but simultaneous with it. There is no such construction as the participle of subsequent action. The spirit of Christ did not die when his flesh did, but "was endued with new and greater powers of life" (Thayer). See I Cor. 15:22 for the use of the verb for the resurrection of the body. But the use of the word *pneumati* (locative case) in contrast with *sarki* starts Peter's mind off in a long comparison by way of illustration that runs from verses 19 to 22. The following verses have caused more controversy than anything in the Epistle.

19. *In which also (en hōi kai)*. That is, in spirit (relative referring to *pneumati*. But, a number of modern scholars

have followed Griesbach's conjecture that the original text
was either *Nōe kai* (Noah also), or *Enōch kai* (Enoch also),
or *en hōi kai Enōch* (in which Enoch also) which an early
scribe misunderstood or omitted *Enōch kai* in copying (*hom-
oioteleuton*). It is allowed in Stier and Theile's *Polyglott*.
It is advocated by J. Cramer in 1891, by J. Rendel Harris
in *The Expositor* (1901), and *Sidelights on N.T. Research*
(p. 208), by Nestle in 1902, by Moffatt's New Translation
of the New Testament. Windisch rejects it as inconsistent
with the context. There is no manuscript for the conjecture, though it would relieve the difficulty greatly. Luther
admits that he does not know what Peter means. Bigg has
no doubt that the event recorded took place between Christ's
death and his resurrection and holds that Peter is alluding
to Christ's *Descensus ad Inferos* in Acts 2:27 (with which
he compares Matt. 27:52f.; Luke 23:34; Eph. 4:9). With
this Windisch agrees. But Wohlenberg holds that Peter
means that Christ in his preëxistent state preached to those
who rejected the preaching of Noah who are now in prison.
Augustine held that Christ was in Noah when he preached.
Bigg argues strongly that Christ during the time between
his death and resurrection preached to those who once heard
Noah (but are now in prison) and offered them another
chance and not mere condemnation. If so, why did Jesus
confine his preaching to this one group? So the theories
run on about this passage. One can only say that it is a
slim hope for those who neglect or reject Christ in this life
to gamble with a possible second chance after death which
rests on very precarious exegesis of a most difficult passage
in Peter's Epistle. Accepting the text as we have, what can
we make of it? *He went and preached* (*poreutheis ekēruxen*).
First aorist passive (deponent) participle of *poreuomai* and
first aorist active indicative of *kērussō*, the verb commonly
used of the preaching of Jesus. Naturally the words mean
personal action by Christ "in spirit" as illustration of his

"quickening" (verse 18) whether done before his death or afterwards. It is interesting to observe that, just as the relative *en hōi* here tells something suggested by the word *pneumati* (in spirit) just before, so in verse 21 the relative *ho* (which) tells another illustration of the words *di' hudatos* (by water) just before. Peter jumps from the flood in Noah's time to baptism in Peter's time, just as he jumped backwards from Christ's time to Noah's time. He easily goes off at a word. What does he mean here by the story that illustrates Christ's quickening in spirit? *Unto the spirits in prison (tois en phulakēi pneumasin).* The language is plain enough except that it does not make it clear whether Jesus did the preaching to spirits in prison at the time or to people whose spirits are now in prison, the point of doubt already discussed. The metaphorical use of *en phulakēi* can be illustrated by II Pet. 2:4; Jude 6; Rev. 20:7 (the final abode of the lost). See Heb. 12:23 for the use of *pneumata* for disembodied spirits.

20. *Which aforetime were disobedient (apeithēsasin pote).* First aorist active participle of *apeitheō* (for which verb see 3:20) in the dative plural agreeing with *pneumasin.* These spirits now in prison once upon a time (*pote*) were disobedient (typical rebels, Hart calls them). *Waited (apexedecheto).* Imperfect middle of the double compound *apekdechomai*, late verb, probably first by Paul (I Cor. 1:7), though in the aprocryphal *Acta Pauli* (iii) and other late writings cited by Nägeli (p. 43). Perfective use of the two prepositions (*apo, ek*) to wait out to the end, as for Christ's Second Coming (Phil. 3:20). A hundred years apparently after the warning (Gen. 5:32; 6:3; 7:6) Noah was preparing the ark and Noah as a preacher of righteousness (II Pet. 2:5) forewarned the people, who disregarded it. *While the ark was a preparing (kataskeuazomenēs kibōtou).* Genitive absolute with present passive participle of *kataskeuazō*, old compound (Matt. 11:10), for *kibōtos* (ark) see on Matt.

24:38. *Wherein* (*eis hēn*). "Into which" (the ark'. *That is* (*tout' estin*). Explanatory expression like our English idiom (Rom. 10:6, etc.). *Souls* (*psuchai*). Persons of both sexes (living men) as in Acts 2:41; 27:37, etc. *Were saved* (*diesōthēsan*). First aorist passive indicative of *diasōzō*, old compound, to bring safe through as in Acts 27:44. *Through water* (*di' hudatos*). "By means of water" as the inter- mediate agent, an apparent change in the use of *dia* in composition just before (local use) to the instrumental use here. They came through the water in the ark and so were saved by the water in spite of the flood around them. Peter lays stress (Hart) on the water rather than on the ark (Heb. 11:7) for the sake of the following illustration.

21. *Which also* (*ho kai*). Water just mentioned. *After a true likeness* (*antitupon*). Water in baptism now as an anti- type of Noah's deliverance by water. For *baptisma* see on Matt. 3:7. For *antitupon* see on Heb. 9:24 (only other N.T. example) where the word is used of the earthly tabernacle corresponding (*antitupa*) to the heavenly, which is the pat- tern (*tupon* Heb. 8:5) for the earthly. So here baptism is presented as corresponding to (prefigured by) the deliver- ance of Noah's family by water. It is only a vague parallel, but not over-fanciful. *Doth now save you* (*humas nun sōzei*). Simplex verb (*sōzō*, not the compound *diasōzō*). The sav- ing by baptism which Peter here mentions is only symbolic (a metaphor or picture as in Rom. 6:2–6), not actual as Peter hastens to explain. *Not the putting away of the filth of the flesh* (*ou sarkos apothesis rupou*). *Apothesis* is old word from *apotithēmi* (2:1), in N.T. only here and II Pet. 1:14. *Rupou* (genitive of *rupos*) is old word (cf. *ruparos*, filthy, in James 2:2; Rev. 22:11), here only in N.T. (cf. Is. 3:3; 4:4). Baptism, Peter explains, does not wash away the filth of the flesh either in a literal sense, as a bath for the body, or in a metaphorical sense of the filth of the soul. No ceremonies really affect the conscience (Heb. 9:13f.).

Peter here expressly denies baptismal remission of sin. *But the interrogation of a good conscience toward God (alla suneidēseōs agathēs eperōtēma eis theon).* Old word from *eperōtaō* (to question as in Mark 9:32; Matt. 16:1), here only in N.T. In ancient Greek it never means answer, but only inquiry. The inscriptions of the age of the Antonines use it of the Senate's approval after inquiry. That may be the sense here, that is, avowal of consecration to God after inquiry, having repented and turned to God and now making this public proclamation of that fact by means of baptism (the symbol of the previous inward change of heart). Thus taken, it matters little whether *eis theon* (toward God) be taken with *eperōtēma* or *suneidēseōs. Through the resurrection of Jesus Christ (di' anastaseōs Iēsou Christou).* For baptism is a symbolic picture of the resurrection of Christ as well as of our own spiritual renewal (Rom. 6:2–6). See 1:3 for regeneration made possible by the resurrection of Jesus.

22. *Having gone (poreutheis).* First aorist (deponent) participle (not periphrastic) of *poreuomai. Being made subject (hupotagentōn).* Second aorist passive participle of *hupotassō* (see 2:18; 3:1) in the genitive absolute construction. *Unto him (autōi).* Christ. See I Cor. 15:28.

CHAPTER IV

1. *For as much then as Christ suffered in the flesh* (*Christou oun pathontos sarki*). Genitive absolute with second aorist active participle of *paschō*, to suffer, and the locative case of *sarx* (*flesh*). The *oun* (then, therefore) draws and applies the main lesson of 3:18–22, the fact that Christ suffered for us. *Arm ye yourselves also* (*kai humeis hoplisasthe*). Direct middle first aorist imperative of *hoplizō*, old verb from *hoplon* (weapon, John 18:3), in metaphorical sense, here only in N.T. *With the same mind* (*tēn autēn ennoian*). Accusative of the thing (content), *ennoian*, old word (from *en*, *nous*), putting in mind, thinking, will, in N.T. only here and Heb. 4:12. "Here again *Christus Patiens* is our *hupogrammos*" (Bigg). *For* (*hoti*). Reason for the exhortation. *Hath ceased from sin* (*pepautai hamartias*). Perfect middle indicative of *pauō* to make cease and the ablative singular *hamartias*, but B reads the dative plural *hamartiais* (cf. Rom. 6:1f.). Temptation has lost its appeal and power with such a man.

2. *That ye no longer should live* (*eis to mēketi biōsai*). Purpose clause with *eis to* (negative *mē*) and the first aorist (for the Attic second aorist *biōnai*) active infinitive of *bioō*, old verb, to spend a life (from *bios*, course of life, Luke 8:14), here only in N.T. *The rest of your time in the flesh* (*ton epiloipon en sarki chronon*). Accusative of time (*chronon*, period of time). *Epiloipon* is old adjective (*epi*, *loipos*, remaining in addition), here only in N.T. But *eis to* here can be result (so that) as in Rom. 1:20; 4:18.

3. *Past* (*parelēluthōs*). Perfect active participle of the compound verb *parerchomai*, old verb, to go by (beside) as in Matt. 14:15 with *hōra* (hour). *May suffice* (*arketos*). No

copula in the Greek, probably *estin* (is) rather than *dunatai* (can). Late and rare verbal adjective from *arkeō*, to suffice, in the papyri several times, in N.T. only here and Matt. 6:34; 10:25, apparently referring to Christ's words in Matt. 6:34 (possibly an axiom or proverb). *To have wrought* (*kateirgasthai*). Perfect middle infinitive of *katergazomai*, common compound (*kata, ergon* work) as in I Cor. 5:3. *The desire* (*to boulēma*). Correct text, not *thelēma*. Either means the thing desired, willed. Jews sometimes fell in with the ways of Gentiles (Rom. 2:21–24; 3:9–18; Eph. 2:1–3) as today some Christians copy the ways of the world. *And to have walked* (*peporeumenous*). Perfect middle participle of *poreuomai* in the accusative plural of general reference with the infinitive *kateirgasthai*. Literally, "having walked or gone." *In lasciviousness* (*en aselgeiais*). All these sins are in the locative case with *en*. "In unbridled lustful excesses" (II Pet. 2:7; II Cor. 12:21). *Lusts* (*epithumiais*). Cf. 2:11; 4:2. *Winebibbings* (*oinophlugiais*). Old compound (*oinos*, wine, *phluō*, to bubble up), for drunkenness, here only in N.T. (also in Deut. 21:20). *Revellings* (*komois*). Old word (from *keimai*, to lie down), rioting drinking parties, in N.T. here and Gal. 5:21; Rom. 13:13. *Carousings* (*potois*). Old word for drinking carousal (from *pinō*, to drink), here only in the N.T. In the light of these words it seems strange to find modern Christians justifying their "personal liberty" to drink and carouse, to say nothing of the prohibition law. The Greeks actually carried lust and drunkenness into their religious observances (Aphrodite, for instance). *Abominable idolatries* (*athemitois eidōlolatriais*). To the Christian all "idolatry," (*eidōlon, latreia*), worship of idols, is "abominable," not allowed (alpha privative and *themitos, themistos* the old form, verbal of *themizō*, to make lawful), but particularly those associated with drinking and licentiousness. The only other N.T. example of *athemitos* is by Peter also (Acts 10:28) and about the Mosaic law. That

may be the idea here, for Jews often fell into idolatrous practices (Deissmann, *Bible Studies*, p. 274).

4. *Wherein* (*en hōi*). "In which thing" (manner of life).
They think it strange (*xenizontai*). Present passive indicative
of *xenizō*, old verb (from *xenos*, stranger), to entertain a
guest (Acts 10:23), to astonish (Acts 17:20). See also 4:12.
"They are surprised or astonished." *That ye run not with
them* (*mē suntrechontōn humōn*). Genitive absolute (negative *mē*) with present active participle of *suntrechō*, old compound, to run together like a crowd or a mob as here (just
like our phrase, "running with certain folks"). *Into the
same excess of riot* (*eis tēn autēn tēs asōtias anachusin*).
Anachusin (from *anacheō* to pour forth) is a late and rare
word, our overflowing, here only in N.T. *Asōtias* is the
character of an abandoned man (*asōtos*, cf. *asōtōs* in Luke
15:13), old word for a dissolute life, in N.T. only here,
Eph. 5:18; Titus 1:6. *Speaking evil of you* (*blasphēmountes*).
Present active participle of *blasphēmeō* as in Luke 22:65.
"The Christians were compelled to stand aloof from all the
social pleasures of the world, and the Gentiles bitterly
resented their puritanism, regarding them as the enemies of
all joy, and therefore of the human race" (Bigg).

5. *Who shall give account* (*hoi apodōsousin logon*). Future
active indicative of *apodidōmi*. For this use with *logon*
(account) see Matt. 12:36; Luke 16:2; Acts 19:40; Heb.
13:17. For the sudden use of the relative *hoi* see Rom. 3:8.
To him that is ready to judge (*tōi hetoimōs krinonti*). Dative,
"to the one readily judging," correct text, not *hetoimōs
echonti krinai*, "to the one ready to judge," which "softens
the rugged original" (Hart). That is Christ apparently
(1:13; II Cor. 5:10), but the Father in 1:17. *The quick and
the dead* (*zōntas kai nekrous*). "Living and dead." Those
living at the time and those already dead (I Thess. 4:15).

6. *Was the gospel preached* (*euēggelisthē*). First aorist
passive indicative of *euaggelizō*. Impersonal use. *Even to*

the dead (*kai nekrois*). Does Peter here mean preached to men after they are dead or to men once alive but dead now or when the judgment comes? There are those (Augustine, Luther, etc.) who take "dead" here in the spiritual sense (dead in trespasses and sins as in Col. 2:13; Eph. 2:1), but consider it "impossible" for Peter to use the same word in two senses so close together; but Jesus did it in the same sentence, as in the case of *psuchē* (life) in Matt. 16:25. Bigg takes it to mean that all men who did not hear the gospel message in this life will hear it in the next before the final judgment. *That they might be judged* (*hina krithōsin men*). Purpose clause with *hina* and the first aorist passive subjunctive of *krinō*, to judge, whereas *zōsin de* (by contrast) is the present active subjunctive of *zaō*, to live. There is contrast also between *kata anthrōpous* (according to men) and *kata theon* (according to God).

7. *But the end of all things is at hand* (*pantōn de to telos ēggiken*). Perfect active indicative of *eggizō*, to draw near, common late verb (from *eggus*), same form used by the Baptist of the Messiah's arrival (Matt. 3:2) and by James in 5:8 (of the second coming). How near Peter does not say, but he urges readiness (1:5f.; 4:6) as Jesus did (Mark 14:38) and Paul (I Thess. 5:6), though it is drawing nearer all the time (Rom. 12:11), but not at once (II Thess. 2:2). *Be ye therefore of sound mind* (*sōphronēsate oun*). In view of the coming of Christ. First aorist (ingressive) active imperative of *sōphroneō* (*sōs*, sound, *phrēn*, mind) as in Mark 5:15. *Be sober unto prayer* (*nēpsate eis proseuchas*). First aorist (ingressive of *nēphō* (see 1:13) and plural *proseuchas*, (prayers). Cf. Eph. 6:18.

8. *Above all things* (*pro pantōn*). See this phrase in James 5:12. *Being fervent* (*ektenē echontes*). Present active participle of *echontes* and predicate accusative of adjective *ektenēs* (from *ekteinō*, to stretch out), stretched out, here only in N.T., "holding intent you love among yourselves."

For love covereth a multitude of sins (*hoti agapē kaluptei plēthos hamartiōn*). See James 5:20 for meaning, sins of the one loved, not of the one loving.

9. *Using hospitality* (*philoxenoi*). "Friendly to strangers," old word (from *philos, xenos*), in N.T. only here and I Tim. 3:2; Titus 1:8. No verb here in the Greek. *Without murmuring* (*aneu goggusmou*). Like *chōris goggusmōn* in Phil. 2:14. Complaint spoils hospitality. Jesus enjoined the entertainment of strangers (Matt. 25:35). Inns were rare and very poor. Hospitality made mission work possible (III John 5).

10. *Gift* (*charisma*). Late N.T. word (in late papyri) from *charizomai*, to give graciously. It is used here by Peter as one of the gifts of the Holy Spirit (I Cor. 12:4, 9, 29–31; Rom. 12:6). *Ministering* (*diakonountes*). Present active participle plural of *diakoneō*, common verb (Matt. 20:28), though *hekastos* (each) is singular. *As good stewards* (*hōs kaloi oikonomoi*). For "steward" (*oikonomos*, house-manager) see Luke 16:1 and I Cor. 4:1 (used by Paul of himself) and of any bishop (Titus 1:7), but here of any Christian. See *kalos* used with *diakonos* in I Tim. 4:6. *Of the manifold grace of God* (*poikilēs charitos theou*). For *poikilos* (many-colored) see on 1:6 and James 1:2.

11. *If any man speaketh* (*ei tis lalei*). Condition of first class, assumed as a fact. *Speaking as it were oracles of God* (*hōs logia theou*). No predicate in this conclusion of the condition. For *logia theou* see Acts 7:38 (Mosaic law); Rom. 3:2 (the Old Testament); Heb. 5:12 (the substance of Christian teaching), here of the utterances of God through Christian teachers. *Logion* (old word) is a diminutive of *logos* (speech, word). It can be construed here as nominative or as accusative. The verb has to be supplied. *If any one ministereth* (*ei tis diakonei*). First-class condition again. See Acts 6:2–4 for the twofold division of service involved here. *Which God supplieth* (*hēs chorēgei ho theos*). Ablative

case (*hēs*) of the relative attracted from the accusative *hēn*, object of *chorēgei* (present active indicative of *chorēgeō*, old verb, to supply from *chorēgos*, chorus leader, in N.T. only here and II Cor. 9:10). Peter has the compound *epichorēgeō* in II Pet. 1:5, 11. God is the supplier of strength. *That God may be glorified* (*hina doxazētai ho theos*). Purpose clause with *hina* and the present passive subjunctive of *doxazō*. See John 15:8. *Whose is* (*hōi estin*). "To whom (dative) is," that is to Jesus Christ the immediate antecedent, but in Rom. 16:27 and Jude 25 the doxology is to God through Christ. For other doxologies see I Pet. 5:11; II Pet. 3:18; Gal. 1:5; Rom. 9:5; 11:36; Phil. 4:20; Eph. 3:21; I Tim. 1:17; 6:16; II Tim. 4:18; Heb. 13:21; Rev. 1:6; 5:13; 7:12. The others addressed to Christ are II Pet. 3:18; II Tim. 4:18; Rev. 1:6.

12. *Think it not strange* (*mē xenizesthe*). Prohibition with *mē* and the present passive imperative of *xenizō*, for which verb see 4:4. "Be not amazed." *Concerning the fiery trial among you* (*tei en humin purōsei*). Instrumental case, "by the among you burning," metaphorical sense of old word (since Aristotle), from *puroō*, to burn (*pur* fire). See 1:7 for the metaphor. See Rev. 18:9, 18 only other N.T. examples. It occurs in Prov. 27:21 for the smelting of gold and silver and so in Ps. 56:10 (LXX 65:10): "Thou didst smelt us as silver is smelted" (*epurōsas hēmās hōs puroutai to argurion*). *Which cometh upon you* (*humin ginomenēi*). Present middle participle of *ginomai* (already coming) with dative case *humin*. *To prove you* (*pros peirasmon*). "For testing." *As though a strange thing happened unto you* (*hōs xenou humin sumbainontos*). Genitive absolute with *hōs*, giving the alleged reason, and *humin*, dative case with *sumbainontos* (present active participle of *sumbainō*, to go together, to happen (Mark 10:32), agreeing with *xenou* (strange, Heb. 13:9).

13. *Inasmuch* (*katho*). "In so far forth as" ("according

to which thing"), old conjunction, in N.T. only here and
II Cor. 8:12; Rom. 8:26. *Ye are partakers of (koinōneite).*
Present active indicative of *koinōneō*, old verb (from *koinōnos*, partner), to share in either with genitive (Heb. 2:14)
or dative as here (*pathēmasin*). *That ye may rejoice with
exceeding joy (hina charēte agalliōmenoi).* Purpose clause
with *hina* and second aorist passive subjunctive of *chairō*,
with the present middle participle of *agalliaō* to exult (1:8),
"that ye may rejoice exulting." See 1:6 to 8 for this same
idea associated with the second coming of Christ as here.

14. *If ye are reproached (ei oneidizesthe).* Condition of
first class assumed as true with *ei* and present passive indicative of *oneidizō*, for which verb see James 1:5. *For the name
of Christ (en onomati Christou).* "In the matter of the name
of Christ." For the idea see Matt. 5:11f.; 19:29; Acts 5:41;
9:16; 21:13. This is the only N.T. example of just *onoma
Christou*, here used because of the use of *Christianos* in
verse 16. For the beatitude *makarioi* see Matt. 5:11f. *The
Spirit of glory and the Spirit of God (to tēs doxēs kai to tou
theou pneuma).* Note repetition of the article (*to*) though
pneuma only once. The reference is to the Holy Spirit, who
is the Spirit of Glory and of God. *Resteth upon you (eph'
hēmas anapauetai).* Quotation from Is. 11:2. Present
middle indicative of *anapauō*, to give rest, refresh (Matt.
11:28). "He rests upon the Christian as the Shechinah
rested upon the tabernacle" (Bigg). Cf. 1:8; Matt. 3:16.

15. *Let no one of you suffer (mē tis humōn paschetō).* Prohibition with *mē* and present active imperative (habit pro-
hibited). *As (hōs).* Charged as and being so. Two specific
crimes (murderer, thief) and one general phrase (*kakopoios*,
evildoer, I Pet. 2:12, 14), and one unusual term *allotriepis-
copos* (a meddler in other men's matters). Note *ē hōs* (or as)
=or "also only as" (Wohlenberg). The word was apparently coined by Peter (occurring elsewhere only in Dionys.
Areop. and late eccles. writers) from *allotrios* (belonging to

another, II Cor. 10:15) and *episkopos*, overseer, inspector, I Pet. 2:25). The idea is apparently one who spies out the affairs of other men. Deissmann (*Bible Studies*, p. 224) gives a second-century papyrus with *allotriōn epithumētēs* a *speculator alienorum*. Epictetus has a like idea (iii. 22. 97). Biggs takes it to refer to "things forbidden." Clement of Alexandria tells of a disciple of the Apostle John who became a bandit chief. Ramsay (*Church in the Roman Empire*, pp. 293, 348) thinks the word refers to breaking up family relationships. Hart refers us to the gadders-about in I Thess. 4:11; II Thess. 3:11 and women as gossipers in I Thess. 5:13. It is interesting to note also that *episkopos* here is the word for "bishop" and so suggests also preachers meddling in the work of other preachers.

16. *But if as a Christian* (*ei de hōs Christianos*). Supply the verb *paschei* (condition of first class, "if one suffer as a Christian"). This word occurs only three times in the N.T. (Acts 11:26; 26:28; I Pet. 4:16). It is word of Latin formation coined to distinguish followers of Christ from Jews and Gentiles (Acts 11:26). Each instance bears that idea. It is not the usual term at first like *mathētai* (disciples), saints (*hagioi*), believers (*pisteuontes*), etc. The Jews used *Nazōraioi* (Nazarenes) as a nickname for Christians (Acts 24:5). By A.D. 64 the name Christian was in common use in Rome (Tacitus, *Ann.* XV. 44). Owing to itacism it was sometimes spelled *Chrēstianoi* (*i, ei* and *ē* pronounced alike). *Let him not be ashamed* (*mē aischunesthō*). Prohibition with *mē* and present passive imperative of *aischunō*. Peter had once been ashamed to suffer reproach or even a sneer for being a disciple of Christ (Mark 14:68). See the words of Jesus in Mark 8:38 and Paul's in II Tim. 1:12. Peter is not ashamed now. *In this name* (*en tōi onomati toutōi*). Of Christian as in Mark 9:41, "because ye are Christ's."

17. *For the time is come* (*hoti ho kairos*). No predicate, probably *estin* (is) to be supplied. The phrase that follows

comes from the vision of Ezekiel (chapter 9). The construction is unusual with *tou arxasthai* (genitive articular aorist middle infinitive of *archō*), not exactly purpose or result, and almost in apposition (epexegetic), but note *tou elthein* used as subject in Luke 17:1. The persecution on hand (1:7) was a foretaste of more to come. By "house of God" he can mean the same as the "spiritual house" of 2:5 or a local church. Biggs even takes it to refer to the family. *And if it begin first at us (ei de prōton aph'hēmōn)*. Condition of first class again, with the verb *archetai* understood. "From us" (*aph'hēmōn*) more exactly. *End (telos)*. Final fate. *Of them that obey not the gospel of God (tōn apeithountōn tōi tou theou euaggeliōi)*. "Of those disobeying the gospel of God." See the same idea in Rom. 2:8. See Mark 1:14 for believing in the gospel.

18. *And if the righteous is scarcely saved (kai ei ho dikaios molis sōzetai)*. First-class condition again with *ei* and present passive indicative of *sōzō*. Quotation from Prov. 11:31. See 3:12, 14 and Matt. 5:20. But the Christian is not saved by his own righteousness (Phil. 3:9; Rev. 7:14). For *molis* see Acts 14:18 and for *asebēs* (ungodly, without reverence) see Rom. 4:5; II Pet. 2:5. *Will appear (phaneitai)*. Future middle of *phainō*, to show. For the question see Mark 10:24–26.

19. *Wherefore (hōste)*. Picking up the thread of consolation again (Bigg). *Commit their souls (paratithesthōsan tas psuchas)*. Present (continuous) middle imperative third plural of *paratithēmi*, old word, a banking figure, to deposit, as in I. Tim. 1:18; II Tim. 2:2, the word used by Jesus as he died (Luke 23:46). *In well-doing (en agathopoiiāi)*. Late and rare word, only here in N.T., from *agathopoieō* (I Pet. 2:15, 20).

CHAPTER V

1. *Who am a fellow-elder* (*ho sunpresbuteros*). Earliest use of this compound in an inscription of B.C. 120 for fellow-elders (alderman) in a town, here only in N.T., in eccles. writers. For the word *presbuteros* in the technical sense of officers in a Christian church (like elder in the local synagogues of the Jews) see Acts 11:30; 20:17. It is noteworthy that here Peter the Apostle (1:1) calls himself an elder along with (*sun*) the other "elders." *A witness* (*martus*). This is what Jesus had said they must be (Acts 1:8) and what Peter claimed to be (Acts 3:15; 10:39). So Paul was to be a *martus* (Acts 22:15). *Who am also a partaker* (*ho kai koinōnos*). "The partner also," "the partaker also." See Luke 5:10; II Cor. 1:7; II Pet. 1:4. See same idea in Rom. 8:17. In Gal. 3:23 and Rom. 8:18 we have almost this about the glory about to be revealed to us where *mellō* as here is used with the infinitive.

2. *Tend* (*poimanate*). First aorist active imperative of *poimainō*, old verb, from *poimēn* (shepherd) as in Luke 17:7. Jesus used this very word to Peter in the interview by the Sea of Galilee (John 21:16) and Peter doubtless has this fact in mind here. Paul used the word to the elders at Miletus (Acts 20:28). See 2:25 for the metaphor. *Flock* (*poimnion*). Old word, likewise from *poimēn*, contraction of *poimenion* (Luke 12:32). *Exercising the oversight* (*episkopountes*). Present active participle of *episkopeō*, old word (in Heb. 12:15 alone in N.T.), omitted here by Aleph B. *Not by constraint* (*mē anagkastōs*). Negative *mē* because of the imperative. Old adverb from verbal adjective *anagkastos*, here alone in N.T. *But willingly* (*alla hekousiōs*). By contrast. Old adverb, in N.T. only here and Heb. 10:26. *Nor yet for filthy*

130

lucre (*mēde aischrokerdōs*). A compound adverb not found elsewhere, but the old adjective *aischrokerdēs* is in I Tim. 3:8; Titus 1:7. See also Titus 1:11 "for the sake of filthy lucre" (*aischrou kerdous charin*). Clearly the elders received stipends, else there could be no such temptation. *But of a ready mind* (*alla prothumōs*). Old adverb from *prothumos* (Matt. 26:41), here only in N.T.

3. *Lording it over* (*katakurieuontes*). Present active participle of *katakurieuō*, late compound (*kata, kurios*) as in Matt. 20:25. *The charge allotted to you* (*tōn klērōn*). "The charges," "the lots" or "the allotments." See it in Acts 1:17, 25 in this sense. The old word meant a die (Matt. 27:25), a portion (Col. 1:12; I Pet. 1:4), here the charges assigned (cf. Acts 17:4). From the adjective *klērikos* come our cleric, clerical, clerk. Wycliff translated it here "neither as having lordship in the clergie." *Making yourselves ensamples* (*tupoi ginomenoi*). Present active participle of *ginomai* and predicate nominative *tupoi* (types, models) for which phrase see I Thess. 1:7. Continually becoming. See 2:21 for *hupogrammos* (writing-copy). *To the flock* (*tou poimniou*). Objective genitive.

4. *When the chief Shepherd shall be manifested* (*phanerōthentos tou archipoimenos*). Genitive absolute with first aorist passive participle of *phaneroō*, to manifest, and genitive of *archipoimēn*, a compound (*archi, poimēn*) after analogy of *archiereus*, here only in N.T., but in *Testam. of Twelve Patrs.* (Jud. #8) and on a piece of wood around an Egyptian mummy and also on a papyrus A.D. 338 (Deissmann, *Light*, etc., p. 100). See Heb. 13:20 for *ho poimēn ho megas* (the Shepherd the great). *Ye shall receive* (*komieisthe*). Future of *komizō* (1:9, which see). *The crown of glory that fadeth not away* (*ton amarantinon tēs doxēs stephanon*). For "crown" (*stephanos*) see James 1:12; I Cor. 9:25; II Tim. 4:8; Rev. 2:10; 3:10; 4:4. In the Gospels it is used only of the crown of thorns, but Jesus is crowned with glory and honor (Heb.

2:9). In all these passages it is the crown of victory as it is
here. See 1:4 for *amarantos*, unfading. *Amarantinos* is made
from that word as the name of a flower amaranth (so called
because it never withers and revives if moistened with water
and so used as a symbol of immortality), "composed of amaranth" or "amarantine," "the amarantine (unfading) crown
of glory."

5. *Be subject* (*hopotagēte*). Second aorist passive imperative of *hupotassō*. *Unto the elder* (*presbuterois*). Dative case.
Here the antithesis between younger and elder shows that
the word refers to age, not to office as in 5:1. See a like
change in meaning in I Tim. 5:1, 17. *All* (*pantes*). All ages,
sexes, classes. *Gird yourselves with humility* (*tēn tapeino-
phrosunēn egkombōsasthe*). First aorist middle imperative
of *egkomboomai*, late and rare verb (in Apollodorus, fourth
cent. B.C.), here only in N.T., from *en* and *kombos* (knot, like
the knot of a girdle). *Egkombōma* was the white scarf or
apron of slaves. It is quite probable that Peter here is
thinking of what Jesus did (John 13:4ff.) when he girded
himself with a towel and taught the disciples, Peter in particular (John 13:9ff.), the lesson of humility (John 13:15).
Peter had at last learned the lesson (John 21:15–19). *The
proud* (*huperēphanois*). Dative plural of *huperēphanos* (James
4:6; Rom. 1:30) after *antitassetai* (present middle indicative
of *antitassō* as in James 4:6 (quoted there as here from Prov.
3:34).

6. *Humble yourselves therefore* (*tapeinōthēte oun*). First
aorist passive imperative of *tapeinoō*, old verb, for which
see Matt. 18:4. Peter is here in the rôle of a preacher of
humility. "Be humbled." *Under the mighty hand of God*
(*hupo tēn krataian cheira tou theou*). Common O.T. picture
(Ex. 3:19; 20:33, etc.). *That he may exalt you* (*hina hupsōsēi*).
Purpose clause with *hina* and first aorist active subjunctive
of *hupsoō*. Cf. Luke 14:11; Phil. 2:9. *In due time* (*en kairōi*).
Same phrase in Matt. 24:45.

7. *Casting* (*epiripsantes*). First aorist active participle of *epiriptō*, old verb, to throw upon, in N.T. only here and Luke 19:35 (casting their clothes on the colt), here from Ps. 54 (55):23. For *merimna* see Matt. 6:25, 31, 34. *He careth* (*autōi melei*). Impersonal verb *melei* (present active indicative) with dative *autōi*, "it is a care to him." God does care (Luke 21:18).

8. *Be watchful* (*grēgorēsate*). First aorist active imperative of *grēgoreō*, late present imperative from perfect *egrēgora* (to be awake) from *egeirō* (to arouse), as in Matt. 24:42. For *nēpsate* see 1:13; 4:7. *Your adversary* (*ho antidikos humōn*). Old word for opponent in a lawsuit (Matt. 5:25). *The devil* (*diabolos*). Slanderer. See on Matt. 4:1. *As a roaring lion* (*hōs ōruomenos leōn*). But Jesus is also pictured as the Lion of the tribe of Judah (Rev. 5:5). But Satan *roars* at the saints. Present middle participle *ōruomai*, old verb, here only in N.T., to howl like a wolf, dog, or lion, of men to sing loud (Pindar). See Ps. 21 (22):14. *Whom he may devour* (*katapiein*). Second aorist active infinitive of *katapinō*, to drink down. B does not have *tina*, Aleph has *tina* (somebody), "to devour some one," while A has interrogative *tina*, "whom he may devour" (very rare idiom). But the devil's purpose is the ruin of men. He is a "peripatetic" (*peripatei*) like the peripatetic philosophers who walked as they talked. Satan wants all of us and sifts us all (Luke 22:31).

9. *Whom withstand* (*hōi antistēte*). Imperative second aorist active (intransitive) of *anthistēmi*; same form in James 4:7, which see. Dative case of relative (*hōi*). For the imperative in a subordinate clause see verse 12, II Thess. 3:10; II Tim. 4:15; Heb. 13:7. Cowardice never wins against the devil (II Tim. 1:7), but only courage. *Steadfast in your faith* (*stereoi tēi pistei*). Locative case *pistei*. *Stereos* is old adjective for solid like a foundation (II Tim. 2:19). *The same sufferings* (*ta auta tōn pathēmatōn*). An unusual construc-

tion with the genitive rather than the usual *ta auta pathē-mata*, perhaps as Hofmann suggests, "the same tax of sufferings" ("the same things in sufferings"). Probably this is correct and is like Xenophon's phrase in the *Memorabilia* (IV. 8. 8), *ta tou gērōs epiteleisthai* (to pay the tax of old age). *Are accomplished* (*epiteleisthai*). Present (and so process) middle (you are paying) or passive (is paid) infinitive of *epiteleō*, old verb, to accomplish (II Cor. 7:1). *In your brethren who are in the world* (*tēi en tōi kosmōi humōn adelphotēti*). Associate-instrumental case *adelphotēti* (in N.T. only here and 2:17, which see) after *ta auta* (like I Cor. 11:5) or dative after *epiteleisthai*. Even so *eidotes* (second perfect active participle of *oida*) with an infinitive usually means "knowing how to" (object infinitive) as in Luke 12:56; Phil. 3:18 rather than "knowing that" (indirect assertion) as taken above.

10. *The God of all grace* (*ho theos tēs charitos*). See 4:10 for *poikilēs charitos theou* (of the variegated grace of God). *In Christ* (*en Christōi*). A Pauline phrase (II Cor. 5:17-19), but Petrine also. For God's "calling" us (*kalesas*) see I Thess. 5:23f.; I Cor. 1:8f.; Rom. 8:29f. *After that ye have suffered a little while* (*oligon pathontas*). Second aorist active participle of *paschō*, antecedent to the principal verbs which are future active (*katartisei*, to mend, Mark 1:19; Gal. 6:1, *stērixei*, for which see Luke 9:51 and 22:32, *sthenōsei* from *sthenos* and so far a *hapax legomenon* like *enischuō* according to Hesychius). For *oligon* see 1:6.

11. *To him* (*autōi*). To God (dative case). Note *kratos* in the doxology as in I Tim. 6:16 and briefer than the doxology in I Pet. 4:11, to Christ.

12. *By Silvanus* (*dia Silouanou*). Probably this postscript (12 to 14) is in Peter's own handwriting, as Paul did (II Thess. 3:17f.; Gal. 6:11-18). If so, Silvanus (Silas) was the amanuensis and the bearer of the Epistle. *As I*

account him (hōs logizomai). Peter uses Paul's phrase (I
Cor. 4:1; Rom. 8:18) in giving approval to Paul's former
companion (Acts 15:40). *I have written (egrapsa).* Epistolary aorist applying to this Epistle as in I Cor. 5:11 (not
5:9); 9:15; Gal. 6:11; Rom. 15:15; Philemon 19, 21. *Briefly
(di' oligōn).* "By few words," as Peter looked at it, certainly not a long letter in fact. Cf. Heb. 13:22. *Testifying
(epimarturōn).* Present active participle of *epimartureō,* to
bear witness to, old compound, here alone in N.T., though
the double compound *sunepimartureō* in Heb. 2:4. *That this
is the true grace of God (tautēn einai alēthē charin tou theou).*
Infinitive *einai* in indirect assertion and accusative of general reference (*tautēn*) and predicate accusative *charin.* Peter
includes the whole of the Epistle by God's grace (1:10) and
obedience to the truth (John 1:17; Gal. 2:5; Col. 1:6).
Stand ye fast therein (eis hēn stēte). "In which (grace) take
your stand" (ingressive aorist active imperative of *histēmi*).

13. *She that is in Babylon, elect together with you (hē en
Babulōni suneklektē).* Either actual Babylon or, as most
likely, mystical Babylon (Rome) as in the Apocalypse. If
Peter is in Rome about A.D. 65, there is every reason why
he should not make that fact plain to the world at large
and least of all to Nero. It is also uncertain whether *hē
suneklektē* (found here alone), "the co-elect woman," means
Peter's wife (I Cor. 9:5) or the church in "Babylon." The
natural way to take it is for Peter's wife. Cf. *eklektēi
kuriāi* in II John 1 (also verse 13). *Mark my son (Markos
ho huios mou).* So this fact agrees with the numerous state-
ments by the early Christian writers that Mark, after leaving Barnabas, became Peter's "interpreter" and under his
influence wrote his Gospel. We know that Mark was with
Paul in Rome some years before this time (Col. 4:10).

14. *With a kiss of love (en philēmati agapēs).* As in I Cor.
16:20. The abuse of this custom led to its confinement to

men with men and women with women and to its final abandonment (*Apost. Const.* ii. 57, 12). *That are in Christ* (*tois en Christōi*). This is the greatest of all secret orders and ties, one that is open to all who take Christ as Lord and Saviour.

THE SECOND EPISTLE OF PETER
ABOUT A.D. 66 OR 67

BY WAY OF INTRODUCTION

Most Doubtful New Testament Book

Every book in the New Testament is challenged by some one, as indeed the historicity of Jesus Christ himself is and the very existence of God. But it is true that more modern scholars deny the genuineness of II Peter than that of any single book in the canon. This is done by men like F. H. Chase, J. B. Mayor, and R. D. Strachan, who are followers of Christ as Lord and Saviour. One has to admit that the case concerning II Peter has problems of peculiar difficulty that call for careful consideration and balanced judgment. One other word needs to be said, which is that an adverse decision against the authenticity of II Peter stands by itself and does not affect the genuineness of the other books. It is easy to take an extreme position for or against it without full knowledge of all the evidence.

Slow in General Acceptance

It was accepted in the canon by the council at Laodicea (372) and at Carthage (397). Jerome accepted it for the Vulgate, though it was absent from the Peshito Syriac Version. Eusebius placed it among the disputed books, while Origen was inclined to accept it. Clement of Alexandria accepted it and apparently wrote a commentary on it. It is probable that the so-called Apocalypse of Peter (early second century) used it and the Epistle of Jude either used it or II Peter used Jude. There are undoubted allusions also to phrases in II Peter in Aristides, Justin Martyr, Irenæus, Ignatius, Clement of Rome. When one considers the brevity of the Epistle, the use of it is really as strong as one can expect. Athanasius and Augustine accepted it as genuine, as did Luther, while Calvin doubted and Erasmus rejected it. It may be said for it that it won its way under criticism and was not accepted blindly.

CLAIMS PETRINE AUTHORSHIP

Not only so, but in fuller form than I Peter 1:1, for the writer terms himself "Simon (Symeon in some MSS.) Peter," a fact that has been used against the genuineness. If no claim had been made, that would have been considered decisive against him. Simon (Symeon was the Jewish form as used by James in Acts 15:14) is the real name (John 1:42) and Peter merely the Greek for Cephas, the nickname given by Christ. There is no reason why both could not properly be employed here. But the claim to Petrine authorship, if not genuine, leaves the Epistle pseudonymous. That was a custom among some Jewish writers and even Christian writers, as the spurious Petrine literature testifies (Gospel of Peter, Apocalypse of Peter, etc.), works of a heretical or curious nature. Whatever the motive for such a pious fraud, the fact remains that II Peter, if not genuine, has to take its place with this pseudonymous literature and can hardly be deemed worthy of a place in the New Testament. And yet there is no heresy in this Epistle, no startling new ideas that would lead one to use the name of Simon Peter. It is the rather full of edifying and orthodox teaching.

AND PERSONAL EXPERIENCES OF PETER

The writer makes use of his own contact with Jesus, especially at the Transfiguration of Christ (Mark 9:2-8 = Matt. 17:1-8 = Luke 9:28-36). This fact has been used against the genuineness of the Epistle on the plea that the writer is too anxious, anyhow, to show that he is Symeon Peter (1:1). But Bigg rightly replies that, if he had only given his name with no personal contacts with Jesus, the name would be called "a forged addition." It is possible also that the experience on the Mount of Transfiguration may have been suggested by Peter's use of *exodos* for his own death (1:15), the very word used by Luke (9:31) as the topic of discussion between Jesus and Moses and Elijah. There is also in 1:13 the use of "tent" (*skēnoma*) for the life in the body, like Peter's use of "tents" (*skēnas*) to Jesus at that very time (Mark 9:5 = Matt. 17:4 = Luke 9:33). In 1:14 Peter also refers to the plain words of Jesus about his coming death (John 21:18f.). In 1:15 Peter speaks of his own plan for preserving the knowledge of Jesus when he is gone (possibly by Mark's Gospel). All this is in perfect keeping with Peter's own nature.

And Yet the Epistle Differs in Style from First Peter

This is a fact, though one greatly exaggerated by some scholars. There are many points of similarity, for one thing, like the habit of repeating words (*epichorēgeō* in 1:10 and 19, *bebaios* in 1:12 and 13 and 15, *prophēteia* in 1:20 and 3:3, etc.). These repetitions occur all through the Epistle as in I Peter. "This is a matter of very high importance" (Bigg). Again in both Epistles there is a certain dignity of style with a tendency to iambic rhythm. There is more quotation of the Old Testament in I Peter, but frequent allusion to words and phrases in II Peter. There are more allusions to words and facts in the Gospels in I Peter than in II Peter, though some do occur in II Peter. Besides those already given, note 1:8 (Luke 13:7f.), 2:1 (Matt. 10:33), 2:20 (Matt. 12:45; Luke 11:26), 3:4 (Matt. 24:1ff.), and possibly 1:3 to Christ's calling the apostles. Both appear to know and use the O.T. Apocrypha. Both are fond of the plural of abstract substantives. Both make sparing use of Greek particles. Both use the article similarly, idiomatically, and sometimes not using it. There are some 361 words in I Peter not in II Peter, 231 in II Peter not in I Peter. There are 686 *hapax legomena* in N.T., 54 in II Peter instead of the average of 62, a large number when the brevity of the Epistle is considered. There are several ways of explaining these variations. One way is to say that they are written by different men, but difference of subject has to be borne in mind. All writers and artists have an early and a later manner. Another solution is that Peter employed different amanuenses. Silvanus was the one for I Peter (5:12). Mark was Peter's usual interpreter, but we do not know who was the amanuensis for II Peter, if indeed one was used. We know from Acts 4:13 that Peter and John were considered unlettered men (*agrammatoi kai idiōtai*). II Peter and the Apocalypse illustrate this statement. II Peter may have more of Peter's real style than I Peter.

He Accepts Paul's Epistles as Scripture

This fact (3:15f.) has been used as conclusive proof by Baur and his school that Peter could not have written the Epistle after the stern rebuke from Paul at Antioch (Gal. 2:11f.). But this argument ignores one element in Peter's impulsive nature and that is his coming back as he did with Jesus. Paul after that event in Antioch spoke kindly of Peter (I Cor. 9:5). Neither Peter nor Paul cherished a personal grudge where the Master's work was involved. It is also objected that Peter would not have put Paul's Epistles on the level with the O.T. and call them by implication "Scripture." But Paul claimed the help of the Holy Spirit in his writings and Peter knew the marks of the Holy Spirit's power. Besides, in calling Paul's Epistles Scripture he may not have meant to place them exactly on a par with the Old Testament.

The Resemblance to the Epistle of Jude

This is undoubted, particularly between Jude and the second chapter of II Peter. Kühl argues that II Peter 2:1

to 3:2 is an interpolation, though the same style runs throughout the Epistle. "The theory of interpolation is always a last and desperate expedient" (Bigg). In II Peter 2 we have the fallen angels, the flood, the cities of the plain with Lot, Balaam. In Jude we have Israel in the wilderness, the fallen angels, the cities of the plain (with no mention of Lot, Cain, Balaam, Korah). Jude mentions the dispute between Michael and Satan, quotes Enoch by name. There is rather more freshness in Jude than in II Peter, though II Peter is more intelligible. Evidently one had the other before him, besides other material. Which is the earlier? There is no way to decide this point clearly. Every point is looked at differently and argued differently by different writers. My own feeling is that Jude was before (just before) II Peter, though it is only a feeling and not a conviction.

Anachronisms

It used to be said that it was impossible for II Peter to have been written in the first century, because it had the atmosphere of the second. But one fact is strongly against that argument. In II Pet. 3:8 occurs the quotation of Ps. 90:4 about the thousand years without any chiliastic turn at all, a thing sure to happen in the second century after chiliasm had come to have such a swing. Peter's use of it suits the first century, not the second. As a matter of fact, the false teachers described in II Peter suit the first century precisely if one recalls Paul's troubles with the Judaizers in Galatia and Corinth and with the Gnostics in Colossæ and Ephesus. "Every feature in the description of the false teachers and mockers is to be found in the apostolic age" (Bigg).

The Readers

The author says that this is his second Epistle to them (3:1), and that means that he is writing to the saints in the five Roman provinces in Asia Minor to whom the first Epistle was sent (I Pet. 1:1). Spitta and Zahn deny this on the ground that the two Epistles do not discuss the same subjects, surely a flimsy objection. Zahn even holds that II Peter precedes I Peter and that the Epistle referred to in II Pet. 3:1 has been lost. He holds that II Peter was addressed to the church in Corinth. He considers the readers to be Jews while I Peter was addressed to Gentiles. But "there is nothing in II Peter to differentiate its first readers from those of I Peter" (Bigg).

The Purpose

Certainly Peter is here concerned chiefly with the heresies of that general region in Asia Minor that so disturbed Paul (Colossians, Ephesians, Pastoral Epistles) and John (Gospel, Epistles, Apocalypse). Paul early foresaw at Miletus these wolves that would ravish the sheep (Acts 20:29f.). In I Peter he is concerned chiefly with the fiery persecutions that are upon them, but here with the heretics that threaten to lead them astray.

Balance of Probability

There are difficulties in any decision about the authorship and character of II Peter. But, when all things are considered, I agree with Bigg that the Epistle is what it professes to be by Simon Peter. Else it is pseudonymous. The Epistle more closely resembles the other New Testament books than it does the large pseudepigraphic literature of the second and third centuries.

The Date

If we accept the Petrine authorship, it must come before his death, which was probably A.D. 67 or 68. Hence the Epistle cannot be beyond this date. There are those who argue for A.D. 64 as the date of Peter's death, but on insufficient grounds in my opinion.

BOOKS ON II PETER BESIDES THOSE ON I PETER ALSO

ABBOTT, E. A., *The Expositor* (Jan. to March, 1822).

CHASE, F. H., *Hastings D B* (Second Peter).

DE ZWAAN, *2 Peter en Judas* (1909).

DIETLEIN, W. O., *Der 2 Brief Petri* (1851).

GROSCH, H., *Die Echtheit des zweiten Briefes Petri* (1889).

HENKEL, K., *Der zweite Brief des Apostelfürsten Petrus* (1904).

HOFMANN, J. C., *Der zweite Brief Petri und der Brief Judä* (1875)

HUNDHAUSEN, *Das zweite Pontifkalschreiben des Apostels Petrus* (1873).

JAMES, M. R., *The Second Epistle of Peter and the Epistle of Jude* (Cambridge Greek Testament, 1912).

LUMBY, J. R., *2 Peter and Jude* (in Bible Commentary).

MAYOR, J. B., *The Epistle of St. Jude and the Second Epistle of St. Peter* (1907).

PLUMMER, A., *The Second Epistle of Peter and the Epistle of Jude* (Vol. 3, N.T. Commentary for English Readers by Ellicott).

ROBSON, E. I., *Studies in the Second Epistle of St. Peter* (1915).

SCHOTT, TH., *Der zweite Brief Petri und der Brief Judä* (1863).

SCHOTT, *Der 2 Br. Petri und der Br. Judä Erkl.* (1863).

SCHWEENHORST, H., *Das Verhältnis des Judasbriefes zum zweiten Petrusbriefe* (1904).

SNYMAN, D. R., *The Authenticity of the Second Epistle of Peter* (thesis in 1923 for Th.D. degree at Southern Baptist Theological Seminary).

SPITTA, F, *Der zweite Brief des Petrus und der Brief des Judas* (1885).

STRACHAN, R. D., *Expositor's Greek Testament* (1910).

ULLMAN, C., *Der 2 Brief Petri Krit. untersuch.* (1821).

WARFIELD, B. B., *A Defence of 2 Peter* (*Southern Presbyterian Review*, January, 1882).

————, *Dr. Edwin A. Abbott on the Genuineness of Second Peter* (*Southern Presbyterian Review*, 1883).

WERDERMANN, H., *Die Irrlehrer des Judasbriefes und 2 Petrusbriefes* (1913).

WIESINGER, J. T. A., *Der zweite Brief des Apostels Petrus und der Brief des Judas* (1862).

CHAPTER I

1. *Simon Peter* (*Simōn Petros*). Aleph A K L P have
Symeōn as in Acts 15:14, while B has *Simōn*. The two forms
occur indifferently in I Macc. 2:3, 65 for the same man.
Servant and apostle (*doulos kai apostolos*). Like Rom. 1:1;
Titus 1:1. *To them that have obtained* (*tois lachousin*). Dative plural articular participle second aorist active of *lag-
chanō*, old verb, to obtain by lot (Luke 1:9), here with the
accusative (*pistin*) as in Acts 1:17. *Like precious* (*isotimon*).
Late compound adjective (*isos*, equal, *timē*, honor, price),
here only in N.T. But this adjective (Field) is used in two
ways, according to the two ideas in *timē* (value, honor),
either like in value or like in honor. This second idea is the
usual one with *isotimos* (inscriptions and papyri, Josephus,
Lucian), while *polutimos* has the notion of price like *timē*
in 1:7, 19; 2:4, 6f. The faith which they have obtained is
like in honor and privilege with that of Peter or any of the
apostles. *With us* (*hēmin*). Associative-instrumental case
after *isotimon*. Equal to *tēi hēmōn* (the faith of us). *In the
righteousness* (*en dikaiosunēi*). Definite because of the preposition *en* and the following genitive even though anarthrous. The O.T. sense of *dikaiosunē* applied to God (Rom.
1:17) and here to Christ. *Of our God and Saviour Jesus
Christ* (*tou theou hēmōn kai sōtēros Iēsou Christou*). So the
one article (*tou*) with *theou* and *sōtēros* requires precisely as
with *tou kuriou hēmōn kai sōtēros Iēsou Christou* (of our
Lord and Saviour Jesus Christ), one person, not two, in
1:11 as in 2:20; 3:2, 18. So in I Pet. 1:3 we have *ho theos
kai patēr* (the God and Father), one person, not two. The
grammar is uniform and inevitable (Robertson, *Grammar*,
p. 786), as even Schmiedel (Winer-Schmiedel, *Grammatik*,

147

p. 158) admits: "Grammar demands that one person be meant." Moulton (*Prol.*, p. 84) cites papyri examples of like usage of *theos* for the Roman emperors. See the same idiom in Titus 2:13. The use of *theos* by Peter as a predicate with Jesus Christ no more disproves the Petrine authorship of this Epistle than a like use in John 1:1 disproves the Johannine authorship of the Fourth Gospel and the same use in Titus 2:13 disproves the genuineness of Titus. Peter had heard Thomas call Jesus God (John 20:28) and he himself had called him the Son of God (Matt. 16:16).

2. *Be multiplied* (*plēthuntheiē*). First aorist passive optative of *plēthunō* in a wish for the future (volitive use) as in I Pet. 1:2; Jude 2. *In the knowledge* (*en epignōsei*). Full (additional, *epi*) knowledge as in 1:8 (only *gnōsis* in 1:5, 6; 3:18), but *epignōsin* again in 1:3, 8; 2:20. As in Colossians, so here full knowledge is urged against the claims of the Gnostic heretics to special *gnōsis*. *Of God and of Jesus our Lord* (*tou theou kai Iēsou tou kuriou hēmōn*). At first sight the idiom here seems to require one person as in 1:1, though there is a second article (*tou*) before *kuriou*, and *Iēsou* is a proper name. But the text here is very uncertain. Bengel, Spitta, Zahn, Nestle accept the short reading of P and some Vulgate MSS. and some minuscles with only *tou kuriou hēmōn* (our Lord) from which the three other readings may have come. Elsewhere in II Peter *gnōsis* and *epignōsis* are used of Christ alone. The text of II Peter is not in a good state of preservation.

3. *Seeing that his divine power hath granted unto us* (*hōs hēmin tēs theias dunameōs autou dedōrēmenēs*). Genitive absolute with the causal particle *hōs* and the perfect middle participle of *dōreō*, old verb, to bestow (*dōrea*, gift), usually middle as here, in N.T. elsewhere only Mark 15:45. *Autou* refers to Christ, who has "divine power" (*tēs theias dunameōs*), since he is *theos* (1:1). *Theios* (from *theos*) is an old adjective in N.T. here and verse 4 only, except Acts 17:29,

where Paul uses *to theion* for deity, thus adapting his language to his audience as the papyri and inscriptions show.
The use of *theios* with an imperial connotation is very common in the papyri and the inscriptions. Deissmann (*Bible
Studies*, pp. 360–368) has shown the singular linguistic likeness between II Pet. 1:3 to 11 and a remarkable inscription
of the inhabitants of Stratonicea in Caria to Zeus Pan-
hemerios and Hecate dated A.D. 22 (in full in C I H ii No.
2715 a b). One of the likenesses is the use of *tēs theias
dunameōs*. Peter may have read this inscription (cf. Paul
in Athens) or he may have used "the familiar forms and
formulæ of religious emotion" (Deissmann), "the official
liturgical language of Asia Minor." Peter is fond of *dunamis*
in this Epistle, and the *dunamis* of Christ "is the sword
which St. Peter holds over the head of the False Teachers"
(Bigg). *All things that pertain unto life and godliness* (*panta
ta pros zōēn kai eusebeian*). "All the things for life and
godliness." The new life in Christ who is the mystery of
godliness (I Tim. 3:16). *Eusebeia* with its cognates (*eusebēs,
eusebōs, eusebeō*) occurs only in this Epistle, Acts, and the
Pastoral Epistles (from *eu*, well, and *sebomai*, to worship).
Of him that called us (*tou kalesantos*). Genitive of the articular first aorist active participle of *kaleō*. Christ called
Peter and all other Christians. *By his own glory and virtue*
(*dia doxēs kai aretēs*). So B K L, but Aleph A C P read
idiāi doxēi kai aretēi (either instrumental case "by" or dative "to"). Peter is fond of *idios* (own, I Pet. 3:1, 5; II
Pet. 2:16, 22, etc.). "Glory" here is the manifestation of
the Divine Character in Christ. For *aretē* see on I Pet.
2:9 and Phil. 4:8; II Pet. 1:5.

4. *Whereby* (*di' hōn*). Probably the "glory and virtue"
just mentioned, though it is possible to take it with *panta
ta pros*, etc., or with *hēmin* (unto us, meaning "through
whom"). *He hath granted* (*dedōrētai*). Perfect middle indicative of *dōreō*, for which see verse 3. *His precious and*

exceeding great promises (*ta timia kai megista epaggelmata*). *Epaggelma* is an old word (from *epaggellō*) in place of the common *epaggelia*, in N.T. only here and 3:13. *Timios* (precious, from *timē*, value), three times by Peter (I Pet. 1:7 of faith; 1:19 of the blood of Christ; II Pet. 1:4 of Christ's promises). *Megista* is the elative superlative used along with a positive adjective (*timia*). *That ye may become* (*hina genēsthe*). Purpose clause with *hina* and second aorist middle subjunctive of *ginomai*. *Through these* (*dia toutōn*). The promises. *Partakers* (*koinōnoi*). Partners, sharers in, for which word see I Pet. 5:1. *Of the divine nature* (*theias phuseōs*). This phrase, like *to theion* in Acts 17:29, "belongs rather to Hellenism than to the Bible" (Bigg). It is a Stoic phrase, but not with the Stoic meaning. Peter is referring to the new birth as I Pet. 1:23 (*anagegennēmenoi*). The same phrase occurs in an inscription possibly under the influence of Mithraism (Moulton and Milligan's *Vocabulary*). *Having escaped* (*apophugontes*). Second aorist active participle of *apopheugō*, old compound verb, in N.T. only here and 2:18, 20, with the ablative here (*phthorās*, old word from *phtheirō*, moral decay as in 2:12) and the accusative there. *By lust* (*en epithumiāi*). Caused by, consisting in, lust. "Man becomes either regenerate or degenerate" (Strachan).

5. *Yea, and for this very cause* (*kai auto touto de*). Adverbial accusative (*auto touto*) here, a classic idiom, with both *kai* and *de*. Cf. *kai touto* (Phil. 1:29), *touto men—touto de* (Heb. 10:33). "The soul of religion is the practical part" (Bunyan). Because of the new birth and the promises we have a part to play. *Adding on your part* (*pareisenegkantes*). First aorist active participle of *pareispherō*, old double compound, to bring in (*eispherō*), besides (*para*), here only in N.T. *All diligence* (*spoudēn pāsan*). Old word from *speudō* to hasten (Luke 19:5f.). This phrase (*pāsan spoudēn*) occurs in Jude 3 with *poioumenos* and on the inscription in

Stratonicea (verse 3) with *ispheresthai* (certainly a curious
coincidence, to say the least, though common in the *Koinē*).
In your faith (*en tēi pistei humōn*). Faith or *pistis* (strong
conviction as in Heb. 11:1, 3, the root of the Christian life
Eph. 2:8) is the foundation which goes through various steps
up to love (*agapē*). See similar lists in James 1:30; I Thess.
1:3; II Thess. 1:3f.; Gal. 5:22f.; Rom. 5:3f.; 8:29f. Hermas
(*Vis.* iii. 8. 1–7) has a list called "daughters" of one another. Note the use of *en* (in, on) with each step. *Supply*
(*epichorēgēsate*). First aorist active imperative of *epichorēgeō*, late and rare double compound verb (*epi* and *chorēgeō*
I Pet. 4:11 from *chorēgos*, chorus-leader, *choros* and *hēgeomai*,
to lead), to fit out the chorus with additional (complete)
supplies. Both compound and simplex (more common) occur in the papyri. In 1:11 and already in II Cor. 9:10;
Gal. 3:5; Col. 2:19. *Virtue* (*aretēn*). Moral power, moral
energy, vigor of soul (Bengel). See 3. *Knowledge* (*gnōsin*).
Insight, understanding (I Cor. 16:18; John 15:15).

6. *Temperance* (*tēn egkrateian*). Self-control. Old word
(from *egkratēs*, *en* and *kratos*, one holding himself in as in
Titus 1:8), in N.T. only here, Acts 24:25; Gal. 5:23. The
opposite of the *pleonexia* of the heretics. *Patience* (*tēn
hupomonēn*). For which see James 1:3. *Godliness* (*tēn
eusebeian*). For which see verse 3.

7. *Love of the brethren* (*tēn philadelphian*). See I Pet. 1:22.
Love (*tēn agapēn*). By deliberate choice (Matt. 5:44). Love
for Christ as the crown of all (I Pet. 1:8) and so for all men.
Love is the climax as Paul has it (I Cor. 13:13).

8. *For if these things are yours and abound* (*tauta gar humin
huparchonta kai pleonazonta*). Present active circumstantial
(conditional) participles neuter plural of *huparchō* and *ple-
onazō* (see I Thess. 3:12) with dative case *humin*, "these
things existing for you (or in you) and abounding." *They
make you to be* (*kathistēsin*). "Render" (present active indicative of *kathistēmi*, old verb, James 3:6), singular because

tauta neuter plural. *Not idle nor unfruitful* (*ouk argous oude akarpous*). Accusative predicative plural with *humas* understood, both adjectives with alpha privative, for *argos* see James 2:20 and for *akarpos* Matt. 13:22. *Knowledge* (*epignōsin*). "Full (additional) knowledge" as in 1:2.

9. *He that lacketh these things* (*hōi mē parestin tauta*). "To whom (dative case of possession) these things are not (*mē* because a general or indefinite relative clause)." *Seeing only what is near* (*muōpazōn*). Present active participle of *muōpazō*, a rare verb from *muōps* (in Aristotle for a near-sighted man) and that from *mueō tous ōpas* (to close the eyes in order to see, not to keep from seeing). The only other instance of *muōpazō* is given by Suicer from Ps. Dion. Eccl. Hier. ii. 3 (*muōpasousēi kai apostrephomenēi*) used of a soul on which the light shines (blinking and turning away). Thus understood the word here limits *tuphlos* as a short-sighted man screwing up his eyes because of the light. *Having forgotten* (*lēthēn labōn*). "Having received forgetfulness." Second aorist active participle of *lambanō* and accusative *lēthēn*, old word, from *lēthomai*, to forget, here only in N.T. See II Tim. 1:5 for a like phrase *hupomnēsin labōn* (having received remembrance). *The cleansing* (*tou katharismou*). See Heb. 1:3 for this word for the expiatory sacrifice of Christ for our sins as in I Pet. 1:18; 2:24; 3:18. In I Pet. 3:21 Peter denied actual cleansing of sin by baptism (only symbolic). If there is a reference to baptism here, which is doubtful, it can only be in a symbolic sense. *Old* (*palai*). Of the language as in Heb. 1:1.

10. *Wherefore* (*dio*). Because of the exhortation and argument in verses 5–9. *Give the more diligence* (*māllon spoudasate*). "Become diligent (first aorist ingressive active imperative of *spoudazō* as in II Tim. 2:15; II Pet. 1:15) the more" (*mallon*, not less). *To make* (*poieisthai*). Present middle infinitive of *poieō*, to make for yourselves. *Calling and election* (*klēsin kai eklogēn*). Both words (*klēsin*, the

invitation, *eklogēn*, actual acceptance). See for *eklogē* I Thess. 1:4; Rom. 9:11. *If ye do* (*poiountes*). Present active circumstantial (conditional) participle of *poieō*, "doing." *Ye shall never stumble* (*ou mē ptaisēte pote*). Strong double negative (*ou mē pote*) with first aorist active subjunctive of *ptaiō*, old verb to stumble, to fall as in James 2:10; 3:2.

11. *Thus* (*houtōs*). As shown in verse 10. *Shall be supplied* (*epichorēgēthēsetai*). Future passive of *epichorēgeō*, for which see verse 5. You supply the virtues above and God will supply the entrance (*hē eisodos*, old word already in I Thess. 1:9, etc.). *Richly* (*plousiōs*). See Col. 3:16 for this adverb. *Into the eternal kingdom* (*eis tēn aiōnion basileian*). The believer's inheritance of I Pet. 1:4 is here termed kingdom, but "eternal" (*aiōnion* feminine same as masculine). Curiously again in the Stratonicea inscription we find *tēs aiōniou archēs* (of the eternal rule) applied to "the lords of Rome." But this is the spiritual reign of God in men's hearts here on earth (I Pet. 2:9) and in heaven. *Of our Lord and Saviour Jesus Christ* (*tou kuriou hēmōn kai sōtēros Iēsou Christou*). For which idiom see on 1:1.

12. *Wherefore* (*dio*). Since they are possessed of faith that conduces to godliness which they are diligently practising now he insists on the truth and proposes to do his part by them about it. *I shall be ready always* (*mellēsō aei*). Future active of *mellō* (Matt. 24:6), old verb, to be on the point of doing and used with the infinitive (present, aorist, or future). It is not here a periphrastic future, but rather the purpose of Peter to be ready in the future as in the past and now (Zahn). *To put you in remembrance* (*humas hupomimnēskein*). Present active infinitive of *hupomimnēskō*, old causative compound (*hupo, mimnēskō*, like our suggest), either with two accusatives (John 14:26) or *peri* with the thing as here), "to keep on reminding you of those things" (*peri toutōn*). *Though ye know them* (*kaiper eidotas*). Second perfect active concessive participle of *oida*, agreeing (acc.

plural), with *humas*. Cf. Heb. 5:8. *Are established* (*estērig-menous*). Perfect passive concessive participle of *stērizō* (I Pet. 5:10). The very verb (*stērison*) used by Jesus to Peter (Luke 22:32). *In the truth which is with you* (*en tēi parousēi alētheiāi*). "In the present truth" (the truth present to you), *parousēi* present active participle of *pareimi*, to be beside one. See Col. 1:6 for this use of *parōn*. Firmly established in the truth, but all the same Peter is eager to make them stronger.

13. *I think it right* (*dikaion hēgoumai*). Peter considers this to be his solemn duty, "right" (*dikaion*). Cf. Phil. 3:1; Eph. 6:1. *So long as* (*eph' hoson*). For this phrase see Matt. 9:15; Rom. 11:13. *Tabernacle* (*skēnōmati*). Old word, in literal sense in Deut. 33:18 for the usual *skēnē* (Peter's word at the Transfiguration, Mark 9:5), earliest use (in N.T. only here, verse 14; Acts 7:46 of the tabernacle of the covenant) in this metaphorical sense of life as a pilgrimage (I Pet. 1:1; 2:11), though Paul has *skēnos*, so in II Cor. 5:1, 4. Peter feels the nearness of death and the urgency upon him. *To stir you up* (*diegeirein humas*). Present active infinitive of *diegeirō*, late (Arist., Hippocr., Herodian, papyri), perfective (*dia* = thoroughly) compound, to wake out of sleep (Mark 4:39), "to keep on rousing you up." *By putting you in remembrance* (*en hupomnēsei*). Old word, from *hupomimnēskō* (verse 12), in N.T. only here, 3:1; II Tim. 15. "By way of reminding you."

14. *The putting off of my tabernacle* (*hē apothesis tou skēn-nōmatos mou*). For *apothesis* see on I Pet. 3:21 and for *skēnōma* verse 13. For the metaphor see II Cor. 5:3f. *Cometh swiftly* (*tachinē estin*). Late adjective (Theocritus, LXX, inscription), in N.T. only here and 2:1. It is not clear whether *tachinos* means soon or speedy as in Is. 59:7 and like *tachus* in James 1:19, or sudden, like *tachus* in Plato (*Republ.* 553 D). Either sense agrees with the urgent tone of Peter here, whether he felt his death to be near or

violent or both. *Signified unto me (edēlōsen moi)*. First aorist active indicative of *dēloō*, old verb (from *delos*), as in I Pet. 1:11. Peter refers to the incident told in John 21:18f., which he knew by personal experience before John wrote it down.

15. Peter may also have had an intimation by vision of his approaching death (cf. the legend *Domine quo vadis*) as Paul often did (Acts 16:9; 18:9; 21:11; 23:11; 27:23). *At every time (hekastote)*. As need arises, old adverb, here alone in N.T. *After my decease (meta tēn emēn exodon)*. For *exodos* meaning death see Luke 9:31, and for departure from Egypt (way out, *ex, hodos*) see Heb. 11:22, the only other N.T. examples. Here again Peter was present on the Transfiguration mount when the talk was about the "exodus" of Jesus from earth. *That ye may be able (echein humas)*. Literally, "that ye may have it," the same idiom with *echō* and the infinitive in Mark 14:8; Matt. 18:25. It is the object-infinitive after *spoudasō* (I will give diligence, for which see verse 10). *To call these things to remembrance (tēn toutōn mnēmēn poieisthai)*. Present middle infinitive of *poieō* (as in verse 10). *Mnēmē* is an old word (from *mnaomai*), here alone in N.T. This idiom, like the Latin *mentionem facere*, is common in the old writers (papyri also both for "mention" and "remembrance"), here only in N.T., but in Rom. 1:20 we have *mneian poioumai* (I make mention). Either sense suits here. It is possible, as Irenæus (iii. 1. 1) thought, that Peter had in mind Mark's Gospel, which would help them after Peter was gone. Mark's Gospel was probably already written at Peter's suggestion, but Peter may have that fact in mind here.

16. *We did not follow (ouk exakolouthēsantes)*. First aorist active participle of *exakoloutheō*, late compound verb, to follow out (Polybius, Plutarch, LXX, papyri, inscriptions as of death following for any Gentile in the temple violating the barrier), with emphatic negative *ouk*, "not having fol-

lowed." See also 2:2 for this verb. *Cunningly devised fables* (*sesophismenois muthois*). Associative instrumental case of *muthos* (old term for word, narrative, story, fiction, fable, falsehood). In N.T. only here and the Pastoral Epistles (I Tim. 1:4, etc.). Perfect passive participle of *sophizō*, old word (from *sophos*), only twice in N.T., in causative sense to make wise (II Tim. 3:15), to play the sophist, to invent cleverly (here) and so also in the old writers and in the papyri. Some of the false teachers apparently taught that the Gospel miracles were only allegories and not facts (Bigg). Cf. 2:3 for "feigned words." *When we made known unto you* (*egnōrisamen humin*). First aorist active indicative of *gnōrizō*, to make known unto you. Possibly by Peter himself. *The power and coming* (*tēn dunamin kai parousian*). These words can refer (Chase) to the Incarnation, just as is true of *epiphaneia* in II Tim. 1:10 (second coming in I Tim. 6:14), and is true of *parousia* (II Cor. 7:6 of Titus). But elsewhere in the N.T. *parousia* (technical term in the papyri for the coming of a king or other high dignitary), when used of Christ, refers to his second coming (II Pet. 3:4, 12). *But we were eye-witnesses* (*all' epoptai genēthentes*). First aorist passive participle of *ginomai*, "but having become eye-witnesses." *Epoptai*, old word (from *epoptō* like *epopteuō* in I Pet. 2:12; 3:2), used of those who attained the third or highest degree of initiates in the Eleusinian mysteries (common in the inscriptions). Cf. *autoptēs* in Luke 1:2. *Of his majesty* (*tēs ekeinou megaleiotētos*). Late and rare word (LXX and papyri) from *megaleios* (Acts 2:11), in N.T. only here, Luke 9:43 (of God); Acts 19:27 (of Artemis). Peter clearly felt that he and James and John were lifted to the highest stage of initiation at the Transfiguration of Christ. Emphatic *ekeinou* as in II Tim. 2:26.

17. *For he received* (*labōn gar*). Second aorist active participle nominative singular of *lambanō*, "he having received," but there is no finite verb, anacoluthon, changing in verse

19 (after parenthesis in 18) to *echomen bebaioteron* rather than *ebebaiōsen*. *When there came such a voice to him* (*phōnēs enechtheisēs autōi toiasde*). Genitive absolute with first aorist passive participle feminine singular of *pherō* (cf. I Pet. 1:13), repeated *enechtheisan* in verse 18. *Phōnē* (voice) is used also of Pentecost (Acts 2:6). *Toiosde* (classical demonstrative) occurs here alone in the N.T. *From the excellent glory* (*hupo tēs megaloprepous doxēs*). "By the majestic glory." *Megaloprepēs*, old compound (*megas*, great, *prepei*, it is becoming), here only in N.T., several times in O.T., Apocr. (II Macc. 8:15), adverb in the inscriptions. Probably a reference to *nephelē phōteinē* (bright cloud, shekinah) in Matt. 17:5. The words given here from the "voice" agree exactly with Matt. 17:5 except the order and the use of *eis hon* rather than *en hōi*. Mark (9:7) and Luke (9:35) have *akouete*. But Peter did not need any Gospel for his report here.

18. *This voice* (*tautēn tēn phōnēn*). The one referred to in verse 17. *We heard* (*ēkousamen*). First aorist active indicative of *akouō*, a definite experience of Peter. *Brought* (*enechtheisan*). "Borne" as in verse 17. *When we were with him* (*sun autōi ontes*). Present active participle of *eimi*, "being with him." *In the holy mount* (*en tōi hagiōi orei*). Made holy by the majestic glory. See Ezek. 28:14 for "holy mount of God," there Sinai, this one probably one of the lower slopes of Hermon. Peter's account is independent of the Synoptic narrative, but agrees with it in all essentials.

19. *The word of prophecy* (*ton prophētikon logon*). "The prophetic word." Cf. I Pet. 1:10, a reference to all the Messianic prophecies. *Made more sure* (*bebaioteron*). Predicate accusative of the comparative adjective *bebaios* (II Pet. 1:10). The Transfiguration scene confirmed the Messianic prophecies and made clear the deity of Jesus Christ as God's Beloved Son. Some with less likelihood take Peter

to mean that the word of prophecy is a surer confirmation of Christ's deity than the Transfiguration. *Whereunto* (*hōi*). Dative of the relative referring to "the prophetic word made more sure." *That ye take heed* (*prosechontes*). Present active participle with *noun* (mind) understood, "holding your mind upon" with the dative (*hōi*). *As unto a lamp* (*hōs luchnōi*). Dative also after *prosechontes* of *luchnos*, old word (Matt. 5:15). *Shining* (*phainonti*). Dative also present active participle of *phainō*, to shine (John 1:5). So of the Baptist (John 5:35). *In a dark place* (*en auchmērōi topōi*). Old adjective, parched, squalid, dirty, dark, murky, here only in N.T., though in Aristotle and on tombstone for a boy. *Until the day dawn* (*heōs hou hēmera diaugasēi*). First aorist active subjunctive of *diaugazō* with temporal conjunction *heōs hou*, usual construction for future time. Late compound verb *diaugazō* (Polybius, Plutarch, papyri) from *dia* and *augē*, to shine through, here only in N.T. *The day-star* (*phōsphoros*). Old compound adjective (*phōs*, light, *pherō*, to bring), light-bringing, light-bearer (Lucifer) applied to Venus as the morning star. Our word *phosphorus* is this word. In the LXX *heōsphoros* occurs. Cf. Mal. 4:2 and Luke 1:76–79; Rev. 22:16 for "dawn" applied to the Messiah. *Arise* (*anateilēi*). First aorist active subjunctive of *anatellō* (James 1:11; Matt. 5:45).

20. *Knowing this first* (*touto prōton ginōskontes*). Agreeing with *poieite* like *prosechontes* in verse 19. *No prophecy of Scripture* (*pāsa prophēteia ou*). Like the Hebrew *lo-kōl*, but also in the papyri as in I John 2:21 (Robertson, *Grammar*, p. 753). *Is* (*ginetai*). Rather "comes," "springs" (Alford), not "is" (*estin*). *Of private interpretation* (*idias epiluseōs*). Ablative case of origin or source in the predicate as with *gnōmēs* in Acts 20:3 and with *tou theou* and *ex hēmōn* in II Cor. 4:7. "No prophecy of Scripture comes out of private disclosure," not "of private interpretation." The usual meaning of *epilusis* is explanation, but the word does

not occur elsewhere in the N.T. It occurs in the papyri in the sense of solution and even of discharge of a debt. Spitta urges "dissolved" as the idea here. The verb *epiluō*, to unloose, to untie, to release, occurs twice in the N.T., once (Mark 4:34) where it can mean "disclose" about parables, the other (Acts 19:39) where it means to decide. It is the prophet's grasp of the prophecy, not that of the readers that is here presented, as the next verse shows.

21. *For* (*gar*). The reason for the previous statement that no prophet starts a prophecy himself. He is not a self-starter. *Came* (*ēnechthē*). First aorist passive indicative of *pherō* (verses 17f.). *By the will of man* (*thelēmati anthrōpou*). Instrumental case of *thelēma*. Prophecy is of divine origin, not of one's private origination (*idias epiluseōs*). *Moved by the Holy Ghost* (*hupo pneumatos hagiou pheromenoi*). Present passive participle of *pherō*, moved from time to time. There they "spoke from God." Peter is not here warning against personal interpretation of prophecy as the Roman Catholics say, but against the folly of upstart prophets with no impulse from God.

CHAPTER II

1. *But there arose (egenonto de).* Second aorist middle indicative of *ginomai* (cf. *ginetai* in 1:20). *False prophets also (kai pseudoprophētai).* In contrast with the true prophets just pictured in 1:20f. Late compound in LXX and Philo, common in N.T. (Matt. 7:15). Allusion to the O.T. times like Balaam and others (Jer. 6:13; 28:9; Ezek. 13:9). *False teachers (pseudodidaskaloi).* Late and rare compound (*pseudēs, didaskalos*) here alone in N.T. Peter pictures them as in the future here (*esontai*, shall be) and again as already present (*eisin*, are, verse 17), or in the past (*eplanēthēsan*, they went astray, verse 15). *Shall privily bring in (pareisaxousin).* Future active of *pareisagō*, late double compound *pareisagō*, to bring in (*eisagō*), by the side (*para*), as if secretly, here alone in N.T., but see *pareisaktous* in Gal. 2:4 (verbal adjective of this same verb). *Destructive heresies (haireseis apōleias).* Descriptive genitive, "heresies of destruction" (marked by destruction) as in Luke 16:8. *Hairesis* (from *haireō*) is simply a choosing, a school, a sect like that of the Sadducees (Acts 5:17), of the Pharisees (Acts 15:5), and of Christians as Paul admitted (Acts 24:5). These "tenets" (Gal. 5:20) led to destruction. *Denying (arnoumenoi).* Present middle participle of *arneomai*. This the Gnostics did, the very thing that Peter did, alas (Matt. 26:70) even after Christ's words (Matt. 10:33). *Even the Master (kai ton despotēn).* Old word for absolute master, here of Christ as in Jude 4, and also of God (Acts 4:24). Without the evil sense in our "despot." *That bought them (ton agorasanta autous).* First aorist active articular participle of *agorazō*, same idea with *lutroō* in I Pet. 1:18f. These were professing Christians, at any rate, these heretics.

Swift destruction (*tachinēn apōleian*). See 1:14 for *tachinēn* and note repetition of *apōleian*. This is always the tragedy of such false prophets, the fate that they bring on (*epagontes*) themselves.

2. *Lascivious doings* (*aselgeiais*). Associative instrumental case after *exakolouthēsousin* (future active, for which verb see 1:16). See I Pet. 4:3 for this word. *By reason of whom* (*di' hous*). "Because of whom" (accusative case of relative, referring to *polloi*, many). *Autōn* (their) refers to *pseudodidaskaloi* (false teachers) while *polloi* to their deluded followers. See Rom. 2:23f. for a picture of such conduct by Jews (quotation from Is. 52:5, with *blasphēmeō* used as here with *di' humas*, because of you). *The way of truth* (*hē hodos tēs alētheias*). *Hodos* (way) occurs often in N.T. for Christianity (Acts 9:2; 16:17; 18:25; 22:4; 24:14). This phrase is in Gen. 24:48 as "the right road," and that is what Peter means here. So Ps. 119:30. See again 2:15, 21.

3. *In covetousness* (*en pleonexiāi*). As did Balaam (verse 15). These licentious Gnostics made money out of their dupes. A merely intellectual Gnosticism had its fruit in immorality and fraud. *With feigned words* (*plastois logois*). Instrumental case. *Plastos* is verbal adjective (from *plassō*, to mould as from clay, for which see Rom. 9:20), here only in N.T. "With forged words." See sample in 3:4. *Shall make merchandise of you* (*humas emporeusontai*). Future middle of *emporeuomai* (from *emporos*, a travelling merchant), old word, to go in for trade, in N.T. only here and James 4:13, which see. Cf. our emporium (John 2:16, market house). *Whose sentence* (*hois to krima*). "For whom (dative case) the sentence" (verdict, not process *krisis*). *Now from of old* (*ekpalai*). Late and common compound adverb, in N.T. only here and 3:5. *Lingereth not* (*ouk argei*). "Is not idle," old verb, *argeō* (from *argos* not working, alpha privative and *ergon*), here only in N.T. *Slumbereth not* (*ou nustazei*). Old and common verb (from *nuō* to nod), in

N.T. only here and Matt. 25:5. Note *apōleia* (destruction) three times in verses 1 to 3.

4. *For if God spared not* (*ei gar ho theos ouk epheisato*). First instance (*gar*) of certain doom, that of the fallen angels. Condition of the first class precisely like that in Rom. 11:21 save that here the normal apodosis (*humōn ou pheisetai*) is not expressed as there, but is simply implied in verse 9 by *oiden kurios ruesthai* (the Lord knows how to deliver) after the parenthesis in verse 8. *Angels when they sinned* (*aggelōn hamartēsantōn*). Genitive case after *epheisato* (first aorist middle indicative of *pheidomai*) and anarthrous (so more emphatic, even angels), first aorist active participle of *hamartanō*, "having sinned." *Cast them down to hell* (*tartarōsas*). First aorist active participle of *tartaroō*, late word (from *tartaros*, old word in Homer, Pindar, LXX Job 40:15; 41:23, Philo, inscriptions, the dark and doleful abode of the wicked dead like the Gehenna of the Jews), found here alone save in a scholion on Homer. *Tartaros* occurs in Enoch 20:2 as the place of punishment of the fallen angels, while Gehenna is for apostate Jews. *Committed* (*paredōken*). First aorist active indicative of *paradidōmi*, the very form solemnly used by Paul in Rom. 1:21, 26, 28. *To pits of darkness* (*seirois zophou*). *Zophos* (kin to *gnophos*, *nephos*) is an old word, blackness, gloom of the nether world in Homer, in N.T. only here, verse 17; Jude 13; Heb. 12:18. The MSS. vary between *seirais* (*seira*, chain or rope) and *seirois* (*seiros*, old word for pit, underground granary). *Seirois* is right (Aleph A B C), dative case of destination. *To be reserved unto judgment* (*eis krisin tēroumenous*). Present (linear action) passive participle of *tēreō*. "Kept for judgment." Cf. I Pet. 1:4. Aleph A have *kolazomenous tērein* as in verse 9. Note *krisis* (act of judgment).

5. *The ancient world* (*archaiou kosmou*). Genitive case after *epheisato* (with *ei* understood) repeated (the second example, the deluge). This example not in Jude. Absence

of the article is common in the prophetic style like II Peter. For *archaios* see Luke 9:8. *Preserved* (*ephulaxen*). Still part of the long protasis with *ei*, first aorist active indicative of *phulassō*. *With seven others* (*ogdoon*). "Eighth," predicate accusative adjective (ordinal), classic idiom usually with *auton*. See I Pet. 3:20 for this same item. Some take *ogdoon* with *kēruka* (eighth preacher), hardly correct. *A preacher of righteousness* (*dikaiosunēs kēruka*). "Herald" as in I Tim. 2:7; II Tim. 1:11 alone in N.T., but *kērussō* is common. It is implied in I Pet. 3:20 that Noah preached to the men of his time during the long years. *When he brought* (*epaxas*). First aorist active participle (instead of the common second aorist active *epagagōn*) of *eisagō*, old compound verb to bring upon, in N.T. only here and Acts 5:28 (by Peter here also). *A flood* (*kataklusmon*). Old word (from *katakluzō*, to inundate), only of Noah's flood in N.T. (Matt. 24:38ff.; Luke 17:27; II Pet. 2:5). *Upon the world of the ungodly* (*kosmoi asebōn*). Anarthrous and dative case *kosmōi*. The whole world were "ungodly" (*asebeis* as in I Pet. 4:18) save Noah's family of eight.

6. *Turning into ashes* (*tephrōsas*). First aorist participle of *tephroō*, late word from *tephra*, ashes (in Dio Cassius of an eruption of Vesuvius, Philo), here alone in N.T. *The cities of Sodom and Gomorrah* (*poleis Sodomōn kai Gomorrās*). Genitive of apposition after *poleis* (cities), though it makes sense as possessive genitive, for Jude 7 speaks of the cities around these two. The third example, the cities of the plain. See Gen. 19:24f. *Condemned them* (*katekrinen*). First aorist active indicative of *katakrinō*, still part of the protasis with *ei*. *With an overthrow* (*katastrophēi*). Instrumental case or even dative like *thanatōi* with *katakrinō* in Matt. 20:18. But Westcott and Hort reject the word here because not in B C Coptic. *Having made them* (*tetheikōs*). Perfect active participle of *tithēmi*. *An example* (*hupodeigma*). For which see James 5:10; John 13:15. Cf. I Pet. 2:21. *Unto those*

that should live ungodly (*mellontōn asebesin*). Rather, "unto ungodly men of things about to be" (see Heb. 11:20 for this use of *mellontōn*). But Aleph A C K L read *asebein* (present active infinitive) with *mellontōn* = *asebēsontōn* (future active participle of *asebeō*), from which we have our translation.

7. *And delivered* (*kai erusato*). First aorist middle of *ruomai* as in Matt. 6:13, still part of the protasis with *ei*. *Righteous Lot* (*dikaion Lot*). This adjective *dikaios* occurs three times in verses 7 and 8. See Wisdom 10:6. *Sore distressed* (*kataponoumenon*). Present passive participle of *kataponeō*, late and common verb, to work down, to exhaust with labor, to distress, in N.T. only here and Acts 7:24. *By the lascivious life of the wicked* (*hupo tēs tōn athesmōn en aselgeiāi anastrophēs*). "By the life in lasciviousness of the lawless." *Athesmos* (alpha privative and *thesmos*), late and common adjective (cf. *athemitos* I Pet. 4:3) for rebels against law (of nature and conscience here). *Anastrophē* is frequent in I Peter.

8. *For* (*gar*). Parenthetical explanation in verse 8 of the remark about Lot. *Dwelling* (*enkatoikōn*). Present active participle of *enkatoikeō*, old but rare double compound, here only in N.T. *In seeing and hearing* (*blemmati kai akoēi*). "By sight (instrumental case of *blemma*, old word, from *blepō* to see, here only in N.T.) and hearing" (instrumental case of *akoē* from *akouō*, to hear, common as Matt. 13:14). *From day to day* (*hēmeran ex hēmerās*). "Day in day out." Accusative of time and ablative with *ex*. Same idiom in Ps. 96:2 for the more common *ex hēmeras eis hēmeran*. *Vexed* (*ebasanizen*). Imperfect active (kept on vexing) of *basanizō*, old word, to test metals, to torment (Matt. 8:29). *With their lawless deeds* (*anomois ergois*). Instrumental case of cause, "because of their lawless (contrary to law) deeds." For *anomos* see II Thess. 2:8.

9. *The Lord knoweth how* (*oiden kurios*). The actual apodosis of the long protasis begun in verse 4. God can

deliver his servants as shown by Noah and Lot and he will deliver you. The idiomatic use of *oida* and the infinitive (*ruesthai* present middle and see verse 7) for knowing how as in Matt. 7:11; James 4:17. *The godly* (*eusebeis*). Old anarthrous adjective (from *eu* and *sebomai*, to worship), in N.T. only here and Acts 10:2, 7 (by Peter). For *temptation* (*peirasmou*) see James 1:2, 12; I Pet. 1:6. *To keep* (*tērein*). Present active infinitive of *tēreō* after *oiden*. *Unrighteous* (*adikous*). As in I Pet. 3:18. *Under punishment* (*kolazomenous*). Present passive participle of *kolazō*, old verb (from *kolos*, lopped off), in N.T. only here and Acts 4:21. Present tense emphasises continuity of the punishment. See *kolasin aiōnion* in Matt. 25:46.

10. *Chiefly* (*malista*). Especially. He turns now to the libertine heretics (verses 2, 7). *After the flesh* (*opisō sarkos*). Hebraistic use of *opisō* as with *hamartiōn* (sins) in Is. 65:2. Cf. Matt. 4:19; I Tim. 5:15. *Of defilement* (*miasmou*). Old word (from *miainō* Tit. 1:15), here only in N.T. *Despise dominion* (*kuriotētos kataphronountas*). *Kuriotēs* is late word for lordship (perhaps God or Christ) (from *Kurios*), in Col. 1:16; Eph. 1:21; Jude 8. Genitive case after *kataphrountas* (thinking down on, Matt. 6:24). *Daring* (*tolmētai*). Old substantive (from *tolmaō*, to dare), daring men, here only in N.T. *Self-willed* (*authadeis*). Old adjective (from *autos* and *hēdomai*), self-pleasing, arrogant, in N.T. only here and Titus. 1:7. *They tremble not to rail at dignities* (*doxas ou tremousin blasphēmountes*). "They tremble not blaspheming dignities." *Tremō* is old verb (Mark 5:33), used only in present as here and imperfect. Here with the complementary participle *blasphēmountes* rather than the infinitive *blasphēmein*. See Jude 8. Perhaps these dignities (*doxas*) are angels (*evil*).

11. *Whereas* (*hopou*). Loose use of *hopou* (in Xenophon) = "wherein." *Though greater* (*meizones ontes*). Than the evil *doxai*. Concessive participle and comparative adjective. *In*

might and strength (*ischui kai dunamei*). Locative case. Both indwelling strength (*ischus,* Mark 12:30) and ability (*dunamis,* Matt. 25:15). *Railing judgment* (*blasphemon krisin*). "Blasphemous accusation." *Against them* (*kat' autōn*). The evil angels (*doxai*). *Before the Lord* (*para kuriōi*). In God's presence. See Jude 9 and possibly Enoch 9.

12. *But these* (*houtoi de*). The false teachers of verse 1. *As creatures* (*zōa*). Living creatures, old word, from *zōos* (alive), Jude 10; Rev. 4, 6–9. *Without reason* (*aloga*). Old adjective, in N.T. only here, Jude 10; Acts 25:27. Brute beasts like *thēria* (wild animals). *Born* (*gegennēmena*). Perfect passive participle of *gennaō. Mere animals* (*phusika*). Old adjective in *-ikos* (from *phusis,* nature), natural animals, here only in N.T. *To be taken* (*eis halōsin*). "For capture" (old substantive, from *haloō,* here only in N.T.). *And destroyed* (*kai phthoran*). "And for destruction" just like a beast of prey caught. See 1:4. *In matters whereof they are ignorant* (*en hois agnoousin*). "In which things they are ignorant." Here *en hois = en toutois ha* (in those things which), a common Greek idiom. For *agnoeō* (present active indicative) see I Thess. 4:13 and I Tim. 1:7 for a like picture of loud ignoramuses posing as professional experts. *Shall in their destroying surely be destroyed* (*en tēi phthorāi autōn phtharēsontai*). Second future passive of *phtheirō.* Rhetorical Hebraism in the use of *en phthorāi* (same root as *phtheirō*), word four times in II Peter. See Jude 10.

13. *Suffering wrong* (*adikoumenoi*). Present middle or passive participle of *adikeō* to do wrong. So Aleph B P, but A C K L have *komioumenoi* (future middle participle of *komizō*), shall receive. *As the hire of wrong-doing* (*misthon adikias*). The Elephantine papyrus has the passive of *adikeō* in the sense of being defrauded, and that may be the idea here. Peter plays on words again here as often in II Peter. The picture proceeds now with participles like *hēgoumenoi* (counting). *Pleasure* (*hēdonēn*). See James 4:1, 3.

To revel in the daytime (*tēn en hēmerāi truphēn*). "The in the daytime revel" (old word *truphē* from *thruptō*, to enervate, in N.T. only here and Luke 7:25). *Spots* (*spiloi*). Old word for disfiguring spot, in N.T. only here and Eph. 5:27. *Blemishes* (*mōmoi*). Old word for blot (kin to *muō*), only here in N.T. See I Pet. 1:19 for *amōmos kai aspilos*. *Revelling* (*entruphōntes*). Present active participle of *entruphaō*, old compound for living in luxury, only here in N.T. *In their love-feasts* (*en tais agapais*). So B Sah, but Aleph A C K L P read *apatais* (in their deceivings). If *agapais* is genuine as it is in Jude 12, they are the only N.T. examples of this use of *agapē*. *While they feast with you* (*suneuōchoumenoi*). Present passive participle of late and rare verb *suneuōcheō* (*sun*, together, and *euōcheō*, to feed abundantly) to entertain with. Clement of Alex. (*Paed.* ii. 1. 6) applies *euōchia* to the *agapē*.

14. *Of adultery* (*moichalidos*). Rather, "of an adulteress," like James 4:4. Vivid picture of a man who cannot see a woman without lascivious thoughts toward her (Mayor). Cf. Matt. 5:28. *That cannot cease* (*akatapastous*). Reading of A B in place of *akatapaustous* (alpha privative and verbal of *katapauō*, to cease). "Unable to stop." This a late verbal, only here in N.T. It is probable that *akatapastous* is merely a misspelling of *akatapaustous*. *From sin* (*hamartias*). Ablative case as in I Pet. 4:1 (*hamartias*). Insatiable lust. *Enticing* (*deleazontes*). Present active participle of *deleazō*, to catch by bait as in verse 18 and James 1:14. *Unsteadfast* (*astēriktous*). Late verbal adjective (alpha privative and *stērizō*), in Longinus and Vettius Valens, here alone in N.T. *Exercised* (*gegumnasmenēn*). Perfect passive predicate participle with *echontes*, from *gumnazō* precisely as in Heb. 5:14. Rhetorical metaphor from the gymnasium. *In covetousness* (*pleonexias*). Genitive case after the participle. *Children of cursing* (*kataras tekna*). Hebraism like *tekna hupakoēs* in I Pet. 1:14 = accursed (*kataratoi*).

15. *Forsaking* (*kataleipontes*). Present active participle of *kataleipō* (continually leaving) or *katalipontes* (second aorist active), having left. *The right way* (*eutheian hodon*). "The straight way" of I Sam. 12:23 (cf. Matt. 7:13f. for this use of *hodos*), "the way of truth" (2:2). *They went astray* (*eplanēthēsan*). First aorist passive indicative of *planaō*, like Mark 12:24. *The way of Balaam* (*tēi hodōi tou Balaam*). Associative instrumental case after *exakolouthēsantes*, for which verb see 1:16; 2:2. These false teachers, as shown in verse 13, followed the way of Balaam, "who loved the hire of wrong-doing" (*hos misthon adikias ēgapēsen*).

16. *But he was rebuked* (*elegxin de eschen*). "But he had rebuke." Second aorist active indicative of *echō* and accusative of *elegxis* (late word from *elegchō*, a periphrasis for *elegchō*, here only in N.T. *For his own transgression* (*idias paranomias*). Objective genitive of *paranomia*, old word (from *paranomos* lawbreaker), here only in N.T. *A dumb ass* (*hupozugion aphōnon*). Dumb is without voice, old word for idols and beasts. The adjective *hupozugios* (*hupo zugon on*) "being under a yoke," is applied to the ass as the common beast of burden (papyri, Deissmann, *Bible Studies*, p. 160), in N.T. only here and Matt. 21:5. *Spake* (*phthegxamenon*). First aorist middle participle of *phtheggomai*, old verb, to utter a sound, in N.T. only here, verse 18, Acts 4:18. *Stayed* (*ekōlusen*). First aorist active indicative of *kōluō*, to hinder. *Madness* (*paraphronian*). Only known example of this word instead of the usual *paraphrosunē* or *paraphronēsis*. It is being beside one's wits.

17. *Without water* (*anudroi*). As in Matt. 12:43; Luke 11:24. Old word for common and disappointing experience of travellers in the orient. *Mists* (*homichlai*). Old word for fog, here alone in N.T. *Driven by a storm* (*hupo lailapos elaunomenai*). *Lailaps* is a squall (Mark 4:37; Luke 8. 23, only other N.T. examples). See James 3:4 for another example of *elaunō* for driving power of wind and waves. *For

whom (*hois*). Dative case of personal interest. *The blackness* (*ho zophos*). See verse 4 for this word. *Hath been reserved* (*tetērētai*). Perfect passive participle of *tēreō*, for which see verses 4 and 9.

18. *Great swelling words* (*huperogka*). Old compound adjective (*huper* and *ogkos*, a swelling, swelling above and beyond), in N.T. only here and Jude 16. *Of vanity* (*mataiotētos*). Late and rare word (from *mataios*, empty, vain), often in LXX, in N.T. here, Rom. 8:20; Eph. 4:17. *By lasciviousness* (*aselgeiais*). Instrumental plural, "by lascivious acts." Note asyndeton as in 1:9, 17. *Those who are just escaping* (*tous oligōs apopheugontas*). So A B read *oligōs* (slightly, a little), while Aleph C K L P read *ontōs* (actually). *Oligōs* late and rare, only here in N.T. So again the Textus Receptus has *apophugontas* (second aorist active participle, clean escaped) while the correct text is the present active *apopheugontas*. *From them that live in error* (*tous en planēi anastrephomenous*). Accusative case after *apopheugontas* (escaping from) according to regular idiom. Peter often uses *anastrephō* and *anastrophē*.

19. *Liberty* (*eleutherian*). Promising "personal liberty," that is license, after the fashion of advocates of liquor today, not the freedom of truth in Christ (John 8:32; Gal. 5:1, 13). *Themselves bondservants* (*autoi douloi*). "Themselves slaves" of corruption and sin as Paul has it in Rom. 6:20. *Of whom* (*hōi*). Instrumental case, but it may mean "of what." *Is overcome* (*hēttētai*). Perfect passive indicative of *hēttaō* (from *hēttōn*, less) old verb, in N.T. only here, verse 20; II Cor. 12:13. *Of the same* (*toutōi*). "By this one (or thing)." *Is brought into bondage* (*dedoulōtai*). Perfect passive indicative of *douloō*. Like Paul again (Rom. 6:16, 18; 8:21).

20. *After they have escaped* (*apophugontes*). Second aorist active participle here (see verse 18). *The defilements* (*ta miasmata*). Old word miasma, from *miainō*, here only in

N.T. Our "miasma." The body is sacred to God. Cf. *miasmou* in verse 10. *They are again entangled* (*palin emplakentes*). Second aorist passive participle of *emplekō*, old verb, to inweave (noosed, fettered), in N.T. only here and II Tim. 2:4. *Overcome* (*hēttōntai*). Present passive indicative of *hēttaoō*, for which see verse 19, "are repeatedly worsted." Predicate in the condition of first class with *ei*. It is not clear whether the subject here is "the deluded victims" (Bigg) or the false teachers themselves (Mayor). See Heb. 10:26 for a parallel. *Therein* (*toutois*). So locative case (in these "defilements"), but it can be instrumental case ("by these," Strachan). *With them* (*autois*). Dative of disadvantage, "for them." *Than the first* (*tōn prōtōn*). Ablative case after the comparative *cheirona*. See this moral drawn by Jesus (Matt. 12:45; Luke 11:26).

21. *It were better* (*kreitton ēn*). Apodosis of a condition of second class without *an*, as is usual with clauses of possibility, propriety, obligation (Matt. 26:24; I Cor. 5:10; Rom. 7:7; Heb. 9:26). *Not to have known* (*mē epegnōkenai*). Perfect active infinitive of *epiginōskō* (cf. *epignōsei*, verse 20) to know fully. *The way of righteousness* (*tēn hodon tēs dikaiosunēs*). For the phrase see Matt. 21:33, also the way of truth (2:2), the straight way (2:15). *After knowing it* (*epignousin*). Second aorist active participle of *epiginōskō* (just used) in the dative plural agreeing with *autois* (for them). *To turn back* (*hupostrepsai*). First aorist active infinitive of *hupostrephō*, old and common verb, to turn back, to return. *From* (*ek*). Out of. So in Acts 12:25 with *hupostrephō*. With ablative case. See Rom. 7:12 for *hagia* applied to *hē entolē* (cf. I Tim. 6:14). II Peter strikes a high ethical note (1:5ff.). *Delivered* (*paradotheisēs*). First aorist passive participle feminine ablative singular of *paradidōmi*.

22. *It has happened* (*sumbebēken*). Perfect active indicative of *sumbainō*, for which see I Pet. 4:12. *According to*

the true proverb (*to tēs alēthous paroimias*).   "The word (*to* used absolutely, the matter of, as in Matt. 21:21; James 4:14) of the true proverb" (*paroimia* a wayside saying, for which see John 10:6; 16:25, 29).   The first proverb here given comes from Prov. 26:11.   *Exerama* is a late and rare word (here only in N.T., in Diosc. and Eustath.) from *exeraō*, to vomit.   *The sow that had washed* (*hūs lousamenē*).   *Hūs*, old word for hog, here only in N.T.   Participle first aorist direct middle of *louō* shows that it is feminine (anarthrous).   This second proverb does not occur in the O.T., probably from a Gentile source because about the habit of hogs.   Epictetus and other writers moralize on the habit of hogs, having once bathed in a filthy mud-hole, to delight in it.   *To wallowing* (*eis kulismon*).   "To rolling."   Late and rare word (from *kuliō*, Mark 9:20), here only in N.T.   *In the mire* (*borborou*). Objective genitive, old word for dung, mire, here only in N.T.   J. Rendel Harris (*Story of Ahikar*, p. LXVII) tells of a story about a hog that went to the bath with people of quality, but on coming out saw a stinking drain and went and rolled himself in it.

CHAPTER III

1. *Beloved* (*agapētoi*). With this vocative verbal (four times in this chapter), Peter "turns away from the Libertines and their victims" (Mayor). *This is now the second epistle that I write unto you* (*tautēn ēdē deuteran humin graphō epistolēn*). Literally, "This already a second epistle I am writing to you." For *ēdē* see John 21:24. It is the predicate use of *deuteran epistolēn* in apposition with *tautēn*, not "this second epistle." Reference apparently to I Peter. *And in both of them* (*en hais*). "In which epistles." *I stir up* (*diegeirō*). Present active indicative, perhaps conative, "I try to stir up." See 1:13. *Mind* (*dianoian*). Understanding (Plato) as in I Pet. 1:13. *Sincere* (*eilikrinē*). Old adjective of doubtful etymology (supposed to be *heilē*, sunlight, and *krinō*, to judge by it). Plato used it of ethical purity (*psuchē eilikrinēs*) as here and Phil. 1:10, the only N.T. examples. *By putting you in remembrance* (*en hupomnēsei*). As in 1:13.

2. *That ye should remember* (*mnēsthēnai*). First aorist passive (deponent) infinitive of *mimnēskō*, to remind. Purpose (indirect command) is here expressed by this infinitive. Imperative in Jude 17. *Spoken before* (*proeirēmenōn*). Perfect passive participle of *proeipon* (defective verb). Genitive case *rēmatōn* after *mnēsthēnai*. *And the commandment* (*kai tēs entolēs*). Ablative case with *hupo* (agency). *Of the Lord and Saviour through your apostles* (*tōn apostolōn humōn tou kuriou kai sōtēros*). *Humōn* (your) is correct, not *hēmōn* (our). But the several genitives complicate the sense. If *dia* (through) occurred before *tōn apostolōn*, it would be clear. It is held by some that Peter would not thus speak of the twelve apostles, including himself, and that the forger

172

here allows the mask to slip, but Bigg rightly regards this
a needless inference. The meaning is that they should remember the teaching of their apostles and not follow the
Gnostic libertines.

3. *Knowing this first* (*touto prōton ginōskontes*). Present
active participle of *ginōskō*. See 1:20 for this identical
phrase. Nominative absolute here where accusative *ginōs-*
kontas would be regular. Peter now takes up the *parousia*
(1:16) after having discussed the *dunamis* of Christ. *In*
the last days (*ep' eschatōn tōn hēmerōn*). "Upon the last of
the days." Jude 18 has it *ep' eschatou chronou* (upon the
last time). In I Pet. 1:5 it is *en kairōi eschatōi* (in the last
time), while I Pet. 1:20 has *ep' eschatou tōn chronōn* (upon
the last of the times). John has usually *tēi eschatēi hēmerāi*
(on the last day, 6:39f.). Here *eschatōn* is a predicate adjective like *summus mons* (the top of the mountain). *Mock-*
ers with mockery (*empaigmonēi empaiktai*). Note Peter's
play on words again, both from *empaizō* (Matt. 2:16), to
trifle with, and neither found elsewhere save *empaiktēs* in
Jude 18 and Is. 3:4 (playing like children).

4. *Where is the promise of his coming?* (*pou estin hē epag-*
gelia tēs parousias autou;). This is the only sample of the
questions raised by these mockers. Peter had mentioned
this subject of the *parousia* in 1:16. Now he faces it squarely.
Peter, like Paul (I Thess. 5:1f.; II Thess. 2:1f.), preached
about the second coming (1:16; Acts 3:20f.), as Jesus himself did repeatedly (Matt. 24:34) and as the angels promised
at the Ascension (Acts 1:11). Both Jesus and Paul (II
Thess. 2:1f.) were misunderstood on the subject of the time
and the parables of Jesus urged readiness and forbade setting
dates for his coming, though his language in Matt. 24:34
probably led some to believe that he would certainly come
while they were alive. *From the day that* (*aph' hēs*). "From
which day." See Luke 7:45. *Fell asleep* (*ekoimēthēsan*).
First aorist passive indicative of *koimaō*, old verb, to put

sleep, classic euphemism for death (John 11:11) like our cemetery (sleeping-place). *Continue (diamenei).* Present active indicative of *diamenō*, to remain through (Luke 1:22). *In statu quo. As they were (houtōs).* "Thus." *From the beginning of creation (ap' archēs ktiseōs).* Precisely so in Mark 10:6, which see.

5. *For this they wilfully forget (lanthanei gar autous touto thelontas).* Literally, "for this escapes them being willing." See this use of *lanthanō* (old verb, to escape notice of, to be hidden from) in Acts 26:26. The present active participle *thelontas* (from *thelō*, to wish) has almost an adverbial sense here. *Compacted (sunestōsa).* See Paul's *sunestēken* (Col. 1:17) "consist." Second perfect active (intransitive) participle of *sunistēmi*, feminine singular agreeing with *gē* (nearest to it) rather than with *ouranoi* (subject of *ēsan* imperfect plural). There is no need to make Peter mean the Jewish mystical "seven heavens" because of the plural which was used interchangeably with the singular (Matt. 5:9f.). *Out of water and amidst water (ex hudatos kai di' hudatos).* Out of the primeval watery chaos (Gen. 1:2), but it is not plain what is meant by *di' hudatos,* which naturally means "by means of water," though *dia* with the genitive is used for a condition or state (Heb. 12:1). The reference may be to Gen. 1:9, the gathering together of the waters. *By the word of God (tōi tou theou logōi).* Instrumental case *logōi,* "by the fiat of God" (Gen. 1:3; Heb. 11:3 *rēmati theou*).

6. *By which means (di' hōn).* The two waters above or the water and the word of God. Mayor against the MSS. reads *di' hou* (singular) and refers it to *logōi* alone. *Being overflowed (kataklustheis).* First aorist passive participle of *katakluzō*, old compound, here only in N.T., but see *kataklusmos* in 2:5. *With water (hudati).* Instrumental case of *hudōr. Perished (apōleto).* Second aorist middle indicative of *apollumi.*

7. *That now are (nun).* "The now heavens" over against

"the then world" (*ho tote kosmos* verse 6). *By the same word* (*tōi autōi logōi*). Instrumental case again referring to *logōi* in verse 6. *Have been stored up* (*tethēsaurismenoi eisin*). Perfect passive indicative of *thēsaurizō*, for which verb see Matt. 6:19; Luke 12:21. *For fire* (*puri*). Dative case of *pur*, not with fire (instrumental case). The destruction of the world by fire is here pictured as in Joel 2:30f.; Ps. 50:3. *Being reserved* (*tēroumenoi*). Present passive participle of *tēreō*, for which see 2:4. *Against* (*eis*). Unto. As in 2:4, 9 and see I Pet. 1:4 for the inheritance reserved for the saints of God.

8. *Forget not this one thing* (*hen touto mē lanthanetō humas*). Rather, "let not this one thing escape you." For *lanthanetō* (present active imperative of *lanthanō*) see verse 5. The "one thing" (*hen*) is explained by the *hoti* (that) clause following. Peter applies the language of Ps. 89 (90):4 about the eternity of God and shortness of human life to "the impatience of human expectations" (Bigg) about the second coming of Christ. "The day of judgment is at hand (I Pet. 4:7). It may come tomorrow; but what is tomorrow? What does God mean by a day? It may be a thousand years" (Bigg). Precisely the same argument applies to those who argue for a literal interpretation of the thousand years in Rev. 20:4–6. It may be a day or a day may be a thousand years. God's clock (*para kuriōi*, beside the Lord) does not run by our timepieces. The scoffers scoff ignorantly.

9. *Is not slack concerning his promise* (*ou bradunei tēs epaggelias*). Ablative case *epaggelias* after *bradunei* (present active indicative of *bradunō*, from *bradus*, slow), old verb, to be slow in, to fall short of (like *leipetai sophias* in James 1:5), here and I Tim. 3:15 only in N.T. *Slackness* (*bradutēta*). Old substantive from *bradus* (James 1:19), here only in N.T. God is not impotent nor unwilling to execute his promise. *To youward* (*eis humas*). Pros rather than *eis* after *makrothumei* in I Thess. 5:14 and *epi* in James 5:7,

etc. *Not wishing (mē boulomenos)*. Present middle participle of *boulomai*. Some will perish (verse 7), but that is not God's desire. *Any (tinas)*. Rather than "some" *(tines)* above. Accusative with the infinitive *apolesthai* (second aorist middle of *apollumi*. God wishes "all" *(pantas)* to come *(chōrēsai* first aorist active infinitive of *chōreō*, old verb, to make room). See Acts 17:30; Rom. 11:32; I Tim. 2:4; Heb. 2:9 for God's provision of grace for all who will repent.

10. *The day of the Lord (hēmera kuriou)*. So Peter in Acts 2:20 (from Joel 3:4) and Paul in I Thess. 5:2, 4; II Thess. 2:2; I Cor. 5:5; and day of Christ in Phil. 2:16 and day of God in 2:12 and day of judgment already in 2:9; 3:7. This great day will certainly come *(hēxei)*. Future active of *hēkō*, old verb, to arrive, but in God's own time. *As a thief (hōs kleptēs)*. That is suddenly, without notice. This very metaphor Jesus had used (Luke 12:39; Matt. 24:43) and Paul after him (I Thess. 5:2) and John will quote it also (Rev. 3:3; 16:15). *In the which (en hēi)*. The day when the Lord comes. *Shall pass away (pareleusontai)*. Future middle of *parerchomai*, old verb, to pass by. *With a great noise (roizēdon)*. Late and rare adverb (from *roizeō, roizos)*—Lycophron, Nicander, here only in N.T., onomatopoetic, whizzing sound of rapid motion through the air like the flight of a bird, thunder, fierce flame. *The elements (ta stoicheia)*. Old word (from *stoichos* a row), in Plato in this sense, in other senses also in N.T. as the alphabet, ceremonial regulations (Heb. 5:12; Gal. 4:3; 5:1; Col. 2:8). *Shall be dissolved (luthēsetai)*. Future passive of *luō*, to loosen, singular because *stoicheia* is neuter plural. *With fervent heat (kausoumena)*. Present passive participle of *kausoō*, late verb (from *kausos*, usually medical term for fever) and nearly always employed for fever temperature. Mayor suggests a conflagration from internal heat. Bigg thinks it merely a vernacular (Doric) future for *kausomena*

(from *kaiō*, to burn). *Shall be burned up* (*katakaēsetai*). Repeated in verse 12. Second future passive of the compound verb *katakaiō*, to burn down (up), according to A L. But Aleph B K P read *heurethēsetai* (future passive of *heuriskō*, to find) "shall be found." There are various other readings here. The text seems corrupt.

11. *To be dissolved* (*luomenōn*). Present passive participle (genitive absolute with *toutōn pantōn*, these things all) of *luō*, either the futuristic present or the process of dissolution presented. *What manner of persons* (*potapous*). Late qualitative interrogative pronoun for the older *podapos* as in Matt. 8:27, accusative case with *dei huparchein* agreeing with *humās* (you). See 1:8 for *huparchō*. *In all holy living and godliness* (*en hagiais anastrophais kai eusebeiais*). "In holy behaviours and pieties" (Alford). Plural of neither word elsewhere in N.T., but a practical plural in *pāsa anastrophē* in I Pet. 1:15.

12. *Looking for* (*prosdokōntas*). Present active participle of *prosdokaō* (Matt. 11:3) agreeing in case (accusative plural) with *humās*. *Earnestly desiring* (*speudontas*). Present active participle, accusative also, of *speudō*, old verb, to hasten (like our speed) as in Luke 2:16, but it is sometimes transitive as here either (preferably so) to "hasten on the parousia" by holy living (cf. I Pet. 2:12), with which idea compare Matt. 6:10 and Acts 3:19f., or to desire earnestly (Is. 16:5). *Being on fire* (*puroumenoi*). Present passive participle of *puroō*, old verb (from *pur*), same idea as in verse 10. *Shall melt* (*tēketai*). Futuristic present passive indicative of *tēkō*, old verb, to make liquid, here only in N.T. Hort suggests *tēxetai* (future middle), though Is. 34:4 has *takēsontai* (second future passive). The repetitions here make "an effective refrain" (Mayor).

13. *Promise* (*epaggelma*). As in 1:4. The reference is to Is. 65:17f.; 66:22. See also Rev. 21:1. For *kainos* (new) see on Matt. 26:29. For the expectant attitude in *pros-*

dokōmen (we look for) repeated from verse 12 and again in verse 14, see *apekdechometha* (we eagerly look for) in Phil. 3:20. *Wherein* (*en hois*). The new heavens and earth. *Dwelleth* (*katoikei*). Has its home (*oikos*). Certainly "righteousness" (*dikaiosunē*) is not at home in this present world either in individuals, families, or nations.

14. *Wherefore* (*dio*). As in 1:10, 12. *Give diligence* (*spoudasate*). As in 1:10. *That ye may be found* (*heurethēnai*). First aorist passive infinitive (cf. *heurethēsetai* in verse 10). For this use of *heuriskō* about the end see II Cor. 5:3; Phil. 3:9; I Pet. 1:7. *Without spot and blameless* (*aspiloi kai amōmētoi*). Predicate nominative after *heurethēnai*. See 2:13 for position words *spiloi kai mōmoi* and I Pet. 1:19 for *amōmos* (so Jude 24) *kai aspilos* (so James 1:27). *Amōmētos* (old verbal of *mōmaomai*) only here in N.T. save some MSS. in Phil. 2:15.

15. *In his sight* (*autōi*). Ethical dative. Referring to Christ. *Is salvation* (*sōtērian*). Predicate accusative after *hēgeisthe* in apposition with *makrothumian* (long-suffering), an opportunity for repentance (cf. I Pet. 3:20). The Lord here is Christ. *Our beloved brother Paul* (*ho agapētos adelphos Paulos*). Paul applies the verbal *agapētos* (beloved) to Epaphras (Col. 1:7), Onesimus (Col. 4:9; Philem. 16), to Tychicus (Col. 4:7; Eph. 6:21), and to four brethren in Rom. 16 (Epainetus 5, Ampliatus 8, Stachys 9, Persis 12). It is not surprising for Peter to use it of Paul in view of Gal. 2:9f., in spite of Gal. 2:11-14. *Given to him* (*dotheisan autōi*). First aorist passive participle of *didōmi* with dative case. Peter claimed wisdom for himself, but recognises that Paul had the gift also. His language here may have caution in it as well as commendation. "St. Peter speaks of him with affection and respect, yet maintains the right to criticise" (Bigg).

16. *As also in all his epistles* (*hōs kai en pasais epistolais*). We do not know to how many Peter here refers. There is

no difficulty in supposing that Peter "received every one of St. Paul's Epistles within a month or two of its publication" (Bigg). And yet Peter does not here assert the formation of a canon of Paul's Epistles. *Speaking in them of these things* (*lalōn en autais peri toutōn*). Present active participle of *laleō*. That is to say, Paul also wrote about the second coming of Christ, as is obviously true. *Hard to be understood* (*dusnoēta*). Late verbal from *dus* and *noeō* (in Aristotle, Lucian, Diog. Laert.), here only in N.T. We know that the Thessalonians persisted in misrepresenting Paul on this very subject of the second coming as Hymenaeus and Philetus did about the resurrection (II Tim. 2:17) and Spitta holds that Paul's teaching about grace was twisted to mean moral laxity like Gal. 3:10; Rom. 3:20, 28; 5:20 (with which cf. 6:1 as a case in point), etc. Peter does not say that he himself did not understand Paul on the subject of faith and freedom. *Unlearned* (*amatheis*). Old word (alpha privative and *manthanō* to learn), ignorant, here only in N.T. *Unsteadfast* (*astēriktoi*). See on 2:14. *Wrest* (*streblousin*). Present active indicative of *strebloō*, old verb (from *streblos* twisted, *strephō*, to turn), here only in N.T. *The other scriptures* (*tas loipas graphas*). There is no doubt that the apostles claimed to speak by the help of the Holy Spirit (I Thess. 5:27; Col. 4:16) just as the prophets of old did (II Pet. 1:20f.). Note *loipas* (rest) here rather than *allas* (other). Peter thus puts Paul's Epistles on the same plane with the O.T., which was also misused (Matt. 5:21–44; 15:3–6; 19:3–10).

17. *Knowing these things beforehand* (*proginōskontes*). Present active participle of *proginōskō* as in I Pet. 1:20. Cf. *prōton ginōskō* (1:20; 3:1). Hence they are without excuse for misunderstanding Peter or Paul on this subject. *Beware* (*phulassesthe*). Present middle imperative of *phulassō*, common verb, to guard. *Lest* (*hina mē*). Negative purpose, "that not." *Being carried away* (*sunapachthentes*). First

aorist passive participle of *sunapagō*, old verb double compound, to carry away together with, in N.T. only here and Gal. 2:13. *With the error* (*tēi planēi*). Instrumental case, "by the error" (the wandering). *Of the wicked* (*tōn athesmōn*). See on 2:7. *Ye fall from* (*ekpesēte*). Second aorist active subjunctive with *hina mē* of *ekpiptō*, old verb, to fall out of, with the ablative here (*stērigmou*, steadfastness, late word from *stērizō*, here alone in N.T.) as in Gal. 5:4 (*tēs charitos exepesate*, ye fell out of grace).

18. *But grow* (*auxanete de*). Present active imperative of *auxanō*, in contrast with such a fate pictured in verse 17, "but keep on growing." *In the grace and knowledge* (*en chariti kai gnōsei*). Locative case with *en*. Grow in both. Keep it up. See on 1:1 for the idiomatic use of the single article (*tou*) here, "of our Lord and Saviour Jesus Christ." *To him* (*autōi*). To Christ. *For ever* (*eis hēmeran aiōnos*). "Unto the day of eternity." So Sirach 18:9f. One of the various ways of expressing eternity by the use of *aiōn*. So *eis ton aiōna* in John 6:5; 12:34.

THE EPISTLE OF JUDE
ABOUT A.D. 65 TO 67

BY WAY OF INTRODUCTION

The Author

He calls himself Judas, but this was a very common name. In the N.T. itself we have Judas Iscariot and Judas not Iscariot (John 14:22; also called Judas of James, son or brother, Luke 6:6), Judas a brother of our Lord (Matt. 13:55), Judas of Galilee (Acts 5:37), Judas of Damascus (Acts 9:11), Judas Barsabbas (Acts 15:22). The author explains that he is a "slave" of Jesus Christ as James did (1:1), and adds that he is also a brother of James. Clement of Alexandria thinks that, like James, he deprecated being called the brother of the Lord Jesus (as by Hegesippus later) as claiming too much authority. Keil identifies him with Jude the Apostle (not Iscariot), but that is most unlikely. The Epistle is one of the disputed books of Eusebius. It was recognized in the canon in the Third Council of Carthage (A.D. 397). It appears in the Muratorian Canon (A.D. 170).

The Relation to II Peter

Beyond a doubt one of these Epistles was used by the other, as one can see by comparing particularly Jude 3–18 and II Peter 2:1–18. As already said concerning II Peter, scholars are greatly divided on this point, and in our present state of knowledge it does not seem possible to reach a solid conclusion. The probability is that not much time elapsed between them. Mayor devotes a whole chapter to the discussion of the relation between II Peter and Jude and reaches the conclusion "that in Jude we have the first thought, in Peter the second thought." That is my own feeling, but it is all so subjective that I have no desire to urge the point unduly. Bigg is equally positive that II Peter comes before Jude.

THE USE OF APOCRYPHAL BOOKS

Jude (verse 14) quotes from "Enoch" by name and says that he "prophesied." What he quotes is a combination of various passages in the Book of Enoch as we have it now. It used to be held that part of Enoch was later than Jude, but Charles seems to have disproved that, though the book as we have it has many interpolations. Tertullian wanted to canonise Enoch because of what Jude says, whereas Chrysostom says that the authenticity of Jude was doubted because of the use of Enoch. In verse 9 there seems to be an allusion to the *Assumption of Moses*, another apocryphal book, but it is the use of "prophesied" in verse 14 about Enoch that gave most offence. It is possible, of course, that Jude did not attach the full sense to that term.

THE STYLE

It is terse and picturesque, with a fondness for triplets. The use of the O.T. is very much like that in II Peter. Alford notes that it is impassioned invective with epithet on epithet, image on image. Bigg remarks on the stern and unbending nature of the author, with no pathos and a harsh view of things and with frequent use of Pauline phraseology. There are some fifteen words not in the rest of the N.T. The grammar is less irregular than that of II Peter. There is often a poetic ring in his words.

THE PURPOSE

The author undoubtedly has the Gnostics in mind and is seeking to warn his readers against them, as is true of II Peter. This same purpose appears in the Johannine Epistles, as was true also of Colossians, Ephesians, the Pastoral Epistles.

The Readers

Of this we know nothing at all. Dr. Chase believes that the Epistle was sent to Antioch in Syria. That may be true, though it is mere conjecture. Any place or places in Asia Minor would suit so far as we know. The readers were probably both Jewish and Gentile Christians. Jerusalem and Alexandria are urged as the place of composition, but of that we have no real information.

The Date

This really turns on the genuineness of the Epistle. Ther is no clear indication of the date, for the Gnostics describeᴄ can belong to the first or to the second century. If it wa used by II Peter, that would place it slightly before tha' Epistle. The date suggested, 65 to 67 A.D., is purely coɪ jectural.

SPECIAL BOOKS ON JUDE

(Apart from those on II Peter or the Catholic Epistles⁾
CHASE, F. H., *Jude in Hastings D B* (1899).
ERMONI, V., *L'épître de Jude* (1903, in Vigoroux, Dictioɪ naire de la Bible).
GEORGHIN, B., *Der Brief Judas* (1901).
KASTEREN, J. P., *De brief van den apostel Judas* (1916).
MAIER, F., *Der Judasbrief* (1906).
MAYOR, J. B., *The Epistle of Jude* (in Expositor's Greeɭ Testament, 1910).
PLUMMER, A., *St. James and St. Jude* (Expositor's Bible).
RAMPF, M. F., *Der Brief Juda* (1854).
STIER, R., *Der Brief Judas, des Bruders des Herrn* (1850).
WANDEL, G., *Der Brief des Judas* (1898).

1. *Servant* (*doulos*). Precisely as James (1:1), only James added *kuriou* (Lord). *Brother of James* (*adelphos Iakōbou*). Thus Jude identifies himself. But not the "Judas of James" (Luke 6:16; Acts 1:13). *To them that are called* (*tois—klētois*). But this translation (treating *klētois* as a substantive like Rom. 1:6; I Cor. 1:24) is by no means certain as two participles come in between *tois* and *klētois*. *Klētois* may be in the predicate position (being called), not attributive. But see I Pet. 1:1. *Beloved in God the Father* (*en theōi patri ēgapēmenois*). Perfect passive participle of *agapaō*, but no precise parallel to this use of *en* with *agapaō*. *Kept for Jesus Christ* (*Iēsou Christōi tetērēmenois*). Perfect passive participle again with dative, unless it is the instrumental, "kept by Jesus Christ," a quite possible interpretation.

2. *Be multiplied* (*plēthuntheiē*). First aorist passive optative of *plēthunō* as in I Pet. 1:2 and II Pet. 1:2.

3. *Beloved* (*agapētoi*). As in III John 2. *All diligence* (*pāsan spoudēn*). As in II Pet. 1:5. *Of our common salvation* (*peri tēs koinēs hēmōn sōtērias*). See this use of *koinos* (common to all) in Titus 1:4 with *pistis*, while in II Pet. 1:1 we have *isotimon pistin*, which see. *I was constrained* (*anagkēn eschon*). "I had necessity" like Luke 14:18; Heb. 7:27. *To contend earnestly* (*epagōnizesthai*). Late and rare (in Plutarch, inscriptions) compound, here only in N.T. A little additional (*epi*) striving to the already strong *agōnizesthai* (*agōn* contest). Cf. I Tim. 6:12 *agōnizou ton kalon agōna*. *For the faith* (*tēi—pistei*). Dative of advantage. Here not in the original sense of trust, but rather of the thing believed as in verse 20 and in Gal. 1:23; 3:23; Phil. 1:27. *Once for all delivered* (*hapax paradotheisēi*). First

186

aorist passive participle feminine dative singular of *paradi-dōmi*, for which see II Pet. 2:21. See also II Thess. 2:15; I Cor. 11:2; I Tim. 6:20.

4. *Are crept in* (*pareiseduēsan*). Second aorist passive indicative of *pareisduō* (*-nō*), late (Hippocrates, Plutarch, etc.) compound of *para* (beside) and *eis* (in) and *duō* to sink or plunge, so to slip in secretly as if by a side door, here only in N.T. *Set forth* (*progegrammenoi*). Perfect passive participle of *prographō*, to write of beforehand, for which verb see Gal. 3:1; Rom. 15:4. *Unto this condemnation* (*eis touto to krima*). See II Pet. 2:3 for *krima* and *ekpalai*. *Palai* here apparently alludes to verses 14 and 15 (Enoch). *Ungodly men* (*asebeis*). Keynote of the Epistle (Mayor), in 15 again as in II Pet. 2:5; 3:7. *Turning* (*metatithentes*). Present active participle of *metatithēmi*, to change, for which verb see Gal. 1:6. For the change of "grace" (*charita*) into "lasciviousness (*eis aselgeian*) see I Pet. 2:16; 4:3; II Pet. 2:19; 3:16. *Our only Master and Lord* (*ton monon despotēn kai kurion hēmōn*). For the force of the one article for one person see on II Pet. 1:1. For *despotēn* of Christ see II Pet. 2:1. *Denying* (*arnoumenoi*). So II Pet. 2:1. See also Matt. 10:33; I Tim. 5:8; Titus 1:16; I John 2:22.

5. *To put you in remembrance* (*hupomnēsai*). See II Pet. 1:12 *hupomimnēskein* (present active infinitive there, first aorist active infinitive here). *Though ye know all things once for all* (*eidotas hapax panta*). Concessive perfect (sense of present) active participle as in II Pet. 1:12, but without *kaiper*. *The Lord* (*kurios*). Some MSS. add *Iēsous*. The use of *kurios* here is usually understood to mean the Lord Jesus Christ, as Clement of Alex. (*Adumbr.* p. 133) explains, Ex. 23:20, by *ho mustikos ekeinos aggelos Iēsous* (that mystical angel Jesus). For the mystic reference to Christ see I Cor. 10:4, 9; Heb. 11:26. Some MSS. here add *theos* instead of *Iēsous*. *Afterward* (*to deuteron*). Adverbial accusative, "the second time." After having saved the people out

of Egypt. *Destroyed* (*apōlesen*). First aorist active indicative of *apollumi*, old verb, to destroy. *Them that believed not* (*tous mē pisteusantas*). First aorist active articular participle of *pisteuō*. The reference is to Numb. 14:27–37, when all the people rescued from Egypt perished except Caleb and Joshua. This first example by Jude is not in II Peter, but is discussed in I Cor. 10:5–11; Heb. 3:18–4:2.

6. *And angels* (*aggelous de*). The second example in Jude, the fallen angels, accusative case after *tetērēken* (perfect active indicative of *tēreō*, for which verb see II Pet. 2:4, 7) at the end of the verse (two emphatic positions, beginning and end of the clause). *Kept not* (*mē tērēsantas*). First aorist active participle with negative *mē*, with play on "kept not" and "he hath kept." *Principality* (*archēn*). Literally, "beginning," "rule," (first place of power as in I Cor. 15:24; Rom. 8:38). In Acts 10:11 it is used for "corners" (beginnings) of the sheet. In Eph. 6:12 the word is used for evil angels. See Deut. 32:8. Both Enoch and Philo (and Milton) discuss the fallen angels. *But left* (*alla apolipontas*). Second aorist active participle of *apoleipō*, old verb, to leave behind (II Tim. 4:13, 20). *Their own proper habitation* (*to idion oikētērion*). Old word for dwelling-place (from *oikētēr*, dweller at home, from *oikos*), in N.T. only here and II Cor. 5:2 (the body as the abode of the spirit). *In everlasting bonds* (*desmois aidiois*). Either locative (in) or instrumental (by, with). *Aidios* (from *aei*, always), old adjective, in N.T. only here and Rom. 1:20 (of God's power and deity). It is synonymous with *aiōnios* (Matt. 25:46). Mayor terms *aidios* an Aristotelian word, while *aiōnios* is Platonic. *Under darkness* (*hupo zophon*). See II Pet. 2:4 for *zophos*. In Wisd. 17:2 we find *desmioi skotous* (prisoners of darkness). *Great* (*megalēs*). Not in II Pet. 2:9, which see for discussion.

7. *Even as* (*hōs*). Just "as." The third instance (Jude passes by the deluge) in Jude, the cities of the plain. *The cities about them* (*hai peri autas poleis*). These were also

included, Admah and Zeboiim (Deut. 29:23; Hos. 11:8).
Zoar, the other city, was spared. *In like manner (ton
homoion tropon)*. Adverbial accusative (cf. *hōs*). Like the
fallen angels. *Having given themselves over to fornication
(ekporneusasai)*. First aorist active participle feminine plural of *ekporneuō*, late and rare compound (perfective use of
ek, outside the moral law), only here in N.T., but in LXX
(Gen. 38:24; Ex. 34:15f., etc.). Cf. *aselgeian* in verse 4.
Strange flesh (sarkos heteras). Horrible licentiousness, not
simply with women not their wives or in other nations, but
even unnatural uses (Rom. 1:27) for which the very word
"sodomy" is used (Gen. 19:4–11). The pronoun *heteras*
(other, strange) is not in II Pet. 2:10. *Are set forth (pro-
keintai)*. Present middle indicative of *prokeimai*, old verb,
to lie before, as in Heb. 12:1f. *As an example (deigma)*.
Predicate nominative of *deigma*, old word (from *deiknumi*
to show), here only in N.T., sample, specimen. II Pet. 2:6
has *hupodeigma* (pattern). *Suffering (hupechousai)*. Present
active participle of *hupechō*, old compound, to hold under,
often with *dikēn* (right, justice, sentence II Thess. 1:9) to
suffer sentence (punishment), here only in N.T. *Of eternal
fire (puros aiōniou)*. Like *desmois aidiois* in verse 7. Cf.
the hell of fire (Matt. 5:22) and also Matt. 25:46. Jude has
no mention of Lot.

8. *Yet (mentoi)*. See John 4:27. In spite of these warnings. *In like manner (homoiōs)*. Like the cities of the plain.
These also (kai houtoi). The false teachers of verse 4. *In
their dreamings (enupniazomenoi)*. Present middle participle
of *enupniazō*, to dream (from *enupnion* dream, Acts 2:17,
from *en* and *hupnos*, in sleep), in Aristotle, Hippocrates,
Plutarch, papyri, LXX (Joel 2:28), here only in N.T. Cf.
Col. 2:18. *Defile (miainousin)*. Present active indicative
of *minainō*, old verb, to stain, with sin (Titus 1:15) as here.
II Pet. 2:10 has *miasmou*. *Set at nought (athetousin)*. Present active indicative of *atheteō*, to annul. Both *kuriotēs*

(dominion) and *doxai* (dignities) occur in II Pet. 2:10, which see for discussion.

9. *Michael the archangel* (*ho Michaēl ho archaggelos*). Michael is mentioned also in Dan. 10:13, 21; 12:1; Rev. 12:7. *Archaggelos* in N.T. occurs only here and I Thess. 4:16, but in Dan. 10:13, 20; 12:1. *Contending with the devil* (*tōi diaboloi diakrinomenos*). Present middle participle of *diakrinō*, to separate, to strive with as in Acts 11:2. Dative case *diaboloi*. *When he disputed* (*hote dielegeto*). Imperfect middle of *dialegomai* as in Mark 9:34. *Concerning the body of Moses* (*peri tou Mōuseōs sōmatos*). Some refer this to Zech. 3:1, others to a rabbinical comment on Deut. 34:6. There is a similar reference to traditions in Acts 7:22; Gal. 3:19; Heb. 2:2; II Tim. 3:8. But this explanation hardly meets the facts. *Durst not bring* (*ouk etolmēsen epenegkein*). "Did not dare (first aorist active indicative of *tolmaō*), to bring against him" (second aorist active infinitive of *epipherō*). *A railing accusation* (*krisin blasphēmias*). "Charge of blasphemy" where II Pet. 2:11 has "*blasphēmon krisin.*" Peter also has *para kuriōi* (with the Lord), not in Jude. *The Lord rebuke thee* (*epitimēsai soi kurios*). First aorist active optative of *epitimaō*, a wish about the future. These words occur in Zech. 3:1–10 where the angel of the Lord replies to the charges of Satan. Clement of Alex. (*Adumb. in Ep. Judae*) says that Jude quoted here the *Assumption of Moses*, one of the apocryphal books. Origen says the same thing. Mayor thinks that the author of the *Assumption of Moses* took these words from Zechariah and put them in the mouth of the Archangel Michael. There is a Latin version of the *Assumption*. Some date it as early as B.C. 2, others after A.D. 44.

10. *Whatsoever things they know not* (*hosa ouk oidasin*). Here II Pet. 2:12 has *en hois agnoousin*. The rest of the sentence is smoother than II Pet. 2:12. *Naturally* (*phusikōs*). Here only in N.T. II Pet. 2:12 has *gegennēmena phusika*.

Jude has the article *ta* with *aloga zōa* and the present passive *phtheirontai* instead of the future passive *phtharēsontai*.

11. *Woe to them* (*ouai autois*). Interjection with the dative as is common in the Gospels (Matt. 11:21). *Went* (*eporeuthēsan*). First aorist passive (deponent) indicative of *poreuomai*. *In the way of Cain* (*tēi hodōi tou Kain*). Locative case *hodōi*. Cain is Jude's fourth example. Not in II Peter, but in Heb. 11:4; I John 3:11f. From Gen. 4:7. *Ran riotously* (*exechuthēsan*). First aorist passive indicative of *ekcheō*, to pour out, "they were poured out," vigorous metaphor for excessive indulgence. But it is used also of God's love for us (Rom. 5:5). *In the error of Balaam* (*tēi planēi tou Balaam*). The fifth example in Jude. In II Peter also (2:15). Either locative case (in) or instrumental (by). *Planē* (in Peter also) is the common word for such wandering (Matt. 24:4ff., etc.). *Perished* (*apōlonto*). Second aorist middle (intransitive) of *apollumi*. *In the gainsaying of Korah* (*tēi antilogiāi tou Kore*). Again either locative or instrumental. The word *antilogia* is originally answering back (Heb. 6:16), but it may be by act also (Rom. 10:21) as here. This is the sixth example in Jude, not in II Peter.

12. *Hidden rocks* (*spilades*). Old word for rocks in the sea (covered by the water), as in Homer, here only in N.T. II Pet. 2:13 has *spiloi*. *Love-feasts* (*agapais*). Undoubtedly the correct text here, though A C have *apatais* as in II Pet. 2:14. For disorder at the Lord's Supper (and love-feasts?) see I Cor. 11:17–34. The Gnostics made it worse, so that the love-feasts were discontinued. *When they feast with you* (*suneuōchoumenoi*). See II Pet. 2:13 for this very word and form. Masculine gender with *houtoi hoi* rather than with the feminine *spilades*. Cf. Rev. 11:4. Construction according to sense. *Shepherds that feed themselves* (*heautous poimainontes*). "Shepherding themselves." Cf. Rev. 7:17 for this use of *poimainō*. *Clouds without water* (*nephelai anudroi*). *Nephelē* common word for cloud (Matt. 24:30). II

Pet. 2:17 has *pēgai anudroi* (springs without water) and then *homichlai* (mists) and *elaunomenai* (driven) rather than *peripheromenai* here (borne around, whirled around, present passive participle of *peripherō* to bear around), a powerful picture of disappointed hopes. *Autumn trees* (*dendra phthino-pōrina*). Late adjective (Aristotle, Polybius, Strabo) from *phthinō*, to waste away, and *opōra*, autumn, here only in N.T. For *akarpa* (without fruit) see II Pet. 1:8. *Twice dead* (*dis apothanonta*). Second aorist active participle of *apothnēskō*. Fruitless and having died. Having died and also "uprooted" (*ekrizōthenta*). First aorist passive participle of *ekrizoō*, late compound, to root out, to pluck up by the roots, as in Matt. 13:29.

13. *Wild waves* (*kumata agria*). Waves (Matt. 8:24, from *kueō*, to swell) wild (from *agros*, field, wild honey Matt. 3:4) like untamed animals of the forest or the sea. *Foaming out* (*epaphrizonta*). Late and rare present active participle of *epaphrizō*, used in Moschus for the foaming waves as here. Cf. Is. 57:20. *Shame* (*aischunas*). Plural "shames" (disgraces). Cf. Phil. 3:19. *Wandering stars* (*asteres plan-ētai*). "Stars wanderers." *Planētēs*, old word (from *planaō*), here alone in N.T. Some refer this to comets or shooting stars. See Is. 14:12 for an allusion to Babylon as the day-star who fell through pride. *For ever* (*eis aiōna*). The rest of the relative clause exactly as in II Pet. 2:17.

14. *And to these also* (*de kai toutois*). Dative case, for these false teachers as well as for his contemporaries. *Enoch the seventh from Adam* (*hebdomos apo Adam Henōch*). The genealogical order occurs in Gen. 5:4–20, with Enoch as seventh. He is so termed in Enoch 60:8; 93:3. *Prophesied* (*eprophēteusen*). First aorist active indicative of *prophēteuō*. If the word is given its ordinary meaning as in I Pet. 1:10, then Jude terms the Book of Enoch an inspired book. The words quoted are "a combination of passages from Enoch" (Bigg), chiefly from Enoch 1:9. *With ten thousand of his*

holy ones (*en hagiais muriasin autou*). "With (*en* of accompaniment, Luke 14:31) his holy ten thousands" (*murias* regular word, feminine gender, for ten thousand, Acts 19:19, there an unlimited number like our myriads, Luke 12:1).

15. *To execute judgment* (*poiēsai krisin*). "To do justice." *To convict* (*elegxai*). First aorist (effective) active infinitive like *poiēsai* before it. *Ungodly* (*asebeis*). See verse 4 and end of this verse. *Of ungodliness* (*asebeias*). Old word as in Rom. 1:18, plural in Jude 18 as in Rom. 11:26. *Which* (*hōn*). Genitive by attraction from *ha* (cognate accusative with *ēsebēsan*, old verb, to act impiously, here alone in N.T. save some MSS. in II Pet. 2:6) to agree with the antecedent *ergōn* (deeds). *Hard things* (*sklērōn*). Harsh, rough things as in John 6:60. *Which* (*hōn*). Genitive by attraction from *ha* (object of *elalēsan*, first aorist active indicative of *laleō*) to the case of the antecedent *sklērōn*. Four times in this verse as a sort of refrain *asebeis* (twice), *asebeias*, *ēsebēsan*.

16. *Murmurers* (*goggustai*). Late onomatopoetic word for agent, from *gogguzō* (Matt. 20:11; I Cor. 10:10) in the LXX (Ex. 16:8; Numb. 11:1, 14–29). *Complainers* (*mempsimoiroi*). Rare word (Isocrates, Aristotle, Plutarch) from *memphomai* to complain and *moira* lot or fate. Here alone in N.T. *Lusts* (*epithumias*). As in II Pet. 3:3. *Swelling* (*huperogka*). So in II Pet. 2:18 (big words). *Showing respect of persons* (*thaumazontes prosōpa*). Present active participle of *thaumazō* to admire, to wonder at. Nowhere else in N.T. with *prosōpa*, but a Hebraism (in Lev. 19:15; Job 13:10) like *lambanein prosōpon* (Luke 20:21) and *blepein prosōpon* (Matt. 22:16) and *prosopōlempteō* (James 2:9). Cf. James 2:1. *For the sake of advantage* (*ōpheleias charin*). To themselves. See also verse 11. The covetousness of these Gnostic leaders is plainly shown in II Pet. 2:3, 14. For *charin* as preposition with genitive see Eph. 3:1, 14.

17. *Remember ye* (*humeis mnēsthēte*). First aorist passive

(deponent) imperative of *mimnēskō* with genitive *rēmatōn* (words). In II Pet. 3:2 we have the indirect form (infinitive *mnēsthēnai*). The rest as in II Peter, but in simpler and more exact structure and with the absence of *tōn hagiōn prophētōn* (the holy prophets).

18. *How that* (*hoti*). Declarative *hoti* as in verse 5. See discussion of II Pet. 3:3 for differences, no *en empaigmonēi* here and no *tōn asebeiōn* there.

19. *They who make separations* (*hoi apodiorizontes*). Present active articular participle of the double compound *apodiorizō* (from *apo, dia, horizō, horos*, boundary, to make a horizon), rare word, in Aristotle for making logical distinctions, here only in N.T. *Diorizō* occurs in Lev. 20:24 and *aphorizō* in Matt. 25:32, etc. See *haireseis* in II Pet. 2:1. *Sensual* (*psuchikoi*). Old adjective from *psuchē* as in I Cor. 2:14; 15:44; James 3:15. Opposed to *pneumatikos*. Not used by Peter. *Having not the Spirit* (*pneuma mē echontes*). Usual negative *mē* with the participle (present active of *echō*). Probably *pneuma* here means the Holy Spirit, as is plain in verse 20. Cf. Rom. 8:9.

20. *Building up* (*epoikodomountes*). Present active participle of *epoikodomeō*, old compound with metaphor of a house (*oikos*), common in Paul (I Cor. 3:9–17; Col. 2:7; Eph. 2:20). *On your most holy faith* (*tēi hagiōtatēi humōn pistei*). For the spiritual temple see also I Pet. 2:3–5. See *pistis* (faith) in this sense (cf. Heb. 11:1) in II Pet. 1:5 with the list of graces added. A true superlative here *hagiōtatēi*, not elative. *Praying in the Holy Spirit* (*en pneumati hagiōi proseuchomenoi*). This is the way to build themselves up on their faith.

21. *Keep yourselves* (*heautous tērēsate*). First aorist active imperative (of urgency) of *tēreō*. In verse 1 they are said to be kept, but note the warning in verse 5 from the angels who did not keep their dominion. See also James 1:27. In Phil. 2:12 both sides (human responsibility and

divine sovereignty are presented side by side). *Looking for* (*prosdechomenoi*). Present middle participle of *prosdecho-mai*, the very form in Titus 2:13. The same idea in *pros-dokōntes* in II Pet. 3:14.

22. *And on some* (*kai hous men*). Demonstrative plural of *hos men—hos de* (*hous de*, below), not the relative *hous*, but by contrast (*men*, *de*). So Matt. 13:8. *Have mercy* (*eleāte*). Present active imperative of *eleaō* (rare form in Rom. 9:16 also for the usual *eleeō* Matt. 9:27). But A C read *elegchete*, refute, in place of *eleāte*. The text of this verse is in much confusion. *Who are in doubt* (*diakrino-menous*). Present middle participle of *diakrinō*, in the accusative case agreeing with *hous men*, though K L P have the nominative. If the accusative and *eleate* is read, see James 1:6 for the idea (doubters). If *elegchete* is read, see Jude 9 for the idea (disputers).

23. *And some save* (*hous de sōzete*). B omits *hous de*. *Snatching them out of the fire* (*ek puros harpazontes*). Present active participle of *harpazō*, old verb, to seize. Quotation from Amos 4:11 and Zech. 3:3. Cf. Ps. 106:18. Firemen today literally do this rescue work. Do Christians? *And on some have mercy with fear* (*hous de eleāte en phobōi*). In fear "of the contagion of sin while we are rescuing them" (Vincent). For this idea see I Pet. 1:17; 3:15; II Cor. 7:1; Phil. 2:12. *Spotted* (*espilōmenon*). Perfect passive participle of *spiloō*, late and common verb (from *spilos*, spot, II Pet. 2:13), in N.T. only here and James 3:6.

24. *From stumbling* (*aptaistous*). Verbal from *ptaiō*, to stumble (James 3:2; II Pet. 1:10), sure-footed as of a horse that does not stumble (Xenophon), and so of a good man (Epictetus, Marcus Antoninus). *Before the presence of his glory* (*katenōpion tēs doxēs autou*). Late compound preposition (*kata*, *en*, *ōps*), right down before the eye of his glory as in Eph. 1:4. Cf. Matt. 25:31–33; Col. 1:22, where Paul has *parastēsai* like *stēsai* here (first aorist active infinitive)

and also *amōmous* as here, but *amōmētos* in II Pet. 3:14.
In exceeding joy (*en agalliasei*). See Luke 1:14.

25. *To the only God our Saviour* (*monōi theōi sōtēri hēmōn*).
Dative in the noble doxology. See Rom. 16:27, *monōi
sophōi theōi* (to the alone wise God), where also we have *dia
Iēsou Christou,* but without *tou kuriou hēmōn* (our Lord)
as here. *Sōtēr* is used of God eight times in the N.T., six
of them in the Pastoral Epistles. *Doxa* (glory) to God or
Christ in all the doxologies except I Tim. 6:16. *Megalosunē*
(Majesty) is a late LXX word, in N.T. only here and Heb.
1:3; 8:1. *Before all time* (*pro pantos tou aiōnos*). Eternity
behind us. See same idea in I Cor. 2:7 *pro tōn aiōnōn. Now*
(*nun*). The present. *For ever more* (*eis pantas tous aiōnas*).
"Unto all the ages." All the future. As complete a statement of eternity as can be made in human language.

THE FIRST EPISTLE OF JOHN

ABOUT A.D. 85 TO 90

BY WAY OF INTRODUCTION

RELATION TO THE FOURTH GOSPEL

There are few scholars who deny that the Epistles of John and the Fourth Gospel are by the same writer. As a matter of fact "in the whole of the First Epistle there is hardly a single thought that is not found in the Gospel" (Schulze). H. J. Holtzmann (*Jahrbuch für Protestantische Theologie*, 1882, p. 128) in a series of articles on the "Problem of the First Epistle of St. John in its Relation to the Gospel" thinks that the similarities are closer than those between Luke's Gospel and the Acts. Baur argued that this fact was explained by conscious imitation on the part of one or the other, probably by the author of the Epistle. The solution lies either in identity of authorship or in imitation. If there is identity of authorship, Holtzmann argues that the Epistle is earlier, as seems to me to be true, while Brooke holds that the Gospel is the earlier and that the First Epistle represents the more complete ideas of the author. Both Holtzmann and Brooke give a detailed comparison of likenesses between the First Epistle and the Fourth Gospel in vocabulary, syntax, style, ideas. The arguments are not conclusive as to the priority of Epistle or Gospel, but they are as to identity of authorship. One who accepts, as I do, the Johannine authorship of the Fourth Gospel for the reasons given in Volume V of this series, does not feel called upon to prove the Johannine authorship of the three Epistles that pass under the Apostle's name. Westcott suggests that one compare John 1:1–18 with I John 1:1–4 to see how the same mind deals with the same ideas in different connections. "No theory of conscious imitation can reasonably explain the subtle coincidences and differences in these two short crucial passages."

GNOSTICISM

The Epistle is not a polemic primarily, but a letter for the edification of the readers in the truth and the life in Christ. And yet the errors of the Gnostics are constantly before John's mind. The leaders had gone out from among the true Christians, but there was an atmosphere of sympathy that constituted a subtle danger. There are only two passages (2:18f.; 4:1–6) in which the false teachers are specifically denounced, but "this unethical intellectualism" (Robert Law) with its dash of Greek culture and Oriental mysticism and licentiousness gave a curious attraction for many who did not know how to think clearly. John, like Paul in Colossians, Ephesians, and the Pastoral Epistles, foresaw this dire peril to Christianity. In the second century it gave pure Christianity a gigantic struggle. "The great Gnostics were the first Christian philosophers" (Robert Law, *The Tests of Life*, p. 27) and threatened to undermine the Gospel message by "deifying the devil" (*ib.*, p. 31) along with dethroning Christ. There were two kinds of Gnostics, both agreeing in the essential evil of matter. Both had trouble with the Person of Christ. The Docetic Gnostics denied the actual humanity of Christ, the Cerinthian Gnostics distinguished between the man Jesus and the *æon* Christ that came on him at his baptism and left him on the Cross. Some practised asceticism, some licentiousness. John opposes both classes in his Epistles. They claimed superior knowledge (*gnōsis*) and so were called Gnostics (*Gnōstikoi*). Nine times John gives tests for knowing the truth and uses the verb *ginōskō* (know) each time (2:3, 5; 3:16, 19, 24; 4:2, 6, 13; 5:2). Some of the leaders he calls antichrists. There are stories about John's dread of Cerinthus and his unwillingness to be seen in the same public bath with him. The Apostle of love, as he is, is a real son of thunder when Gnosticism shows its head. Westcott thinks that the Fourth Gospel was written to prove the deity of Christ, assuming his humanity, while I John was written to prove the humanity of Christ, assuming his deity. Certainly both ideas appear in both books.

DESTINATION

It is not clear to whom the Epistle is addressed. Like the Gospel, the Epistle of John came out of the Asiatic circle with Ephesus as the centre. Augustine has the strange statement that the Epistle was addressed to the Parthians. There are other ingenious conjectures which come to nothing. The Epistle was clearly sent to those familiar with John's message, possibly to the churches of the Province of Asia (cf. the Seven Churches in Revelation).

THE DATE

The time seems to be considerably removed from the atmosphere of the Pauline and Petrine Epistles. Jerusalem has been destroyed. If John wrote the Fourth Gospel by A.D. 95, then the First Epistle would come anywhere from A.D. 85 to 95. The tone of the author is that of an old man. His urgent message that the disciples, his "little children," love one another is like another story about the aged John, who, when too feeble to stand, would sit in his chair and preach "Little children, love one another." The Muratorian Fragment accepts the First Epistle and Origen makes full use of it, as does Clement of Alexandria. Irenæus quotes it by name. Polycarp shows knowledge of it also.

BIBLIOGRAPHY

ALEXANDER, *Epistles of John* (Speaker's Comm., 1889).
BARRETT, *Devotional Comm. on I John* (1910).
BAUMGARTNER, *Die Schriften des N.T.* (IV. 3, 1918).

BELSER, *Komm.* (1906).

BENNETT, *New-Century Bible.*

BROOKE, *Int. Crit. Comm.* (Johannine Epistles, 1912).

COX, *Private Letters of St. Paul and St. John* (1887).

EBRARD, *Die Briefe Johannis* (1859).

EWALD, *Die Johanneischen Schriften* (1861).

FINDLAY, *Fellowship in the Life Eternal* (1909).

GIBBON, *Eternal Life* (1890).

GORE, *Epistles of John* (1921).

GREEN, *Ephesian Canonical Writings* (1910).

HÄRING, *Die Johannesbriefe* (1927).

HAUPT, *I John* (1869).

HILGENFELD, *Das Evangelium und die Briefe Johannis nach ihrem Lehrbegriff dargestellt* (1849).

HOLTZMANN-BAUER, *Hand-Comm. sum N.T.* (1908).

HOLTZMANN, *Das Problem des 1 Johannesbr. in seinem Verhältniss zum Evang.* (Jahrbuch für Prot. Theologie, 1881, 1882).

HUTHER, *Crit. and Exeget. to the General Eps. of James and John* (1882).

KARL, *Johanneische Studien* (der 1er Johannes Brief, 1898).

LAW, *The Tests of Life* (1909).

LIAS, *Epistles of John* (1887).

LOISY, *Les épîtres dites de Jean* (1921) in le quatrième évangile.

LÜCKE, *Comm. on Epistles of John* (1837).

LUTHARDT, *Strack-Zoeckler Komm.* (1895).

MAURICE, *The Epistles of St. John* (1857).

PLUMMER, *Cambridge Greek Test* (1886).

RAMSAY, A., *Westminster N.T.* (1910).

RITTER, *Die Gemeinschaft der Heiligen* (1929).

ROBERTSON, J. A., *The Johannine Epistles* (1920).

ROTHE, *Der erste Brief Johannis* (1878).

SAWTELLE, *American Comm.* (1890).

SMITH, DAVID, *The Expositor's Greek Testament* (1910).

WATSON, *Epistles of John* (1910).

WEISS, B., *Die drei Briefe des Apostels Johannis* (Meyer Komm. 1900).

WENDT, *Die Johannesbriefe und das Johanneische Christentum* (1925).

WESTCOTT, *The Epistles of St. John.* 3rd ed. (1892).

WINDISCH, *Die Katholischer Briefe* (Handbuch zum N.T., 2 Aufl., 1930).

WREDE, *In Die Heiligen Schriften des N.T.* (2 Aufl., 1924).

WURM, *Die Irrlehrer im I^{ten} Johannes Brief* (1903).

CHAPTER I

1. *That which* (*ho*). Strictly speaking, the neuter relative here is not personal, but the message "concerning the Word of life" (*peri tou logou tēs zōēs*), a phrase that reminds one at once of the Word (*Logos*) in John 1:1, 14; Rev. 19:14 (an incidental argument for identity of authorship for all these books). For discussion of the *Logos* see on John 1:1–18 (Vol. V). Here the *Logos* is described by *tēs zōēs* (of life), while in John 1:4 he is called *hē zōē* (the Life) as here in verse 2 and as Jesus calls himself (John 11:25; 14:6), an advance on the phrase here, and in Rev. 19:14 he is termed *ho logos tou theou* (the Word of God), though in John 1:1 the *Logos* is flatly named *ho theos* (God). John does use *ho* in a collective personal sense in John 6:37, 39. See also *pan ho* in I John 5:4. *From the beginning* (*ap' archēs*). Anarthrous as in John 1:1; 6:64; 16:4. See same phrase in 2:7. The reference goes beyond the Christian dispensation, beyond the Incarnation, to the eternal purpose of God in Christ (John 3:16), "coeval in some sense with creation" (Westcott). *That which we have heard* (*ho akēkoamen*). Note fourfold repetition of *ho* (that which) without connectives (asyndeton). The perfect tense (active indicative of *akouō*) stresses John's equipment to speak on this subject so slowly revealed. It is the literary plural unless John associates the elders of Ephesus with himself (Lightfoot) the men who certified the authenticity of the Gospel (John 21:24). *That which we have seen* (*ho heōrakamen*). Perfect active, again, of *horaō*, with the same emphasis on the possession of knowledge by John. *With our eyes* (*tois ophthalmois hēmōn*). Instrumental case and showing it was not imagination on John's part, not an optical illusion as the Docetists claimed,

for Jesus had an actual human body. He could be heard and seen. *That which we beheld* (*ho etheasametha*). Repetition with the aorist middle indicative of *theaomai* (the very form in John 1:14), "a spectacle which broke on our astonished vision" (D. Smith). *Handled* (*epsēlaphēsan*). First aorist active indicative of *psēlaphaō*, old and graphic verb (from *psaō*, to touch), the very verb used by Jesus to prove that he was not a mere spirit (Luke 24:39). Three senses are here appealed to (hearing, sight, touch) as combining to show the reality of Christ's humanity against the Docetic Gnostics and the qualification of John by experience to speak. But he is also "the Word of life" and so God Incarnate.

2. *Was manifested* (*ephanerōthē*). First aorist passive indicative of *phaneroō*, to make known what already exists, whether invisible (B. Weiss) or visible, "intellectual or sensible" (Brooke). In Col. 3:4 Paul employs it of the second coming of Christ. Verse 2 here is an important parenthesis, a mark of John's style as in John 1:15. By the parenthesis John heaps reassurance upon his previous statement of the reality of the Incarnation by the use of *heōrakamen* (as in verse 1) with the assertion of the validity of his "witness" (*marturoumen*) and "message" (*apaggellomen*), both present active indicatives (literary plurals), *apaggellō* being the public proclamation of the great news (John 16:25). *The life, the eternal life* (*tēn zōēn tēn aiōnion*). Taking up *zōē* of verse 1, John defines the term by the adjective *aiōnios*, used 71 times in the N.T., 44 times with *zōē* and 23 in John's Gospel and Epistles (only so used in these books by John). Here it means the divine life which the Logos was and is (John 1:4; I John 1:1). *Which* (*hētis*). Qualitative relative, "which very life." *Was with the Father* (*ēn pros ton patera*). Not *egeneto*, but *ēn*, and *pros* with the accusative of intimate fellowship, precisely as in John 1:1 *ēn pros ton theon* (was

with God). Then John closes the parenthesis by repeating *ephanerōthē*.

3. *That which we have seen* (*ho heōrakamen*). Third use of this form (verses 1, 2, 3), this time resumption after the parenthesis in verse 2. *And heard* (*kai akēkoamen*). Second (verse 1 for first) use of this form, a third in verse 5. Emphasis by repetition is a thoroughly Johannine trait. *Declare we* (*apaggellomen*). Second use of this word (verse 2 for first), but *aggelia* (message) and *anaggellomen* (announce) in verse 5. *That ye also may have* (*hina kai humeis echēte*). Purpose clause with *hina* and present active subjunctive of *echō* (may keep on having). "Ye also" who have not seen Jesus in the flesh as well as those like John who have seen him. Like *kai humin* (to you also) just before. *Fellowship with us* (*koinōnian meth' hēmōn*). Common word in this Epistle, from *koinōnos*, partner (Luke 5:10), and *koinōneō*, to share, in (I Pet. 4:13), with *meta* emphasising mutual relationship (Acts 2:42). This Epistle often uses *echō* with a substantive rather than a verb. *Yea, and our fellowship* (*kai hē koinōnia de hē hēmetera*). Careful explanation of his meaning in the word "fellowship" (partnership), involving fellowship with the Father and with his Son Jesus Christ and only possible in Christ.

4. *We write* (*graphomen hēmeis*). Literary plural present active indicative of *graphō*, which see in the singular in 2:12–14. *May be fulfilled* (*ēi peplērōmenē*). Periphrastic perfect passive subjunctive of *pleroō*, stressing the state of completion in the purpose (*hina*), remain full, precisely as in John 16:24. See aorist subjunctive in John 15:11 and perfect indicative in John 17:13. The MSS. differ as often between *hēmōn* (our) and *humōn* (your).

5. *And* (*kai*). Mutual fellowship depends on mutual knowledge (Westcott). *Message* (*aggelia*). Old word (from *aggelos*, messenger), in N.T. only here and 3:11, and note *ap' autou* (from God like *apaggellō* in verse 3) and *anag-*

gellomen, to announce, to disclose, here as in John 4:25. *God is light* (*ho theos phōs estin*). Precisely so the *Logos* is light (John 1:4-9) and what Jesus claimed to be (John 8:12). John repeats it in negative form as he often does (John 1:3).

6. *If we say* (*ean eipōmen*). Condition of third class with *ean* and second aorist (ingressive, up and say) active subjunctive. Claiming fellowship with God (see verse 3) involves walking in the light with God (verse 5) and in the darkness (*skotos* here, but *skotia* in John 1:5). See 2:11 also for *en tēi skotiāi peripateō*. We lie (pseudometha). Present middle indicative, plain Greek and plain English like that about the devil in John 8:44. *Do not the truth* (*ou poioumen tēn alētheian*). Negative statement of the positive *pseudometha* as in John 8:44. See John 3:21 for "doing the truth," like Neh. 9:33.

7. *If we walk* (*ean peripatōmen*). Condition of third class also with *ean* and present active subjunctive (keep on walking in the light with God). *As he* (*hōs autos*). As God is light (verse 5) and dwells in light unapproachable (I Tim. 6:16). *One with another* (*met' allēlōn*). As he has already said in verse 3. But we cannot have fellowship with one another unless we have it with God in Christ, and to do that we must walk in the light with God. *And the blood of Jesus his Son cleanseth us from all sin* (*kai to haima Iēsou tou huiou autou katharizei hēmās apo pāsēs hamartias*). This clause with *kai* in true Johannine style is coördinate with the preceding one. Walking in the light with God makes possible fellowship with one another and is made possible also by the blood of Jesus (real blood and no mere phantom, atoning blood of the sinless Son of God for our sins). John is not ashamed to use this word. It is not the mere "example" of Jesus that "cleanses" us from sin. It does cleanse the conscience and life and nothing else does (Heb. 9:13f.;

Titus 2:14). See in verse 9 both forgiveness and cleansing. Cf. I John 3:3.

8. *If we say* (*ean eipōmen*). See verse 6. *We have no sin* (*hamartian ouk echomen*). For this phrase see John 9:41; 15:22, 24. That is, we have no personal guilt, no principle of sin. This some of the Gnostics held, since matter was evil and the soul was not contaminated by the sinful flesh, a thin delusion with which so-called Christian scientists delude themselves today. *We deceive ourselves* (*heautous planōmen*). Present active indicative of *planaō*, to lead astray. We do not deceive others who know us. Negative statement again of the same idea, "the truth is not in us."

9. *If we confess* (*ean homologōmen*). Third-class condition again with *ean* and present active subjunctive of *homologeō*, "if we keep on confessing." Confession of sin to God and to one another (James 5:16) is urged throughout the N.T. from John the Baptist (Mark 1:5) on. *Faithful* (*pistos*). Jesus made confession of sin necessary to forgiveness. It is God's promise and he is "righteous" (*dikaios*). *To forgive* (*hina aphēi*). Sub-final clause with *hina* and second aorist active subjunctive of *aphiēmi*. *And to cleanse* (*kai hagiasei*). So again with *hina* and the first aorist active subjunctive of *katharizō* (verse 7).

10. *If we say* (*ean eipōmen*). As in verses 6, 8. *We have not sinned* (*ouch hamartēkamen*). Perfect active indicative of *hamartanō*. This is a denial of any specific acts of sin, while in verse 8 we have the denial of the principle of sin. David Smith observes that the claim to personal perfectionism has two causes, one the stifling of conscience in making God a liar (*pseustēn*, the word used of the devil by Jesus in John 8:44), and the other ignorance of God's word, which is not in us, else we should not make such a claim.

CHAPTER II

1. *My little children* (*teknia mou*). Tender tone with this diminutive of *teknon* (child), again in 2:12 and 3:18, but *paidia* in 2:14. John is now an old man and regards his readers as his little children. That attitude is illustrated in the story of his visit to the robber to win him to Christ. *That ye may not sin* (*hina mē hamartēte*). Purpose (negative) clause with *hina mē* and the second aorist (ingressive, commit sin) active subjunctive of *hamartanō*, to sin. John has no patience with professional perfectionists (1:8–10), but he has still less with loose-livers like some of the Gnostics who went to all sorts of excesses without shame. *If any man sin* (*ean tis hamartēi*). Third-class condition with *ean* and second aorist (ingressive) active subjunctive again, "if one commit sin." *We have* (*echomen*). Present active indicative of *echō* in the apodosis, a present reality like *echomen* in II Cor. 5:1. *An advocate* (*paraklēton*). See on John 14:16, 26; 15:26; 16:7 for this word, nowhere else in the N.T. The Holy Spirit is God's Advocate on earth with men, while Christ is man's Advocate with the Father (the idea, but not the word, in Rom. 8:31–39; Heb. 7:25). As *dikaios* (righteous) Jesus is qualified to plead our case and to enter the Father's presence (Heb. 2:18).

2. *And he* (*kai autos*). He himself in his own person, both priest and sacrifice (Heb. 9:14). *The propitiation* (*hilasmos*). Late substantive from *hilaskomai* (Luke 18:13; Heb. 2:17), in LXX, Philo, Plutarch, in N.T. only here and 4:10. Christ himself is the means of propitiation for (*peri* concerning) our sins. See *hilastērion* in Rom. 3:25. *For the whole world* (*peri holou tou kosmou*). It is possible to supply the ellipsis here of *tōn hamartiōn* (the sins of) as we have it

in Heb. 7:27, but a simpler way is just to regard "the whole world" as a mass of sin (5:19). At any rate, the propitiation by Christ provides for salvation for all (Heb. 2:9) if they will only be reconciled with God (II Cor. 5:19–21).

3. *Hereby* (*en toutōi*). See this phrase also in 2:5; 3:16, 19, 24; 4:2, 13; 5:2. That is explained by the *ean* clause, "if we keep his commandments" (*ean tērōmen*, condition of the third class, *ean* with present active subjunctive, "if we keep on keeping"), the clause itself in apposition with *toutōi* (locative case). *Know we that we know him* (*ginoskomen hoti egnōkamen auton*). "Know we that we have come to know and still know him," *egnōkamen* the perfect active indicative of *ginōskō*. The Gnostics boasted of their superior knowledge of Christ, and John here challenges their boast by an appeal to experimental knowledge of Christ which is shown by keeping his (*autou*, Christ's) commandments, thoroughly Johannine phrase (12 times in the Gospel, 6 in this Epistle, 6 in the Apocalypse).

4. *I know him* (*Egnōka auton*). Perfect active indicative with recitative *hoti* like quotation marks just before it. This is one of the pious platitudes, cheap claptrap of the Gnostics, who would bob up in meetings with such explosions. John punctures such bubbles with the sharp addition "and keepeth not" (*ho mē tērōn*, present active linear participle). "The one who keeps on saying: 'I have come to know him,' and keeps on not keeping his commandments is a liar" (*pseustēs*, just like Satan, John 8:44 and like I John 1:8, 10), followed by the negative statement as in 1:8 and 10. There is a whip-cracker effect in John's words.

5. *But whoso keepeth* (*hos d' an tērēi*). Indefinite relative clause with modal *an* and the present active subjunctive, "whoever keeps on keeping." *Verily* (*alēthōs*). Truly, of a truth. This prize is open to all, not confined to a few initiated Gnostic intellectuals or pneumatics. *Hath the love of God been perfected* (*hē agapē tou theou teteleiōtai*). Perfect

passive indicative of *teleioō*, stands completed. Probably
objective genitive, our love for God, which is realized in
absolute obedience (Brooke). *Hereby* (*en toutōi*). That is
by continuous keeping of Christ's commandments, not by
loud talk and loose living.

6. *Himself also to walk* (*kai autos peripatein*). Present
active infinitive after *opheilei* (ought), "Himself also to keep
on walking," a continuous performance, not a spasmodic
spurt. *Even as he walked* (*kathōs ekeinos periepatēsen*). Constative aorist active indicative summing up the life of Christ
on earth with the emphatic use of the demonstrative *ekeinos*
in reference to Christ as in 3:3, 5, 7, 16; 4:17 and John 7:11;
9:12, 28; 19:21.

7. *Beloved* (*agapētoi*). First instance of this favourite
form of address in these Epistles (3:2, 21; 4:1, 7; III John
1, 2, 5, 11). No *new commandment* (*ouk entolēn kainēn*).
Not novel or new in kind (*kainēn* as distinct from *neos*, new
in time, for which distinction see Luke 5:33–38). *But an
old commandment* (*all' entolēn palaian*). Ancient as opposed
both to *kainos* and *neos*. The Mosaic law taught love for
one's neighbours and Christ taught love even of enemies.
Which ye had (*hēn eichete*). Imperfect active, reaching back
to the beginning of their Christian lives (*ap' archēs*). They
had heard it expressly from Jesus (John 13:34), who, however, calls it "a new commandment."

8. *Again a new commandment* (*palin entolēn kainēn*).
Paradox, but truth. Old in teaching (as old as the story of
Cain and Abel, 3:11f.), but new in practice. For this use
of *palin* for a new turn see John 16:28. To walk as Christ
walked is to put in practice the old commandment and so
make it new (ever new and fresh), as love is as old as man
and fresh in every new experience. *True in him and in you*
(*alēthes en autōi kai en humin*). This newness is shown
supremely in Christ and in disciples when they walk as Jesus
did (verse 6). *Because* (*hoti*). Explanation of the paradox.

Is passing away (*paragetai*). Present middle indicative of *paragō*, old verb, to lead by, to go by (intransitive), as in Matt. 20:30. Night does pass by even if slowly. See this verb in verse 17 of the world passing by like a procession. *True* (*alēthinon*). Genuine, reliable, no false flicker. *Already shineth* (*ēdē phainei*). Linear present active, "is already shining" and the darkness is already passing by. Dawn is here. Is John thinking of the second coming of Christ or of the victory of truth over error, of light over darkness (cf. John 1:5–9), the slow but sure victory of Christ over Satan as shown in the Apocalypse? See 1:5.

9. *And hateth his brother* (*kai ton adelphon autou misōn*). Sharp contrast between the love just described and hate. The only way to walk in the light (1:7) is to have fellowship with God who is light (1:3, 5). So the claim to be in the light is nullified by hating a brother. *Even until now* (*heōs arti*). Up till this moment. In spite of the increasing light and his own boast he is in the dark.

10. *Abideth* (*menei*). Present active indicative, continues in the light and so does not interrupt the light by hating his brother. *Occasion of stumbling* (*skandalon*). See on Matt. 13:41; 16:23 for this interesting word. It is a stumbling-block or trap either in the way of others (its usual sense), as in Matt. 18:7, or in one's own way, as is true of *proskoptō* in John 11:9 and in verse 11 here. But, as Westcott argues, John may very well have the usual meaning here and the other in verse 11.

11. *Blinded* (*etuphlōsen*). First aorist active indicative of *tuphloō*, the very verb and form used in II Cor. 4:4 of the god of this age to keep men from beholding the illumination of the gospel of the glory of Christ who is the image of God. The first part of the verse repeats verse 9, but adds this vivid touch of the blinding power of darkness. In the Mammoth Cave of Kentucky the fish in Echo River have eye-sockets, but no eyes.

12. *I write* (*graphō*). Present active indicative, repeated three times, referring to this Epistle. For "the name" see 3:23 and III John 7. They were loyal to the name of Christ (Matt. 10:22). *Are forgiven* (*apheōntai*). Doric perfect passive indicative of *aphiēmi* (seen also in Luke 5:20, 23) for the usual *apheintai*. *Teknia* (little children) probably includes all, as in verse 1.

13. *Fathers* (*pateres*). Those mature believers with long and rich experience (*egnōkate*, ye have come to know and still know). *Him which is from the beginning* (*ton ap' archēs*). See 1:1 as explaining this crisp description of the Word of life (cf. John 1:1–18). *Young men* (*neaniskoi*). The younger element in contrast to the fathers, full of vigor and conflict and victory. *Ye have overcome the evil one* (*nenikēkate ton ponēron*). Perfect active indicative of *nikaō*, a permanent victory after conflict. The masculine article *ton* shows that the prince of darkness is the one defeated in this struggle, the devil plain in 3:8, 10 (John 8:44; 13:2).

14. *I have written* (*egrapsa*). Repeated three times. Epistolary aorist referring to this Epistle, not to a previous Epistle. Law (*Tests of Life*, p. 309) suggests that John was interrupted at the close of verse 13 and resumes here in verse 14 with a reference to what he had previously written in verse 13. But that is needless ingenuity. It is quite in John's style to repeat himself with slight variations. *The Father* (*ton patera*). The heavenly Father as all of God's children should come to know him. He repeats from verse 13 what he said to "fathers." To the young men he adds *ischuroi* (strong) and the word of God abiding in them. That is what makes them powerful (*ischuroi*) and able to gain the victory over the evil one.

15. *Love not the world* (*mē agapāte ton kosmon*). Prohibition with *mē* and the present active imperative of *agapaō*, either stop doing it or do not have the habit of doing it. This use of *kosmos* is common in John's Gospel (1:10;

17:14ff.) and appears also in I John 5:19. In epitome the Roman Empire represented it. See it also in James 4:4. It confronts every believer today. *If any man love (ean tis agapāi).* Third-class condition with *ean* and present active subjunctive of *agapaō* (same form as indicative), "if any keep on loving the world." *The love of the Father (hē agapē tou patros).* Objective genitive, this phrase only here in N.T., with which compare "love of God" in 2:5. In antithesis to love of the world.

16. *All that (pān to).* Collective use of the neuter singular as in 5:4, like *pān ho* in John 6:37, 39. Three examples, not necessarily covering all sins, are given in the nominative in apposition with *pān to.* "The lust of the flesh" (*hē epithumia tēs sarkos,* subjective genitive, lust felt by the flesh) may be illustrated by Mark 4:19 and Gal. 5:17. So the genitive with *hē epithumia tōn ophthalmōn* (the lust of the eyes) is subjective, lust with the eyes as organs as shown by Jesus in Matt. 5:28. The use of the "movies" today for gain by lustful exhibitions is a case in point. For *alazoneia* see on James 4:16, the only other N.T. example. *Alazōn* (a boaster) occurs in Rom. 1:30; II Tim. 3:2. *Bios* (life) as in 3:17 is the external aspect (Luke 8:14), not the inward principle (*zōē*). David Smith thinks that, as in the case of Eve (Gen. 3:1–6) and the temptations of Jesus (Matt. 4:1–11), these three sins include all possible sins. But they are all "of the world" (*ek tou kosmou*) in origin, in no sense "of the Father" (*ek tou patros*). The problem for the believer is always how to be in the world and yet not of it (John 17:11, 14ff.).

17. *Passeth away (paragetai).* "Is passing by" (linear action, present middle indicative), as in verse 8. There is consolation in this view of the transitoriness of the conflict with the world. Even the lust which belongs to the world passes also. The one who keeps on doing (*poiōn* present active participle of *poieō*) the will of God "abides for ever"

(*menei eis ton aiōna*) "amid the flux of transitory things" (D. Smith).

18. *It is the last hour* (*eschatē hōra estin*). This phrase only here in N.T., though John often uses *hōra* for a crisis (John 2:4; 4:21, 23; 5:25, 28, etc.). It is anarthrous here and marks the character of the "hour." John has seven times "the last day" in the Gospel. Certainly in verse 28 John makes it plain that the *parousia* might come in the life of those then living, but it is not clear that here he definitely asserts it as a fact. It was his hope beyond a doubt. We are left in doubt about this "last hour" whether it covers a period, a series, or the final climax of all just at hand. *As ye heard* (*kathōs ēkousate*). First aorist active indicative of *akouō*. *Antichrist cometh* (*antichristos erchetai*). "Is coming." Present futuristic or prophetic middle indicative retained in indirect assertion. So Jesus taught (Mark 13:6, 22; Matt. 24:5, 15, 24) and so Paul taught (Acts 20:30; II Thess. 2:3). These false Christs (Matt. 24:24; Mark 13:22) are necessarily antichrists, for there can be only one. *Anti* can mean substitution or opposition, but both ideas are identical in the word *antichristos* (in N.T. only here, 2:22; 4:3; II John 7). Westcott rightly observes that John's use of the word is determined by the Christian conception, not by the Jewish apocalypses. *Have there arisen* (*gegonasin*). Second perfect active indicative of *ginomai*. *Many antichrists* (*antichristoi polloi*). Not just one, but the exponents of the Gnostic teaching are really antichrists, just as some modern deceivers deserve this title. *Whereby* (*hothen*). By the fact that these many antichrists have come.

19. *From us* (*ex hēmōn*)—*of us* (*ex hēmōn*). The same idiom, *ex* and the ablative case (*hēmōn*), but in different senses to correspond with *exēlthan* (they went out from our membership) and *ouk ēsan* (they were not of us in spirit and life). For *ex* in the sense of origin see John 17:15, for *ex* in the sense of likeness, John 17:14. *For if they had been of us*

(*ei gar ex hēmōn ēsan*). Condition of second class with *ei* and imperfect tense (no aorist for *eimi*). *They would have continued* (*memenēkeisan an*). Past perfect of *menō*, to remain, without augment, with *an* in apodosis of second-class condition. *With us* (*meth' hēmōn*). In fellowship, for which see *meta* in 1:3. They had lost the inner fellowship and then apparently voluntarily broke the outward. *But they went* (*all'*). Ellipsis of the verb *exēlthan* above, a common habit (ellipse) in John's Gospel (1:8; 9:3; 13:18; 15:25). *That they might be made manifest* (*hina phanerōthōsin*). Purpose clause with *hina* and the first aorist passive subjunctive of *phaneroō*, for which verb see John 21:1; Col. 3:4. See II Cor. 3:3 for the personal construction with *hoti* as here. *They all are not* (*ouk eisin pantes*). Not just some, but all, as in 2:21; 3:5. These antichrists are thus revealed in their true light.

20. *Anointing* (*chrisma*). Old word for result (*mat*) and for the material, from *chriō*, to anoint, perhaps suggested by the use of *antichristoi* in verse 18. Christians are "anointed ones," *christoi* in this sense, with which compare Ps. 105:15: "Touch not my anointed ones" (*mē hapsēsthe tōn christōn mou*). These antichrists posed as the equals of or even superior to Christ himself. But followers of Christ do have "the oil of anointing" (*to elaion tou chrismatos*, Ex. 29:7), the Holy Spirit. This word in the N.T. only here and verse 27. Later the term was applied to baptism after baptismal remission came to be taught (Tertullian, etc.). *From the Holy One* (*apo tou hagiou*). They receive this anointing of the Holy Spirit from the Anointed One, Jesus Christ (the Holy One). Cf. John 6:69; Acts 3:14. *And ye know all things* (*kai oidate panta*). But the best MSS. read *pantes* rather than *panta*, "Ye all know it." This anointing is open to all Christians, not just a select few.

21. *I have not written* (*ouk egrapsa*). Not epistolary aorist (2:14), but a reference to what he has just said. *And be-*

cause no lie is of the truth (kai hoti pān pseudos ek tēs alētheias ouk estin). Not certain whether *hoti* here is causal (because) or declarative (that). Either makes sense. Note the idiomatic use of *ek* and *pān—ouk = ouden* (no) as in verse 19.

22. *The liar (ho pseustēs).* The liar (with the article) *par excellence.* Rhetorical question to sharpen the point made already about lying in 1:6, 10; 2:4, 21. See 5:5 for a like rhetorical question. *But (ei mē).* Except, if not. *That denieth that Jesus is the Christ (ho arnoumenos hoti Iēsous ouk estin ho Christos).* Common Greek idiom for *ouk* to appear after *arneomai* like redundant *mē* in Luke 20:27 and Heb. 12:19. The old Latin retains *non* here as old English did (Shakespeare, *Comedy of Errors* IV. ii. 7, "He denied you had in him no right"). The Cerinthian Gnostics denied the identity of the man Jesus and Christ (an *æon*, they held) like the modern Jesus or Christ controversy. *This is the antichrist (houtos estin ho antichristos).* The one just mentioned, Cerinthus himself in particular. *Even he that denieth the Father and the Son (ho arnoumenos ton patera kai ton huion).* This is the inevitable logic of such a rejection of the Son of God. Jesus had himself said this very same thing (John 5:23f.).

23. *Hath not the Father (oude ton patera echei).* "Not even does he have the Father" or God (II John 9). *He that confesseth the Son (ho homologōn ton huion).* Because the Son reveals the Father (John 1:18; 14:9). Our only approach to the Father is by the Son (John 14:6). Confession of Christ before men is a prerequisite for confession by Christ before the Father (Matt. 10:32 = Luke 12:8).

24. *As for you (humeis).* Emphatic proleptic position before the relative *ho* and subject of *ēkousate*, a familiar idiom in John 8:45; 10:29, etc. Here for emphatic contrast with the antichrists. See 1:1 for *ap' archēs* (from the beginning). *Let abide in you (en humin menetō).* Present active impera-

tive of *menō*, to remain. Do not be carried away by the new-fangled Gnostic teaching.

25. *And this is the promise* (*kai hautē estin hē epaggelia*). See 1:5 for the same idiom with *aggelia* (message). This is the only instance of *epaggelia* in the Johannine writings. Here "the promise" is explained to be "the life eternal" (1:2). In Acts 1:4 the word is used for the coming of the Holy Spirit. *He promised* (*autos epēggeilato*). First aorist middle indicative of *epaggellō*. *Autos* (he) is Christ as is seen in 3:3 by *ekeinos*.

26. *Concerning them that would lead you astray* (*peri tōn planōntōn humas*). "Concerning those that are trying to lead you astray" (conative use of the present active articular participle of *planaō*. See 1:8 for this verb. John is doing his part to rescue the sheep from the wolves, as Paul did (Acts 20:29).

27. *And as for you* (*kai humeis*). Prolepsis again as in verse 24. *Which ye received of him* (*ho elabete ap' autou*). Second aorist active indicative of *lambanō*, a definite experience, this anointing (*chrisma*), from Christ himself as in verse 20. This Paraclete was promised by Christ (John 14:26; 16:13ff.) and came on the great Pentecost, as they knew, and in the experience of all who yielded themselves to the Holy Spirit. *That any one teach you* (*hina tis didaskēi humas*). Sub-final use of *hina* and the present active subjunctive of *didaskō*, "that any one keep on teaching you." *Teacheth you* (*didaskei humas*). Present active indicative. The Holy Spirit was to bring all things to their remembrance (John 14:26) and to bear witness concerning Christ (John 15:26; 16:12–15). Yet they need to be reminded of what they already know to be "true" (*alēthes*) and "no lie" (*ouk estin pseudos*), according to John's habit of positive and negative (1:5). So he exhorts them to "abide in him" (*menete en autōi*, imperative active, though same form as

the indicative). Precisely so Jesus had urged that the disciples abide in him (John 15:4f.).

28. *And now (kai nun).* John tenderly repeats the exhortation, "keep on abiding in him." *If he shall be manifested (ean phanerōthēi).* Condition of third class with *ean* and first aorist passive subjunctive as in verse 19 and Col. 3:3. A clear reference to the second coming of Christ which may be at any time. *That we have boldness (hina schōmen parrēsian).* Purpose clause with *hina* and the ingressive second aorist active subjunctive of *echō,* "that we may get boldness." *And not be ashamed (kai mē aischunthōmen).* Likewise negative purpose (after John's fashion) with *mē* and the first aorist passive subjunctive of *aischunō,* to put to shame. *Before him (ap' autou).* "From him," as if shrinking away from Christ in guilty surprise. See II Thess. 1:9 for this use of *apo* (from the face of the Lord).

29. *If ye know (ean eidēte).* Third-class condition again with *ean* and second perfect active subjunctive of *oida.* If ye know by intuitive or absolute knowledge that Christ (because of verse 28) is righteous, then "ye know" or "know ye" *(ginōskete* either indicative or imperative) by experimental knowledge (so *ginōskō* means in contrast with *oida).* *Is begotten (gegennētai).* Perfect passive indicative of *gennaō,* stands begotten, the second birth (regeneration) of John 3:3–8. *Of him (ex autou).* Plainly "of God" in verse 9 and so apparently here in spite of *dikaios* referring to Christ. Doing righteousness is proof of the new birth.

CHAPTER III

1. *What manner of love* (*potapēn agapēn*). Qualitative interrogative as in II Pet. 3:11; Matt. 8:27. Only here in John's writings. Originally of what country or race. *Hath bestowed* (*dedōken*). Perfect active indicative of *didōmi*, state of completion, "the endowment of the receiver" (Vincent). *That we should be called* (*hina klēthōmen*). Sub-final use of *hina* with the first aorist passive subjunctive of *kaleō*, to call or name, as in Matt. 2:23. *Children* (*tekna*). As in John 1:12 and with an allusion to *gegennētai* in 2:29 in an effort "to restore the waning enthusiasm of his readers, and to recall them to their first love" (Brooke). *And such we are* (*kai esmen*). "And we are." A parenthetical reflection characteristic of John (*kai nun estin* in John 5:25 and *kai ouk eisin* in Rev. 2:2; 3:9) omitted by Textus Receptus, though, in the old MSS. *Because it knew him not* (*hoti ouk egnō auton*). Second aorist active indicative of *ginōskō*, precisely the argument in John 15:18f.

2. *Now* (*nun*). Without waiting for the *parousia* or second coming. We have a present dignity and duty, though there is greater glory to come. *It is not yet made manifest* (*oupō ephanerōthē*). First aorist passive indicative of *phaneroō*. For the aorist indicative with *oupō* with a future outlook Brooke notes Mark 11:2; I Cor. 8:2; Heb. 12:4; Rev. 17:10, 12. *What we shall be* (*ti esometha*). Not *tines* (who), but *ti* (what) neuter singular predicate nominative. "This *what* suggests something unspeakable, contained in the likeness of God" (Bengel). *If he shall be manifested* (*ean phanerōthēi*). As in 2:28, which see. The subject may be Christ as in verse 9, or the future manifestation just mentioned. Either makes sense, probably "it" here

220

better than "he." *Like him (homoioi autōi)*. *Autōi* is associative instrumental case after *homoioi*. This is our destiny and glory (Rom. 8:29), to be like Jesus who is like God (II Cor. 4:6). *We shall see him even as he is (opsometha auton kathōs estin)*. Future middle indicative of *horaō*. The transforming power of this vision of Christ (I Cor. 13:12) is the consummation of the glorious process begun at the new birth (II Cor. 3:18).

3. *Set on him (ep' autōi)*. Resting upon (*epi*) with locative rather than *eis*, looking to, Acts 24:15. That is upon Christ (Brooke), upon God (D. Smith), upon God in Christ (Westcott). *Purifieth himself (hagnizei heauton)*. Present active indicative of *hagnizō*, old verb, from *hagnos* (pure from contamination), used of ceremonial purifications (John 11:55; Acts 21:24, 26 as in Ex. 19:10) and then of personal internal cleansing of heart (James 4:8), soul (I Pet. 1:22), self (here). Cf. Phil. 2:12f. the work of both God and man. *As he is pure (kathōs ekeinos hagnos estin)*. As in 2:6 and 3:9 *ekeinos* (emphatic demonstrative) refers to Christ. Christ can be termed *hagnos* "in virtue of the perfection of his humanity" (Westcott). Our destiny is to be conformed to the image of God in Christ (Rom. 8:29).

4. *Sin is lawlessness (hē hamartia estin hē anomia)*. The article with both subject and predicate makes them coextensive and so interchangeable. Doing sin is the converse of doing righteousness (2:29). The present active participle (*poiōn*) means the habit of doing sin.

5. *He (ekeinos)*. As in verse 3 and John 1:18. *Was manifested (ephanerōthē)*. Same form as in verse 2, but here of the Incarnation as in John 21:1, not of the second coming (I John 2:28). *To take away sins (hina tas hamartias arēi)*. Purpose clause with *hina* and first aorist active subjunctive of *airō* as in John 1:29. In Is. 53:11 we have *anapherō* for bearing sins, but *airō* properly means to lift up and carry away (John 2:16). So in Heb. 10:4 we find

aphaireō and Heb. 10:11 *periaireō*, to take away sins completely (the complete expiation wrought by Christ on Calvary). The plural *hamartias* here, as in Col. 1:14, not singular (collective sense) *hamartian* as in John 1:29. *And in him is no sin (kai hamartia en autōi ouk estin)*. "And sin (the sinful principle) in him is not." As Jesus had claimed about himself (John 7:18; 8:46) and as is repeatedly stated in the N.T. (II Cor. 5:21; Heb. 4:15; 7:26; 9:13).

6. *Sinneth not (ouch hamartanei)*. Linear present (linear *menōn*, keeps on abiding) active indicative of *hamartanō*, "does not keep on sinning." For *menō* (abide) see 2:6 and John 15:4-10. *Whosoever sinneth (ho hamartanōn)*. Present (linear) active articular participle like *menōn* above, "the one who keeps on sinning" (lives a life of sin, not mere occasional acts of sin as *hamartēsas*, aorist active participle, would mean). *Hath not seen him (ouch heōraken auton)*. Perfect active indicative of *horaō*. The habit of sin is proof that one has not the vision or the knowledge (*egnōken*, perfect active also) of Christ. He means, of course, spiritual vision and spiritual knowledge, not the literal sense of *horaō* in John 1:18; 20:29.

7. *Let no man lead you astray (mēdeis planātō humas)*. Present active imperative of *planaō*, "let no one keep on leading you astray." See 1:8 and 2:26. Break the spell of any Gnostic charmer. *He that doeth righteousness (ho poiōn tēn dikaiosunēn)*. "He that keeps on doing (present active participle of *poieō*) righteousness." For this idiom with *poieō* see 1:6; 3:4. *He (ekeinos)*. Christ as in verse 5.

8. *He that doeth sin (ho poiōn tēn hamartian)*. "He that keeps on doing sin" (the habit of sin). *Of the devil (ek tou diabolou)*. In spiritual parentage as Jesus said of the Pharisees in John 8:44. When one acts like the devil he shows that he is not a true child of God. *Sinneth from the beginning (ap' archēs hamartanei)*. Linear progressive present active indicative, "he has been sinning from the beginning"

of his career as the devil. This is his normal life and those who imitate him become his spiritual children. *That he might destroy* (*hina lusēi*). Purpose clause with *hina* and the first aorist active subjunctive of *luō*. This purpose (*eis touto*) Jesus had and has. There is eternal conflict, with final victory over Satan certain.

9. *Doeth no sin* (*hamartian ou poiei*). Linear present active indicative as in verse 4 like *hamartanei* in verse 8. The child of God does not have the habit of sin. *His seed* (*sperma autou*). God's seed, "the divine principle of life" (Vincent). Cf. John 1. *And he cannot sin* (*kai ou dunatai hamartanein*). This is a wrong translation, for this English naturally means "and he cannot commit sin" as if it were *kai ou dunatai hamartein* or *hamartēsai* (second aorist or first aorist active infinitive). The present active infinitive *hamartanein* can only mean "and he cannot go on sinning," as is true of *hamartanei* in verse 8 and *hamartanōn* in verse 6. For the aorist subjunctive to commit a sin see *hamartēte* and *hamartēi* in 2:1. A great deal of false theology has grown out of a misunderstanding of the tense of *hamartanein* here. Paul has precisely John's idea in Rom. 6:1 *epimenōmen tēi hamartiāi* (shall we continue in sin, present active linear subjunctive) in contrast with *hamartēsōmen* in Rom. 6:15 (shall we commit a sin, first aorist active subjunctive).

10. *In this* (*en toutōi*). As already shown. A life of sin is proof that one is a child of the devil and not of God. This is the line of cleavage that is obvious to all. See John 8:33–39 for the claim of the Pharisees to be the children of Abraham, whereas their conduct showed them to be children of the devil. This is not a popular note with an age that wishes to remove all distinctions between Christians and the world. *Doeth not righteousness* (*ho mē poiōn dikaiosunēn*). Habit (linear present participle) again of not doing righteousness, as in verse 7 of doing it. Cf. *poiei* and *mē poiōn*

(doing and not doing) in Matt. 7:24, 26. *Neither* (*kai*). Literally, "and," but with the ellipsis of *ouk estin ek tou theou* (is not of God). The addition here of this one item about not loving (*mē agapōn*) one's brother is like Paul's summary in Rom. 13:9, a striking illustration of the general principle just laid down and in accord with 2:9–11.

11. *Message* (*aggelia*). In N.T. only here and 1:5, but *epaggelia* (promise) fifty-one times. *From the beginning* (*ap' archēs*). See 1:1 for this phrase and 2:7 for the idea. They had the message of love for the brotherhood from the beginning of the gospel and it goes back to the time of Cain and Abel (verse 12). *That we should love one another* (*hina agapōmen allēlous*). Sub-final clause (content of the *aggelia*) with *hina* and present active subjunctive. John repeats the message of 2:7f.

12. *Of the evil one* (*ek tou ponērou*). Ablative case and the same for neuter and masculine singular, but verse 10 makes it clear that the reference is to the devil. *Slew* (*esphaxen*). First aorist active indicative of *sphazō*, old verb, to slay, to butcher, to cut the throat (Latin *jugulare*) like an ox in the shambles, in N.T. only here and Rev. (5:6, 9, 12, etc.). *Wherefore?* (*charin tinos;*). "For the sake of what?" Postpositive preposition (Eph. 3:1, 14) except here. The interpretation of the act of Cain (Gen. 4:8ff.) is an addition to the narrative, but in accord with Heb. 11:4. Jealousy led to murder.

13. *If* (*ei*). Common construction after *thaumazō* (wonder) rather than *hoti* (that, because). Present imperative here with *mē* means "cease wondering." Note *mē thaumasēis* (do not begin to wonder) in John 3:6 (an individual case). See this same condition and language in John 15:18.

14. *We know* (*hēmeis oidamen*). Emphatic expression of *hēmeis* (we) in contrast to the unregenerate world, the Christian consciousness shared by writer and readers. *We have passed* (*metabebēkamen*). Perfect active indicative of

metabainō, old compound to pass over from one place to another (John 7:3), to migrate, out of death into life. We have already done it while here on earth. *Because (hoti).* Proof of this transition, not the ground of it. *We love the brethren (agapōmen tous adelphous).* Just this phrase (plural) here alone, but see 2:9 for the singular. *He that loveth not (ho mē agapōn).* "The not loving man," general picture and picture of spiritual death.

15. *A murderer (anthrōpoktonos).* Old compound (Euripides) from *anthrōpos* (man) and *kteinō* (to kill), a man-killer, in N.T. only here and John 8:44 (of Satan). *No (pās—ou).* According to current Hebraistic idiom = *oudeis* as in 2:19, 21. *Abiding (menousan).* Present active feminine accusative predicate participle of *menō,* "a continuous power and a communicated gift" (Westcott).

16. *Know we (egnōkamen).* Perfect active indicative, "we have come to know and still know." See 2:3 for "hereby" (*en toutōi*). *Love (tēn agapēn).* "The thing called love" (D. Smith). *He for us (ekeinos huper hēmōn). Ekeinos* as in 2:6; 3:3, 5, *huper* here alone in this Epistle, though common in John's Gospel (10:11, 15; 11:50, etc.) and in III John 7. *Laid down his life (tēn psuchēn autou ethēken).* First aorist active indicative of *tithēmi,* the very idiom used by Jesus of himself in John 10:11, 17f. *We ought (hēmeis opheilomen).* Emphatic *hēmeis* again. For *opheilō* see 2:6. Of course our laying down our lives for the brethren has no atoning value in our cases as in that of Christ, but is a supreme proof of one's love (John 13:37f.; 15:13), as often happens.

17. *Whoso hath (hos an echēi).* Indefinite relative clause with modal *an* with *hos* and the present active subjunctive of *echō. The world's goods (ton bion tou kosmou).* "The living or livelihood (not *zōē,* the principle of life, and see 2:16 for *bios*) of the world" (not in the sense of evil or wicked, but simply this mundane sphere). *Beholdeth (the-*

ōrei). Present active subjunctive of *theōreō*, like *echei* just before. *In need* (*chreian echonta*). "Having need" (present active predicate participle of *echō*, agreeing with *adelphon*). See the vivid picture of a like case in James 2:15f. *Shutteth up* (*kleisēi*). First aorist (effective) active subjunctive of *kleiō*, to close like the door, changed on purpose from present tense to aorist (graphic slamming the door of his compassion, *splagchna*, common in LXX and N.T. for the nobler viscera, the seat of the emotions, as in Phil. 2:11; Col. 3:12). Only here in John. *How* (*pōs*). Rhetorical question like that in James 2:16 (what is the use?). It is practical, not speculative, that counts in the hour of need.

18. *In word, neither with the tongue* (*logōi mēde tēi glōssēi*). Either instrumental or locative makes sense. What John means is "not merely by word or by the tongue." He does not condemn kind words which are comforting and cheering, but warm words should be accompanied by warm deeds to make real "in deed and in truth" (*en ergōi kai alētheiāi*). Here is a case where actions do speak louder than mere words.

19. *Shall we know* (*gnōsometha*). Future middle indicative of *ginōskō*, at any future emergency, we shall come to know by this (*en toutōi*) "that we are of the truth" (*hoti ek tēs alētheias esmen*). *Before him* (*emprosthen autou*). In the very presence of God we shall have confident assurance (*peisomen tēn kardian hēmōn*, either we shall persuade our heart or shall assure our heart) because God understands us.

20. *Whereinsoever our heart condemn us* (*hoti ean kataginōskēi hēmōn hē kardia*). A construction like *hoti an*, whatever, in John 2:5; 14:13. *Kataginōskō* occurs only three times in the N.T., here, verse 21, Gal. 2:11. It means to know something against one, to condemn. *Because God is greater than our heart* (*hoti meizōn estin tēs kardias hēmōn*). Ablative *kardias* after the comparative *meizōn*. *And knoweth all things* (*kai ginōskei panta*). Just so Peter replied to

Jesus in spite of his denials (John 21:17). God's omniscience is linked with his love and sympathy. God knows every secret in our hearts. This difficult passage strikes the very centre of Christian truth (Brooke).

21. *If our heart condemn us not* (*ean hē kardia mē kataginōskēi*). Condition of third class with *ean mē* and present active subjunctive. The converse of the preceding, but not a claim to sinlessness, but the consciousness of fellowship in God's presence. *Boldness toward God* (*parrēsian pros ton theon*). Even in prayer (Heb. 4:16). See also 2:28.

22. *Whatsoever we ask* (*ho ean aitōmen*). Indefinite relative clause with modal *an* and the present active subjunctive, like *hoti ean kataginōskēi* in verse 20. In form no limitations are placed here save that of complete fellowship with God, which means complete surrender of our will to that of God our Father. See the clear teaching of Jesus on this subject in Mark 11:24; Luke 11:9; John 14:12f.; 16:23 and his example (Mark 14:36 = Matt. 26:39 = Luke 22:42). The answer may not always be in the form that we expect, but it will be better. *We receive of him* (*lambanomen ap' autou*). See 1:5 for *ap' autou* (from him). *Because* (*hoti*). Twofold reason why we receive regularly (*lambanomen*) the answer to our prayers (1) "we keep" (*tēroumen*, for which see 2:3) his commandments and (2) "we do" (*poioumen*, we practise regularly) "the things that are pleasing" (*ta aresta*, old verbal adjective from *areskō*, to please, with dative in John 8:29 with same phrase; Acts 12:3 and infinitive in Acts 6:2, only other N.T. examples) "in his sight" (*enōpion autou*, common late vernacular preposition in papyri, LXX, and in N.T., except Matthew and Mark, chiefly by Luke and in the Apocalypse), in God's eye, as in Heb. 13:21.

23. *His commandment* (*hē entolē autou*). *That* (*hina*). Subfinal use of *hina* in apposition with *entolē* (commandment) and explanatory of it, as in John 15:12 (*entolē hina*).

See Christ's summary of the commandments (Mark 12:28–31 = Matt. 22:34–40). So these two points here (1) *We should believe* (*pisteusōmen*, first aorist active subjunctive according to B K L, though Aleph A C read the present subjunctive *pisteuōmen*) either in a crisis (aorist) or the continuous tenor (present) of our lives. The "name" of Jesus Christ here stands for all that he is, "a compressed creed" (Westcott) as in 1:3. Note dative *onomati* here with *pisteuō* as in 5:10, though *eis onoma* (on the name) in 5:13; John 1:12; 2:23; 3:18. But (2) "we should love one another" (*agapōmen allēlous*), as he has already urged (2:7f.; 3:11) and as he will repeat (4:7, 11f.; II John 5) as Jesus (even as he gave us commandment, that is Christ) had previously done (John 13:34; 15:12, 17). There are frequent points of contact between this Epistle and the words of Jesus in John 13 to 17.

24. *And he in him* (*kai autos en autōi*). That is "God abides in him" as in 4:15. We abide in God and God abides in us through the Holy Spirit (John 14:10, 17, 23; 17:21). "Therefore let God be a home to thee, and be thou the home of God: abide in God, and let God abide in thee" (Bede). *By the Spirit* (*ek tou pneumatos*). It is thus (by the Holy Spirit, first mention in this Epistle and "Holy" not used with "Spirit" in this Epistle or the Apocalypse) that we know that God abides in us. *Which* (*hou*). Ablative case by attraction from accusative *ho* (object of *edōken*) to agree with *pneumatos* as often, though not always. It is a pity that the grammatical gender (which) is retained here in the English instead of "whom," as it should be.

CHAPTER IV

1. *Beloved* (*agapētoi*). Three times in this chapter (1, 7, 11) we have this tender address on love. *Believe not every spirit* (*mē panti pneumati pisteuete*). "Stop believing," as some were clearly carried away by the spirits of error rampant among them, both Docetic and Cerinthian Gnostics. Credulity means gullibility and some believers fall easy victims to the latest fads in spiritualistic humbuggery. *Prove the spirits* (*dokimazete ta pneumata*). Put them to the acid test of truth as the metallurgist does his metals. If it stands the test like a coin, it is acceptable (*dokimos*, II Cor. 10:18), otherwise it is rejected (*adokimos*, I Cor. 9:27; II Cor. 13:5–7). *Many false prophets* (*polloi pseudoprophētai*). Jesus had warned people against them (Matt. 7:15), even when they as false Christs work portents (Matt. 24:11, 24; Mark 13:22). It is an old story (Luke 6:26) and recurs again and again (Acts 13:6; Rev. 16:13; 19:20; 20:10) along with false teachers (II Pet. 2:1). *Are gone out* (*exelēluthasin*). Perfect active indicative of *exerchomai*. Cf. aorist in 2:19. They are abroad always.

2. *Hereby know ye* (*en toutōi ginōskete*). Either present active indicative or imperative. The test of "the Spirit of God" (*to pneuma tou theou*) here alone in this Epistle, save verse 13. With the clamour of voices then and now this is important. The test (*en toutōi*, as in 3:19) follows. *That Jesus Christ is come in the flesh* (*Iēsoun Christon en sarki elēluthota*). The correct text (perfect active participle predicate accusative), not the infinitive (*elēluthenai*, B Vg). The predicate participle (see John 9:22 for predicate accusative with *homologeō*) describes Jesus as already come in the flesh (his actual humanity, not a phantom body as the

229

Docetic Gnostics held). See this same idiom in II John 7 with *erchomenon* (coming). A like test is proposed by Paul for confessing the deity of Jesus Christ in I Cor. 12:3 and for the Incarnation and Resurrection of Jesus in Rom. 10:6–10.

3. *Confesseth not* (*mē homologei*). Indefinite relative clause with the subjective negative *mē* rather than the usual objective negative *ou* (verse 6). It is seen also in II Pet. 1:9 and Titus 1:11, a survival of the literary construction (Moulton, *Prolegomena*, p. 171). The Vulgate (along with Irenæus, Tertullian, Augustine) reads *solvit* (*luei*) instead of *mē homologei*, which means "separates Jesus," apparently an allusion to the Cerinthian heresy (distinction between Jesus and Christ) as the clause before refers to the Docetic heresy. Many MSS. have here also *en sarki elēluthota* repeated from preceding clause, but not A B Vg Cop. and not genuine. *The spirit of the antichrist* (*to tou antichristou*). *Pneuma* (spirit) not expressed, but clearly implied by the neuter singular article *to*. It is a repetition of the point about antichrists made in 2:18–25. *Whereof* (*ho*). Accusative of person (grammatical neuter referring to *pneuma*) with *akouō* along with accusative of the thing (*hoti erchetai*, as in 2:18, futuristic present middle indicative). Here the perfect active indicative (*akēkoate*), while in 2:18 the aorist (*ēkousate*). *And now already* (*kai nun ēdē*). As in 2:18 also (many have come). "The prophecy had found fulfilment before the Church had looked for it" (Westcott). It is often so. For *ēdē* see John 4:35; 9:27.

4. *Have overcome them* (*nenikēkate autous*). Perfect active indicative of *nikaō*, calm confidence of final victory as in 2:13 and John 16:33. The reference in *autous* (them) is to the false prophets in 4:1. *Because* (*hoti*). The reason for the victory lies in God, who abides in them (3:20, 24; John 14:20; 15:4f.). God is greater than Satan, "he that is in the world" (*ho en tōi kosmōi*), the prince of this world

(John 12:31; 14:30), the god of this age (II Cor. 4:4), powerful as he seems.

5. *Of the world* (*ek tou kosmou*). As Jesus is not and as the disciples are not (John 17:14ff.). *As of the world* (*ek tou kosmou*). No "as" (*hōs*), but that is the idea, for their talk proceeds from the world and wins a ready hearing. The false prophets and the world are in perfect unison.

6. *We* (*hēmeis*). In sharp contrast with the false prophets and the world. We are in tune with the Infinite God. Hence "he that knoweth God" (*ho ginōskōn ton theon*, present active articular participle, the one who keeps on getting acquainted with God, growing in his knowledge of God) "hears us" (*akouei hēmōn*). This is one reason why sermons are dull (some actually are, others so to dull hearers) or inspiring. There is a touch of mysticism here, to be sure, but the heart of Christianity is mysticism (spiritual contact with God in Christ by the Holy Spirit). John states the same idea negatively by a relative clause parallel with the preceding articular participle, the negative with both clauses. John had felt the cold, indifferent, and hostile stare of the worldling as he preached Jesus. *By this* (*ek toutou*). "From this," deduction drawn from the preceding; only example in the Epistle for the common *en toutōi* as in 4:2. The power of recognition (*ginōskomen*, we know by personal experience) belongs to all believers (Westcott). There is no reason for Christians being duped by "the spirit of error" (*to pneuma tēs planēs*), here alone in the N.T., though we have *pneumasin planois* (misleading spirits) in I Tim. 4:1. Rejection of the truth may be due also to our not speaking the truth in love (Eph. 4:15).

7. *Of God* (*ek tou theou*). Even human love comes from God, "a reflection of something in the Divine nature itself" (Brooke). John repeats the old commandment of 2:7f. Persistence in loving (present tense *agapōmen* indicative and *agapōn* participle) is proof that one "has been begotten of

God" (*ek tou theou gegennētai* as in 2:29) and is acquainted with God. Otherwise mere claim to loving God accompanied by hating one's brother is a lie (2:9–11).

8. *He that loveth not* (*ho mē agapōn*). Present active articular participle of *agapaō* "keeps on not loving." *Knoweth not God* (*ouk egnō ton theon*). Timeless aorist active indicative of *ginōskō*, has no acquaintance with God, never did get acquainted with him. *God is love* (*ho theos agapē estin*). Anarthrous predicate, not *hē agapē*. John does not say that love is God, but only that God is love. The two terms are not interchangeable. God is also light (1:5) and spirit (John 4:24).

9. *Was manifested* (*ephanerōthē*). First aorist passive indicative of *phaneroō*. The Incarnation as in 3:5. Subjective genitive as in 2:5. *In us* (*en hēmin*). In our case, not "among us" nor "to us." Cf. Gal. 1:16. *Hath sent* (*apestalken*). Perfect active indicative of *apostellō*, as again in verse 14, the permanent mission of the Son, though in verse 10 the aorist *apesteilen* occurs for the single event. See John 3:16 for this great idea. *His only-begotten Son* (*ton huion autou ton monogenē*). "His Son the only-begotten" as in John 3:16. John applies *monogenēs* to Jesus alone (John 1:14, 18), but Luke (7:12; 8:42; 9:38) to others. Jesus alone completely reproduces the nature and character of God (Brooke). *That we might live through him* (*hina zēsōmen di' autou*). Purpose clause with *hina* and the first aorist (ingressive, get life) active subjunctive of *zaō*. "Through him" is through Christ, who is the life (John 14:6). Christ also lives in us (Gal. 2:20). This life begins here and now.

10. *Not that* (*ouch hoti*)—*but that* (*all' hoti*). Sharp contrast as in John 7:22; II Cor. 7:9; Phil. 4:17. *We loved* (*ēgapēsamen*). First aorist active indicative, but B reads *ēgapēkamen* (perfect active, we have loved). *He* (*autos*). Emphatic nominative (God). *To be the propitiation* (*hilasmon*). Merely predicate accusative in apposition with **huion**

(Son). For the word see 2:2 and Rom. 3:25 for *hilastērion*, and for *peri* see also 2:2.

11. *If God so loved us* (*ei houtōs ho theos ēgapēsen hēmas*). Condition of first class with *ei* and the first aorist active indicative. As in John 3:16, so here *houtōs* emphasises the manifestation of God's love both in its manner and in its extent (Rom. 8:32). *Ought* (*opheilomen*). As in 2:6. *Noblesse oblige*. "Keep on loving," (*agapāin*) as in 3:11.

12. *No one hath beheld God at any time* (*theon oudeis pōpote tetheātai*). Perfect middle indicative of *theaomai* (John 1:14). Almost the very words of John 1:18 *theon oudeis pōpote heōraken* (instead of *tetheātai*). *If we love one another* (*ean agapōmen allēlous*). Third-class condition with *ean* and the present active subjunctive, "if we keep on loving one another." *God abideth in us* (*ho theos en hēmin menei*). Else we cannot go on loving one another. *His love* (*hē agapē autou*). More than merely subjective or objective (2:5; 4:9). "Mutual love is a sign of the indwelling of God in men" (Brooke). *Is perfected* (*teteleiōmenē estin*). Periphrastic (see usual form *teteleiōtai* in 2:5 and 4:17) perfect passive indicative of *teleioō* (cf. 1:4). See verse 18 for "perfect love."

13. *Hereby know we* (*en toutōi ginōskomen*). The Christian's consciousness of the fact of God dwelling in him is due to the Spirit of God whom God has given (*dedōken*, perfect active indicative here, though the aorist *edōken* in 3:24). This gift of God is proof of our fellowship with God.

14. *We have beheld* (*tetheāmetha*). Perfect middle of *theaomai* as in verse 12, though the aorist in 1:1 and John 1:14 (*etheāsametha*). John is qualified to bear witness (*marturoumen* as in 1:2) as Jesus had charged the disciples to do (Acts 1:8). *Hath sent* (*apestalken*). As in verse 9, though *apesteilen* in verse 10. *To be the Saviour of the world* (*sōtēra tou kosmou*). Predicate accusative of *sōtēr* (Saviour), like *hilasmon* in verse 10. This very phrase occurs elsewhere only in

John 4:42 as the confession of the Samaritans, but the idea is in John 3:17.

15. *Whosoever shall confess* (*hos ean homologēsēi*). Indefinite relative clause with modal *ean* (=*an*) and the first aorist active subjunctive, "whoever confesses." See 2:23 and 4:2f. for *homologeō*. *That* (*hoti*). Object clause (indirect assertion) after *homologeō*. This confession of the deity of Jesus Christ implies surrender and obedience also, not mere lip service (cf. I Cor. 12:3; Rom. 10:6–12). This confession is proof (if genuine) of the fellowship with God (1:3f.; 3:24).

16. *We know* (*egnōkamen*). Perfect active indicative, "we have come to know and still know" as in John 6:9, only there order is changed (*pepisteukamen* coming before *egnōkamen*). Confession (*homologeō*) follows experimental knowledge (*ginōskō*) and confident trust (*pisteuō*). Believers are the sphere (*en hēmin*, in our case) in which the love of God operates (Westcott). See John 13:35 for "having love." *God is love* (*ho theos agapē estin*). Repeated from verse 8. So he gathers up the whole argument that one who is abiding in love is abiding in God and shows that God is abiding in him. Thoroughly Johannine style.

17. *Herein* (*en toutōi*). It is not clear whether the *hina* clause (sub-final use) is in apposition with *en toutōi* as in John 15:8 or the *hoti* clause (because) with the *hina* clause as parenthesis. Either makes sense. Westcott argues for the latter idea, which is reinforced by the preceding sentence. *With us* (*meth' hēmōn*). Construed with the verb *teteleiōtai* (is perfected). In contrast to *en hēmin* (verses 12, 16), emphasising coöperation. "God works with man" (Westcott). For boldness (*parrēsian*) in the day of judgment (only here with both articles, but often with no articles as in II Pet. 2:9) see 2:28. *As he is* (*kathōs ekeinos estin*). That is Christ as in 2:6; 3:3, 5, 7, 16. Same tense (present) as in 3:7. "Love is a heavenly visitant" (David Smith). We are in this world to manifest Christ.

18. *Fear* (*phobos*). Like a bond-slave (Rom. 8:15), not the reverence of a son (*eulabeia*, Heb. 5:7f.) or the obedience to a father (*en phoboi*, I Pet. 1:17). This kind of dread is the opposite of *parrēsia* (boldness). *Perfect love* (*hē teleia agapē*). There is such a thing, perfect because it has been perfected (verses 12, 17). Cf. James 1:4. *Casteth out fear* (*exō ballei ton phobon*). "Drives fear out" so that it does not exist in real love. See *ekballō exō* in John 6:37; 9:34f.; 12:31; 15:6 to turn out-of-doors, a powerful metaphor. Perfect love harbours no suspicion and no dread (I Cor. 13). *Hath punishment* (*kolasin echei*). Old word, in N.T. only here and Matt. 25:46. *Timōria* has only the idea of penalty, *kolasis* has also that of discipline, while *paideia* has that of chastisement (Heb. 12:7). The one who still dreads (*phoboumenos*) has not been made perfect in love (*ou teteleiōtai*). Bengel graphically describes different types of men: "*sine timore et amore; cum timore sine amore; cum timore et amore; sine timore cum amore.*"

19. *He first* (*autos prōtos*). Note *prōtos* (nominative), not *prōton*, as in John 20:4, 8. God loved us *before* we loved him (John 3:16). Our love is in response to his love for us. *Agapōmen* is indicative (we love), not subjunctive (let us love) of the same form. There is no object expressed here.

20. *If a man say* (*ean tis eipēi*). Condition of third class with *ean* and second aorist active subjunctive. Suppose one say. Cf. 1:6. *I love God* (*Agapō ton theon*). Quoting an imaginary disputant as in 2:4. *And hateth* (*kai misei*). Continuation of the same condition with *ean* and the present active subjunctive, "and keep on hating." See 2:9 and 3:15 for use of *miseō* (hate) with *adelphos* (brother). *A liar* (*pseustēs*). Blunt and to the point as in 1:10; 2:4. *That loveth not* (*ho mē agapōn*). "The one who does not keep on loving" (present active negative articular participle). *Hath seen* (*heōraken*). Perfect active indicative of *horaō*, the form in John 1:18 used of seeing God. *Cannot love* (*ou dunatai*

agapāin). "Is not able to go on loving," with which compare 2:9, *ou dunatai hamartanein* (is not able to go on sinning). The best MSS. do not have *pōs* (how) here.

21. *That* (*hina*). Sub-final object clause in apposition with *entolēn* as in John 13:34; 15:13. *From him* (*ap' autou*). Either God or Christ. See Mark 12:29–31 for this old commandment (2:7f.).

CHAPTER V

1. *That Jesus is the Christ* (*hoti Iēsous estin ho Christos*).
The Cerinthian antichrist denies the identity of Jesus and
Christ (2:22). Hence John insists on this form of faith
(*pisteuōn* here in the full sense, stronger than in 3:23; 4:16,
seen also in *pistis* in verse 4, where English and Latin fall
down in having to use another word for the verb) as he
does in verse 5 and in accord with the purpose of John's
Gospel (20:31). Nothing less will satisfy John, not merely
intellectual conviction, but full surrender to Jesus Christ as
Lord and Saviour. "The Divine Begetting is the antecedent,
not the consequent of the believing" (Law). For "is begotten of God" (*ek tou theou gegennētai*) see 2:29; 3:9; 4:7;
5:4, 18. John appeals here to family relationship and family
love. *Him that begat* (*ton gennēsanta*). First aorist active
articular participle of *gennaō*, to beget, the Father (our
heavenly Father). *Him also that is begotten of him* (*ton
gegennēmenon ex autou*). Perfect passive articular participle
of *gennaō*, the brother or sister by the same father. So
then we prove our love for the common Father by our conduct towards our brothers and sisters in Christ.

2. *Hereby* (*en toutōi*). John's usual phrase for the test of
the sincerity of our love. "The love of God and the love
of the brethren do in fact include each the other" (Westcott). Each is a test of the other. So put 3:14 with 5:2.
When (*hotan*). "Whenever" indefinite temporal clause with
hotan and the present active subjunctive (the same form
agapōmen as the indicative with *hoti* (that) just before,
"whenever we keep on loving God." *And do* (*kai poiōmen*)
"and whenever we keep on doing (present active subjunc-

tive of *poieō*) his commandments." See 1:6 for "doing the truth."

3. *This* (*hautē*)—*that* (*hina*). Explanatory use of *hina* with *hautē*, as in John 17:3, to show what "the love of God" (4:9, 12) in the objective sense is, not mere declamatory boasting (4:20), but obedience to God's commands, "that we keep on keeping (present active subjunctive as in 2:3) his commandments." This is the supreme test. *Are not grievous* (*bareiai ouk eisin*). "Not heavy," the adjective in Matt. 23:4 with *phortia* (burdens), with *lupoi* (wolves) in Acts 20:29, of Paul's letters in II Cor. 10:10, of the charges against Paul in Acts 25:7. Love for God lightens his commands.

4. *For* (*hoti*). The reason why God's commandments are not heavy is the power that comes with the new birth from God. *Whatsoever is begotten of God* (*pān to gegennēmenon ek tou theou*). Neuter singular perfect passive participle of *gennaō* rather than the masculine singular (verse 1) to express sharply the universality of the principle (Rothe) as in John 3:6, 8; 6:37, 39. *Overcometh the world* (*nikāi ton kosmon*). Present active indicative of *nikaō*, a continuous victory because a continuous struggle, "keeps on conquering the world" ("the sum of all the forces antagonistic to the spiritual life," D. Smith). *This is the victory* (*hautē estin hē nikē*). For this form of expression see 1:5; John 1:19. *Nikē* (victory, cf. *nikaō*), old word, here alone in N.T., but the later form *nikos* in Matt. 12:20 and I Cor. 15:54f., 57. *That overcometh* (*hē nikēsasa*). First aorist active articular participle of *nikaō*. The English cannot reproduce the play on the word here. The aorist tense singles out an individual experience when one believed or when one met temptation with victory. Jesus won the victory over the world (John 16:33) and God in us (I John 4:4) gives us the victory. *Even our faith* (*hē pistis hēmōn*). The only instance of *pistis* in the Johannine Epistles (not in

John's Gospel, though in the Apocalypse). It is our faith in Jesus Christ as shown by our confession (verse 1) and by our life (verse 2).

5. *And who is he that overcometh?* (*tis estin de ho nikōn?*). Not a mere rhetorical question (2:22), but an appeal to experience and fact. Note the present active articular participle (*nikōn*) like *nikāi* (present active indicative in verse 4), "the one who keeps on conquering the world." See I Cor. 15:57 for the same note of victory (*nikos*) through Christ. See verse 1 for *ho pisteuōn* (the one who believes) as here. *Jesus is the Son of God* (*Iēsous estin ho huios tou theou*). As in verse 1 save that here *ho huios tou theou* in place of *Christos* and see both in 2:22f. Here there is sharp antithesis between "Jesus" (humanity) and "the Son of God" (deity) united in the one personality.

6. *This* (*houtos*). Jesus the Son of God (verse 5). *He that came* (*ho elthōn*). Second aorist active articular participle of *erchomai*, referring to the Incarnation as a definite historic event, the preëxistent Son of God "sent from heaven to do God's will" (Brooke). *By water and blood* (*di' hudatos kai haimatos*). Accompanied by (*dia* used with the genitive both as instrument and accompaniment, as in Gal. 5:13) water (as at the baptism) and blood (as on the Cross). These two incidents in the Incarnation are singled out because at the baptism Jesus was formally set apart to his Messianic work by the coming of the Holy Spirit upon him and by the Father's audible witness, and because at the Cross his work reached its culmination ("It is finished," Jesus said). There are other theories that do not accord with the language and the facts. It is true that at the Cross both water and blood came out of the side of Jesus when pierced by the soldier, as John bore witness (John 19:34), a complete refutation of the Docetic denial of an actual human body for Jesus and of the Cerinthian distinction between Jesus and Christ. There is thus a threefold witness to the

fact of the Incarnation, but he repeats the twofold witness before giving the third. The repetition of both preposition (*en* this time rather than *dia*) and the article (*tōi* locative case) argues for two separate events with particular emphasis on the blood ("not only" *ouk monon*, "but" *all*') which the Gnostics made light of or even denied. *It is the Spirit that beareth witness* (*to pneuma estin to marturoun*). Present active articular participle of *martureō* with article with both subject and predicate, and so interchangeable as in 3:4. The Holy Spirit is the third and the chief witness at the baptism of Jesus and all through his ministry. *Because* (*hoti*). Or declarative "that." Either makes sense. In John 15:26 Jesus spoke of "the Spirit of truth" (whose characteristic is truth). Here John identifies the Spirit with truth as Jesus said of himself (John 14:6) without denying personality for the Holy Spirit.

7. *For there are three who bear witness* (*hoti treis eisin hoi marturountes*). At this point the Latin Vulgate gives the words in the Textus Receptus, found in no Greek MS. save two late cursives (162 in the Vatican Library of the fifteenth century, 34 of the sixteenth century in Trinity College, Dublin). Jerome did not have it. Cyprian applies the language of the Trinity and Priscillian has it. Erasmus did not have it in his first edition, but rashly offered to insert it if a single Greek MS. had it and 34 was produced with the insertion, as if made to order. The spurious addition is: *en tōi ouranōi ho patēr, ho logos kai to hagion pneuma kai houtoi hoi treis hen eisin kai treis eisin hoi marturountes en tēi gēi* (in heaven, the Father, the Word, and the Holy Ghost: and these three are one. And there are three that bear witness in earth). The last clause belongs to verse 8. The fact and the doctrine of the Trinity do not depend on this spurious addition. Some Latin scribe caught up Cyprian's exegesis and wrote it on the margin of his text, and

so it got into the Vulgate and finally into the Textus Receptus by the stupidity of Erasmus.

8. *The Spirit and the water and the blood* (*to pneuma kai to hudōr kai to haima*). The same three witnesses of verses 6 and 7 repeated with the Spirit first. *The three* (*hoi treis*). The resumptive article. *Agree in one* (*eis to hen eisin*). "Are for the one thing," to bring us to faith in Jesus as the Incarnate Son of God, the very purpose for which John wrote his Gospel (20:31).

9. *If we receive* (*ei lambanomen*). Condition of first class with *ei* and the present active indicative, assumed as true. The conditions for a legally valid witness are laid down in Deut. 19:15 (cf. Matt. 18:16; John 8:17f.; 10:25; II Cor. 13:1). *Greater* (*meizōn*). Comparative of *megas*, because God is always true. *For* (*hoti*). So it applies to this case. *That* (*hoti*). Thus taken in the declarative sense (the fact that) as in John 3:19, though it can be causal (because) or indefinite relative with *memarturēken* (what he hath testified, perfect active indicative of *martureō*, as in John 1:32; 4:44, etc.), a harsh construction here because of *marturia*, though some MSS. do read *hen* to agree with it (cf. verse 10). See *hoti ean* in 3:20 for that idiom. Westcott notes the Trinity in verses 6 to 9: the Son comes, the Spirit witnesses, the Father has witnessed.

10. *Believeth on* (*pisteuōn eis*). John draws a distinction between "not believing God" (*mē pisteuōn tōi theōi*) in next clause, the testimony of God about his Son, and surrender to and reliance on the Son as here (*eis* and the accusative). See the same distinction less clearly drawn in John 6:30f. See also *eis tēn marturian* after *pepisteuken* in this same verse and John 2:23. *In him* (*en hautōi*). "In himself," though the evidence is not decisive between *hautōi* and *autōi*. *Hath made* (*pepoiēken*). Perfect active indicative of *poieō* like *memarturēken* and *pepisteuken*, permanent state. *A liar* (*pseustēn*). As in 1:10, which see. *Because he hath not be-*

lieved (*hoti ou pepisteuken*). Actual negative reason with negative *ou*, not the subjective reason as in John 3:18, where we have *hoti mē pepisteuken*). The subjective negative is regular with *ho mē pisteuōn*. Relative clause here repeats close of verse 9.

11. *That God gave* (*hoti edōken ho theos*). Declarative *hoti* in apposition with *marturia* as in verse 14 and John 3:19. Note aorist active indicative *edōken* (from *didōmi*) as in 3:23f., the great historic fact of the Incarnation (John 3:16), but the perfect *dedōken* in I John 3:1 to emphasize the abiding presence of God's love. *Eternal life* (*zōēn aiōnion*). Anarthrous emphasizing quality, but with the article in 1:2. *In his Son* (*en tōi huiōi autou*). This life and the witness also. This is why Jesus who is life (John 14:6) came to give us abundant life (John 10:10).

12. *Hath the life* (*echei tēn zōēn*). The life which God gave (verse 11). This is the position of Jesus himself (John 5:24; 14:6).

13. *I have written* (*egrapsa*). Not epistolary aorist, but refers to verses 1 to 12 of this Epistle as in 2:26 to the preceding verses. *That ye may know* (*hina eidēte*). Purpose clause with *hina* and the second perfect active subjunctive of *oida*, to know with settled intuitive knowledge. He wishes them to have eternal life in Christ (John 20:31) and to know that they have it, but not with flippant superficiality (2:3ff.). *Unto you that believe on* (*tois pisteuousin eis*). Dative of the articular present active participle of *pisteuō* and *eis* as in verse 10. For this use of *onoma* (name) with *pisteuō* see 3:23; John 2:23.

14. *Toward him* (*pros auton*). Fellowship with (*pros*, face to face) Christ. For boldness see 2:28. *That* (*hoti*). Declarative again, as in verse 11. *If we ask anything* (*ean ti aitōmetha*). Condition of third class with *ean* and present middle (indirect) subjunctive (personal interest as in James 4:3, though the point is not to be pressed too far, for see

Matt. 20:20, 22; John 16:24, 26). *According to his will (kata to thelēma autou)*. This is the secret in all prayer, even in the case of Jesus himself. For the phrase see I Pet. 4:19; Gal. 1:4; Eph. 1:5, 11. *He heareth us (akouei hēmōn)*. Even when God does not give us what we ask, in particular then (Heb. 5:7f.).

15. *And if we know (kai ean oidamen)*. Condition of first class with *ean* (usually *ei*) and the perfect active indicative, assumed as true. See I Thess. 3:8 and Acts 8:31 for the indicative with *ean* as in the papyri. "An amplification of the second limitation" (D. Smith). *Whatsoever we ask (ho ean aitōmetha)*. Indefinite relative clause with modal *ean* (*=an*) and the present middle (as for ourselves) subjunctive of *aiteō*. This clause, like *hēmōn*, is also the object of *akouei*. *We know that we have (oidamen hoti echomen)*. Repetition of *oidamen*, the confidence of possession by anticipation. *The petitions (ta aitēmata)*. Old word, from *aiteō*, requests, here only in John, elsewhere in N.T. Luke 23:24; Phil. 4:6. We have the answer already as in Mark 11:24. *We have asked (ēitēkamen)*. Perfect active indicative of *aiteō*, the asking abiding.

16. *If any man see (ean tis idēi)*. Third-class condition with *ean* and second aorist active subjunctive of *eidon (horaō)*. *Sinning a sin (hamartanonta hamartian)*. Present active predicate (supplementary) participle agreeing with *adelphon* and with cognate accusative *hamartian*. *Not unto death (mē pros thanaton)*. Repeated again with *hamartanousin* and in contrast with *hamartia pros thanaton* (sin unto death). Most sins are not mortal sins, but clearly John conceives of a sin that is deadly enough to be called "unto death." This distinction is common in the rabbinic writings and in Numb. 18:22 the LXX has *labein hamartian thanatēphoron* "to incur a death-bearing sin" as many crimes then and now bear the death penalty. There is a distinction in Heb. 10:26 between sinning wilfully after full knowledge and sins of

ignorance (Heb. 5:2). Jesus spoke of the unpardonable sin (Mark 3:29; Matt. 12:32; Luke 12:10), which was attributing to the devil the manifest work of the Holy Spirit. It is possible that John has this idea in mind when he applies it to those who reject Jesus Christ as God's Son and set themselves up as antichrists. *Concerning this (peri ekeinēs).* This sin unto death. *That he should make request (hina erōtēsēi).* Sub-final use of *hina* with the first aorist active subjunctive of *erōtaō*, used here as in John 17:15 and 20 (and often) for request rather than for question. John does not forbid praying for such cases; he simply does not command prayer for them. He leaves them to God.

17. *All unrighteousness is sin (pāsa adikia hamartia estin).* Unrighteousness is one manifestation of sin as lawlessness (3:4) is another (Brooke). The world today takes sin too lightly, even jokingly as a mere animal inheritance. Sin is a terrible reality, but there is no cause for despair. Sin not unto death can be overcome in Christ.

18. *We know (oidamen).* As in 3:2, 14; 5:15, 19, 20. He has "ye know" in 2:20; 3:5, 15. *Sinneth not (ouch hamartanei).* Lineal present active indicative, "does not keep on sinning," as he has already shown in 3:4–10. *He that was begotten of God (ho gennētheis ek tou theou).* First aorist passive articular participle referring to Christ, if the reading of A B is correct (*tērei auton,* not *tērei heauton*). It is Christ who keeps the one begotten of God (*gegennēmenos ek tou theou* as in 3:9 and so different from *ho gennētheis* here). It is a difficult phrase, but this is probably the idea. Jesus (John 18:37) uses *gegennēmai* of himself and uses also *tēreō* of keeping the disciples (John 17:12, 15; Rev. 3:10). *The evil one (ho ponēros).* Masculine and personal as in 2:13, not neuter, and probably Satan as in Matt. 6:13, not just any evil man. *Touchest him not (ouch haptetai autou).* Present middle indicative of *haptō,* elsewhere in John only John 20:17. It means to lay hold of or to grasp rather than

a mere superficial touch (*thiggano*, both in Col. 2:21). Here
the idea is to touch to harm. The devil cannot snatch such
a man from Christ (John 6:38f.).

19. *Of God* (*ek tou theou*). See 3:10 and 4:6 for this idiom.
Lieth in the evil one (*en tōi ponērōi keitai*). Present middle
indicative of the defective verb *keimai*, to lie, as in Luke
2:12. *Ponērōi* is masculine, like *ho ponēros* in verse 18.
This is a terrible picture of the Graeco-Roman world of the
first century A.D., which is confirmed by Paul in Romans
1 and 2 and by Horace, Seneca, Juvenal, Tacitus.

20. *Is come* (*hēkei*). Present active indicative, but the
root has a perfect sense, "has come." See *exēlthon kai hēkō*
in John 8:42. *An understanding* (*dianoian*). Here alone in
John's writings, but in Paul (Eph. 4:18) and Peter (I Pet.
1:13). John does not use *gnōsis* (knowledge) and *nous*
(mind) only in Rev. 13:18; 17:9. *That we know* (*hina ginōskomen*). Result clause with *hina* and the present active
indicative, as is common with *hina* and the future indicative
(John 7:3). It is possible that here *o* was pronounced *ō* as
a subjunctive, but many old MSS. have *hina ginōskousin*
(plainly indicative) in John 17:3, and in many other places
in the N.T. the present indicative with *hina* occurs as a
variant reading as in John 5:20. *Him that is true* (*ton alēthinon*). That is, God. Cf. 1:8. *In him that is true* (*en tōi
alēthinōi*). In God in contrast with the world "in the evil
one" (verse 19). See John 17:3. *Even in his Son Jesus
Christ* (*en tōi huiōi autou Iēsou Christōi*). The *autou* refers
clearly to *en tōi alēthinōi* (God). Hence this clause is not in
apposition with the preceding, but an explanation as to how
we are "in the True One" by being "in his Son Jesus Christ."
This (*houtos*). Grammatically *houtos* may refer to Jesus
Christ or to "the True One." It is a bit tautological to
refer it to God, but that is probably correct, God in Christ,
at any rate. God is eternal life (John 5:26) and he gives it
to us through Christ.

21. *Yourselves* (*heauta*). Neuter plural reflexive because of *teknia*. The active voice *phulassete* with the reflexive accents the need of effort on their part. Idolatry was everywhere and the peril was great. See Acts 7:41: I Thess. 1:9 for this word.

SECOND JOHN
ABOUT A.D. 85 TO 90

BY WAY OF INTRODUCTION

There is little to add to what was said about the First Epistle except that here the author terms himself "the elder" (*ho presbuteros*) and writes to "the elect lady" (*eklektēi kuriāi*). There is dispute about both of these titles. Some hold that it is the mythical "presbyter John" of whom Papias may speak, if so understood, but whose very existence is disproved by Dom Chapman in *John the Presbyter and the Fourth Gospel* (1911). Peter the apostle (I Pet. 1:1) calls himself "fellow-elder" (*sunpresbuteros*) with the other elders (I Pet. 5:1). The word referred originally to age (Luke 15:25), then to rank or office as in the Sanhedrin (Matt. 16:21; Acts 6:12) and in the Christian churches (Acts 11:30; 20:17; I Tim. 5:17, 19) as here also. A few even deny that the author is the same as in the First Epistle of John, but just an imitator. But the bulk of modern scholarly opinion agrees that the same man wrote all three Epistles and the Fourth Gospel (the Beloved Disciple, and many still say the Apostle John) whatever is true of the Apocalypse. There is no way of deciding whether "the elect lady" is a woman or a church. The obvious way of taking it is to a woman of distinction in one of the churches, as is true of "the co-elect lady in Babylon" (I Pet. 5:13), Peter's wife, who travelled with him (I Cor. 9:5). Some even take *kuria* to be the name of the lady (Cyria). Some also take it to be "Eklecta the lady." Dr. Findlay (*Fellowship in the Life Eternal*, p. 31) holds that Pergamum is the church to which the letter was sent. The same commentaries treat I, II, and III John as a rule, though Poggel has a book on II, III John (1896) and Bresky (1906) has *Das Verhaltnis des Zweiten Johannesbriefes zum dritten*. Dr. J. Rendel Harris has an interesting article in *The Expositor* of London for March, 1901, on "The Problem of the Address to the Second Epistle of John," in which he argues from papyri examples that *kuria* here means "my dear" or "my lady." But Findlay (*Fellowship in the Life Eternal*, p. 26) argues that "the qualifying adjunct 'elect' lifts us into the region of Christian calling and dignity." It is not certain that II John was written after I John, though probable. Origen rejected it and the Peshitta Syriac does not have II and III John.

1. *And her children* (*kai tois teknois autēs*). As with *eklektē kuria*, so here *tekna* may be understood either literally as in I Tim. 3:4, or spiritually, as in Gal. 4:19, 25; I Tim. 1:2. For the spiritual sense in *teknia* see I John 2:1, 12. *Whom* (*hous*). Masculine accusative plural, though *teknois* is neuter plural (dative), construction according to sense, not according to grammatical gender, "embracing the mother and the children of both sexes" (Vincent). See thus *hous* in Gal. 4:19. *I* (*Egō*). Though *ho presbuteros* is third person, he passes at once after the Greek idiom to the first and there is also special emphasis here in the use of *agapō* with the addition of *en alētheiāi* (in truth, in the highest sphere, as in John 17:19 and III John 1) and *ouk egō monos* (not I only, "not I alone"). Brooke argues that this language is unsuitable if to a single family and not to a church. But Paul employs this very phrase in sending greetings to Prisca and Aquila (Rom. 16:4). *That know* (*hoi egnōkotes*). Perfect active articular participle of *ginōskō*, "those that have come to know and still know."

2. *For the truth's sake* (*dia tēn alētheian*). Repetition of the word, one of which John is very fond (I John 1:6, "the truth, as revealed by the Christ, and gradually unfolded by the Spirit, who is truth" (Brooke). *Which abideth in us* (*tēn menousan en hēmin*). See John 17:19 for "sanctified in truth" and I John 2:6 for abiding in Christ, and so it includes all who are in Christ. *It shall be with us* (*meth'*

hēmōn estai). Confident assertion, not a mere wish. Note the order of the words, "With us it shall be" (*estai* future middle of *eimi*).

3. *Shall be with us (estai meth' hēmōn).* He picks up the words before in reverse order. Future indicative here, not a wish with the optative (*eie*) as we have in I Pet. 1:2; II Pet. 1:2. The salutation is like that in the Pastoral Epistles: "*Charis,* the wellspring in the heart of God; *eleos,* its outpourings; *eirēnē,* its blessed effect" (David Smith). *And from Jesus Christ (kai para Iēsou Christou).* The repetition of *para* (with the ablative) is unique. "It serves to bring out distinctly the twofold personal relation of man to the Father and to the Son" (Westcott). "The Fatherhood of God, as revealed by one who being His Son *can* reveal the Father, and who as man (*Iēsou*) can make him known to men" (Brooke).

4. *I rejoice (echarēn).* Second aorist passive of *chairō* as in III John 3, "of a glad surprise" (D. Smith), as in Mark 14:11, over the discovery about the blessing of their godly home on these lads. *Greatly (lian).* Only here and III John 3 in John's writings. *I have found (heurēka).* Perfect active indicative of *heuriskō* as in John 1:41, our "eureka," here with its usual force, a continued discovery. "He sits down at once and writes to Kyria. How glad she would be that her lads, far away in the great city, were true to their early faith" (David Smith). *Certain of thy children (ek tōn teknōn).* No *tinas* as one would expect before *ek,* a not infrequent idiom in the N.T. (John 16:17). *Walking (peripatountas).* Present active accusative supplementary participle agreeing with *tinas* understood. Probably members of the church off here in Ephesus. *In truth (en alētheiāi).* As in verse 1 and III John 4. *We received (elabomen).* Second aorist active (possibly, though not certainly, literary plural) of *lambanō.* This very idiom (*entolēn lambanō*)

in John 10:18; Acts 17:15; Col. 4:10. Perhaps the reference here is to I John 2:7f.; 3:23.

5. *Beseech* (*erōtō*). For pray as in I John 5:16. *Lady* (*kuria*). Vocative case and in the same sense as in 1. *As though I wrote* (*hōs graphōn*). Common idiom *hōs* with the participle (present active) for the alleged reason. *New* (*kainēn*). As in I John 2:7f., which see. *We had* (*eichamen*). Imperfect active (late -*a* form like *eichan* in Mark 8:7) of *echō* and note *eichete* with *ap' archēs* in I John 2:7. Not literary plural, John identifying all Christians with himself in this blessing. *That we love one another* (*hina agapōmen allēlous*). Either a final clause after *erōtō* as in John 17:15 or an object clause in apposition with *entolēn*, like I John 2:27; 3:23 and like verse 6.

6. *Love* (*hē agapē*). The love just mentioned. *That we should walk* (*hina peripatōmen*). Object clause in nominative case in apposition with *agapē*, with *hina* and the present active subjunctive of *peripateō*, "that we keep on walking." *The commandment* (*hē entolē*). The one just mentioned with the same construction with *hina* as in I John 3:23. John changes from the first person plural to the second (*ēkousate* as in I John 2:7, *peripatēte*) as in I John 2:5, 7. *In it* (*en autēi*). Either to *alētheiāi* (truth) of verse 4, *agapē* of this verse, or *entolē* of this verse. Either makes good sense, probably "in love." With *peripateō* (walk) we have often *en* (I John 1:7, 11, etc.) or *kata* (according to) as in Mark 7:5; I Cor. 3:3; II Cor. 10:2, etc.

7. *Deceivers* (*planoi*). Late adjective (Diodorus, Josephus) meaning wandering, roving (I Tim. 4:1). As a substantive in N.T. of Jesus (Matt. 27:63), of Paul (II Cor. 6:8), and here. See the verb (*tōn planontōn humās*) in I John 2:26 of the Gnostic deceivers as here and also of Jesus (John 7:12). Cf. I John 1:8. *Are gone forth* (*exēlthan*, alpha ending). Second aorist active indicative of *exerchomai*, perhaps an allusion to the crisis when they left the churches

(I John 2:19, same form). *Even they that confess not* (*hoi mē homologountes*). "The ones not confessing" (*mē* regular negative with the participle). The articular participle describes the deceivers (*planoi*). *That Jesus Christ cometh in the flesh* (*Iēsoun Christon erchomenon en sarki*). "Jesus Christ coming in the flesh." Present middle participle of *erchomai* treating the Incarnation as a continuing fact which the Docetic Gnostics flatly denied. In I John 4:2 we have *elēluthota* (perfect active participle) in this same construction with *homologeō*, because there the reference is to the definite historical fact of the Incarnation. There is no allusion here to the second coming of Christ. *This* (*houtos*). See I John 2:18, 22; 5:6, 20. *The deceiver and the antichrist* (*ho planos kai ho antichristos*). Article with each word, as in Rev. 1:17, to bring out sharply each separate phrase, though one individual is referred to. The one *par excellence* in popular expectation (I John 2:22), though many in reality (I John 2:18; III John 7).

8. *Look to yourselves* (*blepete heautous*). Imperative active with reflexive pronoun as in Mark 13:9. The verb often used absolutely (Phil. 3:2) like our "look out." *That ye lose not* (*hina mē apolesēte*). Negative purpose with *hina mē* and first aorist active subjunctive of *apollumi*. This is the correct text (B), not *apolesōmen* (we). Likewise *apolabēte* (that ye receive), not *apolabōmen* (we). *Which we have wrought* (*ha ērgasametha*). This is also correct, first aorist middle indicative of *ergazomai*, to work (John 6:27f.). John does not wish his labour to be lost. See Rom. 1:27 for this use of *apolambanō* for receiving. See John 4:36 for *misthos* in the harvest. The "full reward" (*misthon plērē*) is the full day's wages which each worker will get (I Cor. 3:8). John is anxious that they shall hold on with him to the finish.

9. *Whosoever goeth onward* (*pās ho proagōn*). "Every one who goes ahead. *Proagō* literally means to go on before

(Mark 11:9). That in itself is often the thing to do, but here the bad sense comes out by the parallel clause. *And abideth not in the teaching of Christ* (*kai mē menōn en tēi didachēi tou Christou*). Not the teaching about Christ, but that of Christ which is the standard of Christian teaching as the walk of Christ is the standard for the Christian's walk (I John 2:6). See John 7:16; 18:19. These Gnostics claimed to be the progressives, the advanced thinkers, and were anxious to relegate Christ to the past in their onward march. This struggle goes on always among those who approach the study of Christ. Is he a "landmark" merely or is he our goal and pattern? Progress we all desire, but progress toward Christ, not away from him. Reactionary obscurantists wish no progress toward Christ, but desire to stop and camp where they are. "True progress includes the past" (Westcott). Jesus Christ is still ahead of us all calling us to come on to him.

10. *If any one cometh and bringeth not* (*ei tis erchetai kai ou pherei*). Condition of first class with *ei* and two present indicatives (*erchetai, pherei*). *This teaching* (*tautēn tēn didachēn*). This teaching of Christ of verse 9, which is the standard by which to test Gnostic deceivers (verse 7). John does not refer to entertaining strangers (Heb. 13:2; I Tim. 5:10), but to the deceiving propagandists who were carrying dissension and danger with them. *Receive him not* (*mē lambanete auton*). Present active imperative with *mē*. For *lambanō* in this sense see John 1:12; 6:21; 13:20. *Into your house* (*eis oikian*). Definite without the article like our at home, to town. *Give him no greeting* (*chairein autōi mē legete*). "Say not farewell to him." Apparently *chairein* here (present active infinitive, object of *legete* present active imperative with negative *mē*) is used of farewell as in II Cor. 13:11, though usually in the N.T. (Acts 15:23; 23:26; James 1:1) of the salutation. But here the point turns on the stranger bringing into the house (or trying to do so)

his heretical and harmful teaching which seems to be after
the salutation is over. The usual greeting to a house is
given in Luke 10:5. On the other hand, if *chairein* means
greeting, not farewell, here, it can very well be understood
of the peril of allowing these Gnostic propagandists to
spread their pernicious teachings (cf. Mormons or Bolshe-
vists) in home and church (usually meeting in the home).
This is assuming that the men were known and not mere
strangers.

11. *Partaketh in his evil works (koinōnei tois ergois autou
tois ponērois)*. Associative instrumental case with *koinōnei*
as in I Tim. 5:22, common verb from *koinōnos* (partner).
It is to be borne in mind that the churches often met in
private homes (Rom. 16:5; Col. 4:15), and if these travelling
deceivers were allowed to spread their doctrines in these
homes and then sent on with endorsement as Apollos was
from Ephesus to Corinth (Acts 18:27), there was no way
of escaping responsibility for the harm wrought by these
propagandists of evil. It is not a case of mere hospitality
to strangers.

12. *I would not (ouk eboulēthēn)*. Epistolary aorist (first
passive indicative). *With paper and ink (dia chartou kai
melanos)*. The *chartēs* was a leaf of papyrus prepared for
writing by cutting the pith into strips and pasting together,
old word (Jer. 43:23), here only in N.T. *Melas* is old adjective for black (Matt. 5:36; Rev. 6:5, 12), and for black
ink here, III John 13; II Cor. 3:3. Apparently John wrote
this little letter with his own hand. *To come (genesthai)*.
Second aorist middle infinitive of *ginomai* after *elpizō*, I
hope. *Face to face (stoma pros stoma)*. "Mouth to mouth."
So in III John 14 and Numb. 12:8. "Face to face" (*prosōpon pros prosōpon*) we have in I Cor. 13:12. *Your (humōn)*.
Or "our" (*hēmōn*). Both true. *That may be fulfilled (hina
peplērōmenē ēi)*. Purpose clause with *hina* and the peri-

phrastic perfect passive subjunctive of *plēroō*, as in I John 1:4, which see.

13. *Of thine elect sister* (*tēs adelphēs sou tēs eklektēs*). Same word *eklektē* as in verse 1 and Rev. 17:4. Apparently children of a deceased sister of the lady of verse 1 who lived in Ephesus and whom John knew as members of his church there.

THIRD JOHN

ABOUT A.D. 85 TO 90

BY WAY OF INTRODUCTION

Certainly III John is addressed to an individual, not to a church, though which Gaius we do not know. There are three friends of Paul with this name; Gaius of Corinth (I Cor. 1:14), Gaius of Macedonia (Acts 19:29), Gaius of Derbe (Acts 20:4), but it is unlikely that this Gaius of Pergamum (Findlay would call him) is either of these, though the *Apostolical Constitutions* does identify him with Gaius of Derbe. It is possible that in III John 9 there is an allusion to II John and, if so, then both letters went to individuals in the same church (one a loyal woman, the other a loyal man). Three persons are sharply sketched in III John (Gaius, Diotrephes, Demetrius). Gaius is the dependable layman in the church, Diotrephes the dominating official, Demetrius the kindly messenger from Ephesus with the letter, a vivid picture of early church life and missionary work. John is at Ephesus, the last of the apostles, and with an eagle's eye surveys the work in Asia Minor. The same Gnostic deceivers are at work as in the other Johannine Epistles. Pergamum is described in Rev. 2:13 as the place "where Satan's throne is."

1. *The beloved* (*tōi agapētōi*). Four times in this short letter this verbal adjective is used of Gaius (here, 2, 5, 11). See II John 1 for the same phrase here, "whom I love in truth."

2. *I pray* (*euchomai*). Here only in John's writings. See Rom. 9:3. *In all things* (*peri pantōn*). To be taken with *euodousthai* and like *peri* in I. Cor. 16:1, "concerning all things." *Thou mayest prosper* (*se euodousthai*). Infinitive in indirect discourse (object infinitive) after *euchomai*, with accusative of general reference *se* (as to thee). *Euodoō* is old

259

verb (from *euodos*, *eu* and *hodos*, prosperous in a journey), to have a good journey, to prosper, in LXX, in N.T. only this verse (twice), I Cor. 16:2; Rom. 1:10. *Be in health* (*hugiainein*). In Paul this word always means sound teaching (I Tim. 1:10; 6:3), but here and in Luke 5:31; 7:10; 15:27, of bodily health. Brooke wonders if Gaius' health had caused his friends anxiety. *Even as thy soul prospereth* (*kathōs euodoutai sou hē psuchē*). A remarkable comparison which assumes the welfare (present middle indicative of *euodoō*) of his soul (*psuchē* here as the principle of the higher life as in John 12:27, not of the natural life as in Matt. 6:25).

3. *I rejoiced greatly* (*echarēn lian*). As in II John 4 and Phil. 4:10, not epistolary aorist, but reference to his emotions at the good tidings about Gaius. *When brethren came* (*erchomenōn adelphōn*). Genitive absolute with present middle participle of *erchomai*, and so with *marturountōn* (bare witness, present active participle of *martureō*). Present participle here denotes repetition, from time to time. *To the truth* (*tēi alētheiāi*). Dative case. "As always in the Johannine writings, 'truth' covers every sphere of life, moral, intellectual, spiritual" (Brooke). *Even as thou walkest in truth* (*kathōs su en alētheiāi peripateis*). "Thou" in contrast to Diotrephes (verse 9) and others like him. On *peripateō* see I John 1:6 and on *en alētheiāi* see II John 4.

4. *Greater* (*meizoteran*). A double comparative with *-teros* added to *meizōn*, like our "lesser" and like *mallon kreisson* (more better) in Phil. 1:23. In Eph. 3:8 we have *elachistoterōi*, a comparative on a superlative. Like forms occur in the vernacular papyri and even in Homer (*cheiroteros*, more worse) as also in Shakespeare. *Joy* (*charan*). B reads *charin* (grace). *Than this* (*toutōn*). Ablative neuter plural after the comparative. *To hear of* (*hina akouō*). Object clause (epexegetic) with *hina* and *akouō*, the present active subjunctive (keep on hearing of) in apposition with *toutōn*. *Walking in truth* (*en alētheiāi peripatounta*). As in II John

4, which see. By the use of *tekna* John may mean that Gaius is one of his converts (I Tim. 1:1).

5. *A faithful work* (*piston*). Either thus or "thou makest sure," after an example in Xenophon quoted by Wettstein (*poiein pista*) and parallel to *kaina poieō* in Rev. 21:5. But it is not certain. *In whatsoever thou doest* (*ho ean ergasēi*). Indefinite relative with modal *ean* (=*an*) and the first aorist middle subjunctive of *ergazomai*. See Col. 3:23 for both *poieō* and *ergazomai* in the same sentence. *And strangers withal* (*kai touto xenous*). "And that too" (accusative of general reference as in I Cor. 6:6; Phil. 1:28; Eph. 2:8). This praise of hospitality (Rom. 12:13; I Pet. 4:9; I Tim. 3:2; 5:10; Titus 1:8; Heb. 13:2) shows that in II John 10 John has a peculiar case in mind.

6. *Before the church* (*enōpion ekklēsias*). Public meeting as the anarthrous use of *ekklēsia* indicates, like *en ekklēsiāi* in I Cor. 14:19, 35. *Thou wilt do well* (*kalōs poiēseis*). Future active of *poieō* with adverb *kalōs*, a common polite phrase in letters (papyri) like our "please." See also Acts 10:33; James 2:19; I Cor. 7:37f.; Phil. 4:14; II Pet. 1:19. *To set forward on their journey* (*propempsas*). First aorist active participle (simultaneous action) of *propempō*, to send forward, "sending forward," old word, in N.T. in Acts 15:3; 20:38; 21:5; I Cor. 16:6, 11; II Cor. 1:16; Rom. 15:24; Titus 3:13. *Worthily of God* (*axiōs tou theou*). Precisely this phrase in I Thess. 2:12 and the genitive with *axiōs* also in Rom. 16:2; Phil. 1:27; Col. 1:10; Eph. 4:1. See John 13:20 for Christ's words on the subject. "Since they are God's representatives, treat them as you would God" (Holtzmann). From Homer's time (*Od*. XV. 74) it was customary to speed the parting guest, sometimes accompanying him, sometimes providing money and food. Rabbis were so escorted and Paul alludes to the same gracious custom in Rom. 15:24 and Titus 3:13.

7. *For the sake of the Name* (*huper tou onomatos*). The

name of Jesus. See Acts 5:4; Rom. 1:5 for *huper tou onomatos* and James 2:7 for the absolute use of "the name" as in I Pet. 4:16. "This name is in essence the sum of the Christian creed" (Westcott) as in I Cor. 12:3; Rom. 10:9. It is like the absolute use of "the Way" (Acts 9:2; 19:9, 23; 24:22). *Taking nothing (mēden lambanontes)*. Present active participle with the usual negative with participles (I John 2:4). *Of the Gentiles (apo tōn ethnikōn)*. Instead of the usual *ethnōn* (Luke 2:32), late adjective for what is peculiar to a people (*ethnos*) and then for the people themselves (Polybius, Diodorus, not in LXX), in N.T. only here, Matt. 5:47; 6:7; 18:17. Like our heathen, pagan. John is anxious that Christian missionaries receive nothing from the heathen, as our missionaries have to watch against the charge of being after money. There were many travelling lecturers out for money. Paul in I Cor. 9 defends the right of preachers to pay, but refuses himself to accept it from Corinth because it would be misunderstood (cf. I Thess. 2:6ff.; II Cor. 12:16ff. 12:16ff.). Note *apo* here as in collecting taxes (Matt. 17:25) rather than *para*, which may be suggestive.

8. *Ought (opheilomen)*. See for this word I John 2:6; 3:16; 4:11. *To welcome (hupolambanein)*. Present active infinitive (habit of welcoming) of *hupolambanō*, old word, to take up under, to carry off (Acts 1:9), to reply (Luke 10:30), to suppose (Acts 2:15), only here in N.T. in this sense of receiving hospitably or to take under one's protection like *hupodechomai* (Luke 10:38). *Such (tous toioutous)*. "The such" according to the Greek idiom (I Cor. 16:16, 18). *That we may be (hina ginōmetha)*. Purpose clause with *hina* and the present middle subjunctive of *ginomai*, "that we may keep on becoming." *Fellow-workers (sunergoi)*. Old compound (*sun, ergon*). *With the truth (tēi alētheiāi)*. So associative instrumental case with *sun* in *sunergoi*, but it is not certain that this is the idea, though *sunergeō* is so used with *ergois* in James 2:22. *Sunergos* itself occurs with the genitive of

the person as in *theou sunergoi* (I Cor. 3:9) or with genitive of the thing *tēs charās* (I Cor. 3:9). So then here the meaning may be either "co-workers with such brethren for the truth" (dative of advantage) or "co-workers with the truth" (associative instrumental case).

9. *I wrote somewhat unto the church* (*egrapsa ti tēi ekklēsiāi*). A few MSS. add *an* to indicate that he had not written (conclusion of second-class condition), clearly spurious. Not epistolary aorist nor a reference to II John as Findlay holds, but an allusion to a brief letter of commendation (Acts 18:27; II Cor. 3:1; Col. 4:10) sent along with the brethren in verses 5 to 7 or to some other itinerant brethren. Westcott wrongly thinks that *ti* is never used of anything important in the N.T. (Acts 8:9; Gal. 6:3), and hence that this lost letter was unimportant. It may have been brief and a mere introduction. *Diotrephes* (*Dios* and *trephō*, nourished by Zeus). This ambitious leader and sympathiser with the Gnostics would probably prevent the letter referred to being read to the church, whether it was II John condemning the Gnostics or another letter commending Demetrius and John's missionaries. Hence he sends Gaius this personal letter warning against Diotrephes. *Who loveth to have the preëminence among them* (*ho philoprōteuōn autōn*). Present active articular participle of a late verb, so far found only here and in ecclesiastical writers (the example cited by Blass being an error, Deissmann, *Light* etc., p. 76), from *philoprōtos*, fond of being first (Plutarch), and made like *philoponeō* (papyri), to be fond of toil. This ambition of Diotrephes does not prove that he was a bishop over elders, as was true in the second century (as Ignatius shows). He may have been an elder (bishop) or deacon, but clearly desired to rule the whole church. Some forty years ago I wrote an article on Diotrephes for a denominational paper. The editor told me that twenty-five deacons stopped the paper to show their resentment against being personally attacked in the paper. *Re-*

ceiveth us not (*ouk epidechetai hēmās*). Present active indicative of this old compound, in N.T. only here and verse 10. Diotrephes refused to accept John's authority or those who sided with him, John's missionaries or delegates (cf. Matt. 10:40).

10. *If I come* (*ean elthō*). Condition of third class with *ean* and second aorist active subjunctive of *erchomai*. He hopes to come (verse 14), as he had said in II John 12 (one argument for identifying II John with the letter in III John 9). *I will bring to remembrance* (*hupomnēsō*). Future active indicative of *hupomimnēskō*, old compound (John 14:26; II Pet. 1:12). The aged apostle is not afraid of Diotrephes and here defies him. *Which he doeth* (*ha poiei*). Present active indicative, "which he keeps on doing." *Prating against us* (*phluarōn hēmās*). Present active participle of old verb (from *phluaros*, babbling I Tim. 5:13), to accuse idly and so falsely, here only in N.T. with accusative *hēmās* (us). *With wicked words* (*logois ponērois*). Instrumental case. Not simply foolish chatter, but malevolent words. *Not content* (*mē arkoumenos*). Present passive participle of *arkeō* with usual negative *mē*. For this verb in this sense see I Tim. 6:8 and Heb. 13:5, only there *epi* is absent. John knows that the conduct of Diotrephes will not stand the light. See Paul's threats of exposure (I Cor. 4:21; II Cor. 10:11; 13:1–3). And John is the apostle of love all the same. *He himself* (*autos*). That was bad enough. *Them that would* (*tous boulomenous*). "Those willing or wishing or receive the brethren" from John. *He forbiddeth* (*kōluei*). "He hinders." Present active indicative of *kōluō* and means either actual success in one case (punctiliar use of the present indicative) or repetition in several instances (linear action) or conative action attempted, but not successful as in Matt. 3:14 (this same verb) and John 10:32. *Casteth them out of the church* (*ek tēs ekklēsias ekballei*). Here again *ekballei* can be understood in various ways, like *kōluei*.

This verb occurs in John 2:15 for casting out of the temple the profaners of it and for casting the blind man out of the synagogue (John 9:34f.). If this ancient "church-boss" did not succeed in expelling John's adherents from the church, he certainly tried to do it.

11. *Imitate not* (*mē mimou*). Present middle imperative in prohibition (do not have the habit of imitating) of *mimeomai* (from *mimos*, actor, mimic), old word, in N.T. only here, II Thess. 3:7, 9; Heb. 13:7. *That which is evil* (*to kakon*). "The bad," as in Rom. 12:21 (neuter singular abstract). *But that which is good* (*alla to agathon*). "But the good." As in Rom. 12:21 again. Probably by the contrast between Diotrephes and Demetrius. *He that doeth good* (*ho agathopoiōn*). Articular present active participle of *agathopoieō*, late and rare verb, in contrast with *ho kakopoiōn* (old and common verb) as in Mark 3:4; Luke 6:9; I Pet. 3:17. *Is of God* (*ek tou theou estin*). As in I John 3:9f. *Hath not seen God* (*ouch heōraken ton theon*). As in I John 3:6. He does not say *ek tou diabolou* as Jesus does in John 8:44, but he means it.

12. *Demetrius hath the witness of all men* (*Dēmētriōi memartyrētai hupo pantōn*). Perfect passive indicative of *martureō*, "it has been witnessed to Demetrius (dative case) by all." We know nothing else about him, unless, as is unlikely, he be identified with Demas as a shortened form (Philemon 24; Col. 4:4; II Tim. 4:10), who has come back after his desertion or with the Ephesian silversmith (Acts 19:21ff.), who may have been converted under John's ministry, which one would like to believe, though there is no evidence for it. He may indeed be the bearer of this letter from Ephesus to Gaius and may also have come under suspicion for some reason and hence John's warm commendation. *And of the truth itself* (*kai hupo autēs tēs alētheias*). A second commendation of Demetrius. It is possible, in view of I John 5:6 (the Spirit is the truth), that John means the Holy Spirit and not a mere

personification of the truth. *Yea we also* (*kai hēmeis de*). A third witness to Demetrius, that is John himself (literary plural). *Thou knowest* (*oidas*). "The words in John 21:24 sound like an echo of this sentence" (Westcott). John knew Demetrius well in Ephesus.

13. *I had* (*eichon*). Imperfect active of *echō*, when I began to write (*grapsai*, ingressive aorist active infinitive of *graphō*). *I am unwilling to write* (*ou thelō graphein*). "I do not wish to go on writing them. *With ink and pen* (*dia melanos kai kalamou*), "by means of (*dia*) black (ink) and reed (used as pen)." See II John 12 for *melanos* and Matt. 11:7 for *kalamos*, used for papyrus and parchment, as *grapheion* (a sharp stilus) for wax tablets.

14. *I hope* (*elpizō*)—*We shall speak* (*lalēsomen*). Literary plural really singular like *elpizō*. *Face to face* (*stoma pros stoma*). As in II John 12.

15. *Peace to thee* (*eirēnē soi*). *Pax tibi* like the Jewish greeting *shalōm* (Luke 10:5; 24:36; John 20:19, 21). *The friends* (*hoi philoi*). Those in Ephesus. *By name* (*kat' onoma*). John knew the friends in the church (at Pergamum or wherever it was) as the good shepherd calls his sheep by name (John 10:3, the only other N.T. example of *kat' onoma*). The idiom is common in the papyri letters (Deissmann, *Light*, etc., p. 193, note 21).

THE REVELATION OF JOHN
ABOUT A.D. 95

BY WAY OF INTRODUCTION

DIFFICULTY IN THE PROBLEM

Perhaps no single book in the New Testament presents so many and so formidable problems as the Apocalypse of John. These difficulties concern the authorship, the date, the apocalyptic method, the relation to the other Johannine books, the purpose, the historical environment, the reception of the book in the New Testament canon, the use and misuse of the book through the ages, etc. In the eastern churches the recognition of the Apocalypse of John was slower than in the west, since it was not in the Peshitta Syriac Version. Caius of Rome attributed the book to Cerinthus the Gnostic, but he was ably answered by Hippolytus, who attributed it to the Apostle John. The Council of Laodicea (about A.D. 360) omitted it, but the third Council of Carthage (A.D. 397) accepted it. The dispute about millenarianism led Dionysius of Alexandria (middle of the third century, A.D.) to deny the authorship to the Apostle John, though he accepted it as canonical. Eusebius suggested a second John as the author. But finally the book was accepted in the east as Hebrews was in the west after a period of doubt.

POOR STATE OF THE TEXT

There are only five uncials that give the text of John's Apocalypse (Aleph A C P Q). Of these Aleph belongs to the fourth century, A and C to the fifth, Q (really B_2, B ending with Heb. 9:13, both in the Vatican Library) to the eighth, P to the ninth. Only Aleph A Q (=B_2) are complete, C lacking 1:1, 3:19–5:14, 7:14–17, 8:5–9:16, 10:10–11:3, 14:13–18:2, 19:5–21, P lacking 16:12–17:1, 19:21–20:9,

22:6–21. Both C and P are palimpsests. In the 400 verses of the book "over 1,600 variants have been counted" (Moffatt). Erasmus had only one cursive (of the twelfth century numbered 1r) for his first edition, and the last six verses of the Apocalypse, save verse 20, were a translation from the Vulgate. The result is that the versions are of special importance for the text of the book, since in no single MS. or group of MSS. do we have a fairly accurate text, though Aleph A C and A C Vulgate are the best two groups.

The Apocalyptic Style

The book claims to be an apocalypse (1:1) and has to be treated as such. It is an unveiling (*apokalupsis*, from *apokaluptō*) or revelation of Jesus Christ, a prophecy, in other words, of a special type, like Ezekiel, Zechariah, and Daniel in the Old Testament. There was a considerable Jewish apocalyptic literature by this time when John wrote, much of it B.C., some of it A.D., like the Book of Enoch, the Apocalypse of Baruch, the Book of Jubilees, the Assumption of Moses, the Psalms of Solomon, the Testaments of the Twelve Patriarchs, the Sibylline Oracles, some of them evidently "worked over by Christian hands" (Swete). Jesus himself used the apocalyptic style at times (Mark 13 = Matt. 24 and 25 = Luke 21). Paul in I Cor. 14 spoke of the unpremeditated apocalyptic utterances in the Christian meetings and suggested restraints concerning them. "The Revelation of John is the only written apocalypse, as it is the only written prophecy of the Apostolic age. . . . The first Christian apocalypse came on the crest of this long wave of apocalyptic effort" (Swete). The reason for this style of writing is usually severe persecution and the desire to deliver a message in symbolic form. The effort of Antiochus Epiphanes, who claimed to be "a god manifest," to hellenize the Jews aroused violent opposition and occasioned many apocalypses to cheer the persecuted Jews.

EMPEROR WORSHIP AS THE OCCASION FOR JOHN'S APOCALYPSE

There is no doubt at all that the emperor cult (emperor worship) played a main part in the persecution of the Christians that was the occasion for this great Christian apocalypse. The book itself bears ample witness to this fact, if the two beasts refer to the Roman power as the agent of Satan. It is not possible to single out each individual emperor in the graphic picture. Most would take the dragon to be Satan and the first and the second beasts to be the imperial and provincial Roman power. The Roman emperors posed as gods and did the work of Satan. In particular there were two persecuting emperors (Nero and Domitian) who were responsible for many martyrs for Christ. But emperor worship began before Nero. Julius Cæsar was worshipped in the provinces. Octavius was called Augustus (*Sebastos*, Reverend). The crazy Emperor Caius Caligula not simply claimed to be divine, but actually demanded that his statue be set up for worship in the Holy of Holies in the Temple in Jerusalem. He was killed in January A.D. 41 before he could execute his dire purpose. But the madcap Nero likewise demanded worship and blamed in A.D. 64 the burning of Rome on the Christians, though guilty of it himself. He set the style for persecuting Christians, which slumbered on and burst into flames again under Domitian, who had himself commonly termed *Dominus ac Deus noster* (Our Lord and God). The worship of the emperor did not disturb the worshippers of other gods save the Jews and the Christians, and in particular the Christians were persecuted after the burning of Rome when they were distinguished from the Jews. Up till then Christians were regarded (as by Gallio in Corinth) as a variety of Jews and so entitled to tolerance as a *religio licita*, but they had no standing in law by themselves and their refusal to worship the emperor early gave offence, as Paul indicates in I Cor. 12:3. It was *Kurios Iēsous* or *Kurios Kaisar*. On this very issue Polycarp lost his life. The emperors as a rule were tolerant about it, save Nero and Domitian, who was called Nero *redivivus*, or Nero back again. Trajan in his famous letter to Pliny advised tolerance except in stubborn cases, when the Christians had to be put to death. After Nero it was a crime to be a Christian and all sorts of slanders about them were circulated. We have seen already in II Thess. 2:3ff., the man of sin who sets himself above God as the object of worship. We have seen also in I John 2:18, 22; 4:3; II John 7 the term antichrist applied apparently to Gnostic heretics. One may wonder if, as Beckwith argues, in the Apocalypse the man of sin and the antichrist are united in the beast.

The Author

The writer calls himself John (1:1, 4, 9; 22:8). But what John? The book can hardly be pseudonymous, though, with the exception of the Shepherd of Hermas, that is the rule with apocalypses. There would have been a clearer claim than just the name. The traditional and obvious way to understand the name is the Apostle John, though Dionysius of Alexandria mentions John Mark as held by some and he himself suggests another John, like the so-called Presbyter John of Papias as quoted by Eusebius. The uncertain language of Papias has raised a deal of questioning. Swete thinks that the majority of modern critics ascribe the Apocalypse to this Presbyter John, to whom Moffatt assigns probably II and III John. Irenæus represents the Apostle John as having lived to the time of Trajan, at least to A.D. 98. Most ancient writers agree with this extreme old age of John. Justin Martyr states expressly that the Apostle John wrote the Apocalypse. Irenæus called it the work of a disciple of Jesus. In the ninth century lived

Georgius Hamartolus, and a MS. of his alleges that Papias says that John the son of Zebedee was beheaded by the Jews and there is an extract in an Oxford MS. of the seventh century which alleges that Papias says John and James were put to death by the Jews. On the basis of this slim evidence some today argue that John did not live to the end of the century and so did not write any of the Johannine books. But a respectable number of modern scholars still hold to the ancient view that the Apocalypse of John is the work of the Apostle and Beloved Disciple, the son of Zebedee.

RELATION TO THE FOURTH GOSPEL

Here scholars divide again. Many who deny the Johannine authorship of the Fourth Gospel and the Epistles accept the apostolic authorship of the Apocalypse, Baur, for instance. Hort, Lightfoot, and Westcott argued for the Johannine authorship on the ground that the Apocalypse was written early (time of Nero or Vespasian) when John did not know Greek so well as when the Epistles and the Gospel were written. There are numerous grammatical laxities in the Apocalypse, termed by Charles a veritable grammar of its own. They are chiefly retention of the nominative case in appositional words or phrases, particularly participles, many of them sheer Hebraisms, many of them clearly intentional (as in Rev. 1:4), all of them on purpose according to Milligan (*Revelation* in Schaff's Pop. Comm.) and Heinrici (*Der Litterarische Charakter der neutest. Schriften*, p. 85). Radermacher (*Neutestamentliche Grammatik*, p. 3) calls it "the most uncultured literary production that has come down to us from antiquity," and one finds frequent parallels to the linguistic peculiarities in later illiterate papyri. J. H. Moulton (*Grammar*, Vol. II, Part I, p. 3) says: "Its grammar is perpetually stumbling, its idiom is that of a foreign language, its whole style that of a writer who neither knows nor cares for literary form." But we shall see that the best evidence is for a date in Domitian's reign and not much later than the Fourth Gospel. It is worth noting that in Acts 4:13 Peter and John are both termed by the Sanhedrin *agrammatoi kai idiōtai* (unlettered and unofficial men). We have seen the possibility that II Peter represents Peter's real style or at least that of a different amanuensis from Silvanus in I Pet. 5:12. It seems clear that the Fourth Gospel underwent careful scrutiny and possibly by the elders in Ephesus (John 21:24). If John wrote the Apocalypse while in Patmos and so away from Ephesus, it seems quite possible that here we have John's own uncorrected style more than in the Gospel and Epistles. There is also the added consideration that the excitement of the visions played a part along with a certain element of intentional variations from normal grammatical sequence. An old man's excitement would bring back his early style. There are numerous coincidences in vocabulary and style between the Fourth Gospel and the Apocalypse.

THE UNITY OF THE APOCALYPSE

Repeated efforts have been made to show that the Apocalypse of John is not the work of one man, but a series of Jewish and Christian apocalypses pieced together in a more or less bungling fashion. Spitta argued for this in 1889. Vischer was followed by Harnack in the view there was a Jewish apocalypse worked over by a Christian. Gunkel (*Creation and Chaos*, 1895) argued for a secret apocalyptic tradition of Babylonian origin. In 1904 J. Weiss carried on the argument for sources behind the Apocalypse. Many of the Jewish apocalypses do show composite authorship. There was a current eschatology which may have been drawn on without its being a written source. It is in chapter 12 where the supposed Jewish source is urged more vigorously about the woman, the dragon, and the man child. There are no differences in language (vocabulary or grammar) that argue for varied sources. The author may indeed make use of events in the reign of Nero as well as in the reign of Domitian, but the essential unity of the book has stood the test of the keenest criticism.

THE DATE

There are two chief theories, the Neronic, soon after Nero's death, the other in the reign of Domitian. Irenæus is quoted by Eusebius as saying expressly that the Apocalypse of John was written at the close of the reign of Domitian. This testimony is concurred in by Clement of Alexandria, by Origen, by Eusebius, by Jerome. In harmony with this clear testimony the severity of the persecutions suit the later date better than the earlier one. There is, besides, in Rev. 17:11f. an apparent reference to the story that Nero would return again. The fifth king who is one of the seven is an eighth. There was a Nero legend, to be sure, that Nero either was not dead but was in Parthia, or would be *redivivus* after death. Juvenal termed Domitian "a bald Nero" and others called Domitian "a second Nero." But in spite of all this Hort, Lightfoot, Sanday, Westcott have argued strongly for the Neronic era. Peake is willing to admit allusions to the Neronic period as Swete is also, but both consider the Domitianic date the best supported. Moffatt considers any earlier date than Domitian "almost impossible."

THE VISIONS

No theory of authorship, sources, or date should ignore the fact that the author claims to have had a series of visions in Patmos. It does not follow that he wrote them down at once and without reflection, but it seems hardly congruous to think that he waited till he had returned from exile in Patmos to Ephesus before writing them out. In fact, there is a note of sustained excitement all through the book, combined with high literary skill in the structure of the book in spite of the numerous grammatical lapses. The series of sevens bear a relation to one another, but more in the fashion of a kaleidoscope than of a chronological panorama. And yet there is progress and power in the arrangement and the total effect. There is constant use of Old Testament language and imagery, almost a mosaic, but without a single formal quotation. There is constant repetition of words and phrases in true Johannine style. Each of the messages to the seven churches picks out a metaphor in the first picture of Christ in chapter 1 and there are frequent other allusions to the language in this picture. In fact there is genuine artistic skill in the structure of the book, in spite of the deflections from ordinary linguistic standards. In the visions and all through the book there is constant use of symbols, as is the fashion in apocalypses like the beasts, the scorpions, the horses, etc. These symbols probably were understood by the first readers of the book, though the key to them is lost to us. Even the numbers in the book (3½, 7, 3, 4, 12, 24, 1000) cannot be pressed, though some do so. Even Harnack called the Apocalypse the plainest book in the New Testament, by using Harnack's key for the symbols.

THEORIES OF INTERPRETATION

They are literally many. There are those who make the book a chart of Christian and even of human history even to the end. These divide into two groups, the continuous and the synchronous. The continuous historical theory takes each vision and symbol in succession as an unfolding panorama. Under the influence of this theory there have been all sorts of fantastic identifications of men and events. The synchronous theory takes the series of sevens (seals, trumpets, bowls) as parallel with each other, each time going up to the end. But in neither case can any satisfactory program be arranged. Another historical interpretation takes it all as over and done, the preterist theory. This theory again breaks into two, one finding the fulfilment all in the Neronic period, the other in the Domitianic era. Something can be said for each view, but neither satisfies the whole picture by any means. Roman Catholic scholars have been fond of the preterist view to escape the Protestant interpretation of the second beast in chapter 13 as papal Rome. There is still another interpretation, the futurist, which keeps the fulfilment all in the future and which can be neither proved nor disproved. There is also the purely spiritual theory which finds no historical allusion anywhere. This again can be neither proved nor disproved. One of the lines of cleavage is the millennium in chapter 20. Those who take the thousand years literally are either premillennialists who look for the second coming of Christ to be followed by a thousand years of personal reign here on earth or the postmillennialists who place the thousand years before the second coming. There are others who turn to II Pet. 3:8 and wonder if, after all, in a book of symbols this thousand years has any numerical value at all. There seems abundant evidence to believe that this apocalypse, written during the stress and storm of Domitian's persecution, was intended to cheer the persecuted Christians with a view of certain victory at last, but with no scheme of history in view.

A Practical Purpose

So considered, this vision of the Reigning Christ in heaven with a constant eye on the suffering saints and martyrs is a guarantee of certain triumph in heaven and ultimate triumph on earth. The picture of Christ in heaven is a glorious one. He is the Lamb that was slain, the Lion of the tribe of Judah, the Word of God, the Victor over his enemies, worshipped in heaven like the Father, the Light and Life of men. Instead of trying to fit the various symbols on particular individuals one will do better to see the same application to times of persecution from time to time through the ages. The same Christ who was the Captain of salvation in the time of Domitian is the Pioneer and Perfecter of our faith today. The Apocalypse of John gives glimpses of heaven as well as of hell. Hope is the word that it brings to God's people at all times.

The Readers of the Book

The whole book is sent to the seven churches in Asia (1:4). There is a special message to each of the seven (chapters 2 and 3), suited to the peculiar needs of each church and with a direct reference to the geography and history of each church and city, so Ramsay holds (*The Letters to the Seven Churches*). The book is to be read aloud in each church (1:3). One can imagine the intense interest that the book would arouse in each church. Children are charmed to hear the Apocalypse read. They do not understand the symbols, but they see the pictures in the unfolding panorama. There were other churches in the Province of Asia besides these seven, but these form a circle from Ephesus where John had lived and wrought. They do present a variety of churches, not necessarily all types, and by no means a chart of seven dispensations of Christian history.

A BRIEF BIBLIOGRAPHY (ONLY BOOKS SINCE 1875)

ABBOTT, E. A., *Johannine Grammar* (1906).
————, *Notes on New Testament Criticism* (Part VII of Diatessarica, 1907).
ALLO, E. B., *L'apocalypse et l'époque de la parousia* (1915).
————, *Saint Jean. L'apocalypse* (1921).
BALDENSPERGER, *Messian. Apok. Hoffnung.* 3rd ed. (1903).
BALJON, J. M. S., *Openbaring van Johannes* (1908).

BECKWITH, J. T., *The Apocalypse of John* (1919).
BENSON, E. W., *The Apocalypse* (1900).
BERG, *The Drama of the Apocalypse* (1894).
BLEEK, F., *Lectures on the Apocalypse* (1875).
BOLL, *Aus der Offenbarung Johannis* (1914).
BOUSSET, W., *Die Offenbarung Johannis.* 2 Aufl. (1906).
————, *Zur Textkritik der Apokalypse* (1894).
BROWN, CHARLES, *Heavenly Visions* (1911).
BROWN, D., *The Structure of the Apocalypse* (1891).
BULLINGER, *Die Apokalypse* (1904).
BUNGEROTH, *Schlüssel zur Offenbarung Johannis* (1907).
BURGER, C. H. A., *Offenbarung Johannis* (1877).
CADWELL, *The Revelation of Jesus Christ* (1920).
CALMES, *L'Apokalypse devant la Critique* (1907).
CAMPBELL, *The Patmos Letters Applied to Modern Criticism*
    (1908).
CARRINGTON, P., *The Meaning of the Revelation* (1931).
CASE, S. J., *The Millennial Hope* (1918).
————, *The Revelation of John* (1920).
CHARLES, R. H., *Studies in the Apocalypse* (1913).
————, *The Revelation of St. John.* 2 vols. (1921).
CHEVALIN, *L'apocalypse et les temps presents* (1904).
CRAMPON, *L'Apocalypse de S. Jean* (1904).
DEAN, J. T., *The Book of Revelation* (1915).
DEISSMANN, A., *Light from the Ancient East.* Tr. by Strachan
    (1927).
DELAPORT, *Fragments sahidiques du N.T. Apocalypse* (1906).
DOUGLAS, C. E., *New Light on the Revelation of St. John the
    Divine* (1923).
DÜSTERDIECK, *Offenbarung Johannis.* 4 Aufl. (1887).
ECKMAN, *When Christ Comes Again* (1917).
ERBES, *Offenbar. Johan. Kritischuntersucht* (1891).
FORBES, H. P., *International Handbook on the Apocalypse*
    (1907).
GEBHARDT, *Doctrine of the Apocalypse* (1878).

Geil, W. E., *The Isle That Is Called Patmos* (1905).

Gibson, E. C. S., *The Revelation of St. John* (1910).

Gigot, *The Apocalypse of St. John* (1915).

Glazebrook, *The Apocalypse of St. John* (1924).

Gunkel, H., *Schöpfung und Chaos* (1895).

Gwynn, *The Apocalypse of St. John* (1897).

Harnack, A., *Die Chronologie der altchristlichen Litteratur.* Bd I (1897).

Henderson, B. W., *The Life and Principate of the Emperor Nero* (1903).

Hill, *Apocalyptic Problems* (1916).

Hill, Erskine, *Mystic Studies in the Apocalypse* (1931).

Hirscht, *Die Apokalypse und ihre neueste Kritik* (1895).

Holtzmann, H. J., *Die Offenbarung Johannis* (1891).

Holtzmann-Bauer, *Hand-Comm., Offenbarung des Johannis.* 3 Aufl. (1908).

Horne, *The Meaning of the Apocalypse* (1916).

Hort, F. J. A., *The Apocalypse of St. John, Chs. 1–3* (1908).

James, M. R., *The Apocalypse in Art* (1931).

Jowett, G. T., *The Apocalypse of St. John* (1910).

Kübel, *Offenbarung Johannis* (1893).

Laughlin, *The Solecisms of the Apocalypse* (1902).

Lee, S., *Revelation in Speaker's Comm.* (1881).

Linder, *Die Offenbarung des Johannis aufgeschlossen* (1905).

Llwyd, J. P. D., *The Son of Thunder* (1932).

Lohmeyer, E., *Die Offenbarung des Johannes.* Handbuch zum N.T. (1926).

Loisy, A., *L'Apocalypse de Jean* (1923).

Matheson, *Sidelights upon Patmos.*

Milligan, W., *The Revelation of St. John.* Schaff's Popular Comm. (1885).

————, *The Book of Revelation.* Expositor's Bible (1889).

————, *Lectures on the Apocalypse* (1892).

————, *Discussions on the Apocalypse* (1893).

Moffatt, James, *Intr. to Literature of the N.T.* (1911).

MOFFATT, JAMES, *Revelation in Expos. Greek Testament* (1910).

MOULE, H. C., *Some Thoughts on the Seven Epistles* (1915).

MOZLEY, *The Christian's Hope in the Apocalypse* (1915).

OMAN, JOHN, *The Book of Revelation* (1923).

————, *The Text of Revelation* (1928).

OSBORN, *The Lion and the Lamb* (1922).

PALMER, *The Drama of the Apocalypse* (1902).

PAUL, *Latter Day Light on the Apocalypse* (1898).

PEAKE, A. S., *The Revelation of John* (1921).

PORTER, F. C., *The Messages of the Apocalyptic Writers* (1905).

POUNDER, *Historical Notes on the Book of Revelation* (1912).

PRAGER, L., *Die Offenbarung Johannis* (1901).

RAMSAY, A., *Revelation in Westminster N.T.* (1910).

RAMSAY, W. M., *The Letters to the Seven Churches of Asia* (1904).

RAUCH, *Offenbarung des Johannis* (1894).

REYMOND, *L'apocalypse* (1908).

ROSS, J. J., *Pearls from Patmos* (1923).

RUSSELL, J. S., *The Parousia* (1878).

SABATIER, *Les Origines Littéraires et la Comp. de l'Apoc.* (1888).

SCHLATTER, *Der Evangelist Johannes* (1931).

SCHOEN, *L'Origine de l'Apocalypse* (1887).

SCOTT, C. ANDERSON, *Revelation in New Century Bible* (1902).

SCOTT, C. A., *Revelation in Devot. Comm.* (1906).

SCOTT, J. J., *Lectures on the Apocalypse* (1909).

SELWYN, E. C., *The Christian Prophets and the Prophetic Apocalypse* (1901).

SHEPHERD, W. J. L., *The Revelation of St. John the Divine.* 2 vols. (1923).

SIMCOX, W. H., *Revelation in Cambridge Greek Testament* (1893).

SMITH, J. A., *Revelation in American Comm.* (1888).

SMITH, J. A., *The World Lighted* (1890).

————, *The Divine Parable of History* (1901).

SPITTA, F., *Die Offenbarung des Johannis* (1889).

STRANGE, *Instructions on the Revelation of St. John the Divine* (1900).

SWETE, H. B., *The Apocalypse of St. John* (1906). 2nd ed. 1907.

TURNER, C. H., *Studies in Early Church History* (1912).

VISCHER, *Die Offenb. Johan. eine jüdische Apok* (1886).

VÖLTER, *Offenb. Johannis.* 2 Aufl. (1911).

————, *Das Problem der Apok.* (1893).

WEISS, B., *Die Johannes-Apokalypse.* Textkrit. (1891, 2 Aufl. 1902).

WEISS, J., *Offenb. Johannis* (1904).

WELLHAUSEN, J., *Analyse der Offenb.* (1907).

WEYLAND, *Omwerkings-en Compilatie-Hupothesen Toegepast op de Apok.* (1888).

WHITING, *The Revelation of John* (1918).

ZAHN, *Introduction to the N.T.* 3 vols. (1909).

————, *Komm.* (1926).

CHAPTER I

1. *The Revelation* (*apokalupsis*). Late and rare word outside of N.T. (once in Plutarch and so in the vernacular *Koiné*), only once in the Gospels (Luke 2:32), but in LXX and common in the Epistles (II Thess. 1:7), though only here in this book besides the title, from *apokaluptō*, old verb, to uncover, to unveil. In the Epistles *apokalupsis* is used for insight into truth (Eph. 1:17) or for the revelation of God or Christ at the second coming of Christ (II Thess. 1:7; I Pet. 1:7). It is interesting to compare *apokalupsis* with *epiphaneia* (II Thess. 2:8) and *phanerōsis* (I Cor. 12:7). The precise meaning here turns on the genitive following. *Of Jesus Christ* (*Iēsou Christou*). Hort takes it as objective genitive (revelation about Jesus Christ), but Swete rightly argues for the subjective genitive because of the next clause. *Gave him* (*edōken autoi*). It is the Son who received the revelation from the Father, as is usual (John 5:20f., 26, etc.). *To shew* (*deixai*). First aorist active infinitive of *deiknumi*, purpose of God in giving the revelation to Christ. *Unto his servants* (*tois doulois autou*). Believers in general and not just to officials. Dative case. God's servants (or Christ's). *Must shortly come to pass* (*dei genesthai en tachei*). Second aorist middle infinitive of *ginomai* with *dei*. See this same adjunct (*en tachei*) in Luke 18:8; Rom. 16:20; Rev. 22:6. It is a relative term to be judged in the light of II Pet. 3:8 according to God's clock, not ours. And yet undoubtedly the hopes of the early Christians looked for a speedy return of the Lord Jesus. This vivid panorama must be read in the light of that glorious hope and of the blazing fires of persecution from Rome. *Sent and signified* (*esēmanen aposteilas*). "Having sent (first aorist active participle of *apo-*

stellō, Matt. 10:16 and again in Rev. 22:6 of God sending his angel) signified" (first aorist active indicative of *sēmainō*, from *sēma*, sign or token, for which see John 12:33; Acts 11:28). See 12:1 for *sēmeion*, though *sēmainō* (only here in the Apocalypse) suits admirably the symbolic character of the book. *By his angel (dia tou aggelou autou)*. Christ's angel as Christ is the subject of the verb *esēmanen*, as in 22:16 Christ sends his angel, though in 22:6 God sends. *Unto his servant John (tōi doulōi autou Iōanei)*. Dative case. John gives his name here, though not in Gospel or Epistles, because "prophecy requires the guarantee of the individual who is inspired to utter it" (Milligan). "The genesis of the Apocalypse has now been traced from its origin in the Mind of God to the moment when it reached its human interpreter" (Swete). "Jesus is the medium of all revelation" (Moffatt).

2. *Bare witness (emarturēsen)*. First aorist active indicative of *martureō*, which, along with *martus* and *marturia*, is common in all the Johannine books (cf. 22:18, 20), usually with *peri* or *hoti*, but with cognate accusative as here in 22:16, 20; I John 5:10. Epistolary aorist here, referring to this book. *The word of God (ton logon tou theou)*. Subjective genitive, given by God. The prophetic word as in 1:9; 6:9; 20:4, not the personal Word as in 19:14. *The testimony of Jesus Christ (tēn marturian Iēsou Christou)*. Subjective genitive again, borne witness to by Jesus Christ. *Even of all the things that he saw (hosa eiden)*. Relative clause in apposition with *logon* and *marturian*.

3. *Blessed (makarios)*. As in Matt. 5:3ff. This endorses the book as a whole. *He that readeth (ho anaginōskōn)*. Present active singular articular participle of *anaginōskō* (as in Luke 4:16). Christians in their public worship followed the Jewish custom of public reading of the Scriptures (II Cor. 3:14f.). The church reader (*anagnōstēs*, *lector*) gradually acquired an official position. John expects this book to

be read in each of the seven churches mentioned (1:4) and elsewhere. Today the public reading of the Bible is an important part of worship that is often poorly done. *They that hear* (*hoi akouontes*). Present active plural articular participle of *akouō* (the audience). *And keep* (*kai tērountes*). Present active participle of *tēreō*, a common Johannine word (I John 2:4, etc.). Cf. Matt. 7:24. "The content of the Apocalypse is not merely prediction; moral counsel and religious instruction are the primary burdens of its pages" (Moffatt). *Written* (*gegrammena*). Perfect passive participle of *graphō*. *For the time is at hand* (*ho gar kairos eggus*). Reason for listening and keeping. On *kairos* see Matt. 12:1, time of crisis as in I Cor. 7:29. How near *eggus* (at hand) is we do not know any more than we do about *en tachei* (shortly) in 1:1.

4. *To the seven churches which are in Asia* (*tais hepta ekklēsiais tais en tēi Asiāi*). Dative case as in a letter (Gal. 1:1). John is writing, but the revelation is from God and Christ through an angel. It is the Roman province of Asia which included the western part of Phrygia. There were churches also at Troas (Acts 20:5ff.) and at Colossæ and Hierapolis (Col. 1:1; 2:1; 4:13) and possibly at Magnesia and Tralles. But these seven were the best points of communication with seven districts (Ramsay) and, besides, seven is a favorite number of completion (like the full week) in the book (1:4, 12, 16; 4:5; 5:1, 6; 8:2; 10:3; 11:13; 12:3; 13:1; 14:6f.). *From him which is* (*apo ho ōn*). This use of the articular nominative participle of *eimi* after *apo* instead of the ablative is not due to ignorance or a mere slip (*lapsus pennae*), for in the next line we have the regular idiom with *apo tōn hepta pneumatōn*. It is evidently on purpose to call attention to the eternity and unchangeableness of God. Used of God in Ex. 3:14. *And which was* (*kai ho ēn*). Here again there is a deliberate change from the articular participle to the relative use of *ho* (used in place of *hos* to preserve identity of

form in the three instances like Ionic relative and since no aorist participle of *eimi* existed). The oracle in Pausanias X. 12 has it: *Zeus ēn, Zeus esti, Zeus essetai* (Zeus was, Zeus is, Zeus will be). *Which is to come* (*ho erchomenos*). "The Coming One," futuristic use of the present participle instead of *ho esomenos*. See the same idiom in verse 8 and 4:8 and (without *ho erchomenos*) in 11:17; 16:5. *From the seven spirits* (*apo tōn hepta pneumatōn*). A difficult symbolic representation of the Holy Spirit here on a par with God and Christ, a conclusion borne out by the symbolic use of the seven spirits in 3:1; 4:5; 5:6 (from Zech. 4:2–10). There is the one Holy Spirit with seven manifestations here to the seven churches (Swete, *The Holy Spirit in the N.T.*, p. 374), unity in diversity (I Cor. 12:4). *Which are* (*tōn* article Aleph A, *ha* relative P). *Before his throne* (*enōpion tou thronou autou*). As in 4:5f.

5. *Who is the faithful witness* (*ho martus ho pistos*). "The witness the faithful," nominative in apposition like *prōtotokos* and *archōn* with the preceding ablative *Iēsou Christou* with *apo*, a habit of John in this book (apparently on purpose) as in 2:13, 20; 3:12, etc. See this same phrase in 2:13; 3:14. The use of *martus* of Jesus here is probably to the witness (1:1) in this book (22:16f.), not to the witness of Jesus before Pilate (I Tim. 6:13). *The first-born of the dead* (*ho prōtotokos tōn nekrōn*). A Jewish Messianic title (Ps. 88:28) and as in Col. 1:18 refers to priority in the resurrection to be followed by others. See Luke 2:7 for the word. *The ruler of the kings of the earth* (*ho archōn tōn basileōn tēs gēs*). Jesus by his resurrection won lordship over the kings of earth (17:14; 19:16), what the devil offered him by surrender (Matt. 4:8f.). *Unto him that loveth us* (*tōi agapōnti hēmās*). Dative of the articular present (not aorist *agapēsanti*) active participle of *agapaō* in a doxology to Christ, the first of many others to God and to Christ (1:6; 4:11; 5:9, 12f.; 7:10, 12, etc.). For the thought see John 3:16. *Loosed*

(*lusanti*). First aorist active participle of *luō* (Aleph A C),
though some MSS. (P Q) read *lousanti* (washed), a manifest
correction. Note the change of tense. Christ loosed us once
for all, but loves us always. *By his blood (en tōi haimati
autou*). As in 5:9. John here as in the Gospel and Epistles
states plainly and repeatedly the place of the blood of
Christ in the work of redemption.

6. *And he made (kai epoiēsen*). Change from the participle construction, which would be *kai poiēsanti* (first
aorist active of *poieō*) like *lusanti* just before, a Hebraism
Charles calls it, but certainly an anacoluthon of which John
is very fond, as in 1:18; 2:2, 9, 20; 3:9; 7:14; 14:2f.; 15:3.
Kingdom (basileian). So correctly Aleph A C, not *basileis*
(P cursives). Perhaps a reminiscence of Ex. 19:6, a kingdom
of priests. In 5:10 we have again "a kingdom and priests."
The idea here is that Christians are the true spiritual Israel
in God's promise to Abraham as explained by Paul in Gal.
3 and Rom. 9. *To be priests (hiereis*). In apposition with
basileian, but with *kai* (and) in 5:10. Each member of this
true kingdom is a priest unto God, with direct access to
him at all times. *Unto his God and Father (tōi theōi kai
patri autou*). Dative case and *autou* (Christ) applies to
both *theōi* and *patri*. Jesus spoke of the Father as his God
(Matt. 27:46; John 20:17) and Paul uses like language (Eph.
1:17), as does Peter (I Pet. 1:3). *To him (autōi*). Another
doxology to Christ. "The adoration of Christ which vi-
brates in this doxology is one of the most impressive features of the book" (Moffatt). Like doxologies to Christ
appear in 5:13; 7:10; I Pet. 4:11; II Pet. 3:18; II Tim. 4:18;
Heb. 13:21. These same words (*hē doxa kai to kratos*) in
I Pet. 4:11, only *hē doxa* in II Pet. 3:18 and II Tim. 4:18,
but with several others in Rev. 5:13 and 7:10.

7. *Behold, he cometh with the clouds (idou erchetai meta tōn
nephelōn*). Futuristic present middle indicative of *erchomai*,
a reminiscence of Dan. 7:13 (Theodotion). "It becomes a

common eschatological refrain" (Beckwith) as in Mark 13:26; 14:62; Matt. 24:30; 26:64; Luke 21:27. "Compare the manifestation of God in the clouds at Sinai, in the cloudy pillar, the Shekinah, at the transfiguration" (Vincent). *Shall see* (*opsetai*). Future middle of *horaō*, a reminiscence of Zech. 12:10 according to the text of Theodotion (Aquila and Symmachus) rather than the LXX and like that of Matt. 24:30 (similar combination of Daniel and Zechariah) and 26:64. This picture of the victorious Christ in his return occurs also in 14:14, 18–20; 19:11–21; 20:7–10. *And they which* (*kai hoitines*). "And the very ones who," Romans and Jews, all who shared in this act. *Pierced* (*exekentēsan*). First aorist active indicative of *ekkenteō*, late compound (Aristotle, Polybius, LXX), from *ek* and *kenteō* (to stab, to pierce), in N.T., only here and John 19:37, in both cases from Zech. 12:10, but not the LXX text (apparently proof that John used the original Hebrew or the translation of Theodotion and Aquila). *Shall mourn* (*kopsontai*). Future middle (direct) of *koptō*, old verb, to cut, "they shall cut themselves," as was common for mourners (Matt. 11:17; Luke 8:52; 23:27). From Zech. 12:12. See also Rev. 18:9. *Tribes* (*phulai*). Not just the Jewish tribes, but the spiritual Israel of Jews and Gentiles as in 7:4–8. No nation had then accepted Christ as Lord and Saviour, nor has any yet done so.

8. *The Alpha and the Omega* (*to Alpha kai to Ō*). The first and the last letters of the Greek alphabet, each with its own neuter (grammatical gender) article. This description of the eternity of God recurs in 21:6 with the added explanation *hē archē kai to telos* (the Beginning and the End) and of Christ in 22:13 with the still further explanation *ho prōtos kai ho eschatos* (the First and the Last). This last phrase appears also in 1:17 and 2:8 without *to Alpha kai to Ō*. The change of speaker here is unannounced, as in 16:15; 18:20. Only here and 21:5f. is God introduced as

the speaker. The eternity of God guarantees the prophecy just made. *The Lord God* (*Kurios ho theos*). "The Lord the God." Common phrase in Ezekiel (6:3, 11; 7:2, etc.) and in this book (4:8; 11:17; 15:3; 16:7; 19:6; 21:22). See 1:4 and 4:8 for the triple use of *ho*, etc. to express the eternity of God. *The Almighty* (*ho pantokratōr*). Late compound (*pās* and *krateō*), in Cretan inscription and a legal papyrus, common in LXX and Christian papyri, in N.T. only in II Cor. 6:18 (from Jer. 38:35) and Rev. 1:8; 4:8; 11:17; 15:3; 16:7, 14; 19:6, 15; 21:22.

9. *I John* (*Egō Iōanēs*). So 22:8. In apocalyptic literature the personality of the writer is always prominent to guarantee the visions (Dan. 8:1; 10:2). *Partaker with you* (*sunkoinōnos*). See already I Cor. 9:23. "Co-partner with you" (Rom. 11:17). One article with *adelphos* and *sunkoinōnos* unifying the picture. The absence of *apostolos* here does not show that he is not an apostle, but merely his self-effacement, as in the Fourth Gospel, and still more his oneness with his readers. So there is only one article (*tēi*) with *thlipsei* (tribulation), *basileiāi* (kingdom), *hupomonēi* (patience), ideas running all through the book. Both the tribulation (see Matt. 13:21 for *thlipsis*) and the kingdom (see Matt. 3:2 for *basileia*) were present realities and called for patience (*hupomonē* being "the spiritual alchemy" according to Charles for those in the kingdom, for which see Luke 8:15; James 5:7). All this is possible only "in Jesus" (*en Iēsou*), a phrase on a par with Paul's common *en Christōi* (in Christ), repeated in 14:13. Cf. 3:20 and II Thess. 3:5. *Was* (*egenomēn*). Rather, "I came to be," second aorist middle indicative of *ginomai*. *In the isle that is called Patmos* (*en tēi nēsōi tēi kaloumenēi Patmōi*). Patmos is a rocky sparsely settled island some ten miles long and half that wide, one of the Sporades group in the Ægean Sea, south of Miletus. The present condition of the island is well described by W. E. Geil in *The Isle That Is Called*

Patmos (1905). Here John saw the visions described in the book, apparently written while still a prisoner there in exile. *For the word of God and the testimony of Jesus (dia ton logon tou theou kai tēn marturian Iēsou).* The reason for (*dia* and the accusative) John's presence in Patmos, naturally as a result of persecution already alluded to, not for the purpose of preaching there or of receiving the visions. See verse 2 for the phrase.

10. *I was in the Spirit (egenomēn en pneumati).* Rather, "I came to be (as in 1:9) in the Spirit," came into an ecstatic condition as in Acts 10:10f.; 22:17, not the normal spiritual condition (*einai en pneumati,* Rom. 8:9). *On the Lord's Day (en tēi kuriakēi hēmerāi).* Deissmann has proven (*Bible Studies,* p. 217f.; *Light,* etc., p. 357ff.) from inscriptions and papyri that the word *kuriakos* was in common use for the sense "imperial" as imperial finance and imperial treasury and from papyri and ostraca that *hēmera Sebastē* (Augustus Day) was the first day of each month, Emperor's Day on which money payments were made (cf. I Cor. 16:1f.). It was easy, therefore, for the Christians to take this term, already in use, and apply it to the first day of the week in honour of the Lord Jesus Christ's resurrection on that day (*Didache* 14, Ignatius *Magn.* 9). In the N.T. the word occurs only here and I Cor. 11:20 (*kuriakon deipnon* the Lord's Supper). It has no reference to *hēmera kuriou* (the day of judgment, II Pet. 3:10). *Behind me (opisō mou).* "The unexpected, overpowering entrance of the divine voice" (Vincent). Cf. Ezek. 3:12. *Voice (phōnēn).* Of Christ, as is plain in verses 12f. *As of a trumpet (hōs salpiggos).* So in 4:1 referring to this. *Saying (legousēs).* Present active participle genitive case agreeing with *salpiggos* rather than *legousan,* accusative agreeing with *phōnēn.* So on purpose, as is clear from 4:1, where *lalousēs* also agrees with *salpiggos.*

11. *Write in a book (grapson eis biblion).* First aorist ac-

tive imperative of *grapho* for instantaneous action. The commission covers the whole series of visions which all grow out of this first vision of the Risen Christ. *Send* (*pempson*). First aorist active imperative of *pempo*. Part of the commission from Christ. The names of the seven churches of 1:4 are now given, and the particular message to each church comes in chapters 2 and 3 and in the same order, the geographical order going north from Ephesus, then east and south to Laodicea. But apparently the whole book was to be read to each of the seven churches. It would probably also be copied at each church.

12. *To see the voice* (*blepein tēn phōnēn*). The voice put for the person speaking. *Having turned* (*epistrepsas*). First aorist active participle of *epistrephō*, from which also *epestrepsa*, just before, for which verb see Acts 15:36; 16:18. *Seven golden candlesticks* (*hepta luchnias chrusas*). See Matt. 5:15 for *luchnia* (lampstand). Symbols of the seven churches as explained in verse 20. See Ex. 25:35ff. for description of a seven-branched candlestick, but here the lampstands are separate.

13. *One like unto a son of man* (*homoion huion anthrōpou*). Note accusative here with *homoion* (object of *eidon*) as in 14:14 and not the associative-instrumental as is usual (1:15; 4:3, 6). Charles holds that *homoion* here has the sense of *hōs* (as) and compares 4:6 with 22:1 for proof. The absence of the article here shows also (Charles) that the idea is not "like the Son of man" for Christ *is* the Son of man. He is like "a son of man," but not a man. *Clothed* (*endedumenon*). Perfect passive participle of *enduō*, accusative case agreeing with *homoion*. *A garment down to the foot* (*podērē*). Old adjective *podērēs* (from *pous*, foot, and *airō*), here only in N.T., accusative singular retained with the passive participle as often with verbs of clothing. Supply *chitōna* or *esthēta* (garment). *Girt about* (*periezōsmenon*). Perfect passive participle of *perizōnnumi*, accusative singular agreeing

with *homoion*. *At the breasts* (*pros tois mastois*). Old word
for breasts of a woman (Luke 11:27; 23:29) and nipples of
a man, as here. High girding like this was a mark of dignity
as of the high priest (Josephus, *Ant.* III. 7. 2). For *pros*
with the locative see Mark 5:11. *With a golden girdle*
(*zōnēn chrusān*). Accusative case again retained with the
passive participle (verb of clothing). Note also *chrusān*
(vernacular *Koiné*) rather than the old form, *chrusēn*.

14. *As white wool* (*hōs erion leukon*). *Erion* (wool) in
N.T. only here and Heb. 9:19, though old word. The person of the Lord Jesus is here described in language largely
from Dan. 7:9 (the Ancient of Days). *White as snow* (*hōs
chiōn*). Just "as snow," also in Dan. 7:9. In N.T. only
here and Matt. 28:3. *As a flame of fire* (*hōs phlox puros*).
In Dan. 7:9 the throne of the Ancient of Days is *phlox puros*,
while in Dan. 10:6 the eyes of the Ancient of Days are
lampades puros (lamps of fire). See also 2:18 and 19:12 for
this bold metaphor (like Heb. 1:7).

15. *Burnished brass* (*chalkolibanōi*). Associative-instrumental case after *homoioi*. This word has so far been found
nowhere else save here and 2:18. Suidas defines it as an
ēlecktron (amber) or a compound of copper and gold and
silver (*aurichalcum* in the Latin Vulgate). It is in reality
an unknown metal. *As if it had been refined* (*hōs pepuro-
menēs*). Perfect passive participle of *puroō*, old verb, to
set on fire, to glow, as in Eph. 6:16; Rev. 3:18. The feminine gender shows that *hē chalkolibanos* is referred to with
tēs chalkolibanou understood, for it does not agree in case
with the associative-instrumental *chalkolibanōi* just before.
Some would call it a slip for *pepuromenoi* as Aleph, and some
cursives have it (taking *chalkolibanōi* to be neuter, not
feminine). But P Q read *pepurōmenoi* (masculine plural),
a correction, making it agree in number and gender with
podes (feet). *In a furnace* (*en kaminōi*). Old word, in
N.T. also 9:2; Matt. 13:42, 50. *As the voice of many waters*

(*hōs phōnē hudatōn pollōn*). So the voice of God in the Hebrew (not the LXX) of Ezek. 43:2. Repeated in 14:2; 19:6.

16. *And he had* (*kai echōn*). "And having," present active participle of *echō*, loose use of the participle (almost like *eiche*, imperfect) and not in agreement with *autou*, genitive case. This is a common idiom in the book; a Hebraism, Charles calls it. *In his right hand* (*en tēi dexiāi cheiri*). For safe keeping as in John 10:28. *Seven stars* (*asteras hepta*). Symbols of the seven churches (verse 20), seven planets rather than Pleiades or any other constellation like the bear. *Proceeded* (*ekporeuomenē*). Present middle participle of *ekporeuomai*, old compound (Matt. 3:5) used loosely again like *echōn*. *A sharp two-edged sword* (*romphaia distomos oxeia*). "A sword two-mouthed sharp." *Romphaia* (as distinct from *machaira*) is a long sword, properly a Thracian javelin, in N.T. only Luke 2:35 and Rev. 1:16; 2:12; Heb. 4:12. See *stoma* used with *machairēs* in Luke 21:24 (by the mouth of the sword). *Countenance* (*opsis*). Old word (from *optō*), in N.T. only here, John 7:24; 11:44. *As the sun shineth* (*hōs ho hēlios phainei*). Brachylogy, "as the sun when it shines." For *phainei* see John 1:5.

17. *I fell* (*epesa*). Late form for the old *epeson* (second aorist active indicative of *piptō*, to fall). Under the overpowering influence of the vision as in 19:10. *He laid* (*ethēken*). First aorist active indicative of *tithēmi*. The act restored John's confidence. *Fear not* (*mē phobou*). Cf. Luke 1:13 to Zacharias to give comfort. *I am the first and the last* (*egō eimi ho prōtos kai ho eschatos*). Used in Is. 44:6 and 48:12 of God, but here, 2:8; 22:13 of Christ. *And the Living One* (*kai ho zōn*). Present active articular participle of *zaō*, another epithet of God common in the O.T. (Deut. 32:40; Is. 49:18, etc.) and applied purposely to Jesus, with which see John 5:26 for Christ's own words about it.

18. *And I was dead* (*kai egenomēn nekros*). "And I became dead" (aorist middle participle of *ginomai* as in 1:9, 10, definite reference to the Cross). *I am alive* (*zōn eimi*). Periphrastic present active indicative, "I am living," as the words *ho zōn* just used mean. *Forevermore* (*eis tous aiōnas tōn aiōnōn*). "Unto the ages of the ages," a stronger expression of eternity even than in 1:6. *The keys* (*tas kleis*). One of the forms for the accusative plural along with *kleidas*, the usual one (Matt. 16:19). *Of death and of Hades* (*tou thanatou kai tou hāidou*). Conceived as in Matt. 16:18 as a prison house or walled city. The keys are the symbol of authority, as we speak of honouring one by giving him the keys of the city. Hades here means the unseen world to which death is the portal. Jesus has the keys because of his victory over death. See this same graphic picture in 6:8; 20:13f. For the key of David see 3:7, for the key of the abyss see 9:1; 20:1.

19. *Therefore* (*oun*). In view of Christ's words about himself in verse 18 and the command in verse 11. *Which thou sawest* (*ha eides*). The vision of the Glorified Christ in verses 13–18. *The things which are* (*ha eisin*). Plural verb (individualising the items) though *ha* is neuter plural, certainly the messages to the seven churches (1:20 to 3:22) in relation to the world in general, possibly also partly epexegetic or explanatory of *ha eides*. *The things which shall come to pass hereafter* (*ha mellei ginesthai meta tauta*). Present middle infinitive with *mellei*, though both aorist and future are also used. Singular verb here (*mellei*) blending in a single view the future. In a rough outline this part begins in 4:1 and goes to end of chapter 22, though the future appears also in chapters 2 and 3 and the present occurs in 4 to 22 and the elements in the vision of Christ (1:13–18) reappear repeatedly.

20. *The mystery of the seven stars* (*to mustērion tōn hepta asterōn*). On the word *mustērion* see on Matt. 13:11; II

Thess. 2:7; Col. 1:26. Here it means the inner meaning (the secret symbol) of a symbolic vision (Swete) as in 10:7; 13:18; 17:7, 9 and Dan. 2:47. Probably the accusative absolute (Charles), "as for the mystery" (Robertson, *Grammar*, pp. 490, 1130), as in Rom. 8:3. This item is picked out of the previous vision (1:16) as needing explanation at once and as affording a clue to what follows (2:1, 5). *Which* (*hous*). Masculine accusative retained without attraction to case of *asterōn* (genitive, *hōn*). *In my right hand* (*epi tēs dexias mou*). Or "upon," but *en tēi*, etc., in verse 16. *And the seven golden candlesticks* (*kai tas hepta luchnias tas chrusās*). "The seven lampstands the golden," identifying the stars of verse 16 with the lampstands of verse 12. The accusative case here is even more peculiar than the accusative absolute *mustērion*, since the genitive *luchniōn* after *mustērion* is what one would expect. Charles suggests that John did not revise his work. *The angels of the seven churches* (*aggeloi tōn hepta ekklēsiōn*). Anarthrous in the predicate (angels of, etc.). "The seven churches" mentioned in 1:4, 11. Various views of *aggelos* here exist. The simplest is the etymological meaning of the word as messenger from *aggellō* (Matt. 11:10) as messengers from the seven churches to Patmos or by John from Patmos to the churches (or both). Another view is that *aggelos* is the pastor of the church, the reading *tēn gunaika sou* (thy wife) in 2:20 (if genuine) confirming this view. Some would even take it to be the bishop over the elders as *episcopos* in Ignatius, but a separate *aggelos* in each church is against this idea. Some take it to be a symbol for the church itself or the spirit and genius of the church, though distinguished in this very verse from the churches themselves (the lampstands). Others take it to be the guardian angel of each church assuming angelic patrons to be taught in Matt. 18:10; Acts 12:15. Each view is encompassed with difficulties, perhaps fewer belonging to the view that the "angel" is the pastor. *Are seven churches (hepta ekklēsiai eisin).* These seven churches (1:4, 11) are themselves lampstands (1:12) reflecting the light of Christ to the world (Matt. 5:14–16; John 8:12) in the midst of which Christ walks (1:13).

CHAPTER II

1. *In Ephesus* (*en Ephesōi*). Near the sea on the river Cayster, the foremost city of Asia Minor, the temple-keeper of Artemis and her wonderful temple (Acts 19:35), the home of the magic arts (Ephesian letters, Acts 19:19) and of the mystery-cults, place of Paul's three years' stay (Acts 19:1–10; 20:17–38), where Aquila and Priscilla and Apollos laboured (Acts 18:24–28), where Timothy wrought (I and II Tim.), where the Apostle John preached in his old age. Surely it was a place of great privilege, of great preaching. It was about sixty miles from Patmos and the messenger would reach Ephesus first. It is a free city, a seat of proconsular government (Acts 19:38), the end of the great road from the Euphrates. The port was a place of shifting sands, due to the silting up of the mouth of the Cayster. Ramsay (*Letters to the Seven Churches*, p. 210) calls it "the City of Change." *These things* (*tade*). This demonstrative seven times here, once with the message to each church (2:1, 8, 12, 18; 2:1, 7, 14), only once elsewhere in N.T. (Acts 21:11). *He that holdeth* (*ho kratōn*). Present active articular participle of *krateō*, a stronger word than *echōn* in 1:16, to which it refers. *He that walketh* (*ho peripatōn*). Present active articular participle of *peripateō*, an allusion to 1:13. These two epithets are drawn from the picture of Christ in 1:13–18, and appropriately to conditions in Ephesus describe Christ's power over the churches as he moves among them.

2. *I know* (*oida*). Rather than *ginōskō* and so "emphasizes better the absolute clearness of mental vision which photographs all the facts of life as they pass" (Swete). So also in 2:9, 13, 19; 3:1, 8, 15. For the distinction see John 21:17, "where the universal knowledge passes into the field

of special observation." *Works* (*erga*). The whole life and conduct as in John 6:29. *And thy toil and patience* (*kai ton kopon kai tēn hupomonēn sou*). "Both thy toil and patience," in explanation of *erga*, and see I Thess. 1:3, where all three words (*ergon, kopos, hupomonē*) occur together as here. See 14:13 for sharp distinction between *erga* (activities) and *kopoi* (toils, with weariness). Endurance (*hupomonē*) in hard toil (*kopos*). *And that* (*kai hoti*). Further explanation of *kopos* (hard toil). *Not able* (*ou dunēi*). This *Koiné* form for the Attic *dunasai* (second person singular indicative middle) occurs also in Mark 9:22; Luke 16:2. *Bear* (*bastasai*). First aorist active infinitive of *bastazō*, for which verb see John 10:31; 12:6; Gal. 6:2. These evil men were indeed a heavy burden. *And didst try* (*kai epeirasas*). First aorist active indicative of *peirazō*, to test, a reference to a recent crisis when these Nicolaitans (verse 6) were condemned. The present tenses (*dunēi, echeis*) indicate the continuance of this attitude. Cf. I John 4:1. *Which call themselves apostles* (*tous legontas heautous apostolous*). Perhaps itinerant missionaries of these Nicolaitans who posed as equal to or even superior to the original apostles, like the Judaizers so described by Paul (II Cor. 11:5, 13; 12:11). Paul had foretold such false teachers (Gnostics), grievous wolves, in Acts 20:29; in sheep's clothing, Jesus had said (Matt. 7:15). *And they are not* (*kai ouk eisin*). A parenthesis in Johannine style (John 2:9; 3:9; I John 3:1) for *kai ouk ontas* to correspond to *legontas*. *And didst find* (*kai heures*). Second aorist active indicative of *heuriskō*. Dropping back to the regular structure parallel with *epeirasas*. *False* (*pseudeis*). Predicate accusative plural of *pseudēs*, self-deceived deceivers as in 21:8.

3. *Thou hast* (*echeis*). Continued possession of patience. *Didst bear* (*ebastasas*). First aorist indicative of *bastazō*, repeated reference to the crisis in verse 2. *And hast not grown weary* (*kai ou kekopiakes*). Perfect active indicative of

kopiaō, old verb, to grow weary (Matt. 6:28), play on the word *kopos*, late form in *-es*, for the regular *-as* (*lelukas*), like *aphēkes* (verse 4) and *peptōkes* (verse 5). "Tired in loyalty, not of it. The Ephesian church can bear anything except the presence of impostors in her membership" (Moffatt).

4. *This against thee, that* (*kata sou hoti*). For the phrase "have against" see Matt. 5:23. The *hoti* clause is the object of *echō*. *Thou didst leave* (*aphēkes*). First aorist active (kappa aorist, but with *-es* instead of *-as*) of *aphiēmi*, a definite and sad departure. *Thy first love* (*tēn agapēn sou tēn prōtēn*). "Thy love the first." This early love, proof of the new life in Christ (I John 3:13f.), had cooled off in spite of their doctrinal purity. They had remained orthodox, but had become unloving partly because of the controversies with the Nicolaitans.

5. *Remember* (*mnēmoneue*). Present active imperative of *mnēmoneuō*, "continue mindful" (from *mnēmōn*). *Thou art fallen* (*peptōkes*). Perfect active indicative of *piptō*, state of completion. Down in the valley, look up to the cliff where pure love is and whence thou hast fallen down. *And repent* (*kai metanoēson*). First aorist active imperative of *metanoeō*, urgent appeal for instant change of attitude and conduct before it is too late. *And do* (*kai poiēson*). First aorist active imperative of *poieō*, "Do at once." *The first works* (*ta prōta erga*). Including the first love (Acts 19:20; 20:37; Eph. 1:3ff.) which has now grown cold (Matt. 24:12). *Or else* (*ei de mē*). Elliptical condition, the verb not expressed (*metanoeis*), a common idiom, seen again in verse 16, the condition expressed in full by *ean mē* in this verse and verse 22. *I come* (*erchomai*). Futuristic present middle (John 14:2f.). *To thee* (*soi*). Dative, as in 2:16 also. *Will move* (*kinēsō*). Future active of *kineō*. In Ignatius' Epistle to Ephesus it appears that the church heeded this warning. *Except thou repent* (*ean mē metanoēsēis*). Condition of third

class with *ean mē* instead of *ei mē* above, with the first
aorist active subjunctive of *metanoeō*.

6. *That thou hatest* (*hoti miseis*). Accusative object clause
in apposition with *touto* (this). Trench tells of the words
used in ancient Greek for hatred of evil (*misoponēria*) and
misoponēros (hater of evil), neither of which occurs in the
N.T., but which accurately describe the angel of the church
in Ephesus. *Of the Nicolaitans* (*tōn Nikolaitōn*). Mentioned
again in verse 15 and really meant in verse 2. Irenæus and
Hippolytus take this sect to be followers of Nicolaus of
Antioch, one of the seven deacons (Acts 6:5), a Jewish
proselyte, who is said to have apostatized. There was such
a sect in the second century (Tertullian), but whether de-
scended from Nicolaus of Antioch is not certain, though
possible (Lightfoot). It is even possible that the Balaamites
of verse 14 were a variety of this same sect (verse 15).
Which I also hate (*ha kagō misō*). Christ himself hates the
teachings and deeds of the Nicolaitans (*ha*, not *hous*, deeds,
not people), but the church in Pergamum tolerated them.

7. *He that hath an ear* (*ho echōn ous*). An individualizing
note calling on each of the hearers (1:3) to listen (2:7, 11,
17, 28; 3:3, 6, 13, 22) and a reminiscence of the words of
Jesus in the Synoptics (Matt. 11:15; 13:9, 43; Mark 4:9,
23; Luke 8:8; 14:35), but not in John's Gospel. *The spirit*
(*to pneuma*). The Holy Spirit as in 14:13; 22:17. Both
Christ and the Holy Spirit deliver this message. "The
Spirit of Christ in the prophet is the interpreter of Christ's
voice" (Swete). *To him that overcometh* (*tōi nikōnti*). Dative of the present (continuous victory) active articular participle of *nikaō*, a common Johannine verb (John 16:33;
I John 2:13f.; 4:4; 5:4f.; Rev. 2:7, 11, 17, 26; 3:5, 12, 21;
5:5; 12:11; 15:2; 17:14; 21:7). Faith is dominant in Paul,
victory in John, faith is victory (I John 5:4). So in each
promise to these churches. *I will give* (*dōsō*). Future active of *didōmi* as in 2:10, 17, 23, 26, 28; 3:8, 21; 6:4; 11:3;

21:6. *To eat* (*phagein*). Second aorist active infinitive of *esthiō*. *Of the tree of life* (*ek tou xulou tēs zōēs*). Note *ek* with the ablative with *phagein*, like our "eat of" (from or part of). From Gen. 2:9; 3:22. Again in Rev. 22:2, 14 as here for immortality. This tree is now in the Garden of God. For the water of life see 21:6; 22:17 (Cf. John 4:10, 13f.). *Which* (*ho*). The *xulon* (tree). *In the Paradise of God* (*en tōi paradeisōi tou theou*). Persian word, for which see Luke 23:43; II Cor. 12:4. The abode of God and the home of the redeemed with Christ, not a mere intermediate state. It was originally a garden of delight and finally heaven itself (Trench), as here.

8. *In Smyrna* (*en Smurnēi*). North of Ephesus, on a gulf of the Ægean, one of the great cities of Asia (province), a seat of emperor-worship with temple to Tiberius, with many Jews hostile to Christianity who later join in the martyrdom of Polycarp, poor church (rich in grace) which receives only praise from Christ, scene of the recent massacre of Greeks by the Turks. Ramsay (*op. cit.*, p. 251) terms Smyrna "the City of Life." Christianity has held on here better than in any city of Asia. *The first and the last* (*ho prōtos kai ho eschatos*). Repeating the language of 1:17. *Which was dead* (*hos egeneto nekros*). Rather, "who became dead" (second aorist middle indicative of *ginomai*) as in 1:18. *And lived again* (*kai ezēsen*). First aorist (ingressive, came to life) active of *zaō* (*ho zōn* in 1:18). Emphasis on the resurrection of Christ.

9. *Thy tribulation and thy poverty* (*sou tēn thlipsin kai ptōcheian*). Separate articles of same gender, emphasizing each item. The tribulation was probably persecution, which helped to intensify the poverty of the Christians (James 2:5; I Cor. 1:26; II Cor. 6:10; 8:2). In contrast with the wealthy church in Laodicea (3:17). *But thou art rich* (*alla plousios ei*). Parenthesis to show the spiritual riches of this church in contrast with the spiritual poverty in Lao-

dicea (3:17), this a rich poor church, that a poor rich church. Rich in grace toward God (Luke 12:21) and in good deeds (I Tim. 6:18). Perhaps Jews and pagans had pillaged their property (Heb. 10:34), poor as they already were. *Blasphemy* (*blasphēmian*). Reviling believers in Christ. See Mark 7:22. The precise charge by these Jews is not indicated, but see Acts 13:45. *Of them which say* (*ek tōn legontōn*). "From those saying" (*ek* with the ablative plural of the present active articular participle of *legō*). *They are Jews* (*Ioudaious einai heautous*). This is the accusative of general reference and the infinitive in indirect discourse after *legō* (Acts 5:36; 8:9) even though *legontōn* is here ablative (cf. 3:9), common idiom. These are actual Jews and only Jews, not Christians. *And they are not* (*kai ouk eisin*). Another parenthesis like that in 2:2. These are Jews in name only, not spiritual Jews (Gal. 6:15f., Rom. 2:28). *A synagogue of Satan* (*sunagōgē tou Satanā*). In 3:9 again and note 2:13, 24, serving the devil (John 8:44) instead of the Lord (Numb. 16:3; 20:4).

10. *Fear not* (*mē phobou*). As in 1:17. Worse things are about to come than poverty and blasphemy, perhaps prison and death, for the devil "is about to cast" (*mellei ballein*), "is going to cast." *Some of you* (*ex humōn*). Without *tinas* (some) before *ex humōn*, a common idiom as in 3:9; 11:19; Luke 11:49. *That ye may be tried* (*hina peirasthēte*). Purpose clause with *hina* and the first aorist passive subjunctive of *peirazō*. John himself is in exile. Peter and John had often been in prison together. James the brother of John, Paul, and Peter had all suffered martyrdom. In 3:10 a general persecution is outlined by *peirasmos*. *Ye shall have* (*hexete*). Future active, but some MSS. read *echēte* (present active subjunctive with *hina*, "that ye may have"). *Tribulation ten days* (*thlipsin hēmerōn deka*). "Tribulation of ten days" (or "within ten days"). It is unwise to seek a literal meaning for ten days. Even ten days of suffering might

seem an eternity while they lasted. *Be thou faithful* (*ginou pistos*). "Keep on becoming faithful" (present middle imperative of *ginomai*), "keep on proving faithful unto death" (Heb. 12:4) as the martyrs have done (Jesus most of all). *The crown of life* (*ton stephanon tēs zōēs*). See this very image in James 1:12, a familiar metaphor in the games at Smyrna and elsewhere in which the prize was a garland. See also 3:11. The crown consists in life (2:7). See Paul's use of *stephanos* in I Cor. 9:25; II Tim. 4:8.

11. *Shall not be hurt* (*ou mē adikēthēi*). Strong double negative with first aorist passive subjunctive of *adikeō*, old verb, to act unjustly (from *adikos*), here to do harm or wrong to one, old usage as in 6:6; 7:2f.; 9:4, 10; 11:5. *Of the second death* (*ek tou thanatou tou deuterou*). *Ek* here used for the agent or instrument as often (3:18; 9:2; 18:1). See 20:6, 14; 21:8 where "the second death" is explained as "the lake of fire." The idea is present in Dan. 12:3 and John 5:29 and is current in Jewish circles as in the Jerusalem Targum on Deut. 33:6 and in Philo. It is not annihilation. The Christians put to death in the persecution will at least escape this second death (eternal punishment).

12. *In Pergamum* (*en Pergamōi*). In a north-easterly direction from Smyrna in the Caicus Valley, some fifty-five miles away, in Mysia, on a lofty hill, a great political and religious centre. Ramsay (*op. cit.*, p. 281) calls it "the royal city, the city of authority." Eumenes II (B.C. 197–159) extended it and embellished it with many great buildings, including a library with 200,000 volumes, second only to Alexandria. The Kingdom of Pergamum became a Roman province B.C. 130. Pliny termed it the most illustrious city of Asia. Parchment (*charta Pergamena*) derived its name from Pergamum. It was a rival of Ephesus in the temples to Zeus, Athena, Dionysos, in the great grove Nicephorium (the glory of the city). Next to this was the grove and temple of Asklepios, the god of healing, called the god of

Pergamum, with a university for medical study. Pergamum was the first city in Asia (A.D. 29) with a temple for the worship of Augustus (Octavius Cæsar). Hence in the Apocalypse Pergamum is a very centre of emperor-worship "where Satan dwells" (2:13). Here also the Nicolaitans flourished (2:15) as in Ephesus (2:6) and in Thyatira (2:20f.). Like Ephesus this city is called temple-sweeper (*neōkoros*) for the gods. *The sharp two-edged sword* (*tēn romphaian tēn distomon tēn oxeian*). This item repeated from 1:16 in the same order of words with the article three times (the sword the two-mouthed the sharp) singling out each point.

13. *Where* (*pou—hopou*). *Pou* is interrogative adverb used here in an indirect question as in John 1:39. *Hopou* is relative adverb referring to *pou*. *Satan's throne* (*ho thronos tou Satanā*). Satan not simply resided in Pergamum, but his "throne" or seat of power of king or judge (Matt. 19:28; Luke 1:32, 52). The symbol of Asklepios was the serpent as it is of Satan (12:9; 20:2). There was, besides, a great throne altar to Zeus cut on the Acropolis rock, symbol of "rampant paganism" (Swete) and the new Cæsar-worship with the recent martyrdom of Antipas made Pergamum indeed a very throne of Satan. *Holdest fast my name* (*krateis to onoma sou*). Present active indicative of *krateō*, "dost keep on holding," as in 2:25, 3:11. This church refused to say *Kurios Kaisar* (*Martyrd. Polyc.* 8f.) and continued to say *Kurios Iēsous* (I Cor. 12:3). They stood true against the emperor-worship. *Didst not deny* (*ouk ērnēsō*). First aorist middle second person singular of *arneomai*. Reference to a specific incident not known to us. *My faith* (*tēn pistin mou*). Objective genitive, "thy faith in me." *Of Antipas* (*Antipas*). Indeclinable in this form. It is possible that *Antipa* (genitive) was really written, though unimportant as the nominative follows in apposition. Nothing is really known of this early martyr in Pergamum before the writing of the Apocalypse. One legend is that he was burnt

to death in a brazen bull.   Other martyrs followed him at
Pergamum (Agathonice, Attalus, Carpus, Polybus).   *My
witness* (*ho martus mou*).   Nominative in apposition with a
genitive as in 1:5 (with ablative), common solecism in the
Apocalypse.   "Witness" as Jesus had said they should be
(Acts 1:8) and Stephen was (Acts 22:20) and others were
(Rev. 17:6).   The word later (by third century) took on the
modern meaning of martyr.   *My faithful one* (*ho pistos mou*).
Nominative also, with *mou* also.   Jesus gives Antipas his
own title (Swete) as in 1:5; 3:14.   Faithful unto death.   *Was
killed* (*apektanthē*).   First aorist passive indicative of *apokteinō*, this passive form common in the Apocalypse (2:13;
6:11; 5:9, 13; 13:10, 15; 18, 20; 19:21).   *Among you* (*par'
humin*).   By your side.   Proof of the throne of Satan,
"where Satan dwells" (*hopou ho Satanās katoikei*), repeated
for emphasis.

14. *There* (*ekei*).   That is *par' humin* (among you).   A
party in the church that resisted emperor-worship, to the
death in the case of Antipas, yet were caught in the insidious
wiles of the Nicolaitans which the church in Ephesus with-
stood.   *Some that hold* (*kratountas*).   "Men holding" (present active participle of *krateō*).   *The teaching of Balaam* (*tēn
didachēn Balaam*).   Indeclinable substantive Balaam (Numb.
25:1–9; 31:15f.).   The point of likeness of these heretics
with Balaam is here explained.   *Taught Balak* (*edidasken
tōi Balak*).   Imperfect indicative of *didaskō*, Balaam's habit,
"as the prototype of all corrupt teachers" (Charles).   These
early Gnostics practised licentiousness as a principle since
they were not under law, but under grace (Rom. 6:15).   The
use of the dative with *didaskō* is a colloquialism rather than
a Hebraism.   Two accusatives often occur with *didaskō*.
To cast a stumbling-block (*balein skandalon*).   Second aorist
active infinitive (accusative case after *edidasken*) of *ballō*,
regular use with *skandalon* (trap) like *tithēmi skandalon* in
Rom. 14:13.   Balaam, as Josephus and Philo also say,

showed Balak how to set a trap for the Israelites by beguiling them into the double sin of idolatry and fornication, which often went together (and do so still). *To eat things sacrificed to idols* (*phagein eidōlothuta*). Second aorist active infinitive of *esthiō* and the verbal adjective (from *eidōlon* and *thuō*), quoted here from Numb. 25:1f., but in inverse order, repeated in other order in verse 20. See Acts 15:29; 21:25; I Cor. 8:1ff. for the controversy over the temptation to Gentile Christians to do what in itself was harmless, but which led to evil if it led to participation in the pagan feasts. Perhaps both ideas are involved here. Balaam taught Balak how to lead the Israelites into sin in both ways.

15. *So thou also* (*houtōs kai su*). Thou and the church at Pergamum as Israel had the wiles of Balaam. *The teaching of the Nicolaitans likewise* (*tēn didachēn tōn Nikolaitōn homoiōs*). See on 1:6 for the Nicolaitans. The use of *homoiōs* (likewise) here shows that they followed Balaam in not obeying the decision of the Conference at Jerusalem (Acts 15:20, 29) about idolatry and fornication, with the result that they encouraged a return to pagan laxity of morals (Swete). Some wrongly hold that these Nicolaitans were Pauline Christians in the face of Col. 3:5–8; Eph. 5:3–6.

16. *Repent therefore* (*metanoēson oun*). First aorist (tense of urgency) active imperative of *metanoeō* with the inferential particle *oun* (as a result of their sin). *I come* (*erchomai*). Futuristic present middle indicative, "I am coming" (imminent), as in 2:5 with *tachu* as in 3:11; 11:14; 22:7, 12, 20. As with *en tachei* (1:1), we do not know how soon "quickly" is meant to be understood. But it is a real threat. *Against them* (*met' autōn*). This proposition with *polemeō* rather than *kata* (against) is common in the LXX, but in the N.T. only in Rev. 2:16; 12:7; 13:4; 17:14 and the verb itself nowhere else in N.T. except James 4:2. "An eternal roll of thunder from the throne" (Renan). "The glorified Christ is in this book a Warrior, who fights with the sharp sword of

the word" (Swete). *With* (*en*). Instrumental use of *en*. For the language see 1:16; 2:12; 19:15.

17. *Of the hidden manna* (*tou manna tou kekrummenou*). "Of the manna the hidden" (perfect passive articular participle of *kruptō*). The partitive genitive, the only N.T. example with *didōmi*, though Q reads *to* (accusative) here. For examples of the ablative with *apo* and *ek* see Robertson, *Grammar*, p. 519. See John 6:31, 49 for the indeclinable word *manna*. The golden pot of manna was "laid up before God in the ark" (Ex. 16:23). It was believed that Jeremiah hid the ark, before the destruction of Jerusalem, where it would not be discovered till Israel was restored (II Macc. 2:5ff.). Christ is the true bread from heaven (John 6:31–33, 48–51) and that may be the idea here. Those faithful to Christ will have transcendent fellowship with him. Swete takes it to be "the life-sustaining power of the Sacred Humanity now hid with Christ in God." *A white stone* (*psēphon leukēn*). This old word for pebble (from *psaō*, to rub) was used in courts of justice, black pebbles for condemning, white pebbles for acquitting. The only other use of the word in the N.T. is in Acts 26:10, where Paul speaks of "depositing his pebble" (*katēnegka psēphon*) or casting his vote. The white stone with one's name on it was used to admit one to entertainments and also as an amulet or charm. *A new name written* (*onoma kainon gegrammenon*). Perfect passive predicate participle of *graphō*. Not the man's own name, but that of Christ (Heitmüller, *Im Namen Jēsu*, p. 128–265). See 3:12 for the name of God so written on one. The man himself may be the *psēphos* on which the new name is written. "The true Christian has a charmed life" (Moffatt). *But he that receiveth it* (*ei mē ho lambanōn*). "Except the one receiving it." See Matt. 11:27 for like intimate and secret knowledge between the Father and the Son and the one to whom the Son wills to reveal the Father. See also Rev. 19:12.

18. *In Thyatira* (*en Thuateirois*). Some forty miles southeast of Pergamum, a Lydian city on the edge of Mysia, under Rome since B.C. 190, a centre of trade, especially for the royal purple, home of Lydia of Philippi (Acts 16:14f.), shown by inscriptions to be full of trade guilds, Apollo the chief deity with no emperor-worship, centre of activity by the Nicolaitans with their idolatry and licentiousness under a "prophetess" who defied the church there. Ramsay calls it "Weakness Made Strong" (*op. cit.*, p. 316). *The Son of God* (*ho huios tou theou*). Here Jesus is represented as calling himself by this title as in John 11:4 and as he affirms on oath in Matt. 26:63f. "The Word of God" occurs in 19:13. *His eyes like a flame of fire* (*tous ophthalmous autou hōs phloga puros*). As in 1:14. *His feet like burnished brass* (*hoi podes autou homoioi chalkolibanōi*). As in 1:15.

19. *Thy works* (*sou ta erga*). As in 2:2 and explained (explanatory use of *kai* = namely) by what follows. Four items are given, with separate feminine article for each (*tēn agapēn, tēn pistin, tēn diakonian, tēn hupomonēn*), a longer list of graces than in 2:2 for Ephesus. More praise is given in the case of Ephesus and Thyatira when blame follows than in the case of Smyrna and Philadelphia when no fault is found. Love comes first in this list in true Johannine fashion. Faith (*pistin*) here may be "faithfulness," and ministry (*diakonian*) is ministration to needs of others (Acts 11:29; I Cor. 16:15). *And that* (*kai*). Only *kai* (and) in the Greek, but doubtless *hoti* (that) is understood. *Than the first* (*tōn prōtōn*). Ablative after the comparative *pleiona* (more).

20. *Thou sufferest* (*apheis*). Late vernacular present active indicative second person singular as if from a form *apheō* instead of the usual *aphiēmi* forms. *The woman Jezebel* (*tēn gunaika Iezabel*). Symbolical name for some prominent woman in the church in Thyatira, like the infamous wife of Ahab who was guilty of whoredom and witchcraft (I Kings

16:31; II Kings 9:22) and who sought to drive out the worship of God from Israel. Some MSS. here (A Q 40 min.s) have *sou* (thy wife, thy woman Ramsay makes it), but surely Aleph C P rightly reject *sou*. Otherwise she is the pastor's wife! *Which calleth herself a prophetess (hē legousa heautēn prophētin)*. Nominative articular participle of *lego* in apposition with the accusative *gunaika* like *ho martus* in apposition with *Antipas* in 2:13. *Prophētis* is an old word, feminine form for *prophētēs*, in N.T. only here and Luke 2:36 (Anna), two extremes surely. See Acts 21:9 for the daughters of Philip who prophesied. *And she teacheth and seduceth (kai didaskei kai planāi)*. A resolution of the participles (*didaskousa kai planōsa*) into finite verbs (present active indicatives) as in 1:5f. This woman was not a real prophetess, but a false one with loud claims and loose living. One is puzzled to know how such a woman had so much shrewdness and sex-appeal as to lead astray the servants of God in that church. The church tolerated the Nicolaitans and this leader whose primary object was sexual immorality (Charles) and became too much involved with her to handle the heresy.

21. *I gave her time (edōka autēi chronon)*. First aorist active indicative of *didōmi*, allusion to a definite visit or message of warning to this woman. *That she should repent (hina metanoēsēi)*. Sub-final use of *hina* with first aorist active subjunctive of *metanoeō*. *And she willeth not (kai ou thelei)*. "And she is not willing." Blunt and final like Matt. 23:37. *To repent of (metanoēsai ek)*. First aorist (ingressive) active infinitive with *ek*, "to make a change out of," the usual construction with *metanoeō* in this book (2:22; 9:20ff.; 16:11), with *apo* in Acts 8:22. *Porneia* (fornication) here, but *moicheuō* (to commit adultery) in verse 22.

22. *I do cast (ballō)*. Futuristic present active indicative rather than the future *balō*, since judgment is imminent. *Into a bed (eis klinēn)*. "A bed of sickness in contrast with the bed of adultery" (Beckwith). *Them that commit adultery*

with her (*tous moicheuontas met' autēs*). Present active articular participle accusative plural of *moicheuō*. The actual paramours of the woman Jezebel, guilty of both *porneia* (fornication, verse 21) and *moicheia* (adultery), works of Jezebel of old and of this Jezebel. There may be also an allusion to the spiritual adultery (II Cor. 11:2) towards God and Christ as of old (Jer. 3:8; 5:7; Ezek. 16:22). *Except they repent* (*ean mē metanoēsousin*). Condition of first class with *ean mē* and the future active indicative of *metanoeō*, put in this vivid form rather than the aorist subjunctive (*-ōsin*) third-class condition. *Of her works* (*ek tōn ergōn autēs*). *Autēs* (her) correct rather than *autōn* (their). Jezebel was chiefly responsible.

23. *I will kill with death* (*apoktenō en thanatōi*). Future (volitive) active of *apokteinō* with the tautological (cognate) *en thanatōi* (in the sense of pestilence) as in Ezek. 33:27. *Her children* (*ta tekna autēs*). Either her actual children, like the fate of Ahab's sons (II Kings 10:7) or "her spiritual progeny" (Swete) who have completely accepted her Nicolaitan practices. *Shall know* (*gnōsontai*). Future (ingressive punctiliar) middle of *ginōskō*, "shall come to know." "The doom of the offenders was to be known as widely as the scandal had been" (Charles). *Searcheth* (*eraunōn*). Present active articular participle of *eraunaō*, to follow up, to track out, late form for *ereunaō*, from Jer. 17:10. *Reins* (*nephrous*). Old word for kidneys, here only in N.T., quoted also with *kardias* from Jer. 17:10. See 22:17 for the reward of punishment.

24. *To you the rest* (*humin tois loipois*). Dative case. Those who hold out against Jezebel, not necessarily a minority (9:20; 19:21; I Thess. 4:13). *As many as* (*hosoi*). Inclusive of all "the rest." *This teaching* (*tēn didachēn tautēn*). That of Jezebel. *Which* (*hoitines*). "Which very ones," generic of the class, explanatory definition as in 1:7. *Know not* (*ouk egnōsan*). Second aorist (ingressive) active of

ginōskō, "did not come to know by experience." *The deep things of Satan (ta bathea tou Satanā).* The Ophites (worshippers of the serpent) and other later Gnostics (Cainites, Carpocratians, Naassenes) boasted of their knowledge of "the deep things," some claiming this very language about Satan (the serpent) as Paul did of God (I Cor. 2:10). It is not clear whether the words here quoted are a boast of the Nicolaitans or a reproach on the other Christians for not knowing the depths of sin. Some even claimed that they could indulge in immorality without sinning (I John 1:10; 3:10). Perhaps both ideas are involved. *As they say (hōs legousin).* Probably referring to the heretics who ridicule the piety of the other Christians. *None other burden (ou— allo baros). Baros* refers to weight (Matt. 20:12), *phortion,* from *pherō,* to bear, refers to load (Gal. 6:5), *ogkos* to bulk (Heb. 12:1). Apparently a reference to the decision of the Jerusalem Conference (Acts 15:28) where the very word *baros* is used and mention is made about the two items in verse 20 (fornication and idolatry) without mentioning the others about things strangled, etc. See the Pharisaic narrowness in Matt. 23:4.

25. *Howbeit (plēn).* Common after *ouk allo* as a preposition with the ablative (Mark 12:32), but here a conjunction as in Phil. 1:18. *Hold fast (kratēsate).* First aorist active imperative of *krateō,* either ingressive (get a grip on) or constative (hold on as a single decisive effort). See present imperative *kratei* in 3:11 (keep on holding). *Till I come (achri hou an hēxō).* Indefinite temporal clause with *achri hou* (until which time) with modal *an* and either the future active indicative or the first aorist active subjunctive of *hēkō* (usual idiom with *achri* in Revelation as in 7:3; 15:8; 20:3, 5).

26. *He that overcometh and he that keepeth (ho nikōn kai ho tērōn).* Present active articular participles of *nikaō* and *tēreō* in the nominative absolute (*nominativus pendens*) as in 3:12, 21, resumed by the dative *autōi* (to him), as in verses 7, 17.

Unto the end (achri telous). That is, *achri hou an hēxo* above. *Authority over the nations (exousian epi tōn ethnōn).* From Ps. 2:8f. The followers of the Messiah will share in his victory over his enemies (1:6; 12:5; 19:15).

27. *He shall rule (poimanei).* Future active of *poimainō,* to shepherd (from *poimēn,* shepherd), also from Ps. 2:8f. See again Rev. 7:17; 12:5; 19:15. *With a rod of iron (en rabdōi siderāi).* Continuing the quotation. Instrumental use of *en.* *Rabdos* (feminine) is the royal sceptre and indicates rigorous rule. *The vessels of the potter (ta skeuē ta keramika).* Old adjective, belonging to a potter (*kerameus, keramos*), here only in N.T. *Are broken to shivers (suntribetai).* Present passive indicative of *suntribō,* old verb, to rub together, to break in pieces (Mark 14:3).

28. *As I also have received (hōs kágō eilēpha).* Perfect active indicative of *lambanō.* Christ still possesses the power from the Father (Acts 2:33; Ps. 2:7). *The morning star (ton astera ton prōinon).* "The star the morning one." In 22:16 Christ is the bright morning star. The victor will have Christ himself.

CHAPTER III

1. *In Sardis (en Sardesin).* Some thirty miles south-east of Thyatira, old capital of Lydia, wealthy and the home of Crœsus, conquered by Cyrus and then by Alexander the Great, in B.C. 214 by Antiochus the Great, at the crossing of Roman roads, in a plain watered by the river Pactolus, according to Pliny the place where the dyeing of wool was discovered, seat of the licentious worship of Cybele and the ruins of the temple still there, called by Ramsay (*op. cit.*, p. 354) "the city of Death," city of softness and luxury, of apathy and immorality, "a contrast of past splendour and present unresting decline" (Charles). Along with Laodicea it was blamed most of all the seven churches. *That hath the seven Spirits of God (ho echōn ta hepta pneumata tou theou).* For which picture of the Holy Spirit see 1:4. *And the seven stars (kai tous hepta asteras).* As in 1:16, 20. *A name that thou livest (onoma hoti zēis).* A name in contrast with reality. The *hoti* clause in apposition with *onoma*. *And thou art dead (kai nekros ei).* "The paradox of death under the name of life" (Swete). Not complete (a nucleus of life) death (verse 2), but rapidly dying. See the picture in James 2:17; II Cor. 6:9; II Tim. 3:5.

2. *Be thou watchful (ginou grēgorōn).* Periphrastic imperative with present middle of *ginomai* (keep on becoming) and present active participle of *grēgoreō* (late present from perfect *egrēgora* and that from *egeirō*, as in Matt. 24:42) and see 16:15 for *grēgoreō* also. He does not say "Arise from the dead" (Eph. 5:14), for there are vestiges of life. Those still alive are addressed through the angel of the church. *Stablish the things that remain (stērison ta loipa).* First aorist active imperative of *stērizō*, to make stable.

Those not actually dead, but in grave peril. See a like command to Titus in Crete (1:5). Every new pastor faces such a problem. *Which were ready to die* (*ha emellon apothanein*). Imperfect active plural because the individuals, though neuter plural, are regarded as living realities. The imperfect looking on the situation "with a delicate optimism" (Swete) as having passed the crisis, a sort of epistolary imperfect. *For I have found no works of thine* (*ou gar heurēka sou erga*). "For I have not found any works of thine." Perfect active indicative of *heuriskō*. The church as a whole represented by *sou* (thy). *Fulfilled* (*peplērōmena*). Perfect passive predicate participle of *plēroō*. Their works have not measured up to God's standard (*enōpion tou theou mou*).

3. *Remember* (*mnēmoneue*). "Keep in mind," as in 2:5. *Therefore* (*oun*). Resumptive and coördinating as in 1:19; 2:5. *Thou hast received* (*eilēphas*). Perfect active indicative of *lambanō*, "as a permanent deposit" (Vincent). *Didst hear* (*ēkousas*). First aorist active indicative, the act of hearing at the time. *And keep it* (*kai tērei*). Present active imperative of *tēreō*, "hold on to what thou hast." *And repent* (*kai metanoēson*). First aorist active imperative of *metanoeō*, "Turn at once." *If therefore thou shalt not watch* (*ean oun mē grēgorēseis*). Condition of third class with *ean mē* and the first aorist (ingressive) active subjunctive of *grēgoreō*, "if then thou do not wake up." *I will come* (*hēxō*). Certainly future active here, though probably aorist subjunctive in 2:25. *As a thief* (*hōs kleptēs*). As Jesus had already said (Matt. 24:43; Luke 12:39), as Paul had said (I Thess. 5:2), as Peter had said (II Pet. 3:10), as Jesus will say again (Rev. 16:15). *Thou shalt not know* (*ou mē gnōis*). Strong double negative *ou mē* with second aorist active subjunctive of *ginōskō*, though some MSS. have the future middle indicative *gnōsei*. *What hour* (*poian hōran*). A rare classical idiom (accusative) surviving in the *Koiné* rather than the genitive of time, somewhat like John 4:52;

Acts 20:16 (Robertson, *Grammar*, p. 470f.). Indirect question with *poian*.

4. *A few names* (*oliga onomata*). This use of *onoma* for persons is seen in the *Koiné* (Deissmann, *Bible Studies*, p. 196f.) as in Acts 1:15; Rev. 11:13. *Did not defile* (*ouk emolunan*). First aorist active indicative of *moluno* (I Cor. 8:7; I Pet. 1:4), pollution. *They shall walk* (*peripatesousin*). Future active of *peripateo*, promise of fellowship with Christ (*met' emou*, with me) "in white" (*en leukois*), as symbols of purity (7:9, 13) like the angel (Matt. 28:3), with possibly a reference to Enoch (Gen. 5:22). *For they are worthy* (*hoti axioi eisin*). To walk with Christ, not worthy in the same sense as God and Christ (4:11; 5:9), but in a relative sense. See Rev. 16:6 for bad sense of *axios*.

5. *Shall be arrayed* (*peribaleitai*). Future middle indicative of *periballo*, to fling around one, here and in 4:4 with *en* and the locative, but usually in this book with the accusative of the thing, retained in the passive or with the middle (7:9, 13; 10:1; 11:3; 12:1; 17:4; 18:16; 19:8, 13). *In white garments* (*en himatiois leukois*). Apparently the spiritual bodies in the risen life as in II Cor. 5:1, 4 and often in Revelation (3:4, 5; 6:11; 7:9, 13f.; 19:8). *I will in no wise blot out* (*ou me exaleipso*). Strong double negative *ou me* and the first aorist active (or future) of *exaleipho*, old word, to wipe out (Acts 3:19). *Of the book of life* (*ek tes biblou tes zoes*). Ablative case with *ek*. This divine register first occurs in Ex. 32:32f. and often in the O.T. See Luke 10:20; Phil. 4:3; Rev. 13:8; 20:15; 21:27. The book is in Christ's hands (13:8; 21:27). *His name* (*to onoma autou*). The name of the one who overcomes (*ho nikon*). Clear reminiscence of the words of Christ about confessing to the Father those who confess him here (Matt. 10:32; Mark 8:38; Luke 9:26; 12:8). Whether John knew the Synoptic Gospels (and why not?) he certainly knew such sayings of Jesus.

7. *In Philadelphia (en Philadelphiāi)*. Some twenty-eight miles south-east of Sardis, in Lydia, subject to earthquakes, rebuilt by Tiberius after the great earthquake of A.D. 17, for a time called in coins Neo-Cæsarea, in wine-growing district with Bacchus (Dionysos) as the chief deity, on fine Roman roads and of commercial importance, though not a large city, called by Ramsay (*op. cit.*, p. 392) "the Missionary City" to promote the spread of the Græco-Roman civilization and then of Christianity, later offering stubborn resistance to the Turks (1379–90 A.D.) and now called Ala-Sheher (reddish city, Charles, from the red hills behind it). The chief opposition to the faithful little church is from the Jews (cf. Rom. 9–11). There are some 1,000 Christians there today. *The holy, he that is true (ho hagios, ho alēthinos).* Separate articles (four in all) for each item in this description. "The holy, the genuine." Asyndeton in the Greek. Latin Vulgate, *Sanctus et Verus. Ho hagios* is ascribed to God in 4:8; 6:10 (both *hagios* and *alēthinos* as here), but to Christ in Mark 1:24; Luke 4:34; John 6:69; Acts 4:27, 30; I John 2:20, a recognized title of the Messiah as the consecrated one set apart. Swete notes that *alēthinos* is *verus* as distinguished from *verax (alēthēs)*. So it is applied to God in 6:10 and to Christ in 3:14; 19:11 as in John 1:9; 6:32; 15:1. *He that hath the key of David (ho echōn tēn klein Daueid).* This epithet comes from Is. 22:22, where Eliakim as the chief steward of the royal household holds the keys of power. Christ as the Messiah (Rev. 5:5; 22:16) has exclusive power in heaven, on earth, and in Hades (Matt. 16:19; 28:18; Rom. 14:9; Phil. 2:9f.; Rev. 1:18). Christ has power to admit and exclude of his own will (Matt. 25:10f.; Eph. 1:22; Rev. 3:21; 19:11–16; 20:4; 22:16). *And none shall shut (kai oudeis kleisei).* Charles calls the structure Hebrew (future active indicative of *kleiō*), and not Greek because it does not correspond to the present articular participle just before *ho anoigōn* (the one opening), but

it occurs often in this book as in the very next clause, "and none openeth" (*kai oudeis anoigei*) over against *kleiōn* (present active participle, opening) though here some MSS. read *kleiei* (present active indicative, open).

8. *I have set* (*dedōka*). Perfect active indicative of *didōmi*, "I have given" (a gift of Christ, this open door). See Luke 12:51 for a like use of *didōmi*. *A door .opened* (*thuran ēneōigmenēn*). Perfect (triple reduplication) passive predicate participle of *anoigō* (verse 7) accusative feminine singular. The metaphor of the open door was a common one (John 10:7-9; Acts 14:27; I Cor. 16:9; II Cor. 2:12; Col. 4:3; Rev. 3:20; 4:1). Probably it means here a good opportunity for missionary effort in spite of the Jewish hostility. *Which* (*hēn—autēn*). Pleonastic vernacular and Hebrew repetition of the personal pronoun *autēn* (it) after the relative *hēn* (which). Direct reference to the statement in verse 7. *That* (*hoti*). This conjunction resumes the construction of *oida sou ta erga* (I know thy works) after the parenthesis (*idou—autēn*, Behold—shut). *A little power* (*mikran dunamin*). Probably "little power," little influence or weight in Philadelphia, the members probably from the lower classes (I Cor. 1:26f.). *And didst keep* (*kai etērēsas*). "And yet (adversative use of *kai*) didst keep" (first aorist active indicative of *tēreō*) my word in some crisis of trial. See John 17:6 for the phrase "keeping the word." *Didst not deny* (*ouk ērnēsō*). First aorist middle indicative second person singular of *arneomai*. The issue was probably forced by the Jews (cf. 2:9), but they stood true.

9. *I give* (*didō*). Late omega form for *didōmi*, but the -*mi* form in 17:13 (*didoasin*). These Jewish converts are a gift from Christ. For this use of *didōmi* see Acts 2:27; 10:40; 14:3. There is ellipse of *tinas* before *ek* as in 2:10 (*ex humōn*) and see 2:9 for "the synagogue of Satan." *Of them which say* (*tōn legontōn*). Ablative plural in apposition with *sunagōgēs*. On the construction of *heautous Ioudaious*

einai see on 2:9 (*Ioudaious einai heautous*, the order of words being immaterial). *But do lie* (*alla pseudontai*). Present middle indicative of *pseudomai*, explanatory positive, addition here to *kai ouk eisin* of 2:9, in contrast also with *ho alēthinos* of verse 7 and in Johannine style (John 8:44; I John 1:10; 2:4). *I will make them* (*poiēsō autous*). Future active indicative of *poieō*, resuming the prophecy after the parenthesis (*tōn*—*pseudontai*, which say—but do lie). *To come and worship* (*hina hēxousin kai proskunēsousin*). "That they come and worship" (final clause, like *facio ut* in Latin, with *hina* and the future active of *hēkō* and *proskuneō*). The language is based on Is. 45:14; 60:14. The Jews expected homage (not worship in the strict sense) from the Gentiles, but it will come to the Christians at last (I Cor. 14:24). Later Ignatius (*Philad.* 6) warns this church against Judaizing Christians, perhaps one result of an influx of Jews. *And to know* (*kai gnōsin*). Continuation of the purpose clause with *hina*, but with the second aorist active subjunctive rather than the less usual future indicative. See both constructions also with *hina* in 22:14. Probably a reminiscence of Is. 43:4 in *egō ēgapēsa se* (I loved thee), first aorist active indicative.

10. *Patience* (*hupomenēs*). "Endurance" as in 13:10; 14:12 as also in II Thess. 3:5. *Thou didst keep* (*etērēsas*)—*I also will keep* (*kagō tērēsō*). Aorist active indicative and future active corresponding to each other. For a like play on the tenses of this verb by Christ see John 17:6 (*tetērēkan*), 11 (*tērēson*), 12 (*etēroun*). *From the hour of trial* (*ek tēs hōras tou peirasmou*). This use of *ek* after *tēreō* in John 17:15, *apo* in James 1:27. Trial brings temptation often (James 1:2, 13). Jesus endured (Heb. 12:1f.) and he will help them. There is still a church in Philadelphia in spite of the Turks. *Which is to come* (*tēs mellousēs erchesthai*). Agreeing with *hōras* (feminine), not with *peirasmou* (masculine). *Upon the whole world* (*epi tēs epoikoumenēs holēs*). The inhabited

earth (*gēs*) as in Rev. 12:19; Luke 2:1; Acts 16:6, etc.), not the physical earth, but the world of men as explained by the next clause. *To try* (*peirasai*). First aorist active infinitive of purpose from *peirazō*, probably to tempt (cf. the demons in 9:1–21), not merely to afflict (2:10). *That dwell upon the earth* (*tous katoikountas epi tēs gēs*). Present active articular participle of *katoikeō*, explaining "the whole world" just before.

11. *I come quickly* (*erchomai tachu*). As in 2:16; 22:7, 12, 20. "The keynote of the book" (Beckwith). But allow the author's own meaning of "quickly." *Hold fast that which thou hast* (*kratei ho echeis*). Sort of motto for each church (2:25). *That no one take* (*hina mēdeis labēi*). Purpose clause with *hina* and second aorist active subjunctive of *lambanō*. Here to take away "thy crown" (2:10) which will be thine if really won and not forfeited by failure (II Tim. 4:8). In that case it will go to another (Matt. 25:28; Rom. 11:17f.).

12. *He that overcometh* (*ho nikōn*). Nominative absolute as in 2:26, resumed by the accusative *auton* (him). *A pillar* (*stulon*). Old word for column, in N.T. only here, 10:1; Gal. 2:9; I Tim. 3:15. Metaphorical and personal use with a double significance of being firmly fixed and giving stability to the building. Philadelphia was a city of earthquakes. "Temple" (*naos*) here is also metaphorical (7:15), as in I Tim. 3:15 for the people of God. In 21:22 we read that there is no temple in the heavenly Jerusalem (21:10–22:5) descending as the new Jerusalem with God himself as the temple, though the metaphorical temple is mentioned in 7:15. *He shall go out thence no more* (*exō ou mē elthēi*). Strong double negative *ou mē* with the second aorist active subjunctive of *erchomai*. The subject is *ho nikōn* (the one overcoming). "Fixity of character is at last achieved" (Charles). He, like the *stulos* (pillar), remains in place. *Upon him* (*ep' auton*). Upon *ho nikōn* (the victor), not upon the pillar

(*stulos*). He receives this triple name (of God, of the city of God, of Christ) on his forehead (14:1; 7:3; 17:5; 22:4) just as the high-priest wore the name of Jehovah upon his forehead (Ex. 28:36, 38), the new name (2:17), without any magical or talismanic power, but as proof of ownership by God, as a citizen of the New Jerusalem, with the new symbol of the glorious personality of Christ (Rev. 19:12), in contrast with the mark of the beast on others (13:17; 14:17). For citizenship in God's city see Gal. 4:26; Phil. 3:20; Heb. 11:10; 12:22; 13:14. *The new Jerusalem* (*tēs kainēs Ierousalēm*). Not *neas* (young), but *kainēs* (fresh). See also 21:2, 10 and already Gal. 4:26 and Heb. 12:22. Charles distinguishes between the Jerusalem before the final judgment and this new Jerusalem after that event. Perhaps so! In the Apocalypse always this form *Ierousalēm* (3:12; 21:2, 10), but in John's Gospel *Hierosoluma* (1:19, etc.). *Which cometh down* (*hē katabainousa*). Nominative case in apposition with the preceding genitive *poleōs* as in 1:5; 2:20, etc. *Mine own new name* (*to onoma mou to kainon*). For which see 2:17; 19:12, 16. Christ himself will receive a new name along with all else in the future world (Gressmann).

14. *In Laodicea* (*en Laodikiāi*). Forty miles south-east of Philadelphia and some forty miles east of Ephesus, the last of the seven churches addressed with special messages, on the river Lycus on the border of Phrygia, near Colossæ and Hierapolis, recipient of two letters by Paul (Col. 4:16), on the great trade-route from Ephesus to the east and seat of large manufacturing and banking operations (especially of woollen carpets and clothing, Ramsay, *Cities and Bishoprics of Phrygia*, p. 40ff.), centre of the worship of Asklepios and seat of a medical school and also of a provincial court where Cicero lived and wrote many of his letters, home of many Jews, called by Ramsay (*op. cit.*, p. 413) "the City of Compromise," the church here founded apparently by Epaphras (Col. 1:7; 4:12f.), now a deserted ruin, one of six cities with

this name (meaning justice of the people). No praise is bestowed on this church, but only blame for its lukewarmness. *The Amen* (*ho Amēn*). Personal (masculine article) name here alone, though in Is. 65:16 we have "the God of Amen" understood in the LXX as "the God of truth" (*ton theon ton alēthinon*). Here applied to Christ. See 1:5 for *ho martus ho pistos* (the faithful witness) and 3:7 for *ho alēthinos* (the genuine), "whose testimony never falls short of the truth" (Swete). *The beginning of the creation of God* (*hē archē tēs ktiseōs tou theou*). Not the first of creatures as the Arians held and Unitarians do now, but the originating source of creation through whom God works (Col. 1:15, 18, a passage probably known to the Laodiceans, John 1:3; Heb. 1:2, as is made clear by 1:18; 2:8; 3:21; 5:13).

15. *Neither cold* (*oute psuchros*). Old word from *psuchō*, to grow cold (Matt. 24:12), in N.T. only Matt. 10:42 and this passage. *Nor hot* (*oute zestos*). Late verbal from *zeō*, to boil, (Rom. 12:11), boiling hot, here only in N.T. *I would thou wert* (*ophelon ēs*). Wish about the present with *ophelon* (really *ōphelon*, second aorist active indicative of *opheilō*, without augment) with the imperfect *ēs* (instead of the infinitive) as in II Cor. 11:1, when the old Greek used *eithe* or *ei gar*. See I Cor. 4:8 for the aorist indicative and Gal. 5:12 for the future.

16. *Lukewarm* (*chliaros*). Tepid. Old adjective from *chliō*, to liquefy, to melt, here alone in N.T. *I will* (*mellō*). "I am about to," on the point of. *Spew thee* (*se emesai*). First aorist active infinitive of *emeō*, old verb to vomit, to reject with extreme disgust, here alone in N.T.

17. *I am rich* (*hoti plousios eimi*). Recitative *hoti* like quotation marks before direct quotation. Old adjective from *ploutos*, riches, wealth. Laodicea was a wealthy city and the church "carried the pride of wealth into its spiritual life" (Swete). *Have gotten riches* (*peploutēka*). Perfect active indicative of *plouteō*, old verb from *ploutos*, used

here of imagined spiritual riches which the church did not possess, just the opposite of church in Smyrna (poor in wealth, rich in grace). This church was in a rich city and was rich in pride and conceit, but poor in grace and ignorant of its spiritual poverty (*ouk oidas*, knowest not). *The wretched one* (*ho talaipōros*). Old adjective from *tlaō*, to endure, and *pōros*, a callus, afflicted, in N.T. only here and Rom. 7:24. Note the one article in the predicate with all these five adjectives unifying the picture of sharp emphasis on "thou" (*su*), "thou that boastest." *Miserable* (*eleeinos*). Pitiable as in I Cor. 15:19. *Poor* (*ptōchos*). See 2:9 for spiritual poverty. Perhaps some local example of self-complacency is in mind. *Blind* (*tuphlos*). Spiritual blindness as often (Matt. 23:17), and note "eye-salve" in verse 18. *Naked* (*gumnos*). "The figure completes the picture of actual poverty" (Beckwith). See 15 and 16.

18. *I counsel* (*sumbouleuō*). Present active indicative, old compound from *sumboulos*, counsellor (Rom. 11:34), as in John 18:14. Almost ironical in tone. *To buy* (*agorasai*). First aorist active infinitive of *agorazō* (from *agora*, marketplace), rich as they think themselves to be. *From me* (*par' emou*). From my side, emphatic. *Refined by fire* (*pepurōmenon ek puros*). Perfect passive participle of *puroō* (as in 1:15) and the metaphor carried on by *ek puros*, "fired by fire." Purity by removing dross (Ps. 66:10) like I Pet. 1:7. *That thou mayest become rich* (*hina ploutēsēis*). Purpose clause with *hina* and the ingressive first aorist active of *plouteō*, spiritual riches. *That thou mayest clothe thyself* (*hina peribalēi*). Purpose clause with *hina* and second aorist middle (direct) subjunctive of *periballō*, to fling round one as in 3:5. *Be not made manifest* (*mē phanerōthēi*). Continued purpose clause with negative *mē* and first aorist passive subjunctive of *phaneroō*. *Nakedness* (*gumnotētos*). Late and rare word from *gumnos*, naked, in N.T. only here, II Cor. 11:27; Rom. 8:35. Cf. Rev. 16:15; 20:13; II Cor. 5:2f. *Eye-*

salve (*kollourion*). Diminutive of *kollura* (coarse bread of cylindrical shape), object of *agorasai*, name for a famous Phrygian powder for the eyes made in Laodicea (Charles), Latin *collyrium* (used for eye-salve by Horace and Juvenal). *To anoint* (*egchrisai*). First aorist active infinitive (epexegetic) of *egchriō*, late compound (*en*, *chriō*, Strabo, Epictetus), to rub in, here only in N.T. *That thou mayest see* (*hina blepēis*). Another purpose clause with *hina* and the present active subjunctive (keep on seeing).

19. Free rendering of Prov. 3:12 (in Heb. 12:6), but with *hous ean* (indefinite relative plural) for *hon* (definite relative singular), with *philō* instead of *agapāi* and with the first person *paideuō for paideuei* (the Lord chastens, from *pais*, child, training a child) and with *elegchō* (reprove) added. *Be zealous* (*zēleue*). Present active imperative of *zēleuō*, in good sense (from *zēlos*, *zeō*, to boil), in opposition to their lukewarmness, here only in N.T. (elsewhere *zēloō*), "keep on being zealous." *Repent* (*metanoēson*). Ingressive first aorist active imperative of *metanoeō*.

20. *I stand at the door* (*hestēka epi tēn thuran*). Perfect active of *histēmi* (intransitive). Picture of the Lord's advent as in Matt. 24:33; James 5:9, but true also of the individual response to Christ's call (Luke 12:36) as shown in Holman Hunt's great picture. Some see a use also of Song of Solomon 5:2. *If any man hear—and open* (*ean tis akousēi kai anoixēi*). Condition of third class with *ean* and first aorist (ingressive) active subjunctive of *akouō* and *anoigō*. See John 10:3; 18:37. See the picture reversed (Swete) in Luke 13:25 and Matt. 25:10. *I will come in to him* (*eiseleusomai*). Future middle of *eiserchomai*. See Mark 15:43; Acts 11:3 for *eiserchomai pros*, to go into a man's house. Cf. John 14:23. *Will sup* (*deipnēsō*). Future active of *deipneō*, old verb, from *deipnon* (supper), as in Luke 17:8. Fellowship in the Messianic kingdom (Luke 22:30; Mark 14:25; Matt. 26:29). Purely metaphorical, as is plain from I Cor. 6:13.

21. *He that overcometh* (*ho nikōn*). Absolute nominative again as in 3:12, but resumed this time by the dative *autōi* as in 2:26. *To sit* (*kathisai*). First aorist active infinitive of *kathizō*. This promise grows out of the prophecy that the saints will share in the Messiah's rule, made to the twelve (Matt. 19:28; Luke 22:29f.), repeated by Paul (I Cor. 6:2f.), enlarged in Rev. 22:1–5 (to last forever, II Tim. 2:11f.). James and John took this hope and promise literally (Mark 10:40) not metaphorically. *As I also overcame* (*hōs kagō enikēsa*). First aorist active indicative of *nikaō*, looking back on the victory as over in the past. In John 16:33 before the Cross Jesus says *Egō nenikēka ton kosmon* (perfect active), emphasizing the abiding effect of the victory. *Sat down* (*ekathisa*). "I took my seat" (Heb. 1:3) where Christ is now (Rev. 22:3; Col. 3:1). Cf. I John 5:4; Rev. 2:27f. Each of these seven messages begins alike and ends alike. Each is the message of the Christ and of the Holy Spirit to the angel of the church. Each has a special message suited to the actual condition of each church. In each case the individual who overcomes has a promise of blessing. Christ the Shepherd knows his sheep and lays bare the particular peril in each case.

CHAPTER IV

1. *After these things* (*meta tauta*). Change in the pano-- rama, not chronology (7:1, 9; 15:5; 18:1; 19:1). This vision is of heaven, not of earth as was true of chapters 1 and 2. The first vision of Christ and the messages to the seven churches began in 1:12f. This new vision of the throne in heaven (4:1–11) succeeds that to which it here alludes. *I saw* (*eidon*). Second aorist active indicative of *horaō*. *Behold* (*idou*). Exclamation of vivid emotion as John looked. No effect on the structure and nominative case *thura* (door) follows it. *Opened* (*ēneōigmenē*). Perfect (triple reduplication) passive participle of *anoigō* as in 3:8 (door of opportunity) and 3:20 (door of the heart), here the door of revelation (Swete). *In heaven* (*en tōi ouranōi*). As in Ezek. 1:1; Mark 1:10; John 1:51. In Revelation always in singular except 12:12. *The first* (*hē prōtē*). Reference is to 1:10. *Speaking* (*lalousēs*). From *laleō*, rather *legousēs* of 1:10 from *legō*, both agreeing with *salpiggos* (trumpet). *Saying* (*legōn*). Present active participle of *legō* repeating the idea of *lalousēs*, but in the nominative masculine singular construed with *phōnē* (feminine singular), construction according to sense because of the person behind the voice as in 11:15; 19:14. *Come up* (*anaba*). Short *Koinē* form for *anabēthi* (second aorist active imperative second person singular of *anabainō*). *Hither* (*hōde*). Originally "here," but vernacular use (John 6:25; 10:27). *I will show* (*deixō*). Future active of *deiknumi* in same sense in 1:1. *Hereafter* (*meta tauta*). Some editors (Westcott and Hort) connect these words with the beginning of verse 2.

2. *Straightway I was in the Spirit* (*eutheōs egenomēn en pneumati*). But John had already "come to be in the

325

Spirit" (1:10, the very same phrase). Perhaps here effective aorist middle indicative while ingressive aorist in 1:10 (sequel or result, not entrance), "At once I found myself in the Spirit" (Swete), not "I came to be in the Spirit" as in 1:10. *Was set* (*ekeito*). Imperfect middle of *keimai*, old verb, used as passive of *tithēmi*. As the vision opens John sees the throne already in place as the first thing in heaven. This bold imagery comes chiefly from I Kings 22:19; Is. 6:1ff.; Ezek. 1:26–28; Dan. 7:9f. One should not forget that this language is glorious imagery, not actual objects in heaven. God is spirit. The picture of God on the throne is common in the O.T. and the N.T. (Matt. 5:34f.; 23:22; Heb. 1:3 and in nearly every chapter in the Revelation, 1:4, etc.). The use of *kathēmenos* (sitting) for the name of God is like the Hebrew avoidance of the name *Jahweh* and is distinguished from the Son in 6:16 and 7:10. *Upon the throne* (*epi ton thronon*). *Epi* with the accusative, as in 4:4; 6:2, 4f.; 11:16; 20:4, but in verses 9 and 10, 4:1, 7, 13; 6:16; 7:15 we have *epi tou thronou* (genitive), while in 7:10; 19:14; 21:5 we have *epi tōi thronōi* (locative) with no great distinction in the resultant idea.

3. *To look upon* (*horasei*). Locative case of *horasis*, old word (from *horaō*, to see) for appearance (in appearance) as in Ezek. 1:5, 26. *Like a jasper stone* (*homoios iaspidi*). Associative-instrumental case of *iaspis*, old word (Persian), used for stones of different colors, one opaque like opal, one translucent (21:11, 18f., possibly here, only N.T. examples), one a red or yellow stone (Is. 54:12). Some even take it for the diamond. Certainly not our cheap modern jasper. *A sardius* (*sardiōi*). Old word, in N.T. only here and 21:20. The carnelian or other red stone, derived from Sardis (Pliny). *Rainbow* (*iris*). Old word, in N.T. only here and 10:1. From Ezek. 1:28. *An emerald* (*smaragdinōi*). Adjective (from *smaragdos*, Rev. 21:19), of emerald (supply *lithōi*), in associative instrumental case after *homoios*. John sees no

form for God (Ex. 24:10), but only the brilliant flashing gems. "In the vision the flashing lustre of the *iaspis* and the fiery red of the *sard* are relieved by the halo (*iris*) of emerald which encircled the Throne" (Swete). A complete circle.

4. *Round about the throne* (*kuklothen tou thronou*). Here as a preposition with the genitive, though only adverb in 4:8 (only N.T. examples save Textus Rec. in 5:11). *Four and twenty thrones* (*thronoi eikosi tessares*). So P Q, but Aleph A have accusative *thronous* (supply *eidon* from 4:1) and *tessares* (late accusative in *-es*). This further circle of thrones beyond the great throne. *I saw four and twenty elders* (*eikosi tessaras presbuterous*). No *eidon* in the text, but the accusative case calls for it. Twenty-four as a symbolic number occurs only in this book and only for these elders (4:4, 10; 5:8; 11:16; 19:4). We do not really know why this number is chosen, perhaps two elders for each tribe, perhaps the twelve tribes and the twelve apostles (Judaism and Christianity), perhaps the twenty-four courses of the sons of Aaron (I Chron. 24:1–19), perhaps some angelic rank (Col. 1:16) of which we know nothing. Cf. Eph. 2:6. *Sitting* (*kathēmenous*). Upon their thrones. *Arrayed* (*peribeblēmenous*). Perfect passive participle of *periballō* (to throw around). *In white garments* (*himatiois leukois*). Locative case here as in 3:5 (with *en*), though accusative in 7:9, 13. *Crowns of gold* (*stephanous chrusous*). Accusative case again like *presbuterous* after *eidon* (4:1), not *idou*. In 19:14 *echōn* (having) is added. John uses *diadēma* (diadem) for the kingly crown in 12:3; 13:1; 19:12, but it is not certain that the old distinction between *diadem* as the kingly crown and *stephanos* as the victor's wreath is always observed in late Greek.

5. *Out of the throne* (*ek tou thronou*). Back to the throne itself. The imagery is kin to that in Ex. 19:16; 24:9f.; Ezek. 1:22, 27. *Proceed* (*ekporeuontai*). Graphic historical

present. *Lightnings and voices and thunders (astrapai kai phōnai kai brontai).* So exactly in 11:19; 16:18, but in 8:5 with *brontai* first, *astrapai* last, all old and common words. "The thunderstorm is in Hebrew poetry a familiar symbol of the Divine power: cf., e.g., I Sam. 2:10; Ps. 18:9f.; Job 37:4f." (Swete). *Seven lamps of fire (hepta lampades puros).* Return to the nominative (*idou*, not *eidon*) with *ēsan* (were) understood. Metaphor drawn from Ezek. 1:13 and Zech. 4:12ff. Our word "lamp," but here a torch as in 8:10, identified with the Holy Spirit (the Seven Spirits of God) as in 1:4; 3:1, not *luchniai* (lampstands) as in 1:12, 20, nor *luchnos* a hand-lamp with oil (Matt. 5:15). "These torches blaze perpetually before the throne of God" (Swete).

6. *As it were a glassy sea (hōs thalassa hualinē).* Old adjective (from *hualos*, glass, 21:18, 21), in N.T. only here and 15:2. Possibly from *huei* (it rains), like a raindrop. At any rate here it is the appearance, not the material. Glass was made in Egypt 4,000 years ago. In Ex. 24:10 the elders see under the feet of God in the theophany a paved work of sapphire stone (cf. Ezek. 1:26). The likeness of the appearance of sky to sea suggests the metaphor here (Beckwith). *Like crystal (homoia krustallōi).* Associative-instrumental case after *homoia*. Old word, from *kruos* (ice and sometimes used for ice), in N.T. only here and 22:1, not semiopaque, but clear like rock-crystal. *In the midst of the throne (en mesōi tou thronou).* As one looks from the front, really before. *Round about the throne (kuklōi tou thronou).* Merely an adverb in the locative case (Rom. 15:19), as a preposition in N.T. only here, 5:11; 7:11. This seems to mean that on each of the four sides of the throne was one of the four living creatures either stationary or moving rapidly round (Ezek. 1:12f.). *Four living creatures (tessera zōa).* Not *thēria* (beasts), but living creatures. Certainly kin to the *zōa* of Ezek. 1 and 2 which are cherubim (Ezek. 10:2, 20), though here the details vary as to faces

and wings with a significance of John's own, probably representing creation in contrast with the redeemed (the elders). *Full of eyes* (*gemonta ophthalmōn*). Present active participle of *gemō*, to be full of, with the genitive, signifying here unlimited intelligence (Beckwith), the ceaseless vigilance of nature (Swete).

7. *Like a lion* (*homoion leonti*). Associative-instrumental case again. In Ezek. (1:6, 10) each *zōon* has four faces, but here each has a different face. "The four forms represent whatever is noblest, strongest, wisest, and swiftest in nature" (Swete). But it is not necessary to try to find a symbolism in each face here like the early baseless identification with the Four Evangelists (the lion for Mark, the man for Matthew, the calf for Luke, the eagle for John). *Moschos* is first a sprout, then the young of animals, then a calf (bullock or heifer) as in Luke 15:23, 27, 30, or a full-grown ox (Ezek. 1:10). *Had* (*echōn*). Masculine singular (some MSS. *echon* neuter singular agreeing with *zōon*) present active participle of *echō*, changing the construction with the *triton zōon* almost like a finite verb as in verse 8. *A face as of a man* (*prosōpon hōs anthrōpou*). Shows that the likeness in each instance extended only to the face. *Like an eagle flying* (*homoion aetōi petomenōi*). Present middle participle of *petomai*, to fly, old verb, in N.T. only in Rev. 4:7; 8:13; 12:14; 14:6; 19:17. The *aetos* in Matt. 24:28 and Luke 17:37 may be a form of vulture going after carrion, but not in Rev. 8:13; 12:14.

8. *Each one of them* (*hen kath' hen autōn*). "One by one of them," a vernacular idiom like *heis kata heis* in Mark 14:19. *Having* (*echōn*). Masculine participle again as in verse 7, though *zōon* neuter. *Six wings* (*ana pterugas hex*). Distributive use of *ana*, "six wings apiece" as in Luke 10:1 (*ana duo*, by twos). Like Is. 6:2, not like Ezek. 1:6, where only four wings are given apiece. *Are full of* (*gemousin*). Plural verb, though *zōa* neuter, to individualize each one.

Round about and within (*kuklothen kai esōthen*). Perhaps before and behind (4:6) and under the wings, "pointing to the secret energies of nature" (Swete). *Rest* (*anapausin*). See also 14:11. Old word (from *anapauō*, to relax), as in Matt. 11:29. God and Christ cease not their activity (John 5:17). "This ceaseless activity of nature under the hand of God is a ceaseless tribute of praise" (Swete). *Day and night* (*hēmeras kai nuktos*). Genitive of time, by day and by night. *Holy, holy, holy* (*hagios, hagios, hagios*). "The task of the Cherubim together with the Seraphim and Ophannim is to sing the praises of God" (Charles) in the *trisagion* (triple repetition of *hagios*). *Is the Lord God* (*Kurios ho theos*). See Is. 6:3. The copula *estin* (is) is not expressed, but is implied. *The Almighty* (*ho pantokratōr*). See on 1:8. *Which was and which is and which is to come* (*ho ēn kai ho ōn kai ho erchomenos*). Just as in 1:4, 8, but with the order changed.

9. *When the living creatures shall give* (*hotan dōsousin ta zōa*). Indefinite temporal clause with *hotan* and the future active indicative (*dōsousin*) rather than the more common second aorist active subjunctive (*dōsin*) with the notion of repetition rather than unbroken continuance, "whenever they give." The giving of praise and glory to God by the four living creatures (representatives of nature) is met by corresponding worship by the redeemed (the four and twenty elders). "Created life adores the Uncreated" (Swete), "to the one living for ages of ages."

10. *Shall fall down* (*pesountai*, future middle of *piptō*), *shall worship* (*proskunēsousin*, future active of *proskuneō*), *shall cast their crowns* (*balousin tous stephanous*, future active of *ballō*). The two actions by the two groups (living creatures, elders) are coördinated (simultaneous in the repetition). They thus acknowledge that all this kingly dignity comes from God, who is King of kings and Lord of

lords. Charles takes the elders, however, to be angels, not redeemed men.

11. *Our Lord and our God* (*ho kurios kai ho theos hēmōn*). The nominative form here used as vocative as in John 20:28 and often. *To receive* (*labein*). Epexegetic second aorist active infinitive of *lambanō* with *axios* (worthy). *The glory* (*tēn doxan*). The article referring to *doxan* in verse 9 and so with *tēn timēn* (the honour), though *tēn dunamin* (the power) is not in verse 9, but is the power due to be ascribed to God. *Thou didst create* (*su ektisas*). Emphasis on *su* (thou), first aorist active indicative of *ktizō*, the verb used about the act of creation by Paul in Col. 1:16 (*ektisthē*, *ektistai*), constative aorist giving a summary picture of the whole (not as a process). *Because of thy will* (*dia to thelēma sou*). Reason for creation of the universe as in Heb. 2:10 (*di' hon*). *They were* (*ēsan*). Imperfect tense with a cursory glance at the universe as a fact, possibly a potential existence in God's purpose in the eternal past before the actual creation in time. *And were created* (*kai ektisthēsan*). First aorist passive indicative of the same verb, *ktizō*, just used and in the plural, while Paul (Col. 1:16) uses the singular *ektisthē*. See I Cor. 8:6. God's will wrought through the Logos (Christ).

CHAPTER V

1. *In the right hand* (*epi tēn dexian*). "Upon the right hand" (*epi*, not *en*), the open palm. Anthropomorphic language drawn from Ezek. 2:9f. *A book* (*biblion*). Diminutive of *biblos*, but no longer so used, *biblaridion* occurring instead (10:2). *Written* (*gegrammenon*). Perfect passive predicate participle of *graphō*. *Within and on the back* (*esōthen kai opisthen*). "Within and behind." Description of a roll like that in Luke 4:17, not a codex as some scholars think. Usually these papyrus rolls were written only on the inside, but this one was so full of matter that it was written also on the back side (*opisthen*), and so was an *opisthographon* like that in Ezek. 2:10. There are many allegorical interpretations of this fact which are all beside the point. *Sealed* (*katesphragismenon*). Perfect passive predicate participle of *katasphragizō*, old compound (perfective use of *kata*), to seal up (down), here only in N.T. *With seven seals* (*sphragisin hepta*). Instrumental case of *sphragis*, old word used in various senses, proof or authentication (I Cor. 9:2; Rom. 4:11), signet-ring (Rev. 7:2), impression made by the seal (Rev. 9:4; II Tim. 2:19), the seal on books closing the book (Rev. 5:1, 2, 5, 9; 6:1, 3, 5, 7, 9, 12; 8:1). "A will in Roman law bore the seven seals of the seven witnesses" (Charles). But this sealed book of doom calls for no witnesses beyond God's own will. Alford sees in the number seven merely the completeness of God's purposes.

2. *A strong angel* (*aggelon ischuron*). One needed (10:1; 18:21) "whose call could reach to the farthest limits of the universe" (Beckwith) and so "with a great voice" (*en phōnēi megalēi*, in a great voice, as in 14:7, 9, 15, and without *en* 5:12; 6:10; 7:2, 10; 8:13; 10:3, etc.). See *en ischurāi*

phōnēi (18:2). *Proclaiming* (*kērussonta*). Present active predicate participle of *kērussō*, to herald, to preach. *Worthy to open and to loose* (*axios anoixai kai lusai*). Worthy by rank and character (cf. John 1:27) as well as by ability (*edunato*, verse 3), followed by two infinitives (first aorist active) of *anoigō* and *luō*, though *hina* and the subjunctive can be used after *axios* as in John 1:27. Here *axios* is like *hikanos* (capable, qualified) as in Matt. 8:8. The articles here (*to, tas*) refer to the book and the seals in verse 1. It is a husteron-proteron, since the loosing of the seals precedes the opening of the book.

3. *En* (in) with locative (*ouranōi*), *epi* (upon) with genitive (*gēs*), *hupokatō* (under) with ablative (*gēs*), as in verse 13, including the whole universe, as in Ex. 20:4 (Phil. 2:10). The MSS. vary in the negative conjunctions after *oudeis* (no one) between *oude—oude* (continuative, and not—nor) and *oute—oute* (disjunctive, neither—nor). *To look thereon* (*blepein auto*). Into the contents of the book. The universe declines the challenge.

4. *I wept much* (*egō eklaion polu*). Imperfect active of *klaiō*, picturesque, descriptive, I kept on weeping much; natural tense in these vivid visions (1:12; 2:14; 5:4, 14; 6:8, 9; 10:10; 19:14; 21:15). Perhaps weeping aloud. *Was found* (*heurethē*). First aorist passive indicative of *heuriskō*. *Worthy* (*axios*). Predicative nominative after *heurethē*.

5. *One of the elders* (*heis ek tōn presbuterōn*). "One from among the elders" of 4:4, 10 (*ek* with the ablative 8 times in the Apocalypse, 12 in the Fourth Gospel, 10 in rest of the N.T., in place of the mere partitive genitive). No particular reason for one elder as the agent over another (7:13). *Saith* (*legei*). Dramatic vivid present. *Weep not* (*mē klaie*). "Cease weeping" (prohibition with *mē* and the present active imperative of *klaiō*. *The Lion* (*ho leōn*). Satan is called a lion by Peter (I Pet. 5:8), but the metaphor belongs to Jesus also. Judah is called a lion in the blessing of Jacob

(Gen. 49:9) and Jesus as the greatest of the tribe of Judah, "the Root of David" (*hē riza Daueid*, Is. 11:1, 10) or the Branch from this root (the Messiah). *Hath overcome* (*enikēsen*). First aorist active indicative of *nikaō*, "did overcome," coming first in the sentence as "the great historical fact of the victory of the Christ" (Swete).

6. *And I saw* (*kai eidon*). Stirred by the words of the elder in verse 5 (*idou*, behold). "I beheld." *In the midst* (*en mesōi*). See 4:6 for this idiom. It is not quite clear where the Lamb was standing in the vision, whether close to the throne or in the space between the throne and the elders (perhaps implied by "came" in verse 7, but nearness to the throne is implied by 14:1 and Acts 7:56; Heb. 10:11). *A Lamb* (*arnion*). Elsewhere in the N.T. *ho amnos* is used of Christ (John 1:29, 36; Acts 8:32; I Pet. 1:19 like Is. 53:7), but in the Apocalypse *to arnion* occurs for the Crucified Christ 29 times in twelve chapters. *Standing* (*hestēkos*). Second perfect active (intransitive of *histēmi*) neuter accusative singular (grammatical gender like *arnion*), though some MSS. read *hestēkōs* (natural gender masculine and nominative in spite of *eidon* construction according to sense). *As though it had been slain* (*hōs esphagmenon*). Perfect passive predicate participle of *sphazō*, old word, in N.T. only in Rev. 5:6, 9, 12; 6:4, 9; 13:3; 18:24; and I John 3:12. *Hōs* (as if) is used because the Lamb is now alive, but (in appearance) with the marks of the sacrifice. The Christ as the Lamb is both sacrifice and Priest (Heb. 9:12f.; 10:11). *Having* (*echōn*). Construction according to sense again with masculine nominative participle instead of *echonta* (masculine accusative singular) or *echon* (neuter accusative singular). Seven horns (*keras*) is a common symbol in the O.T. for strength and kingly power (I Sam. 2:10; I Kings 22:11; Ps. 112:9; Dan. 7:7, 20ff.) and often in Rev. (12:3; 13:1; 17:3, 12). Fulness of power (the All-powerful one) is symbolized by seven. *Seven eyes* (*ophthalmous hepta*). Like Zech. 3:9;

4:10 and denotes here, as there, omniscience. Here they are identified with the seven Spirits of Christ, while in 1:4 the seven Spirits are clearly the Holy Spirit of God (3:1), and blaze like torches (4:5), like the eyes of Christ (1:14). The Holy Spirit is both Spirit of God and of Christ (Rom. 8:9). *Sent forth* (*apestalmenoi*). Perfect passive predicate participle of *apostellō*, masculine plural (agreeing with *hoi* and *ophthalmous* in gender), but some MSS. have *apestalmena* agreeing with the nearer *pneumata*.

7. *He taketh* (*eilēphen*). Perfect active indicative of *lambanō*, not used for the aorist (cf. *ēlthen*, he came), but vivid dramatic picture of the actual scene, "he has taken it."

8. *He had taken* (*elaben*). Here John drops back to the narrative tense (the second aorist active indicative of *lambanō*), not the past perfect as the English rendering might indicate, merely "when he took." For like vivid variation (not confusion) of tenses with *eilēphen* see 3:3; 8:5; 11:17 and with *eirēka* in 7:13f.; 19:3. *Fell down* (*epesan*). Second aorist active indicative of *piptō* with first aorist (-*an*) ending, just "fell." *Having* (*echontes*). "Holding." *A harp* (*kitharan*). Old word, the traditional instrument (lyre or zithern) for psalmody (Ps. 33:2; 98:5, etc.). *Golden bowls* (*phialas chrusās*). Broad shallow saucers, old word, in N.T. only in Rev. 5:8; 15:7; 16:1-4, 8, 10, 12, 17; 17:1; 21:9. *Of incense* (*thumiamatōn*). Old word from *thumiaō*, to burn incense (Luke 1:9), as in Luke 1:10. *Which are* (*hai eisin*). "Which (these bowls of incense) symbolize the prayers of the saints" as in Ps. 140:2; Luke 1:10.

9. *They sing* (*āidousin*). Present active indicative of *āidō*. Old verb, to chant with lyrical emotion (Col. 3:16. *A new song* (*ōidēn kainēn*). Cognate accusative for *oide* (*ōidē*, song) is *āoide* from *āeidō*, that is *āidō* (the verb used), old word already used (Col. 3:16; Eph. 5:19), called *kainēn* because a fresh song for new mercies (Is. 42:10; Ps. 33:3; 40:3, etc.), here in praise of redemption to Christ (14:3) like

the new name (2:17; 3:12), the new Jerusalem (3:12; 21:2), the new heaven and the new earth (21:1), not the old song of creation (4:8, 11) to God. *For thou wast slain* (*hoti esphagēs*). Second aorist passive indicative of *sphazō*. *Agorazō* used by Paul and Peter of our purchase from sin by Christ (I Cor. 6:20; 7:23; Gal. 3:13; 4:5; II Pet. 2:1; cf. I Pet. 1:18f.). *Unto God* (*tōi theōi*). Dative case of advantage as also in verse 10. *With thy blood* (*en tōi haimati sou*). Instrumental use of *en* as in 1:5. The blood of Christ as the price of our redemption runs all through the Apocalypse. This is the reason why Christ is worthy to "take the book and open its seals." That is, he is worthy to receive adoration and worship (4:11) as the Father does. *Men of every* (*ek pasēs*). No *anthrōpous* (men) or *tinas* (some) before *ek* in the Greek. See a like ellipsis in 11:9 with a like grouping of words for all mankind, representatives of all races and nations (7:9; 13:7; 14:6).

10. *Madest* (*epoiēsas*). First aorist active indicative of *poieō*, a prophetic use anticipating the final result. *A kingdom and priests* (*basileian kai hiereis*). As the correct text in 1:6. *They reign* (*basileuousin*). Present active indicative, futuristic use, though Aleph P have the future *basileusousin* (shall reign) as in 20:6.

11. *And I saw* (*kai eidon*). A new feature introduced by the outer and vaster circle (*kuklōi*) of angels who catch up the new song of redemption in antiphonal singing, answering the song of the four living creatures and the twenty-four elders. Some MSS. read *hōs* (as if) before *phōnēn* (voice). *Ten thousand times ten thousand* (*muriades muriadōn kai chiliades chiliadōn*). Literally, "myriads of myriads and thousands of thousands," a mild husteron-proteron. The regular order in I Enoch 40:1. See Dan. 7:10 for *chiliai chiliades* (thousand thousands) and *muriai muriades* (countless myriads). They are all efforts to express the innumerable hosts of the angels.

12. *Worthy* (*axion*). Agreeing in gender (grammatical neuter) with *arnion*, but some MSS. have *axios* (masculine, natural gender). Note change to third person *estin* instead of second *ei*. The point of the song is the same as that in verses 9 and 10, but the language differs. Note the repeated article *to* (the lamb the slain) referring to verses 6 and 9. Note also the one article *tēn* before *dunamin* for all the seven grounds of praise (*dunamin*, power, *plouton*, wealth, *sophian*, wisdom, *ischun*, strength, *timēn*, honor, *doxan*, glory, *eulogian*, blessing), though *plouton* is masculine, in contrast with separate article for each item (all three feminine) in 4:11, here grouping them all together, "a heptad of praise" (Swete).

13. *Every created thing* (*pān ktisma*). Every creature in a still wider antiphonal circle beyond the circle of angels (from *ktizō*, for which see I Tim. 4:4; James 1:18), from all the four great fields of life (in heaven, upon the earth, under the earth as in verse 3, with on the sea *epi tēs thalassēs* added). No created thing is left out. This universal chorus of praise to Christ from all created life reminds one of the profound mystical passage in Rom. 8:20–22 concerning the sympathetic agony of creation (*ktisis*) in hope of freedom from the bondage of corruption. If the trail of the serpent is on all creation, it will be ultimately thrown off. *Saying* (*legontas*). Masculine (construction according to sense, personifying the created things) if genuine, though some MSS. have *legonta* (grammatical gender agreeing with *panta*) present active participle of *legō*, to say. *And to the Lamb* (*kai tōi arniōi*). Dative case. Praise and worship are rendered to the Lamb precisely as to God on the throne. Note separate articles here in the doxology as in 4:11 and the addition of *to kratos* (active power) in place of *ischus* (reserve of strength) in 5:12.

14. *Amen* (*Amēn*). The four living creatures give their approval to the doxology after the antiphonal songs *Fell*

down and worshipped (*epesan kai prosekunēsan*). In silent adoration that closes the whole service of praise to the One upon the throne and to the Lamb. As in 4:10 so here the representatives of the redeemed bow in silent worship. Pliny says that the Christians sing a song to Christ as to God. He is here worshipped by the universe (Phil. 2:10f.).

CHAPTER VI

1. *And I saw* (*kai eidon*). As in 4:1; 5:1. The vision unfolds without anything being said about opening the book and reading from it. In a more vivid and dramatic fashion the Lamb breaks the seals one by one and reveals the contents and the symbolism. The first four seals have a common note from one of the four *zōa* and the appearance of a horse. No effort will be made here to interpret these seals as referring to persons or historical events in the past, present, or future, but simply to relate the symbolism to the other symbols in the book. It is possible that there is some allusion here to the symbolism in the so-called "Little Apocalypse" of Mark 13 = Matt. 24f. = Luke 21. The imagery of the four horses is similar to that in Zech. 1:7–11; 6:1–8 (cf. Jer. 14:12; 24:10; 42:17). In the Old Testament the horse is often the emblem of war (Job 39:25; Ps. 76:6; Prov. 21:31; Ezek. 26:10). "Homer pictures the horses of Rhesus as whiter than snow, and swift as the wind" (Vincent). *When the Lamb opened* (*hote ēnoixen to arnion*). First aorist active indicative of *anoigō*. This same phrase recurs in rhythmical order at the opening of each seal (6:1, 3, 5, 7, 9, 12) till the last (8:1), where we have *hotan ēnoixen* (*hotan* rather than *hote* calling particular attention to it). *One* (*mian*). Probably used here as an ordinal (the first) as in Matt. 28:1. See Robertson, *Grammar*, p. 671f. *Of* (*ek*). This use of *ek* with the ablative in the partitive sense is common in the Apocalypse, as twice in this verse (*ek tōn*, etc.). So *henos ek tōn* (one of the four living creatures) is "the first of," etc. *In a voice of thunder* (*en phōnēi brontēs*). Old word used of John and James (Mark 3:17) and elsewhere in N.T. only John 12:29 and a dozen times in the Apocalypse.

Come (*Erchou*). Present middle imperative of *erchomai*, but with exclamatory force (not strictly linear). The command is not addressed to the Lamb nor to John (the correct text omits *kai ide* "and see") as in 17:1; 21:9, but to one of the four horsemen each time. Swete takes it as a call to Christ because *erchou* is so used in 22:17, 20, but that is not conclusive.

2. *And I saw and behold* (*kai eidon kai idou*). This combination is frequent in the Apocalypse (4:1; 6:2, 5, 8; 14:1, 14; 19:11). *A white horse* (*hippos leukos*). In Zech. 6:1–8 we have red, black, white, and grizzled bay horses like the four winds of heaven, ministers to do God's will. White seems to be the colour of victory (cf. the white horse of the Persian Kings) like the white horse ridden by the Roman conqueror in a triumphant procession. *Had* (*echōn*). Agreeing in gender and case with *ho kathēmenos*. *A bow* (*toxon*). Old word (Zech. 9:13f. of a great bow), here only in N.T. *Was given* (*edothē*). First aorist passive indicative of *didōmi*. *A crown* (*stephanos*). See on 4:4 for this word. *He came forth* (*exēlthen*). Second aorist active indicative of *exerchomai*, either to come out or to go out (went forth). *Conquering* (*nikōn*). Present active participle of *nikaō*. *And to conquer* (*kai hina nikēsēi*). Purpose clause with *hina* and the first aorist active subjunctive of *nikaō*. Here *hōs nikēsōn* (future active participle with *hōs*) could have been used. The aorist tense here points to ultimate victory. Commentators have been busy identifying the rider of the white horse according to their various theories. "It is tempting to identify him with the Rider on the white horse in 19:11f., whose name is 'the Word of God'" (Swete). Tempting, "but the two riders have nothing in common beyond the white horse."

3. *The second seal* (*tēn sphragida tēn deuteran*). "The seal the second." The white horse with his rider vanished from the scene, bent on his conquering career.

4. *A red horse* (*hippos purros*). Old adjective from *pur* (fire), flame-coloured, blood-red (II Kings 3:22), in N.T. only here and 12:3, like Zech. 1:8; 6:2 (roan horse). *To take peace from the earth* (*labein tēn eirēnēn ek tēs gēs*). Second aorist active infinitive of *lambanō*, and here the nominative case, the subject of *edothē* (see verse 2), "to take peace out of the earth." Alas, how many red horses have been ridden through the ages. *And that they should slay one another* (*kai hina allēlous sphaxousin*). Epexegetical explanatory purpose clause with *hina* and the future active of *sphazō* (5:6) instead of the more usual subjunctive (verse 2). Cf. Robertson, *Grammar*, p. 998f. This is what war does to perfection, makes cannon fodder (cf. John 14:27) of men. *A great sword* (*machaira megalē*). *Machaira* may be a knife carried in a sheath at the girdle (John 18:10) or a long sword in battle as here. *Romphaia*, also a large sword, is the only other word for sword in the N.T. (Rev. 1:16; 2:12, 16; 6:8; 19:15, 21).

5. *A black horse* (*hippos melas*). Lust of conquest brings bloodshed, but also famine and hunger. "The colour of mourning and famine. See Jer. 4:28; 8:21; Mal. 3:14, where *mournfully* is, literally, in black" (Vincent). *Had* (*echōn*) as in verse 2. *A balance* (*zugon*). Literally, a yoke (old word from *zeugnumi*, to join), of slavery (Acts 15:10; Gal. 5:1), of teaching (Matt. 11:29), of weight or measure like a pair of scales evenly balancing as here (Ezek. 5:1; 45:10). The rider of this black horse, like the spectral figure of hunger, carries in his hand a pair of scales. This is also one of the fruits of war.

6. *As it were a voice* (*hōs phōnēn*). "This use of *hōs*, giving a certain vagueness or mysteriousness to a phrase, is one of the characteristics of the writer's style, e.g., 8:1; 14:3; 19:1, 6" (Beckwith). This voice comes from the midst of the four living creatures, "the protest of nature against the horrors of famine" (Swete). *A measure* (*choinix*). Old word

for less than a quart with us, here only in N.T. *Of wheat* (*sitou*). Old word for wheat, a number of times in N.T., in Rev. only here and 18:13. This was enough wheat to keep a man of moderate appetite alive for a day. *For a penny* (*dēnariou*). Genitive of price, the wages of a day laborer (Matt. 20:2), about eighteen cents in our money today. *Of barley* (*krithōn*). Old word *krithē*, usually in plural as here. Barley was the food of the poor and it was cheaper even in the famine and it took more of it to support life. Here the proportion is three to one (cf. II Kings 7:18). The proclamation forbids famine prices for food (solid and liquid). *Hurt thou not* (*mē adikēsēis*). Prohibition with *mē* and the ingressive first aorist active subjunctive of *adikeō*. See 7:3 and 9:4 for *adikeō* for injury to vegetable life. "The prohibition is addressed to the nameless rider who represents Dearth" (Swete). Wheat and barley, oil and the vine, were the staple foods in Palestine and Asia Minor.

8. *A pale horse* (*hippos chlōros*). Old adjective. Contracted from *chloeros* (from *chloē*, tender green grass) used of green grass (Mark 6:39; Rev. 8:7; 9:4), here for yellowish, common in both senses in old Greek, though here only in N.T. in this sense, greenish yellow. We speak of a sorrel horse, never of a green horse. Zechariah (6:3) uses *poikilos* (grizzled or variegated). Homer used *chlōros* of the ashen colour of a face blanched by fear (pallid) and so the pale horse is a symbol of death and of terror. *His name was Death* (*onoma autōi ho thanatos*). Anacoluthon in grammatical structure like that in John 3:1 (cf. Rev. 2:26) and common enough. Death is the name of this fourth rider (so personified) and there is with Death "his inseparable comrade, Hades (1:16; 20:13f.)" (Swete). Hades (*hāidēs*, alpha privative, and *idein*, to see, the unseen) is the abode of the dead, the keys of which Christ holds (Rev. 1:18). *Followed* (*ēkolouthei*). Imperfect active of *akoloutheō*, kept step with death, whether on the same horse or on another horse by

his side or on foot John does not say. *Over the fourth part
of the earth* (*epi to tetarton tēs gēs*). Partitive genitive *gēs*
after *tetarton*. Wider authority (*exousia*) was given to this
rider than to the others, though what part of the earth is
included in the fourth part is not indicated. *To kill* (*apok-
teinai*). First aorist active infinitive of *apokteinō*, explanation of the *exousia* (authority). The four scourges of Ezek.
14:21 are here reproduced with instrumental *en* with the
inanimate things (*romphaiāi, limōi thanatōi*) and *hupo* for
the beasts (*thēriōn*). Death here (*thanatōi*) seems to mean
pestilence as the Hebrew does (*loimos*—cf. *limos* famine).
Cf. the "black death" for a plague.

9. *Under the altar* (*hupokatō tou thusiastēriou*). "Under"
(*hupokatō*), for the blood of the sacrifices was poured at the
bottom of the altar (Lev. 4:7). The altar of sacrifice (Ex.
39:39; 40:29), not of incense. The imagery, as in Hebrews,
is from the tabernacle. For the word see Matt. 5:23f., often
in Rev. (8:3, 5; 9:13; 11:1; 14:18; 16:7). This altar in
heaven is symbolic, of course, the antitype for the tabernacle
altar (Heb. 8:5). The Lamb was slain (5:6, 9, 12) and these
martyrs have followed the example of their Lord. *The souls*
(*tas psuchas*). The lives, for the life is in the blood (Lev.
17:11), were given for Christ (Phil. 2:17; II Tim. 4:6). *Of
the slain* (*tōn esphagmenōn*). See 5:6. Christians were slain
during the Neronian persecution and now again under Domitian. A long line of martyrs has followed. *For the word
of God* (*dia ton logon tou theou*). As in 1:9, the confession of
loyalty to Christ as opposed to emperor-worship. *And for
the testimony which they held* (*kai dia tēn marturian hēn
eichon*). See also 1:9. Probably *kai* equals "even" here,
explaining the preceding. The imperfect tense *eichon* suits
the repetition of the witness to Christ and the consequent
death.

10. *How long* (*heōs pote*). "Until when." Cf. Matt. 7:17;
John 10:24. *O Master* (*ho despotēs*). Nominative articular

form, but used as vocative (*despota*) as in 4:11 (John 20:28).
On *despotēs* (correlative of *doulos*) see Luke 2:29. Here
(alone in the Apocalypse) it is applied to God as in Luke
2:29; Acts 4:24, but to Christ in Jude 4; II Pet. 2:1. *The
holy and true* (*ho hagios kai alēthinos*). See 3:7 for these
attributes of God. *Avenge our blood on them that dwell upon
the earth* (*ekdikeis to haima hēmōn ek tōn katoikountōn epi tēs
gēs*). This same idiom in 19:2 and see it also in Luke 18:7f.,
"a passage which goes far to answer many questions in the-
odicy" (Swete). We find *ekdikeō*, late compound, used with
ek as here in Deut. 18:19; I Sam. 24:13, but with *apo* in
Luke 18:3. For *epi tēs gēs* (upon the earth) see 3:10.

11. *A white robe* (*stolē leukē*). Old word from *stellō*, to
equip, an equipment in clothes, a flowing robe (Mark 12:38).
For the white robe for martyrs see 3:4f.; 4:4; 7:9, 13; 19:14.
That they should rest (*hina anapausontai*). Sub-final clause
with *hina* and the future indicative (as in 3:9; 6:4) middle
rather than the aorist middle subjunctive *anapausōntai* of
Aleph C. *Yet for a little time* (*eti chronon mikron*). Accusative of extension of time as in 20:3. Perhaps rest from their
cry for vengeance and also rest in peace (14:13). For the
verb *anapauō* see on Matt. 11:28. *Until should be fulfilled*
(*heōs plērōthōsin*). Future indefinite temporal clause with
heōs and the first aorist passive subjunctive of *plēroō*, to fill
full (Matt. 23:32; Col. 2:10), "until be filled full" (the number
of), regular Greek idiom. *Which should be killed* (*hoi mel-
lontes apoktennesthai*). Regular construction of articular
present active participle of *mellō* (about to be, going to be)
with the present passive infinitive of *apoktennō*, Æolic and
late form for *apokteinō*, to kill (also in Mark 12:5). John
foresees more persecution coming (2:10; 3:10).

12. *There was a great earthquake* (*seismos megas egeneto*).
"There came a great earthquake." Jesus spoke of earth-
quakes in his great eschatological discourse (Mark 13:8).
In Matt. 24:29 the powers of the heavens will be shaken.

Seismos is from *seiō*, to shake, and occurs also in Rev. 8:5; 11:13, 19; 16:18. The reference is not a local earthquake like those so common in Asia Minor. *As sackcloth of hair* (*hōs sakkos trichinos*). *Sakkos* (Attic *sakos*), Latin *saccus*, English *sack*, originally a bag for holding things (Gen. 42:25, 35), then coarse garment of hair (trichinos, old word from *thrix*, here only in N.T.) clinging to one like a sack, of mourners, suppliants, prophets leading austere lives (Matt. 3:4; 11:21; Luke 10:13). Here the hair is that of the black goat (Is. 50:3). Cf. Joel 2:10; Ezek. 32:7f.; Is. 13:10; Mark 13:24f. See Eccl. 12:2 for eclipses treated as symbols of old age. Apocalyptic pictures all have celestial phenomena following earthquakes. *As blood* (*hōs haima*). In Acts 2:20 we find Peter interpreting the apocalyptic eschatological language of Joel 2:31 about the sun being turned into darkness and the moon into blood as pointing to the events of the day of Pentecost as also "the great day of the Lord." Peter's interpretation of Joel should make us cautious about too literal an exegesis of these grand symbols.

13. *Her unripe figs* (*tous olunthous autēs*). An old word (Latin *grossi*) for figs that grow in winter and fall off in the spring without getting ripe (Song of Solomon 2:11f.), here only in N.T. Jesus used the fig tree (Mark 13:28) as a sign of the "end of the world's long winter" (Swete). Cf. Is. 34:4; Nah. 3:12. *When she is shaken of a great wind* (*hupo anemou megalou seiomenē*). Present passive participle of *seiō*, "being shaken by a great wind." See Matt. 11:7 for the reed so shaken.

14. *Was removed* (*apechōristhē*). First aorist passive indicative of *apochōrizō*, to separate, to part (Acts 15:39). "The heaven was parted." *As a scroll when it is rolled up* (*hōs biblion helissomenon*). Present passive participle of *helissō*, old verb, to roll up, in N.T. only here (from Is. 34:4) and Heb. 1:12 (from Ps. 102:27). Vivid picture of the expanse of the sky rolled up and away as a papyrus roll

(Luke 4:17). *Were moved* (*ekinēthēsan*). First aorist passive indicative of *kineō*, to move. *Out of their places* (*ek tōn topōn autōn*). See also 16:20 for these violent displacements in the earth's crust. Cf. Nah. 1:5 and Jer. 4:24. Jesus spoke of faith removing mountains (of difficulty) as in Mark 11:23 (cf. I Cor. 13:2).

15. *The princes* (*hoi megistānes*). Late word from the superlative *megistos*, in LXX, Josephus, papyri, in N.T. only in Mark 6:21; Rev. 6:15; 18:23, for the grandees, the persecuting proconsuls (Swete). *The chief captains* (*hoi chiliarchoi*). The commanders of thousands, the military tribunes (Mark 6:21; 19:18). *The rich* (*hoi plousioi*). Not merely those in civil and military authority will be terror-stricken, but the self-satisfied and complacent rich (James 5:4f.). *The strong* (*hoi ischuroi*). Who usually scoff at fear. See the list in 13:16 and 19:18. Cf. Luke 21:26. *Every bondman* (*pās doulos*) *and freeman* (*kai eleutheros*). The two extremes of society. *Hid themselves in the caves and in the rocks of the mountains* (*ekrupsan heautous eis ta spēlaia kai eis tas petras tōn oreōn*). Based on Is. 2:10, 18f. First aorist active indicative of *kruptō* with the reflexive pronoun. For the old word *spēlaion* see Matt. 21:13; Heb. 11:38. *Oreōn* is the uncontracted Ionic form (for *orōn*) of the genitive plural of *oros* (mountain).

16. *They say* (*legousin*). Vivid dramatic present active indicative, as is natural here. *Fall on us* (*Pesate eph' hēmās*). Second aorist (first aorist ending) imperative of *piptō*, tense of urgency, do it now. *And hide us* (*kai krupsate hēmās*). Same tense of urgency again from *kruptō* (verb in verse 15). Both imperatives come in inverted order from Hos. 10:8 with *kalupsate* (cover) in place of *krupsate* (hide), quoted by Jesus on the way to the Cross (Luke 23:30) in the order here, but with *kalupsate*, not *krupsate*. *From the face of him that* (*apo prosōpou tou*, etc.). "What sinners dread most is not death, but the revealed Presence of God" (Swete). Cf. Gen.

3:8. *And from the wrath of the Lamb* (*kai apo tēs orgēs tou arniou*). Repetition of "the grave irony" (Swete) of 5:5f. The Lamb is the Lion again in the terribleness of his wrath. Recall the mourning in 1:7. See Matt. 25:41ff. where Jesus pronounces the woes on the wicked.

17. *The great day* (*hē hēmera hē megalē*). The phrase occurs in the O.T. prophets (Joel 2:11, 31; Zeph. 1:14. Cf. Jude 6) and is here combined with "of their wrath" (*tēs orgēs autōn*) as in Zeph. 1:15, 18; 2:3; Rom. 2:5. "Their" (*autōn*) means the wrath of God and of the Lamb put here on an equality as in 1:17f., 22:3, 13; as in I Thess. 3:11; II Thess. 2:16. Beckwith holds that this language about the great day having come "is the mistaken cry of men in terror caused by the portents which are bursting upon them." There is something, to be sure, to be said for this view which denies that John commits himself to the position that this is the end of the ages. *And who is able to stand?* (*kai tis dunatai stathēnai?*). Very much like the words in Nah. 1:6 and Mal. 3:2. First aorist passive infinitive of *histēmi*. It is a rhetorical question, apparently by the frightened crowds of verse 15. Swete observes that the only possible answer to that cry is the command of Jesus in Luke 21:36: "Keep awake on every occasion, praying that ye may get strength to stand (*stathēnai*, the very form) before the Son of Man."

CHAPTER VII

1. *After this* (*meta touto*). Instead of the seventh seal (8:1) being opened, two other episodes or preliminary visions occupy chapter 7 (the sealing of the servants of God 7:1–8 and the vision of the redeemed before the throne 7:9–17). *Standing* (*hestōtas*). Second perfect predicate participle of *histēmi*, intransitive and followed by *epi* and the accusative case *gōnias* as already in 3:20 (*epi thurian*) and often again (8:3 some MSS., others genitive; 11:11; 12:18; 14:1; 15:2), but note *epi* with genitive *thalassēs* in the next clause, like *epi kephalēs* in 12:1 and in 7:3. *Corners* (*gōnias*). Old word for angle (Matt. 6:5), also in 20:8. *Holding* (*kratountas*). Present active participle of *krateō*, to hold fast (Mark 7:3; John 20:23). The four winds (cf. Matt. 24:31) are held prisoner by angels at each of the four corners. Some Jews held the winds from due north, south, east, west to be favourable, while those from the angles (see Acts 27:14) were unfavourable (Charles). There is an angel of the fire (14:18) and an angel of the waters (16:5). *That no wind should blow* (*hina mē pneēi anemos*). Negative purpose clause with *hina mē* and the present active subjunctive, "lest a wind keep on blowing." *Upon any tree* (*epi pan dendron*). Accusative case here with *epi* rather than the preceding genitives (*gēs, thalassēs*), "upon the land or upon the sea," but "against any tree" (picture of attack on the tree like a tornado's path).

2. *Ascend* (*anabainonta*). Present active participle of *anabainō*, "ascending," "going up," picturing the process. *From the sun-rising* (*apo anatolēs hēliou*). Same phrase in 16:12. From the east, though why is not told. Swete suggests it is because Palestine is east of Patmos. The plural

apo anatolōn occurs in Matt. 2:1 without *hēliou* (sun). *The seal of the living God* (*sphragida theou zōntos*). Here the signet ring, like that used by an Oriental monarch, to give validity to the official documents. The use of *zōntos* with *theou* accents the eternal life of God (1:18; 10:6; 15:7) as opposed to the ephemeral pagan gods. *To whom it was given* (*hois edothē autois*). For *edothē* see on 6:2, 4, etc. The repetition of *autois* in addition to *hois* (both dative) is a redundant Hebraism (in vernacular *Koiné* to some extent) often in the Apocalypse (3:8). The angels are here identified with the winds as the angels of the churches with the churches (1:20). *To hurt* (*adikēsai*). First aorist active infinitive of *adikeō*, subject of *edothē*, common use of *adikeō* in this sense of to hurt in the Apocalypse (2:11; 6:6 already), in Luke 10:19 also. The injury is to come by letting loose the winds, not by withholding them.

3. *Hurt not* (*mē adikēsēte*). Prohibition with *mē* and the ingressive aorist active subjunctive of *adikeō*, not to begin to hurt. *Till we shall have sealed* (*achri sphragisōmen*). Temporal clause of indefinite action for the future with *achri* (sometimes *achris hou* or *achris hou an*) and the aorist sub-junctive as in 15:8; 20:3, 5 or the future indicative (17:7), usually with the notion of ascent (up to) rather than extent like *mechri*. *An* (modal) sometimes occurs, but it is not necessary. But there is no *futurum exactum* idea in the aorist subjunctive, simply "till we seal," not "till we shall have sealed." *Upon their foreheads* (*epi tōn metōpōn*). From Ezek. 9:4. Old word (*meta*, *ōps*, after the eye, above the eye, the space above or between the eyes), in N.T. only in the Apocalypse (7:3; 9:4; 13:16; 14:1, 9; 17:5; 20:4; 22:4). For "the servants of God" (*tous doulous tou theou*) who are to be thus marked linked with angels in the service of God see Rev. 1:1; 2:20; 19:2, 5; 22:3, 6.

4. *The number of the sealed* (*ton arithmon tōn esphragis-menōn*). Accusative case object of *ēkousa* and genitive of

the perfect passive articular participle of *sphragizō*. He did not see the sealing or count them himself, but only heard. *A hundred and forty and four thousand (hekaton tesserakonta tessares chiliades)*. Symbolical, of course, and not meant to be a complete number of the sealed (or saved) even in that generation, let alone for all time. The number connotes perfection (Alford), $12 \times 12 \times 1000 = $ a hundred and forty-four thousands (*chiliades*, 5:11). Nominative absolute, not agreeing in case either with *arithmon* (accusative) or *esphragismenōn* (genitive). So as to the case of *esphragismenoi*. *Out of every tribe of the children of Israel (ek pāsēs phulēs huiōn Israēl)*. There are two opposite views here, one taking the sealed as referring only to Jews (either actual Jews as a remnant or just Jewish Christians), the other including Gentiles as well as Jewish Christians, that is the true Israel as in 2:9; 3:9ff. and like Paul in Galatians and Romans. This is the more probable view and it takes the twelve tribes in a spiritual sense. But in either view there remains the difficulty about names of the tribes. The list is not geographical, since Levi is included, but Dan is omitted and Manasseh put in his place, though he as the son of Joseph is included in Joseph. Irenæus suggested that Antichrist was expected to come from the tribe of Dan and hence the omission here. There are various lists of the tribes in the O.T. (Gen. 35:22f.; 46:8ff., 49; Ex. 1:1ff.; Num. 1:2; 13:4ff.; 26:34; Deut. 27:11f.; 33:6ff.; Josh. 13–22; Judges 5; I Chron. 2–8; 12:24ff.; 27:16ff.; Ezek. 48) and given in various orders. In I Chron. 7:12 both Dan and Zebulon are omitted. Joseph is given here in place of Ephraim. The distribution is equal (12,000) to each tribe.

9. *Which no man could number (hon arithmēsai auton oudeis edunato)*. Redundant repetition of the pronoun *auton* after the relative *hon* as in 7:5 and 3:8. *Edunato* imperfect indicative and *arithmēsai* first aorist active infinitive of *arithmeō*, old verb, in N.T. only here, Matt. 10:30; Luke

12:7. See 5:9 (also 11:9; 13:7; 14:10; 17:15) for the list of words after *ek* (the spiritual Israel carried on all over the world), "a polyglott cosmopolitan crowd" (Swete). *Standing (hestōtes)*. Same form in 7:1, only nominative masculine plural referring to *ochlos* (masculine singular), construction according to sense like the plural *legontōn* with *ochlou* in 19:1. *Arrayed (peribeblēmenous)*. Perfect passive participle of *periballō*, but in the accusative plural (not nominative like *hestōtes*), a common variation in this book when preceded by *eidon* and *idou* as in 4:4 (*thronoi, presbuterous*). Charles regards this as a mere slip which would have been changed to *peribeblēmenoi* if John had read the MS. over. *In white robes (stolas leukas)*. Predicate accusative retained with this passive verb of clothing as in 7:13; 10:1; 11:3; 12:1; 17:4; 18:16; 19:13. *Palms (phoinikes)*. Nominative again, back to construction with *idou*, not *eidon*. Old word, in N.T. only here for palm branches and John 12:13 for palm trees. Both these and the white robes are signs of victory and joy.

10. *They cry (krazousi)*. Vivid dramatic present. *With a great voice (phōnēi megalēi)*. As in 6:10; 7:2. "The polyglott multitude shouts its praises as with one voice" (Swete). *Salvation (hē sōtēria)*. As in 12:10; 19:1. Nominative absolute. Salvation here is regarded as an accomplished act on the part of those coming out of the great tribulation (verse 14) and the praise for it is given to God (*tōi theōi*, dative case) and to the Lamb (*tōi arniōi*, dative also). Both God and Christ are thus called *sōtēr* as in the Pastoral Epistles, as to God (I Tim. 1:1; 2:3; Titus 1:3; 3:4) and to Christ (Titus 1:4; 2:13; 3:6). For *hē sōtēria* see John 4:22; Acts 4:12; Jude 3.

11. *Were standing (histēkeisan)*. Past perfect active of *histēmi* intransitive and used like an imperfect as in John 19:25. *Round about (kuklōi)*. Preposition (in a circle) with genitive as in 4:6; 5:11. The angels here rejoice in the sal-

vation of men (Luke 15:7, 10; I Pet. 1:12). *Upon their faces* (*epi ta prosōpa autōn*). In reverential worship of God as in 11:16. For this worship (fell and worshipped) see also 4:10; 5:14; 11:16; 19:4, 10; 22:8. The dative *tōi theōi* (God) with *proskuneō* (to worship) is the usual construction for that meaning. When it means merely to do homage the accusative case is usual in this book (Charles). But in the Fourth Gospel the reverse order is true as to the cases with *proskuneō* (Abbott, *Joh. Vocab.* pp. 138–142).

12. Note *amēn* at the beginning and the close of the doxology. Note also separate feminine article with each of the seven attributes given God, as in 4:11; 5:12, 13.

13. *Answered* (*apekrithē*). First aorist passive (deponent) of *apokrinomai* with *legōn* (saying), a common (only here in the Apocalypse) Hebrew redundancy in the Gospels (Mark 9:5). An elder intervenes, though no question has been asked to interpret the vision (Swete). *These* (*houtoi*). Prophetic predicate nominative put before *tines eisin* (who are they). Note article repeated with *stolas* pointing to verse 9, and accusative also retained after *peribeblēmenoi* as there. Both "who" and "whence" as in Josh. 9:8.

14. *I say* (*eirēka*). Perfect active indicative of *eipon*, "I have said." "To the Seer's mind the whole scene was still fresh and vivid" (Swete) like *kekragen* in John 1:15 and *eilēphen* in Rev. 5:7, not the so-called "aoristic perfect" which even Moulton (*Prol.* p. 145) is disposed to admit. *My lord* (*Kurie mou*). "An address of reverence to a heavenly being" (Vincent), not an act of worship on John's part. *Thou knowest* (*su oidas*). "At once a confession of ignorance, and an appeal for information" (Swete), not of full confidence like *su oidas* in John 21:15ff. *They which come out of the great tribulation* (*hoi erchomenoi ek tēs thlipseōs tēs megalēs*). Present middle participle with the idea of continued repetition. "The martyrs are still arriving from the scene of the great tribulation" (Charles). Apparently

some great crisis is contemplated (Matt. 13:19ff.; 24:21; Mark 13:10), though the whole series may be in mind and so may anticipate final judgment. *And they washed* (*kai eplunan*). First aorist active indicative of *plunō*, old verb, to wash, in N.T. only Luke 5:2; Rev. 7:14; 22:14. This change of construction after *hoi erchomenoi* from *hoi plunēsantes* to *kai eplunan* is common in the Apocalypse, one of Charles's Hebraisms, like *kai epoiēsen* in 1:6 and *kai planāi* in 2:20. *Made them white* (*eleukanan*). First aorist active indicative of *leukainō*, to whiten, old verb from *leukos* (verse 13), in N.T. only here and Mark 9:3. "Milligan remarks that *robes* are the expression of character, and compares the word *habit* used of dress" (Vincent). The language here comes partly from Gen. 49:11 and partly from Ex. 19:10, 14. For the cleansing power of Christ's blood see also Rom. 3:25; 5:9; Col. 1:20; Eph. 1:7; I Pet. 1:2; Heb. 9:14 and I John 1:7; Rev. 1:5; 5:9; 22:14. "The aorists look back to the life on earth when the cleansing was effected" (Swete). See Phil. 2:12f. for both divine and human aspects of salvation. *In the blood of the Lamb* (*en tōi haimati tou arniou*). There is power alone in the blood of Christ to cleanse from sin (I John 1:7), not in the blood of the martyrs themselves. The result is "white," not "red," as one might imagine.

15. *Therefore* (*dia touto*). Because of the washing described in verse 14. *They serve him* (*latreuousin autōi*). Dative case with *latreuō* (present active indicative, old verb, originally to serve for hire *latron*, then service in general, then religious service to God, Matt. 4:10, then in particular ritual worship of the priests, Heb. 8:5). All the redeemed are priests (Rev. 16:5, 10) in the heavenly temple (6:9) as here. But this service is that of spiritual worship, not of external rites (Rom. 12:1; Phil. 3:3). *Day and night* (*hēmeras kai nuktos*). Genitive of time, "by day and night," as in 4:8 of the praise of the four living creatures. *Shall*

spread his tabernacle over them (*skēnōsei ep' autous*). Future (change of tense from present in *latreuousin*) active of *skēnoō*, old verb from *skēnos* (tent, tabernacle), used in John 1:14 of the earthly life of Christ, elsewhere in N.T. only in Rev. (7:14; 12:12; 13:6; 21:3). In 12:12 and 13:6 of those who dwell in tents, here of God spreading his tent "over" (*ep' autous*) the redeemed in heaven, in 21:3 of God tabernacling "with" (*met' autōn*) the redeemed, in both instances a picture of sacred fellowship, and "the further idea of God's Presence as a protection from all fear of evil" (Swete) like the overshadowing of Israel by the Shekinah and a possible allusion also to the tents (*skēnai*) of the feast of tabernacles and to the tent of meeting where God met Moses (Ex. 33:7–11).

16. *They shall hunger no more* (*ou peinasousin eti*). Future tense of *peinaō*, old verb with late form instead of *peinēsousin* like Luke 6:25. It is a free translation of Is. 49:10 (not quotation from the LXX). *Neither thirst any more* (*oude dipsēsousin eti*). Future tense of *dipsaō*, the two strong human appetites will be gone, a clear refutation of a gross materialistic or sensual conception of the future life. Cf. John 6:35. *Neither shall strike* (*oude mē pesēi*). Strong double negative *oude mē* with second aorist active subjunctive of *piptō*, to fall. They will no longer be under the rays of the sun as upon earth. *Nor any heat* (*oude pān kauma*). Old word from *kaiō*, to burn, painful and burning heat, in N.T. only here and 16:9 (picture of the opposite condition). The use of the negative with *pān* (all) for "not any" is common in N.T. Cf. Ps. 121:6.

17. *In the midst* (*ana meson*). In 5:6 we have *en mesōi tou thronou* as the position of the Lamb, and so that is apparently the sense of *ana meson* here as in Matt. 13:25, though it can mean "between," as clearly so in I Cor. 6:5. *Shall be their shepherd* (*paimanei autous*). "Shall shepherd them," future active of *poimainō* (from *poimēn*, shepherd),

in John 21:16; Acts 20:28; I Pet. 5:2; Rev. 2:27; 7:17; 12:5; 19:15. Jesus is still the Good Shepherd of his sheep (John 10:11, 14ff.). Cf. Ps. 23:1. *Shall guide them (hodē-gēsei autous).* Future active of *hodēgeō*, old word (from *hodēgos*, guide, Matt. 15:14), used of God's guidance of Israel (Ex. 15:13), of God's guidance of individual lives (Ps. 5:9), of the guidance of the Holy Spirit (John 16:13), of Christ's own guidance here (cf. John 14:4; Rev. 14:4). *Unto fountains of waters of life (epi zōēs pēgas hudatōn).* The language is like that in Is. 49:10 and Jer. 2:13. Note the order, "to life's water springs" (Swete) like the Vulgate *ad vitæ fontes aquarum,* with emphasis on *zōēs* (life's). For this idea see also John 4:12, 14; 7:38f.; Rev. 21:6; 22:1, 17. No special emphasis on the plural here or in 8:10; 14:7; 16:4. *And God shall wipe away (kai exaleipsei ho theos).* Repeated in 21:4 from Is. 25:8. Future active of *exaleiphō,* old compound, to wipe out (*ex*), off, away, already in 3:5 for erasing a name and in Acts 3:19 for removing the stain (guilt) of sin. *Every tear (pān dakruon).* Old word, with other form, *dakru,* in Luke 7:38, 44. Note repetition of *ek* with *ophthalmōn* (out of their eyes). "Words like these of vv. 15–17 must sound as a divine music in the ears of the persecuted. God will comfort as a mother comforts" (Baljon).

CHAPTER VIII

1. *And when he opened* (*kai hotan ēnoixen*). Here modal *an* is used with *hote* (used about the opening of the preceding six seals), but *hotan* is not here rendered more indefinite, as is sometimes true (Mark 3:11; Rev. 4:9), but here and possibly (can be repetition) in Mark 11:19 it is a particular instance, not a general rule (Robertson, *Grammar*, p. 973). *There followed a silence* (*egeneto sigē*). Second aorist middle of *ginomai*. "There came silence." Dramatic effect by this profound stillness with no elder or angel speaking, no chorus of praise nor cry of adoration, no thunder from the throne (Swete), but a temporary cessation in the revelations. See 10:4. *About the space of half an hour* (*hōs hēmiōron*). Late and rare word (*hēmi*, half, *hōra*, hour), here only in N.T. Accusative of extent of time.

2. *Stand* (*hestēkasin*). Perfect active of *histēmi* (intransitive). Another "hebdomad" so frequent in the Apocalypse. The article (the seven angels) seems to point to seven well-known angels. In Enoch 20:7 the names of seven archangels are given (Uriel, Raphael, Raguel, Michael, Sariel, Gabriel, Remiel) and "angels of the Presence" is an idea like that in Is. 63:9. We do not know precisely what is John's idea here. *Seven trumpets* (*hepta salpigges*). We see trumpets assigned to angels in Matt. 24:31; I Thess. 4:16; I Cor. 15:52; Rev. 4:1, 4. See also the use of trumpets in Josh. 6:13; Joel 2:1. These seven trumpets are soon to break the half-hour of silence. Thus the seven trumpets grow out of the opening of the seventh seal, however that fact is to be interpreted.

3. *Another angel* (*allos aggelos*). Not one of the seven of verse 2 and before they began to sound the trumpets. This

preliminary incident of the offering of incense on the altar
covers verses 3 to 6. *Stood* (*estathē*). Ingressive first aorist
passive of *histēmi* (intransitive), "took his place." *Over the
altar* (*epi tou thusiastēriou*). See 6:9 for the word for the
burnt-offering, here apparently the altar of incense (clearly
so in Luke 1:11; possibly also Rev. 9:13), but it is not clear
that in apocalyptic the distinction between the two altars
of the tabernacle and temple is preserved. Aleph C Q have
the genitive, while A P have the accusative *epi to thusiastērion*. *A golden censer* (*libanōton chrusoun*). Old word for
frankincense (from *libanos*, Matt. 2:11; Rev. 18:13), but here
alone in N.T. and for censer, as is plain by the use of *chrusoun*
(golden) with it. Cf. I Kings 7:50. *Much incense* (*thumiamata polla*). See 5:8 for *thumiama* (the aromatic substance
burnt, also in 18:13), but here for the live coals on which
the incense falls. *That he should add* (*hina dōsei*). Sub-final
clause (subject of *edothē*, was given, singular because *thumiamata* neuter plural) with *hina* and the future active indicative of *didōmi*, to give, instead of *dōi*, the second aorist
subjunctive. *Unto the prayers* (*tais proseuchais*). Dative
case. In 5:18 the *thumiamata* are the prayers. *Upon the
golden altar* (*epi to thusiastērion to chrusoun to*). Accusative
case here, not genitive as above, and apparently the altar
of incense as indicated by the word golden (Ex. 30:1ff.; Lev.
4:17). Note triple article here *to* (once before the substantive, once before the adjective, once before the adjunct "the
one before the throne").

4. *The smoke* (*ho kapnos*). Old word, in N.T. only Acts
2:19 and Rev. 8:4; 9:2f., 17f.; 14:11; 15:8; 18:9, 18; 19:3.
Here from the incense in the angel's hand. *With the prayers
(*tais proseuchais*). So associative-instrumental case, but it
may be dative as in verse 3 (for).

5. *Taketh* (*eilēphen*). Vivid dramatic perfect active indicative of *lambanō* as in 5:7, "has taken." The angel had
apparently laid aside the censer. Hardly merely the pleo-

nastic use of *lambanō* (John 19:23). John pictures the scene for us. *Filled* (*egemisen*). He drops back to the narrative use of the first aorist active indicative of *gemizō*. *With the fire* (*ek tou puros*), live coals from the altar (cf. Is. 6:6). *Cast* (*ebalen*). Second aorist active indicative of *ballō*. See Gen. 19:24 (Sodom); Ezek. 10:2 and Christ's bold metaphor in Luke 12:49. See this use of *ballō* also in Rev. 8:7; 12:4, 9, 13; 14:19. *Followed* (*egenonto*). Came to pass naturally after the casting of fire on the earth. Same three elements in 4:5, but in different order (lightnings, voices, thunders), lightning naturally preceding thunder as some MSS. have it here. Perhaps *phōnai*, the voices of the storm (wind, etc.).

6. *Prepared themselves* (*hētoimasan hautous*). First aorist active indicative of *hetoimazō*. They knew the signal and got ready. *To sound* (*hina salpisōsin*). Sub-final (object) clause with *hina* and the first aorist ingressive active subjunctive of *salpizō*. The infinitive could have been used.

7. *Sounded* (*esalpisen*). First aorist active indicative of *salpizō*, repeated with each angel in turn (8:8, 10, 12; 9:1, 13; 11:15). *Hail and fire mingled with blood* (*chalaza kai pur memigmena en haimati*). Like the plague of hail and fire in Ex. 9:24. The first four trumpets are very much like the plagues in Egypt, this one like a semitropical thunderstorm (Swete) with blood like the first plague (Ex. 7:17ff.; Ps. 106:35). The old feminine word *chalaza* (hail) is from the verb *chalaō*, to let down (Mark 2:4), in N.T. only in Rev. 8:7; 11:19; 16:21. The perfect passive participle *memigmena* (from *mignumi*, to mix) is neuter plural because of *pur* (fire). *Were cast* (*eblēthē*). First aorist passive singular because *chalaza* and *pur* treated as neuter plural. "The storm flung itself on the earth" (Swete). *Was burnt up* (*katekaē*). Second aorist (effective) passive indicative of *katakaiō*, old verb to burn down (effective use of *kata*, *up*, we say). Repeated here three times for dramatic effect. See 7:1–3 about the

trees and 9:4 where the locusts are forbidden to injure the grass.

8. *As it were* (*hōs*). "As if," not a great mountain, but a blazing mass as large as a mountain. *Burning with fire* (*puri kaiomenon*). Present middle participle of *kaiō*. Somewhat like Enoch 18:13, but perhaps with the picture of a great volcanic eruption like that of Vesuvius in A.D. 79. Strabo tells of an eruption B.C. 196 which made a new island (Palæa Kaumene). *Became blood* (*egeneto haima*). Like the Nile in the first plague (Ex. 7:20ff.). Cf. also 16:3.

9. *Of the creatures* (*tōn ktismatōn*). See 5:13 for this word *ktisma*. *Even they that had life* (*ta echonta psuchas*). Here the nominative articular participle is in apposition with the genitive *ktismatōn*, as often in this book. See Ex. 7:20 for the destruction of fish, and Zeph. 1:3. *Was destroyed* (*diephtharēsan*). Second aorist passive indicative of *diaphtheirō*, old compound, to corrupt, to consume, to destroy (perfective use of *dia*), also 11:18. The plural *ploion* just before the verb makes the idea plural.

10. *Burning as a torch* (*kaiomenos hōs lampas*). See 4:5 and Matt. 2:2, perhaps a meteor, striking at the fresh-water supply (rivers *potamōn*, springs *pēgas*) as in the first Egyptian plague also.

11. *Wormwood* (*ho Apsinthos*). Absinthe. Usually feminine (*hē*), but masculine here probably because *astēr* is masculine. Only here in N.T. and not in LXX (*pikria*, bitterness, *cholē*, gall, etc.) except by Aquila in Prov. 5:4; Jer. 9:15; 23:15. There are several varieties of the plant in Palestine. *Became wormwood* (*egeneto eis apsinthon*). This use of *eis* in the predicate with *ginomai* is common in the LXX and the N.T. (16:19; John 16:20; Acts 5:36). *Of the waters* (*ek tōn hudatōn*). As a result of (*ek*) the use of the poisoned waters. *Were made bitter* (*epikranthēsan*). First aorist passive indicative of *pikrainō*. Old verb (from

pikros, bitter), as in 10:9f. In a metaphorical sense to embitter in Col. 3:19.

12. *Was smitten* (*eplēgē*). Second aorist passive indicative of *plēssō*, old verb (like *plēgē* plague), here only in N.T. *That should be darkened* (*hina skotisthēi*). Purpose clause with *hina* and the first aorist passive subjunctive of *skotizō*, from *skotos* (darkness) as in Matt. 24:29, but *skotoō* in Rev. 9:2. *And the day should not shine* (*kai hē hēmera mē phanēi*). Negative purpose clause with *hina mē* and the first aorist active subjunctive of *phainō*, to shed light upon, as in 18:23, not the second aorist passive subjunctive *phanēi* with different accent. The eclipse here is only partial and is kin to the ninth Egyptian plague (Ex. 10:21).

13. *An eagle* (*henos aetou*). "One eagle," perhaps *henos* (*heis*) used as an indefinite article (9:13; 18:21; 19:17). See 4:7 also for the flying eagle, the strongest of birds, sometimes a symbol of vengeance (Deut. 28:49; Hos. 8:1; Hab. 1:8). *Flying in mid-heaven* (*petomenou en mesouranēmati*). Like the angel in 14:6 and the birds in 19:17. *Mesouranēma* (from *mesouraneō* to be in mid-heaven) is a late word (Plutarch, papyri) for the sun at noon, in N.T. only these three examples. This eagle is flying where all can see, and crying so that all can hear. *Woe, woe, woe* (*ouai, ouai, ouai*). Triple because three trumpets yet to come. In 18:10, 16, 19 the double *ouai* is merely for emphasis. *For them that dwell on the earth* (*tous katoikountas*). Accusative of the articular present active participle of *katoikeō*, is unusual (Aleph Q here and also in 12:12) as in Matt. 11:21. There is even a nominative in 18:10. *By reason of the other voices* (*ek tōn loipōn phōnōn*). "As a result of (*ek*) the rest of the voices." There is more and worse to come, "of the three angels who are yet to sound" (*tōn triōn aggelōn tōn mellontōn salpizein*).

CHAPTER IX

1. *Fallen* (*peptōkota*). Perfect active participle of *piptō*, already down. In Luke 10:18 note *pesonta* (constative aorist active, like a flash of lightning) after *etheōroun* and in Rev. 7:2 note *anabainonta* (present active and linear, coming up, picturing the process) after *eidon*. *Of the pit of the abyss* (*tou phreatos tēs abussou*). *Abussos* is an old adjective (alpha privative and *buthos*, depth, without depth), but *hē abussos* (supply *chōra* place), the bottomless place. It occurs in Rom. 10:7 for the common receptacle of the dead for Hades (Sheol), but in Luke 8:31 a lower depth is sounded (Swete), for the abode of demons, and in this sense it occurs in Rev. 9:1, 2, 11; 11:7; 17:8; 20:1, 3. *Phrear* is an old word for well or cistern (Luke 14:5; John 4:11f.) and it occurs in Rev. 9:1f. for the mouth of the abyss which is pictured as a cistern with a narrow orifice at the entrance and this fifth angel holds the key to it.

2. *Opened* (*ēnoixen*). First aorist active indicative of *anoignumi*. With the "key" (*kleis*). *As the smoke of a great furnace* (*hōs kapnos kaminou megalēs*). The plague of demonic locusts is here turned loose. *Kaminos* is old word for a smelting-furnace, already in 1:15. *Were darkened* (*eskotōthē*). First aorist passive indicative of *skotoō*, old causative verb from *skotos*, in N.T. only here, 16:10; Eph. 4:18. *By reason of* (*ek*). "Out of," as a result of (8:13).

3. *Locusts* (*akrides*). Also verse 7 and already in Matt. 3:4; Mark 1:6 (diet of the Baptist). The Israelites were permitted to eat them, but when the swarms came like the eighth Egyptian plague (Ex. 10:13ff.) they devoured every green thing. The smoke was worse than the fallen star and the locusts that came out of the smoke were worse

361

still, "a swarm of hellish locusts" (Swete). *The scorpions* (*hoi skorpioi*). Old name for a little animal somewhat like a lobster that lurks in stone walls in warm regions, with a venomous sting in its tail, in N.T. in Luke 10:19; 11:12; Rev. 9:3, 5, 10. The scorpion ranks with the snake as hostile to man.

4. *It was said* (*errethē*). First aorist passive indicative of *eipon*. *That they should not hurt* (*hina mē adikēsousin*). Sub-final (object clause subject of *errethē*) with *hina mē* and the future active of *adikeō* as in 3:9; 8:3. Vegetation had been hurt sufficiently by the hail (8:7). *But only such men as* (*ei mē tous anthrōpous hoitines*). "Except (elliptical use of *ei mē*, if not, unless) the men who (the very ones who)." For this use of *hostis* see 1:7; 2:24; 20:4. *The seal of God upon their foreheads* (*tēn sphragida tou theou epi tōn metōpōn*). Provided for in 7:3ff. "As Israel in Egypt escaped the plagues which punished their neighbours, so the new Israel is exempted from the attack of the locusts of the Abyss" (Swete).

5. *That they should not kill them* (*hina mē apokteinōsin autous*). Sub-final object clause (subject of *edothē*) with *hina mē* and the subjunctive of *apokteinō* either present (continued action) or aorist (constative, form the same), the usual construction with *hina*. The locusts are charged to injure men, but not to kill them. *But that they should be tormented* (*all' hina basanisthēsontai*). Sub-final clause again with *hina*, but this time with the first future passive indicative (like 3:9; 6:4; 8:3; 13:12) of *basanizō*, old verb, to test metals (from *basanos*, Matt. 4:24) by touchstone, then to torture like Matt. 8:29, further in Rev. 11:10; 12:2; 14:10; 20:10. *Five months* (*mēnas pente*). Accusative of extent of time. The actual locust is born in the spring and dies at the end of summer (about five months). *Torment* (*basanismos*). Late word for torture, from *basanizō*, in N.T. only in Rev. 9:5; 14:11; 18:7, 10, 15. The wound of the scorpion

was not usually fatal, though exceedingly painful. *When it striketh a man* (*hotan paisēi anthrōpon*). Indefinite temporal clause with *hotan* and the first aorist active subjunctive of *paiō* (Matt. 26:51), old verb, to smite, "whenever it smites a man."

6. *Men* (*hoi anthrōpoi*). Generic use of the article (men as a class). *Shall not find it* (*ou mē heurēsousin auton*). Strong double negative *ou mē* with the future active indicative according to Aleph Q, but *heurōsin* (second aorist active subjunctive) according to A P (either construction regular). The idea here is found in Job 3:21 and Jer. 8:3. "Such a death as they desire, a death which will end their sufferings, is impossible; physical death is no remedy for the *basanismos* of an evil conscience" (Swete). *They shall desire to die* (*epithumēsousin apothanein*). Future active of *epithumeō*, a climax to *zētēsousin* (they shall seek), to desire vehemently. Paul in Phil. 1:23 shows a preference for death if his work is done, in order to be with Christ, a very different feeling from what we have here. *Fleeth* (*pheugei*). Vivid futuristic present active indicative of *pheugō*. Even death does not come to their relief.

7. *The shapes* (*ta homoiōmata*). Old word from *homoioō*, to make like (from *homoios*, like), likeness, in N.T. only here, Rom. 5:14; Phil. 2:7, "the likenesses were like" (*homoia*). *Homoiōma* is "midway between *morphē* and *schēma*" (Lightfoot). *Unto horses* (*hippois*). Associative-instrumental case, as is the rule with *homoios* (1:15; 2:18; 4:6ff.; 9:10, 19; 11:1; 13:2, 11), but with the accusative in 1:13; 14:14. So also *homoioi chrusōi* (like gold) in this same verse. *Prepared for war* (*hētoimasmenois eis polemon*). Perfect passive participle of *hetoimazō*. This imagery of war-horses is like that in Joel 2:4f. "The likeness of a locust to a horse, especially to a horse equipped with armour, is so striking that the insect is named in German *Heupferd* (hay-horse), and in Italian *cavalett a little horse*" (Vincent).

As it were crowns (*hos stephanoi*). Not actual crowns, but what looked like crowns of gold, as conquerors, as indeed they were (4:4; 6:2; 12:1; 14:14). These locusts of the abyss have another peculiar feature. *As men's faces* (*hōs prosōpa anthrōpōn*). Human-looking faces in these demonic locusts to give added terror, "suggesting the intelligence and capacity of man" (Swete). Vincent actually sees "a distinct resemblance to the human countenance in the face of the locust."

8. *They had* (*eichan*). Imperfect active, late form as in Mark 8:7 in place of the usual *eichon*. *As hair of women* (*hōs trichas gunaikōn*). That is long hair (I Cor. 11:15), with no reference to matters of sex at all, for *anthrōpōn* just before is used, not *andrōn* (men as distinct from women). Perhaps the antennæ of the locust were unusually long. *As the teeth of lions* (*hōs leontōn*). Supply *hoi odontes* (the teeth) before *leontōn*. See Joel 1:6. The locust is voracious.

9. *As it were breastplates of iron* (*hōs thōrakas siderous*). The *thōrax* was originally the breast (from the neck to the navel), then the breastplate, only N.T. usage (Rev. 9:9, 17; I Thess. 5:8; Eph. 6:14). The armour for the breastplate was usually of iron (*siderous*, Rev. 2:27), but with the locusts it only seemed to be so (*hōs*). However, the scaly backs and flanks of the locusts do resemble coats of mail. "The locusts of the Abyss may be the memories of the past brought home at times of Divine visitation" (Swete). *The sound of their wings* (*hē phōnē tōn pterugōn*). Graphic picture of the onrush of the swarms of demonic locusts and the hopelessness of resisting them. *As the sound of chariots, of many horses rushing to war* (*hōs phōnē harmatōn hippōn pollōn trechontōn eis polemon*). Both metaphors here, the clatter and clangour of the chariot wheels and the prancing of the horses are found in Joel 2:4f. *Trechontōn* is present active predicate participle of *trechō*, to run. Cf. II Kings 7:6; Jer. 47:3.

10. *Tails* (*ouras*). Old word, in N.T. only in Rev. 9:10, 19; 12:4. *Like unto scorpions* (*homoias skorpiois*). Aleph A wrongly have *homoiois* (agreeing with *skorpiois* instead of with *ouras*). It is a condensed idiom for "like unto the tails of the scorpions" as we have it in 13:11 (cf. Matt. 5:20; I John 2:2). *Stings* (*kentra*). Old word from *kentreō* (to prick, to sting), in N.T. only here, Acts 26:14 (about Paul); I Cor. 15:55 (about death). It is used "of the spur of a cock, the quill of the porcupine, and the stings of insects" (Vincent). It was the goad used for oxen (Prov. 26:3; Acts 26:14). *In their tails* (*en tais ourais autōn*). This locates "their power to hurt" (*hē exousia autōn adikēsai*, infinitive here, *hina adikēsousin* in 9:4) in their tails. It might have been in other organs.

11. *As king* (*basilea*). Predicate accusative and anarthrous. In Prov. 30:27 it is stated that the locust has no king, but this is not true of these demonic locusts. Their king is "the angel of the abyss (verse 1) whose orders they obey." *His name is* (*onoma autōi*). "Name to him" (nominative absolute and dative, as in 6:8). *In Hebrew* (*Ebraisti*). Adverb as in 16:16; John 5:2; 19:13, 17, 20; 20:16. *Abaddōn.* A word almost confined to the Wisdom books (Job 26:6; Ps. 88:11; Prov. 15:11). It is rendered in the LXX by *Apōleia*, destruction. *In the Greek tongue* (*en tēi Hellēnikēi*). With *glōssēi* or *dialektōi* understood. As usual, John gives both the Hebrew and the Greek. *Apollyon* (*Apolluōn*). Present active masculine singular participle of *apolluō*, meaning "destroying," used here as a name and so "Destroyer," with the nominative case retained though in apposition with the accusative *onoma*. The personification of Abaddon occurs in the Talmud also. It is not clear whether by Apollyon John means Death or Satan. Bousset even finds in the name Apollyon an indirect allusion to Apollo, one of whose symbols was the locust, a doubtful point assuredly.

12. *The first woe* (*hē ouai hē mia*). Note feminine gender

ascribed to the interjection *ouai* as in 11:14, perhaps because *thlipsis* is feminine, though we really do not know. Note also the ordinal use of *mia* (one) like *prōtē* (first) as in 6:1; Mark 16:2. *There come yet two Woes* (*erchetai eti duo Ouai*). Singular number *erchetai* instead of *erchontai*, though *duo ouai*. It is true that *ouai* is an interjection and indeclinable, but it is here used with *duo* and is feminine just before, and not neuter.

13. *A voice* (*phōnēn mian*). For *mian* as indefinite article see 8:13. Accusative case here after *ēkousa*, though genitive in 8:13, a distinction between sound and sense sometimes exists (Acts 9:7; 22:9), but not here as the words are clearly heard in both instances. *From* (*ek*). "Out of the horns." Note triple use of the genitive article here as of the accusative article with this identical phrase in 8:3 ("the altar the golden the one before the throne").

14. *One saying to the sixth angel* (*legonta tōi hektōi*). Accusative masculine singular active participle of *legō*, personifying *phōnēn* and agreeing with it in case, though not in gender. This voice speaks to the sixth angel (dative case). *Which had the trumpet* (*ho echōn tēn salpigga*). Nominative case in apposition with *aggelōi* (dative), the same anomalous phenomenon in 2:20; 3:12; 14:12. Swete treats it as a parenthesis, like 4:1; 11:15. *Loose* (*luson*). First aorist (ingressive) active imperative of *luō*, "let loose." Another group of four angels (7:1) like Acts 12:4, described here "which are bound" (*tous dedemenous*). Perfect passive articular participle of *deō*, evidently the leaders of the demonic horsemen (9:15ff.) as the four angels let loose the demonic locusts (7:1ff.), both quaternions agents of God's wrath. *At the great river Euphrates* (*epi tōi potamōi tōi megalōi Euphratēi*). A regular epithet of the Euphrates (16:12; Gen. 15:18; Deut. 1:7). It rises in Armenia and joins the Tigris in lower Babylonia, a total length of nearly 1800 miles, the eastern boundary of the Roman Empire next to Parthia.

15. *Were loosed* (*eluthēsan*). First aorist (ingressive) passive indicative of *luō*, "were let loose." *Which had been prepared* (*hoi hētoimasmenoi*). Perfect passive articular participle of *hetoimazō*, to make ready (*hetoimos*), in a state of readiness prepared by God (12:6; 16:12; Matt. 25:34). *For the hour and day and month and year* (*eis tēn hōran kai hēmeran kai mēna kai eniauton*). For this use of *eis* with *hētoimasmenon* see II Tim. 2:21. All preparation over, the angels are waiting for the signal to begin. *That they should kill* (*hina apokteinōsin*). The same idiom in verse 5 about the fifth trumpet, which brought torture. This one brings death.

16. *Of the horsemen* (*tou hippikou*). Old adjective *hippikos* from *hippos* (horse), equestrian. The neuter articular singular *to hippikon*, the horse or the cavalry in contrast with *to pezikon* (the infantry), here only in N.T. For the numbers here see on 5:11; 7:4.

17. *And thus I saw in the vision* (*kai houtōs eidon en tēi horasei*). Nowhere else does John allude to his own vision, though often in Dan. (7:2; 8:2, 15; 9:21). *Having* (*echontas*). Accusative masculine plural of *echō*, probably referring to the riders (*tous kathēmenous ep' autōn*) rather than to the horses (*tous hippous*). *Breastplates as of fire and of hyacinth and of brimstone* (*thōrakas purinous kai huakinthinous kai theiōdeis*). There is no *hōs* (as) in the Greek, but that is the idea of these three adjectives which are only metaphors. *Purinos* is an old adjective (from *pur*, fire), here only in N.T. *Huakinthos* is also an old word (from *huakinthos*, hyacinth, then of a sapphire stone Rev. 21:20), of a red color bordering on black, here only in the N.T. *Theiōdēs* is a late word (from *theion*, brimstone), sulphurous, here only in N.T. *As the heads of lions* (*hōs kephalai leontōn*). This of the horses, war-horses as always in the Bible except in Is. 28:28. These horses likewise have "fire and smoke and brimstone" (*theion*, brimstone, is old word, in N.T. only

in Rev. and Luke 17:29) proceeding (*ekporeuetai*, singular because it comes first and the subjects afterwards) out of their mouths. Both rider and horse are terrible.

18. *By these three plagues* (*apo tōn triōn plēgōn toutōn*). Our "plague" or stroke from *plēssō*, as in Luke 10:30 and often in Rev. (9:20; 11:6; 15:1, 6, 8; 16:9; 18:4, 8; 22:18). It is used in Ex. 11:1ff. for the plagues in Egypt. The three plagues here are the fire, smoke, and brimstone which proceed from the mouths of the horses. *Was killed* (*apektanthēsan*). First aorist passive indicative of *apokteinō*, to kill, third person plural, though *to triton* is neuter singular because a collective idea. See same form in verse 20.

19. *The power* (*hē exousia*). As in 2:26; 6:8. This power of the horses is both in their mouths (because of the fire, smoke, brimstone) and in their tails, "for their tails are like unto serpents" (*hai gar ourai autōn homoiai ophesin*). Associative-instrumental case *ophesin* after *homoiai*. *Ophis* is old word for snake (Matt. 7:10). *Having heads* (*echousai kephalas*). Feminine present active participle of *echō*, agreeing with *ourai* (tails). *With them* (*en autais*). Instrumental use of *en*. Surely dreadful monsters.

20. *Repented not* (*ou metenoēsan*). First aorist active indicative of *metanoeō*. The two-thirds of mankind still spared did not change their creed or their conduct. *Of the works* (*ek tōn ergōn*). For this use of *ek* after *metanoeō* see 2:21; 9:21; 16:11. By "works" (*ergōn*) here idolatries are meant, as the next verse shows. *That they should not worship* (*hina mē proskunēsousin*). Negative purpose clause with *hina mē* and the future active of *proskuneō* as in 9:5. *Devils* (*ta daimonia*). Both in the O.T. (Deut. 32:17; Ps. 96:5; 106:37) and in the N.T. (I Cor. 10:21) the worship of idols is called the worship of unclean spirits. Perhaps this is one explanation of the hideous faces given these images. "The idols" (*ta eidōla* I John 5:21, from *eidos*, form, appearance) represented "demons," whether made of gold (*ta chrusā*) or of

silver (*ta argurā*) or of brass (*ta chalkā*) or of stone (*ta lithina*) or of wood (*ta xulina*). See Dan. 5:23 for this picture of heathen idols. The helplessness of these idols, "which can neither see nor hear nor walk" (*ha oute blepein dunantai oute akouein oute peripatein*), is often presented in the O.T. (Ps. 113:12ff.; 115:4).

21. *Of their murders* (*ek tōn phonōn autōn*). Heads the list, but "sorceries" (*ek tōn pharmakōn*) comes next. *Pharmakon* was originally enchantment, as also in Rev. 21:8, then drug. For *pharmakia* see Rev. 18:34; Gal. 5:20. The two other items are fornication (*porneias*) and thefts (*klemmatōn*, old word from *kleptō*, here alone in N.T.), all four characteristic of demonic worship and idolatry. See other lists of vices in Mark 7:21; Gal. 5:20; Rev. 21:8; 22:15. Our word "pharmacy" as applied to drugs and medicine has certainly come a long way out of a bad environment, but there is still a bad odour about "patent medicines."

CHAPTER X

1. *Another strong angel (allon aggelon ischuron)*. But the seventh trumpet does not sound till 11:15. This angel is not one of the seven or of the four, but like the other strong angel in 5:2 and 18:21 or the other angel in 14:6, 15. The sixth trumpet of 9:13 ends in 9:21. The opening of the seventh seal was preceded by two visions (chapter 7) and so here the sounding of the seventh trumpet (11:15) is preceded by a new series of visions (10:1 to 11:14). *Coming down out of heaven (katabainonta ek tou ouranou)*. Present active participle of *katabainō* picturing the process of the descent as in 20:1 (cf. 3:12). *Arrayed with a cloud (peribeblēmenon nephelēn)*. Perfect passive participle of *periballō* with accusative case retained as in 7:9, 13. Not proof that this angel is Christ, though Christ will come on the clouds (1:7) as he ascended on a cloud (Acts 1:9). God's chariot is in the clouds (Ps. 104:3), but this angel is a special messenger of God's. *The rainbow (hē iris)*. See 4:3 for this word. The construction here is changed from the accusative to the nominative. *As the sun (hōs ho hēlios)*. The very metaphor applied to Christ in 1:16. *As pillars of fire (hōs stuloi puros)*. Somewhat like the metaphor of Christ in 1:15, but still no proof that this angel is Christ. On *stulos* see 3:12 and Gal. 2:9.

2. *And he had (kai echōn)*. This use of the participle in place of *eichen* (imperfect) is like that in 4:7f.; 12:2; 19:12; 21:12, 14, a Semitic idiom (Charles), or as if *katabainōn* (nominative) had preceded in place of *katabainonta*. *A little book (biblaridion)*. A diminutive of *biblarion* (papyri), itself a diminutive of *biblion* (5:1) and perhaps in contrast with it, a rare form in Hermas and Rev. 10:2, 9, 10. In

10:8 Tischendorf reads *biblidarion*, diminutive of *biblidion*
(Aristophanes) instead of *biblion* (Westcott and Hort). The
contents of this little book are found in 11:1–13. *Open*
(*eneōigmenon*). See Ezek. 2:9f. Perfect (triple reduplication) passive participle of *anoigō*, in contrast to the closed
book in 5:1. There also we have *epi* (upon) *tēn dexian* (the
right hand), for it was a large roll, but here the little open
roll is held in the hand (*en tēi cheiri*), apparently the left
hand (verse 5). *He set* (*ethēken*). First aorist active indicative of *tithēmi*. The size of the angel is colossal, for he be-
strides both land and sea. Apparently there is no special
point in the right foot (*ton poda ton dexion*) being on the
sea (*epi tēs thalassēs*) and the left (*ton euōnumon*) upon the
land (*epi tēs gēs*). It makes a bold and graphic picture.
As a lion roareth (*hōsper leōn mukātai*). Only instance of
hōsper in the Apocalypse, but *hōs* in the same sense several
times. Present middle indicative of *mukaomai*, an old
onomatopoetic word from *mu* or *moo* (the sound which a
cow utters), common for the lowing and bellowing of cattle,
Latin *mugire*, but in Theocritus for the roaring of a lion
as here, though in I Pet. 5:8 we have *ōruomai*. Homer uses
mukaomai for the clangour of the shield and Aristophanes
for thunder. It occurs here alone in the N.T. It does not
mean that what the angel said was unintelligible, only loud.
Cf. 1:10; 5:2, 12; 6:10; 7:2, 10, etc.

3. *The seven thunders* (*hai hepta brontai*). A recognized
group, but not explained here, perhaps John assuming them
to be known. For *brontai* see already 4:5; 6:1; 8:5. In Ps.
29 the Lord speaks in the sevenfold voice of the thunderstorm upon the sea. *Their voices* (*tas heautōn phōnas*).
Cognate accusative with *elalēsan* and *heautōn* (reflexive)
means "their own." In John 12:28 the voice of the Father
to Christ was thought by some to be thunder.

4. *I was about to write* (*ēmellon graphein*). Imperfect ac-

tive of *mellō* (double augment as in John 4:47; 12:33; 18:32) and the present (inchoative) active infinitive of *graphō*, "I was on the point of beginning to write," as commanded in 1:11, 19. *Seal up* (*sphragison*). Aorist active imperative of *sphragizō*, tense of urgency, "seal up at once." *And write them not* (*kai mē auta grapseis*). Prohibition with *mē* and the ingressive aorist active subjunctive of *graphō*, "Do not begin to write." It is idle to conjecture what was in the utterances. Compare Paul's silence in II Cor. 12:4.

5. *Standing* (*hestōta*). Second perfect active participle of *histēmi* (intransitive). John resumes the picture in verse 2. *Lifted up* (*ēren*). First aorist active indicative of *airō*, to lift up. *To heaven* (*eis ton ouranon*). Toward heaven, the customary gesture in taking a solemn oath (Gen. 14:22; Deut. 32:40; Dan. 12:7).

6. *Sware* (*ōmosen*). First aorist indicative of *omnuō* to swear. *By him that liveth* (*en tōi zōnti*). This use of *en* after *omnuō* instead of the usual accusative (James 5:12) is like the Hebrew (Matt. 5:34, 36). "The living one for ages of ages" is a common phrase in the Apocalypse for God as eternally existing (1:18; 4:9, 10; 15:7). This oath proves that this angel is not Christ. *Who created* (*hos ektisen*). First aorist active indicative of *ktizō*, a reference to God's creative activity as seen in Gen. 1:1ff.; Ex. 20:11; Is. 37:16; 42:5; Ps. 33:6; 145:6, etc. *That there shall be time no longer* (*hoti chronos ouketi estai*). Future indicative indirect discourse with *hoti*. But this does not mean that *chronos* (time), Einstein's "fourth dimension" (added to length, breadth, height), will cease to exist, but only that there will be no more delay in the fulfillment of the seventh trumpet (verse 7), in answer to the question, "How long?" (6:10).

7. *When he is about to sound* (*hotan mellēi salpizein*). Indefinite temporal clause with *hotan* and the present active

subjunctive of *mellō* and the present (inchoative) active infinitive of *salpizō*, "whenever he is about to begin to sound" (in contrast to the aorist in 11:15). *Then* (*kai*). So in apodosis often (14:10). *Is finished* (*etelesthē*). First aorist passive indicative of *teleō*, proleptic or futuristic use of the aorist as in I Cor. 7:28. So also 15:1. *The mystery of God* (*to mustērion tou theou*). This same phrase by Paul in I Cor. 2:1; Col. 2:2. Here apparently the whole purpose of God in human history is meant. *According to the good tidings which he declared* (*hōs euēggelisen*). "As he gospelized to," first aorist active indicative of *euaggelizō*, a rare use of the active as in 14:6 with the accusative. See the middle so used in Gal. 1:9; I Pet. 1:12. See Amos 3:7; Jer. 7:25; 25:4 for this idea in the O.T. prophets who hoped for a cleaning up of all mysteries in the last days.

8. *Again speaking and saying* (*palin lalousan kai legousan*). Present active predicate participles feminine accusative singular agreeing with *hēn* (object of *ēkousa*), not with *phōnē* (nominative) as most of the cursives have it (*lalousa kai legousa*). Ordinarily it would be *elalei kai elegen*. See 4:1 for like idiom. This is the voice mentioned in verse 4. No great distinction is to be made here between *laleō* and *legō*. *Go, take* (*Hupage labe*). Present active imperative of *hupagō* and second aorist active imperative of *lambanō*. The use of *hupage* (exclamation like *ide*) is common in N.T. (Matt. 5:24; 8:4; 19:21; John 4:16; 9:7). Charles calls it a Hebraism (16:1). Note the repeated article here (*to*) referring to the open book in the hand of the angel (verse 2), only here *biblion* is used, not the diminutive of *biblaridion* of verses 2, 9, 10.

9. *I went* (*apēltha*). Second aorist active indicative (*-a* form), "I went away" (*ap-*) to the angel. John left his position by the door of heaven (4:1). *That he should give* (*dounai*). Second aorist active infinitive of *didōmi*, indirect

command after *legōn* (bidding) for *dos* in the direct discourse (second aorist active imperative second person singular). This use of *legō* to bid occurs in 13:14; Acts 21:21. *He saith* (*legei*). Dramatic vivid present active indicative of *legō*. *Take it and eat it up* (*labe kai kataphage auto*). Second aorist (effective) active imperatives of *lambanō* and *katesthiō* (perfective use of *kata*, "eat down," we say "eat up"). See the same metaphor in Ezek. 3:1–3; Jer. 15:6f. The book was already open and was not to be read aloud, but to be digested mentally by John. *It shall make thy belly bitter* (*pikranei sou tēn koilian*). Future active of *pikrainō*, for which verb see 8:11; 10:10; and Col. 3:19. There is no reference in Ezekiel or Jeremiah to the bitterness here mentioned. *Sweet as honey* (*gluku hōs meli*). For the sweetness of the roll see Ps. 19:10f.; 119:103. "Every revelation of God's purposes, even though a mere fragment, a *biblaridion*, is 'bitter-sweet,' disclosing judgement as well as mercy" (Swete). Deep and bitter sorrows confront John as he comes to understand God's will and way.

10. *I took—and ate it up* (*elabon—kai katephagon auto*). Second aorist active indicatives of the same verbs to show John's prompt obedience to the command. The order of the results is here changed to the actual experience (sweet in the mouth, bitter in the belly). The simplex verb *ephagon* (I ate) is now used, not the compound *katephagon* (I ate up).

11. *They say* (*legousin*). Present active of vivid dramatic action and the indefinite statement in the plural as in 13:16; 16:15. It is possible that the allusion is to the heavenly voice (10:4, 8) and to the angel (10:9). *Thou must prophesy again* (*dei se palin prophēteusai*). Not a new commission (1:19), though now renewed. Cf. Ezek. 4:7; 6:2; Jer. 1:10. The *palin* (again) points to what has preceded and also to what is to come in 11:15. Here it is predictive prophecy (*prophēteusai*, first aorist active infinitive of *prophēteuō*).

Over (*epi*). In the case, in regard to as in John 12:16 (with *graphō*), not in the presence of (*epi* with genitive, Mark 13:9) nor against (*epi* with the accusative, Luke 22:53). For this list of peoples see 5:9, occurring seven times in the Apocalypse.

CHAPTER XI

1. *A reed* (*kalamos*). Old word for a growing reed (Matt. 11:7) which grew in immense brakes in the Jordan valley, a writer's reed (III John 7), a measuring-rod (here, 21:15f.; Ezek. 40:3–6; 42:16–19). *Like a rod* (*homoios rabdōi*). See 2:27; Mark 6:8 for *rabdos*. *And one said* (*legōn*). "Saying" (present active masculine participle of *legō*) is all that the Greek has. The participle implies *edōken* (he gave), not *edothē*, a harsh construction seen in Gen. 22:20; 38:24, etc. *Rise and measure* (*egeire kai metrēson*). Present active imperative of *egeirō* (intransitive, exclamatory use as in Mark 2:11) and first aorist active imperative of *metreō*. In Ezek. 42:2ff. the prophet measures the temple and that passage is probably in mind here. But modern scholars do not know how to interpret this interlude (11:1–13) before the seventh trumpet (11:15). Some (Wellhausen) take it to be a scrap from the Zealot party before the destruction of Jerusalem, which event Christ also foretold (Mark 13:2 = Matt. 24:2 = Luke 21:6) and which was also attributed to Stephen (Acts 6:14). Charles denies any possible literal interpretation and takes the language in a wholly eschatological sense. There are three points in the interlude, however understood: the chastisement of Jerusalem or Israel (verses 1 and 2), the mission of the two witnesses (3–12), the rescue of the remnant (13). There is a heavenly sanctuary (7:15; 11:19; 14:15, etc.), but here *naos* is on earth and yet not the actual temple in Jerusalem (unless so interpreted). Perhaps here it is the spiritual (3:12; II Thess. 2:4; I Cor. 3:16f.; II Cor. 6:16; Eph. 2:19ff.). For altar (*thusiastērion*) see 8:3. Perhaps measuring as applied to "them that worship therein"

376

(*tous proskunountas en autōi*) implies a word like numbering, with an allusion to the 144,000 in chapter 7 (a zeugma).

2. *The court* (*tēn aulēn*). The uncovered yard outside the house. There were usually two, one between the door and the street, the outer court, the other the inner court surrounded by the buildings (Mark 14:66). This is here the outer court, "which is without the temple" (*tēn exōthen tou naou*), outside of the sanctuary, but within the *hieron* where the Gentiles could go (carrying out the imagery of the Jerusalem temple). *Leave without* (*ekbale exōthen*). Literally, "cast without" (second aorist active imperative of *ekballō*. *Do not measure it* (*mē autēn metrēsēis*). Prohibition with *mē* and the first aorist active (ingressive) subjunctive of *metreō*. This outer court is left to its fate. In Herod's temple the outer court was marked off from the inner by "the middle wall of partition" (*to mesoitoichon tou phragmou*, Eph. 2:15), beyond which a Gentile could not go. In this outer court was a house of prayer for the Gentiles (Mark 11:17), but now John is to cast it out and leave to its fate (given to the Gentiles in another sense) to be profaned by them. *They shall tread under foot* (*patēsousin*). Future active of *pateō*, here to trample with contempt as in Luke 21:24, even the holy city (Matt. 4:5; Is. 48:2; Neh. 11:1). Charles thinks that only the heavenly city can be so called here (21:2, 10; 22:19) because of 11:8 (Sodom and Gomorrah). But the language may be merely symbolical. See Dan. 9:24. *Forty and two months* (*mēnas tesserakonta kai duo*). Accusative of extent of time. This period in Dan. 7:25; 12:7. It occurs in three forms in the Apocalypse (forty-two months, here and 13:5; 1260 days, 11:3 and 12:6; time, times and half a time or 3½ years, 12:14 and so in Daniel). This period, however its length may be construed, covers the duration of the triumph of the Gentiles, of the prophesying of the two witnesses, of the sojourn of the woman in the wilderness.

3. *I will give* (*dōsō*). Future active of *didōmi*. The speaker may be God (Beckwith) or Christ (Swete) as in 2:13; 21:6 or his angel representative (22:7, 12ff.). The idiom that follows is Hebraic instead of either the infinitive after *didōmi* as in 2:7; 3:21; 6:4; 7:2; 13:7, 15; 16:8 or *hina* with the subjunctive (9:5; 19:8) we have *kai prophēteusousin* (and they shall prophesy). *Unto my two witnesses* (*tois dusin martusin mou*). Dative case after *dōsō*. The article seems to point to two well-known characters, like Elijah, Elisha, but there is no possible way to determine who they are. All sorts of identifications have been attempted. *Clothed* (*periblēmenous*). Perfect passive participle of *periballō* as often before (7:9, 13; 10:1, etc.). But Aleph A P Q here read the accusative plural in -*ous*, while C has the nominative in -*oi*. Charles suggests a mere slip for the nominative, but Hort suggests a primitive error in early MSS. for the dative *peribeblemenois* agreeing with *martusin*. *In sackcloth* (*sakkous*). Accusative retained with this passive verb as in 7:9, 13. See 6:12 for *sakkos* and also Matt. 3:4. The dress suited the message (Matt. 11:21).

4. *The two olive trees* (*hai duo elaiai*). The article seems to point to what is known. For this original use of *elaia* see Rom. 11:17, 24. In Zech. 4:2, 3, 14 the lampstand or candlestick (*luchnia*) is Israel, and the two olive trees apparently Joshua and Zerubbabel, but John makes his own use of this symbolism. Here the two olive trees and the candlesticks are identical. *Standing* (*hestōtes*). Masculine perfect active participle agreeing with *houtoi* instead of *hestōsai* (read by P and cursives) agreeing with *elaiai kai luchniai*, even though *hai* (feminine plural article) be accepted before *enōpion tou kuriou* (before the Lord).

5. *If any man desireth to hurt them* (*ei tis autous thelei adikēsai*). Condition of first class, assumed to be true, with *ei* and present active indicative (*thelei*) "if any one wants to hurt" (*adikēsai* first aorist active infinitive). It is impos-

sible to hurt these two witnesses till they do their work. The fire proceeding out of the mouths of the witnesses is like Elijah's experience (II Kings 1:10). *Devoureth (katesthiei)*. "Eats up (down)," present active indicative of *katesthiō*. *If any man shall desire (ei tis thelēsēi)*. Condition of third class with *ei* and first aorist active subjunctive of *thelō* as in Luke 9:13; Phil. 3:12, but MSS. also read either *thelei* (present active indicative) or *thelēsei* (future active, condition of the first class like the preceding one. The condition is repeated in this changed form, as less likely to happen and with inevitable death (*dei auton apoktanthēnai*, must be killed, first aorist passive infinitive of *apokteinō* with *dei*).

6. *To shut the heaven (kleisai ton ouranon)*. First aorist active infinitive of *kleiō*. As Elijah did by prayer (I Kings 17:1; Luke 4:25; James 5:17). *That it rain not (hina mē huetos brechēi)*. Sub-final use of *hina mē* with the present active subjunctive of *brechō*, old verb to rain (Matt. 5:45), here with *huetos* as subject. *During the days (tas hēmeras)*. Accusative of extent of time. In Luke 4:25 and James 5:17 the period of the drouth in Elijah's time was three and a half years, just the period here. *Of their prophecy (tēs prophēteias autōn)*. Not here the gift of prophecy (I Cor. 12:10) or a particular prophecy or collection of prophecies (Rev. 1:3; 22:7f.), but "the execution of the prophetic office" (Swete). *Over the waters (epi tōn hudatōn)*. "Upon the waters." As Moses had (Ex. 7:20). *Into blood (eis haima)*. As already stated in 8:8 about the third trumpet and now again here. *To smite (pataxai)*. First aorist active infinitive of *patassō*, used here with *exousian echousin* (they have power), as is *strephein* (to turn). *With every plague (en pasēi plēgēi)*. In I Kings 4:8, but with reference to the plagues in Egypt. *As often as they shall desire (hosakis ean thelēsōsin)*. Indefinite temporal clause with *hosakis* and

modal *ean* (=*an*) and the first aorist active subjunctive of *thelō*, "as often as they will."

7. *When they shall have finished* (*hotan telesōsin*). Merely the first aorist active subjunctive of *teleō* with *hotan* in an indefinite temporal clause with no *futurum exactum* (future perfect), "whenever they finish." *The beast* (*to thērion*). "The wild beast comes out of the abyss" of 9:1f. He reappears in 13:1; 17:8. In Dan. 7:3 *thēria* occurs. Nothing less than antichrist will satisfy the picture here. Some see the abomination of Dan. 7:7 and Matt. 24:15. Some see Nero *redivivus*. *He shall make war with them* (*poiēsei met' autōn polemon*). This same phrase occurs in 12:17 about the dragon's attack on the woman. It is more the picture of single combat (2:16). *He shall overcome them* (*nikēsei autous*). Future active of *nikaō*. The victory of the beast over the two witnesses is certain, as in Dan. 7:21. *And kill them* (*kai apoktenei*). Future active of *apokteinō*. Without attempting to apply this prophecy to specific individuals or times, one can agree with these words of Swete: "But his words cover in effect all the martyrdoms and massacres of history in which brute force has seemed to triumph over truth and righteousness."

8. *Their dead bodies lie* (*to ptōma autōn*). Old word from *piptō* (to fall), a fall, especially of bodies slain in battle, a corpse, a carcase (Matt. 14:12), here the singular (some MSS. *ptōmata*, plural) as belonging to each of the *autōn* (their) like *stomatos autōn* (their mouth) in verse 5. So also in verse 9. No word in the Greek for "lie." *In* (*epi*). "Upon," as in verse 6, with genitive (*tēs plateias*), the broad way (*hodou* understood), from *platus* (broad) as in Matt. 6:5, old word (Rev. 21:21; 22:2). *Of the great city* (*tēs poleōs tēs megalēs*). Clearly Jerusalem in view of the closing clause (*hopou—estaurōthē*), though not here called "the holy city" as in verse 2, and though elsewhere in the Apocalypse Babylon (Rome) is so described (14:8; 16:19; 17:5; 18:2,

10, 16, 18, 19, 21). *Which* (*hētis*). "Which very city," not
"whichever." *Spiritually* (*pneumatikōs*). This late adverb
from *pneumatikos* (spiritual) occurs in the N.T. only twice,
in I Cor. 2:14 (13) for the help of the Holy Spirit in interpreting God's message and here in a hidden or mystical
(allegorical sense). For this use of *pneumatikos* see I Cor.
10:3f. Judah is called Sodom in Is. 1:9f.; Ezek. 16:46, 55.
See also Matt. 10:15; 11:23. Egypt is not applied to Israel
in the O.T., but is "an obvious symbol of oppression and
slavery" (Swete). *Where also their Lord was crucified* (*hopou
kai ho kurios autōn estaurōthē*). First aorist passive indicative of *stauroō*, to crucify, a reference to the fact of Christ's
crucifixion in Jerusalem. This item is one of the sins of
Jerusalem and the disciple is not greater than the Master
(John 15:20).

9. *Men from among* (*ek tōn etc.*). No word for "men"
(*anthrōpoi* or *polloi*) before *ek tōn*, but it is implied (partitive
use of *ek*) as in 2:10 and often. See also 5:9; 7:9 for this
enumeration of races and nations. *Do look upon* (*blepousin*).
Present (vivid dramatic) active indicative of *blepō*. *Three
days and a half* (*hēmeras treis kai hēmisu*). Accusative of
extent of time. *Hēmisu* is neuter singular though *hēmeras*
(days) is feminine as in Mark 6:23; Rev. 12:14. The days
of the gloating over the dead bodies are as many as the
years of the prophesying by the witnesses (11:3), but there
is no necessary correspondence (day for a year). This delight of the spectators "is represented as at once fiendish
and childish" (Swete). *Suffer not* (*ouk aphiousin*). Present
active indicative of *aphiō*, late form for *aphiēmi*, as in
Mark 1:34 (cf. *apheis* in Rev. 2:20). This use of *aphiēmi*
with the infinitive is here alone in the Apocalypse, though
common elsewhere (John 11:44, 48; 12:7; 18:8). *Their dead
bodies* (*ta ptōmata autōn*). "Their corpses," plural here,
though singular just before and in verse 8. *To be laid in a
tomb* (*tethēnai eis mnēma*). First aorist passive of *tithēmi*,

to place. *Mnēma* (old word from *mimnēskō*, to remind) is a memorial, a monument, a sepulchre, a tomb (Mark 5:3). "In a country where burial regularly took place on the day of death the time of exposure and indignity would be regarded long" (Beckwith). See Tobit 1:18ff.

10. *They that dwell upon the earth* (*hoi katoikountes epi tēs gēs*). Present active articular participle of *katoikeō*, "an Apocalyptic formula" (Swete) for the non-Christian world (3:10; 6:10; 8:13; 13:8, 12, 14; 17:8). *Rejoice* (*chairousin*). Present active indicative of *chairō*. *Over them* (*ep' autois*). Locative (or dative) case with *epi* as in 10:11. *Make merry* (*euphrainontai*). Present middle indicative of *euphrainō*, old verb (*eu, phrēn*, jolly mind), as in Luke 15:32; Rev. 12:12; 18:20. Jubilant jollification over the cessation of the activity of the two prophets. *They shall send gifts to one another* (*dōra pempsousin allēlois*). Future active of *pempō* with dative *allēlois*. Just as we see it done in Esther 9:19, 22; Neh. 8:10, 12. *Tormented* (*ebasanisan*). First aorist active indicative of *basanizō*, for which see 9:5. This is the reason (*hoti*) of the fiendish glee of Jew and Gentile, who no longer will have to endure the prophecies (11:3f.) and dread miracles (11:5f.) of these two prophets. "Such a sense of relief is perhaps not seldom felt today by bad men when a preacher of righteousness or a signal example of goodness is removed" (Swete).

11. *After the* (*meta tas etc.*). The article *tas* (the) points back to 11:9. *The breath of life from God* (*pneuma zōēs ek tou theou*). This phrase (*pneuma zōēs*) occurs in Gen. 6:17; 7:15, 22 of the lower animals, but here there is clearly an allusion to Ezek. 37:5, 10 (also II Kings 13:21), where the dead bones lived again. *Entered into them* (*eisēlthen en autois*). Second aorist active indicative of *eiserchomai* with *en* rather than *eis* after it (cf. Luke 9:46). The prophecy has here become fact (change from future *pempsousin* to aorist *eisēlthen*). *They stood upon their feet* (*estēsan epi tous*

podas autōn). Ingressive second aorist active indicative of
histēmi (intransitive). Reference to Ezek. 37:10, but with
the accusative in place of genitive there after *epi* as in II
Kings 13:21. *Fell upon* (*epepesen epi*). Second aorist active indicative of *epipiptō* with repetition of *epi*. The same
prophetic use of the aorist as in *eisēlthen* and *estēsan*. *Beheld* (*theōrountas*). Present active articular participle of
theōreō. "The spectators were panic-stricken" (Swete).

12. *Saying* (*legousēs*). Present active predicate participle
of *legō*, feminine genitive agreeing with *phōnēs*, though some
MSS. have the accusative *phōnēn legousan*, either construction being proper after *ēkousan* (they heard). There is a
little evidence for *ēkousa* like 12:10 (24 times in the book).
Cf. John 5:28. *Come up hither* (*anabate hōde*). Second
aorist active imperative of *anabainō*. The ascension of these
two witnesses is in full view of their enemies, not just in
the presence of a few friends as with Christ (Acts 1:9).
They went up (*anebēsan*). Second aorist active indicative
of *anabainō*. *In the cloud* (*en tēi nephelēi*). As Jesus did
(Acts 1:9) and like Elijah (II Kings 2:11). Their triumph
is openly celebrated before their enemies and is like the
rapture described by Paul in I Thess. 4:17.

13. *There was* (*egeneto*). "There came to pass" (second
aorist middle indicative of *ginomai*). Earthquakes are often
given as a symbol of great upheavals in social and spiritual
order (Swete) as in Ezek. 37:7; 38:19; Hagg. 2:6; Mark
13:8; Heb. 12:26f.; Rev. 6:12; 16:18. *Fell* (*epesen*). Second
aorist active indicative of *piptō*, to fall. Only the tenth (*to
dekaton*) of the city fell. Cf. *to triton* (the third) in 8:7–12,
perhaps a conventional number. *Were killed* (*apektanthēsan*).
First aorist passive indicative of *apokteinō* as in 9:18. *Seven
thousand persons* (*onomata anthrōpōn chiliades hepta*). This
use of *onomata* (names of men here) is like that in 3:4; Acts
1:15 and occurs in the papyri (Deissmann, *Bible Studies*, p.
196f.). *Were affrighted* (*emphoboi egenonto*). "Became ter-

rified," old adjective (*en, phobos*, fear) as in Luke 24:5; Acts 10:4; 24:25. "A general movement toward Christianity, induced by fear or despair—a prediction fulfilled more than once in ecclesiastical history" (Swete). *Gave glory* (*edōkan doxan*). First aorist active indicative of *didōmi*, when they saw the effect of the earthquake, recognition of God's power (John 9:24; Acts 12:23; Rom. 4:20).

14. *Is past* (*apēlthen*). Second aorist active indicative of *aperchomai*. See 9:12 for this use and 21:1, 4. The second woe (*hē ouai hē deutera*) is the sixth trumpet (9:12) with the two episodes attached (10:1–11:13). *The third woe* (*hē ouai hē tritē*, feminine as in 9:12) is the seventh trumpet, which now "cometh quickly" (*erchetai tachu*), for which phrase see 2:16; 3:11; 22:7, 12, 20. Usually pointing to the Parousia.

15. *There followed* (*egenonto*). "There came to pass." There was silence in heaven upon the opening of the seventh seal (8:1), but here "great voices." Perhaps the great voices are the *zōa* of 4:6ff.; 5:8. *Saying* (*legontes*). Construction according to sense; *legontes*, masculine participle (not *legousai*), though *phōnai*, feminine. John understood what was said. *Is become* (*egeneto*). "Did become," prophetic use of the aorist participle, already a fact. See *egeneto* in Luke 19:9. *The kingdom of our Lord and of his Christ* (*tou kuriou hēmōn kai tou Christou autou*). Repeat *hē basileia* from the preceding. God the Father is meant here by *kuriou* (Lord), as *autou* (his) shows. This is the certain and glorious outcome of the age-long struggle against Satan, who wields the kingdom of the world which he offered to Christ on the mountain for one act of worship. But Jesus scorned partnership with Satan in the rule of the world, and chose war, war up to the hilt and to the end. Now the climax has come with Christ as Conqueror of the kingdom of this world for his Father. This is the crowning lesson of the Apocalypse. *He shall reign* (*basileusei*). Future active of *basileuō*. God shall reign, but the rule of God and

of Christ is one as the kingdom is one (I Cor. 15:27). Jesus is the Lord's Anointed (Luke 2:26; 9:20).

16. *The four and twenty elders* (*hoi eikosi tessares presbuteroi*). They follow the living creatures (verse 15, if correctly interpreted) in their adoration, as in 4:9ff. Though seated on thrones of their own (4:4), yet they fall upon their faces in every act of worship to God and Christ (4:10; 5:8, 14; 19:4). Here *epi ta prosōpa autōn* (upon their faces) is added as in 7:11 about the angels. The elders here again represent the redeemed, as the four living creatures the forces of nature, in the great thanksgiving here (*eucharistoumen*, present active indicative of *eucharisteō*).

17. *O Lord God* (*Kurie ho theos*). Vocative form *kurie* and nominative form *ho theos* (vocative in use). See 1:8; 4:8 for this combination with *ho pantokratōr* (the Almighty). For *ho ōn kai ho ēn* (which art and which wast) see 1:4, 8; 4:8; 16:5. *Thou hast taken* (*eilēphes*). Perfect active indicative of *lambanō*, emphasizing the permanence of God's rule, "Thou hast assumed thy power." *Didst reign* (*ebasileusas*). Ingressive first aorist active indicative of *basileuō*, "Didst begin to reign." See this combination of tenses (perfect and aorist) without confusion in 3:3; 5:7; 8:5.

18. *Were wroth* (*ōrgisthēsan*). Ingressive first aorist active indicative of *orgizomai*, "became angry." The culmination of wrath against God (16:13ff.; 20:8f.). Cf. Ps. 2:1, 5, 12; 99:1; Acts 4:25ff. John sees the hostility of the world against Christ. *Thy wrath came* (*ēlthen hē orgē sou*). Second aorist active indicative of *erchomai*, the prophetic aorist again. The *Dies Iræ* is conceived as already come. *The time of the dead to be judged* (*ho kairos tōn nekrōn krithēnai*). For this use of *kairos* see Mark 11:13; Luke 21:24. By "the dead" John apparently means both good and bad (John 5:25; Acts 24:21), coincident with the resurrection and judgment (Mark 4:29; Rev. 14:15ff.; 20:1–15). The infinitive *krithēnai* is the first aorist passive of *krinō*, epexegetic use

with the preceding clause, as is true also of *dounai* (second aorist active infinitive of *didōmi*), to give. *Their reward* (*ton misthon*). This will come in the end of the day (Matt. 20:8), from God (Matt. 6:1), at the Lord's return (Rev. 22:12), according to each one's work (I Cor. 3:8). *The small and the great* (*tous mikrous kai tous megalous*). The accusative here is an anacoluthon and fails to agree in case with the preceding datives after *dounai ton misthon*, though some MSS. have the dative *tois mikrois*, etc. John is fond of this phrase "the small and the great" (13:16; 19:5, 18; 20:12). *To destroy* (*diaphtheirai*). First aorist active infinitive of *diaphtheirō*, carrying on the construction with *kairos*. Note *tous diaphtheirontas*, "those destroying" the earth (corrupting the earth). There is a double sense in *diaphtheirō* that justifies this play on the word. See 19:2. In I Tim. 6:5 we have those "corrupted in mind" (*diaphtharmenoi ton noun*). God will destroy the destroyers (I Cor. 3:16f.).

19. *Was opened* (*ēnoigē*). Second aorist passive indicative of *anoigō*, with augment on the preposition as in 15:5. For the sanctuary (*naos*) of God in heaven see 3:12; 7:15; 15:5ff.; 21:22. *Was seen* (*ōphthē*). First aorist passive indicative of *horaō*. *The ark of his covenant* (*hē kibōtos tēs diathēkēs autou*). The sacred ark within the second veil of the tabernacle (Heb. 9:4) and in the inner chamber of Solomon's temple (I Kings 8:6) which probably perished when Nebuchadrezzar burnt the temple (II Kings 25:9; Jer. 3:16). For the symbols of majesty and power in nature here see also 6:12; 8:5; 11:13; 16:18, 21.

CHAPTER XII

1. *A great sign* (*sēmeion mega*). The first of the visions to be so described (13:3; 15:1), and it is introduced by *ōphthē* as in 11:19 and 12:3, not by *meta tauto* or by *eidon* or by *eidon kai idou* as heretofore. This "sign" is really a *teras* (wonder), as it is so by association in Matt. 24:24; John 4:48; Acts 2:22; 5:12. The element of wonder is not in the word *sēmeion* as in *teras*, but often in the thing itself as in Luke 21:11; John 9:16; Rev. 13:13ff.; 15:1; 16:14; 19:20. *A woman* (*gunē*). Nominative case in apposition with *sēmeion*. "The first 'sign in heaven' is a Woman—the earliest appearance of a female figure in the Apocalyptic vision" (Swete). *Arrayed with the sun* (*peribeblēmenē ton hēlion*). Perfect passive participle of *periballō*, with the accusative retained as so often (9 times) in the Apocalypse. Both Charles and Moffatt see mythological ideas and sources behind the bold imagery here that leave us all at sea. Swete understands the Woman to be "the church of the Old Testament" as "the Mother of whom Christ came after the flesh. But here, as everywhere in the Book, no sharp dividing line is drawn between the Church of the Old Testament and the Christian Society." Certainly she is not the Virgin Mary, as verse 17 makes clear. Beckwith takes her to be "the heavenly representative of the people of God, the *ideal* Zion, which, so far as it is embodied in concrete realities, is represented alike by the people of the Old and the New Covenants." John may have in mind Is. 7:14 (Matt. 1:23; Luke 1:31) as well as Mic. 4:10; Is. 26:17f.; 66:7 without a definite picture of Mary. The metaphor of childbirth is common enough (John 16:21; Gal. 4:19). The figure is a bold one with the moon "under her feet" (*hupokatō tōn*

podōn autēs) and "a crown of twelve stars" (*stephanos asterōn dōdeka*), a possible allusion to the twelve tribes (James 1:1; Rev. 21:12) or to the twelve apostles (Rev. 21:14).

2. *And she was with child* (*kai en gastri echousa*). Perhaps *estin* to be supplied or the participle used as a finite verb as in 10:2. This is the technical idiom for pregnancy as in Matt. 1:18, 23, etc. *Travailing in birth* (*ōdinousa*). Present active participle of *ōdinō*, old verb (from *ōdin* birth-pangs I Thess. 5:3), in N.T. only here and Gal. 4:27. *And in pain* (*kai basanizomenē*). "And tormented" (present passive participle of *basanizō*, for which see already 9:5; 11:10), only here in N.T. in sense of childbirth. *To be delivered* (*tekein*). Second aorist active infinitive of *tiktō*, to give birth, epexegetical use. Also in verse 4.

3. *Another sign* (*allo sēmeion*). "A second tableau following close upon the first and inseparable from it" (Swete). *And behold* (*kai idou*). As often (4:1; 6:2, 5, 8, etc.). *A great red dragon* (*drakōn megas purros*). Homer uses this old word (probably from *derkomai*, to see clearly) for a great monster with three heads coiled like a serpent that ate poisonous herbs. The word occurs also in Hesiod, Pindar, Æschylus. The Babylonians feared a seven-headed hydra and Typhon was the Egyptian dragon who persecuted Osiris. One wonders if these and the Chinese dragons are not race memories of conflicts with the diplodocus and like monsters before their disappearance. Charles notes in the O.T. this monster as the chief enemy of God under such title as Rahab (Is. 51:9f.; Job 26:12f.), Behemoth (Job 40:15–24), Leviathan (Is. 27:1), the Serpent (Amos 9:2ff.). In Ps. 74:13 we read of "the heads of the dragons." On *purros* (red) see 6:4. Here (12:9) and in 20:2 the great dragon is identified with Satan. See Dan. 7 for many of the items here, like the ten horns (Dan. 7:7) and hurling the stars (Dan. 8:10). The word occurs in the Apocalypse alone in

the N.T. *Seven diadems* (*hepta diadēmata*). Old word from
diadeō (to bind around), the blue band marked with white
with which Persian kings used to bind on the tiara, so a
royal crown in contrast with *stephanos* (chaplet or wreath
like the Latin *corona* as in 2:10), in N.T. only here, 13:1;
19:12. If Christ as Conqueror has "many diadems," it is
not strange that Satan should wear seven (ten in 13:1).

4. *His tail* (*hē oura autou*). See 9:10, 19. *Draweth* (*surei*).
Present active indicative of *surō*, old verb, to drag, here
alone in the Apocalypse, but see John 21:8. *The third part
of the stars* (*to triton tōn asterōn*). Like a great comet is this
monster. See Dan. 8:10. Perhaps only the third is meant
to soften the picture as in Rev. 8:7f. *Did cast them* (*ebalen
autous*). Second aorist active indicative. Charles takes this
to refer to a war in heaven between the good angels and
Satan, with the fall of some angels (Jude 6). But John
may have in mind the martyrs before Christ (Heb. 11:32f.)
and after Christ's ascension (Matt. 23:35). *Stood* (*estēken*).
Imperfect active of a late verb, *stēkō*, from the perfect
hestēka of *histēmi*, graphic picture of the dragon's challenge
of the woman who is about to give birth. *When she was
delivered* (*hotan tekēi*). Indefinite temporal clause with *hotan*
and the second aorist active subjunctive of *tiktō*, "whenever
she gives birth." *That he might devour* (*hina kataphagēi*).
Purpose clause with *hina* and the second aorist active subjunctive of *katesthiō*, to eat up (down). Cf. Jer. 28:34.
This is what Pharaoh did to Israel (Ex. 1:15–22; Ps. 85:13;
Is. 27:1; 51:9; Ezek. 29:3). Precisely so the devil tried to
destroy the child Jesus on his birth.

5. *She was delivered of a son* (*eteken huion*). Literally,
"she bore a son" (second aorist active indicative of *tiktō*).
A man child (*arsen*). So A C with the neuter *teknon* or
paidion in mind, as often in O.T. (*eteken arsen*, Ex. 1:16ff.;
2:2; Lev. 12:2, 7; Is. 66:7; Jer. 20:15, etc.), but P and some
cursives read *arsena* (masculine accusative), as in verse 13

(*ton arsena*), while Aleph Q have *arrena*. The word is old (either *arsēn* or *arrēn*), as in Matt. 19:4, only in this chapter in the Apocalypse. It is really redundant after *huion* (son), as in Tob. 6:12 (Aleph). *Who is to rule all the nations with a rod of iron* (*hos mellei poimainein panta ta ethnē en rabdōi sidērāi*). See 2:27 for these words (from Ps. 2:9) applied there to victorious Christians also, and in 19:15 to the triumphant Christian. His rule will go beyond the Jews (Matt. 2:6). There is here, of course, direct reference to the birth of Jesus from Mary, who thus represented in her person this "ideal woman" (God's people). *Was caught unto God* (*hērpasthē*). First aorist passive indicative of *harpazō*, old verb for seizing or snatching away, as in John 10:12, here alone in the Apocalypse. Reference to the ascension of Christ, with omission of the ministry, crucifixion, and resurrection of Christ because he is here simply showing that "the Dragon's vigilance was futile" (Swete). "The Messiah, so far from being destroyed, is caught up to a share in God's throne" (Beckwith).

6. *Fled into the wilderness* (*ephugen eis tēn erēmon*). Second aorist active indicative of *pheugō*. Here, of course, not Mary, but "the ideal woman" (God's people) of the preceding verses, who fled under persecution of the dragon. God's people do not at once share the rapture of Christ, but the dragon is unable to destroy them completely. The phrases used here seem to be reminiscent of Deut. 8:2ff. (wanderings of Israel in the wilderness), I Kings 17:2f. and 19:3f. (Elijah's flight), I Macc. 2:29 (flight of the Jews from Antiochus Epiphanes), Matt. 2:13 (flight of Joseph and Mary to Egypt), Mark 13:14 (the flight of Christians at the destruction of Jerusalem). *Where* (*hopou—ekei*). Hebrew redundancy (where—there) as in 3:8; 8:2, 9; 13:8, 12; 17:9; 20:8. *Prepared* (*hētoimasmenon*). Perfect passive predicate participle of *hetoimazō*, for which verb see Matt. 20:23; Rev. 8:6; 9:7, 15; 16:12; 19:7; 21:2, and for its use

with *topos* John 14:2f. and for the kind of fellowship meant by it (Ps. 31:21; II Cor. 13:13; Col. 3:3; I John 1:3). *Of God (apo tou theou)*. "From (by) God," marking the source as God (9:18; James 1:13). This anticipatory symbolism is repeated in 12:13f. *That there they may nourish her (hina ekei trephōsin autēn)*. Purpose clause with *hina* and the present for continued action: active subjunctive according to A P though C reads *trephousin*, present active indicative, as is possible also in 13:17 and certainly so in I John 5:20 (Robertson, *Grammar*, p. 984), a solecism in late vernacular Greek. The plural is indefinite "they" as in 10:11; 11:9. One MSS. has *trephetai* (is nourished). The stereotyped phrase occurs here, as in 11:2f., for the length of the dragon's power, repeated in 12:14 in more general terms and again in 13:5.

7. *There was war in heaven (egeneto polemos en tōi ouranōi)*. "There came to be war in heaven" (*egeneto*, not *ēn*). "Another *tableau*, not a *sēmeion* (vv. 1, 3), but consequent upon the two *sēmeia* which precede it. The birth and rapture of the Woman's Son issue in a war which invades the *epourania*" (Swete). The reference is not to the original rebellion of Satan, as Andreas held. As the coming of Christ brought on fresh manifestations of diabolic power (Mark 1:13; Luke 22:3, 31; John 12:31; 14:30; 16:11), just so Christ's return to heaven is pictured as being the occasion of renewed attacks there. We are not to visualize it too literally, but certainly modern airplanes help us to grasp the notion of battles in the sky even more than the phalanxes of storm-clouds (Swete). John even describes this last conflict as in heaven itself. Cf. Luke 10:18; I Kings 22:1ff.; Job 1 and 2; Zech. 3:1ff. *Michael and his angels (ho Michaēl kai hoi aggeloi autou)*. The nominative here may be in apposition with *polemos*, but it is an abnormal construction with no verb, though *egeneto* (arose) can be understood as repeated. Michael is the champion of the Jewish people

(Dan. 10:13, 21; 12:1) and is called the archangel in Jude 9. *Going forth to war* (*tou polemēsai*). This genitive articular infinitive is another grammatical problem in this sentence. If *egeneto* (arose) is repeated as above, then we have the infinitive for purpose, a common enough idiom. Otherwise it is anomalous, not even like Acts 10:25. *With the dragon* (*meta tou drakontos*). On the use of *meta* with *polemeō* see 2:16; 13:4; 17:14 (nowhere else in N.T.). The devil has angels under his command (Matt. 25:41) and preachers also (II Cor. 11:14f.). *Warred* (*epolemēsen*). Constative aorist active indicative of *polemeō*, picturing the whole battle in one glimpse.

8. *And they prevailed not* (*kai ouk ischusan*). Here *kai* equals "and yet" or "but." A few MSS. read the singular *ischusen* like *epolemēsen*, but wrongly so. *Neither was their place found any more* (*oude topos heurethē autōn eti*). First aorist passive indicative of *heuriskō*, to find. Probably *autōn* is the objective genitive (place for them), just as in 20:11 *autois* (dative, for them) is used with *topos ouch heurethē*. The phrase occurs in Dan. 2:35 Theod. and Zech. 10:10. The dragon is finally expelled from heaven (cf. Job 1:6), though to us it seems a difficult conception to think of Satan having had access to heaven.

9. *Was cast down* (*eblēthē*). Effective first aorist passive indicative of *ballō*, cast down for good and all, a glorious consummation. This vision of final victory over Satan is given by Jesus in Luke 10:18; John 12:31. It has not come yet, but it is coming, and the hope of it should be a spur to missionary activity and zeal. The word *megas* (great) occurs here with *drakōn* as in 12:3, and the whole picture is repeated in 20:2. The dragon in both places is identified with the old serpent (Gen. 3:1ff.) and called *archaios* (from *archē*, beginning), as Jesus said that the devil was a murderer "from the beginning" (John 8:44). Both diabolos (*slanderer*) and Satan (*Satanās*) are common in N.T. for

this great dragon and old serpent, the chief enemy of man-kind. See on Matt. 4:1 and Rev. 2:10 for *diabolos* and Luke 10:18 for *Satanās*. *The deceiver of the whole world* (*ho planōn tēn oikoumenēn holēn*). This is his aim and his oc-cupation, pictured here by the nominative articular present active participle of *planaō*, to lead astray. For "the in-habited world" see Luke 2:1; Rev. 3:10; 16:14. Satan can almost "lead astray" the very elect of God (Matt. 24:24), so artful is he in his beguilings as he teaches us how to de-ceive ourselves (I John 1:8). *He was cast down to the earth* (*eblēthē eis tēn gēn*). Effective aorist repeated from the be-ginning of the verse. "The earth was no new sphere of Satan's working" (Swete). *Were cast down* (*eblēthēsan*). Triple use of the same verb applied to Satan's minions. The expulsion is complete.

10. *A great voice saying* (*phōnēn megalēn legousan*). Ac-cusative after *ēkousa* in this phrase as in 5:11; 10:4; 14:2; 18:4, but the genitive *phōnēs legousēs* in 11:12; 14:13. We are not told whence this voice or song comes, possibly from one of the twenty-four elders (Swete) or some other heavenly beings (11:15) who can sympathize with human beings (19:10), the martyrs in heaven (Charles). *Now is come* (*arti egeneto*). *Arti* (John 13:33) shows how recent the downfall of Satan here proleptically pictured as behind us in time (aorist tense *egeneto*). *The salvation* (*hē sōtēria*). Here "the victory" as in 7:10; 19:1. *The power* (*hē dunamis*). God's power over the dragon (cf. 7:12; 11:17; 19:1). *The kingdom* (*hē basileia*). "The empire of God" as in 11:15. *The authority of his Christ* (*hē exousia tou Christou autou*). Which Christ received from the Father (Matt. 28:18; John 17:2). See 11:15 (Ps. 2:2) for "his Anointed." *The accuser* (*ho katēgōr*). The regular form, *katēgoros*, occurs in John 8:10; Acts 23:30, 35; 25:16, 18 and in many MSS. here in Rev. 12:10, but A reads *katēgōr*, which Westcott and Hort accept. It was once considered a Greek transliteration of a Hebrew

word, but Deissmann (*Light*, etc., p. 93f.) quotes it from a vernacular magical papyrus of the fourth century A.D. with no sign of Jewish or Christian influence, just as *diakōn* appears as a vernacular form of *diakonos*. Only here is the word applied to Satan in the N.T. In late Judaism Satan is the accuser, and Michael the defender, of the faithful. *Of our brethren* (*tōn adelphōn hēmōn*). The saints still on earth battling with Satan and his devices. *Which accuseth them* (*ho katēgorōn autous*). Articular present active participle of *katēgoreō*, old verb, to accuse, usually with the genitive of the person (John 5:45), but here with the accusative. This is the devil's constant occupation (Job 1:6f.). *Day and night* (*hēmeras kai nuktos*). Genitive of time. "By day and by night."

11. *They overcame him* (*autoi enikēsan*). First aorist active indicative of *nikaō*, the verb used by Jesus of his own victory (John 16:33) and about him (Rev. 3:21; 5:5). "The victory of the martyrs marks the failure of Satan's endeavours" (Swete). *Because of the blood of the Lamb* (*dia to haima tou arniou*). As in 1:5; 5:6, 9; 7:14. The blood of Christ is here presented by *dia* as the ground for the victory and not the means, as by *en* in 1:5; 5:9. Both ideas are true, but *dia* with the accusative gives only the reason. The blood of Christ does cleanse us from sin (John 1:29; I John 1:7). Christ conquered Satan, and so makes our victory possible (Luke 11:21f.; Heb. 2:18). "Thus the Lamb is the true *sunēgoros* [like Michael] of the New Israel, its *paraklētos pros ton patera* (I John 2:1)" (Swete). *Because of the Word of their testimony* (*dia ton logon tēs marturias autōn*). The same use of *dia*, "because of their testimony to Jesus" as in John's own case in 1:9. These martyrs have been true to their part. *They loved not their life even unto death* (*ouk ēgapēsan tēn psuchēn autōn achri thanatou*). First aorist active indicative of *agapaō*. They did resist "unto blood" (*mechris haimatos* Heb. 12:4) and did not put

their own lives before loyalty to Christ. There is a direct
reference to the words of Jesus in John 12:25 as illustrated
also in Mark 8:35; Matt. 10:39; 16:25; Luke 9:24; 17:33.
Paul's own example is pertinent (Acts 21:13; Phil. 1:20ff.).
Jesus himself had been "obedient unto death" (Phil. 2:8).
These martyrs seem to be still alive on earth, but their
heroism is proleptically pictured.

12. *Therefore* (*dia touto*). "For this reason" as in 7:15;
18:8 (15 times in John's Gospel, Charles notes). It points
back to verse 10. *Rejoice* (*euphrainesthe*). Present middle
imperative of *euphrainō* as in 11:10; 18:20. *O heavens* (*hoi
ouranoi*). Plural here alone in the Apocalypse, though common elsewhere in the N.T. Satan is no longer in the heavens.
They that dwell therein (*hoi en autois skēnountes*). Present
active articular participle of *skēnoō* (see 7:15 and 13:6) to
dwell (tabernacle) as of Christ in John 1:14 and of God in
Rev. 21:3. The inhabitants of heaven (angels and saints)
have cause to rejoice, and earth reason to mourn. *Woe for
the earth and for the sea* (*ouai tēn gēn kai tēn thalassan*).
The accusative after *ouai* as in 8:13, but nominative in
18:10, 16, 19 in place of the usual dative (Matt. 11:21;
18:7, etc.). *Is gone down* (*katebē*). Second aorist (effective)
active indicative of *katabainō*, "did go down." *But a short
time* (*oligon kairon*). Accusative of extent of time, "a little
time." The devil's departure from his warfare in the heavens
reveals (*eidōs*, knowing, perfect active participle) to him
that his time for doing harm to men is limited, and hence
his great wrath (*thumon*, boiling rage).

13. *He persecuted* (*ediōxen*). First aorist active participle
of *diōkō*, to pursue, to chase, hostile pursuit here as in
Matt. 5:10f.; 10:23, etc. John now, after the "voice" in
10 to 13, returns to the narrative in verse 9. The child was
caught away in verse 5, and now the woman (the true Israel
on earth) is given deadly persecution. Perhaps events since
A.D. 64 (burning of Rome by Nero) amply illustrated this

vision, and they still do so. *Which* (*hētis*). "Which very one."

14. *There were given* (*edothēsan*). As in 8:2; 9:1, 3. *The two wings of the great eagle* (*hai duo pteruges tou aetou tou megalou*). Not the eagle of 8:13, but the generic use of the article. Every eagle had two wings. Probably here, as in Matt. 24:28, the griffon or vulture rather than the true eagle is pictured. For the eagle in the O.T. see Ex. 19:4; Is. 40:31; Job 9:26; Prov. 24:54. *That she might fly* (*hina petētai*). Purpose clause with *hina* and present middle subjunctive of *petomai*, old verb, to fly, in N.T. only in the Apocalypse (4:7; 8:13; 12:14; 14:6; 19:17). Resumption of the details in verse 6 (which see) about the "wilderness," her "place," the redundant *ekei* with *hopou*, the "time and times, and half a time" (*kairon kai kairous kai hēmisu*), 1260 days, but with *trephetai* (present passive indicative) instead of *trephōsin* (general plural of the present active subjunctive), and with the addition of "from the face of the serpent" (*apo prosōpou tou opheōs*), because the serpent rules the earth for that period. "To the end of the present order the Church dwells in the wilderness" (Swete), and yet we must carry on for Christ.

15. *Water as a flood* (*hudōr hōs potamon*). "Water as a river," accusative case after *ebalen* (cast). The serpent could not follow the woman or stop her flight and so sought to drown her. *That he might cause her to be carried away by the stream* (*hina autēn potamophorēton poiēsēi*). Purpose clause with *hina* and the first aorist active subjunctive of *poieō*. For this use of *poieō* see 17:16. This compound verbal *potamophorēton* in the predicate accusative (*potamos*, river, *phorēton* from *phoreō*, to bear) was not coined by John, but occurs in a papyrus of B.C. 110 and in several others after N.T. times. It means simply "carried away by the river."

16. *Helped the woman* (*eboēthēsen tēi gunaiki*). First aorist

active indicative of *boētheō*, old verb with the dative as in Heb. 2:18, which see. Herodotus tells of the Lycus disappearing underground near Colossae. But this vivid symbol is not dependent on historical examples. *Swallowed up* (*katepien*). Second aorist active indicative of *katapinō*, literally "drank down."

17. *Waxed wroth* (*ōrgisthē*). First aorist (ingressive) passive indicative of *orgizomai*, "became angry." *With the woman* (*epi tēi gunaiki*). "At the woman," "because of the woman." *Went away* (*apēlthen*). "Went off" in his rage to make war with the scattered followers of the Lamb not in the wilderness, perhaps an allusion to Gen. 3:15. The devil carries on relentless war with all those "which keep the commandments of God and hold the testimony of Jesus" (*tōn tērountōn tas entolas tou theou kai echontōn tēn marturian Iēsou*). These two marks excite the wrath of the devil then and always. Cf. 1:9; 6:9; 14:12; 19:10; 20:4.

18. *He stood* (*estathē*). First aorist passive indicative of *histēmi* (intransitive), as in 8:3. "He stopped" on his way to war with the rest of the woman's seed. P Q read here *estathēn* (I stood) when it has to be connected with chapter 13. *Upon the sand* (*epi tēn ammon*). The accusative case as in 7:1; 8:3, etc. *Ammos* is an old word for sand, for innumerable multitude in 20:8.

CHAPTER XIII

1. *Out of the sea (ek tēs thalassēs)*. See 11:7 for "the beast coming up out of the abyss." The imagery comes from Dan. 7:3. See also Rev. 17:8. This "wild beast from the sea," as in Dan. 7:17, 23, is a vast empire used in the interest of brute force. This beast, like the dragon (12:3), has ten horns and seven heads, but the horns are crowned, not the heads. The Roman Empire seems to be meant here (17:9, 12). On "diadems" (*diadēmata*) see 12:3, only ten here, not seven as there. *Names of blasphemy (onomata blasphēmias)*. See 17:3 for this same phrase. The meaning is made plain by the blasphemous titles assumed by the Roman emperors in the first and second centuries, as shown by the inscriptions in Ephesus, which have *theos* constantly applied to them.

2. *Like unto a leopard (homoion pardalei)*. Associative-instrumental case of *pardalis*, old word for panther, leopard, here only in N.T. The leopard (*leo, pard*) was considered a cross between a panther and a lioness. *As the feet of a bear (hōs arkou)*. Old word, also spelled *arktos*, here only in N.T. From Dan. 7:4. No word in the Greek for "feet" before "bear." *As the mouth of a lion (hōs stoma leontos)*. From Dan. 7:4. This beast combines features of the first three beasts in Dan. 7:2ff. The strength and brutality of the Babylonian, Median, and Persian empires appeared in the Roman Empire. The catlike vigilance of the leopard, the slow and crushing power of the bear, and the roar of the lion were all familiar features to the shepherds in Palestine (Swete). *The dragon gave him (edōken autōi ho drakōn)*. First aorist active indicative of *didōmi* (to give) and dative case *autōi* (the beast). The dragon works through this beast.

The beast is simply Satan's agent. Satan claimed this power to Christ (Matt. 4:9; Luke 4:6) and Christ called Satan the prince of this world (John 12:31; 14:30; 16:11). So the war is on.

3. *And I saw* (*kai*). No verb (*eidon*) in the old MSS., but clearly understood from verse 2. *As though it had been smitten* (*hōs esphagmenēn*). Perfect passive participle of *sphazō*, as in 5:6, accusative singular agreeing with *mian* (one of the heads), object of *eidon* understood, "as though slain" (so the word means in seven other instances in the book). There is a reference to the death and new life of the Lamb in 5:6. *And his death-stroke was healed* (*kai hē plēgē autou etherapeuthē*). First aorist passive indicative of *therapeuō*. "The stroke of death" (that led to death). Apparently refers to the death of Nero in June 68 A.D. by his own hand. But after his death pretenders arose claiming to be Nero *redivivus* even as late as 89 (Tacitus, *Hist.* i. 78, ii. 8, etc.). John seems to regard Domitian as Nero over again in the persecutions carried on by him. The distinction is not always preserved between the beast (Roman Empire) and the seven heads (emperors), but in 17:10 the beast survives the loss of five heads. Here it is the death-stroke of one head, while in verses 12, 14 the beast himself receives a mortal wound. *Wondered after the beast* (*ethaumasthē opisō tou thēriou*). First aorist passive (deponent) indicative of *thaumazō*, to wonder at, to admire, as in 17:8. For this pregnant use of *opisō* see John 12:9; Acts 5:37; 20:30; I Tim. 5:15. "All the earth wondered at and followed after the beast," that is Antichrist as represented by Domitian as Nero *redivivus*. But Charles champions the view that Caligula, not Nero, is the head that received the death-stroke and recovered and set up statues of himself for worship, even trying to do it in Jerusalem.

4. *They worshipped the dragon* (*prosekunēsan tōi drakonti*). First aorist active indicative of *proskuneō*, with dative case

drakonti (from *drakōn*). They really worshipped Satan (the dragon) when "they worshipped the beast" (*prosekunēsan tōi thēriōi*) or any one of the heads (like Caligula, Nero, Domitian) of the beast. The beast is merely the tool of the devil for worship. Recall the fact that the devil even proposed that Jesus worship him. Emperor-worship, like all idolatry, was devil-worship. The same thing is true today about self-worship (humanism or any other form of it). *Who is like unto the beast?* (*tis homoios tōi thēriōi;*). Associative-instrumental case after *homoios*. An echo, perhaps parody, of like language about God in Ex. 15:11; Ps. 35:10; 113:5. "The worship of such a monster as Nero was indeed a travesty of the worship of God" (Swete). *And who is able to war with him?* (*kai tis dunatai polemēsai met' autou;*). Worship of the devil and the devil's agent is justified purely on the ground of brute force. It is the doctrine of Nietzsche that might makes right.

5. *There was given to him* (*edothē autōi*). First aorist passive indicative of *didōmi*, to give, as in next line and verse 7. Perhaps a reference to *edōken* (he gave) in verse 4, where the dragon (Satan) gave the beast his power. The ultimate source of power is God, but the reference seems to be Satan here. *Speaking great things and blasphemies* (*laloun megala kai blasphēmias*). Present active participle of *laleō*, agreeing with *stoma* (nominative neuter singular and subject of *edothē*). The words are like Daniel's description of the Little Horn (7:8, 20, 25) and like the description of Antiochus Epiphanes (I Macc. 1:24). Cf. II Pet. 2:11. *To continue* (*poiēsai*). First aorist active infinitive (epexegetic use) of *poieō*, either in the sense of working (signs), as in Dan. 8:12, 14, with the accusative of duration of time (*mēnas* months), or more likely in the sense of doing time, with *mēnas* as the direct object as in Matt. 20:12; Acts 20:3; James 4:13.

6. *For blasphemies* (*eis blasphēmias*). "For the purpose

of blasphemies." *Against God* (*pros ton theon*). "Face to face with God" in sheer defiance, like Milton's picture of Satan in *Paradise Lost*. See Dan. 7:25; 8:10. The aorist *ēnoixen* is probably constative, for he repeated the blasphemies, though the phrase (*anoigō to stoma*, to open the mouth) is normally ingressive of the beginning of an utterance (Matt. 5:2; Acts 8:35). This verse explains verse 5. The Roman emperors blasphemously assumed divine names in public documents. They directed their blasphemy against heaven itself ("his tabernacle," *tēn skēnēn autou*, 7:15; 12:12; 21:3) and against "them that dwell in the heaven" (*tous en tōi ouranōi skēnountas*), the same phrase of 12:12 (either angels or the redeemed or both).

7. *To make war with the saints and to overcome them* (*poiēsai polemon meta tōn hagiōn kai nikēsai autous*). This clause with two epexegetical first aorist active infinitives (*polemēsai* and *nikēsai*) is omitted in A C P, but probably by *homœoteleuton* (like ending) because of the repetition of *edothē*. The words seem to come from Dan. 7:21, 23. There was no escape from the beast's rule in the Mediterranean world. See 5:9 for the phrases here used, there for praise to the Lamb.

8. *Shall worship him* (*proskunēsousin auton*). Future active of *proskuneō* with the accusative here as some MSS. in 13:4 (*to thērion*), both constructions in this book. *Whose* (*hou—autou*). Redundant use of genitive *autou* (his) with *hou* (whose) as common in this book, and singular instead of plural *hōn* with antecedent *pantes* (all, plural), thus calling attention to the responsibility of the individual in emperor-worship. *Hath not been written* (*ou gegraptai*). Perfect passive indicative of *graphō*, permanent state, stands written. *In the book of life of the Lamb* (*en tōi bibliōi tēs zōēs tou arniou*). See 3:5 for this phrase and the O.T. references. It occurs again in 17:8; 20:12, 15; 21:27. "Here and in 21:27, the Divine Register is represented as belong-

ing to 'the Lamb that was slain'" (Swete). *That hath been slain from the foundation of the world* (*tou esphagmenou* (for which see 5:6) *apo katabolēs kosmou*). For the phrase *apo katabolēs kosmou* (not in the LXX) there are six other N.T. uses (Matt. 13:35 without *kosmou*; 25:34; Luke 11:50; Heb. 4:3; 9:26; Rev. 17:8), and for *pro katabolēs kosmou* three (John 17:24; Eph. 1:4; I Pet. 1:20). It is doubtful here whether it is to be taken with *tou esphagmenou* (cf. I Pet. 1:20) or with *gegraptai* as in Rev. 17:8. Either makes sense, and here the most natural use is with *esphagmenou*. At any rate the death of Christ lies in the purpose of God, as in John 3:16.

9. *If any one hath an ear* (*ei tis echei ous*). Condition of first class, repetition of the saying in 2:7, 11, 17, 29, etc.

10. *If any man is for captivity* (*ei tis eis aichmalōsian*). Condition of first class, but with no copula (*estin*) expressed. For *aichmalōsian* (from *aichmalōtos* captive) see Eph. 4:8, only other N.T. example. Apparently John means this as a warning to the Christians not to resist force with force, but to accept captivity as he had done as a means of grace. Cf. Jer. 15:2. The text is not certain, however. *If any man shall kill with the sword* (*ei tis en machairēi apoktenei*). First-class condition with future active of *apokteinō*, not future passive, for it is a picture of the persecutor drawn here like that by Jesus in Matt. 26:52. *Must he be killed* (*dei auton en machairēi apoktanthēnai*). First aorist passive infinitive of *apokteinō*. The inevitable conclusion (*dei*) of such conduct. The killer is killed. *Here* (*hōde*). In this attitude of submission to the inevitable. For *hōde* see 13:18; 14:12; 17:9. "Faith" (*pistis*) here is more like faithfulness, fidelity.

11. *Another beast* (*allo thērion*). Like the first beast (verse 1), not a *heteron thērion* (a different beast). *Out of the earth* (*ek tēs gēs*). Not "out of the sea" as the first (verse 1), perhaps locating him in Asia Minor without world-wide

scope, but plainly the agent of the first beast and so of the dragon. *He had* (*eichen*). Imperfect active of *echō*. Only two horns (not ten like the first, verse 1). *Like unto a lamb* (*homoia arniōi*). Usual construction. Only the two horns of a young lamb and without the ferocity of the other beast, but "he spake as a dragon" (*elalei hōs drakōn*). Gunkel and Charles confess their inability to make anything out of this item. But Swete thinks that he had the roar of a dragon with all the looks of a lamb (weakness and innocence). Cf. the wolves in sheep's clothing (Matt. 7:15).

12. *He exerciseth* (*poiei*). Present active dramatic present of *poieō*. *In his sight* (*enōpion autou*). In the eye of the first beast who gets his authority from the dragon (13:2). The second beast carries on the succession of authority from the dragon and the first beast. It has been a common Protestant interpretation since the Reformation of Luther to see in the first beast Pagan Rome and in the second beast Papal Rome. There is undoubted verisimilitude in this interpretation, but it is more than doubtful if any such view comes within the horizon of the imagery here. Ramsay takes the first beast to be the power of imperial Rome and the second beast to be the provincial power which imitated Rome in the persecutions. *To worship the first beast* (*hina proskunēsousin to thērion to prōton*). Sub-final clause with *hina* after *poiei* seen in John 11:37; Col. 4:16; Rev. 3:9, usually with the subjunctive, but here with the future indicative as in 3:9. Note the accusative after *proskuneō* as in verse 8. Here the death-stroke of one of the heads (verse 3) is ascribed to the beast. Clearly the delegated authority of the provincial priests of the emperor-worship is rigorously enforced, if this is the correct interpretation.

13. *That he should even make fire come down out of heaven* (*hina kai pur poiēi ek tou ouranou katabainein*). Purpose clause again with *hina* and the present active subjunctive of *poieō* and the object infinitive of *katabainō* after *poiei*.

Christ promised great signs to the disciples (John 14:12), but he also warned them against false prophets and false christs with their signs and wonders (Mark 13:22). So also Paul had pictured the power of the man of sin (II Thess. 2:9). Elijah had called down fire from heaven (I Kings 18:38; II Kings 1:10) and James and John had once even urged Jesus to do this miracle (Luke 9:54).

14. *And he deceiveth (kai planāi).* Present active (dramatic) indicative of *planaō,* the very thing that Jesus had said would happen (Matt. 24:24, "So as to lead astray" *hōste planāsthai,* the word used here, if possible the very elect). It is a constant cause for wonder, the gullibility of the public at the hands of new charlatans who continually bob up with their pipe-dreams. *That they should make an image to the beast (poiēsai eikona tōi thēriōi).* Indirect command (this first aorist active infinitive of *poieō*) after *legōn* as in Acts 21:21, not indirect assertion. This "image" (*eikōn,* for which word see Matt. 22:20; Col. 1:15) of the emperor could be his head upon a coin (Mark 12:16), an *imago* painted or woven upon a standard, a bust in metal or stone, a statue, anything that people could be asked to bow down before and worship. This test the priests in the provinces pressed as it was done in Rome itself. The phrase "the image of the beast," occurs ten times in this book (13:14, 15 *ter*; 14:9, 11; 15:2; 16:2; 19:20; 20:4). Emperor-worship is the issue and that involves worship of the devil. *The stroke of the sword (tēn plēgēn tēs machairēs).* This language can refer to the death of Nero by his own sword. *And lived (kai ezēsen).* "And he came to life" (ingressive first aorist active indicative of *zaō*). Perhaps a reference to Domitian as a second Nero in his persecution of Christians.

15. *To give breath to it (dounai pneuma autēi).* This second beast, probably a system like the first (not a mere person), was endowed with the power to work magical tricks, as was true of Simon Magus and Apollonius of Tyana

and many workers of legerdemain since. *Pneuma* here has its original meaning of breath or wind like *pneuma zōēs* (breath of life) in 11:11. *Even to the image* (*tēi eikoni*). No "even" in the Greek, just apposition with *autēi* (her). *That should both speak and cause* (*hina kai lalēsēi kai poiēsēi*). Final clause with *hina* and the first aorist active subjunctive of *laleō* and *poieō*. Ventriloquism like that in Acts 16:16. *That should be killed* (*hina apoktanthōsin*). Sub-final clause with *hina* and the first aorist passive subjunctive of *apokteinō*, after *poiēsēi*, as in verse 12 (future indicative). *As many as should not worship* (*hosoi ean mē proskunēsōsin*). Indefinite relative clause with modal *ean* (=*an*) and the first aorist active subjunctive of *proskuneō* with the accusative *tēn eikona* (some MSS. the dative). Note the triple use of "the image of the beast" in this sentence. "That refusal to worship the image of the emperor carried with it capital punishment in Trajan's time is clear from Pliny's letter to Trajan (X. 96)" (Charles).

16. *He causeth all* (same use of *poieō* as in 12 and 15). Note article here with each class (the small and the great, etc.). *That there be given them* (*hina dōsin autois*). Same use of *hina* after *poieō* as in 12 and 15, only here with indefinite plural *dōsin* (second aorist active subjunctive), "that they give themselves," as in 10:11; 12:6; 16:15. *A mark* (*charagma*). Old word from *charassō*, to engrave, in Acts 17:29 of idolatrous images, but in Rev. (13:16, 17; 14:9, 11; 16:2; 19:20; 20:4) of the brand of the beast on the right hand or on the forehead or on both. Deissmann (*Bible Studies*, pp. 240ff.) shows that in the papyri official business documents often have the name and image of the emperor, with the date as the official stamp or seal and with *charagma* as the name of this seal. Animals and slaves were often branded with the owner's name, as Paul (Gal. 6:17) bore the *stigmata* of Christ. Ptolemy Philadelphus compelled some Alexandrian Jews to receive the mark of Dionysus

as his devotees (III Macc. 3:29). The servants of God receive on their foreheads the stamp of the divine seal (Rev. 7:3). Charles is certain that John gets his metaphor from the *tephillin* (phylacteries) which the Jew wore on his left hand and on his forehead. At any rate, this "mark of the beast" was necessary for life and all social and business relations. On the right hand, that is in plain sight. *Upon their forehead* (*epi to metōpon autōn*). Accusative with *epi*, though genitive just before with *cheiros* (hand). See already 7:3; 9:4 (genitive *epi tōn metōpōn*). Only in the Apocalypse in N.T.

17. *That no man should be able to buy or to sell* (*hina mē tis dunētai agorasai ē pōlēsai*). Final clause with *hina* and present middle subjunctive of *dunamai* with aorist active infinitives. This is a regular boycott (Ramsay, *Seven Letters*, p. 106f.) against all not worshippers of the emperor. *Save* (*ei mē*). "If not," "except." *Even the name* (*to onoma*). No "even," just apposition with *charagma* (the mark). *Or the number* (*ē ton arithmon*). The stamp (the mark) may bear either the name or the number of the beast. The name and the number are one and the same. They could write the name in numerals, for numbers were given by letters. Swete suggests that it was "according to a sort of *gematria* known to the Apocalyptist and his Asian readers, but not generally intelligible."

18. *Here is wisdom* (*hōde hē sophia*). The puzzle that follows as in 17:9. See Eph. 1:17 for "a spirit of wisdom and of understanding." *He that understands* (*ho echōn noun*). "The one having intelligence" in such matters. Cf. the adverb *nounechōs* (discreetly) in Mark 12:34. *Let him count* (*psēphisatō*). First active imperative of *psēphizō*, old verb (from *psēphos* pebble), to count, in N.T. only here and Luke 14:28. *The number of a man* (*arithmos anthrōpou*). "A man's number." But what man and what name? *Six hundred and sixty-six* (*hexakosioi hexēkonta hex*). Unfor-

tunately some MSS. here read 616 instead of 666. All sorts of solutions are offered for this conundrum. Charles is satisfied with the Hebrew letters for Nero Cæsar, which give 666, and with the Latin form of Nero (without the final n), which makes 616. Surely this is ingenious and it may be correct. But who can really tell?

CHAPTER XIV

1. *The Lamb* (*to arnion*). See 5:6; 7:17; 12:11; 13:8 and is in contrast with the anarthrous *arnion* in 13:11. This proleptic vision of the Lamb "standing on the mount Zion" (*hestos epi to oros Siōn*, second perfect active participle neuter of *histēmi* with *epi* and accusative) is reasoning after the visions of the two beasts. Mount Zion is the site of the new city of God (Heb. 12:22), the Jerusalem above (Gal. 4:26), the seat of the Messianic Kingdom whether heaven or the new earth (Rev. 21 and 22). These victors have the name of the Lamb and God upon their foreheads as in 3:12 and 22:4, in place of the mark of the beast above (13:16; 14:11). This seal protects them (9:4). *A hundred and forty and four thousand* (*hekaton tesserakonta tessares chiliades*). "Thousands" literally (*chilias* feminine word for a thousand and so *echousai* feminine plural). For the 144,000 see 7:5, 8, though some scholars seek a distinction somehow.

2. *As a voice of many waters* (*hōs phōnēn hudatōn pollōn*). For which see 1:15. *Of a great thunder* (*brontēs megalēs*). For which see 6:1; 19:6. For this voice out of heaven see 10:4; 14:15; 18:4 and note accusative with *ēkousa*. *As the voice of harpers harping with their harps* (*hōs kitharōidōn kitharizontōn en tais kitharais autōn*). Triple use of *kithara* (5:8), *kitharōidōn* (18:22), *kitharizontōn* (old verb *kitharizō*, in N.T. only here and I Cor. 14:7). Wonderful melody in this chorus by the angels, not by the 144,000.

3. *They sing as it were a new song* (*aidousin hōs ōidēn kainēn*). See 5:9 for this phrase (cognate accusative) save that here *hōs* (as if) is added. There the new song was sung by the four living creatures and the elders, but here "before" (*enōpion*) them and so apparently by the throng

who were themselves redeemed by the Lamb. *No man could learn the song save* (*oudeis edunato mathein tēn ōidēn ei mē*). Imperfect (*edunato*) of *dunamai* and second aorist (ingressive) active infinitive of *manthanō*. In 5:9–12 the angels join in the song. In 15:3 it is the Song of Moses and the Lamb. *Even they that had been purchased out of the earth* (*hoi ēgorasmenoi apo tēs gēs*). Perfect passive articular participle of *agorazō*, purchased by the blood of the Lamb (5:9), masculine plural in apposition with *chiliades* (thousands) feminine plural (7:5, 8; 14:1). *Apo* (from) here, though *ek* (out of) in 5:9. The 144,000 are not yet separated from the earth (John 17:15). Whether the 144,000 here are identical with that number in 7:4–8 or not, they must embrace both men and women.

4. *Were not defiled with women* (*meta gunaikōn ouk emolunthēsan*). First aorist passive indicative of *molunō*, old verb, to stain, already in 3:4, which see. The use of this word rules out marriage, which was not considered sinful. *For they are virgins* (*parthenoi gar eisin*). *Parthenos* can be applied to men as well as women. Swete takes this language "metaphorically, as the symbolical character of the Book suggests." Charles considers it an interpolation in the interest of celibacy for both men and women. If taken literally, the words can refer only to adultery or fornication (Beckwith). Jesus recognised abstinence only for those able to receive it (Matt. 19:12), as did Paul (I Cor. 7:1, 8, 32, 36). Marriage is approved by Paul in I Tim. 4:3 and by Heb. 13:4. The New Testament exalts marriage and this passage should not be construed as degrading it. *Whithersoever he goeth* (*hopou an hupagei*). Indefinite local clause with modal *an* and the present active indicative of *hupagō*. The Christian life is following the Lamb of God as Jesus taught (Mark 2:14; 10:21; Luke 9:59; John 1:43; 21:19, etc.) and as Peter taught (I Pet. 2:21) and John (I John 2:6). *Were purchased from among men* (*ēgorasthēsan apo tōn anthrōpōn*).

First aorist passive indicative of *agorazō*, repeating the close of verse 3. *First fruits* (*aparchē*). See for this word I Cor. 16:15; Rom. 11:16; 16:5. This seems to mean that the 144,000 represent not the whole, but only a portion of the great harvest to come (Matt. 9:37), not only the first instalment, but those marked by high spiritual service to God and the Lamb (Rom. 12:1; Heb. 13:15; I Pet. 2:5).

5. *Was found no lie* (*ouch heurethē pseudos*). First aorist passive indicative of *heuriskō*. In I Pet. 2:23 this passage (Is. 53:9) is quoted with *dolos* (deceit, guile) instead of *pseudos* (lie), but the difference is not great. *Without blemish* (*amōmoi*). Alpha privative and *mōmos* (blemish, spot). As Christ the Paschal Lamb is (I Pet. 1:19; Heb. 9:14), so the followers of the Lamb are to be in the end (Phil. 2:15).

6. *Another angel* (*allon aggelon*). A new turn in the drama comes with each angel (7:2; 8:3, 13; 10:1). Here the angel is seen "flying in mid heaven" (*petomenon en mesouranēmati*), while in 8:13 John heard him "flying in mid heaven" (genitive case of same participle, which see). This one is in the sight and hearing of all. *Having* (*echonta*). Accusative singular agreeing with *aggelon* like *petomenon* (flying), but *legōn* in verse 7 is nominative, as if a new sentence like *legōn* in 4:1. *An eternal gospel* (*euaggelion aiōnion*). The only use of *euaggelion* in John's writings, though the verb *euaggelisai* (first aorist active infinitive epexegetical with *echonta* like John 16:12) occurs here and in 10:7. Here it is not *to euaggelion* (the gospel), but merely a proclamation of God's eternal (*aiōnios* here alone in the Apocalypse, though common in the Fourth Gospel and I John) purpose. Origen even took this "eternal gospel" to be another book to be written! Note the double use of *epi* (with accusative after *euaggelisai* and the genitive with *gēs*). See 5:9 for the races, etc.

7. *And he saith* (*legōn*). See above. *Fear God* (*phobēthēte*

ton theon). First aorist passive (deponent) imperative of *phobeomai*, here transitive with the accusative as in Luke 12:5. It is a call to judgment with no hope offered except by implication (Acts 14:15ff.). *Give him glory* (*dote autōi doxan*). Second aorist active indicative of *didōmi*. For the phrase see 11:13. *The hour is come* (*hē hōra ēlthen*). Second aorist (prophetic use) active indicative of *erchomai*. Common idiom in John's Gospel (2:4; 4:21, 23; 5:25, 28; 7:30, etc.). *Worship* (*proskunēsate*). First aorist active imperative of *proskuneō* with the dative case. Solemn call to the pagan world to worship God as Creator (4:11; 10:6), as in Ps. 96:6; Acts 14:15. For "the fountains of waters" see 8:10.

8. *Another, a second angel* (*allos deuteros aggelos*). This second angel "followed" (*ēkolouthēsen*, first aorist active indicative of *akoloutheō*) and interpreted in part the first one. *Fallen, fallen* (*epesen, epesen*). Prophetic aorist active indicative of *piptō*, repeated as a solemn dirge announcing the certainty of the fall. The English participle "fallen, fallen" is more musical and rhythmical than the literal rendering "fell, fell." The language is an echo of Is. 21:9, though B in the LXX has *peptōken, peptōken* (perfect). *Babylon the great* (*Babulōn hē magalē*). The adjective *megalē* occurs with *Babulōn* each time in the Apocalypse (14:8; 16:19; 17:5; 18:2, 10, 21) as a reminder of Nebuchadrezzar. There is no doubt that Rome is meant by Babylon, as is probably seen already in I Pet. 5:13. As a prisoner in Patmos John can speak his mind by this symbolism. *Hath made to drink* (*pepotiken*). Perfect active indicative of *potizō*, old causative verb (from *potos* drinking, I Pet. 4:3), as in Matt. 25:35. The remarkable phrase that follows seems based on Jer. 51:8 (25:15). It is a combination also of Rev. 14:10 (the wine of God's wrath, also in 16:19; 19:15) and 17:2. There is no doubt of the dissoluteness of the old Babylon of Jeremiah's day as of the Rome of John's

time. Rome is pictured as the great courtesan who intoxicates and beguiles the nations to fornication (17:2, 4, 6), but the cup of God's wrath for her and her paramours is full (14:10; 16:19; 18:2).

9. *A third* (*tritos*). "The third of this succession of herald angels denounces the Cæsar-worshippers" (Swete). Cf. 13:12ff. This counter proclamation (verses 9–12) warns those tempted to yield to the threats of the second beast about boycott and death (13:11–17). *If any man worshippeth the beast and his image* (*ei tis proskunei to thērion kai tēn eikona autou*). Condition of first class challenging those afraid of the beast. Note accusative (*thērion*) after *proskunei*, not dative as in verse 7. *And receiveth a mark* (*kai lambanei charagma*). Carries on the same condition and picks up the very language of 13:16. These Cæsar-worshippers are guilty of an "eternal sin" (Mark 3:29).

10. *He also shall drink* (*kai autos pietai*). Future middle of *pinō*. Certainty for him as for Babylon and her paramours (16:17). *Of the wine of the wrath of God* (*ek tou oinou tou thumou tou theou*). Note *ek* (partitive) after *pietai*. In 16:19 and 19:15 we have both *thumou* and *orgēs* (wrath of the anger of God). The white heat of God's anger, held back through the ages, will be turned loose. *Prepared unmixed* (*tou kekerasmenou akratou*). A bold and powerful oxymoron, "the mixed unmixed." *Akratos* is an old adjective (alpha privative and *kerannumi* to mix) used of wine unmixed with water (usually so mixed), here only in N.T. So it is strong wine mixed (perfect passive participle of *kerannumi*) with spices to make it still stronger (cf. Ps. 75:9). *In the cup of his anger* (*en tōi potēriōi tēs orgēs autou*). Both *thumos* (vehement fury) and *orgē* (settled indignation). *He shall be tormented* (*basanisthēsetai*). Future passive of *basanizō*. See 9:5; 11:10. *With fire and brimstone* (*en puri kai theiōi*). See 9:17 for fire and brimstone and also 19:20; 20:10; 21:8. The imagery is already in Gen. 19:24; Is.

30:33; Ezek. 38:22. *In the presence of the holy angels and in the presence of the Lamb* (*enōpion aggelōn hagiōn kai enōpion tou arniou*). This holy environment adds to the punishment.

11. *The smoke of their torment* (*ho kapnos tou basanismou autōn*). See 9:5 for *basanismos*, only there it was a limited penalty, here it is "for ever and ever" (*eis aiōnas aiōnōn*, unto ages of ages). See also 18:9; 19:3; 20:10. *They have no rest* (*ouk echousin anapausin*). The very language used in 4:8 of the four living creatures in praising God. "Those who desert Christ for Cæsar will be the victims of a remorse that never dies or sleeps" (Swete). The rest of the verse repeats the solemn challenge of verse 9.

12. *Here is the patience of the saints* (*Hōde hē hupomonē tōn hagiōn estin*). John's own comment as in 13:10; 17:9. In this struggle against emperor worship lay their opportunity (Rom. 5:3). It was a test of loyalty to Christ. *They that keep* (*hoi tērountes*). In apposition with *tōn hagiōn* (genitive), though nominative, a frequent anacoluthon in this book (2:20, etc.). Cf. 12:17. *The faith of Jesus* (*tēn pistin Iēsou*). "The faith in Jesus" (objective genitive) as in 2:13; Mark 11:22; James 2:1.

13. *Write* (*Grapson*). First aorist active imperative of *graphō* as in 1:11. John's meditation is broken by this command. This new beatitude (*makarioi*, Blessed) for the Christian dead goes farther than Paul's words (I Thess. 4:14–16; I Cor. 15:18). Probably "from henceforth" (*ap' arti*) goes with "those who die in the Lord," giving comfort to those facing persecution and death. *That they may rest* (*hina anapaēsontai*). Purpose clause with *hina* and the second future passive of *anapauō*. *From their labours* (*ek tōn kopōn autōn*). From the toils, the wearinesses, but not from the activities (*erga*), for these "follow with them." There is this to comfort us for all our growth here. Even

if cut short, it can be utilized in heaven, which is not a place of idleness, but of the highest form of spiritual service.

14. *A white cloud* (*nephelē leukē*). Like the "bright cloud" of Matt. 17:5 (Transfiguration), a familiar object in the Mediterranean lands. See Dan. 7:13; Matt. 24:30; 26:64; Acts 1:9, 11 for the picture of Christ's return. *I saw one sitting* (*kathēmenon*). No *eidon* here, but the accusative follows the *eidon* at the beginning, as *nephelē* is nominative after *idou*, as in 4:1, 4. *Like unto a son of man* (*homoion huion anthrōpou*). Accusative here after *homoion* as in 1:13, instead of the usual associative instrumental (13:4). *Having* (*echōn*). Nominative again after the *idou* construction, just before, not after, *eidon*. *A golden crown* (*stephanon chrusoun*). Here a golden wreath, not the diadems of 19:12. *A sharp sickle* (*drepanon oxu*). Old form *drepanē* (from *drepō*, to pluck), pruning-hook, in N.T. only in this chapter and Mark 4:29. Christ is come for reaping this time (Heb. 9:28) for the harvesting of earth (verses 15–17). The priesthood of Christ is the chief idea in 1:12–20 and "as the true *Imperator*" (Swete) in chapter 19.

15. *Send forth* (*pempson*). First aorist (urgency) active imperative of *pempō*. "Thrust in thy sickle now," this angel urges Christ. *And reap* (*kai therison*). First aorist (urgency) active imperative of *therizō*, old verb (from *theros*, summer), as in Matt. 6:26. See verse 7 for "the hour is come." *Therisai* (to reap) is epexegetical infinitive (first aorist active of *therizō*). *The harvest* (*ho therismos*). Old, but rare word (from *therizō*, to harvest), as in Matt. 13:30; John 4:35, here only in Revelation. *Is over-ripe* (*exēranthē*). First aorist (prophetic as in 10:17; 15:1) passive of *xērainō* (cf. James 1:11), to wither, to dry up. Perhaps just "ripe," not "over-ripe." Cf. Joel 1:17.

16. *Cast* (*ebalen*). Second aorist active indicative of *ballō*. No violence by the use of *ebalen* as is seen in Matt. 10:34 (*balein eirēnēn*, to bring peace). *Was reaped* (*etheristhē*).

First aorist passive indicative of *therizō*. Both prophetic aorists again. Christ puts in the sickle as he wills with his own agents (Matt. 9:37f.; 13:39, 41).

17. *He also* (*kai autos*). As well as the Reaper on the cloud. This is the fifth angel who is God's messenger from heaven (temple where God dwells). This fifth angel with his sharp sickle is to gather the vintage (18–20) as Christ did the wheat.

18. *Another angel* (*allos aggelos*). The fifth angel above Swete terms "the Angel of vengeance." He responds to the call of the sixth angel here as Christ does to the call of the fourth angel in verse 15. *Out from the altar* (*ek tou thusiastēriou*). From the altar of incense where he is in charge of the fire (*exousian epi tou puros*). If it is the altar of burnt offering (6:9; 11:1), we are reminded of the blood of the martyrs (Swete), but if the altar of incense (8:3, 5; 9:13; 16:7), then of the prayers of the saints. *The sharp sickle* (*to drepanon to oxu*). Useful for vintage as for harvesting. So "send forth" (*pempson*) as in verse 15. *Gather* (*trugēson*). First aorist active imperative of *trugaō*, old verb (from *trugē* dryness, ripeness), in N.T. only Rev. 15:18f. and Luke 6:44. *The clusters* (*tous botruas*). Old word *botrus*, here only in N.T. (Gen. 40:10). *Her grapes* (*hai staphulai autēs*). Old word again for grapes, bunch of grapes, in N.T. only here, Matt. 7:16; Luke 6:44. *Are fully ripe* (*ēkmasan*). Old and common verb (from *akmē*, Matt. 15:16), to come to maturity, to reach its acme, here only in N.T.

19. *Cast* (*ebalen*). As in verse 16. *Gathered* (*etrugēsen*). Like *etheristhē* in verse 16, in obedience to the instructions in verse 18 (*trugēson*). *The vintage of the earth* (*tēn ampelon tēs gēs*). "The vine of the earth." Here *ampelos* is used for the enemies of Christ collectively pictured. *And cast it* (*ebalen*). Repeating *ebalen* and referring to *ampelon* (vintage) just before. *Into the winepress the great winepress* (*eis tēn lēnon ton megan*). *Lēnos* is either feminine as in verse

20 and 19:15, or masculine sometimes in ancient Greek. Here we have both genders, a solecism frequent in the Apocalypse (21:14 *to teichos echōn*). See Matt. 21:33. For this metaphor of God's wrath see 14:10; 15:1, 7; 16:1, 19; 19:15.

20. *Was trodden* (*epatēthē*). First aorist passive indicative of *pateō*, to tread. The image of treading out the grapes is a familiar one in the East. Perhaps Is. 63:3 is in mind. *Without the city* (*exōthen tēs poleōs*). Ablative case with *exōthen* (like *exō*). This was the usual place (Heb. 13:12). See *exōthen* in 11:2. Joel (3:12) pictures the vally of Jehoshaphat as the place of the slaughter of God's enemies. Cf. Zech. 14:4. *Blood from the winepress* (*haima ek tēs lēnou*). Bold imagery suggested by the colour of the grapes. *Unto the bridles* (*achri tōn chalinōn*). Old word (from *chalaō* to slacken), in N.T. only here and James 3:3. Bold picture. *As far as a thousand and six hundred furlongs* (*apo stadiōn chiliōn hexakosiōn*). A peculiar use of *apo*, for "distance from (of)" as also in John 11:18; 21:8, somewhat like the use of *pro* in John 12:1. The distance itself covers the length of Palestine, but it is more likely that "the metaphor is worked out with the exuberance of apocalyptic symbolism" (Swete) for the whole earth.

CHAPTER XV

1. *Another sign in heaven* (*allo sēmeion en tōi ouranōi*). Looking back to 12:1, 3, after the series intervening. The Seven Bowls are parallel with the Seven Seals (ch. 6) and the Seven Trumpets (chapters 8 to 11), but there is an even closer connection with chapters 12 to 14, "the drama of the long conflict between the church and the world" (Swete). *Great and marvellous* (*mega kai thaumaston*). *Thaumastos* is an old verbal adjective (from *thaumazō*, to wonder) and is already in Matt. 21:42. The wonder extends to the end of this vision or sign (16:21). *Seven angels* (*aggelous hepta*). Accusative case in apposition with *sēmeion* after *eidon*. Cf. 8:2. *Which are the last* (*tas eschatas*). "Seven plagues the last." As in 21:9, "the final cycle of such visitations" (Swete). *Is finished* (*etelesthē*). Proleptic prophetic first aorist passive indicative of *teleō* as in 10:7. The number seven seems particularly appropriate here for finality and completeness.

2. *As it were a glassy sea* (*hōs thalassan hualinēn*). Accusative case after *eidon* and *hōs* here, not in 4:6, which see for the symbol. *Mingled with fire* (*memigmenēn puri*). Perfect passive participle of *mignumi*, to mix, and the associative instrumental case *puri*. This item not in 4:6 (a vision of peace), but here it adds to the splendour of the vision. This parenthesis (2 to 4) gives a picture of the martyrs in their state of bliss. *Them that come off victorious* (*tous nikōntas*). Present active articular participle of *nikaō*, accusative after *eidon*, "those that come off victorious" (14:4). *From the beast and from his image* (*ek tou thēriou kai ek tēs eikonos autou*). This use of *ek* after *nikaō* is unusual, also with *ek tou arithmou*. For these items see 13:1, 14, 17;

14:9, 11; 19:20; 20:4. *By the glassy sea (epi tēn thalassan tēn hualinēn).* Or "upon" more likely (4:6) with the accusative as in Matt. 14:25ff. *Harps of God (kitharas tou theou).* Objective genitive, for the worship of God (5:8; 14:2; I Chron. 16:42).

3. *The song of Moses (tēn ōidēn tou Mōuseōs).* Ex. 14:31; 15:1–19. A song of victory like that of Moses after crossing the Red Sea. *And the song of the Lamb (tēn ōidēn tou arniou).* A separate note of victory like that of Moses, though one song, not two. Charles finds it impossible to reconcile the two expressions, if genuine, but it is a needless objection. The words come from the O.T.: "great" (*megala*) from Ps. 111:2, "wonderful" (*thaumasta*) from Ps. 139:14, "O Lord God the Almighty" (*Kurie ho theos ho pantokratōr*) from Amos 4:13 (Rev. 4:8), "righteous and true" (*dikaiai kai alēthinai*) from Deut. 32:4, "Thou King of the ages" (*ho basileus tōn aiōnōn*) like Jer. 10:10 and I Tim. 1:17. Some MSS. have "the king of the saints" and some "the king of the nations," like Jer. 10:7. John thus combines in Hebraic tone the expressions of the old and the new in the song to the Glorified Messiah.

4. *Who shall not fear? (tis ou mē phobēthēi;).* Rhetorical question with *ou mē* (double negative) and first aorist passive subjunctive of *phobeomai* (future passive in Jer. 10:7). *And glorify (kai doxasei).* Change here to the future indicative instead of the aorist subjunctive, as often. Cf. Ps. 86:9. *Thou only art holy (monos hosios).* Both predicate adjectives, "Thou art alone holy." God alone is perfectly holy (16:5). *Shall come (hēxousin).* Future active of *hēkō*. *And worship (kai proskunēsousin).* Future active of *proskuneō*. Both from Ps. 86:9. *Have been made manifest (ephanerōthēsan).* Prophetic first aorist passive indicative of *phaneroō*. This martyr's song has the ring of great poetry.

5. *The temple of the tabernacle of the testimony (ho naos*

tēs skēnēs tou marturiou). Charles calls this "strange" language. Probably the tabernacle or tent of witness (Numb. 9:15; 17:7) is in mind and the tent of meeting (Ex. 27:21) rather than the temple in Jerusalem. *Was opened (ēnoigē)*. Second aorist passive indicative of *anoigō* as in 11:19. For *naos* see 3:12; 7:15; 14:15, 17; 16:1, 17.

6. *There came out (exēlthan)*. Second aorist active indicative of *exerchomai* with *-an* rather than *-on*. Proleptic and prophetic aorist. *The seven angels (hoi hepta aggeloi)*. Those in verse 1. *The seven plagues (tas hepta plēgas)*. The bowls are not given them till verse 7. *Arrayed (endedumenoi)*. Perfect passive participle of *enduō*. *With precious stone pure and bright (lithon katharon lampron)*. Accusative case retained with verb of clothing as so often, literally "with a stone pure bright." For both adjectives together see 19:8, 14. Some MSS. read *linon* (linen). For *lithon* see 17:4; 18:16; Ezek. 28:13. *Girt (periezōsmenoi)*. Perfect passive participle of *perizōnnuō*. See 1:13 for both participles. For *stēthos* (breast) see Luke 18:13. *With golden girdles (zōnas chrusās)*. Accusative case after the perfect passive participle *periezōsmenoi* as in 1:13.

7. *Seven golden bowls (hepta phialas chrusās)*. Golden saucers, but not full of incense as in 5:8, but "full (*gemousas* for which see 5:8) of the wrath of God who liveth for ever and ever" (*tou thumou tou theou tou zōntos eis tous aiōnas tōn aiōnōn*). Portents of dreadful events.

8. *Was filled with smoke (egemisthē kapnou)*. First aorist passive indicative of *gemizō* (from *gemō*), to fill full, and with the genitive *kapnou* (smoke). Smoke is here the symbol of God's presence (Ex. 19:18; Is. 6:5). *Till should be finished (achri telesthōsin)*. Temporal clause for future time with *achri* (equal to *heōs* in import) and the first aorist passive subjunctive of *teleō*, a metaphorical and symbolic "smoke screen" to keep all out of the sanctuary for the time being.

CHAPTER XVI

1. *A great voice* (*megalēs phōnēs*). Not an angel as in
5:2; 7:2; 10:3; 14:7, 9, 15, 18, but of God as 15:8 shows,
since no one could enter the *naos*. *Pour out* (*ekcheete*).
Second aorist active imperative of *ekcheō* (same form as
present active imperative). Blass would change to *ekcheate*
(clearly aorist) as in verse 6. *The seven bowls* (*tas hepta
phialas*). The article points to verse 7.

2. *Went and poured out* (*apēlthen kai execheen*). Second
aorist active indicative of *aperchomai* (redundant use like
hupagete with *ekcheete*, "go and pour out," in verse 1) and
of *ekcheō*. Each angel "went off" to perform his task.
For *execheen* see it repeated in verses 3, 4, 8, 10, 12, 17. *Into
the earth* (*eis tēn gēn*). This same use of *eis* after *execheen*
in verses 3, 4. *It became* (*egeneto*). "There came" (second
aorist middle indicative of *ginomai*). *A noisome and grievous sore* (*helkos kakon kai ponēron*). "Bad and malignant
sore." *Helkos* is old word for a suppurated wound (Latin
ulcus), here, verse 11, and Luke 16:21. See the sixth Egyptian plague (Ex. 9:10; Deut. 28:27, 35) and Job 2:7. The
magicians were attacked in Egypt and the worshippers of
Cæsar here (13:17; 14:9, 11; 19:20).

3. *Into the sea* (*eis tēn thalassan*). Like the first Egyptian
plague (Ex. 7:12–41) though only the Nile affected then.
Blood as of a dead man (*haima hōs nekrou*). At the trumpet
(8:11) the water becomes wormwood. Here *hōs nekrou* is
added to Ex. 7:19, "the picture of a murdered man welter-
ing in his blood" (Swete). "Coagulated blood, fatal to
animal life" (Moffatt). *Every living soul* (*pāsa psuchē zōēs*).
"Every soul of life" (Hebraism, Gen. 1:21, marked by life).
Even the things that were in the sea (*ta en tēi thalassēi*). "The

things in the sea," in apposition with *psuchē*. Complete destruction, not partial as in 8:9.

4. *Into the rivers and the fountains of waters* (*eis tous potamous kai tas pēgas tōn hudatōn*). See 8:10 for this phrase. Contamination of the fresh-water supply by blood follows that of the sea. Complete again.

5. *The angel of the waters* (*tou aggelou tōn hudatōn*). Genitive case object of *ēkousa*. See 7:1 for the four angels in control of the winds and 14:18 for the angel with power over fire. The rabbis spoke also of an angel with power over the earth and another over the sea. *Which art and which wast* (*ho ōn kai ho ēn*). See this peculiar idiom for God's eternity with *ho* as relative before *ēn* in 1:4, 8; 4:8, but without *ho erchomenos* (the coming on, the one who is to be) there for the future as in 11:17. *Thou Holy One* (*ho hosios*). Nominative form, but vocative case, as often. Note both *dikaios* and *hosios* applied to God as in 3:1 and 15:3f. *Because thou didst thus judge* (*hoti tauta ekrinas*). Reason for calling God *dikaios* and *hosios*. The punishment on the waters is deserved. First aorist active indicative of *krinō*, to judge.

6. *For* (*hoti*). Second causal conjunction (*hoti*) explanatory of the first *hoti*, like the two cases of *hoti* in 15:4. *They poured out* (*exechean*). Second aorist active indicative of *ekcheō* with -*an* instead of -*on*. *Blood hast thou given them to drink* (*haima autois dedōkas pein*). *Haima* (blood) is the emphatic word, measure for measure for shedding the blood of saints and prophets (11:18; 18:24). Perfect active indicative of *didōmi*, and so a permanent and just punishment. *Pein* is the abbreviated second aorist active infinitive of *pinō* for *piein* (*epion*). It is the epexegetical infinitive after *dedōkas*. There was no more drinking-water, but only this coagulated blood. *They are worthy* (*axioi eisin*). "Terrible antithesis" (Swete) to 3:4. The asyndeton adds to it (Alford).

7. *O Lord God, the Almighty* (*Kurie ho theos ho pantokratōr*).

Just as in 15:3 in the Song of Moses and of the Lamb, vocative with the article *ho*. "Judgments" (*kriseis*) here instead of "ways" (*hodoi*) there, and with the order of the adjectives reversed (*alēthinai kai dikaiai*, true and righteous).

8. *Upon the sun* (*epi ton hēlion*). Not *eis* (into) as in verses 2, 3, 4. The fourth trumpet (8:12) affected a third of the sun, moon, and stars with a plague of darkness, but here it is a plague of extreme heat. *To scorch with fire* (*kaumatisai en puri*). First aorist active infinitive of *kaumatizō*, late (Plutarch, Epictetus) causative verb (from *kauma*, heat), in N.T. only here and verse 9, Matt. 13:6; Mark 4:6. The addition of *en puri* (in fire, with fire) intensifies the picture.

9. *Were scorched* (*ekaumatisthēsan*). First aorist passive indicative of same verb. *With great heat* (*kauma mega*). Cognate accusative retained with the passive verb. Old word (from *kaiō* to burn), in N.T. only 7:16 and here. For blaspheming the name of God see 13:6; James 2:7; Rom. 2:24; I Tim. 6:1. They blamed God for the plagues. *They repented not* (*ou metenoēsan*). This solemn negative aorist of *metanoeō* is a refrain like a funeral dirge (9:20f.; 16:11). In 11:13 some did repent because of the earthquake. Even deserved punishment may harden the heart. *To give him glory* (*dounai autōi doxan*). Second aorist active infinitive of *didōmi*, almost result. For the phrase see 11:13; 14:7; 19:7.

10. *Upon the throne of the beast* (*epi ton thronon tou thēriou*). That is Rome (13:2). The dragon gave the beast his throne (2:13). *Was darkened* (*egeneto eskotōmenē*). Periphrastic past perfect passive with *ginomai* and *skotoō* (9:2). Like the darkness of the Egyptian plague (Ex. 10:22) and worse, for the effects of the previous plagues continue. *They gnawed their tongues* (*emasōnto tas glōssas autōn*). Imperfect middle of *masaomai*, old verb (to chew), from *maō* (to knead), only here in N.T. *For pain* (*ek tou ponou*).

"Out of distress" (cf. *ek* in 8:13), rare sense of old word (from *penomai* to work for one's living), in N.T. only here, 21:4; Col. 4:13. See Matt. 8:12.

11. *They blasphemed* (*eblasphēmēsan*) *and they repented not* (*kai ou metenoēsan*). Precisely as in verse 9, which see. Not just because of the supernatural darkness, but also "because of their pains" (*ek tōn ponōn autōn*, plural here and same use of *ek*) and their sores (*kai ek tōn helkōn autōn*, as in verse 2, only plural, and same use of *ek*). *Of their works* (*ek tōn ergōn autōn*). "Out of their deeds," and addition to verse 9. *The God of heaven* (*ton theon tou ouranou*). As in Dan. 2:44. Like the pride of Nebuchadrezzar against Jehovah.

12. *Upon the great river, the river Euphrates* (*epi ton potamon ton megan ton Euphratēn*). The sixth trumpet brings up the river Euphrates also (9:14), only there *epi* with the locative, while here *epi* with the accusative. Note triple use of the article *ton* here. *Was dried up* (*exēranthē*). First aorist (prophetic) passive of *xērainō* (14:15). Cf. Zech. 10:11. *That may be made ready* (*hina hetoimasthēi*). Purpose clause with *hina* and the first aorist passive of *hetoimazō*. Common verb in Rev. (8:6; 9:7, 15; 12:6; 19:7; 21:2). *The way for the kings* (*hē hodos tōn basileōn*). Objective genitive *basileōn*. *That come from the sunrising* (*tōn apo anatolēs hēliou*). "Those from the rising of the sun," the kings from the east (cf. Matt. 2:2) in their march against Rome. Parthia in particular resisted Rome before Trajan's day.

13. *Coming out of* (*ek* alone, no participle *erchomena*). *Of the dragon* (*tou drakontos*). That is Satan (12:3, 9). *Of the beast* (*tou thēriou*). The first beast (13:1, 12) and then just "the beast" (13:14ff.; 14:9, 11; 15:2; 16:2, 10), "the brute force of the World-power represented by the Roman Empire" (Swete). *Of the false prophet* (*tou pseudoprophētou*). Cf. Matt. 7:15; Acts 13:6; I John 2:22; 4:3; II John 7.

Identified with the second beast (13:11–14) in 19:20; 20:10. So the sixth bowl introduces the dragon and his two sub-alterns of chapters 12 and 13 (the two beasts). *Three unclean spirits* (*pneumata tria akatharta*). Out of the mouths of each of the three evil powers (the dragon and the two beasts) comes an evil spirit. See the use of mouth in 1:16 (9:17f.; 11:5; 12:15; 19:15, 21) as a chief seat of influence. In II Thess. 2:8 we have "the breath of his mouth" (the other sense of *pneuma*). For *akatharton* (unclean) with *pneuma* see Mark 1:23f.; 3:11; 5:2ff.; Acts 5:16; 8:7. "Christ expelled unclean spirits, but His enemies send them forth" (Swete). See Zech. 13:2 "the false prophets and the unclean spirits." *As it were frogs* (*hōs batrachoi*). Cf. Ex. 8:5; Lev. 11:10ff. Old word, here alone in N.T. Like loathsome frogs in form.

14. *Spirits of devils* (*pneumata daimoniōn*). "Spirits of demons." Explanation of the simile *hōs batrachoi*. See I Tim. 4:1 about "deceiving spirits and teachings of demons." *Working signs* (*poiounta sēmeia*). "Doing signs" (present active participle of *poieō*). The Egyptian magicians wrought "signs" (tricks), as did Simon Magus and later Apollonius of Tyana. Houdini claimed that he could reproduce every trick of the spiritualistic mediums. *Which go forth* (*ha ekporeuetai*). Singular verb with neuter plural (collective) subject. *Unto the kings* (*epi tous basileis*). The three evil spirits (dragon and the two beasts) spur on the kings of the whole world to a real world war. "There have been times when nations have been seized by a passion for war which the historian can but imperfectly explain" (Swete). *To gather them together* (*sunagagein*). Second aorist active infinitive of *sunagō*, to express purpose (that of the unclean spirits). *Unto the war of the great day of God, the Almighty* (*eis ton polemon tēs hēmeras tēs megalēs tou theou tou pantokratoros*). Some take this to be war between nations, like Mark 13:8, but it is more likely war against God (Ps. 2:2)

and probably the battle pictured in 17:14 and 19:19. Cf.
II Pet. 3:12, "the day of God," his reckoning with the na-
tions. See Joel 2:11; 3:4. Paul uses "that day" for the
day of the Lord Jesus (the Parousia) as in I Thess. 5:2;
II Thess. 1:10; 2:2; I Cor. 1:8; II Cor. 1:14; Phil. 1:6; 2:16;
II Tim. 1:12, 18; 4:8.

15. *Behold, I come as a thief* (*idou erchomai hōs kleptēs*).
The voice of Christ breaks in with the same metaphor as
in 3:3, which see. There comes one of seven beatitudes in
Rev. (1:3; 14:13; 16:15; 19:9; 20:6; 22:7, 14). For *grēgorōn*
(watching) see 3:2, and for *tērōn* (keeping), 1:3. *Lest he
walk naked* (*hina mē gumnos peripatēi*). Negative purpose
clause with *hina mē* and the present active subjunctive of
peripateō, and note predicate nominative *gumnos* (naked).
And they see his shame (*kai blepōsin tēn aschēmosunēn autou*).
Continuation of the final clause with present active subjunctive of *blepō*. *Aschēmosunēn* is old word (from *aschēmōn*,
indecent, I Cor. 12:23), in N.T. only here and Rom. 1:27,
a euphemism for *tēn aischunēn* (Rev. 3:18).

16. *They gathered* (*sunēgagen*). Second aorist active indicative of *sunagō*, singular (the three unclean spirits), like
ekporeuetai in verse 14. *Har-Magedon* (*Har-Magedōn*). John
proceeds now after the interruption in verse 15. Perhaps
"the mountains of Megiddo" though not certain. Megiddo
is in the valley of Esdraelon, and by the waters of Megiddo
(the Kishon) Israel gained a decisive victory over Sisera
(Judges 5:19), celebrated in Deborah's song. See also Rev.
20:8ff. and Ezek. 39:2, 4.

17. *Upon the air* (*epi ton aera*). All men breathe the air
and this is worse than the smiting of the earth (verse 2),
the sea (3), the fresh waters (4), the sun (8). *A great voice*
(*phōnē megalē*). The voice of God as in 16:1. *It is done*
(*Gegonen*). Perfect active indicative of *ginomai*. Like
Gegonan in 21:6. The whole series of plagues is now complete.

18. *And there were* (*kai egenonto*). "And there came" (same verb *ginomai*). See 8:5; 11:19 for this list of terrible sounds and lightnings, and for the great earthquake (*seismos megas*) see 6:12; 11:13 (cf. Luke 21:11). *Such as was not* (*hoios ouk egeneto*). Qualitative relative with *ginomai* again, "such as came not." *Since there were men* (*aph' hou anthrōpoi egenonto*). "Since which time (*chronou* understood) men came." *So great an earthquake, so mighty* (*tēlikoutos seismos houtō megas*). Quantitative correlative *tēlikoutos* rather than the qualitative *toioutos*, to correspond with *hoios* (not *hosos*). And then *houtō megas* repeats (redundant) *tēlikoutos*. Cf. Mark 13:19 for *hoia—toiautē* about like tribulation (*thlipsis*).

19. *Was divided into three parts* (*egeneto eis tria merē*). "Came into three parts" (*ginomai* again). In 11:3 a tenth part of the city fell. Babylon (Rome) is meant (17:18). *Fell* (*epesan*). Second aorist active indicative of *piptō* (*-an* form in place of *-on*). *Was remembered* (*emnēsthē*). First aorist (prophetic) passive indicative of *mimnēskō*. Babylon (Rome) had not been overlooked. God was simply biding his time with Rome. *To give unto her* (*dounai autēi*). Second aorist active infinitive of *didōmi*, epexegetic use as in 11:18; 16:9. *The cup of the wine of the fierceness of his wrath* (*to potērion tou oinou tou thumou tēs orgēs autou*). "The cup of the wine of the wrath of his anger," using both *thumos* (boiling rage) and *orgē* (settled anger). See both in Jer. 37 (30): 24.

20. *Fled* (*ephugen*). Second aorist active indicative of *pheugō*. Islands sometimes sink in the sea in earthquakes (6:14). *Were not found* (*ouch heurethēsan*). First aorist passive indicative of *heuriskō*. See 20:11 for the same idea.

21. *Hail* (*chalaza*). As in 8:17; 11:19. *Every stone about the weight of a talent* (*hōs talantiaia*). Old adjective (from *talanton*), here only in N.T., but in Polybius and Josephus. See Ex. 9:24 for the great hail in Egypt and also Josh. 10:11;

Is. 28:2; Ezek. 38:22 for hail as the symbol of God's wrath. In the LXX a *talanton* ranged in weight from 108 to 130 pounds. *Because of the plague of hail* (*ek tēs plēgēs tēs chalazēs*). "As a result of the plague of hail." This punishment had the same effect as in verses 9 and 11. *Exceeding great* (*Megalē—sphrodra*). Emphatic positions at ends of the clause (great—exceedingly).

CHAPTER XVII

1. *I will show thee* (*deixō soi*). Future active of *deiknumi*. It is fitting that one of the seven angels that had the seven bowls should explain the judgment on Babylon (16:19) already pronounced (14:8). That is now done in chapters 17 and 18. *The judgment of the great harlot* (*to krima tēs pornēs tēs megalēs*). The word *krima* is the one used about the doom of Babylon in Jer. 28(51):9. Already in 14:8 Babylon is called the harlot. *Pornēs* is the objective genitive, "the judgment on the great harlot." *That sitteth upon many waters* (*tēs kathēmenēs epi hudatōn pollōn*). Note triple use of the article *tēs*. In Jer. 28(51):13 we have *eph' hudasi pollois* (locative in place of genitive as here). Babylon got its wealth by means of the Euphrates and the numerous canals for irrigation. Rome does not have such a system of canals, but this item is taken and applied to the New Babylon in 17:15. Nahum (3:4) calls Nineveh a harlot, as Isaiah (23:16f.) does Tyre.

2. *The kings of the earth* (*hoi basileis tēs gēs*). Repeated in 1:5; 6:15; 17:18; 18:3, 9; 19:19; 21:24 and "the kings of the inhabited earth" (16:14) either for human rulers in general or the vassal kings absorbed by the Roman Empire. *Committed fornication* (*eporneusan*). First aorist active indicative of *porneuō*. "In purchasing the favour of Rome by accepting her suzerainty and with it her vices and idolatries" (Swete). *Were made drunken* (*emethusthēsan*). First aorist passive indicative of *methuskō*, old verb (from *methu*), as in Luke 12:45, here only in the Apocalypse. Cf. Is. 51:7 and *pepotiken* in Rev. 14:8. See 18:3.

3. *He carried me away* (*apēnegken me*). Second aorist active indicative of *apopherō*, to bear away, prophetic aorist.

This verb is used of angels at death (Luke 16:22) or in an ecstasy (Rev. 21:10 and here). *In the Spirit* (*en pneumati*). Probably his own spirit, though the Holy Spirit is possible (1:10; 4:2; 21:10), without Paul's uncertainty (II Cor. 12:2). Cf. Ezek. 3:14f.; 8:3; 11:24. *Into a wilderness* (*eis erēmon*). In Is. 21 there is *to horama tēs erēmou* (the vision of the deserted one, Babylon), and in Is. 14:23 Babylon is called *erēmon.* John may here picture this to be the fate of Rome or it may be that he himself, in the wilderness (desert) this side of Babylon, sees her fate. In 21:10 he sees the New Jerusalem from a high mountain. *Sitting* (*kathēmenēn*). Present middle participle of *kathēmai* as in verse 1. "To manage and guide the beast" (Vincent). *Upon a scarlet-coloured beast* (*epi thērion kokkinon*). Accusative with *epi* here, though genitive in verse 1. Late adjective (from *kokkos*, a parasite of the *ilex coccifera*), a crimson tint for splendour, in Rev. 17:3, 4; 18:12, 16 and Matt. 27:28; Heb. 9:19. *Full of names of blasphemy* (*gemonta onomata blasphēmias*). See 13:1 for "names of blasphemy" on the seven heads of the beast, but here they cover the whole body of the beast (the first beast of 13:1; 19:20). The harlot city (Rome) sits astride this beast with seven heads and ten horns (Roman world power). The beast is here personified with masculine participles instead of neuter, like *thērion* (*gemonta* accusative singular, *echōn* nominative singular, though some MSS. read *echonta*), construction according to sense in both instances. The verb *gemō* always has the genitive after it in the Apocalypse (4:6, 8; 5:8; 15:7; 17:4; 21:9) save here and apparently once in 17:4.

4. *Was arrayed* (*ēn peribeblēmenē*). Periphrastic past perfect indicative of *periballō*, to fling round one. *In purple and scarlet* (*porphuroun kai kokkinon*). Accusative retained after this passive verb of clothing, as so often. *Porphurous* is old adjective for purple (from *porphura*), in N.T. only here and John 19:2, 5. See preceding verse for *kokkinos.*

Decked (*kechrusōmenē*). Perfect passive participle of *chrusoō*, old verb, to gild, to adorn with gold, here alone in N.T. *With gold and precious stone and pearls* (*chrusiōi kai lithōi timiōi kai margaritais*). Instrumental case. *Chrusiōi* is cognate with the participle. *Lithōi timiōi* is collective (18:12, 16; 21:19). There is a *zeugma* also with *margaritais* (18:12, 16; 21:21), for which word see Matt. 7:6. Probably John is thinking of the finery of the temple prostitutes in Asia Minor. *Full of abominations* (*gemon bdelugmatōn*). Agreeing with *potērion*, "cup" (neuter singular accusative). Some MSS. read *gemōn* (nominative masculine like *echōn* in verse 3, quite irregular). For *bdelugmatōn* (genitive after *gemon*) see Matt. 24:15; (Mark 13:14), common in the LXX for idol worship and its defilements (from *bdelussō*, to render foul), both ceremonial and moral. See Jer. 15:7. *Even the unclean things of her fornication* (*kai ta akatharta tēs porneias autēs*). Either the accusative after *gemon* as in verse 3 (and full of the unclean things of her fornication) or the object of *echousa*, like *potērion*.

5. *Upon her forehead a name written* (*epi to metōpon autēs onoma gegrammenon*). Roman harlots wore a label with their names on their brows (Seneca, *Rhet.* I. 2. 7; Juvenal VI. 122f.), and so here. In 19:16 Christ has a name on his garments and on his thigh, while in 14:1 and 22:4 the redeemed have the name of God on their foreheads. There is undoubtedly a contrast between this woman here and the woman in chapter 12. *Mystery* (*mustērion*). Either in apposition with *onoma* or as part of the inscription on her forehead. In either case the meaning is the same, that the name Babylon is to be interpreted mystically or spiritually (cf. *pneumatikōs* 11:8) for Rome. *The Mother of the Harlots and of the Abominations of the Earth* (*Hē Mētēr tōn Pornōn kai tōn Bdelugmatōn tēs Gēs*). The Metropolis of the Empire is the mother of harlotry and of the world's idolatries. Charles quotes Tacitus (*Ann.* XV. 44) about Rome as the

city "*quo cuncta undique atrocia aut pudenda confluunt celebranturque.*"

6. *Drunken with the blood of the saints* (*methuousan ek tou haimatos tōn hagiōn*). Present active feminine accusative singular participle of *methuō*, old verb, to be drunk (Matt. 24:49). *Of the martyrs of Jesus* (*tōn marturōn Iēsou*). "Witnesses" (2:13) for Jesus (objective genitive) unto blood (16:6; 18:24) and so martyrs in the modern sense of the word. "Drunk with blood" is a common idea with the ancients (Euripides, Josephus, Philo, Cicero, Pliny). *With a great wonder* (*thauma mega*). Cognate accusative with *ethaumasa*.

7. *I will tell thee the mystery* (*egō erō soi to mustērion*). The angel gives his interpretation of the woman and the beast (17:7–18). *Erō* is the future active of *eipon* (defective verb), to tell, to say.

8. *Was and is not* (*ēn kai ouk estin*). Imperfect and present of *eimi*, an apparent antithesis to *ho ēn kai ho ōn* of 1:4. This is a picture of the beast of 13:1ff. which the woman is riding, but no longer just the empire, but one of the emperors who died (*ouk estin*, is not). *And is about to come up out of the abyss* (*kai mellei anabainein ek tēs abussou*). That is, he is going to come to life again. *And to go into perdition* (*kai eis apōleian hupagei*). So (and he goes into perdition) the best MSS. read rather than the infinitive *hupagein*. Most interpreters see here an allusion to the "Nero *redivivus*" expectancy realized in Domitian, who was ruling when John wrote and who was called Nero *redivivus*. *Shall wonder* (*thaumasthēsontai*). First future passive (deponent) of *thaumazō*, with which compare *ethaumasthē* in 13:3. John had wondered (*ethaumasa*) in verse 6 "with the amazement of a horrible surprise; the world will wonder and admire" (Swete). *Whose name* (*hōn onoma*). Singular *onoma*, like *ptōma* in 11:8. See 13:8 for the same description of those who worship the beast and for discussion of details. *When*

they behold (blepontōn). Genitive plural of the present active participle of *blepō,* agreeing with *hōn* (genitive relative) rather than with *hoi katoikountes* (nominative just before *hōn*). *How that (hoti).* "Namely that." *He was, and is not, and shall come (ēn kai ouk estin kai parestai).* Repetition of what is in verse 7 with *parestai* (future of *pareimi,* from which *parousia* comes) in place of *mellei,* "parody of the divine name" (Charles) in 1:4, 8; 4:8, "as the hellish antitype of Christ." The Neronic Antichrist has also a *parousia.*

9. *Here is the mind which hath wisdom (Hōde ho nous ho echōn sophian).* "Here is the intelligence which has wisdom" (Charles). A variation of 13:18, but the same idea. *Seven mountains (hepta orē).* Rome was known as the city on seven hills (Vergil, Horace, Ovid, Cicero, etc.). *On which (hopou—ep' autōn).* "Where—upon them." Pleonasm like *hopou—ekei* in 12:6. In 13:1ff. it is the beast that has the seven heads, while here the woman riding the beast has seven heads, a slight change in the symbolism, and the heads are further identified as kings.

10. *Seven kings (basileis hepta).* This is another change in the symbolism. The identification of these seven kings is one of the puzzles of the book. *The five are fallen (hoi pente epesan).* Second aorist active indicative of *piptō* with the *-an* ending. Common for the downfall of kings (Ezek. 29:5; 30:6; Is. 21:9, etc.). See II Sam. 3:38. *The one is (ho heis estin).* The one when this vision is dated. *The other is not yet come (ho allos oupō ēlthen).* Prophetic second aorist active of *erchomai.* Charles takes this as the date of this "source" or part of the Apocalypse. But John could himself have used this language in the time of Domitian even if he was the one who had not yet come. The difficulty about counting these emperors is that Galba, Otho, Vitellius reigned so briefly that they hardly merit being included. *When he cometh (hotan elthēi).* Indefinite temporal clause for the future, with *hotan* and the second aorist active sub-

junctive of *erchomai*, "whenever he comes." *He must continue a little while* (*oligon auton dei meinai*). Swete takes this to be Titus, who died September 13, 81, after a short reign.

11. *Is himself also an eighth and is of the seven* (*kai autos ogdoos kai ek tōn hepta*). This is the angel's interpretation and it looks like a reference to Domitian as the eighth, who is regarded as one of the seven because he was considered a second Nero (Nero *redivivus*). For *ek tōn hepta* see Acts 21:8. John may have used *ek tōn* instead of *heis ek tōn* to avoid absolute identity between Domitian and Nero (Beckwith). *And he goeth unto perdition* (*kai eis apōleian hupagei*). As in verse 8. "Domitian was assassinated (September 18, 96), after a terrible struggle with his murderers. The tyrant's end was a symbol of the end to which the Beast which he personated was hastening" (Swete). Cf. 19:11–21.

12. *Which have received no kingdom as yet* (*hoitines basileian oupō elabon*). Second aorist (proleptic and prophetic) active indicative of *lambanō*. The heads are emperors and the horns are kings (both called *basileis*). *As kings* (*hōs basileis*). Compared to kings (see *hōs* in 1:10; 4:6; 9:7; 13:3; 14:3; 16:21) without identification with the emperors, though succeeding them with "quasi-imperial powers" with the beast. *For one hour* (*mian hōran*). Accusative of extent of time, and that a brief time (18:10, 16, 19) in comparison with the beast (13:2).

13. *Have one mind* (*mian gnōmēn echousin*). "One purpose" (*gnōmē* from *ginōskō*) as in Acts 20:3 and I Cor. 1:10. The new powers are allies of the beast. *They give their power and authority unto the beast* (*tēn dunamin kai tēn exousian autōn tōi thēriōi didoasin*). Present active indicative of *didōmi*. Just as the dragon gave both power and authority to the beast (13:2), so they are wholly at the service of the beast.

14. *These* (*houtoi*). These ten kings. *Shall war against the Lamb* (*meta tou thēriou polemēsousin*). Future active of

polemeo, to war. As allies of the beast (the servant of the dragon, 12:7) they will wage war with the Lamb (the enemy of the dragon). These kings gather for battle as in 16:13f. *And the Lamb shall overcome them (kai to arnion nikēsei autous).* Future active of *nikaō*. This is the glorious outcome, victory by the Lamb over the coalition of kings as against the beast before. *For he is Lord of lords and King of kings (hoti Kurios kuriōn estin kai Basileus basileōn).* The same words are again descriptive of Christ in 19:16, as of God in Deut. 10:17 (God of gods and Lord of lords) and Dan. 10:17 (God of gods and Lord of kings). Cf. also I Tim. 6:15 and Rev. 1:5. Crowned heads are Christ's subjects. *And they also shall overcome that are with him (kai hoi met' autou).* "And those with him shall also overcome" (supply *nikēsousin*, not *eisin*). They will share in the triumph of the Lamb, as they shared in the conflict. Cf. *meta tou thēriou* in verse 12. *Called and chosen and faithful (klētoi kai eklektoi kai pistoi).* These are the three notes of those who share in the victory. For *klētos* and *eklektos* see Matt. 22:14 (contrasted); Rom. 8:28ff.; II Pet. 1:10; Rev. 2:10, 13. The elect are called and prove faithful.

15. *Where the harlot sitteth (hou hē pornos kathētai).* Relative adverb *hou* (where) referring to the waters (*hudata*) of verse 1 on which the harlot sits. Present middle indicative of *kathēmai*. *Are peoples, and multitudes, and nations, and tongues (laoi kai ochloi eisin kai ethnē kai glōssai).* The O.T. uses "waters" as symbol for "peoples" (Is. 8:7; Jer. 47:2; Ps. 29:10, etc.). "Rome's greatest danger lay in the multitudes which were under her sway" (Swete).

16. *These shall hate the harlot (houtoi misēsousin tēn pornēn).* Future active of *miseō*. *Houtoi* is resumptive demonstrative pronoun (masculine) referring to the ten horns and the beast (neuter); construction according to sense. The downfall of Rome will come from the sudden change in subject peoples. *Shall make her desolate and naked*

(*erēmōmenēn poiēsousin autēn kai gumnēn*). Future active of *poieō* and perfect passive predicate accusative participle of *erēmoō*, old verb (from *erēmos* desolate), again in 18:16, 19. *Gumnēn* (naked) is predicate adjective. *Shall eat her flesh* (*tas sarkas autēs phagontai*). Future middle of the defective verb *esthiō*, to eat. Note plural *sarkas*, portions of flesh (James 5:3) as in Ps. 27:2 and Mic. 3:3. *Shall burn her utterly with fire* (*autēn katakausousin en puri*). Future active of *katakaiō*, to burn down (perfective use of *kaiō*). John wrote before the days of Alaric, Genseric, Ricimer, Totila, with their hordes which devastated Rome and the west in the fifth and sixth centuries. "No reader of the *Decline and Fall* can be at a loss for materials which will at once illustrate and justify the general trend of St. John's prophecy" (Swete).

17. *Did put* (*edōken*). "Did give" (first aorist active of *didōmi*. *To do his mind* (*poiēsai tēn gnōmēn autou*). Epexegetic first aorist active infinitive of *poieō* after *edōken*, as often in this book. They are of one mind (verse 13) because God put them up to it, clear statement of God's overruling hand among the nations. *Until the words of God should be accomplished* (*achri telesthēsontai hoi logoi tou theou*). Temporal clause about the future with *achri* (like *heōs*), with the future indicative of *teleō*, but with aorist passive subjunctive *telesthōsin* in 15:8. For *teleō* see also 10:7. For "the words of God" see 19:9. They will be fulfilled.

18. *The woman* (*hē gunē*). She is now explained after the beast has been interpreted. Verse 9 made it plain enough, but this verse demonstrates that the woman is the city of Rome "which reigneth (*hē echousa basileian*, the one having a kingdom) over the kings of the earth (*epi tōn basileōn tēs gēs*)." Rome followed Babylon, and other cities may follow in their train.

CHAPTER XVIII

1. *Coming down out of heaven* (*katabainonta ek tou ouranou*).
Present active predicate participle. Not the angel of 17:1,
7, 15 (John's guide), but one announcing the doom of Babylon (Rome). As in 10:1; 20:1. *Was lightened* (*ephōtisthē*).
First aorist passive of *phōtizō*, old causative verb (from
phōs, light), common in N.T. as in Rev. 18:1; 21:23; 22:5.
With his glory (*ek tēs doxēs autou*). "By reason of (*ek* as in
8:13; 16:10) his glory." "So recently has he come from
the Presence that in passing he flings a broad belt of light
across the dark earth" (Swete).

2. *Fallen, fallen is Babylon the great* (*epesen, epesen Babulōn hē megalē*). The very words of 14:8: "Did fall, did fall
Babylon the great." Prophetic aorists of *piptō* repeated like
a solemn dirge of the damned. *Is become* (*egeneto*). Prophetic aorist middle. *A habitation of devils* (*katoikētērion*).
Late word (from *katoikeō*, to dwell), in N.T. only here and
Eph. 2:22. Devils should be demons, of course. So Isaiah
prophesied of Babylon (12:21f.) and also Jeremiah (50:39)
and Zephaniah of Nineveh (2:14). Both Babylon and Nineveh are ruins. *A hold of every unclean spirit* (*phulakē pantos
pneumatos akathartou*). *Phulakē* is garrison or watch-tower
as in Hab. 2:1, rather than a prison (20:7). *A hold of every
unclean and hateful bird* (*phulakē pantos orneou akathartou
kai memisēmenou*). *Orneou* is old word for bird, in N.T.
only Rev. 18:2; 19:17, 21. "The evil spirits, watching over
fallen Rome like night-birds or harpies that wait for their
prey, build their eyries in the broken towers which rise from
the ashes of the city" (Swete). Long ago true of Babylon
and Nineveh, some day to be true of Rome.

3. *By* (*ek*). "As a result of." Some MSS. omit "of the

wine" (*tou oinou*). Cf. 14:10; 16:10. *Have fallen* (*peptōkan*).
Perfect active third personal of *piptō* for usual *peptōkasi*.
Some MSS. read *pepōkan* (have drunk), from *pinō* like the
metaphor in 14:8, 10; 16:19; 17:2. See 17:2 for the same
charge about the kings of the earth. *The merchants of the
earth* (*hoi emporoi tēs gēs*). Old word for one on a journey
for trade (from *en, poros*), like drummers, in N.T. only
Matt. 13:45; Rev. 18:3, 11, 15, 23. Like *emporion* (John
2:16) and *emporeuomai* (James 4:13). *Waxed rich* (*eplou-
tēsan*). First ingressive aorist active indicative of *plouteō*,
to be rich (cf. 3:17). Here alone in the N.T. do we catch
a glimpse of the vast traffic between east and west that made
Rome rich. *Of her wantonness* (*tou strēnous autēs*). Late
word for arrogance, luxury, here alone in N.T. See *strēniaō*
in verses 7 and 9, to live wantonly.

4. *Come forth, my people, out of her* (*exelthate, ho laos mou,
ex autēs*). Second aorist (urgency) active imperative (-*a*
form) of *exerchomai*. Like Is. 48:20; 52:11; Jer. 50:8; 51:6
(about Babylon). See also the call of Abram (Gen. 12:1),
the rescue of Lot (Gen. 19:12ff.). In the N.T. see Mark
13:4; II Cor. 6:14; Eph. 5:11; I Tim. 5:11. *Ho laos* is vocative with the form of the nominative. *That ye have no
fellowship with her sins* (*hina mē sunkoinōnēsēte tais hamar-
tais autēs*). Purpose clause with *hina mē* and the first aorist
active subjunctive of *sunkoinōneō*, old compound (*sun*, together, *koinōnos*, partner), in N.T. only here, Phil. 4:14;
Eph. 5:11. With associative instrumental case *hamartiais*.
And that ye receive not of her plagues (*kai ek tōn plēgōn autēs
hina mē labēte*). Another purpose clause dependent on the
preceding, with *hina mē* and the second aorist active subjunctive of *lambanō*, and with proleptic emphatic position of
ek tōn plēgōn autēs before *hina mē*.

5. *Have reached* (*ekollēthēsan*). First aorist passive (deponent) indicative of *kollaō*, old verb (from *kolla*, gluten,
glue), to cleave to, to join one another in a mass "up to

heaven" (*achri tou ouranou*). Cf. Jer. 51:9; Zech. 14:5. *Hath remembered* (*emnēmoneusen*). First aorist (prophetic) active indicative of *mnēmoneuō*, here with the accusative (*adikēmata*, iniquities) instead of the genitive (Col. 4:18).

6. *Render as she rendered* (*apodote hōs apedōken*). Second aorist (effective) active imperative and first aorist (effective) active of *apodidōmi*, old and common verb for requital, to give back, the *lex talionis* which is in the O.T. (Jer. 50:15, 29; 51:24, 56; Ps. 137:8), and in the N.T. also (Matt. 7:2). Here the reference is to persecutions by Rome, particularly the martyrdom of the saints (18:24; 19:2). *Double the double* (*diplōsate ta dipla*). First aorist imperative of *diploō*, old verb (from *diploos*, double, Matt. 23:15), here only in N.T. *Diplā* is simply the neuter plural accusative (cognate) contract form for *diploa* (not *diplō*). Requite here in double measure, a full requital (Ex. 22:4, 7, 9; Is. 40:2; Jer. 16:18; 17:18; Zech. 9:12). The double recompense was according to the Levitical law. *Which she mingled* (*hōi ekerasen*). First aorist active indicative of *kerannumi*. The relative *hōi* is attracted to the locative case of its antecedent *potēriōi* (cup), for which see 14:8, 10; 17:4; 18:3. *Mingle unto her double* (*kerasate autēi diploun*). First aorist active imperative of the same verb *kerannumi*, with the same idea of double punishment.

7. *How much soever* (*hosa*). Indefinite quantitative relative pronoun *hosos* in the accusative (cognate) neuter plural object of *edoxasen* (first aorist active indicative of *doxazō*). *Herself* (*hautēn*). Reflexive pronoun, accusative also with *edoxasen*. *Waxed wanton* (*estrēniasen*). First aorist (ingressive) active indicative of *strēniaō* (to live luxuriously), verb in late comedy instead of *truphaō* (James 5:5), from *strēnos* (Rev. 18:3), only here in N.T. *So much give her of torment and mourning* (*tosouton dote autēi basanismon kai penthos*). Second aorist active imperative of *didōmi*, to give. The correlative pronoun *tosouton* is masculine singular accusative,

agreeing with *basanismon*, for which see 9:5 and 14:11, and
is understood with the neuter word *penthos* (mourning), in
N.T. only in James 4:9; Rev. 18:7ff.; 21:4 (kin to *pathos*,
penomai). *I sit a queen* (*kathēmai basilissa*). Predicate nominative for the old form *basileia* (*basilis*), as in Matt. 12:42.
Babylon and Tyre had preceded Rome in such boasting (Is.
47:7–9; Ezek. 27:3; 28:2; Zeph. 2:15). *And am no widow*
(*kai chēra ouk eimi*). Feminine of the adjective *chēros* (barren), old word (Mark 12:40). *Shall in no wise see mourning*
(*penthos ou mē idō*). Confident boast of security with emphatic position of *penthos* (see above) and double negative
ou mē with the second aorist active subjunctive of *horaō*
(defective verb).

8. *Therefore* (*dia touto*). Because of her presumption
added to her crimes. *In one day* (*en miāi hēmerāi*). Symbolical term for suddenness like *miāi hōrāi*, in one hour
(18:10, 16, 19). John has in mind still Is. 47:7–9. *Shall
come* (*hēxousin*). Future active of *hēkō*. Her plagues are
named (death, mourning, famine). *She shall be utterly
burned* (*katakauthēsetai*). Future passive of *katakaiō* (perfective use of *kata*). *With fire* (*en puri*). "In fire," as in
17:16. *Which judged her* (*ho krinas autēn*). Articular first
aorist active participle of *krinō* referring to *kurios ho theos*
(the Lord God). The doom of Babylon is certain because
of the power of God.

9. *Shall weep* (*klausousin*). Future active of *klaiō*, middle *klausontai* in Attic, as in John 16:20. *And wail over her*
(*kai kopsontai ep' autēn*). Future direct middle of *koptō*,
old verb, to beat, to cut, middle to beat oneself (Rev. 1:7).
For combination with *klaiō* as here see Luke 8:52. See
17:2; 18:3, 7 for *hoi porneusantes kai strēniasantes*). *When
they look upon* (*hotan blepōsin*). Indefinite temporal clause
with *hotan* and the present active subjunctive of *blepō*.
The smoke of her burning (*ton kapnon tēs purōseōs autēs*).
Purōsis is an old word (from *puroō* to burn), in N.T. only

I Pet. 4:12; Rev. 18:9, 18. See verse 8 for other plagues on Rome, but fire seems to be the worst (17:16; 18:8, 9, 17; 19:3).

10. *Standing afar off* (*apo makrothen hestēkotes*). Perfect active (intransitive) participle of *histēmi*. Vivid picture of the terrible scene, fascinated by the lurid blaze (cf. Nero's delight in the burning of Rome in A.D. 64), and yet afraid to draw near. On *apo makrothen* see Mark 5:6. There is a weird charm in a burning city. They feared the same fate (cf. verse 7 for *basanismou*, torment). *Woe, woe, the great city* (*ouai, ouai, hē polis hē megalē*). Only example in the Apocalypse of the nominative with *ouai* except verses 16, 19, though in Luke 6:25 and common in LXX (Is. 5:7, 11, etc.). For the dative see Rev. 8:13, once so "strong" (*hē ischura*)! *In one hour* (*miāi hōrāi*). Repeated in verses 16, 19, and like *miāi hēmerāi* (in one day) in verse 8. Some MSS. have here *mian hōran*, like *poian hōran* (accusative of extent of time) in 3:3. See verse 8 (*ho krinas*) for *hē krisis sou* (thy judgment). This is the dirge of the kings.

11. *The merchants* (*hoi emporoi*). As in 18:3, 15, 23. The dirge of the merchants follows the wail of the kings. *Weep and mourn* (*klaiousin kai penthousin*). Present active indicatives of *klaiō* and *pentheō* as in verses 9 (for *klaiō*), 15, 19. *For no man buyeth their merchandise any more* (*hoti ton gomon autōn oudeis agorazei ouketi*). Reason enough for their sorrow over Rome's fall. *Gomos* is old word (from *gemō* to be full) for a ship's cargo (Acts 21:3) and then any merchandise (Rev. 18:11f.). Galen, Pliny, Aristides tell of the vastness of the commerce and luxury of Rome, the world's chief market. Many of the items here are like those in the picture of the destruction of Tyre in Ezek. 26 and 27. There are twenty-nine items singled out in verses 12 and 13 of this merchandise or cargo (*gomon*), imports into the port of Rome. Only a few need any comment.

12. *Of fine linen* (*bussinou*). Genitive case after *gomon*,

as are all the items to *kokkinou*. Old adjective from *bussos* (linen, Luke 16:19), here a garment of linen, in N.T. only Rev. 18:12, 16; 19:8, 14. *Purple* (*porphuras*). Fabric colored with purple dye (*porphureos*, 17:4; 18:16), as in Mark 15:17, 20; Luke 16:19. *Silk* (*sirikou*). So the uncials here. *To sērikon* (the silken fabric) occurs in Plutarch, Strabo, Arrian, Lucian, only here in N.T. Probably from the name of the Indian or Chinese people (*hoi Sēres*) from whom the fabric came after Alexander invaded India. Silk was a costly article among the Romans, and for women as a rule. *Scarlet* (*kokkinou*). See 17:4 and 18:16. *All thyine wood* (*pan xulon thuinon*). Now accusative again without *gomon* dependence. An odoriferous North African citrus tree, prized for the colouring of the wood for dining-tables, like a peacock's tail or the stripes of a tiger or panther. Here only in N.T. *Of ivory* (*elephantinon*). Old adjective (from *elephas* elephant) agreeing with *skeuos* (vessel), here only in N.T. Cf. Ahab's ivory palace (I Kings 22:39). *Of marble* (*marmarou*). Old word (from *marmairō*, to glisten), genitive after *skeuos* (vessel), here only in N.T.

13. *Cinnamon* (*kinnamōmon*). Old word transliterated into English, here only in N.T. Of Phœnician origin (Herodotus) as to name and possibly from South China. *Spice* (*amōmon*). A fragrant plant of India, *amomum*, for perfume. *Incense* (*thumiamata*). See 5:8; 8:3. *Ointment* (*muron*). See Matt. 26:7. *Frankincense* (*libanon*). See 8:3. *Fine flour* (*semidalin*). Old word for finest wheaten flour, here only in N.T. *Of horses* (*hippōn*). Here then is a return to the construction of the genitive after *gomon* in verse 12, though not used here, an anomalous genitive construction (Charles). *Of chariots* (*redōn*). A Gallic word for a vehicle with four wheels, here only in N.T. *Of slaves* (*somatōn*). "Of bodies," treated as animals or implements, like the horses and the chariots (cf. *rickshaw* men in China). This use of *sōma* for slave occurs in Gen. 34:29; Tob. 10:11

(*sōmata kai ktēnē*, slaves and cattle); II Macc. 8:11. *Souls of men* (*psuchas anthrōpōn*). Deissmann (*Bible Studies*, p. 160) finds this use of *sōma* for slave in the Egyptian Delta. Return to the accusative *psuchas*. From Numb. 31:35; I Chron. 5:21; Ezek. 27:13. This addition is an explanation of the use of *sōmata* for slaves, "human live stock" (Swete), but slaves all the same. Perhaps *kai* here should be rendered "even," not "and": "bodies even souls of men." The slave merchant was called *sōmatemporos* (body merchant).

14. *The fruits* (*hē opōra*). The ripe autumn fruit (Jer. 40:10, 12). Here only in N.T. Of uncertain etymology (possibly *opos*, sap, *hōra*, hour, time for juicy sap). See Jude 12 for *dendra phthinopōrinos* (autumn trees). *Which thy soul lusteth after* (*sou tēs epithumias tēs psuchēs*). "Of the lusting of thy soul." *Are gone from thee* (*apēlthen apo sou*). Prophetic aorist active indicative of *aperchomai* with repetition of *apo*. *All things that were dainty and sumptuous* (*panta ta lipara kai ta lampra*). "All the dainty and the gorgeous things." *Liparos* is from *lipos* (grease) and so fat, about food (here only in N.T.), while *lampros* is bright and shining (James 2:2f.), about clothing. *Are perished from thee* (*apōleto apo sou*). Prophetic second aorist middle indicative of *apollumi* (intransitive). *Shall find them no more at all* (*ouketi ou mē auta heurēsousin*). Doubled double negative with future active, as emphatic a negation as the Greek can make.

15. *Of these things* (*toutōn*). Listed above in verses 12 to 14. *Who were made rich by her* (*hoi ploutēsantes ap' autēs*). "Those who grew rich (ingressive aorist active participle of *plouteō*, for which see verses 3 and 13) from her." *Shall stand afar off* (*apo makrothen stēsontai*). Future middle of *histēmi*. Repeating the picture in verse 10. Again in verse 17. See verse 11 for the two participles *klaiontes kai penthountes*.

16. For the Woe see verses 10, 19. For the next clause see 17:4 with the addition here of *bussinon* (18:12). *For in one hour so great riches is made desolate* (*hoti miāi hōrāi ērēmōthē ho tosoutos ploutos*). The reason (*hoti*) for the "woe." First aorist passive indicative of *eremoō*, for which verb see 17:16 and 18:19. This is the dirge of the merchants.

17. *Shipmaster* (*kubernētēs*). Old word (from *kubernaō*, to steer), helmsman, sailing-master, in N.T. only here and Acts 27:11. Subordinate to the *nauklēros* (supreme commander). *That saileth any whither* (*ho epi topon pleōn*). "The one sailing to a place." See Acts 27:2, *tous kata tēn Asian pleontas* (those sailing down along Asia). Nestle suggests *ponton* (sea) here for *topon* (place), but it makes sense as it is. *Mariners* (*nautai*). Old word (from *naus*, ship), in N.T. only here and Acts 27:27, 30. *Gain their living by the sea* (*tēn thalassan ergazontai*). "Work the sea." This idiom is as old as Hesiod for sailors, fishermen, etc. See verses 10, 15.

18. *As they looked* (*blepontes*). Present active participle of *blepō*. See *hotan blepōsin* in verse 10. *What city is like the great city?* (*tis homoia tēi polei tēi megalēi;*). No *polis* with *tis*, but implied. Associative instrumental case, as usual, with *homoia*. "The eternal city" is eternal no longer.

19. *They cast dust* (*ebalon choun*). Second aorist active of *ballō*. *Chous* is old word (from *cheō* to pour) for heap of earth, dust, in N.T. only here and Mark 6:11. Cf. Ezek. 27:30; Luke 10:13. This is the dirge of the sea-folk (cf. verses 10, 16). *By reason of her costliness* (*ek tēs timiotētos autēs*). Occasionally in later literary Greek, though here only in N.T. and not in LXX. The same use of *timē* appears in I Pet. 2:7. Common in the papyri as a title like "Your Honor" (Moulton and Milligan's *Vocabulary*).

20. *Rejoice over her* (*Euphrainou ep' autēi*). Present middle imperative of *euphrainō*, for which verb see 11:10, used there of the joy of the wicked over the death of the two

witnesses, just the opposite picture to this. "The song of doom" (Charles) here seems to be voiced by John himself. *God hath judged your judgment* (*ekrinen ho theos to krima*). First aorist (prophetic) active of *krinō* and cognate accusative *krima*, here a case for trial (Ex. 18:22; I Cor. 6:7), not a sentence as in 17:1. God has approved the case of heaven.

21. *A strong angel* (*heis aggelos ischuros*). Here *heis* = a, just an indefinite article, not "one" as a numeral. *Took up* (*ēren*). First aorist active indicative of *airō*. *As it were a great millstone* (*hōs mulinon megan*). Late adjective, in inscriptions, here only in N.T., made of millstone (*mulos*, Matt. 18:6; Rev. 18:22), while *mulikos* (Luke 17:2) means belonging to a mill. This is not a small millstone turned by women (Matt. 24:41), but one requiring an ass to turn it (Mark 9:42), and so "a great" one. *Cast* (*ebalen*). Second aorist active of *ballō*, to hurl. *With a mighty fall* (*hormēmati*). Instrumental case (manner) of *hormēma*, a rush, old word from *hormaō*, to rush (Matt. 8:32), here only in N.T. *Shall be cast down* (*blethēsetai*). Future (first) passive of *ballō*, the same verb (*ebalen*), effective punctiliar future. Like a bowlder hurled into the sea. *Shall be found no more at all* (*ou mē heurethēi eti*). Double negative with first aorist passive subjunctive of *heuriskō*. See 9:6 for *ou mē* with the active voice of *heuriskō*. Already the old Babylon was a desert waste (Strabo, XVI. 1073).

22. *The voice* (*phōnē*). Cf. Ezek. 26:13. Or "sound" as in I Cor. 14:8 with *salpigx* (trumpet). For this song of judgment see Jer. 25:10. *Of harpers* (*kitharōidōn*). Old word (from *kithara*, harp, and *ōidos*, singer) as in 14:2. *Of minstrels* (*mousikōn*). Old word (from *mousa*, music), here only in N.T., one playing on musical instruments. *Of flute-players* (*aulētōn*). Old word (from *auleō*, to play on a flute, Matt. 11:17, *aulos*, flute, I Cor. 14:7), in N.T. only here and Matt. 9:23. *Of trumpeters* (*salpistōn*). Late form

for the earlier *salpigktēs* (from *salpizō*), here only in N.T. *Shall be heard no more at all* (*ou mē akousthēi*). First aorist passive subjunctive of *akouō* with the double negative as below, with *phōnē mulou* (sound of the millstone), and as in verse 21 with *ou me heurethēi* and again with *pās technitēs* (craftsman). This old word is from *technē*, art, as here in some MSS. ("of whatsoever craft," *pasēs technēs*). *Technitēs* occurs also in this sense in Acts 19:24, 38 and in Heb. 11:10 of God as the Architect. There is power in this four-fold sonorous repetition of *ou mē* and the subjunctive with two more examples in verse 23.

23. *Of a lamp* (*luchnou*). Old word (Matt. 5:15), again in Rev. 22:5. *Shall shine no more at all* (*ou mē phanēi*). Fifth instance in these verses of *ou mē* with the aorist subjunctive, here the active of *phainō* as in Rev. 8:12. It is not known whether Rome had street lights or not. *The voice of the bridegroom and of the bride* (*phōnē numphiou kai numphēs*). See John 3:29 and Jer. 7:34; 16:9. "Even the occasional flash of the torches carried by bridal processions (Matt. 25:1ff.) is seen no more" (Swete). The sixth instance of *ou mē*, in verses 21 to 23, occurs with *akousthēi* (third instance of *akousthēi*, two in verse 22). *Were the princes of the earth* (*ēsan hoi megistānes tēs gēs*). For *megistān* see Rev. 6:15, and Mark 6:21. "Thy merchants were the grandees" once, but now these merchant princes are gone. *With thy sorcery* (*en tēi pharmakiāi sou*). *En* (instrumental use) and the locative case of *pharmakia*, old word (from *pharmakeuō*, to prepare drugs, from *pharmakon*, sorcery, Rev. 9:21), in N.T. only here and Gal. 5:20 for sorcery and magical arts. If one is puzzled over the connection between medicine and sorcery as illustrated by this word (our pharmacy), he has only to recall quackery today in medicine (patent medicines and cure-alls), witch-doctors, professional faith-healers, medicine-men in Africa. True medical science has had a hard fight to shake off chicanery and charlatanry. *Were deceived*

(*eplanēthēsan*). First aorist passive indicative of *planaō*. These charlatans always find plenty of victims. See Mark 12:24.

24. *In her* (*en autēi*). In Rome. *Was found* (*heurethē*). First aorist passive indicative of *heuriskō*. See 16:6; 17:6 for the blood already shed by Rome. Rome "butchered to make a Roman holiday" (Dill, *Roman Society*, p. 242) not merely gladiators, but prophets and saints from Nero's massacre A.D. 64 to Domitian and beyond. *Of all that have been slain* (*pantōn tōn esphagmenōn*). Perfect passive articular participle genitive plural of *sphazō*, the verb used of the Lamb slain (5:9, 12; 13:8). Cf. Matt. 23:35 about Jerusalem.

CHAPTER XIX

1. *After these things* (*meta tauta*). Often when a turn comes in this book. But Beckwith is probably correct in seeing in 19:1–5 the climax of chapter 18. This first voice (verses 1 and 2) *hōs phōnēn megalēn ouchlou pollou* (as it were great voice of much multitude) is probably the response of the angelic host (Rev. 5:11; Heb. 12:22). There is responsive singing (grand chorus) as in chapters 4 and 5. *Saying* (*legontōn*). Present active participle of *legō*, genitive plural, though *ochlou* is genitive singular (collective substantive, agreement in sense). *Hallelujah* (*Allēlouia*). Transliteration of the Hebrew seen often in the Psalms (LXX) and in III. Macc. 7:13, in N.T. only in Rev. 19:1, 3, 4, 6. It means, "Praise ye the Lord." Fifteen of the Psalms begin or end with this word. The Great Hallel (a title for "Psalms 104 to 109") is sung chiefly at the feasts of the passover and tabernacles. This psalm of praise uses language already in 12:10.

2. *For* (*hoti*). Because. The reason for God's judgments is given in 15:3; 16:7. The doom of Babylon seen in 14:7 is now realized. *For* (*hoti*). Second use of *hoti*, explaining the first. *He hath judged* (*ekrinen*). First aorist (prophetic and climacteric, effective) active indicative of *krinō*. *Which* (*hētis*). The very one which. *Did corrupt* (*ephtheiren*). This is the terrible fact. First aorist active indicative of *phtheirō*. Cf. 11:18; 14:8; 17:2; 18:3. *And he hath avenged* (*kai exedikēsen*). God has exacted vengeance for the blood of his servants from (*ek*) her. Prophetic aorist again of *ekdikeō* with accusative and *ek* with ablative as in 6:10.

3. *A second time* (*deuteron*). Adverbial accusative, a heavenly encore. *They say* (*eirēkan*). Perfect active indica-

tive of *eipon*. "They have said," not an "aoristic" perfect for "they say," but vivid dramatic perfect as in 5:7 and the form in *-an* instead of *-asin* as in 18:3; 21:6. *Goeth up* (*anabainei*). Linear present active indicative of *anabainō*, "keeps on going up," "a last touch to the description already given (18:21ff.) of Babylon's utter collapse" (Swete). The smoke of the city's ruin (14:11; 18:8f., 18) instead of incense (8:4). Cf. Is. 34:9f.

4. *Fell down and worshipped God* (*epesan kai prosekunēsan tōi theōi*). Precisely as in 7:11, which see. The twenty-four elders and the four living creatures take up the antiphonal chorus of the angels.

5. *A voice from the throne* (*phōnē apo tou thronou*). Not the voice of God, nor of the Lamb, nor *ek tou naou* (16:17), but from an angel of the Presence. This angel summons all the servants of God to join in the antiphonal praise to God. *Give praise to our God* (*aineite tōi theōi hēmōn*). Present active imperative of *aineō*, old verb, with the accusative elsewhere in N.T., but here with the dative as occasionally in the LXX (I Chron. 16:36, etc.).

6. *As it were the voice* (*hōs phōnēn*). Used here three times, as once in verse 1: once of a second great multitude (*ochlou pollou*), not of angels as in verse 1, but the innumerable multitude of the redeemed of 7:9; then "of many waters" (*hudatōn pollōn*) as in 1:15 and 14:2 like "the roar of a cataract" (Swete); and once more "the voice of mighty thunders" (*brontōn ischurōn*) as in 6:1 and 10:3ff. *Saying* (*legontōn*). The best attested reading, genitive plural of *legō*, agreeing with *ochlou* (genitive singular), for roll of the waters and the roar of the thunders were not articulate. Some MSS. have *legontes* (nominative plural) referring also to *ochlou*, though nominative instead of genitive. The fourth "Hallelujah" comes from this vast multitude. *The Lord our God, the Almighty* (*Kurios, ho theos, ho pantokratōr*). For this designation of God see also 1:8; 4:8; 11:17; 15:3; 16:7,

14; 19:15; 21:22. Cf. *deus et dominus noster* used of the Roman emperor. *Reigneth* (*ebasileusen*). First aorist active of *basileuō*. Probably ingressive prophetic aorist, "God became king" in fulness of power on earth with the fall of the world power.

7. *Let us rejoice and be exceeding glad* (*chairōmen kai agalliōmen*). Present active subjunctive (volitive) of *chairō* and *agalliaō* (elsewhere in N.T. in the middle except Luke 1:47; I Pet. 1:8). For both verbs together see Matt. 5:12. *Let us give* (*dōmen*). Second aorist active subjunctive of *didōmi*, but A reads *dōsomen* (future active) and P *dōsōmen*. If the future indicative is read, the tone is changed from exhortation to declaration (we shall give glory unto him). *The marriage of the Lamb* (*ho gamos tou arniou*). In the O.T. God is the Bridegroom of Israel (Hos. 2:16; Is. 54:6; Ezek. 16:7ff.). In the N.T. Christ is the Bridegroom of the Kingdom (the universal spiritual church as seen by Paul, II Cor. 11:2; Eph. 5:25ff., and by John in Rev. 3:20; 19:7, 9; 21:2, 9; 22:17. In the Gospels Christ appears as the Bridegroom (Mark 2:19f.; Matt. 9:15; Luke 5:34f.; John 3:29). The figure of *gamos* occurs in Matt. 22:2–14. Three metaphors of women appear in the Apocalypse (the Mother in chapter 12, the Harlot in 17 to 19, and the Bride of Christ here to the end). "The first and third present the Church under two different aspects of her life, while the second answers to her great rival and enemy" (Swete). *Is come* (*ēlthen*). Prophetic aorist, come at last. *Made herself ready* (*hētoimasen heautēn*). First aorist active indicative of *hetoimazō* and the reflexive pronoun. See 22:2 for *hētoimasmenēn hōs numphēn* (prepared as a bride). There is something for her to do (I John 3:3; Jude 21; II Cor. 7:1), but the chief preparation is the act of Christ (Eph. 5:25ff.).

8. *That she should array herself* (*hina peribalētai*). Subfinal object clause subject of *edothē* (was given to her) with *hina* and the second aorist middle (direct) of *periballō* to

fling around. This bridal dress is a gift from Christ. This form, *edothē* (it was given), occurs some 20 times in this book. *In fine linen, bright and pure (bussinon lampron katharon)*. See 19:14 for the same raiment on those accompanying "The Word of God" and for the seven angels in 15:6. See by contrast the garments of the harlot (17:4; 18:16). For *bussinon* see 18:16. *The righteous acts of the saints (ta dikaiōmata tōn hagiōn)*. This is the explanation (*gar*) of the bridal dress and explains why there is work for the Bride as well as for Christ (Phil. 2:12f.). See 15:4 for *dikaiōma* (also Rom. 5:18).

9. *Write (Grapson)*. First aorist active imperative of *graphō* as in 1:11; 14:13. The speaker may be the angel guide of 17:1. It is another beatitude (*makarioi*, Blessed) like that in 14:13 (fourth of the seven in the book). *They which are bidden (hoi keklēmenoi)*. Articular perfect passive participle of *kaleō*, like Matt. 22:3; Luke 14:17. Cf. Rev. 17:14. This beatitude reminds us of that in Luke 14:15. (Cf. Matt. 8:11; 26:29.) *These are true words of God (Houtoi hoi logoi alēthinoi tou theou eisin)*. Undoubtedly, but one should bear in mind that apocalyptic symbolism "has its own methods and laws of interpretation, and by these the student must be guided" (Swete).

10. *To worship him (proskunēsai autōi)*. First aorist active infinitive of purpose. John either felt that the angel represented God or he was beside himself with excitement over the glorious consummation. He was tempted to worship an angel (Col. 2:18). *See thou do it not (hora mē)*. Repeated in 22:9. Here there is no verb after *mē* (ellipse of *poiēseis touto*) as in Mark 1:44; I Thess. 5:15), the aorist subjunctive of negative purpose with *mē* after *hora* (present active imperative of *horaō*), a common enough idiom. *Fellow-servant (sundoulos)*. The angel refuses worship from John on this ground. All Christians are *sundouloi* (fellow-servants) as Christ taught (Matt. 18:28ff.; 24:49) and as

Paul (Col. 1:7; 4:7) and John (Rev. 6:11) taught. Angels are God's servants also (Heb. 1:4-14). For "the testimony of Jesus" see 1:2, 9; 6:9; 12:17; 22:4. *Worship God (tōi theōi proskunēson)*. And Christ, who is the Son of God (5:13f.). *The spirit of prophecy (to pneuma tēs prophēteias)*. Explanatory use of *gar* (for) here as in 8. The possession of the prophetic spirit shows itself in witness to Jesus. In illustration see Mark 1:10; Matt. 3:16; Luke 3:21; John 1:51; Rev. 4:1; 10:1; 11:19; 14:17; 15:5; 18:1; 19:1, 7-9.

11. *The heaven opened (ton ouranon ēneōigmenon)*. Perfect passive participle (triple reduplication) of *anoigō*. Accusative case after *eidon*. So Ezekiel (1:1) begins his prophecy. See also the baptism of Jesus (Matt. 3:16 = Luke 3:21, but *schizomenous* in Mark 1:10). Jesus predicted the opened heavens to Nathanael (John 1:51). In Rev. 4:1 a door is opened in heaven, the sanctuary is opened (11:19; 15:5), angels come out of heaven (10:1; 14:17; 18:1), and sounds come from heaven (19:1). *Behold, a white horse (idou hippos leukos)*. Nominative case because of *idou*, not *eidon*. Cf. 6:2 for *hippos leukos*. The emblem of victory in both cases, but the riders are very different. Here it is the Messiah who is the Warrior, as is made plain by "Faithful and True" (*pistos kai alēthinos*), epithets already applied to Christ (1:5; 3:7, 14). Cf. also 22:6. *In righteousness he doth judge and make war (en dikaiosunēi krinei kai polemei)*. See Is. 11:3ff. The Messiah is both Judge and Warrior, but he does both in righteousness (15:3; 16:5, 7; 19:2). He passes judgment on the beast (antichrist) and makes war on him. Satan had offered Christ a victory of compromise which was rejected.

12. *A flame of fire (phlox puros)*. As in the opening vision of Christ in 1:14 (2:18). *Many diadems (diadēmata polla)*. A new feature, but the dragon has a diadem on each of his seven heads (12:3) and the first beast one upon each of his ten horns (13:1). So the victorious Messiah will wear

many royal diadems and not mere crowns, because he is King of kings (19:16). *And he hath* (*kai echōn*). Nominative active present participle of *echō* either used absolutely as an independent verb (like indicative) or in an anacoluthon, though *autou* (his) is genitive. *A name written* (*onoma gegrammenon*). Perfect passive participle of *graphō* as in 2:17 (cf. 3:12). *But he himself* (*ei mē autos*). "Except himself" (common ellipsis of the verb after *ei mē*, "if not"). See 2:17 and 3:12 for the new name there described. See 14:1 for the name of Christ on the forehead of the 144,000, and 17:5 for the name on the forehead of the harlot. This word here supplements what Jesus says in Matt. 11:27.

13. *Arrayed* (*peribeblēmenos*). Perfect passive participle of *periballō*, to clothe, often in this book. *In a garment* (*himation*). Accusative case after the passive participle *peribeblēmenos*. *Sprinkled* (*rerantismenon*). Perfect passive participle of *rantizō*, in the predicate accusative case agreeing with *himation*. A Q here read *bebammenon* (perfect passive participle of *baptō*, to dip). Probably *rerantismenon* (sprinkled) is correct, because the picture comes from Is. 63:3, where Aquila and Symmachus use *rantizō*. The use of *bebammenon* (dipped) is a bolder figure and Charles considers it correct. In either case it is the blood of Christ's enemies with which his raiment (*himation*, perhaps a *chlamus* Matt. 27:28, 31) is sprinkled or dipped as the case may be, not his own blood on Calvary (1:5; 5:9; 7:14; 12:11), but proleptically and prophetically the blood of Christ's enemies. *Haimati* can be either locative case with *bebammenon* (dipped in blood) or instrumental with *rerantismenon* (sprinkled with blood). *The Word of God* (*ho Logos tou theou*). Some scholars hold this addition inconsistent with verse 12, but it may be merely the explanation of the secret name or still another name besides that known only to himself. The personal use of the Logos applied to Christ occurs only in the Johannine writings unless that is the idea

in Heb. 4:12. In John 1:1, 14 it is merely *ho Logos* (the Word), in I John 1:1 *ho Logos tēs zōēs* (the Word of Life), while here it is *ho Logos tou theou* (the Word of God), one of the strongest arguments for identity of authorship. The idiom here is one common in Luke and Paul for the teaching of Christ (Luke 5:1; 8:11, etc.; I Cor. 14:36; II Cor. 2:17, etc.). Jesus is himself the final and perfect revelation of God to men (Heb. 1:1f.).

14. *The armies which are in heaven* (*ta strateumata ta en tōi ouranōi*). See 12:7 for Michael and angels warring with the dragon, and also Matt. 26:53 for the angels at Christ's call, not to say Heb. 1:6f., 14; Matt. 13:41; Rev. 5:11f. *Followed* (*ēkolouthei*). Imperfect active and singular (*strateumata*, neuter plural) of *akoloutheō*, graphic picture of the celestial Warrior with his angelic hosts "upon white horses" (*eph' hippois leukois*) like the Leader and, like him "clothed in fine linen white and pure" (*endedumenoi bussinon leukon katharon*) like the Leader again (19:8). Note *endedumenoi* here as in 1:13 and 15:6.

15. *A sharp sword* (*romphaia oxeia*). As in 1:16 and 2:12, 15. *That he should smite* (*hina pataxēi*). Purpose clause with *hina* and the first aorist active subjunctive of *patassō*, old verb already in 11:6 and like Is. 11:4, a figure here for forensic and judicial condemnation. *And he shall rule them* (*kai autos poimanei*). Emphatic use of *autos* twice (he himself). Future active of *poimainō*, to shepherd as in 2:27, and 12:5 "with a rod of iron" (*en rabdōi sidērāi*) as there. See I Pet. 2:25 and Heb. 13:20 for Christ as Shepherd. *And he treadeth* (*kai autos patei*). Change to present tense of *pateō*, to tread (here transitive), with solemn repetition of *kai autos*. *The winepress of the fierceness of the wrath of Almighty God* (*tēn lēnon tou oinou tou thumou tēs orgēs tou theou tou pantokratoros*). Literally, "the winepress of the wine of the wrath of the anger of God the Almighty" (four genitives dependent on one another and on *lēnon*). These

images are here combined from 14:8, 10, 19f.; 16:19. The fact is already in 19:13 after Is. 63:1ff.

16. *And on his thigh* (*kai epi ton mēron autou*). "Even upon his thigh." Old word, here alone in N.T. *King of kings, and Lord of lords* (*Basileus basileōn kai Kurios kuriōn*). The title already given to the Lamb in 17:14, but in reverse order. See the same idea in I Tim. 6:15.

17. *An angel* (*hena aggelon*). Like *heis* in 18:21, just "an," not "one." *Standing in the sun* (*hestōta en tōi hēliōi*). Second perfect active participle of *histēmi* (intransitive). "Where all the birds of prey would behold him" (Beckwith). For *orneois* (birds) see 18:2 and for *en mesouranēmati* (in mid heaven) see 18:13; 14:6. *Come and be gathered together* (*Deute sunachthēte*). *Deute* is the adverb *deurō* (hither), used when two or more are addressed, possibly from *deuro ite* (come here). Asyndeton also without *kai* (and). First aorist passive imperative of *sunagō*. The metaphor is drawn from Ezek. 39:17. *Unto the great supper of God* (*eis to deipnon to mega tou theou*). The habits of vultures are described by Christ in Matt. 24:28. This is a bold and powerful picture of the battlefield after the victory of the Messiah, "a sacrificial feast spread on God's table for all the vultures of the sky" (Swete). Is this battle the same as that of Har Magedon (16:16) and that of Gog and Magog (20:8ff.) mentioned after the thousand years? The language in 20:8ff. seems like this derived from Ezek. 39:17ff., and "in the Apocalypse priority in the order of sequence does not always imply priority in time" (Swete). There seems no way to decide this point save that the end seems to be at hand.

18. *That ye may eat* (*hina phagēte*). Purpose clause with *hina* and the second aorist active subjunctive of *esthiō*. *The flesh of kings* (*sarkas basileōn*). "Pieces of flesh" (plural of *sarx*, flesh) and of all classes and conditions of men who fell in the battle (6:18; 11:13; 13:16; 19:5; 20:12). War is no respecter of persons.

19. *Gathered together* (*sunēgmena*). Perfect passive participle of *sunagō*. *In battle array*. *To make war against* (*poiēsai polemon meta*). First aorist active infinitive of *poieō*, to express purpose. See *polemeō meta* in 12:7 and the use of *sunagō eis polemon* in 16:14; 20:8. The beast (for his army see 16:13f.) led a league of ten kings against Babylon in 17:16f., but with the purpose also of fighting the Lamb (17:14).

20. *Was taken* (*epiasthē*). First aorist (prophetic) passive indicative of the Doric *piazō* (Attic *piezō*). Cf. II Thess. 2:8. *The false prophet* (*ho pseudoprophētēs*). Possibly the second beast of 13:11–17; 16:13; 20:10. Charles takes him to be "the priesthood of the Imperial cult, which practised all kinds of magic and imposture to beguile men to worship the Beast." *That wrought the signs in his sight* (*ho poiēsas ta sēmeia enōpion autou*). As in 13:14. *Wherewith* (*en hois*). "In which" signs. *He deceived* (*eplanēsen*). First aorist active indicative of *planaō*. He was only able to deceive "them that had received" (*tous labontas*, articular second aorist active participle of *lambanō*, "those receiving") "the mark of the beast" (13:16; 14:9ff.; 16:2; 20:4) "and them that worshipped his image" (*tous proskunountas tēi eikoni autou*) as in 13:15. *They twain* (*hoi duo*). "The two." *Were cast* (*eblēthēsan*). First aorist passive indicative of *ballō*. They fall together as they fought together. "The day that sees the end of a false statecraft will see also that of a false priestcraft" (Swete). *Alive* (*zōntes*). Present active participle of *zaō*, predicative nominative, "living." *Into the lake of fire* (*eis tēn limnēn tou puros*). Genitive *puros* describes this *limnēn* (lake, cf. Luke 5:1) as it does *gehenna* in Matt. 5:22. See also 20:10; 21:8. It is a different figure from the "abyss" in 9:1ff. and 20:1ff. This is the final abode of Satan, the beast, the false prophet, and wicked men. *That burneth with brimstone* (*tēs kaiomenēs en theiōi*). Note the genitive here in place of the accusative *limnēn*,

perhaps because of the intervening genitive *puros* (neuter, not feminine). The agreement is regular in 21:8. For *en theiōi* (with brimstone) see 14:10; 20:10; 21:8. The fact of hell is clearly taught here, but the imagery is not to be taken literally any more than that of heaven in chapters 4, 5, 21, 22 is to be so understood. Both fall short of the reality.

21. *The rest* (*hoi loipoi*). Of the enemy (the kings and their hosts of verse 19). *Were killed* (*apektanthēsan*). First aorist (effective) passive indicative of *apokteinō*. Those affected by the Cæsar-worship (14:9ff.) were not at once cast into the lake with the two beasts. *Were filled* (*echortasthēsan*). First aorist (effective) passive of *chortazō*. As they had been invited to do in verse 17.

CHAPTER XX

1. *Coming down out of heaven* (*katabainonta ek tou ouranou*). As in 10:1; 18:1. *The key of the abyss* (*tēn klein tēs abussou*). As in 9:1. *A great chain* (*halusin megalēn*). Paul wore a *halusis* (alpha privative and *luō*, to loose) in Rome (II Tim. 1:16), as did Peter in prison in Jerusalem (Acts 12:6). *In his hand* (*epi tēn cheira autou*). "Upon his hand," ready for use. See *epi* with the genitive in 1:20.

2. *He laid hold on* (*ekratēsen*). First aorist active indicative of *krateō*, to seize. *The dragon* (*ton drakonta*). Accusative after *ekratēsen* instead of the genitive as in 2:1. He has been behind the beast and the false prophet from the start. Now he is seized. *The old serpent* (*ho ophis ho archaios*). Precisely the description in 12:9, only the nominative is here retained, though in apposition with the accusative *ton drakonta*, a frequent anacoluthon in the Apocalypse (1:5, etc.). Swete calls it a parenthesis. *Which is* (*hos estin*). The relative here relieves the construction and takes the place of *ho kaloumenos* in 12:9 before *Diabolos kai ho Satanās*. *And bound him* (*kai edēsen auton*). First aorist active indicative of *deō*. *For a thousand years* (*chilia etē*). Accusative of extent of time. Here we confront the same problem found in the 1260 days. In this book of symbols how long is a thousand years? All sorts of theories are proposed, none of which fully satisfy one. Perhaps Peter has given us the only solution open to us in II Pet. 3:8 when he argues that "one day with the Lord is as a thousand years and a thousand years as one day." It will help us all to remember that God's clock does not run by ours and that times and seasons and programs are with him. This wonderful book

was written to comfort the saints in a time of great trial, not to create strife among them.

3. *Into the abyss* (*eis tēn abusson*). The one in 9:1f. and the one spoken of by the legion of demons in Luke 8:31 under the charge of the angel of the abyss (Apollyon, Rev. 9:11) who is either Satan himself or a kindred power. "Already he has been cast out of Heaven (12:9), now he is cast out of the earth, and returns to his own place" (Swete). *Shut it and sealed it* (*ekleisen kai esphragisen*). Effective first aorists active indicative of *kleiō* and *sphragizō*. *That he should deceive no more* (*hina mē planēsēi*). Negative purpose clause with *hina mē* and the first aorist active subjunctive of *planaō*. Glorious relief after the strain of the previous visions of conflict. Small wonder that Christians today cherish this blessed hope whatever the actual meaning may be. *Until should be finished* (*achri telesthēi*). Temporal clause of future purpose with *achri* (as a conjunction like *heōs*) and the first aorist passive subjunctive of *teleō*. Repeated in verse 5 and see *achri* and the subjunctive in 7:3; 15:8. *He must be loosed* (*dei luthēnai*). Sad necessity, alas, with *dei* and the first aorist passive infinitive of *luō*. *For a little time* (*mikron chronon*). Accusative of time. Whatever the thousand years means, it is here said plainly that after it is over the devil will again have power on earth "for a little time."

4. *And they sat upon them* (*kai ekathisan ep' autous*). First aorist active indicative of *kathizō*. Another period here apparently synchronous (verse 7) with the confinement of Satan in the abyss. No subject is given for this plural verb. Apparently Christ and the Apostles (Matt. 19:28; Luke 22:30) and some of the saints (I Cor. 6:3), martyrs some hold. *Judgment was given unto them* (*krima edothē autois*). First aorist passive of *didōmi*. Picture of the heavenly court of assizes. *The souls* (*tas psuchas*). Accusative after *eidon* at the beginning of the verse. *Of them that*

had been beheaded (*tōn pepelekismenōn*). Genitive of the articular perfect passive participle of *pelekizō*, old word (from *pelekus* an axe, the traditional instrument for execution in republican Rome, but later supplanted by the sword), to cut off with an axe, here only in N.T. See 6:9; 18:24; 19:2 for previous mention of these martyrs for the witness of Jesus (1:9; 12:17; 19:10). Others also besides martyrs shared in Christ's victory, those who refused to worship the beast or wear his mark as in 13:15; 14:9ff.; 16:2; 19:20. *And they lived* (*kai ezēsan*). First aorist active indicative of *zaō*. If the ingressive aorist, it means "came to life" or "lived again" as in 2:8 and so as to verse 5. If it is the constative aorist here and in verse 5, then it could mean increased spiritual life. See John 5:21–29 for the double sense of life and death (now literal, now spiritual) precisely as we have the second death in Rev. 2:11; 20:6, 14. *And reigned with Christ* (*kai ebasileusan meta tou Christou*). Same use of the first aorist active indicative of *basileuō*, but more clearly constative. Beckwith and Swete take this to apply solely to the martyrs, the martyrs' reign with Christ.

5. *The rest of the dead* (*hoi loipoi tōn nekrōn*). "All except the martyrs, both the righteous and the unrighteous" (Beckwith). But some take this to mean only the wicked. *Lived not until the thousand years should be finished* (*ouk ezēsan achri telesthēi ta chilia etē*). See verse 4 for the items here. "To infer from this statement, as many expositors have done, that the *ezēsan* of v. 4 must be understood of bodily resuscitation, is to interpret apocalyptic prophecy by methods of exegesis which are proper to ordinary narrative" (Swete). I sympathize wholly with that comment and confess my own ignorance therefore as to the meaning of the symbolism without any predilections for post-millennialism or premillennialism. *This is the first resurrection* (*hautē hē anastasis hē prōtē*). Scholars differ as to the genuineness of this phrase. Accepting it as genuine, Swete applies it to

"the return of the martyrs and confessors to life at the beginning of the Thousand Years." According to this view the first resurrection is a special incident in the present life before the Parousia. It has no parallel with I Thess. 4:16, where the dead in Christ are raised before those living are changed. Some think that John here pictures the "Regeneration" (*palingenesia*) of Matt. 19:28 and the "Restoration" (*apokatastasis*) of Acts 3:21. No effort is here made to solve this problem, save to call attention to the general judgment out of the books in 20:12 and to the general resurrection in John 5:29 and Acts 24:15.

6. *Blessed and holy* (*makarios kai hagios*). A fifth beatitude (1:3; 14:13; 16:15; 19:9) already and two more to come (22:7, 14, seven in all). Here *hagios* is added to the usual *makarios*. *The second death* (*ho deuteros thanatos*). The spiritual death of 2:11; 20:14; 21:8 in contrast to the first or physical death. This language raises a question about the interpretation of the first and the second resurrections, whether both are of the body or one of the spirit. There seems no way to reach a solid conception about it. In I Cor. 15:23 there is no mention of the resurrection of any save "those of Christ" (*hoi tou Christou*), though the end follows (verse 24). However, Paul elsewhere (Acts 24:15) speaks of the resurrection of the just and of the unjust as if one event. *Priests of God and of Christ* (*hiereis tou theou kai tou Christou*). As in 1:6; 5:10; 22:3, 5. *Shall reign with him* (*basileusousin met' autou*). As promised in the same passages. The servants of God are to be priests with Christ and to reign with him (Matt. 19:28). In 5:10 *epi tēs gēs* (upon earth) occurs, but this item does not appear here. "No hint is given as to where this service is to be rendered and this royalty to be exercised" (Swete).

7. *When are finished* (*hotan telesthēi*). Indefinite future temporal clause with *hotan* and the first aorist passive subjunctive of *teleō*, "whenever are finished." *Shall be loosed*

(*luthēsetai*). Future passive of *luō*, no longer bound as in
20:2f. He uses the future as a prophet in verses 7 and 8,
but in 9 and 10 he uses the aorist as a seer. *Out of his prison*
(*ek tēs phulakēs autou*). For *phulakē* in this sense see 2:10.
Out of the abyss of verses 2 and 3.

8. *To deceive the nations* (*planēsai ta ethnē*). First aorist
active infinitive of purpose of *planaō*, Satan's chief task
(chapters 12 to 18, in particular 12:9; 13:14; 19:20; 20:3,
10). *Which are in the four corners of the earth* (*ta en tais
tessarsi gōniais tēs gēs*). Clearly the reign with Christ, if
on earth, was not shared in by all on earth, for Satan finds
a large and ready following on his release. See 7:1 (Is.
11:12) for "the four corners of the earth." *Gog and Magog*
(*ton Gōg kai Magōg*). Accusative in explanatory apposition
with *ta ethnē* (the nations). Magog is first mentioned in
Gen. 10:2. The reference here seems to be Ezek. 38:2,
where both are mentioned. Josephus (*Ant.* I. 6. 1) identifies Magog with the Scythians, with Gog as their prince.
In the rabbinical writings Gog and Magog appear as the
enemies of the Messiah. Some early Christian writers
thought of the Goths and Huns, but Augustine refuses to
narrow the imagery and sees only the final protest of the
world against Christianity. *To gather them together to the
war* (*sunagagein autous eis ton polemon*). Second aorist active infinitive of purpose of *sunagō*, a congenial task for
Satan after his confinement. See 16:14 for this very phrase
and also 17:14; 19:19. *Of whom* (*hōn—autōn*). Pleonasm
or redundant pronoun as in 3:8 and often (of whom—of
them). *As the sand of the sea* (*hōs hē ammos tēs thalassēs*).
Already in 12:18. Clearly then the millennium, whatever
it is, does not mean a period when Satan has no following
on earth, for this vast host rallies at once to his standard.

9. *They went up* (*anebēsan*). Second aorist active indicative of *anabainō*, a return to the manner of the seer as in
verses 4 and 5. *Over the breadth of the earth* (*epi to platos*

tēs gēs). *Platos* is old word, in N.T. only here, 21:16; Eph. 3:18. The hosts of Satan spread over the earth. *Compassed* (*ekukleusan*). First aorist (prophetic) active indicative of *kukleuō*, to encircle, late verb (Strabo) from *kuklos* (circle), in N.T. only here and margin in John 10:24 (for *ekuklōsan* from *kukloō*). *The camp of the saints* (*tēn parembolēn tōn hagiōn*). *Parembolē* (*para, en, ballō*) is common late word for military camp, in LXX for the Israelites in the desert (Ex. 29:14, etc.), in N.T. for Roman barracks (Acts 24:34, 37) and for an army in line of battle (Heb. 11:34; Rev. 20:9). *The beloved city* (*tēn polin tēn ēgapēmenēn*). Perfect passive participle of *agapaō*, "the city the beloved." See Ps. 78:68; 87:2 for Jerusalem so described. So Charles takes it here, but Swete holds it to be "the Church the New Zion" that is meant. *And fire came down out of heaven* (*kai katebē pur ek tou ouranou*). Second aorist (prophetic) active indicative of *katabainō*. Cf. Gen. 19:24; 39:6; Ezek. 38:22; II Kings 1:10, 12; Luke 9:54 (about John). *Devoured them* (*katephagen autous*). Second aorist (prophetic) active of *katesthiō*, to eat up (down). Vivid climax to this last great battle with Satan.

10. *Was cast* (*eblēthē*). First aorist (prophetic, affective) passive indicative of *ballō* (verse 3). *Into the lake of fire and brimstone* (*eis tēn limnēn tou puros kai theiou*). As in 19:20 with the two beasts, as he adds, "where are also the beast and the false prophet" (*hopou kai to thērion kai ho pseudoprophētēs*). *They shall be tormented* (*basanisthēsontai*). Return to the prophetic future of verses 7 and 8. For *basanizō* see 9:5; 14:10. For "day and night" (*hēmeras kai nuktos*) see 4:8; 7:15; 12:10; 14:11. For "for ever and ever" (*eis tous aiōnas ton aiōnōn*) see 1:6, 18; 4:9, 10; 5:13; 7:12; 10:6; 11:15, etc. The devil was cast down from heaven (12:9), then imprisoned (20:2ff.), now he received his final doom.

11. *A great white throne* (*thronon megan leukon*). Here

megan (great) is added to the throne pictures in 4:4; 20:4. The scene is prepared for the last judgment often mentioned in the N.T. (Matt. 25:31-46; Rom. 14:10; II Cor. 5:10). "The absolute purity of this Supreme Court is symbolized by the colour of the Throne" (Swete) as in Dan. 7:9; Ps. 9:1; 97:2. The name of God is not mentioned, but the Almighty Father sits upon the throne (4:2f., 9; 5:1, 7, 13; 6:16; 7:10, 15; 19:4; 21:5), and the Son sits there with him (Heb. 1:3) and works with the Father (John 5:19-21; 10:30; Matt. 25:31ff.; Acts 17:31; II Cor. 5:10; II Tim. 4:1). *From whose face the earth and the heaven fled away* (*hou apo prosōpou ephugen hē gē kai ho ouranos*). Second aorist (prophetic) active of *pheugō*. See 16:20. The non-eternity of matter is a common teaching in the O.T. (Ps. 97:5; 102:27; Is. 51:6) as in the N.T. (Mark 13:31; II Pet. 3:10). *Was found* (*heurethē*). First aorist passive indicative of *heuriskō*. All is now spiritual. Even scientists today are speaking of the non-eternity of the universe.

12. *The dead, the great and the small* (*tous nekrous tous megalous kai tous mikrous*). The general resurrection of verse 13 is pictured by anticipation as already over. No living are mentioned after the battle of verses 7-10, though some will be living when Jesus comes to judge the quick and the dead (II Tim. 4:1; I Thess. 4:13ff.). All classes and conditions (11:18; 13:16; 19:5, 18) John saw "standing before the throne" (*hestōtas enōpion tou thronou*). *Books were opened* (*biblia ēnoichthēsan*). First aorist passive of *anoigō*. Like Dan. 7:10. The record of each human being has been kept in God's books. *Were judged* (*ekrithēsan*). First aorist passive indicative of *krinō*. The sentence upon each rests upon written evidence. *Another book which is the book of life* (*allo biblion ho estin tēs zōēs*). This book has already been mentioned (3:5; 13:8; 17:8). "It is the roll of living citizens of Jerusalem" (Swete), "the church of the first born enrolled in heaven" (Heb. 12:23). The books are

"the vouchers for the book of life" (Alford). We are saved by grace, but character at last (according to their works) is the test as the fruit of the tree (Matt. 7:16, 20; 10:32f.; 25:31-46; John 15:6; II Cor. 5:10; Rom. 2:10; Rev. 2:23; 20:12; 22:12).

13. *Gave up* (*edōken*). Just "gave" (first aorist active indicative of *didōmi*), but for the sea to give is to give up (effective aorist). Sea as well as land delivers its dead (all kinds of dead, good and bad). Swete notes that accidental deaths will not prevent any from appearing. Milligan is sure that the sea here means "the sea of the troubled and sinful world." *Death and Hades* (*ho thanatos kai ho hāidēs*). "An inseparable pair" (Swete) as in 1:18; 6:8; 20:14. So in Matt. 16:18 "the gates of Hades" means the power of death. Etymologically Hades is the unseen world where all who die are as opposed to this visible world, but in actual use Hades is sometimes treated as the abode of the unrighteous (Luke 16:23). Charles thinks that this is true here, though there is nothing to show it apart from the personification of death and Hades and the casting of both into the lake of fire in verse 14. Here again "each man" (*hekastos*) receives judgment according to his deeds (Matt. 16:27; I Cor. 3:13; II Cor. 5:10; Rom. 2:6; 14:12; I Pet. 1:17; Rev. 2:23).

14. *Were cast* (*eblēthēsan*). As the devil (20:10) followed the two beasts (19:20) into the same dread lake of fire. Death is personified and is disposed of, "the last enemy" (I Cor. 15:26) and Paul sings the pæan of victory over death (I Cor. 15:54f., from Hos. 13:14). Hades has no more terrors, for the saints are in heaven. There is no more fear of death (Heb. 2:15), for death is no more (Rev. 21:4). The second death (2:11; 20:6; 21:8) is here identified as in 21:8 with the lake of fire.

15. *If any was not found written in the book of life* (*ei tis ouch heurethē en tēi biblōi tēs zōēs*). Condition of first class

with *ei* and the first aorist passive indicative of *heuriskō*. In this short sentence the doom is told of all who are out of Christ, for they too follow the devil and the two beasts into the lake of fire (the counterpart of the Gehenna of fire, Matt. 5:22). There is no room here for soul sleeping, for an intermediate state, for a second chance, or for annihilation of the wicked. In Dan. 12:2 there is a resurrection to death as well as to life and so in John 5:29; Acts 24:15.

CHAPTER XXI

1. *A new heaven and a new earth (ouranon kainon kai gēn kainēn)*. This new vision (*eidon*) is the picture of the bliss of the saints. *The first heaven and the first earth (ho prōtos ouranos kai hē prōtē gē) are passed away (apēlthan*, went away, second aorist active indicative of *aperchomai)*. "Fled away" (*ephugen*) in 20:11. *And the sea is no more (kai hē thalassa ouk estin eti)*. The sea had given up its dead (20:13). There were great risks on the sea (18:17ff.). The old physical world is gone in this vision. It is not a picture of renovation of this earth, but of the disappearance of this earth and sky (not heaven where God dwells). It is a glorious picture here in 21:1–8 in sharp contrast to the lake of fire in 20:11–15. The symbolism in neither case is to be pressed too literally, but a stern and a glorious reality exists behind it all.

2. *The holy city, new Jerusalem (tēn polin tēn hagian Ierousalēm kainēn)*. "The New Earth must have a new metropolis, not another Babylon, but another and greater Jerusalem" (Swete), and not the old Jerusalem which was destroyed A.D. 70. It was called the Holy City in a conventional way (Matt. 4:5; 27:53), but now in reality because it is new and fresh (*kainēn*), this heavenly Jerusalem of hope (Heb. 12:22), this Jerusalem above (Gal. 4:26ff.) where our real citizenship is (Phil. 3:20). *Coming down out of heaven from God (katabainousan ek tou ouranou apo tou theou)*. Glorious picture caught by John and repeated from 3:12 and again in 21:10. But Charles distinguishes this new city of God from that in 21:9 to 22:2 because there is no tree of life in this one. But one shrinks from too much manipulation of this symbolism. It is better to see the glorious picture with

466

John and let it tell its own story. *Made ready* (*hētoimas-menēn*). Perfect passive participle of *hetoimazō* as in 19:7. The Wife of the Lamb made herself ready in her bridal attire. *As a bride adorned* (*hōs numphēn kekosmēmenēn*). Perfect passive participle of *kosmeō*, old verb (from *kosmos* ornament like our cosmetics), as in 21:19. Only here the figure of bride is not the people of God as in 19:7, but the abode of the people of God (the New Jerusalem). *For her husband* (*tōi andri autēs*). Dative case of personal interest.

3. *The tabernacle of God is with men* (*hē skēnē tou theou meta tōn anthrōpōn*). It is one of the angels of the Presence (16:17; 19:5) speaking. *And he shall dwell with them* (*kai skēnōsei met' autōn*). Future active of *skēnoō*, already in 7:15 from Ezek. 37:27; Zech. 2:10; 8:8 and used of the Incarnate Christ on earth by John (1:14), now a blessed reality of the Father. The metaphor stands for the Shekinah Glory of God in the old tabernacle (7:15; 13:6; 15:5), the true taber-nacle of which it was a picture (Heb. 8:2; 9:11). God is now Immanuel in fact, as was true of Christ (Matt. 1:23).

4. *Shall wipe away every tear from their eyes* (*exaleipsei pān dakruon ek tōn ophthalmōn autōn*). More exactly, "shall wipe out every tear out of their eyes" (repetition of *ex*) like a tender mother as in 7:17 (Is. 25:8). There is no more that ought to cause a tear, for death (*thanatos*) is no more, mourning (*penthos*), associated with death and crying (*kraugē*, wailing), and pain (*ponos* as in 16:10) are all gone. There is peace and bliss.

5. *Behold, I make all things new* (*Idou kaina poiō panta*). The first time since 1:8 that God has been represented as speaking directly, though voices have come out of the throne before (21:3) and out of the sanctuary (16:1, 17), which may be from God himself, though more likely from one of the angels of the Presence. This message is not addressed to John (7:14; 17:7; 21:6; 22:6), but to the entire world of the blessed. See Is. 43:18f. for the words (*Idou egō poiō kaina*).

The idea of a new heaven and a new earth is in Is. 65:17; 66:22; Ps. 102:25f. For the locative here with *epi* (*epi tōi thronōi*) see 7:10; 19:4 (genitive more usual, 4:9f.; 5:1, 7, 13, etc.). See 20:11 for the picture. *And he saith* (*kai legei*). Probably this means a change of speakers, made plain by *moi* (to me) in many MSS. An angel apparently (as in 14:13; 19:9f.) assures John and urges him to write (*grapson* as in 1:11; 2:1, 8, 12, 18; 3:1, 7, 14; 14:3). The reason given (*hoti*, for) is precisely the saying in 22:6 and he uses the two adjectives (*pistoi kai alēthinoi*) employed in 19:11 about God himself, and 3:14 about Christ. In 19:9 *alēthinoi* occurs also about "the words of God" as here. They are reliable and genuine.

6. *They are come to pass* (*Gegonan*). Second perfect active indicative of *ginomai* with -*an* for -*asi*. See 16:17 for a like use of *gegonen*, "They have come to pass." Here again it is the voice of God because, as in 1:8, He says: *I am the Alpha and the Omega* (*Egō to Alpha kai to Ō*) with the addition "the beginning and the end" (*hē archē kai to telos*), the whole used in 22:13 of Christ. In Is. 44:6 there is something like the addition, and in Col. 1:18 and Rev. 3:14 *hē archē* is applied to Christ, while here God is the First Cause (*archē*) and the Finality (*telos*) as in Rom. 11:36 and Eph. 4:6. But God works through Christ (John 1:3; Heb. 1:2f.; Col. 1:12–20). God is the bountiful Giver (James 1:5, 17) of the Water of Life. See 7:17; 22:1, 17 for this metaphor, which is based on Is. 55:1. It is God's own promise (*Egō dōsō*), "I will give." *Of the fountain* (*ek tēs pēgēs*). For this partitive use of *ek* see Matt. 25:8, without *ek* Rev. 2:17. *Freely* (*dōrean*). See Matt. 10:8; John 4:10; Rom. 3:24; Acts 8:20; Rev. 22:17.

7. *He that overcometh* (*ho nikōn*). Recalls the promises at the close of each of the Seven Letters in chapters 2 and 3. *Shall inherit* (*klēronomēsei*). Future active of *klēronomeō*, word with great history (Mark 10:17; I Pet. 1:4; Gal. 4:7; Rom. 8:17), here interpreted for the benefit of these who

share in Christ's victory. *I will be his God (Esomai autōi theos)*. Repeated Old Testament promise (first to Abraham, Gen. 17:7f.). Cf. Rev. 21:3. *He shall be my son (autos estai moi huios)*. Made first of Solomon (II Sam. 7:14) and applied to David later in Ps. 89:26f.

8. *Their part shall be (to meros autōn)*. In contrast to the state of the blessed (verses 3 to 7) the state of "those who have disfranchised themselves from the Kingdom of God" (Charles) is given. They are with Satan and the two beasts, and are the same with those not in the book of life (20:15) in the lake of fire and brimstone (19:20; 20:10, 14f.), that is the second death (2:11; 20:6, 14). See also 14:10. There are eight epithets here used which apply to various sections of this direful list of the doomed and the damned, all in the dative (case of personal interest). *For the fearful (tois deilois)*. Old word (from *deidō*, to fear) for the cowardly, who recanted under persecution, in N.T. only here, Matt. 8:26; Mark 4:40. *Unbelieving (apistois)*. "Faithless," "untrustworthy," in contrast with Christ *"ho pistos"* (1:5). Cf. 2:10, 13; 3:14; 17:14. Disloyalty is close kin to cowardice. *Abominable (ebdelugmenois)*. Perfect passive participle of *bdelussō*, old verb, in N.T. only here and Rom. 2:22, common in LXX, to pollute (Ex. 5:21). Those who have become defiled by the impurities of emperor-worship (7:4f.; 21:27; Rom. 2:22; Titus 1:16). *Murderers (phoneusin)*. As a matter of course and all too common always (Mark 7:21; Rom. 1:29; Rev. 9:21). *Fornicators (pornois)*. Again all too common always, then and now (I Cor. 5:10; I Tim. 1:9f.). These two crimes often go together. *Sorcerers (pharmakois)*. Old word, in N.T. only here and 22:15. Closely connected with idolatry and magic (9:21; 13:13f.). *Idolaters (eidōlolatrais)*. See I Cor. 5:10f.; 10:7; Eph. 5:5; Rev. 22:15. With a powerful grip on men's lives then and now. *All liars (pasi tois pseudesin)*. Repeated in 22:15

and stigmatized often (2:2; 3:9; 14:5; 21:8, 27; 22:15). Not a "light" sin.

9. *One of the seven angels* (*heis ek tōn hepta aggelōn*). As in 17:1 with the same introduction when the angel made the announcement about the harlot city (Babylon), so here the description of the heavenly city, the New Jerusalem, is given by one of the same group of angels who had the seven bowls. Thus the *numphē* (Bride) is placed in sharp contrast with the *pornē* (Harlot). The New Jerusalem was briefly presented in verse 2, but now is pictured at length (21:9–22:5) in a nearer and clearer vision. *The bride the wife of the Lamb* (*tēn numphēn tēn gunaika tou arniou*). Twice already the metaphor of the Bride has been used (19:7; 21:2), here termed "wife" (*gunaika*), mentioned proleptically as in 19:7 if the marriage is not yet a reality. For the use of the same metaphor elsewhere in the N.T. see on 19:7.

10. *He carried me away in the Spirit* (*apēnegken me en pneumati*). See same language in 17:7 when John received a vision of the Harlot City in a wilderness. Here it is "to a mountain great and high" (*epi oros mega kai hupsēlon*). So it was with Ezekiel (40:2) and so the devil took Jesus (Matt. 4:8). It was apparently not Mount Zion (14:1), for the New Jerusalem is seen from this mountain. "The Seer is carried thither 'in spirit' (cf. 1:10; 4:1); the Angel's *deuro* is a *sursum cor* to which his spirit under the influence of the 'Spirit of revelation' (Eph. 1:17) at once responds" (Swete). *And he shewed me* (*kai edeixen moi*). First aorist active indicative of *deiknumi*, just as he had said he would do in verse 9 (*deixō soi*, I will shew thee). Precisely the same words about Jerusalem as in verse 2, save the absence of *kainēn* (New).

11. *Having the glory of God* (*echousan tēn doxan tou theou*). Syntactically this clause goes with verse 10, the feminine accusative singular participle *echousan* agreeing with *polin*,

the radiance of the dazzling splendour of God as seen in
Is. 60:1; Ezek. 43:5. God's very presence is in the Holy
City (the Bride). *Light* (*phōstēr*). "Luminary," late word
(in LXX, papyri), in N.T. only here and Phil. 2:15. Christ
is the light (*phōs*) of the world (John 8:12) and so are Christians (Matt. 5:14) who have received the illumination
(*phōtismos*) of God in the face of Christ (II Cor. 4:6) and
who radiate it to men (Phil. 2:15). See both words in Gen.
1:3, 14. "The 'luminary' of the Holy City is her witness
to Christ" (Swete). *Like unto a stone most precious* (*homoios
lithōi timiōtatōi*). Associative instrumental case after *homoios*. *Timiōtatōi* is the elative superlative. *As it were a
jasper stone* (*hōs lithōi iaspidi*). As in 4:3, which see. *Clear
as crystal* (*krustallizonti*). Verb not found elsewhere from
krustallos (old word, 4:6; 22:1), "of crystalline brightness
and transparency" (Thayer), "transparent and gleaming as
rock-crystal" (Moffatt).

12. *Having a wall great and high* (*echousa teichos mega kai
hupsēlon*). John returns, after the parenthesis in verse 11,
to the structure in verse 10, only to use the accusative
echousan as before to agree with *polin*, but the nominative
echousa as again with "twelve gates" (*pulōnas dōdeka*).
Pulōn is an old word (from *pulē* gate) for a large gate as in
Luke 16:20 and six times in Rev. for the gate tower of a
city wall (21:12, 13, 15, 21, 25; 22:14) as in I Kings 17:10;
Acts 14:13. See Ezek. 48:31ff. for these twelve gates, one
for each tribe (cf. Rev. 7:1–8). *At the gates* (*epi tois pulōsin*).
"Upon the gate towers." *Twelve angels* (*aggelous dōdeka*).
As *pulōroi* or *phulakes* according to Is. 62:6; II Chron. 8:14.
Names written thereon (*onomata epigegrammena*). Perfect
passive participle of *epigraphō*. *Which are the names* (*ha
estin*). Just as in Ezekiel's vision (48:31ff.), so here the
names of the twelve tribes of Israel appear, one on each
gate.

13. *Three gates* (*pulōnes treis*) on each of the four sides

as in Ezek. 42:16ff.; "on the east" (*apo anatolēs*, as in 16:12, starting from the east), "on the north" (*apo borrā*, from the north, as in Luke 13:29), "on the south" (*apo notou*, from the south, as in Luke 13:29), "on the west" (*apo dusmōn*, from the west, as in Matt. 8:11).

14. *Had* (*echōn*). Masculine present active participle of *echō* instead of *echon* (neuter like *to teichos*), and the participle occurs independently as if a principal verb (*eichen*) as often in this book. *Twelve foundations* (*themelious dōdeka*). Foundation stones, old adjective (from *thema*, from *tithēmi*), here as in I Cor. 3:11ff. and II Tim. 2:19, with *lithous* (stones understood), though often neuter substantive *to themelion* (Luke 6:48f.; Acts 16:26). See Is. 28:16; Heb. 11:10. Twelve because of the twelve apostles as foundation stones (Eph. 2:20). *On them* (*ep' autōn*). On the twelve foundation stones. *Names of the twelve apostles of the Lamb* (*onomata tōn dōdeka apostolōn tou arniou*). Jesus had spoken of twelve thrones for the apostles (Matt. 19:28); names of all twelve are here written, not just that of Peter, as some would argue from Matt. 16:18. As a matter of fact, Christ is the corner stone or *akrogōniaion* (I Pet. 2:6; I Cor. 3:10; Eph. 2:20), though rejected by the Sanhedrin (Matt. 21:42ff.). One may wonder if the name of Judas is on that stone or that of Matthias.

15. *Had* (*eichen*). Regular imperfect here, no longer *echōn*. *For a measure a golden reed* (*metron kalamon chrusoun*). See 11:1 for *kalamos* (reed). *Metron* is an old word, kin to *mētēr* (mother, moulder, manager), an instrument for measuring (*metreō*) as in Matt. 7:2, here in the predicate accusative. *To measure* (*hina metrēsēi*). Purpose clause with *hina* and the first aorist active subjunctive of *metreō*. The rod of gold was in keeping with the dignity of the service of God (1:12; 5:8; 8:3; 9:13; 15:7).

16. *Lieth foursquare* (*tetragōnos keitai*). Present middle indicative of *keimai*. The predicate adjective is from *tetra*

(Æolic for *tessares* four) and *gōnos* (*gōnia* corner, Matt. 6:5)
here only in N.T.   As in Ezek. 48:16, 20.   It is a tetragon
or quadrilateral quadrangle (21:12f.).   *The length thereof is as
great as the breadth* (*to mēkos autēs hoson to platos*).   It is
rectangular, both walls and city within.   Babylon, according
to Herodotus, was a square, each side being 120 stadia.
Diodorus Siculus says that Nineveh was also foursquare.
With the reed (*tōi kalamōi*).   Instrumental case (cf. verse 15
for *kalamos*) and for *metreō* (aorist active indicative here).
Twelve thousand furlongs (*epi stadiōn dōdeka chiliadōn*).   This
use of the genitive *stadiōn* with *epi* is probably correct (reading of Aleph P), though A Q have *stadious* (more usual, but
confusing here with *chiliadōn*).   Thucydides and Xenophon
use *epi* with the genitive in a like idiom (in the matter of).
It is not clear whether the 1500 miles (12,000 furlongs) is
the measurement of each of the four sides or the sum total.
Some of the rabbis argued that the walls of the New Jerusalem of Ezekiel would reach to Damascus and the height
would be 1500 miles high.   *Equal* (*isa*).   That is, it is a
perfect cube like the Holy of Holies in Solomon's temple
(I Kings 6:19f.).   This same measurement (*platos, mēkos,
hupsos*) is applied to Christ's love in Eph. 3:18, with *bathos*
(depth) added.   It is useless to try to reduce the measure-
ments or to put literal interpretations upon this highly
wrought symbolic language.   Surely the meaning is that
heaven will be large enough for all, as Jesus said (John
14:1ff.) without insisting on the materialistic measurement
of a gorgeous apartment house full of inside rooms.

17. *A hundred and forty and four cubits* (*hekaton tesserakonta tessarōn pēchōn*).   Another multiple of 12 (12×12 =
144) as in 7:4; 14:1.   It is not clear whether it is the height
or the breadth of the wall that is meant, though *hupsos*
(height) comes just before.   That would be 216 feet high
(cf. verse 12), not enormous in comparison with the 7,000,000
feet (1500 miles) height of the city.   *According to the measure*

of a man, that is, of an angel (*metron anthrōpou, ho estin aggelou*). No preposition for "according to," just the accusative case of general reference in apposition with the verb *emetrēsen.* Though measured by an angel, a human standard was employed, man's measure which is angel's (Bengel).

18. *The building of the wall* (*hē endōmēsis tou teichous*). Or *endomēsis,* elsewhere so far only in Josephus (*Ant.* XV. 9.6, a mole or breakwater) and in an inscription (*Syll.* 583[31]), apparently from *endomeō,* to build in, and so the fact of building in. The wall had jasper (verse 11) built into it. *Was pure gold* (*chrusion katharon*). No copula *ēn* (was) expressed. The city shone like a mass of gold in contrast with the jasper lustre of the wall. *Pure glass* (*hualōi katharōi*). Associative instrumental case after *homoion. Hualos* (apparently from *huei,* it rains, and so raindrop) in N.T. only Rev. 21:18, 21.

19. *Were adorned* (*kekosmēmenoi*). Perfect passive participle of *kosmeō* as in verse 2, but without the copula *ēsan* (were), followed by instrumental case *lithōi* (stone). *With all manner of precious stones* (*panti lithōi timiōi*). "With every precious stone." The list of the twelve stones in verses 19 and 20 has no necessary mystical meaning. "The writer is simply trying to convey the impression of a radiant and superb structure" (Moffatt). The twelve gems do correspond closely (only eight in common) with the twelve stones on the high priest's breastplate (Ex. 28:17–20; 39:10ff.; Ezek. 28:13; Is. 54:11f.). Charles identifies them with the signs of zodiac in reverse order, a needless performance here. See the stones in Rev. 4:3. These foundation stones are visible. For jasper (*iaspis*) see 4:3; 21:11, 18; Is. 54:12; sapphire (*sappheiros*) see Ex. 24:10; Is. 54:11 (possibly the *lapis lazuli* of Turkestan); chalcedony (*chalkēdōn*) we have no other reference in N.T. or LXX (described by Pliny, H.N. XXXIII.21), possibly a green silicate of

copper from near Chalcedon; emerald (*smaragdos*) here only in N.T., see 4:3 *smaragdinos*, and like it a green stone.

20. Sardonyx (*sardonux*), here only in N.T., white with layers of red, from sardion (red carnelian) and onyx (white); for sardius (*sardion*) see 4:3; chrysolite (*chrusolithos*), here only in N.T. (Ex. 28:20), stone of a golden colour like our topaz or amber or a yellow beryl or golden jasper; beryl (*bērullos*), again here only in N.T. (Ex. 28:20), note the difficulty of identification, much like the emerald according to Pliny; for topaz (*topazion*), here only in N.T. (Ex. 28:17), a golden-greenish stone; chrysoprase (chrusoprasos), here only in N.T. (not in LXX), in colour like a teek, translucent golden-green; jacinth (*huakinthos*), of the colour of the hyacinth, a violet colour (Pliny), already in 9:17 like blue smoke, like achates in LXX; amethyst (*amethustos*), only here in N.T. (Ex. 28:19), of a violet and purple colour, more brilliant than the *huakinthos*. Swete sums up the colours thus: blue (sapphire, jacinth, amethyst), green (jasper, chalcedony, emerald, beryl, topaz, chrysoprase), red (sardonyx, sardius), yellow (chrysolite). But even so there is great variety in hue and brilliancy and in the reaction on each other. Clement of Alexandria argues that this variety illustrates the variety of gifts and graces in the twelve apostles. Possibly so.

21. *Twelve pearls* (*dōdeka margaritai*). These gate towers (*pulōnes*) were mentioned in verses 12f. Each of these (cf. Is. 54:12) is a pearl, one of the commonest of jewels (Matt. 7:6; 13:46; I Tim. 2:9). *Each one* (*ana heis hekastos*). Distributive use of *ana*, but with the nominative (used as adverb, not preposition) rather than the accusative (as a preposition) as appears also in Mark 14:19; John 8:9; with *kata* in Rom. 12:5, "a barbaric construction" according to Charles. *Street* (*plateia*). For which word (broad way, *hodos* understood) see Matt. 6:5, here the singular, but includes all the streets. *Transparent* (*diaugēs*). Old word

(from *dia*, through, *augē*, ray, shining through), here alone in N.T.

22. *I saw no temple therein (naon ouk eidon en autēi).* "Temple I did not see in it." The whole city is a temple in one sense (verse 16), but it is something more than a temple even with its sanctuary and Shekinah Glory in the Holy of Holies. *For the Lord God the Almighty, and the Lamb are the temple thereof (ho gar Kurios ho theos ho pantokratōr, naos autēs estin kai to arnion).* "For the Lord God, the Almighty, is the sanctuary of it and the Lamb." The Eternal Presence is the Shekinah Glory of God (verse 3). In II Cor. 6:16 we are the sanctuary of God here, but now God is our Sanctuary, and so is the Lamb as in chapters 4 and 5. See 1:8 and often for the description of God here.

23. *To shine upon it (hina phainōsin autēi).* Purpose clause with *hina* and the present active subjunctive of *phainō*, to keep on shining. Light is always a problem in our cities. See Is. 60:19ff. *Did lighten it (ephōtisen autēn).* First aorist active indicative of *phōtizō*, to illumine, old verb from *phōs* (Luke 11:36). If the sun and moon did shine, they would give no added light in the presence of the Shekinah Glory of God. See verse 11 for "the glory of God." Cf. 18:1 and 21:3. "Their splendour is simply put to shame by the glory of God Himself" (Charles). *And the lamp thereof is the Lamb (kai ho luchnos autēs to arnion).* Charles takes *ho luchnos* as predicate, "and the Lamb is the lamp thereof." Bousset thinks that John means to compare Christ to the moon the lesser light (Gen. 1:16), but that contrast is not necessary. Swete sees Christ as the one lamp for all in contrast with the many *luchniai* of the churches on earth (1:12, 20). "No words could more clearly demonstrate the purely spiritual character of St. John's conception of the New Jerusalem" (Swete).

24. *Amidst the light thereof (dia tou phōtos autēs).* Rather "by the light thereof." From Is. 60:3, 11, 20. All the

moral and spiritual progress of moderns is due to Christ, and the nations of earth will be represented, including "the kings" (*hoi basileis*), mentioned also in Isaiah 60:3, "do bring their glory into it" (*pherousin tēn doxan autōn eis autēn*). Present active indicative of *pherō*. Swete is uncertain whether this is a picture of heaven itself or "some gracious purpose of God towards humanity which has not yet been revealed" and he cites 22:2 in illustration. The picture is beautiful and glorious even if not realized here, but only in heaven.

25. *Shall in no wise be shut* (*ou mē kleisthōsin*). Double negative with the first aorist passive subjunctive of *kleiō*. *By day* (*hēmeras*). Genitive of time. Mentioned alone without *nuktos* (by night), "for there shall be no night there" (*nux gar ouk estai ekei*). This looks like a continued picture of heaven.

26. *They shall bring* (*oisousin*). Future active indicative of *pherō*. Rome gathered the merchandise of the world (18:11ff.). The City of God will have the best of all the nations (Is. 60:5, 11), an expansion of verse 24.

27. *There shall in no wise enter into it* (*ou mē eiselthēi eis autēn*). Double negative again with the second aorist active subjunctive of *eiserchomai* with *eis* repeated. Like Is. 52:1 and Ezek. 44:9. *Anything unclean* (*pān koinon*). Common use of *pān* with negative like *ouden*, and the use of *koinos* for defiled or profane as in Mark 7:2; Acts 10:14, not just what is common to all (Titus 1:4). *Or he that* (*kai ho*). "And he that." *Maketh an abomination and a lie* (*poiōn bdelugma kai pseudos*). Like Babylon (17:4 which see for *bdelugma*) and 21:8 for those in the lake of fire and brimstone, and 22:15 for "every one loving and doing a lie." These recurrent glimpses of pagan life on earth and of hell in contrast to heaven in this picture raise the question already mentioned whether John is just running parallel pictures of heaven and hell after the judgment or

whether, as Charles says: "The unclean and the abominable and the liars are still on earth, but, though the gates are open day and night, they cannot enter." In apocalyptic writing literalism and chronology cannot be insisted on as in ordinary books. The series of panoramas continue to the end. *But only they which are written (ei mē hoi gegrammenoi).* "Except those written." For "the book of life" see 3:5; 13:8; 20:15. Cf. Dan. 12:1.

CHAPTER XXII

1. *He shewed me* (*edeixen moi*). The angel as in 21:9, 10 (cf. 1:1; 4:1). Now the interior of the city. *A river of water of life* (*potamon hudatos zōēs*). For *hudōr zōēs* (water of life) see 7:17; 21:6; 22:17; John 4:14. There was a river in the Garden of Eden (Gen. 2:10). The metaphor of river reappears in Zech. 14:8; Ezek. 47:9, and the fountain of life in Joel 3:18; Jer. 2:13; Prov. 10:11; 13:14; 14:27; 16:22; Ps. 36:10. *Bright as crystal* (*lampron hōs krustallon*). See 4:6 for *krustallon* and 15:6; 19:8; 22:16 for *lampron*. "Sparkling like rock crystal" (Swete), shimmering like mountain water over the rocks. *Proceeding out of the throne of God and of the Lamb* (*ekporeuomenon ek tou thronou tou theou kai tou arniou*). Cf. Ezek. 47:1; Zech. 14:8. Already in 3:21 Christ is pictured as sharing the Father's throne as in Heb. 1:3. See also 22:3. This phrase has no bearing on the doctrine of the Procession of the Holy Spirit.

2. *In the midst of the street thereof* (*en mesōi tēs plateias autēs*). Connected probably with the river in verse 1, though many connect it with verse 2. Only one street mentioned here as in 21:21. *On this side of the river and on that* (*tou potamou enteuthen kai ekeithen*). *Enteuthen* occurs as a preposition in Daniel 12:5 (Theodoret) and may be so here (post-positive), purely adverbial in John 19:18. *The tree of life* (*xulon zōēs*). For the metaphor see Gen. 1:11f. and Rev. 2:7; 22:14. *Xulon* is used for a green tree in Luke 23:31; Ezek. 47:12. *Bearing* (*poioun*). Neuter active participle of *poieō* (making, producing, as in Matt. 7:17). Some MSS. have *poiōn* (masculine), though *xulon* is neuter. *Twelve manner of fruits* (*karpous dōdeka*). "Twelve fruits." *Yielding* (*apodidoun*). Neuter active participle of *apodidōmi*, to

479

give back, but some MSS. have *apodidous* (masculine) like *poiōn*. *For the healing of the nations* (*eis therapeian tōn ethnōn*). Spiritual healing, of course, as leaves (*phulla*) are often used for obtaining medicines. Here again the problem occurs whether this picture is heaven before the judgment or afterwards. Charles distinguishes sharply between the Heavenly City for the millennial reign and the New Jerusalem that descends from heaven after the judgment. Charles rearranges these chapters to suit his theory. But chronology is precarious here.

3. *There shall be no curse any more* (*pan katathema ouk estai eti*). No other example of *katathema* has been found outside of the *Didache* XVI. 5, though the verb *katathematizō* occurs in Matt. 26:74, meaning to curse, while we have *anathematizō* in Mark 14:71 in the same sense. It may be a syncopated form of *katanathema*. The usual *anathema* (curse) occurs in I Cor. 16:22; Gal. 1:8; Rom. 9:3. For *pan* with *ouk* = *ouden* see 21:27. *Shall do him service* (*latreusousin autōi*). Future active of *latreuō*, linear idea, "shall keep on serving." See 7:15 for present active indicative of this same verb with the dative *autōi* as here, picturing the worship of God in heaven. See 27:1 for "the throne of God and of the Lamb."

4. *They shall see his face* (*opsontai to prosōpon autou*). Future active of *horaō*. This vision of God was withheld from Moses (Ex. 33:20, 23), but promised by Jesus to the pure in heart (Matt. 5:8) and mentioned in Heb. 12:14 as possible only to the holy, and promised in Ps. 17:15. Even here on earth we can see God in the face of Christ (II Cor. 4:6), but now in the New Jerusalem we can see Christ face to face (I Cor. 13:12), even as he is after we are made really like him (II Cor. 3:18; Rom. 8:29; I John 3:2). It is anthropomorphic language, to be sure, but it touches the essential reality of religion. "The supreme felicity is reached, immediate presence with God and the Lamb" (Beckwith).

His name on their foreheads (*to onoma autou epi tōn metōpōn autōn*). As in 3:12; 7:3; 14:1.

5. *Shall be night no more* (*nux ouk estai eti*). As in 21:25. *They need* (*echousin chreian*). Present active indicative, "They have need," though A has *hexousin* (shall have), future like *estai*. Here again there is repetition of part of 21:23, but for the purpose of showing the delightsomeness of the New Jerusalem with no need of lamp or sun (change to *phōs* with *hēliou* instead of *phōtos*, "they have no light of sun"). *Shall give them light* (*phōtisei*). Future active of *phōtizō*, while aorist *ephōtisen* in 21:23. *They shall reign* (*basileusousin*). Future active of *basileuō*. Reign eternally in contrast with the limited millennial reign of 20:4, 6. This glorious eternal reign with Christ occurs repeatedly in the book (1:6; 3:21; 5:10) as in Luke 22:30. Christ's Kingdom is spiritual (John 18:36f.). "The visions of the Apocalypse are now ended; they have reached their climax in the New Jerusalem" (Swete). Now John gives the parting utterances of some of the speakers, and it is not always clear who is speaking.

6. *He said unto me* (*eipen moi*). Apparently the same angel as in 22:1 (21:9, 15). *These words* (*houtoi hoi logoi*). The same words used in 21:5 by the angel there. Whatever the application there, here the angel seems to endorse as "faithful and true" (*pistoi kai alēthinoi*) not merely the preceding vision (21:9–22:5), but the revelations of the entire book. The language added proves this: "Sent his angel to shew unto his servants the things which must shortly come to pass" (*apesteilen ton aggelon autou deixai tois doulois autou ha dei genesthai en tachei*), a direct reference to 1:1 concerning the purpose of Christ's revelation to John in this book. For "the God of the spirits of the prophets" (*ho theos tōn pneumatōn tōn prophētōn*) see 19:10 and I Cor. 14:32. Probably the prophets' own spirits enlightened by the Holy Spirit (10:7; 11:8; 22:9).

7. *And behold, I come quickly* (*kai idou erchomai tachu*). Christ is the speaker, either through this angel or more probably directly from Christ without introduction as in verses 12, 16. About Christ coming quickly see 2:5, 16; 3:11; 16:15, and already in 1:2f. Once more we must recall that *tachu* and *en tachei* are according to God's time, not ours (II Pet. 3:8). *Blessed* (*makarios*). This beatitude is like in substance the first (1:3) and is in Christ's own words like the one in 16:15. This book is here called a "prophecy" (*prophēteias*) as in verses 10, 18, 19. It is Christ's revelation from God, a direct message from God. Part of it is prediction of doom on Christ's enemies, but most of it is a comforting picture of final triumph and bliss for the faithful in a time of great distress and persecution.

8. *And I John* (*Kágō Iōannēs*). Here John the Seer is the speaker. He had already given his name (1:1, 4, 9). Here he claims to be the "one who hears and sees these things" (*ho akouōn kai blepōn tauta*). *I fell down to worship* (*epesa proskunēsai*). Second aorist active indicative of *piptō* (with -*a* form) and the first aorist active infinitive of purpose of *proskuneō*. It was a natural, though a wrong, thing to do, especially after Christ's own voice followed that of the angel "which shewed me these things" (*tou deiknuontos tauta*). Genitive singular of the articular present active participle of *deiknuō*. Cf. 1:1; 4:1; 17:1; 21:9f.; 22:1, 6.

9. *See thou do it not* (*Hora mē*). The angel promptly interposes (*legei*, dramatic present). See 19:10 for discussion of this same phrase *hora mē* when John had once before started to worship the angel in his excitement. Here we have added to the words in 19:10 "the prophets (*tōn prophētōn*) and also "them which keep the words of this book" (*tōn tērountōn tous logous tou bibliou toutou*), the last a repetition from 22:7. In both places we have "Worship God" (*tōi theōi proskunēson*). And not an angel.

10. *And he saith unto me* (*kai legei moi*). The angel re-

sumes as in 19:9. *Seal not up* (*mē sphragiseis*). Prohibition with *mē* and the ingressive first aorist active subjunctive of *sphragizō*. Charles takes this to be the command of Christ because in verses 7 and 18 "the words of the prophecy of this book" come from Christ. But that is not a conclusive argument, though Charles, as already stated, rearranges these chapters to suit his own notion. Once only (10:4) was John directed to seal and not to write. See there for discussion of *sphragizō*. This book is to be left open for all to read (1:3; 13:18; 17:9; 22:7, 18). *At hand* (*eggus*). As in 1:3.

11. *Let him do unrighteousness still* (*adikēsatō eti*). First aorist (constative) active imperative of *adikeō*, viewed here as a whole. The language is probably ironical, with a reminder of Dan. 12:10, in no sense a commendation of their lost estate. Charles rejects this verse as not like John. It is the hopelessness of the final state of the wicked which is here pictured. So as to "Let him be made filthy still" (*rupanthētō eti*). First aorist (constative) passive imperative of *rupainō*, old verb, to make foul or filthy (from *rupos*, filth, I Pet. 3:21, as is *ruparos*, filthy), here only in N.T. The use of *eti* is not perfectly clear, whether "still" or "yet more." It is the time when Christ has shut the door to those outside who are now without hope (Matt. 25:10; Luke 13:25). *Ruparos* occurs elsewhere in N.T. only in James 2:2, and *ruparia* (filthiness) only in James 1:21. So then "the righteous" (*ho dikaios*) is to do righteousness still (*dikaiosunēn poiēsatō eti*, first constative aorist active imperative of *poieō*) and "the holy" (*ho hagios*) to be made holy still (*hagiasthētō eti*, first constative aorist passive imperative of *hagiazō*). The states of both the evil and the good are now fixed forever. There is no word here about a "second chance" hereafter.

12. *My reward is with me* (*ho misthos mou met' emou*). It is Christ speaking again and he repeats his promise of

coming quickly as in verse 7. He speaks now as the Rewarder (*ho misthapodotēs*) of Heb. 11:6. Cf. Rev. 11:18; Is. 40:10; 62:11. *To render* (*apodounai*). Second aorist active infinitive of purpose of *apodidōmi*, to give back. Each will receive the reward according to his own work (Rev. 2:23; II Cor. 5:10; Rom. 2:26).

13. *I am the Alpha and the Omega* (*Egō to Alpha kai to Ō*). Applied to God in 1:8; 21:6, and here alone to Christ, crowning proof in this book of Christ's deity. So in 21:6 God is termed, as Christ is here, *hē archē kai to telos* (the beginning and the end), while *ho prōtos kai ho eschatos* (the first and the last) is applied only to Christ (1:17; 2:8). Solemn assurance is thus given that Christ is qualified to be the Judge of verse 12 (cf. Matt. 25:31-46). In Heb. 12:2 Jesus is the *archēgos kai teleiōtēs tēs pisteōs* (the author and finisher of faith). Christ was the Creator of the universe for the Father. So now he is the Consummation of redemption.

14. *Blessed* (*makarioi*). This is the last beatitude of the book and "deals with the issues of the higher life" (Swete). *They that wash their robes* (*hoi plunontes tas stolas autōn*). Present active articular participle of *plunō*. See 7:14 for this very verb with *stolas*, while in 3:4 the negative statement occurs. Cf. I Cor. 6:11. *That they may have the right* (*hina estai hē exousia autōn*). Purpose clause with *hina* and the future middle of *eimi* (a common construction in this book, 6:4, 11; 9:5, 20; 13:12; 14:13), "that there may be their right." *To come to the tree of life* (*epi to xulon tēs zōēs*). "Over the tree of life." On *exousia epi* = "power over" see 6:8; 13:7; 16:9; Luke 9:1. On "the tree of life" see 2:7; 22:2. *May enter in* (*eiselthōsin*). Purpose clause with *hina* and the second aorist active subjunctive of *eiserchomai* parallel with hina *estai* (future). *By the gates* (*tois pulōsin*). Associative instrumental case of *pulōn* (21:12), "by the gate towers."

15. *Without* (*exō*). Outside the holy city, with which compare 21:8, 27. Düstierdieck supplies an imperative: "Out, ye dogs." *The dogs* (*hoi kunes*). Not literal dogs, but the morally impure (Deut. 23:18; II Kings 8:13; Ps. 22:17, 21; Matt. 7:6; Mark 7:27; Phil. 3:3). Dogs in the Oriental cities are the scavengers and excite unspeakable contempt. *The sorcerers* (*hoi pharmakoi*). As in 21:8, where are listed "the fornicators and the murderers and the idolaters," all "outside" the holy city here as there "in the lake that burns with fire and brimstone, the second death." Both are pictures (symbolic language) of hell, the eternal absence from fellowship with God. Another time Jesus spoke of "the outer darkness" (*eis to skotos to exōteron*, Matt. 8:12; 22:13; 25:30), outside of lighted house, as the abode of the damned. Another symbol is the worm that dies not (Mark 9:48). *Every one that loveth and maketh a lie* (*pās philōn kai poiōn pseudos*). An interpretation of *pāsin tois pseudesin* (all liars) of 21:8 and of *poiōn pseudos* (doing a lie) of 21:27. Satan is the father of lying (John 8:44) and Satan's home is a congenial place for those who love and practise lying (II Thess. 2:12). See I John 1:6 for not doing the truth and see also Rom. 1:25; Eph. 4:25.

16. *I Jesus* (*Egō Iēsous*). The last and most solemn attestation to the book that from Jesus (the historic Jesus known to the churches), in harmony with 1:1f. *Have sent* (*epempsa*). First aorist active indicative of *pempō*, used here in the same sense as *aposteilas* in 1:1 as his personal messenger. It is the Jesus of history here speaking, who is also the Christ of theology and the Lamb of God. *For the churches* (*epi tais ekklēsiais*). For this use of *epi* see 10:11; John 12:16. It is not just for the seven churches (1:4), but for all the churches in the world then and now. *I am the root and the offspring of David* (*Egō eimi hē riza kai to genos Daueid*). See 5:5 for "the root of David," to which John now adds *to genos* in the sense of "offspring"

(Acts 17:28f.), not of family or race (Acts 4:6; 7:13). Cf. Matt. 22:42–45. *The bright, the morning star* (*ho astēr ho lampros ho prōinos*). The Davidic King is called a star in Numb. 24:17; Luke 1:78. This "day-star" (*phōsphoros*) is interpreted as Christ (II Pet. 1:19). In Rev. 2:28 the phrase "the morning star" occurs in Christ's words, which is here interpreted. Christ is the Light that was coming into the world (John 1:9; 8:12).

17. *The Spirit and the bride* (*to pneuma kai hē numphē*). The Holy Spirit, speaking through the prophets or the Spirit of prophecy (2:7; 16:4; 18:24), joins with the bride (21:2), the people of God, in a response to the voice of Jesus just heard. After the picture of heaven in 22:1–5 there is intense longing (19:7) of God's people for the consummation of the marriage of the Lamb and the Bride. So now "the prophets and the saints" (Swete) make a common plea to the Lord Jesus to "come" (*Erchou*, present middle imperative of *erchomai*, Come on) as he has just said twice that he would do (22:1, 12). The call for Christ is to be repeated by every hearer (*ho akouōn*) as in 1:3. *Let him come* (*erchesthō*). Change of person and this verb applied not to Christ as just before, but to the one who wishes to greet Christ. The thirsty man is bidden to come himself before it is too late. See 5:6 for *dipsaō*, used for spiritual thirst, and in particular John 6:35 and 7:37 for one thirsting for the water of life (21:6; 22:1). Cf. Is. 55:1. *He that will* (*ho thelōn*). Even if not yet eagerly thirsting. This one is welcome also. For this use of *thelō* see Phil. 2:13. *Let him take* (*labetō*). Second ingressive aorist active imperative of *lambanō*. In accordance with the free promise in 21:6, "freely" (*dōrean*) here as there. This gracious and wide invitation is cheering after the gloomy picture of the doomed and the damned. The warnings against the dragon and the two beasts with all their dreadful consequences are meant to deter men from falling victims to all the devil's devices then and now. The

door of mercy still stands wide open today, for the end has not yet come. The series of panoramas is over, with the consummation pictured as a reality. Now we drop back to the standpoint before we saw the visions through John's eyes. In verse 17 we hear the voice of the Spirit of God inviting all who hear and see to heed and to come and drink of the water of life freely offered by the Lamb of God.

18. *I testify* (*Egō marturō*). Commentators disagree keenly about the words in verses 18 and 19. Charles rejects them as an interpolation and out of harmony with the rest of the book. Beckwith takes them to be John's own warning, drawn from Deut. 4:2 "to every man that heareth" (*panti tōi akouonti*, dative of the articular present active participle of *akouō*, which compare 1:3). Swete properly holds these verses to be from Jesus himself, still bearing solemn witness to this book, with warning against wilful perversion of its teachings. *If any man shall add* (*ean tis epithēi*). Condition of the third class with *ean* and the second aorist active subjunctive of *epitithēmi*, with *epi* added with *auta*, as also in the conclusion *epithēsei ep' auton* (future active). This warning is directed against perversions of this book, not about the New Testament or the Bible as a whole, though it may be true there also. Surely no warning was more needed when we consider the treatment accorded the Apocalypse, so that Dr. Robert South said that the Apocalypse either found one crazy or left him so.

19. *If any man shall take away* (*ean tis aphelēi*). Also condition of the third class with *ean* and second aorist active subjunctive of *aphaireō*, with *apo* repeated both in the condition and in the conclusion (*aphelei apo*, future active indicative of *aphaireō* for the more usual *aphairēsei*). *Which are written in this book* (*tōn gegrammenōn en tōi bibliōi toutōi*). Ablative neuter plural articular perfect passive participle in apposition with *ek tou xulou tēs zōēs* (from the tree of life)

and *ek tēs poleōs tēs hagias* (out of the holy city). Such a man is unworthy of his inheritance.

20. *He which testifieth* (*ho marturōn*). That is Jesus (1:2) who has just spoken (22:18). *Yea: I come quickly* (*Nai, erchomai tachu*). Affirmation again of the promise in 22:7, 12. On *Nai* (Yes) see 1:7 for the Lord's assent to the call. Then John expresses his absolute belief in the Lord's promise: "Amen: come, Lord Jesus" (*Amēn, erchou, Kurie Iēsou*). On *Amēn* see 1:7. On *erchou* see 22:17. Note *Kurie* with *Iēsou*. As in I Cor. 12:3; Phil. 2:11. For Paul's confidence in the deity of Christ and the certainty of his second coming see Titus 2:13 and II Tim. 4:8. *Marana tha* (I Cor. 16:22).

21. *The grace of the Lord Jesus be with the saints* (*hē charis tou Kuriou Iēsou meta tōn hagiōn*). John's own benediction, an unusual ending for an apocalypse, but suitable for one meant to be read in the churches (1:3f.). Grace is Paul's unvarying word in conclusion of his letters, as is true of Heb. 13:25. "The saints" or the consecrated (*hoi hagioi*) is John's constant word for believers in Christ (8:3f.; 11:18; 13:7, 10; 14:12; 16:6; 17:6; 18:20, 24; 19:8; 20:9). It is a good word for the close of this marvellous picture of God's gracious provision for his people in earth and heaven.